THE
OLD WORLD
KITCHEN

THE OLD WORLD KITCHEN

THE RICH TRADITION OF

EUROPEAN PEASANT COOKING

Elisabeth Luard

BANTAM BOOKS
TORONTO · NEW YORK · LONDON · SYDNEY · AUCKLAND

THE OLD WORLD KITCHEN:
THE RICH TRADITION OF EUROPEAN PEASANT COOKING
A Bantam Book / October 1987

Grateful acknowledgment is made for permission to reprint the following:

Ernest Hemingway, excerpted from DANGEROUS SUMMER. Copyright © 1960 by Ernest Hemingway, copyright © 1985 by Mary Hemingway, John Hemingway, Patrick Hemingway, and Gregory Hemingway. Reprinted with permission from Charles Scribner's Sons.

Library of Congress Cataloging-in-Publication Data

Luard, Elisabeth.
  The old world kitchen.

  Bibliography: p. 524
  Includes index.
  1. Cookery, European.   I. Title.
TX723.5.A1L83   1987   641.594   87-47565
ISBN 0-553-05219-5

Published simultaneously in the United States and Canada

For my children,
Caspar, Francesca, Poppy, and Honey,
without whom there would not have been a book.

ACKNOWLEDGMENTS

Over the years many people from many countries have helped me in many ways with the preparation of this book, notably those whose names appear in the text. In addition to them, I owe particular gratitude for patient assistance in cultural and culinary matters to the staff of the London Library, Betty Molesworth Allen, Maurice de Ponton d'Amecourt, Bernard Augé, Elisabeth and Odbjorn Andreassen, Viviker and Richard Bernstrom, Tomas Bianchi, Mrs. Vasili Frunzete, Alfred Grisel, Christian Hesketh, Vane Ivanovic, Frau Klein, Mitte Lhoest, Cecilia McEwen, Maureen McGlashan, Kiki Munchi, Ilhan and Ruya Nebioglu, May Pocock, Dr. Astri Riddervold, Monica Rawlins, Erzbet Schmidl, Iolanda Tsalas, and Jacqueline Weir. Above all, my thanks to Priscilla Wintringham-White, who valiantly tested the recipes in my kitchen; to Fran McCullough, who has been inspiration, mentor, and midwife to the American edition of this book; and to my beloved husband and companion-at-table, Nicholas.

Contents

Introduction

The market stalls in the southern Spanish port of Algeciras, among which as a young wife and new mother I found myself and my basket one bright June morning in 1965, had very little in common with the shelves of the city supermarkets where I had been accustomed to shop. I was bewildered but intrigued. A childhood spent in several distant parts of the world with my parents, foreign-posted diplomats, had given me an early appetite for street-corner food. This youthful enthusiasm had also left me with an unshakable optimism that I could eat, and usually appreciate, anything that was palatable to any other human. I had discovered a single exception. Monday dinner, at the English boarding school to which I was periodically returned, invariably consisted of mouse-gray mincemeat accompanied by wet toast. I had never managed to stomach that, not even with an appetite sharpened by outdoor swimming at 7 A.M. on an English March morning.

The Algeciras market could not have produced a school dinner in a month of Mondays. The vegetable stalls which formed its outer ring were piled with unfamiliar greenery: a heap of *tagarnina*, thistle stems waving tarantulalike green extremities; bundles of fresh garlic, like ice-white onions; smiling pink segments of watermelon; purple-tipped cardoons tied as rosebud bouquets. Between the stalls little encampments of Gypsy children presided over sacks of tiny snails with translucent bodies and inquiring pin-stalk eyes, flanked by baskets of wild mushrooms and bundles of slender wild asparagus bound with esparto grass. The fish vendors, raised above their customers on a line of white-tiled stalls dripping seawater, bellowed out their wares: octopus, squid, cuttlefish, monkfish, sea bream, bass, anchovies, and sardines. The poultry market was livelier still. There were bunches of chickens squawking on the ends of brawny arms, a blue-eyed goose, and a few mournful turkeys gobbling in one corner—no Andalusian housewife would have trusted a dead barnyard bird as far as she could chase it. The spice lady must have had fifty open sacks around her: almonds, six kinds of tea, bay leaves, dried garlic and paprika, cloves and cinnamon bark, thyme, rosemary, marjoram, coriander, poppy seeds, licorice twigs, pumpkin seeds, dozens more. Often she would be asked to make up a flavoring mix: a paper twist of the herbs to spice four kilos of snails, to prepare a side of pork in paprika lard, to provide the aromatics for ten kilos of olives. Later I learned to rely on her expertise myself.

María, my neighbor up the valley where I and my growing family settled, was my mentor in those first years. "*Así se hace,*" she would patiently explain, "This is how it is done," as I struggled with the ink sacs in the cuttlefish, or attempted to cook the chick-peas without soaking them first. Very often she would come by with gifts of food for my children—honey from her uncle's hives, the first figs, wrapped in one of their own leaves, from the tree in her father's garden, oil biscuits which she had made after bread-baking day.

My family and I saw the seasons pass in the valley. The children went to the local school, where they learned along with the three R's how to trap and skin rabbits, how to stake pastures to hold the forest's hogs, and how to mend a hand-drawn threshing sled made to a design unchanged since the Iron Age. With María's advice and under her tutelage we acquired a donkey, a kitchen garden, and a household pig—the last, I stipulated, only if María helped me at its final hour. The pig thrived mightily on the scraps from my kitchen. Finally, on a late October day deemed suitable, the moon being in the right quarter and the pig having been fattened to the correct weight on acorns from the surrounding cork oaks, María's husband and brother-in-law arrived at sunrise to prepare for the dreaded event. Soon afterwards María, her cousins, and her mother appeared to help with the kitchen labor. The children were packed off to school early, and all day we worked salting hams, seasoning sausages, stuffing black puddings, and spicing *chorizos*. That evening, as she prepared the traditional celebration meal of *chicharros*, pork skin fried crisp; kidneys in sherry; and garlic-fried liver which follows a country *matanza* (butchering), María finally asked the question which made me embark on this book.

"Tell me," she said, her voice sympathetic as she leaned over the table and restored control of the sausage casing to my clumsy fingers for the fifth time, "I have been wanting to ask you ever since you and your family arrived, but I did not wish to seem inquisitive. Please forgive me, but did your mother teach you nothing at all?"

From then on, María became a surrogate mother in the old ways of the countryside to all of us. Seven years later, when we departed for the Languedoc to give the children a year's schooling in France, she came down the hill to see us on our way. As we climbed into our crammed vehicle, she handed a bundle in through the window. Inside was a bag of dried sunflower seeds—the children's favorite *pipas*, to be cracked between the teeth and the shell expertly propelled through the open window—a hank of dried sausage, and a gigantic loaf pricked with the baker's initials, a bread of the size normally baked for a cork tree-stripping gang on a two-week excursion into the hills.

"There," she said. "I could not bear to think you might be hungry on your journey."

Once we were established in the Languedoc, María's role in our lives was taken over by our neighboring farmer's wife, who kept a fine old-fashioned barnyard, pigeon loft, and piggery. Her three strapping sons and burly husband bore visible witness to her culinary skills. From her I learned how to choose a *foie gras* while it was still encased in the goose, how to pot a *confit*, and the correct way to layer a *cassoulet*—even how to bake the goose feathers to sterilize them for stuffing a feather pillow. When the time came in its turn for us to leave the Languedoc to return to England for the children to finish their schooling in a more conventional fashion, she also gave us a picnic basket for our journey. In it, wrapped in wax paper, were thick slices of her special cured ham, a cool square of sweet butter, and a big bunch of radishes from her garden. Nestling in one corner was a small bottle of *eau-de-vie aux cerneaux*—white walnut brandy—which the farmer himself distilled and flavored with leaves from his own tree. She too did not wish to see us leave hungry.

"I shall call peasants those who have, at the least, this in common: their agriculture is a livelihood and a way of life, not a business for profit." Thus Dr. Redfield defined "peasant" in his *Peasant Society and Culture*. Certainly both my neighbors in the Andalusian valley and on the plains of the Languedoc grew or earned a cash crop to supplement their way of life. María's mother told me that her mother used to raise silkworms for money to buy supplies of salt, a little coffee, spices, and a few other things which the household needed and could not make. But the pantries of both families were still filled largely from the fruits of their own labors. Even tea was grown in the garden. Today the pattern of European peasant life is changing swiftly, but throughout Eastern Europe the same pockets of self-sufficiency can still be found.

Peasant cookery must of its nature depend on ingredients which can be easily obtained or grown locally. The glow of embers on the hearth, a savory broth simmering in the cooking pot on its tripod, a flitch of bacon from last autumn's pig smoking in a hollow in the chimney—until very recently these were not nostalgic pleasures; for centuries they were the very stuff of life in Europe. Peasant cooking was always dominated by practical rather than economic factors. There are few peasant recipes for offal, since this was only available in quantity to the poor of the towns. Sugar was an expensive commodity in all but Ottoman-dominated Europe until recently, so there are few high-sugar dishes. Peasant communities had no organized trade. Barter was the chief form of exchange, and there were no regular tradesmen to supply goods or services. Fuel in particular was precious. It needed energy to collect and was often in short supply. In consequence, cooking was usually done on a single heat source.

Possessions were scarce: A medieval peasant kitchen would have been equipped with a boiling pot, a frying pan, and a kettle. As late as the seventeenth and eighteenth centuries the peasant house was only one room, plus barns and a storehouse. The fireplace was the focal point, whether there was a chimney to extract the smoke or not, and there would have been one large table with benches set around it, the benches also being used for sleeping. Early mattresses were of heaped straw and were replaced later by home-produced featherbedding. The whole household gathered together at mealtimes and ate from a communal bowl with wooden spoons—children often took their meals standing up. There were wooden boards for portions of bread, and a knife, often shared, for the meat. It was only after 1800 that sugar, coffee, and tea became widely available and affordable.

The limitations imposed by a single pot, a single heat source, local produce, and little or no access to imports are all characteristic of peasant cooking and give it its particular identity. But in no sense does this mean that the ingredients were necessarily poor or inferior: salmon, oysters, crayfish, snails, excellent cheeses, superb truffles and fungi, and an abundance of poultry and game were all available to local communities. Even the most sophisticated delicacies such as *foie gras* from the favorite table-bird of the peasantry, the goose, were as likely to be found in a French peasant's cupboard as in the kitchen of the Sun King. Each generation in a community might produce perhaps one particularly inspired cook, whose innovations would be added to the repertoire of the immediate area. This has led to variations of local dishes which are peculiar to an individual neighborhood and whose merits are fiercely contested—there are dozens of different recipes for the making of a Spanish *paella*, for instance, each dependent on the local ingredients. There is, however, an underlying philosophy which governs all the recipes for a particular dish, and an understanding of this allows the cook to experiment and adapt the recipe to her own local produce.

The peasant larder varied according to climate and conditions. Northern Europe—Scandinavia, Scotland, and northern Germany—makes good use of its seacoasts: Salted, sometimes smoked, and pickled fish, including salmon, were and are important items of the region's diet, as is dried meat. Barley, oats, and rye are the chief cereal crops. Central Europe is rich in wheat and dairy produce: Cheese, bacon, potatoes, vegetables, and the fruit of the vine are all plentiful, and this is reflected in the peasant cookery of Germany, Austria, Rumania, Hungary, Bulgaria, and northern France. The Mediterranean region, in particular Spain, Portugal, southern France, Italy, Greece, and Yugoslavia, has the advantage of olive oil, abundant vineyards, and citrus fruit to add to good supplies of fish from the long coastline, as well as a temperate climate for the growing of a great many varieties of vegetables.

The ideal of peasant life is probably most nearly represented by the philosophy of the rural Spanish revolutionaries of the 1920s: communal, supportive, and hardworking, yet allowing the individual enough dignity, freedom, and leisure to develop intellectually and physically—a most difficult ideal to achieve. All those who have had first-hand experience of peasant existence hark back to the fundamental issue: survival. In the peasant world, the work is perpetual and the living is hard. Yet most insist that the way of life has its own rewards in the satisfaction of tasks well completed, of responsibilities to the land properly discharged. The earth must be husbanded, coaxed, and cared for; it cannot be exploited or it will take swift revenge. The old peasant kitchen habits of frugality are part of that husbandry—making stock out of bones, pickling and salting in times of glut, stocking the pantry, using diet to care for the sick and the elderly, making good food out of few and simple ingredients.

This concern was reflected in real terms in the life expectancy of the peasantry such as that of England in feudal times who, having survived the dangerous childhood years, were likely to live longer and in better health than their overlord, who dined daily on large quantities of meat and fine white bread. The ordinary diet of the famously long-lived Georgians, listed by F. P.

Armitage in 1922, is quintessential peasant food—black bread, rice, wheat cakes, beans, raw green vegetables, cheese, milk both fresh and soured, and fish—salted, smoked, and dried. In poor communities which could not afford doctors, good health was clearly essential to survival, and country dwellers became extremely knowledgeable about the adjustments in diet necessary for those who were ill, or to combat seasonal maladies. Winter food was well-balanced for the winter months. Store-cupboards were stocked to restore seasonal imbalance. Traditional prejudices about what should be served with what were often based on sound and practical grounds of health. If any one phrase can summarize the peasant cuisine it is precisely that—good health.

"The diet of the European population at the beginning of modern times," says Diedrich Saarfeld, writing of pre-1585 Europe in *The Struggle to Survive*, "can be generally described as simple and nourishing: it consisted chiefly of the natural products of the countryside. The population was still relatively undifferentiated. It is not easy to find records of preparation and meals, but ingredients are listed. This simplicity held until the middle of the 17th century, when improved communication meant items such as grain and such stores could be transported."

The various grains—wheat, rye, and barley in particular—were usually milled and made into bread, sometimes kneaded with whey or milk to give added food value, sometimes mixed with eggs and butter and dried fruit for a special occasion. Most peasant farmers baked their own bread in their own ovens or in the village communal oven. If there was no oven, the milled grain might be eaten as porridge, noodles, or flat cakes and pancakes. During the week this cereal diet would be supplemented with milk products such as butter, curds and cheese, eggs and animal fats, with occasionally some fish and meat. Catholic Europe ate fish, dried and pickled, on fast days and during Lent. The rest of Europe, with the exception of Scandinavia, did not often eat it. Meat was usually cooked in the stock pot which hung permanently over the fire, and eaten either with a dumpling, cloth-wrapped and boiled in the broth, or with bread. Roasting was only for Sunday or special occasions.

Premodern (pre-1585) Mediterranean Europe came under the influence of two major Eastern invaders: the Moorish Muslims, who occupied southern Spain from 711 until Ferdinand and Isabella's campaign of 1492; and the Turks of the Islamic Ottoman Empire, who dominated central and eastern Europe from the dissolution of the Byzantine Empire in the thirteenth century until the early years of the twentieth century.

Both civilizations took a lively interest in the pleasures of the table, and both left their culinary mark on the populations they conquered. Among the skills and refinements learned from the Moors by the Iberian peoples were the art of making sweets and the use of almonds—it was the Moors who planted Jordan almond trees in Andalusia. The Turkish skill in pastry making and the technique of layering fine sheets of filo pastry spread as far north as Austria, where the strudel dumpling became the strudel pastries which today keep such delightful company with that other Turkish introduction, coffee. Turkish *dolmades*—vine leaves stuffed with rice and meat—traveled from the Bosporous, via Bulgaria, Rumania, and Hungary (the Turks planted rice in the Danube basin), as far north as Scandinavia, where the Swedish national dish of stuffed cabbage rolls, *kåldomar*, still keeps its Turkish semantic origin.

After 1492 an astonishing wealth of new ingredients began to arrive from the New World via Spain and Italy. Today it is hard to imagine how Mediterranean and Balkan cooks managed without tomatoes, peppers, eggplants, and beans for their stews and sauces; or indeed how Eastern Europe fared without the corn, pumpkin, and squashes which now fill their collectivized fields; or how the Hungarians survived until the arrival, via the Ottoman Turks, of their beloved paprika. The potato, the most important New World contribution of all, the ingredient which fueled Europe's population explosion of the eighteenth and nineteenth centuries, took longest to achieve acceptance.

By the sixteenth century, the appetites of the increasingly prosperous townfolk had pushed the price of meat beyond the purchasing power of the peasant, leaving him with the products of his pig and his barnyard. By the end of the eighteenth century the population was increasing so rapidly that even the price of bread began to climb steeply. The peasantry had to find a substitute for the daily grain meal: The potato, undemanding of space and labor and thus the ideal poor man's food, came into its own at last. The adaptable new foodstuff was cooked according to the custom of the country in which it found itself, to the extent that the modern traveler will find regional potato recipes a very good indicator of local culinary habits. The Scots make scones with their supplies; the Spanish fry theirs in olive oil; the Hungarians have a delicious paprika potato stew; the Germans make potato dumplings; the Italians make *gnocchi;* the English plain-roast or boil their crop; the French make wonderful *garbures* and gratins with theirs; the Swiss like theirs with melted cheese.

Such a rapidly acquired dependence on one major foodstuff, did, however, leave the peasantry extremely vulnerable. In 1846–47 terrible weather conditions caused the failure of both the potato and the wheat harvests, and brought in its wake the last great European famine. The peasants of Europe suffered appallingly. In Ireland 1 million out of a total population of 8 million died of starvation. Europe now began to import grain from the limitless granaries of the New World. Grain, unlike the potato, has a very long shelf life, is easily stored, and can feed both the urban populations and the domestic animals whose meat is still in such high demand in the cities. European farming was never the same again.

Eastern Europe lagged somewhat behind the rest in its development. By the nineteenth century, peasant communities of the east were at about the same practical level as those of Western Europe had been during the seventeenth and eighteenth centuries. On feast days people still roasted whole animals, stuffed themselves on puddings, and washed it all down with copious supplies of home-brewed alcohol.

Britain was a special case: England began to lose her rural peasant population in medieval times, largely as a result of the land enclosures which proceeded unopposed after the Restoration in 1660 and forced the independent peasantry away from the countryside. In Scotland the same dispossession continued with the Highland Clearances until Victorian times. Insofar as the native British tradition of peasant cooking survived, it was in an amended form in the nurseries of the upper and middle classes.

Throughout Europe during the nineteenth and twentieth centuries large town-based populations of landless workers continued to grow. High-yield farms were necessary to feed them, and the subsistence-farming peasantry, particularly sharecropping tenants, were rapidly squeezed out of their smallholdings by larger and often absentee landowners who farmed exclusively for profit. Only in the most isolated communities, such as those of southern Spain, Greece, southern Italy, and Eastern Europe, could the peasant culture withstand the economic pressures. Even so, the shift to the towns continues to depopulate large areas of previously marginally viable farmland.

European peasant cookery is immensely old. It has evolved, it has been tried and tested, over centuries, perhaps over thousands of years. Throughout its existence the patiently gathered hard-won knowledge it incorporates has been passed on orally. Like all orally transmitted traditions, it is only as strong as the last link in the chain of communication. Today our predominantly urban-dwelling, industrialized population must rely on increasingly mechanized methods of food production: The standard American hot dog is now made from ingredients few people can identify; it is difficult to associate the bread roll which encloses it with the great gray millstones turned by the harnessed power of water or wind which formerly ground the wheat into flour, or the mustard which spices the hot dog itself with the seed of those pretty yellow-blossomed flowers which bloomed in ancient meadows. The home cook is inevitably distanced from the primary products of field and barnyard, dairy, piggery, and kitchen garden—and the checks and balances of season and economy have disappeared. Most peasant meals would have been (and still are in those communities which survive) structured around a single dominant ingredient at a single moment—when the new peas were at their best, the pig had just been slaughtered, the hens' laying was particularly prolific.

For that reason I have arranged this book around ingredients rather than in the more customary soup-fish-meat-sweet divisions. This reflects the central importance of the raw materials—that in the peasant world, the "real" world of climate and season, of mountain and plain, forest, meadow, and shoreline, with all their changing patterns and rhythms, it was not possible simply to go out and buy an ingredient if it was lacking, and that seasonal abundance was far more likely to dictate the composition of the meal than whim. Most of the recipes, therefore, include suggestions for the completion of the meal of which they are the centerpiece—the suggestions, equally, coming from the same ancient tradition of what was available, excellent to the taste, and nutritionally appropriate.

Apart from those leisurely foundation years spent in wild Spain and rural France, my practical research has taken me into markets and kitchens, storehouses and vegetable gardens, farms and vineyards across Europe from the North Cape to the Golden Horn. I have been met everywhere with great courtesy and generosity, although sometimes with surprise that anyone should need to write down things which are so obvious. In those places where the demands of modern life have all but obliterated the traces of the old ways, even the most sophisticated of restaurant chefs still remember with nostalgic pleasure the dishes Mother used to make, and recall their own then-small fingers helping to rub suet or mold dumplings.

Such recipes and methods are best demonstrated, as my Spanish neighbor María knew well, by mothers to daughters, fathers to sons: the moment to pick the plum, the exact brining necessary for a particular ham from a particular pig fattened in a particular oak wood. Even the ancient earthenware *toupin*, whose curve is precisely right for the beans of Soissons, is perhaps an essential part of the "true" recipe. Yet in the course of my travels I became aware that there can be no definitive recipes, just as there are no definitive mothers and fathers. What I am sure of is that there do exist old and exemplary culinary traditions which are passed on by good cooks, working within the boundaries of their own local produce, from one generation to the next.

They are the "mother-recipes" from which all European cookery springs—whether it be bourgeois or haute cuisine, fast food or high-fiber diets. For most of us in the Western world they are as integral a part of our past, and of what shapes and nourishes us today, as our literature and songs, our paintings and technology.

As María would say in the old Spanish greeting to those at table: *"Gracias a Dios—buen provecho."* Thanks be to God—much good may it do you.

Note to the Reader

The recipes in this book, more than five hundred of them, come from twenty-five European countries, ranging from Ireland in the west to Rumania in the east, Iceland in the north to Turkey in the south. The book does not cover Poland and Czechoslovakia, partly because these two cuisines did not come under the immediate influence of the Ottoman Turks, and partly because, particularly in the case of Poland, they derive from a different tradition which looks further east for its inspiration, and which deserves a whole book to itself.

So ancient is European peasant cuisine that attributing recipes on a national basis is always difficult, especially where countries share a common historical past and borders which have moved backwards and forwards with conquest and reconquest. Northern France and southern Germany share with the Low Countries a wide variety of sauerkraut, sausage, and sweet bread recipes which differ only regionally. The Swiss share their *garbures* and melted-cheese recipes with eastern France and northern Italy. The Balkans and Greece have a common culinary heritage left by their lengthy domination by the Turks. The Ottoman Turks were also responsible, through their trade with the Venetians, for the introduction to Eastern Europe of the crops from the New World—the arrival of these vegetables (including potatoes, corn, tomatoes, beans, and the capsicum pepper) in the wake of Christopher Columbus' voyage was the single most revolutionary culinary event of recent times.

Conquest is the most persuasive instructor of all. The Romans replanted the kitchen gardens of Europe in their time. The Moors taught their Iberian servants how to cook new and sophisticated stews, how to prepare sweetmeats, and how to plant and cook rice. The Turks performed a similar service at the other end of the Mediterranean. The English learned to drink gin in Holland during their wars with the Dutch. The returning Crusaders spread the ingredients and recipes of the east throughout their home territories. The exodus of the persecuted Huguenots of France brought not only their skilled workmanship to the countries in which they settled but also their culinary expertise. Many a poor man's pot was tastier after he had married a daughter of the refugees—and that most British of dishes, oxtail stew, appears to owe its inspiration to the impoverished Huguenots.

There were less obvious arteries of culinary exchange, such as the trade routes which supplied the great medieval fairs with their spices and other treasures from the East; or the Venetian trade with China, opened by Marco Polo, which afforded new recipes for pasta and, incidentally, instruction in the use of coal to heat the cooking pot. The pilgrim roads, like the ones which led across the Pyrenees to the great Christian holy place of Santiago de Compostela, kept the culinary lines of communication open: the Hungarians, Yugoslavs, Italians, French, and Basques were all linked across the Pyrenees by these routes. All share many common preparations including tomato-and-pimento sauces and a variety of very similar bean-and-pork dishes such as the Spanish *cocido*, the French *cassoulet*, and the Balkan bean soups. The other dominant traders of Europe in the Middle Ages were the German merchants of the Hanseatic League, who controlled the export of salt cod from Scandinavia to its customers in southern Europe, offering in return salt, grain, and spices. Salt cod provided the raw material for the *brandade de morue* and other Lenten dishes of the Mediterranean, while the rice that went north in exchange was used for the stuffed cabbage leaves and the Christmas porridge which are both considered among Scandinavia's native dishes.

Seamen took their culinary habits with them when they put in to foreign ports: A stew of potatoes and fish or meat which is cooked until dry and then allowed to fry, called "scouse" in Liverpool and *skaus* in the kitchens of Hamburg, appears with minor variations in every seaside hamlet and in the galley of every fishing smack from the North Cape to the Algarve. Sea routes make good highways: the Phoenicians, trading oranges for tin with the Cornish coastal dwellers, left a trail of recipes for fish soup from the straits of the Bosporus to the North Sea. There were many of these points of contact. Until recent times the Norwegians conducted a three-cornered trade exchanging their harvest of wild berries for cloth with the wool merchants of Yorkshire, and sugar and spices with the merchants of Amsterdam. The sailors' girls must surely have discussed recipes for jams to be made with the berries, and found out how Mother made her porridge and oatcakes at home in Bergen, while the Dutch women would certainly have had a few tips for spicing the herring catch.

When I began the on-the-spot research in those countries in which I had not lived, I was delighted to find how accurate my literary mentors had been, and how many of the customs they described were still evident in modern culinary practices. Many of the traditional dishes are now transmuted into the packets and tins of the supermarket shelves, and these can be excellent sources of basic information on local preferences. The herb garden betrays the house-wife's secret ingredients: chives and chervil in a German backyard, parsley and mint in Britain. But the best information source of all is the marketplace, where ingredients for the old recipes are still to be found lined up on a single stall, whose proprietor is often willing and able to explain the use of his or her wares: potatoes and peppers for a Galician stew (a dish which reappears in Hungary, one of whose original tribes, the Ruthenians, came from Galicia long before the arrival of these New World ingredients). In the markets of Tuscany, all the seasonal *minestrone* vegetables are displayed on the same stall. A housewife buying her fish on a Marseilles wharf will look for the crate with the selection of spiny rockfish which go into a *bouillabaisse*. The street food offered for sale to the early-rising housewives when their marketing is done is still true to its customers' ancient tastes: liver and pickles in Hungary, fritters in Spain, stuffed whole roast pig in Italy. Finally, I learned that today as in the past true country people everywhere will still share a meal with a stranger, and explain with tolerance and patience how to cook it.

I found the travels of all these dishes fascinating, and I am only sorry they cannot be explored at more length here. The book should, of course, be many times its present length—but it is already bursting its seams, and, if I were to do the subject the justice it deserves, I would need at least double the twenty-five years already invested in its compilation. Among so much I have reluctantly had to jettison are some of the classic recipes for foods that simply are not available commercially in America—for instance, herring. There are others, particularly from Eastern Europe, where national identities are so blurred by invasion and conquest that some dishes are near-identical but appear under different names. Often I have had to select on the basis of a particular recipe's importance in its national kitchen. Sometimes I have included or rejected a dish on grounds of taste—my children in particular found that they were testers for more than enough northern cabbage recipes, and pleaded for a week or two on the sweet vegetables of Provence.

Perhaps you have a favorite dish that has not surfaced here—I only wish I could have included many, many more. What I can assure you is that every one of these recipes has been tested in my own kitchen—except for a very few, such as the Swedish *surströmming*, which requires the full attentions of the great Scandinavian outdoors. All the recipes tasted very good indeed to both our testers and our families. I hope you have similar success and, every now and then, a revelation. There is a particular pleasure in carrying on this ancient tradition, and in creating once again the delicious and healthy food that has sustained our fellow creatures for so many centuries.

CHAPTER ONE

Vegetable Dishes

A well-tended vegetable patch is the most valuable storehouse a peasant family can have. A tiny plot carefully maintained can keep a family healthy if not wealthy. There is a great feeling of security in fertile earth—my city neighbor, himself two generations away from his Sardinian peasant ancestors, still coaxes his little urban patch into life each spring. His sunflowers, cabbages, potatoes, corn, onions, plums, and apples are available cheaply and for no effort just down the way. He leans over my wall each spring and explains that he does not know why he puts in so much effort for a reward so easily bought with money in our local shops. "I can't help it," he says. "Every year I sow; every year I reap little in this terrible climate of the north. But it makes me feel good; it makes me feel safe to know my sunflower seeds will be ready for drying each September."

The gardens of Eastern Europe fringe the trunk roads which carry quotas—cabbages and seed oils for export only—to the State's collective storehouses. Each peasant farmer guards his own long, thin patch of ground, even if he goes daily to work in the local factory or collective farm. Cabbages, potatoes, maize, pumpkins, garlic, onions, and paprika peppers are his main concern—the good solid staples with no frills which are the preoccupation of those who grow food to survive.

The vegetable gardens of Finland and northern Scandinavia produce those things which can germinate and mature in the short summers available. Potatoes are a reasonably safe crop, although sometimes the ground freezes again before they can be dug. Rhubarb, adapted to a Tibetan climate, gives the first fruit of the spring. Raspberries, strawberries, and currants will ripen, and with luck, cabbage can form good solid heads before the winter closes in. A brief crop of lettuces, little onions, dill, and parsley can be coaxed from the soil in the twenty-four-hour sunlight of the three months of summer.

The south has other concerns: Irrigation is the first priority. The vegetable patch of a Mediterranean family is usually carefully located near the stream so that the young shoots can easily be watered. My neighbors in

Mirabel in the Baronnies of Provence grew garlic and onions, beans and chick-peas, spinach, carrots, potatoes, parsley, cabbage, and chard. Sometimes, if there was time, the father would plant peppers, tomatoes, and eggplant too. The garlic and onions were braided into ropes and hung in the barn. When the dried beans were gathered at the end of the summer, it was the grandfather who sat on the stoop in the autumn sunshine, stripping and podding the winter's supplies.

HOT VEGETABLE SOUPS

MIXED-VEGETABLE SOUP

Minestrone (Italy)

Minestrone should be so thick with vegetables that a wooden spoon will stand up in it. Signor Bertorelli, the famous London restaurateur, recalls that the diet of his family—his father and four brothers—living on the small family farm near Parma during the first half of the twentieth century, was *minestrone* and *polenta*, with one pig slaughtered annually.

The best *minestrone* is made with the stock left over from the boiling of a ham or one of the Italian stuffed sausages such as *zampone*. The vegetables, herbs, and pasta content is open to any variation you please, as long as all three elements are present. If you are using plain water, or if the stock you have is uninteresting, add a few cubes of *prosciutto* or a little chopped lean bacon to the pot.

SERVES: 4 to 6

TIME: 1 hour

2	*large carrots, scraped and sliced*	1	*small bunch of parsley, chopped*
1/3	*cup olive oil*	2	*large potatoes, peeled and cut*
1	*large onion, chopped*		*into small cubes*
2	*celery stalks, chopped*	2	*ounces dried short macaroni or*
2	*large tomatoes, peeled and*		*any medium-sized pasta shape*
	chopped	4	*outside leaves of green cabbage*
1	*quart water or stock*		*Salt and pepper*

You will need a large saucepan. Dice the carrots if they are large. Warm the oil in the saucepan, and then add the carrots, onion and celery. Leave them to stew gently.

Add the tomatoes to the pot, and mash them in as they melt in the heat. Add the water or stock and sprinkle in the parsley. Simmer for 10 minutes. Put in the cubed potatoes. Simmer for 10 minutes longer. Add the pasta. Simmer for another 10 minutes, until the vegetables are soft and the pasta is well cooked.

Taste and adjust the seasoning. Mash in a few of the vegetables to thicken the liquid a little before you serve it. Pass around a bowl of grated cheese.

◆

SUGGESTIONS

Stir in a spoonful of *pesto* (page 3) to make the Provençal *soupe au pistou*.
One 8-ounce can of tomatoes can substitute for the fresh variety.
Four ounces of cooked white *cannellini* beans can replace the pasta.
So indeed can a handful of rice or a few crumbled slices of stale bread.
Swiss chard and zucchini can be added in season.
Use the *tarhonya* noodles (page 163) instead of the macaroni. They work beautifully in this soup.

Leftovers: Toast a piece of bread for each diner, and rub it with garlic. Put the toast into the bottom of each bowl, and pour the hot soup over. Top with a little fresh olive oil and a scattering of chopped chives or scallions before you serve it. Or float the bread on top; then sprinkle it with cheese and brown it under the broiler.

◆

BAVARIAN HERB SOUP

Krautlsuppe (Germany)

Bitter herbs are traditionally eaten at Easter in Christian countries as a sign of penitence. This Bavarian soup is served on Easter Thursday, known as Maundy Thursday. Fresh chervil, easily available in any German market, is usually the dominating flavor. This is a delicate fresh-tasting soup for any time of year.

SERVES: 4

TIME: 30 minutes plus 15 minutes cooking

1 pound herbs: at least three of these: chervil, watercress, spinach, sorrel (dandelion and pimpernel for brave souls)	1 quart water or vegetable stock
	1 large potato, peeled and chopped into small cubes
2 ounces butter (4 tablespoons)	Salt and pepper
1 large onion, chopped	Bread cubes for croutons

You will need a large saucepan. Pick over and wash the herbs, stripping the leaves from those stalks which are too woody. Chop the rest.

Melt the butter in a deep pan and fry the onion gently until transparent. Add the herbs and sweat them for a moment before you pour in the water or broth. Add the potato to the soup. Bring the soup to a boil, and then turn down the heat. Simmer for 20 minutes. Mash the potato in the soup to thicken it a little. Taste, and add salt and freshly milled pepper.

Serve with bread croutons fried in butter or bacon fat (goose fat is even better). They should be so hot that they sizzle when they are added to the hot soup at the table.

SUGGESTIONS

Experiment with your own favorite herbs.

Try young nettle tops in the early spring (just the top four leaves of the spring shoots—don't forget to wear gloves when you pick them).

DILL SOUP

Koper Juba (Yugoslavia)

A wonderfully simple and fresh-tasting recipe from Serbia, the same soup can be made with thyme, tarragon, caraway—any herb which you favor or can grow easily. Keep it to a single herb: this is about the best way to appreciate its individual fragrance.

SERVES: 4

TIME: 20 minutes

1 tablespoon butter	*2 egg yolks*
1 tablespoon flour	*½ cup sour cream*
1 quart chicken stock (homemade	*Salt and pepper*
* from a chicken carcass)*	*Bread cubes for croutons*
1 big handful of fresh dill, chopped	
* fine*	

You will need a medium saucepan. Melt the butter in the saucepan. When it foams, add the flour. Cook the flour until the mixture looks sandy but has not yet browned. Stir in the stock, beating so that no lumps form. Bring to a boil and simmer for 5 to 10 minutes. Stir in the dill and keep stirring for another 5 minutes. Beat the egg yolks and the sour cream together, and pour the mixture into a soup tureen.

Remove the soup from the heat, taste, and adjust the seasoning with salt and pepper. Pour the hot liquid onto the egg yolks and sour cream in the tureen. Pass hot croutons fried in butter. A well-spiced sausage, plain grilled, might follow.

◆

PUMPKIN SOUP

Kuerbissupe (Germany)

Pumpkin is both undemanding in its cultivation and a very convenient vegetable for storage, hence for making a winter soup.

SERVES: 4

TIME: 20 minutes plus 20 to 30 minutes cooking

One 2-pound piece of pumpkin		2	tablespoons wine vinegar
2	cups water	2	ounces butter (4 tablespoons)
6	cloves		Salt, pepper, sugar
1	small piece of cinnamon stick		

Peel the pumpkin and scoop out the seeds and the fibrous middle. Cut the flesh into cubes, and put them in a saucepan with the water (it looks like too little, but the pumpkin itself is full of water). Add the cloves and the cinnamon (tie them into a little cheesecloth bag—easy to remove). Stew the pumpkin gently with the spices for 20 to 30 minutes, until soft.

Take out the spices; then, in a blender, puree the pumpkin with its cooking liquid. Stir in the vinegar. Heat again and beat in the butter. Season with salt, plenty of freshly milled black pepper, and a little sugar to bring out the sweetness of the vegetable. This is a very delicate, amber-clear soup (resist the temptation to stir in cream or it will be cloudy and lose its innocence).

Complete the meal with a sweet dumpling, a strudel, or a fruit tart.

◆

PUMPKIN SOUP

Swp Pwmpen (Wales)

Many peasant communities took advantage of the pumpkin's tractability, as Lady Llanover pointed out in the middle of the last century:

Perhaps Gower in South Wales is the only part of the United Kingdom where pumpkins are grown as an article of diet by the rural population; and there they are to be seen, as on the Continent, hanging from the ceilings for winter store, and any little spare corner in the field or garden is made use of to place the small mound on which to sow a few pumpkin seeds . . . In Gower they are added to hashed meat, made into pies with apples, and put into soup. Pumpkins have one peculiar quality in addition to a good deal of natural sweetness: they will absorb and retain the flavour of whatever they are cooked with. If stewed with plums it tastes exactly like them in puddings and tarts; the same with apples, rhubarb or gooseberries; and for savoury cookery it would be difficult to say in what dish it may not be used with advantage as an addition. [*The First Principles of Good Cookery*, Lady Llanover, 1867]

SERVES: 4 to 6

TIME: 10 minutes plus 3 hours cooking

1 *whole pumpkin, 8 to 12 inches in diameter*	½ *teaspoon salt*
	Pepper
3 *to 4 cups half-and-half*	*Bread cubes for croutons*

Preheat the oven to 300°F. You will need an oven-to-table baking dish and a ricer or a blender.

Cut off a lid from the stalk end of the pumpkin. Scoop out the pith and the seeds. Put the pumpkin in the baking dish. Fill the hollow with the half-and-half (the liquid shouldn't come more than two thirds up the pumpkin, so adjust the quantity according to the size of the hollow) making sure you have room for at least 3 cups. Add the salt and give a few turns of the pepper mill.

Replace the lid on the pumpkin, and then put it in a low oven to bake. A medium-sized pumpkin takes 3 hours at 300°F. At the end of that time the pumpkin flesh will be soft and the skin will still be whole—though somewhat collapsed and fragile. Scoop out the insides—liquid, flesh, and all—taking care not to puncture the pumpkin. Then either push the solids through a ricer or process everything in a blender. Return the soup to the pumpkin and carry it to the table.

Serve the soup straight from the pumpkin into bowls. Who needs a tureen when you can have the natural-grown container? Pass hot croutons fried in butter. You won't need anything heavy after this rich soup—just a simple grilled lamb chop accompanied by a few new potatoes.

◆

CABBAGE SOUP WITH BACON

Ciorba teraneasca (Rumania)

D. J. Hall had a good supper at the village priest's home in pre-Second World War Rumania:

> As we drank our cabbage soup, Stanescu told me of his difficulties in getting the cooking to his taste.
>
> "This now, it is delicious." He pursed his lips. "But most of the peasants throw in a cabbage, boil it, and call it soup. I pick only the finest of my cabbages, choose only the tender leaves, flavour it with green peppers, put in a little bacon and then. You see . . ." Pressing his forefinger to his thumb, he expressed its exquisite delicacy.
>
> So with the fried chicken and the cheese pancakes which followed he told me minutely how they should be cooked. It was certainly a meal such as I had not tasted for a long while. [*Romanian Furrow*, D. J. Hall, 1939]

S E R V E S : 6

T I M E : 20 minutes plus 50 minutes cooking

One 8-ounce slab of bacon, sliced	Several sprigs of dill and savory,
2 onions, sliced	chopped
2 green peppers, hulled and	1½ quarts water
chopped	2 egg yolks
1 cabbage, cut into slices	½ cup heavy cream (sweet or sour)
Salt and pepper	1 tablespoon vinegar

You will need a large soup pot. Chop up one slice of the bacon, and fry it in a heavy stewpan until the fat runs. Fry the onions in the fat until they are golden. Add the peppers and fry them too. Remove the stewpan from the heat. Layer the cabbage and the rest of the bacon into the soup pot. Season between the layers with salt and pepper and the herbs.

Pour the water over it all and bring to a boil. Turn the heat down, and simmer the soup for 40 to 50 minutes, until the vegetables are tender. Remove the soup from the heat.

Beat the egg yolks with the cream and the vinegar in a little bowl. Stir in a ladleful of the hot soup. Whisk well and pour the mixture back into the soup to thicken and enrich it.

Serve in deep bowls accompanied with fresh bread. This soup is a meal in itself, and wants only a piece of cheese and fresh fruit to make it complete.

◆

SIBIU-SAXON SOUP

Eintopfgericht (Rumania)

The Sibiu Saxons, formerly citizens of the Austro-Hungarian Empire and today Rumanian nationals, are still, after eight centuries, blond and blue-eyed and purely Saxon. The Saxons of Sibiu and its seven surrounding villages are very orderly: Their children receive Saxon schooling in the shadow of their austere, cavernous Lutheran church, newly reroofed with beautiful glazed viridian tiles made to the old pattern. The Transylvanian plain on which Sibiu stands beneath the Carpathians has never been a peaceful thoroughfare. The Saxons fortified their churches and defended their own throughout the centuries against would-be conquerors and marauders.

Their cooking is as conservative as their religion, reflecting its German origins. An appetite for Eastern spices in breads, cakes, and dried sausages was supplied until 1980 by the "foreigners' market," held on Tuesdays and Saturdays in a corner of the arcade in the market square. Silks and carpets, coffee and tea also came with the Turkish traders in the old days. The most beautiful carpets went to commemorate prominent Saxon citizens in the Black Church at Brasov—where they still glow like dark jewels. Sadly, there are no more "foreigners' markets" in modern Rumania, and the Saxons have to manage as best they can.

SERVES: 6

TIME: 40 minutes

1 whole cabbage, cut into slices	1 pound onions, sliced
½ pound knockwurst	2 to 3 egg yolks
7 cups water	½ cup heavy cream
1 teaspoon salt	1 tablespoon chopped fresh herbs
4 to 5 slices of day-old bread (black or white)	(marjoram, savory, dill, parsley)
2 tablespoons oil or butter	

You will need a large saucepan, a soup tureen, a frying pan, and a small bowl. Put the cabbage in a deep saucepan with the knockwurst, water, and salt. Bring to a boil, and then turn down the heat. Simmer for 20 minutes, until the cabbage is well cooked and the broth flavored with the sausage.

While the soup is cooking, turn your attention to the rest of the operation: Put the slices of bread into the soup tureen. Heat the oil or butter in a frying pan, and sauté the onions until they are soft and golden. Lay them on the bread. Mix the egg yolks with the cream in a bowl, and then whisk in a spoonful of hot broth from the soup.

By now the soup should be ready, so remove it from the heat, take out the knockwurst, and stir in the egg yolk-and-cream mixture and the herbs. Cut up the knockwurst, and lay the slices on top of the bread and onions in the tureen. Pour the cabbage soup over everything.

Serve a compote of fruit and a slice of cake after the soup, and your meal will be complete.

◆

SIBIU-SAXON SALAD—SOUP

Salatsuppe (Rumania)

Frau Klein, wife of the Lutheran bishop of Sibiu, whose recipe this is, says these soup-stew dishes are typical of the ancient dishes: "Characteristic of the special meals of Transylvania's Saxon peasants is a kind of soup or *eintopfgericht*, one-pan meal, which can be eaten with the spoon. The meat is always cut before, and bread is always used."

SERVES: 6

TIME: 40 minutes

3   firm lettuces (cos or iceberg are best), shredded
1½ quarts water
1   teaspoon salt
One 2-ounce slab of bacon, cubed
1   ounce (2 tablespoons) butter
2   ounces (½ cup) flour

½   cup milk
2 to 3 eggs
1   tablespoon wine vinegar or malt vinegar
Pepper
Several sprigs of dill and savory, chopped

You will need a large soup pot. Put the lettuce to simmer in the soup pot with the water and the salt for 20 minutes.

Meanwhile, put the bacon into a hot dry pan with the butter to fry gently. When the cubes are browned, take them out and add them to the soup. Meanwhile, mix the flour to a thick cream with the milk, and then beat in the eggs. Fry the egg mixture a tablespoonful at a time in the hot bacon fat. Cut these little pancakes into strips and add them to the soup.

Bring the soup to a boil and stir in the vinegar. Taste, and adjust the seasoning with salt and pepper. Sprinkle in the dill and savory. Serve very hot, with dark rye bread. Follow with a dish of *mamaliga* and poppy seeds (page 126).

◆

SPINACH BOUILLABAISSE

Bouillabaisse d'épinards (France)

A very popular country soup and an excellent light lunch, the greens used in it can be varied from Swiss chard through the repertoire of edible green leaves (including cabbage) which the Provençal farmer's wife is likely to grow in her vegetable patch. *Bouillabaisse* is a description of the cooking method rather than the ingredients—the soup is boiled very fast to allow reduction by evaporation.

SERVES: 4

TIME: 40 minutes

2 *pounds spinach (or the equivalent frozen)*	4 *medium potatoes (yellow potatoes are preferable to white for this dish), peeled and sliced*
1 *quart water*	1 *teaspoon salt*
2 *garlic cloves*	½ *teaspoon of saffron*
1 *branch of fennel*	4 *eggs*
1 *tablespoon olive oil*	4 *slices of dry bread*
1 *onion, minced*	

You will need a saucepan and a large soup pot (an earthenware marmite is the proper utensil). Wash the spinach carefully (if it is fresh), and put it in a pan. Cook it in its own moisture for 5 minutes, until the leaves are wilted. Drain and then chop the spinach finely. If you are using frozen spinach, defrost, drain, and chop it.

Put the water to boil. Peel the garlic and crush it—a blow from the flat blade of a heavy knife will serve the purpose. Chop the fennel into short lengths.

Warm the oil in the soup pot. Add the onion and cook it until it is transparent. Push it to one side. Add the spinach and turn it in the oil. Add the potatoes and then the boiling water. Now add the salt, garlic, fennel, and saffron. Bring the soup rapidly to a boil. Simmer for 20 minutes, until the potatoes are cooked. When you are ready to serve, slide 1 egg per person onto the surface of the simmering soup. Poach the eggs gently for 2 to 3 minutes, so that the whites set into a white veil for the soft yolks.

Serve in deep soup plates, with an egg and a slice of dry bread in each. Be careful not to break the eggs as you take them from the broth.

◆

SUGGESTIONS

Make a *bouillabaisse de petits pois* by replacing the spinach with 2 pounds of little shelled peas, possibly even better tasting than the spinach.

Replace the dry bread with little croutons fried in olive oil perfumed with garlic.

◆

GARLIC SOUP

Sopa de ajo (Spain and Mediterranean)

"Gina Ciccia, how often do you bake?"

"Every twelve days."

"How long does it take to heat the oven?"

"Half an hour in August, but in winter, when the walls are damp, perhaps an hour."

A Colonial housewife used to piling wood into her brick oven would have rebelled if expected to bake with no fuel but grape prunings, but in Gina Ciccia's land, these are good fuel; the woman who bakes with thorn twigs or brambles is the one to pity.

"And the bread, does it get dry?"

"Hard as a stone to kill a dog. Too hard to eat without grinding teeth. But at night if there is no cooked food one boils water with a little garlic and dips in the bread. That is good." [*By-Paths in Sicily*, Eliza Putnam Heaton, 1920]

SERVES: 4

TIME: 10 to 15 minutes

8	*garlic cloves*	5	*cups water*
4	*tablespoons olive oil*	½	*teaspoon salt*
4	*slices of stale bread*	4	*eggs*

Peel the garlic cloves and crush them with the flat blade of a knife. Put the oil to warm in a fireproof casserole or roomy saucepan. Add the garlic cloves and the slices of bread. Fry both gently together until they take color. Add the water and the salt, and bring all to the boil. Simmer gently for 10 minutes.

Slip in the four eggs one by one. Allow them to poach gently for 5 minutes. Serve each person with a bowl of soup and an egg.

◆

SUGGESTIONS

Those nervous about poaching eggs may prefer to hard-boil them first and add them quartered or sliced to the finished soup.

A sprinkling of chopped ham can be added.

A very similar soup appears in southern France as *aigo-boulido*. To make the French version, stir the beaten eggs into the soup once you have removed it from the fire so that they cook immediately in the hot liquid and thicken the broth.

◆

ONION SOUP

Soupe à l'oignon (France)

The soup of the market men of Les Halles in Paris, this is very comforting on an icy morning in the French capital, and a universal staple, with minor amendments, throughout the rest of Europe.

SERVES: 4

TIME: 20 minutes plus 20 minutes cooking

3 ounces (6 tablespoons) butter	4 to 8 slices of day-old bread
1½ pounds onions, sliced thin	4 ounces grated cheese (Cantal,
5 cups cold water	Gruyère, cheddar)
Salt and pepper	

Preheat the oven to 300°F. You will need a large saucepan or earthenware marmite. Put the butter to melt in the saucepan and throw in the onions. Cook them gently, stirring every now and then, for 10 minutes, until they are soft and golden. Add the water. Bring the soup to a boil, and season with salt and pepper. Turn down to simmer. Leave on a low heat for 20 minutes.

Meanwhile, put the slices of bread to dry in a low (300°F) oven. Put each slice in the bottom of a soup bowl. Pour the soup over and serve. Pass the cheese separately.

This is a very simple soup, but excellent if prepared with care. If you would like a more dramatic version, let the bread bob to the top of the soup,

sprinkle it with cheese, and flash it under the broiler to melt and gild the
cheese. But do try it once without these refinements.

SUGGESTIONS

Thicken the soup with a couple of eggs beaten first with a tablespoon of
vinegar and a ladleful of the hot soup. Don't reboil it once the eggs have been
stirred in. Or stir in a little cream.

GREEN PEA SOUP WITH DUMPLINGS

Gronaertesuppe mit melboller (Denmark)

Although at its best made with tender young peas, this soup can be made with
peas late in the season, when they are a little too hard for serving unadorned.
Either way it is a delightful dish—emerald green and delicately flavored.

SERVES: 4 to 6

TIME: 1 hour

THE SOUP:

1 pound green peas in their pods	Salt and pepper
1 quart water	1 teaspoon sugar
1 large potato, peeled and cubed	1 ounce (2 tablespoons) butter
1 large onion, chopped fine	

THE DUMPLINGS:

½ cup water	1 large egg
2 ounces (4 tablespoons) butter	Salt and pepper
2 ounces (½ cup) flour	

You will need two saucepans and a strainer. Shell the peas and put them
aside. Put the shells into a saucepan with the water. Bring to a boil and stew
gently until the pods are soft—about 30 minutes. Strain the stock—it will add
plenty of flavor to the soup. Put the shelled peas and the potato, onion, and
pod stock back into the saucepan, and bring to a boil. Lower the heat and
simmer for 20 to 30 minutes, until the vegetables are soft.

Meanwhile, prepare the dumplings. Put the water to boil in a roomy
saucepan. When it is boiling, add the butter and melt it in. Beat in the flour.
Continue to beat out the lumps as the paste cooks. When you have a homoge-

nous mass which leaves the sides of the pan clean, take it off the heat. Allow to cool a little; then beat in the egg. Season with salt and pepper.

The soup should by now be cooked. Mash the vegetables in to thicken it a little, or if you like it very smooth, puree it in a blender. Taste, and season with salt, pepper, and the sugar, and bring it back to a boil. Form the dumplings wth two wet teaspoons and drop them into the soup. The dumplings will puff up and be ready in a few minutes. Just before you serve the soup, float a nugget of cold butter on the surface.

◆

SUGGESTIONS

Instead of the dumplings, serve the soup with sizzling hot croutons fried in bacon fat or butter. Croutons are at their best when they are so hot, they hiss when added to the soup.

The dumplings are made as for a choux paste. They can be sweetened and poached in a fruit soup as well as the more usual meat or vegetable soups.

◆

CHESTNUT SOUP

Puchero de castañas (Spain)

The best dried ham in Spain comes from Jabugo, where the incomparable flavor comes from pigs loosed to roam free in the chestnut woods which clothe the surrounding slopes of the Sierra Morena. The nuts are harvested in the autumn by troops of villagers, who work from the tops of the slopes to the bottom, shaking the trees so that the prickly balls roll down to where they can be gathered easily by the women and children. This rough-and-ready harvesting technique leaves plenty for the four-legged gleaners. The gathered chestnuts are peeled, dried, and stored for the winter, to be cooked either with chick-peas or beans in a *puchero* or stew, or on their own as a soup, enriched with a little ham from the gleaning-fattened porkers.

SERVES: 6

TIME: 90 minutes

2 pounds chestnuts	1 carrot, scrubbed and cubed
1½ quarts homemade stock or water	1 onion, cubed
1 bay leaf	Salt and pepper
One 2-ounce slab of bacon, cubed	1 teaspoon sugar
4 ounces jamón serrano or	
prosciutto, cubed (optional)	

Preheat the oven to 300°F. You will need a saucepan and a frying pan. Roast the chestnuts in the oven for half an hour. Peel them when they are cool enough to handle. Put them in a saucepan and cover them with the stock or water. Put in the bay leaf. Leave to stew gently for another half hour.

Put the bacon in a frying pan and sweat it gently so that the fat runs. Add the ham, carrot, and onion. Cook for 5 minutes; then add the contents of the pan to the stewing chestnuts. Simmer together for another 15 minutes. Taste, and season with salt, freshly ground pepper, and the sugar. Serve in deep bowls, accompanied by good bread and a bottle of dry white wine from the plains of the Guadalquivir below the mountains.

◆

SUGGESTION

An old partridge or a pheasant, roughly jointed and stewed with the chestnuts, improves the dish greatly. The Spanish red-legged partridge is quite common in the area.

◆

CHESTNUT SOUP

Kostanj Juha (Yugoslavia)

The European chestnut has been gathered for food since prehistoric times. The large nuts of *Castanea sativak* were freely available, easy to gather, could be dried and stored for the winter and ground up into a passable flour, and until the New World imports such as maize replaced them, formed the staple diet of the poor of southern Europe. Village stores in Mediterranean and Balkan countries still carry sacks of shelled, dried parchment-colored nuts along with the lentils and beans for sale by weight. Dried chestnuts are included in bean stews to add variety and interest—a convenient addition since they take about the same time to swell up and soften. This soup is made in the autumn with fresh nuts and into the winter with dried ones.

SERVES: 4 to 6

TIME: 1 hour

1½ pounds fresh chestnuts in their skins	1 tablespoon sugar
	2 ounces (4 tablespoons) butter
1 quart homemade chicken stock or water mixed with a glass of white wine	2 egg yolks
	Salt and pepper

You will need a medium saucepan and a sieve or a blender. Put a medium saucepan of water on to boil. Boil the chestnuts in their jackets for 15 minutes. Plunge the nuts into cold water immediately—the skins will then come off easily, both the tough outer shell and the russet inner skin. Put them back in the pan and cover with the stock (or water and wine), sugar, and butter. Bring the soup to a boil and then turn the heat down. Simmer for 30 to 40 minutes, until the chestnuts are soft. Save a dozen whole nuts, and either push the rest through a sieve or put all into a blender and blend until smooth.

Return the soup to the pan and whisk in the egg yolks. Taste, and add salt and freshly milled pepper. Reheat carefully without allowing the soup to reboil. Add the whole chestnuts and serve the soup in small bowls. Bread, a salad, and a piece of cheese complete the meal.

◆

QUINCE SOUP

Kutina Juha (Yugoslavia)

The beautiful downy-yellow quince was until recently widely cultivated all over Europe. Quince trees are still to be found fruiting alongside the silk-worm's mulberry trees in many an abandoned cottage garden. Although to today's palate, overattuned to sweet things, quince is considered too sour to eat raw, it loses its harshness when cooked, and turns a soft and pretty pink. The fruit is mostly used to make a preserve—in France it's a speciality of Orleans called *cotignac*, in Spain *dulce de membrillo*, and in Portugal, where the word for quince is *marmelo*, the same preparation was the ancestor of that British breakfast staple, marmalade. In Croatia this pretty pale and delicately flavored soup is still popular.

SERVES: 4

TIME: 40 minutes

2 pounds ripe quinces	2 egg yolks
2 cups white wine	½ cup heavy cream
Salt and pepper	Bread cubes for croutons
1 teaspoon sugar	

Preheat the oven to 350°F. You will need a baking dish, a blender, and a saucepan. Bake the quinces until soft—30 minutes at 350°F should do the trick. Then peel, core, and put them in a blender with the wine. Blend thoroughly. Pour the mixture back into the pan and heat it gently. Add salt and pepper and the sugar, and simmer for 10 minutes, until the alcohol has evaporated.

Meanwhile, beat the egg yolks and the cream together and pour some into each individual soup bowl. Pour in the hot soup.

Accompany with piping-hot croutons fried golden in butter. A fine fat carp, grilled with fennel, could complete the meal. These giant, firm-fleshed fish are sold live from tanks in Belgrade, the ancient capital of Serbo-Croatia.

◆

COLD VEGETABLE SOUPS

◆

TOMATO-AND-GARLIC SOUP

Gazpacho (Spain)

Gazpacho is a true peasant dish which has become as gentrified as *bouillabaisse*. At its simplest (and probably most ancient), it is a kind of thick bread porridge flavored with olive oil, vinegar, and garlic (the constant factors) with, if possible, a sprinkling of whatever the *huerta*, the vegetable patch, could offer in the way of green peppers, tomatoes, and onions. In winter, the dish can be taken hot; in the summer it is eaten cold. The bread, garlic, vinegar, and water are either pounded in a mortar or merely infused together. The vegetables in the simplest version would have been used as a garnish, rather than as an integral part of the liquid. The modern version concentrates more on the vegetable soup aspect of the dish, and increasingly leaves out the bread and oil altogether. A special Sunday *gazpacho* makes the best compromise.

Gil Lopez, a local landowner in Andalusia interviewed by Ronald Fraser in 1968, remembered:

In our house we ate what everyone in Andalusia eats—bread and tomato soup made with oil and water, fried fish, fried potatoes, pimientos, whatever the land produced. We had money enough to buy meat, but we hardly ever ate it. The Catalans and Basques say they can't understand how the Andalusians have the energy to work eating only "bread and water." That's what they call the soups we eat here. But you go to the largest, wealthiest *cortijo* and that's what you'll find being eaten there.

This was confirmed by Salvador Torres, a day laborer reaping the wheat:

We had a young boy with us who brought us water in the fields and cooked. He had to get up at two or three in the morning to start preparing a soup. We'd eat that at seven, for by then we had been working two or three hours. At noon a *gazpacho*—and then back to work until six. By then the boy had prepared a stew of chick-peas and potatoes . . . at the end of the day's work we'd eat more *gazpacho*. [*The Pueblo*, Ronald Fraser, 1973]

SERVES: 4 to 6

TIME: 30 minutes

3 to 4 slices of day-old bread	*1 small cucumber or half a large*
2 cups cold water	*one (Spanish cucumbers are*
2 tablespoons wine vinegar	*the size of the pickling variety)*
2 garlic cloves, peeled and	*1 cup canned tomato juice (unless*
crushed	*you are making this in Spain,*
2 pounds ripe tomatoes	*when you can use extra water*
2 green peppers	*instead, because the tomatoes*
1 large Spanish onion	*are much more flavorful*
2 tablespoons olive oil	*Salt*

You will need a food processor or a blender, or a pestle and mortar. Put the bread to soak with the garlic in a few tablespoons of the water and all the vinegar, while you prepare the vegetables.

Chop the tomatoes roughly (they may be peeled if you wish—in which case, scald them in boiling water to loosen the skins first). Take the seeds out of the green peppers and chop the flesh roughly. Peel the onion and chop it up. Put aside a quarter of the chopped vegetables in separate dishes, to be passed separately as a garnish.

Either blend the soaked bread and garlic, the rest of the chopped vegetables, and the olive oil in a blender or a food processor, or pound them in a mortar. (If you need to keep the *gazpacho*, omit the onion from the soup—it ferments rather easily.) Add the tomato juice and then the rest of the water until you have the consistency you like. Adjust the seasoning with salt. Put the soup in the refrigerator for an hour at least. Serve as iced as possible (but not with ice cubes in it—ice cubes always seem to taste odd and will dilute the soup).

Pass small bowls of the extra chopped vegetables for each person to sprinkle on his or her own serving—as in the everyday peasant version. Chopped hard-boiled eggs and *hot* croutons fried in olive oil can be included as a special treat. This final garnishing is an integral part of the modern dish.

◆

COLD ALMOND SOUP

Ajo blanco (Spain)

This deliciously refreshing cold soup of the peasant bread-soup family is prepared in the rich *vega*, the great fertile plain of Granada. The inclusion of almonds is a refinement introduced by the Moors. The legacy of six centuries of Moorish occupation did not vanish overnight—nor indeed did the extensive plantations of almond trees brought by the Muslims from the Jordan valley. Almonds are still an important cash crop for the small farmers of Andalusia.

SERVES: 4 to 5

TIME: 30 minutes plus 1 hour cooking

3 to 4 slices of stale bread	1 quart cold water
3 ounces blanched almonds	Salt
4 garlic cloves, peeled	2 tablespoons white wine vinegar
2 tablespoons olive oil	1 handful of small grapes

You will need a pestle and mortar, or a blender. Put the bread, almonds, garlic, oil, and a pint of the water into a blender, and blend thoroughly. In the peasant kitchen, this job would have been done with a pestle and mortar, and there are those who say the soup is finest thus made. Or put all the ingredients except the grapes in the blender and blend them. Add the rest of the water until you have the consistency you like. Season with salt and the vinegar. Cool in the refrigerator to infuse for an hour or so.

Peel and seed the grapes and float them on top of each serving of soup. The patios of rural dwellings in the south are usually shaded by a trellis with a vine which bears grapes long into the winter months, so this ingredient is very much to hand, and is essential to the proper flavoring of the soup.

Little cubes of bread, fried golden in olive oil and served sizzling hot, make an excellent addition.

◆

COLD SOUP MADE WITH YOGURT AND WALNUTS

Tarator (Bulgaria)

This soup is a legacy from the Ottoman Turks, whose officers and governors took pleasure in laying a good table and were more than willing to train servants from their subject nations. As the Romans before them, the Turks planted their favorite ingredients if they were not available locally. Today walnut, hazelnut, and almond trees shade the foothills of Bulgaria's mountain ranges. The woods blaze scarlet and gold in the autumn, towering over the gilded onion domes left behind in the wake of the retreating Ottoman armies.

SERVES: 4 to 6

TIME: 20 minutes plus ½ hour cooking

1 cucumber	4 cups yogurt
2 to 3 garlic cloves	1 small bunch of mint and dill,
½ teaspoon salt	chopped
3 ounces walnuts	

You will need a grater or a food processor, and a colander. Grate or dice the cucumber, salt it, and put it to drain in a colander for half an hour. Peel and crush the garlic with the ½ teaspoon salt. Crush the walnuts.

Rinse the cucumber and stir it into the yogurt with the garlic and the walnuts. Ladle into bowls, and sprinkle the dill and mint over the top. It is deliciously refreshing on a hot day.

VEGETABLE STEWS

VEGETABLE HOT POT

Xhivetch (Bulgaria)

Vegetable gardens are called *bulgaridi* in Rumania, being always kept by immigrant Bulgarians, who grow all the vegetables for the town's supply, the staple produce being melons, water and sugar melons, cucumbers, pimentos, cabbages, vegetable marrows, tomatoes. Potatoes do not yet enjoy much favor with the Rumanian peasant as regular food, but seem to be gaining ground, nevertheless; they are grown in the *bulgaridi*, but still more they are sown between the maize, where one can see no end of pumpkins creeping among the maize in all directions, and also haricot beans, which are grown in great quantities, being the staple food of the Rumanians in fasting times. [*From Carpathian to Pindus*, Theresa Stratilesco, 1906]

SERVES: 6 as a main course; 8 as an accompaniment (omit the lamb)

TIME: 25 to 30 minutes plus 1 hour cooking

1 pound onions	½ cup sunflower oil (or sesame or any seed oil)
2 to 3 small hot red peppers (optional)	1 pound cubed lamb (optional)
4 pounds vegetables (choose at least 4 varieties): potatoes, eggplants, peppers, okra (ladies' fingers), green beans, fava beans, peas, carrots, leeks, zucchini, spinach, Swiss chard	Salt and pepper
	1 pound tomatoes (or a 1-pound can of tomatoes)

TO FINISH:
2   eggs
2   heaping tablespoons chopped Italian parsley
1   cup rich yogurt

Preheat the oven to 300°F. You will need your best large-lidded baking dish for this stew. The ones made in Bulgaria for the purpose are of pale earthenware with a pearly-blue glaze. You may need a frying pan.

Peel and chop the onions. Seed, devein, and crush the red peppers if using. Prepare the rest of the vegetables, peeling only when necessary and cutting them into even-sized cubes.

Heat the oil in the casserole (if it is safe on direct heat—otherwise you will have to start in a frying pan). Fry the onions, then the lamb if you are using it; then add the crushed red peppers. Add the vegetables and toss everything in the hot oil—if you are using a frying pan, transfer the ingredients to the casserole as they are sautéed. Season with salt and pepper and then pour in enough water to cover. Lay the tomatoes over the vegetables. Cover and bake very gently at 300°F for an hour, or equally gently on top of the stove.

Mix the eggs with the parsley and the yogurt, and pour the mixture over the stew after 50 minutes. Allow to cool a little and serve with plenty of good bread.

Finish the meal with a dish of those particularly succulent large white grapes which the Bulgarians grow so well. Grape vines are often trained over a shed-shaped trellis, which provides dappled shade in the summer and autumn for semi-outdoor activities such as fermenting plums for *slivova*, the Bulgarians' favorite liquor, or yogurt and cheese making.

SUGGESTION

Instead of the yogurt-and-egg topping, scatter a handful of little sour grapes over the top of the dish 15 minutes before the end of the cooking time.

GREEN-PEPPER-AND-TOMATO STEW

Letcho (Hungary)

The Hungarians rival the Bulgarians (from whom they learned much, including the cultivation of their beloved paprika) as gardeners and are blessed with the fertile soil of the Danube basin in which to hoe and sow. This very basic and versatile vegetable preparation is Serbian in origin. Hungarian housewives take their vegetables seriously and consider them the central ingredient for main dishes in their own right. No Hungarian cook worth her salt would serve plain-boiled vegetables as a garnish for meat. This basic mixture is also used for flavoring like *ragù* in the Italian kitchen.

SERVES: 4

TIME: 10 minutes plus 20 to 30 minutes cooking

1	pound green peppers (preferably the thin-skinned frying variety)	1 ounce (2 tablespoons) lard
		½ pound onions, chopped fine
1	pound tomatoes or a 1-pound can of tomatoes	1 tablespoon paprika

You will need a heavy frying pan. Hull, seed, and slice the peppers finely. Then chop them—the fatter-fleshed they are, the finer you should chop them. Scald the tomatoes with boiling water to loosen the skins, peel them, and chop them. If the tomatoes are our northern sunless variety, add a tablespoon of tomato puree to the dish together with a teaspoon of sugar.

Put the lard to melt in a heavy pan. Add the onions and stir them in the hot fat until they are golden. Push to one side and add the chopped peppers. Fry gently. Sprinkle in the paprika and add the tomatoes. You may need a little extra liquid if the tomatoes are not very juicy.

Simmer the stew for 20 to 30 minutes. Use as you please, on its own or for flavoring other dishes. Make a double quantity and keep it in the refrigerator to add to other stews and baked dishes.

This is very good served with plain-boiled noodles or *tarhonya* noodle barley (page 162) or with fried eggs or a slice of grilled ham.

SUGGESTION

Add a few slices of smoked sausage to the *letcho* and then scramble four eggs in it. This is almost exactly like the Basque *piperade*.

BAKED VEGETABLES

Briam (Greece)

The selection of vegetables varies according to the season and the gardener, so leave out or add to the list as you please. *Briam* is a very popular dish in Greece and often provides a meal in itself. Fresh vegetables are easily available everywhere—sold in the country villages from the backs of local farmers' trucks, the tailgate swung down to provide a sales counter. City dwellers often buy their vegetables and fruit straight from the producers' roadside stalls. Okra (ladies' fingers) is sold dried as well as fresh, strung like beads on thin cotton thread.

SERVES: 4 to 5 as a main course; 6 to 8 as an accompaniment

TIME: 30 minutes plus 1½ to 2 hours cooking

½ *pound okra*
Lemon juice
½ *cup olive oil*
2 *pounds ripe tomatoes, sliced*
½ *pound potatoes, cut into thick*
    slices
½ *pound eggplant, cut into rounds*

½ *pound zucchini, cut into rounds*
½ *pound green peppers, hulled and*
    sliced
Salt and pepper
2 *onions, chopped*
4 *garlic cloves, chopped*

Preheat the oven to 350°F. You will need a wide shallow casserole. Wash the okra and sprinkle it with lemon juice (okra is a good addition if you can get it—the juice gives a nice gluey texture to the dish).

Trickle a thin layer of the oil over the bottom of a wide, shallow ovenproof dish. Lay half the tomato slices over it. Arrange the rest of the vegetables in layers over the tomatoes, sprinkling with salt and pepper and the onions and the garlic as you go. Lay the second half of the tomato slices on top. Pour the rest of the oil evenly on top.

Bake for 1½ to 2 hours. Serve warm or cool (the Greeks never eat their food piping hot) with plenty of bread to accompany—the juices are delicious. *Briam* makes a wonderful light summer lunch to be taken in the pearl-gray shade of an olive tree beside the Aegean. It will smell as sweet as the drowsy heat of a Greek summer's day.

◆

FAVA BEANS WITH HAM

Habas con jamón (Spain)

One of my favorite Spanish dishes, this is best made when the fava beans are small and tender, and the pods, which are used in the dish, are not stringy. The slightly sticky, velvety texture, not unlike okra in flavor and feel, is surprisingly good. I first had this dish in one of the mountain villages behind Ronda, where the wild sweet pea tangles with the rows of fava bean plants in blossom on the stony terraces. Wild and cultivated crops unite in such primitive fields: round pink heads of the wild garlic, *Allium roseum*, add confusion to the cultivated garlic patch. Wild and domestic animals graze the same meadow flowers. Old men with panniered donkeys collect greens from the side of the road—*tagarnina* thistle rosettes for the evening stew, clover and pea for the rabbits. The dish can be made with shelled old fava beans, or with dried fava beans in the winter. Dried fava beans predated the family of New World beans such as haricots, butter beans, and pinto beans in the stews of Spain, France, Italy, and the Balkans.

SERVES: 4

TIME: 30 minutes plus 1½ to 2 hours cooking

2	*pounds young fava beans in their pods*	1	*small bunch of Italian parsley, chopped*
4	*ounces* jamón serrano, *or any dried ham or fatback*	1	*small glass of dry sherry or white wine*
4	*tablespoons olive oil*	1	*large glass of water*
1	*onion, chopped*		Salt and pepper
3	*garlic cloves, chopped*		Pinch of sugar

You will need a stewpan. Top and tail the beans, and chop them into short lengths—more or less following the swell of each bean. Do not do this in advance or the beans will turn an odd navy blue color at the edges. Slice the ham or bacon into small cubes.

Heat the oil in the stewpan. Add the onion and the garlic, and fry for a moment without allowing them to take color. Add the beans, ham, and parsley. Fry for a moment longer. Add the sherry or the wine, and the water. Cover and stew gently for 1½ to 2 hours. Add salt and pepper and a little sugar when the beans are tender—they will be a blue-gray and completely soft. Cook the stew uncovered for a moment to evaporate the liquid if there is too much juice. Delicious on its own as a first course of a light supper, it is also good served with cubes of fried bread, or *migas*.

SUGGESTION

For a more substantial dish, stir in 2 to 3 eggs beaten together, and scramble them with the juice. Serve with squares of bread fried in olive oil and garlic.

Leftovers: Stir into a *cocido* (page 110) or a lentil stew.

Or reheat with chopped tomatoes and onions which have been stewed together in a little oil.

Reheat as it is, but stir in a spoonful of fresh herbs chopped with garlic just before you serve it.

STEWED ARTICHOKES

Ragoût d'artichaut (France)

One of those simple Provençal vegetable dishes at which the country people excel, this is reminiscent of the Greek vegetable dishes.

SERVES: 4

TIME: 20 minutes plus 1½ hours cooking

8 to 12 small artichokes	Juice of 1 lemon
4 tablespoons olive oil	1 glass of white wine
1 onion or 2 small white new ones, chopped	Salt and pepper
1 branch of thyme or rosemary, or a bay leaf	

Choose a wide stewpan which will allow you to cook the artichokes in a single layer. Trim the artichokes down to their edible parts with a small sharp knife. Make sure you manage to remove the whole choke and trim the tough outer leaves right down. If the artichokes are on the large side, cut them into quarters.

Warm the oil in the pan and add the onion. Let it soften without browning, and then add the artichoke bottoms and the thyme, rosemary, or bay leaf. Cook together gently until the vegetables are impregnated with the oil. Then add the lemon juice, wine, salt, and pepper. Cover tightly and cook very gently for 1½ hours.

◆

SUGGESTION

Serve the artichokes on their own—perhaps to follow or precede a small shoulder of lamb slowly pot-roasted at the same time. Sprinkle the tender little roast with rosemary, and shove in a clove or two of garlic near the bone before you put it in a lidded casserole to roast in its own juices. A glass of white wine poured around it will keep it deliciously moist.

◆

MIXED MEDITERRANEAN VEGETABLES

Ratatouille (France)

The *ratatouille* of Provence is a thorny subject. No family can agree with its neighbor on the correct composition. However, the parameters are well enough defined: Only those vegetables which can readily be found in peak condition simultaneously in the Provençal summer garden will do. To the gardener-cook, the slow, deliberate choosing of the most scarlet tomatoes, the plumpest peppers, the firmest plum-purple eggplants, the sweetest onions, is the primary ingredient in the recipe. This dish is a marriage of cooked vegetables, not a hodgepodge stew. Make it with care and you will be well rewarded.

SERVES: 4

TIME: 1 hour

1	*pound eggplant*	*1*	*pound tomatoes (or a 1-pound*
2	*onions, chopped*		*can of tomatoes)*
2	*garlic cloves, chopped*	*Salt and pepper*	
6	*tablespoons olive oil*		
1	*pound peppers (red, yellow, green), hulled, seeded, and cut into strips*		

You will need a colander, a frying pan, and a casserole. Slice the eggplant finely; salt the slices and leave them to drain in a colander. Fry the onions and the garlic gently in some of the oil until they are soft and lightly golden. Transfer them to the casserole, and keep them warm over very low heat.

Scorch the peppers by turning them in a naked flame. When the skins are charred all over, scrape them off. Cook the peppers gently in oil in the frying pan until they are soft. Transfer them to the casserole—save the oil.

Rinse and pat the eggplant dry, and fry the slices gently in the reserved oil until they are soft and golden. Add more oil if necessary. They drink oil like sponges, so drain them well in a sieve after cooking and before you transfer them to the casserole. Reserve the drained oil.

Plunge the tomatoes into boiling water to loosen the skins. Peel them and chop them (you can take out the seeds, too, if you wish). Let the pulp melt down to a rich sauce in the rest of the oil, including that drained from the eggplant. Transfer the tomato mixture to the casserole.

Heat everything together for a few minutes. Do not cook any further.

Serve the *ratatouille* on its own with plenty of fresh bread, or with eggs fried crisp in hot olive oil so that the yolks still remain runny, or with a plain-grilled steak or chop. Accompany with a bottle of red wine from the Rhône. Finish with fresh walnuts, cheese, and fruit, or, great luxury, a *tarte au citron* (page 447).

SUGGESTIONS

Include 1 pound of zucchini, sliced and fried like the eggplant.

The dish has a close cousin with which it is frequently confused, the *Bohèmienne*, which confines its vegetables to the tomato and the eggplant. The combination also makes a delicious dish.

Note: If you cannot obtain good olive oil, include a few pitted, chopped *black* olives and use the best seed oil you can find.

◆

GARLIC PURÉE

Purée d'ail (France)

The first unformed heads of fresh garlic appear in Mediterranean markets in the spring. This delicate dish is best made a few weeks later when the cloves have just formed. Fresh garlics look like very white onions, and it takes a couple of weeks for the cloves to suck the juice from the onion layers and plump themselves out. Garlic cloves are then at their sweetest and best for this dish, which has a mild flavor quite unlike the fierce raw bulb. If you cannot get the fresh garlic, try it with the usual mature heads. The flavor will be stronger, so exercise caution in your choice of companion.

SERVES: 4

TIME: 20 minutes

10   *heads of fresh garlic*
½   *cup heavy cream*
Salt and pepper

You will need a small pan with a lid, and a sieve or a blender. Peel the garlic cloves, and put them to cook in the pan with enough boiling salted water to cover them. Let them simmer for 10 minutes; then drain them. If the garlic is old, cook it a little longer.

Purée the garlic with the cream. (A blender will do the job swiftly.) Season with salt and pepper.

This purée is irresistible with a dish of fried eggs or a piece of roast pork, or a leg of spring lamb roasted and basted with oil and a few sprigs of thyme or rosemary. This purée is also very good with roast game.

◆

FARMHOUSE PEAS

Petits pois à la fermière (France)

Peas, new carrots, and wild asparagus were the spring vegetables most appreciated by my neighbors in the Languedoc. All through the winter I would cross the farm's snow-covered courtyard in the early dawn, on the way to leave my children in the local village to catch the school bus. French schools start early and finish late, and there was never a sign from the farmhouse's shuttered windows as we passed. Everything changed as soon as the thaw came in early March. Then the courtyard came alive long before we came through. Even the rooster and the rabbits had been fed well before dawn, and Madame Escrieu was out in her garden tending her young vegetables in the first shafts of sunlight. She told me what to do with the basin of peas and herbs she gave me when the plants were at the height of their crop.

SERVES: 4 to 6

TIME: 30 minutes

2 pounds peas, shelled	1 teaspoon sugar
3 ounces (6 tablespoons) butter	1 quart homemade stock or water
½ tablespoon flour	1 bunch of parsley and chervil,
1 lettuce, shredded	chopped
½ pound baby onions, peeled	Salt and pepper

You will need a roomy saucepan or a casserole. Put the peas, 4 tablespoons of the butter, and the flour in the saucepan over low heat. Cook until the butter melts, stirring constantly. Add the lettuce, onions, sugar, and stock or water. Cover and stew gently for half an hour. Stir in the herbs and the rest of the butter. Add salt and pepper to taste.

A pork chop or a piece of black pudding fried with apples might start the meal. Serve the peas as a dish on their own, perhaps with a few small triangles of bread fried golden in butter. A good piece of cheese rounds off the repast.

◆

SUGGESTIONS

Leftovers: Blend into a luscious pale green soup with as much again of creamy milk and a few leaves of parsley and chervil; serve hot or cold.

◆

PEAS WITH HAM

Petits pois au jambon (France)

My Languedoc neighbor also had the benefit of a pantry full of the products of the autumn pig killing. Her family liked their Sunday peas cooked with a thick slice of their own ham.

SERVES: 6

TIME: 20 minutes plus 1 hour cooking

2   ounces (4 tablespoons) butter
One ½-pound piece of raw ham or
    bacon
2 to 3 crisp lettuces (cos or
    iceberg)

1   cup clear stock or water
1½ pounds peas, shelled or 2½
    pounds whole beans
1   teaspoon sugar
Salt and pepper

You will need a roomy stewpot or a casserole. Melt 2 tablespoons of the butter in the stewpot. Slice the ham or bacon into small cubes, and put it to sweat gently in the butter. Wash and chop the lettuce roughly; add it to the pot. Pour in the stock or water, and cover tightly. Leave to cook over low heat for half an hour—lettuce requires either no cooking at all or a very long stewing.

Add the peas after the half hour of cooking, along with the sugar. You may need to add a little more stock or water. Continue to cook over low heat for another half hour. When the peas are ready, stir in the rest of the butter. Add salt and freshly milled pepper to taste.

Serve as a dish on its own. The peas are in no hurry, so you will have plenty of time to make and serve omelets for everyone first. My neighbor made hers with the little spindly wild asparagus (sprue) for which our neighborhood was famous.

◆

SUGGESTIONS

Leftovers: Reheat and stir in a couple of well-beaten eggs and a tablespoon of chopped parsley and chives.

Or drain and put the peas in the bottom of individual earthenware dishes with a teaspoon of heavy cream. Crack an egg or two into each dish. Cook in a hot (400°F) oven or on direct heat until the egg is set.

◆

CATALAN VEGETABLE STEW

Garbure catalane (France)

The *garbure* is the classic peasant dish most likely to be found on the countryman's table on his return from a hard day in the fields. It is neither soup nor stew but something in between. Its ingredients are dependent on the means, the habits, and the origin of the cook and vary widely, from the thick green-vegetable stew of Béarn to the *ratatouille*-like mixtures of Provence. The *garbure* is most probably a reference to the chief ingredients of the dish, *garbe* meaning a branch or sheaf of vegetables. The alternative theory is that the word—and the dish—springs from the Spanish *garbias*, a stew. In its simplest form it is a soup-stew of vegetables, sometimes flavored with a small piece of bacon and thickened with dry bread. I offer here the version which is native to the Catalan border and so spans the two cuisines.

SERVES: 4 to 6

TIME: 30 minutes plus 1½ hours cooking

1 small loaf of stale bread	*2 garlic cloves, peeled and chopped*
1 pound tomatoes	*Salt and pepper*
½ cup olive oil	*3 pounds pumpkin, peeled and*
1 pound onions, sliced	*sliced*
1 handful of herbs: Italian	*1 wine glass of water*
parsley, marjoram, thyme,	
chopped	

Preheat the oven to 300°F. You will need a glazed earthenware pot and a frying pan.

Slice the bread and put it to toast crisp in the oven. Pour boiling water over the tomatoes; peel and slice them.

Put half the olive oil to warm in a frying pan. Add the onions and fry them gently. When they are soft and golden, put a layer of them in the bottom of the earthenware pot. Seasoning with the herbs, garlic, salt, and pepper as you go, continue with a layer of bread, a layer of pumpkin, a layer of tomatoes, a layer of bread, a layer of pumpkin, another of onions, a layer of pumpkin, a layer of tomatoes, and finish with bread. Or in any other order which appeals to you, as long as you finish with a layer of bread. Pour the water over everything, and trickle the rest of the oil over the top.

Cover and bake in a moderate (325°F) oven for 1½ hours. Take the cover off for the last 15 minutes of the cooking time and turn up the oven heat to crisp the top.

Serve with a green salad, a bottle of red wine, and you will need nothing more but the *goudale:* Pour a glass of your wine into the last of your soup and drink it straight from the bowl. Finish with a handful of sweet grapes and a small glass of *eau-de-vie.*

◆

SUGGESTIONS

Garbure provençale has eggplant, peppers, onions, tomatoes, zucchini, and a little garlic layered with toasted bread and olive oil in a deep casserole, with a layer of bread on top. Pour in a glass or two of water or stock. Cover and cook slowly in a 300°F oven for 2 hours—take the lid off for the last 10 minutes and turn up the heat to crisp the top. A few minutes before you serve it, pour half a glass of Armagnac or brandy over it. Whiskey would do also.

Garbure gasconne has turnips, potatoes, cabbage, and onions layered with bread, with a piece of bacon or preserved goose buried in it.

Garbure béarnais is the classic *garbure,* the glory of Béarn, and includes fresh vegetables (cabbage, potatoes, beans, peas), and, in its grandest form, a piece of preserved goose—the whole finished with a *trebuc*—a slice of salt meat. Chestnuts and dried beans are added in the winter months.

FRIED AND ROAST VEGETABLES

ROAST ONIONS

(England)

The English appetite for roasting and the taste of the fire extends to vegetables as well as meat. Vegetables with a high sugar content are the ones to roast, best of all around the meat: potatoes, onions, and parsnips respond particularly well. Carrots and turnips tend to dry out. Roast a panful of the mixed vegetables together in a medium oven, and serve them with Yorkshire pudding (page 359) and gravy (page 361).

SERVES: 4

TIME: 5 minutes plus 2 hours cooking

4   *large or 8 medium onions*

Preheat the oven to 325°F. You will need a roasting pan.

Leave the onions as they are—neither peel them nor cut off the root ends. Put them in the roasting pan, root side down, and put them to bake in the oven for 2 hours. Serve just as they are, in their own golden skins, with salt, freshly ground pepper, and plenty of cold butter to melt into the sweet flesh.

ROAST PARSNIPS

(England)

SERVES: 4

TIME: 10 to 15 minutes plus 1½ hours cooking

4   *large parsnips*
Salt and pepper
4   *tablespoons drippings or lard*

Preheat the oven to 325°F. You will need a roasting pan and a saucepan.

Peel the parsnips, and then boil them for 10 minutes in salted water. Drain and shake them over the heat to dry. Salt and pepper them, and then roast them, well-basted with drippings or lard, in the oven for 1½ hours. They can also be roasted along with your meat.

◆

ROAST POTATOES

(England)

SERVES: 4

TIME: 10 to 15 minutes plus 1 hour and 15 minutes cooking

2   *pounds (6 medium-sized) old,*
floury potatoes, such as
Idahos

1   *ounce (¼ cup) flour*
4   *ounces (½ cup) good beef fat or*
lard

Preheat the oven to 425°F. You will need a saucepan and a roasting pan.

Peel the potatoes and bring them to a boil in a pot of salted water. Cook gently for 15 minutes, until nearly soft. Drain them, shake them over the heat to dry them, and rough up the outsides with a fork. A sprinkling of flour helps them to crisp. Melt some drippings in a roasting pan and turn the potatoes in the very hot fat. Or put them to cook in the hot drippings around the meat as it roasts (put them in their own pan if the meat has been frozen; it will give out too much liquid and make the potatoes soggy). Roast the potatoes, turning and basting them occasionally, in the oven for 1 hour. They should be brown and crisp outside, and soft and fragrant within.

◆

ROAST GARLIC

Ail au four (France)

The people of Provence like their garlic baked long and slow. The baking process tames the fierce tuber into a sweet, mild vegetable—from Shrew to gentle Kate in half an hour.

SERVES: 4

TIME: 30 minutes

8	whole heads of fresh, firm garlic		Salt and pepper
2	tablespoons olive oil		French bread for toasting

Preheat the oven to 400°F. You will need a bowl and a small casserole.

Do not peel or separate the heads of garlic. Put them whole in a bowl and pour boiling water over them. Leave them for 1 minute and then drain them.

Pour the oil over the bottom of a small casserole, and put in the whole heads of garlic. Sprinkle them with salt and pepper, and then put the dish to bake uncovered in the oven for half an hour. Open the oven occasionally and sprinkle the garlic with a little water.

Meanwhile, cut the bread into 1-inch-thick slices. Toast the slices—if possible on the end of a fork over a direct flame (there are wire grids available in Mediterranean countries which assist this). The bread is then singed rather than dried out, and adds its own peculiar pungency to this simple but delicious dish. To eat, squeeze the aromatic contents of each clove of garlic onto a piece of toast, sprinkle with a little salt and pepper, and pop it in your mouth. A quick sip of light rosé from neighboring Tavel helps when you burn your mouth. A salad of *mesclun* and a little goat cheese completes a light meal. Or you might have room for a *clafoutis* (page 448).

◆

PROVENÇAL TOMATOES

Tomates à la provençal (France)

This is another of the Provençal vegetable dishes which achieves its concentrated sweetness through long, slow cooking.

SERVES: 4

TIME: 10 minutes plus 1 hour and 15 minutes cooking

8	large tomatoes (only ripe fresh ones will do)	2	garlic cloves
3	tablespoons olive oil	1	handful of Italian parsley
			Salt

You will need a heavy frying pan. Cut the tomatoes in half and remove the seeds. Warm the oil in a wide shallow pan. Add the tomatoes, cut side down.

Fry them over the gentlest of heat for 40 to 45 minutes, shaking the pan from time to time so that the tomatoes do not stick and burn. It is this slow, patient cooking which gives the dish its unique flavor.

Peel the garlic, crush it, and then mince it very finely with the parsley.

Turn the tomatoes over, and sprinkle them with salt and the minced garlic and parsley. Let them continue to cook very gently on the other side—another half hour is not too long.

Serve the tomatoes after a dish of little fried fish, or a *loup de mer grillé au fenouille*, sea bass, roasted over a fire made aromatic with dried stalks of fennel. Or after a dish of fresh sardines, grilled for no more than 3 minutes a side over hot charcoal and served with a knob of butter pounded with garlic and parsley. There is nothing that can recall more vividly the scents of Provence.

◆

BAKED SPINACH

Tian d'épinards (France)

The *tian* is a wide earthenware baking dish which has given its name to that which is baked in it. The prepared dish would be taken to cook slowly in the local baker's cooling oven. The Provençaux often serve their beautiful vegetables as the main dish of the meal.

SERVES: 4

TIME: 20 minutes plus 1 hour cooking

2	pounds spinach		Salt and pepper
1	garlic clove	2	tablespoons olive oil
8	eggs		
2	ounces strong grated cheese		
	(Parmesan or mature cheddar)		

Preheat the oven to 300°F. You will need a lidded saucepan, a bowl, and a *tian* or a gratin dish.

Wash the spinach and strip off the stalks if it is fresh. Put the leaves in a tightly lidded saucepan to cook in the moisture which clings to them. When they are wilted—which will only take a few minutes—drain them, squeezing hard to extract all the liquid. Mince the spinach with a sharp knife.

Crush the garlic with a little salt and chop it in with the spinach. Beat the eggs in a bowl with the cheese, salt, and pepper. Stir the spinach and garlic into the eggs.

Oil the *tian* and fill it with the mixture. Bake for 1 hour.

Plenty of fresh bread and red wine should accompany this dish. While you are waiting for the *tian*, serve a few slices of one of the delicious rosy dried sausages, a *saucisson d'Arles*, or any *saucisson sec*. Follow the *tian* with a green salad—*mâche* or chicory would be good—dressed with olive oil and wine vinegar in a proportion of four to one, salt, and pepper.

If you were cooking the dish in its native territory, you might finish the meal with a ewe's-milk cheese which comes from the hills behind Nice, La Brousse, eaten with sugar and grappa or orange-flower water.

◆

SUGGESTIONS

Make a *tian de printemps* with spring vegetables replacing the spinach. Choose among young broad beans (pods and all), new carrots, baby green beans, zucchini, and baby artichokes—all cut into fat matchsticks of an even size. Best of all, see if you can find the young shoots of wild asparagus, native throughout central and southern Europe, which appear overnight beneath the parent plant. Like mushrooms, they are a gypsy crop, sold in the spring by dark-eyed girls with wicker baskets over their arms, in the markets of the Mediterranean.

◆

FRIED CAULIFLOWER

Cavolfiore stracciato (Italy)

My favorite way with both cauliflower and cabbage, this makes an excellent light supper dish served with plenty of bread, and a cheese and some fruit to follow.

SERVES: 4

TIME: ½ hour

1 *large cauliflower*
2–4 *garlic cloves*
4–6 *tablespoons olive oil*
Salt and pepper

You will need a medium-sized saucepan with a lid and a wide frying pan. Trim and then cook the cauliflower in boiling salted water until soft—15 to 20 minutes. Drain thoroughly and break it up into florets.

Meanwhile, peel and chop the garlic. Put the olive oil to heat in a roomy frying pan, and when it is hot put in the garlic. Fry for a moment to perfume the oil and gild the garlic; then throw in the cauliflower. Turn up the heat and fry the cauliflower until it is a little crisp and well impregnated with garlic and oil. Salt and pepper with a generous hand. Serve hot, as a course on its own.

SUGGESTIONS

Fry a handful of bread crumbs in with the garlic before you add the cauliflower. Drain them and sprinkle them over the vegetable after it has been fried.

Make the recipe with finely shredded cooked cabbage.

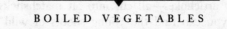

BOILED VEGETABLES

BOILED VEGETABLES WITH WHITE SAUCE

(England)

Vegetables to be sauced in the English style should be well cooked and soft to the fork. If they are crisp, the ingredients will not marry properly. Made with care, the dish can be delicious—adding interest and food value to mature autumn and winter vegetables in particular.

This white sauce is referred to in Victorian cookbooks as "French White Sauce," perhaps to distinguish it from the English "Butter Sauce." This last is the notorious sauce of which Francesco Caraccioli, traveling in England at the end of the eighteenth century, complained: "There are in England sixty different religions, but only one sauce."

SERVES: 4

TIME: 40 minutes

THE VEGETABLES:

1   *pound carrots, scraped and sliced into rings*
(Or) *1 pound leeks, washed thoroughly, topped and tailed and cut into 2-inch lengths*
(Or) *1 pound medium-sized onions, peeled and left whole*
(Or) *1 cauliflower, divided into florets*
(Or) *1 pound shelled fava beans*

(Or) *1 pound beets, to be cooked whole and then peeled and cubed*
(Or) *1 pound spinach, stripped of its stalks and chopped after cooking*
(Or) *1 pound Swiss chard, washed and sliced*
(Or) *1 pound broccoli, washed and separated into florets*
(Or) *1 large head of celery, thoroughly washed*

THE WHITE SAUCE:

2 ounces (4 tablespoons) butter	Salt and pepper
2 ounces (½ cup) flour	Freshly grated nutmeg
2 cups creamy milk or	1 tablespoon heavy cream or
half-and-half	butter

You will need a large and a small saucepan. Bring plenty of salted water to a boil in a roomy saucepan. When it is boiling, throw in the chosen vegetable. Cook for 15 to 20 minutes until the vegetable is soft. Beets and onions will take longer, spinach and chard less time.

Melt the butter in a small pan and stir in the flour. Fry gently until the mixture is sandy but has not yet taken color. Whisk in the milk or half-and-half gradually over the heat, beating to keep it smooth (you can heat the milk first to minimize lumps).

Simmer the sauce gently for 5 to 6 minutes to thicken it and cook the flour (the sauce will taste of raw flour if you omit this step). Add salt and pepper to taste. A sprinkle of grated nutmeg and a spoonful of cream or a nugget of butter stirred in just before you sauce the vegetables will do wonders for the dish.

◆

SUGGESTIONS

I sometimes start the sauce in a blender. Just put in all the ingredients and blend them well. A handful of parsley and chives, or a nugget of cheese and a spoonful of mustard are suitable flavoring extras to include in the blending process. Transfer the mixture to the saucepan and bring the liquid gently to a boil, whisking all the time. Simmer until thick. Proceed according to the recipe.

To convert the ingredients into a vegetable gratin (a cauliflower cheese, perhaps), stir 2 ounces of grated cheese into the sauce, spread the vegetable in a shallow gratin dish, pour the sauce over it, and sprinkle 2 more ounces of cheese over the top. Slip the dish under the broiler for a few minutes to melt and brown the cheese. This quantity will be enough for two as a main dish.

◆

STUFFED VEGETABLES

MIXED STUFFED VEGETABLES

Gemista (Greece)

Vegetables are a very important item of diet among Greek peasants and mountain people. They are eaten fresh in season and dried in the autumn sun for use throughout the winter even today. Big flat earthenware dishes of these stuffed vegetables, rich with oil and scented with herbs, would be cooked in the cooling bread oven after the day's baking. They can be eaten warm or cold. If eaten warm, it is as the main dish of the meal. Served cold, they are a snack or appetizer.

Prepare any selection from the following list for stuffing:

Tomatoes: The big meaty Mediterranean ones called "beefsteak" tomatoes are best. Wash them but do not peel. Cut off a lid from the round end of each, and scoop out the seeds and central pulp. Chop up the pulp and reserve it for the stuffing. Save the lid to put back after stuffing.

Eggplant: Choose firm fruits. Wash and stalk and cut them in half. Scoop out the central pulp, and mince it for the stuffing. Salt the flesh and put the eggplant upside down to drain out some of its juices. This is not a necessary ritual, but it is rather soothing to do things which have been done for centuries. A Greek friend of mine says that our eggplants are soft and dry, and not a patch on those found in Mediterranean markets.

Artichokes: Rinse them and cut off the stalks at the base of the leaves. Peel the stalks and chop them up for the stuffing. Blanch the artichokes in boiling salted water for 10 minutes. Drain them, and then slice off the top part of the leaves. Dig out the hairy chokes in the middle with the point of your knife. Rub the wound with a cut lemon to prevent its turning black.

Zucchini: The little round variety are the only ones worth stuffing. Hull them, wash them, and cut them in half around the equator, or top and tail them so that they can sit on their bottoms. Scoop out the seeds and pulp in the middle, and chop it for the stuffing.

Onions: Choose large firm onions, preferably the Spanish variety. Peel them, and then blanch them in boiling water for 10 to 15 minutes. Cut a lid off the top of each and take out the middle section, leaving three to four layers of flesh to form the cup to be filled. This is a fiddly operation—cut across straight down toward the base with a sharp knive and then chop sideways to release the sections. You are chopping these bits up anyway to use in the stuffing, so it doesn't matter how much they are hacked about. Reserve the top for a lid.

Peppers: Trim off the stalk from each, and cut a lid from the stalk end. Remove the seeds. Since there is no flesh to be scooped out, chop up one of the peppers for use in the stuffing. Reserve the lid so that you can put it back after stuffing. The thin frying variety is delicious stuffed with a finger of strong cheese, dipped whole into a frying batter, and then deep-fried and served with a fresh tomato sauce.

In the peasant kitchen the vegetables are likely to be fried in oil before being stuffed. This makes a rather heavy dish—so unless you intend a long day building a stone wall or harrowing a field by hand, it is probably wise to omit this preliminary and just sprinkle the hollowed-out vegetables with a little oil before you stuff them.

The best stuffings are made with plain and fresh ingredients. The recipe that follows yields enough stuffing for 3 pounds of vegetables.

SERVES: 6

TIME: 1 hour plus 1 hour and 10 minutes cooking

STUFFING:

1 onion	*Water*
½ *cup olive oil*	3 *tablespoons chopped fresh herbs:*
4 *ounces (½ cup) rice*	*oregano, marjoram, Italian*
2 *ounces (¼ cup) pine nuts*	*parsley*
Pulp from the vegetable to be stuffed	*Salt and pepper*
2 *ounces (¼ cup) raisins*	4 *tablespoons fresh lemon juice*

Preheat the oven to 350°F. You will need a frying pan and a wide shallow baking dish.

Peel and mince the onion finely. Heat 4 tablespoons of the oil in a frying pan, stir in the chopped onion, and fry it for a moment. Add the rice, and turn it in the hot oil until it is transparent. Add the nuts and cook for a moment longer. Add the vegetable pulp, the raisins, and a wine glass of water. Cover and leave to simmer for 10 to 15 minutes, until the rice is nearly cooked. Stir in the herbs, and season with salt and pepper.

Stuff the vegetables with the rice-and-vegetable mixture. Put the lids back on those vegetables which have them.

Pour the rest of the oil into a wide (preferably earthenware) gratin dish—it must be large enough to accommodate all the vegetables in a single layer. Put the dish in the oven to heat. When the oil is smoking, add the vegetables. Let them cook in the oil for 10 minutes. Then pour in the lemon juice mixed with an equal amount of water, and cover the dish.

Cook for 40 minutes; then uncover the vegetables and allow them to bake another 20 minutes. The oil will splutter as the liquid evaporates. The total cooking time is 1 hour and 10 minutes, by which time the vegetables should be soft and the juice concentrated to a few tablespoons of well-flavored oil. All this can be done on top of the stove if you prefer.

Have patience and allow the dish to cool down before you serve it—with accompaniments of bread, a side dish of Greek yogurt-and-cucumber salad (page 53), quartered lemons, and a jug of *retsina*.

◆

STUFFED POTATOES

Pommes de terre farcis (France)

The southern French farming communities prefer to live in or close to villages, even the smallest of which has a local baker who bakes the village's bread. Until quite recently many of his customers required the provision of a hot oven, and the housewives themselves would make their own bread from their own flour. So well organized was this in the larger villages that a crier would go round the streets very early in the morning crying *"Mesdames, faites vos pains!*" to warn the good wives it was time to put their loaves to rise. He would wake different streets in rotation according to the baker's list of who was due to bake.

Mlle. Morell, the sister of the curé of Mirabel in the Baronnies of Provence, remembers the crier well. She also remembers that her mother would rise at 2 A.M. on a baking morning to set her leaven to work to be ready for the first shift. Later in the day, great round shallow earthenware dishes of vegetables, stuffed and herbed and shiny with olive oil, would be taken down to the bakery to take advantage of the cooling oven. Roasts of meat, a special treat usually reserved for a Sunday or a day of celebration, would go in at the same time. The food would be ready for the early-evening meal, eaten in the warm kitchen after the day's work in the fields was done. Many of the beautiful slow-baked vegetable dishes of Provence originated with this ritual.

S E R V E S : 4 as a main dish, with 2 other stuffed vegetables

T I M E : 30 minutes plus 1 hour cooking

4 *large baking potatoes*	1 *small bunch of Italian parsley*
1 *onion*	*and 2 sage leaves*
One *2-ounce slab of bacon or* petit	1 *egg*
salé *(page 511)*	*Salt and pepper*
5 *tablespoons oil*	*Water or stock*
4 *ounces chopped cooked meat or*	
dried pork sausage	

Preheat the oven to 350°F. You will need a saucepan, a draining spoon, a shallow baking dish, a frying pan, a small bowl, and foil.

Peel the potatoes, and cut them in two lengthwise to give a thin lid and a thick base. Scoop out the centers to leave a hollow shell for stuffing. Scoop a teaspoon of flesh out of the lid. Chop up the scraped-out potato. Put the hollowed-out potatoes into a pan of cold salted water, and bring it to a boil. Add the potato lids and simmer for 5 minutes. Remove the potatoes carefully with a draining spoon, and arrange the bases in an earthenware gratin dish which will just accommodate them.

Peel and chop the onion very fine. Chop the bacon into small cubes and put it to melt in a tablespoonful of the oil in a frying pan. Add the onion and fry for a moment. Add the chopped potato and the meat. If you are using dried sausage, split the skin and empty out the contents into the pan. Cook until the potato pulp is soft. Tip it all into a bowl.

Chop up the herbs—the sage is very pungent. Mix them into the contents of the bowl, and add the egg lightly beaten. Season with freshly ground pepper. Add salt only if you are not using dried sausage. Work it all well together, and divide the stuffing between the hollowed-out bottom shells of the potatoes. Put on their lids. Trickle the rest of the oil over them, and pour in a glass of water or stock to come halfway up the lower shells.

Cover with foil and bake the stuffed potatoes for 40 to 50 minutes. Uncover for the last 10 minutes of the cooking time.

Serve them piping-hot, with at least one other baked stuffed vegetable. Two would be twice as good.

◆

SUGGESTIONS

If you have fresh cèpes, replace the minced meat or sausage with the mushrooms well cleaned and then chopped, stalks and all. Cèpes have a lovely gluey texture which goes well with potatoes. Dried cèpes can be bought in most Italian delicatessens (2 ounces dried replaces 1 pound fresh), and are a very acceptable substitute after they have been soaked in warm water for 20 minutes (save the soaking liquid for soup).

Any variety of dried sausage can be used.

◆

STUFFED TOMATOES

Tomates farcies (France)

SERVES: 4

TIME: 30 minutes plus 1 hour cooking

4	large firm "beefsteak" tomatoes	4	ounces fresh peas or fava beans, shelled
1	garlic clove	1	egg
1	small onion	1	small bunch of fresh basil and Italian parsley
4	tablespoons olive oil		Salt and pepper
3	ounces (about ⅓ cup) rice		

Preheat the oven to 350°F. You will need a small frying pan, a bowl, and a shallow baking dish.

Cut lids (save them) off the round ends of the tomatoes, and scoop out the seeds and pulp. Salt the shells, and upend them to drain on a plate while you prepare the stuffing.

Peel and chop the garlic and the onion. Warm 2 tablespoons of the oil in a frying pan. Throw in the garlic and the onion, and let them soften. Then stir in the rice. Fry gently together until the rice turns transparent. Add the tomato pulp and a tablespoon of water. Leave to cook on low heat for 15 minutes—the water should be all absorbed and the rice *al dente*. If the mixture looks a little liquid, turn up the heat for a moment to evaporate it. Stir in the peas, and transfer the mixture to a bowl.

Beat the egg lightly, and then mix it into the rice. Sprinkle in 2 table-spoons of the chopped herbs, and season with salt and freshly milled pepper. Pile the stuffing into the tomatoes. Put back the lids.

Arrange the stuffed tomatoes in a baking dish—brown earthenware is prettiest against their scarlet skins. Pour the rest of the oil over them. Bake for 30 to 40 minutes.

Serve in their own dish, accompanied by another stuffed vegetable or two.

◆

STUFFED EGGPLANT
WITH ANCHOVIES

Aubergines farcies aux anchoies (France)

This is a stuffing from the littoral of Provence. Many households salted their own fish, so all these ingredients would be available in the pantry.

SERVES: 4

TIME: 40 minutes plus 40 minutes cooking

4 large eggplants	½ pound tomatoes or an 8-ounce
6 to 8 (1 small can) anchovy	can of tomatoes
fillets	Fresh parsley and thyme, about 2
2 ounces black olives	heaped tablespoonfuls altogether
2 slices of day-old bread	1 egg
2 garlic cloves	½ cup olive oil
1 small onion	Pepper

Preheat the oven to 350°F. You will need a frying pan, a colander, and a wide shallow baking dish.

Hull the eggplants and cut them in half from stalk end to tip. Hollow them out and sprinkle the insides with salt. Put them to drain while you prepare the rest of the ingredients.

Chop up the scooped-out eggplant flesh. Chop up the anchovies finely. Stone and chop the olives finely. Soak the bread in a little water and squeeze out excess moisture. Peel and chop the garlic and the onion. If you are using fresh tomatoes, cover them with boiling water to loosen the skins, and then peel and chop them roughly. Chop the herbs. Beat the egg lightly.

Rinse away all the salt from the eggplant shells. Heat the oil in a small frying pan and fry the eggplant shells, flesh side down, for 5 minutes to soften them. Take them out and put them into a colander to drain (save the oil). Put some more oil in the pan and fry the chopped garlic, onion, and the rest of the eggplant pulp gently for a moment—the vegetables should soften, not take color. Add the tomatoes, the olives, and the anchovies. Simmer gently uncovered for 5 to 10 minutes, until the sauce thickens. Allow it to cool for a moment.

Mix in the soaked bread, the egg, the herbs, and a good sprinkling of freshly ground pepper. Arrange the eggplant shells in a single layer in a baking dish. Divide the stuffing mixture between them. Trickle the oil which drained from the fried eggplants over the top. Bake for 45 minutes.

Serve with plenty of bread—this is a very rich dish—and a green salad including a little sorrel or dandelion or watercress among the leaves. A *vin gris* from the salty flatlands of the Camargue can accompany.

◆

SUGGESTIONS

Anchovies from the barrel need 10 minutes soaking in milk to rid them of excess salt. The canned ones can go in as they are, although the mixture should not be further salted.

◆

STUFFED ZUCCHINI WITH WILD MUSHROOMS

Courgettes farcies aux grisettes (France)

Mediterranean squash grown for stuffing are short and fat like little oval melons. Failing these, fat slices of a larger squash are a better alternative than the long thin zucchini. Their companion in the dish, *grisettes*, are one of the most sought-after mushrooms in the markets of France. Their Latin name is *Amanita vaginata*, perhaps because they drip a milky juice. Found in beech woods in autumn, their pale-gray caps are easily visible among drifts of bronzed leaves.

SERVES: 4

TIME: 30 minutes plus 40 minutes cooking

4	round green squash	2	slices of day-old bread
4	grisettes or 4 ounces cultivated mushrooms		Fresh parsley and thyme, 1 heaped tablespoon each if fresh, or ½ teaspoon dried
2	garlic cloves		
6	tablespoons olive oil		Salt and pepper
2	ounces fatback	1	egg
2	ounces diced ham or cooked chopped meat		

Preheat the oven to 350°F. You will need a large saucepan, a colander, a small frying pan, and a shallow baking dish.

Wipe and cut the squash in half. Hollow them out. Chop up the scooped-out flesh, sprinkle it with a little salt, and put it aside to drain. Put on a pan of salted water; bring it to a boil, and plunge in the squash shells. Bring the water back to a boil, and simmer for 5 minutes. Put the shells hollow side down in a colander, and leave them to drain thoroughly.

Wipe and trim the stalk ends off the mushrooms. Chop them. Peel and chop the garlic. Warm 3 to 4 tablespoons of the oil in a frying pan and put in the fatback and ham, well chopped, or cooked chopped meat. Add the garlic and chopped mushrooms. Stew gently for 5 to 10 minutes, until the mushrooms are tender.

Tear up the bread, soak it in a little water, and then squeeze it dry. Chop the herbs. Add the bread to the mushroom-fatback mixture, along with the herbs, a teaspoon of salt, freshly milled pepper, and the egg, lightly beaten. Mix it all together well. Stuff the squash with the mixture.

Arrange the squash shells in a single layer in a wide earthenware dish. Fill them with the stuffing and trickle the rest of the oil over the top. Bake for 40 to 45 minutes.

◆

SUGGESTIONS

Squash flowers, which appear at the tip of the baby squash (or on masculine stems) early in its development, can be picked without affecting the rest of the plant and stuffed with the same mixture.

Any other wild or cultivated mushroom (known as *champignons de Paris*—the location of the caves where they were first successfully cultivated) can replace the *grisettes* in the recipe—try cultivated mushrooms plus one of the Chinese dried mushrooms such as Wood Ears, *Auricularia polytricha*, well soaked and chopped (use the soaking liquid to dampen the bread crumbs).

◆

STUFFED PEPPERS WITH PINE NUTS

Poivrons farcis (France)

Pine nuts are the little kernels of the nuts which drop out of pinecones. They need plenty of patience to prepare, as they are small and well protected by stone-hard shells. They are an ideal harvest, since time is more available than money in a peasant community. The task of cracking the shells often falls to the children. Pine nuts are sold from open sacks by the spice vendor in Mediterranean markets, along with toasted salted sunflower seeds, pumpkin seeds, and melon seeds which mothers give their children instead of sweets.

SERVES: 4

TIME: 30 to 40 minutes plus 40 minutes cooking

5 peppers	1 egg
4 tablespoons olive oil	4 ounces grated cheese (Cantal,
One 2-ounce slab of bacon or petit	Gruyère, Emmenthaler, ched-
salé, chopped	dar, Grana)
1 garlic clove, chopped	One small bunch of Italian parsley
1 small onion, chopped	2 ounces (¼ cup) pine nuts
4 ounces (½ cup) rice	Salt and pepper

Preheat the oven to 350°F. You will need a frying pan, a bowl, and a wide shallow baking dish.

Cut a lid off the stalk end of four of the peppers and remove the seeds. Put the peppers aside to await the stuffing. Hull, seed, and chop finely the remaining pepper.

Warm 2 tablespoons of the oil in a small frying pan. Add the bacon, garlic, and onion, and fry for a moment. Stir in the rice and fry it gently until it turns transparent. Add the chopped peppers. Pour in a large glass of water. Leave it to simmer for 15 minutes—the water should be all absorbed and the rice *al dente*. If you have any liquid left, give a fierce boil at the end to evaporate it. Leave it to cool a little.

Beat the egg lightly with half the cheese, and then mix it into the cooled rice, along with a tablespoon of chopped parsley and the pine nuts. Season with salt and freshly milled pepper.

Arrange the peppers in a single layer in a wide earthenware dish. Fill them with the stuffing, sprinkle some more cheese on top, and trickle over the rest of the oil. Bake for 40 to 45 minutes.

◆

STUFFED LEAVES

The travels of the Turkish *dolma* are quite remarkable. It would seem that the Ottoman Turks are responsible for the whole gamut of regional stuffed-leaf dishes, ranging from the *avgolemono*-sauced vine leaves of Greece to the braised stuffed cabbage of the Swedish table. The progress of the *dolma* can be traced in the baggage train of the Ottoman Empire, which in its heyday during the sixteenth century under Suleiman the Magnificent stretched across Persia, Egypt, and Arabia, took in most of Greece and the Balkans, and reached as far north as the borders of Austria. Not until the early part of this century did the empire finally shrink within the confines of today's Turkey.

Although *dolma* is a Turkish word meaning "stuffed," wrapped vine leaves feature in both Ancient Greek and Persian writings. The Ottoman

Turks started with a rather poor kitchen themselves, being nomadic Mongolians in origin. Affluence and stability brought new habits, and a natural appetite for pleasure made them very receptive to new ideas. *Dolmades* were originally palace cuisine—they need skill and patience. The sultan's kitchens in Topkapi Palace in Istanbul were entirely staffed by professional male chefs, and although many of the utensils they used were of the mass-catering variety—huge cauldrons and pans—there is a small collection of implements such as Chinese steamers, whisks, and small mixing bowls which indicates a more sophisticated and elegant approach to the royal table.

◆

RICE-STUFFED VINE LEAVES

Dolmades (Greece, Turkey, and Neighbors)

The Rev. W. Denton, writing home to his wife from his travels through Eastern Europe in the 1860s, came across the *dolma*, in company with that other standby of the Greek table, *avgolemono:*

> The traveller then, whether on a visit to a family in Servia or staying at an inn, will almost to a certainty be served with sour soup—that is, with soup flavoured with lemon-juice—and perhaps thickened, as was the case at Swilainatz, with champillons shred into it. Then will come forced meats, or rissoles, dressed in vine leaves or mixed with raisins, followed by a more substantial dish either of lamb or mutton, according to the season. The bread will be of the same dark and sour description to which he has been accustomed in Germany, unless he be fortunate enough to meet with maize bread, which is sweet and agreeable, but is generally rejected as being of too heating a nature to be wholesome. Should a ham make its appearance, he will find it well-flavoured, and partaking of all the excellency of wild-boar.
>
> By the side of one dish or another, but most likely with a plate of soft cheese, will be laid two or three very strong green onions; and the whole meal will invariably close with two eggs, just warmed—and barely warmed though in fact, raw—which, if careful to follow the pactice of the country, he should suck. Good Negotin or some similar wine, of a bright rose-colour, will be placed on the table in decanters holding half a gallon, to be taken—as indeed the size would indicate—ad libitum, and with this a small glass or two of raki or slivovitza. [*Servia and the Servians*, The Rev. W. Denton, 1862]

SERVES: 6

TIME: 40 minutes plus 1 hour cooking

½ *pound vine leaves, fresh or canned*	2 *ounces (¼ cup) pine nuts*
½ *pound onions*	2 *ounces (¼ cup) raisins*
½ *cup olive oil*	*Salt and pepper*
8 *ounces (1 cup) rice*	*Juice of 2 lemons*

You will need a large saucepan, a frying pan, and a shallow heatproof pan. If the vine leaves are fresh, clip off their stalks and lay them in a saucepan. Cover with boiling water and simmer for 5 minutes. Drain, and use when cool enough to handle. If the leaves are canned, they will probably not need this extra preparation.

Peel and mince the onions finely. Put 4 tablespoons of the oil in a frying pan and heat until a faint blue haze rises. Fry the onions lightly and then add the rice. Turn it in the oil to coat the grains and then add the pine nuts, raisins, salt and pepper, and a glass of water. Cook for 10 minutes or so, loosely covered, until the rice has absorbed all the water.

Pick up one leaf at a time in the palm of your hand, shiny side down. Put a teaspoonful of the filling at one end of the leaf. Fold the two sides over and roll it up into a little bolster—not too tightly, as the rice still has to swell a little. Repeat until all the filling is used up. Pack the leaf parcels as close together as possible in a shallow pan—they must not roll around or the filling will fall out. Pour in the rest of the oil, the lemon juice, and another glass of water. Cover and cook them on low heat for 1 hour, or in a preheated 300°F oven for 1 hour.

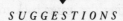

SUGGESTIONS

This rice mixture can be used for the Greek stuffed vegetables (page 37).

Leftovers: Serve the little parcels when cool as a snack or appetizer.

STUFFED CABBAGE

Gefüllter Kohl (Germany)

One of the most universal northern dishes, variations on this recipe are found all around the Baltic, including Scandinavia, and also in Hungary, Bulgaria, Rumania, Yugoslavia, and northern France.

SERVES: 5 to 6

TIME: 40 minutes plus 40 minutes cooking

4	ounces (½ cup) fresh bread crumbs
½	cup milk, stock, or water
1	onion
1	tablespoon fresh marjoram, chopped, or 1 teaspoon dried
1	egg
1	pound minced meat (pork, beef, veal—or all three mixed)

	Salt and pepper
1	fresh white cabbage or 12 to 15 leaves of salted (sauerkraut) cabbage
2	ounces (4 tablespoons) butter
1	cup thick sour cream
1	teaspoon flour

You will need two bowls, a large saucepan, and a shallow casserole with a lid. Soak the bread crumbs in the liquid. Peel and chop the onion finely. Chop the marjoram. Beat the egg.

Squeeze the excess liquid from the bread crumbs, and then mix them with the onion, marjoram, egg, minced meat, and salt and pepper, and work them into a soft dough. Have a bowl of cold water beside you so that you can dip your hands in to stop the mixture's sticking to them.

If you are using fresh cabbage, bring a large pan of salted water to a boil. Trim off any damaged outside leaves, and then plunge the whole head into the boiling water to blanch. Bring the water back to a boil, and then drain the cabbage. This will allow you to separate the leaves.

If you have chosen to use sauerkraut cabbage, rinse it well and then stew it gently for half an hour before draining and stuffing.

Preheat the oven to 350°F. Cut off the larger cabbage leaves and spread them out on the table—you may need to flatten the stalks with the back of a knife. (Shred the rest of the leaves to cook lightly in a little boiling salted water and serve with the stuffed rolls.) Fill each leaf with a teaspoon of stuffing, and then roll it up into a little parcel. Continue until all are finished.

Pack the stuffed leaves in a single layer in a buttered casserole with a lid. Dot with the rest of the butter and trickle in a tablespoon or two of water. Sprinkle with salt and pepper, cover the dish tightly, and bake for 40 minutes.

After 30 minutes, pour the sour cream, mixed with the flour to stabilize it, into the gaps between the rolls. Cook uncovered for the remaining 10 minutes.

Serve hot in its own dish. The lightly cooked shredded cabbage dressed with more sour cream can be passed separately. Alternatively serve with potatoes mashed with cream. This is a wonderfully comforting dish on a cold day.

◆

STUFFED CABBAGE LEAVES

Kaldomar (Sweden)

This is the northern version of the Turkish/Greek stuffed vine-leaf dish, *dolmades*. Cabbage replaces the southerly vine leaf. It seems likely that the dish arrived in Sweden with the creditors of the warrior-king Charles XII. His Majesty had been roundly defeated in 1709 by Czar Peter the Great at the

Battle of Poltava, and the great military adventurer had escaped by the skin of his teeth and without his army. He took refuge in Turkey, where he attempted without success to persuade the sultan to take up arms on his behalf. When, some five years later, Charles set off to ride home, his Turkish creditors and their obligatory retinue of cooks followed. Although Charles (who managed to start another Nordic war on his return) died in 1718, the Turks stayed around for a further fifteen years to collect what they were owed. The first recipe for their favorite dish, Nordicised into *kaldomar*, is to be found in Kajsa Warg's 1765 book on household management.

SERVES: 6

TIME: 30 to 40 minutes plus 20 to 30 minutes cooking

4	ounces (½ cup) fresh bread crumbs	1	teaspoon salt
			Pepper
½	cup milk or cream	1	large white cabbage
1	small onion	4	ounces (½ cup) butter for sauce
1	pound minced meat		(optional)
1	egg		

You will need a bowl, a saucepan, and a shallow pan with a lid. Put the bread crumbs to soak in the milk or cream. Peel and chop the onion finely. Put the minced meat into a bowl with the egg, salt, and freshly milled pepper. Squeeze the excess moisture out of the bread crumbs and add them to the meat, along with the chopped onion. Mix it all together and knead thoroughly.

Break off 16 to 20 outside leaves from the cabbage, and blanch them for a moment in boiling salted water. Place a sausage of the forcemeat in each leaf, tuck the sides over, roll the leaf up with its stuffing inside, and lay the rolls in a single layer in a well-fitting pan. Cover with boiling salted water and poach them gently for 20 to 30 minutes.

These rolls can be served as they are, or browned quickly in butter and then served with a jug of more melted butter.

◆

SUGGESTIONS

Cooked rice often replaces the bread crumbs in the mixture: echoes of the Mediterranean *dolmades*. All the Scandinavian nations love rice.

Use young beech or hazelnut leaves instead of cabbage as the wrapper.

◆
_____

STUFFED LEAVES

Sarmale (Rumania)

The favorite dish of rural Rumania, here the Turkish/Greek *dolmades* are at their most adaptable and it is truly a dish of the crossroads of Europe. The variability of its composition reveals Rumania as a kind of culinary Galápagos Islands. In the late spring and early summer, vine leaves are the preferred wrapping for the stuffing. The late summer and autumn sees cabbage leaves employed for the purpose. By the winter, the *dolma* is well on its way north and appears wrapped in sauerkraut leaves. The Turks established paddy fields to grow their favorite crop, rice, in the fertile Danube delta.

S E R V E S : 4

T I M E : If you salt your own cabbage, start 1 week before; 30 minutes plus 30 to 40 minutes cooking

16 to 20 vine leaves or 1 fresh or salted cabbage	3 tablespoons oil
	1 cup water
8 ounces (1 cup) long-grain rice	Salt, pepper, savory, tarragon, and thyme to taste
2 to 3 scallions with their green leaves	½ pound minced meat

You will need a saucepan, a frying pan, and a shallow casserole with a lid. To salt a whole cabbage, make a brine with 1 ounce of salt to 2 cups of water. Put the cabbage in a deep dish and cover it with brine. Weight it to keep it well under the brine. Cover and leave to ferment for a week in a cool place. Rinse well before using.

If you are using a fresh cabbage, blanch it for 5 minutes in boiling water. Remove any particularly thick ribs from the cabbage, whether salt or fresh. Separate and trim the leaves if you are using vine leaves. Pick over the rice. Peel and chop the scallions finely, leaves and all.

Put the oil to heat in a frying pan. Toss the scallions in it and push to one side. Turn the rice in the oil until it is transparent. Add the water, a little salt, pepper, and chopped herbs. Bring to a boil and simmer for 10 minutes, when the rice will still be chewy.

Put the meat in a bowl and add the rice mixture; turn it with your hand, squeezing and draining to make a firm mixture. Clean hands are the most versatile implements in the kitchen and this is a lovely tranquil job.

Lay out the leaves. Place a small ball of stuffing (about a tablespoon a time) on each leaf, and roll it up neatly, tucking the sides over first to enclose the mixture. Put each little parcel into a shallow casserole as you make it, seam downwards, all the rolls tucked neatly together. Pour enough water in to cover the base of the dish to the depth of one finger. Cover and cook either gently on top of the stove, or in a preheated 350°F oven, for 30 to 40 minutes.

Serve Rumania's favorite dish with *mamaliga* (page 126) and a bowl of thick sour cream.

◆

SUGGESTIONS

Minced bacon, finely chopped vegetables, chopped wild or cultivated mushrooms, or a few chopped fresh herbs can replace the meat. At the Cernice Monastery just outside Bucharest, whose inmates are condemned to a perpetual fast of superb fish, I am told they make excellent *sarmale* with a fish stuffing.

◆

CABBAGE ROLLS
Sarma (Yugoslavia)

This recipe comes from Nada Babich, with help from her husband, Hrvoje, and his sister Lada. Nada says that *sarma*, if prepared in sufficient quantity, can be eaten for three days—better on the second day and best of all on the third. Lada says that although it takes a little time to prepare, this frees the housewife from the obligations of the kitchen for two whole days.

Sour (salt) cabbage, *kisele kupus*, is easily bought in the markets of northern Yugoslavia, and indeed throughout the Balkans and into Germany and Alsace, but many families prefer to make their own when living abroad. They make it by placing fresh cabbage in brine in a closed plastic container and storing it in a cool place. Hrvoje says that the consistency of the brine should be midway between seawater and a soup. *Sarma* is a winter dish, and Hrvoje suggests storing the cabbage on the balcony in the cold winter air—the cabbage should be sour enough, he says, in about two weeks (I find it quite sour enough in one week—but it does improve with the extra keeping).

SERVES: 12

TIME: Start a week or two ahead if you make your own cabbage

1	large onion	1	teaspoon salt
1	tablespoon corn or other vegetable oil	1	teaspoon pepper
1	pound lean ground beef	1	head of sour cabbage, approximately 3 pounds (see previous recipe)
½	pound ground pork		
2	thick slices of bacon	½	pound smoked pork or dried smoked sausage
½	cup rice		
2	garlic cloves		

TO FINISH:

2   *tablespoons corn or vegetable oil*
1   *tablespoon flour*
1   *teaspoon sweet paprika*

You will need a frying pan, a mixing bowl, and a heavy pot or casserole with a lid. Peel the onion and chop it finely. Warm the oil in a frying pan and add the onion. Leave it to fry gently until transparent and golden.

Meanwhile, mix the ground beef and the ground pork with the bacon cut into small squares, the rice, the peeled and finely chopped garlic, and the salt and pepper. Add the fried onion with its oil. Mix all together well.

Remove the core of the cabbage head. Peel off the cabbage leaves and trim off the thick ribs at the base. Save any trimmings. Rinse the leaves and taste a little piece. If it tastes too sour or salty, boil the cabbage leaves for a few minutes.

Form the meat mixture into oblong shapes about 1 to 2 inches long and ¾ to 1 inch thick. The size of the meat shapes should match the size of the cabbage leaves in which they will be rolled, the larger ones being used in the outside leaves and the smaller ones in the inner leaves. Place each meat patty in the center of its appropriate cabbage leaf. Roll the leaf over the meat from the left side, and fold over one end. Finish rolling, and tuck in the free end.

Line the bottom and the sides of a pot or casserole with cabbage leaves, about 2 or 3 leaves thick. Place the cabbage rolls side by side in the pot—like laying bricks, says Hrvoje—to form layers. Between the layers tuck in roughly chopped pieces of the smoked pork or dried sausage. Use finely chopped scraps of cabbage to fill in the voids.

To finish, heat the 2 tablespoons of oil in the frying pan. When it smokes, stir in the flour and the paprika to make a thick paste. Add about a pint of water and pour this sauce over the cabbage rolls. Add water to the pot until the level is about ½ inch below the top layer of rolls.

Bring the liquid to a boil, cover the pot, and simmer slowly for 1½ hours. Serve with bread, and choose a good Yugoslav wine, white or red, to accompany the dish.

◆

SUGGESTIONS

There are many versions of *sarma*. Lada says that perhaps tomatoes should be included, but both Nada and Hrvoje emphatically disagree. Hrvoje explained that although there are indeed many versions of *sarma*, Nada's recipe is second only to that of his mother.

Leftovers: Reheat the dish—you will probably need extra liquid. For a variation, add Lada's pulped tomatoes to the additional cooking liquid.

VEGETABLE SALADS

CUCUMBER-AND-YOGURT SALAD

Tzatziki (Greece)
Cacik (Turkey)

This is a refreshing salad for a hot day which makes use of the excellent Greek yogurt—the most delicious of which is made from sheep's milk. In Greece a special thick yogurt is prepared for this dish—achieved by leaving ordinary yogurt to drain overnight through a jelly cloth. The guiding principle is that the thicker the yogurt, the better.

SERVES: 5 to 6

TIME: If you want to make drained yogurt, start the day before; 25 minutes

1   *large cucumber*
½   *teaspoon salt*
2   *cups thick yogurt (see note below)*
2 to 3 *garlic cloves*

NOTE: If you are making your own drained yogurt, leave it overnight to drip in a cloth pinned onto an upturned stool's legs, or in a jelly bag (the whey will make deliciously light scones—see page 423).

You will need a grater, a sieve, or a colander, and two bowls. Grate or chop the cucumber finely; then put it into a sieve or colander and sprinkle it with the salt. Leave it to drain for 20 minutes or so, while you prepare the rest of the ingredients.

Put the thick yogurt into a deep bowl. Peel and crush the garlic and stir a little of the yogurt into it. Mix well, and then add it to the rest of the yogurt. Fold in the rinsed, drained cucumber. Serve the salad cool, with a dish of black olives and plenty of bread. As a first course, another salad or two can accompany this one—say the *taramasalata* (page 272) and the *melitzanosalata* (page 54).

SUGGESTION

In Turkey and the Middle East chopped fresh mint is often added.

EGGPLANT SALAD

Melitzanosalata (Greece)

This is one of a range of purees which are eaten with bread. More of a dip than a salad, eggplants thus prepared have a peculiarly addictive, slightly bitter, smoky flavor. Similar recipes appear all around the Middle East.

SERVES: 5 to 6

TIME: 20 minutes plus 40 minutes cooking

1½ pounds eggplant	Juice of 1 lemon
1 to 2 garlic cloves	Salt and pepper
⅓ pint (5⅓ ounces) olive oil	

Preheat the oven to 400°F. You will need a food processor or a pestle and mortar.

Wipe the eggplants and put them to roast in the oven until they are soft and the skins have blistered. This will take about 40 minutes. It can also be done on top of a charcoal brazier.

Peel the eggplants and pound the pulp to a paste with the garlic, peeled and crushed. Beat in the oil and lemon juice until you have a thick pale puree. This can be done very successfully in a food processor, adding the oil and lemon in a thin stream. Add salt and pepper to taste.

Serve the purée at room temperature. Garnish with a few black olives, preferably Calamata. Accompany with one or two other salads, perhaps a *taramasalata* (page 272) and a *salata horiatiki* (page 55). Serve with plenty of good Greek bread to scoop up the purée.

SUGGESTION

In Bulgaria the dish is named *zelen haviar*, and is usually spiked with a little chili and some chopped tomato.

GREEK SALAD

Salata horiatiki (Greece)

These simple salads appear on the countryman's board almost automatically, to be eaten with bread as a sop to the appetite while the hot dish is cooking. The salad itself can be as elegant or simple as the habit and means of the housewife dictates, but it is always freshly made from the best ingredients available.

In a household which lives near the sea, there might be a dish of crisp-fried fish to follow. The country people might have a plate of french fries topped by a couple of eggs, the whites fried crisp in olive oil. The meal will be accompanied by a glass of wine for pleasure and water for thirst.

SERVES: 5 to 6

TIME: 20 minutes

4 to 5 large ripe tomatoes	*2 teaspoons salt*
1 cucumber	*1 tablespoon wine vinegar*
3 to 5 green peppers	*4 tablespoons olive oil*
1 bundle of scallions or 2 sweet	*1 tablespoon oregano, chopped*
* Spanish onions*	*1 tablespoon black olives, chopped*
8 ounces feta cheese	

You will need a large flat serving dish. Wash the vegetables and quarter the tomatoes—cut them into chunks if they are the large Mediterranean variety. All the vegetables should be cut into approximately the same size chunks. Cut the cucumber into generous cubes. Seed the peppers and cut the flesh into squares. Peel the scallions or onions and either slice them or chop them roughly. Mix the vegetables and spread them decoratively over a flat plate.

Slice the cheese and cut it into squares. Lay the cheese slices over the top of the salad—they are the most important ingredient, and generous quantities indicate a generous host. Mix the salt and the vinegar together until the salt has dissolved—this makes all the difference to the result—and then mix in the oil. Sprinkle the salad with the oregano and black olives.

BEET SALAD

Patzaria salata (Greece)

This beet salad utilizes both the root and the leaves of the beet. Wide use is made in Greece of wild greens such as *radiki*, dandelion greens, which are particularly important in the early spring. They are the Lenten bitter herbs, most welcome after the winter's shortages. Wild greens are always gathered by the women. *Radiki* leaves are mild in flavor when young, and are even gathered in the cities. They must always be washed very thoroughly. Another of this range of green salads is *vlita*, mustard greens, which are lightly boiled and dressed while still warm with olive oil and chopped raw garlic.

SERVES: 6

TIME: 10 minutes plus 45 minutes cooking

2   *pounds young beets, still crowned with their fresh leaves*
1   *teaspoon salt*
2   *tablespoons wine vinegar*
6   *tablespoons olive oil*

You will need a large saucepan. Cut off the green leaves and the roots of the beets and wash both. Cook the roots, without peeling them, in a roomy pot in plenty of boiling water for 30 minutes (less if the roots are very small). Then add the leaves and stems. Cook for another 15 minutes. Drain.

Peel the beets, keeping them separate, and then slice them. Chop the leaves and stems. Pile the greens in the middle of a flat dish, and surround them with an overlapping circle of the deep-crimson slices of beet. Mix the salt and the vinegar together until the salt crystals dissolve; then stir in the oil. Dress the salad while the beets are still warm.

This salad is served with its favorite accompaniment, a bowl of *skordalia* (the recipe follows). Complete the meal with a dish of plain-grilled meat or fish, served with lemon quarters, salt, and good Greek bread.

◆

SUGGESTION

If you cannot find raw beets, make the dish with 2 pounds of canned beets and a few stalks of Swiss chard—which you will have to slice and then boil in salted water for 10 minutes before you drain and dress them.

◆

GREEK GARLIC SAUCE

Skordalia (Greece)

There is no other garlic sauce which approaches this in drama and pungency. It is only for committed garlic lovers. In Greece, where the sauce is much appreciated, it is pounded in a *goudi*—a special pestle and mortar. It is served with fried fish (particularly salt cod fritters and fried mussels), fritters of eggplant and squash, or fried potatoes. It is also served with beet salad (page 55). *Skordalia* can be made without bread to thicken: It is then spooned directly onto the food rather than being passed separately.

SERVES: 6 to 8

TIME: 20 minutes

1 whole garlic bulb (10 to 12 fat cloves)	1 teaspoon salt
	1 cup olive oil
2 slices of bread	4 tablespoons freshly squeezed lemon juice
4 tablespoons hot water	

You will need a pestle and mortar or a food processor. Peel the garlic cloves. Tear up the bread and mash it thoroughly in the hot water. Add the garlic cloves and the salt, and mash them to a pulp. Gradually trickle in the oil, adding the lemon juice as you go, as if making a mayonnaise, beating vigorously.

The result should be a thick paste which can be used as a dip as well as a sauce. The whole job can be done most effectively in a food processor.

◆

SUGGESTIONS

If the sauce separates, take the easy way out and start again, this time adding an egg yolk, as for a mayonnaise.

Four ounces of ground almonds can be included to make a more elegant sauce. In Turkey, where the sauce is called *tarator*, walnuts replace the almonds. Pine nuts are also used where they are more readily available.

VEGETABLE SALAD

Salata (Bulgaria)

The Ottoman yoke came down on the Bulgarian ox in 1393 when the ancient capital, Turnovo, was captured and destroyed. Today in Bulgaria, the best gardeners in Eastern Europe have plenty of New World vegetables in their kitchen plots, supplied initially by the gourmet Turks anxious for new flavors. The change was chronicled by the meticulous Turkish tax collectors. The vegetables readily available in fifteenth-century Bulgarian markets were sturdy peasant crops: cabbages, cucumbers, spinach, turnips, radishes, broad beans, peas, lentils, melons, onions, and garlic. The Turks were responsible for the introduction of rice, the Damask rose (attar for Turkish beauties and sybaritic sweetmeats), Egyptian maize ("Turkish wheat"), and finally from America came the bean, tomato, capsicum pepper, potato, and pumpkin. The Bulgarians planted and tended them all with enthusiasm. Their reward ever since has been an excellent vegetable supply.

SERVES: 6

TIME: Start 1 hour before; 15 minutes

2　green and 2 red peppers	1　tablespoon fresh lemon juice
2　pounds tomatoes	4　tablespoons sunflower oil or a
½　pound mild onions	light seed oil such as sesame
2　tablespoons pine nuts or almonds	1　tablespoon each chopped Italian
or walnuts	parsley and dill
1　teaspoon salt	

You will need a large bowl.

Stalk, seed, and chop the peppers very fine. Wipe the tomatoes and chop them very fine. Peel and mince the onions. Pound up the nuts. Mix all the ingredients together and leave them for an hour or two for the flavors to develop.

Serve with plenty of rough dark bread (page 407) on which to pile spoonfuls of the salad. In Bulgaria it might come accompanied by a few slices of *sirene*, the local fresh white goat's cheese, for which feta or any strong salty goat's cheese can substitute, or some *kashkaval*, the local cured yellow cheese.

The dish is excellent with a little grilled lamb cutlet or lightly spiced kabob. The Bulgarians make their own variety of minced meat kabobs called *kebapcheta*.

◆

LIMA BEAN SALAD

Koukia (Greece)

Fava beans and their American cousin lima beans have been grown in Greece since Neolithic times; they are one of the most ancient of the European cultivars.

SERVES: 4

TIME: 15 to 20 minutes plus 1½ hours cooking

1	pound young lima beans in the pod	1	sweet onion
6	tablespoons olive oil		Fresh parsley and dill, chopped, about 2 tablespoons or more
1	glass of water		Salt and pepper
1	lemon		

You will need a saucepan or a heatproof casserole. String the beans and then chop them into lengths, pod and all. Later in the year you may have to shell them; later still use them dried.

Put the oil to warm in a pan or casserole. Add the beans and stew them in the oil for a moment before pouring in a glass of water. Cover tightly and simmer very gently for 1½ hours, until the beans are mushy, the juices evaporated, and only oil remains. Take the lid off toward the end of the cooking to assist the evaporation process.

Squeeze the lemon and stir the juice into the beans. Peel and chop the onion finely: Hold it in the palm of your hand and make downward cuts into it (without going all the way through) in a close grid pattern. Now you have but to slice across the cuts and you will have perfectly minced onion. Chop the herbs. Scatter the onion and the herbs over the warm beans. Season with salt and pepper. Serve cool.

Accompany with plenty of good bread and serve with grilled fish or *souvlakia*—cubes of meat threaded on skewers, brushed with oil and lemon juice, and grilled. Finish the meal with a short glass of *ouzo*, a long glass of water, and a tiny cup of thick, sweet Turkish coffee.

◆

SUGGESTIONS

This dish can be made with almost any Mediterranean-grown vegetable: green beans, Swiss chard, spinach, baby artichokes, potatoes, peppers.

Chopped tomatoes (if you use these, leave out the water in the recipe), whole olives, and garlic can be included—and you have a *plaki*.

Leftovers: In a blender, dilute the plain mix with stock or milk to make a light and delicious soup. Sprinkle with chopped onion and mint. Serve hot or cold.

◆

ASPARAGUS VINAIGRETTE

Asperges vinaigrette (France)

After the terrible winter of 1956, when two thirds of the olive trees in Provence had the sap frozen in their taproots, only a few farmers had the courage to replant. The rest spread the risk: apricots, cherries, more vines, asparagus. The asparagus is the most demanding: Seasonal labor must be employed and must be up at five to look in the heaped beds under plastic strip blankets. Mlle. Morell, a resident of the area, and herself as old as the century, told me that she found the fast-growing asparagus magical:

> "You wouldn't believe it. At night there is nothing there, and in the morning, marvelous, a row of little points, ready to be plucked with the special knife that can nip them off down under the earth. Then the sticks must be graded and bundled for market. People today are very demanding. They must have their points just so. Two months only the season lasts, but all that time you must be in the fields with the dew before dawn, every day, and then all day picking and grading, picking and grading."

The fruit of the olive trees which survived the terrible cold of that year still blesses the vegetables which replaced them. Good Provençal olive oil is as sweet and thick as half-melted butter.

SERVES: 4

TIME: 15 to 20 minutes plus 15 to 20 minutes cooking

2   *pounds large white asparagus*
½   *cup extra virgin olive oil*
3   *tablespoons wine vinegar*
Salt and pepper

You will need a very large deep saucepan or an asparagus boiler. Wash and trim the asparagus stalks and tie them into a bundle. Bring a large pan of salted water to a rolling boil and lower the bundles in, feet first. Prop them up so that the stalks are submerged but the tips are only in steam. Bring the water back to a boil, turn the heat down, and boil gently for 15 to 20 minutes, until the stalks are soft. Lift them out, drain them thoroughly, and serve them piping hot on a white napkin.

Accompany with a jug of the best olive oil you can find, mixed with the wine vinegar, with a fork left in the jug so that oil and vinegar can be stirred together again. Put a dish of rough salt and a pepper mill on the table, and plenty of bread. Few French countrymen would enjoy a meal without bread to mop up the juices.

A pork or lamb chop, grilled with rosemary and acompanied by a potato gratin (page 99) could follow this dish. Cheese and fruit or a fresh fruit tart (page 106) complete a perfect Sunday lunch.

SUGGESTIONS

Serve the stalks of the Swiss chard (whose leaves you have used to make a *trouchia*) in the same manner. The hot vegetable and the light vinaigrette are delicious together. The oil must be of the best Provence can offer—and that is very good indeed. Lemon juice can be used instead of the vinegar—citrus and vines grow side by side in the fertile Rhône basin.

MIXED-LEAF SALAD

Salade de Mesclun (France)

This is the mixture of herbs, named from the Latin word *miscellaneus*, long appreciated as a special salad mixture around Nice and lately the darling of nouvelle cuisine. Packets of assorted *mesclun* seeds can be bought from the seedsmen and spice merchants who set up their stalls in the market squares of the villages of Provence. The salad leaves used to be cultivated in the monastery garden of the Franciscan friars at Cimiez in the hills behind Nice, and fetched in special baskets to be presented by children to favored adults. Dandelion, rocket, purslane, and chervil provide the small leaves; red Treviso chicory, white bitter chicory, oak leaf, and cos lettuce the larger. Rub the inside of the salad bowl with a cut clove of garlic, or toss it with a *chapon*—a nugget of stale bread rubbed with garlic—and dress the salad lightly with olive oil, a few drops of vinegar, and salt.

A nut oil makes a delicious dressing, but a blessing of olive oil is more likely in the home territory of this salad, which is at its delicate best after a dish of plain-grilled fish or a beautiful fish soup. Follow with a sharp, salty, dark-rinded little goat's cheese, or a *tarte au citron* (page 447).

FIELD SALAD

Salade des champs (France)

Ensalado champenello in the patois, this is food for the road, to be taken into the fields by harvesters for their midday breakfast. The fish mixture would be made in situ with a salted fish (ramrod straight and known as a *gendarme*) from the barrel in the local shop. The salad would be easily gathered from the kitchen garden or roadside—corn salad (*mâche*) grows anywhere, all year round if the climate is mild.

SERVES: 4

TIME: 10 minutes

1 smoked herring (preferably with roe)
4 tablespoons olive oil
1 tablespoon wine vinegar (red or white)

1 pound corn salad (also called in Provence mâche, doucette, lachugetto) or any tender young lettuce leaves

You will need a pestle and mortar or a food processor. Broil the herring lightly—this can be done on a barbecue with great success. Skin the fish, remove the bones, and pound the flesh in a mortar with the oil and the vinegar (this is easily done in a food processor). Toss the corn salad in this fishy dressing.

Serve in individual bowls, with plenty of bread, a handful of olives, a bottle of red wine, a piece of ripe salty Roquefort from the neighboring Causses, and you will be well satisfied.

◆

SALADE NIÇOISE

(France)

This is one of the most abused salads ever devised. Cooked vegetables, including potatoes, are often and quite wrongly included. On the other hand, prepared correctly with good fresh ingredients and absolutely no cooked vegetables, it provides the most refreshing of light summer lunches, or a delicious entrée to a meal. All the ingredients, with the exception of the comparatively expensive tuna fish, are easily come by in the Mediterranean kitchen garden and cupboard.

SERVES: 4

TIME: 30 minutes

4 to 5 fresh eggs at room temperature
2 pounds tomatoes (plump, firm, and ripe)
Salt
1 cucumber (not too large)
1 small can of anchovies or 12 fillets from the barrel, soaked in milk to remove excess saltiness
1 can of tuna fish

2 green peppers
1 small bundle of scallions or 1 sweet onion
½ pound shelled young raw lima beans or raw baby artichokes
1 garlic clove
1 handful of black olives
A few leaves of fresh basil
Olive oil

You will need a small saucepan for the eggs and a large shallow bowl or dish. To hard-cook the eggs, have them at room temperature, put them in a saucepan, and cover them with cold water. Bring the water to a boil; then cover the pan and turn off the heat. After 10 minutes take them out and plunge them into cold water. When they are cool enough to handle, peel them and quarter them lengthwise.

Quarter the tomatoes, sprinkle them with salt, and put them to drain while you prepare the rest of the ingredients. Wipe and then slice the cucumber (not too finely). Cut the anchovy fillets in half and flake the tuna fish roughly. Wipe, top, and seed the peppers, and cut them into rings. Peel and trim the scallions, or onion, and slice them into rings. Slice the beans or, if you are using baby artichokes, trim off the hard leaf-tops, scoop out the tiny chokes, and slice the rest finely.

Rub thoroughly the inside of a large shallow bowl, preferably made of olive wood, with the cut garlic clove. Arrange all the salad ingredients carefully in the bowl. Sprinkle the olives and a few torn leaves of basil over the top. Sprinkle with olive oil and salt. That's all. Serve immediately.

Accompany with the best fresh bread in the neighborhood and a bottle or two of strong young wine—red or white. Serve a potato gratin after the salad. Finish the meal with a piece of cheese and a bowl of fresh southern fruit—sweet orange-fleshed canteloupe, ripe peaches, apricots, or grapes. Or take the opportunity to make a fruit tart (page 106).

SUGGESTIONS

Leftovers: Make a *pan bagnat* or "wet bread"—there is a special little round loaf baked in the Nice area for this favorite "second breakfast" which is taken to the fields or the workplace. Bread rolls or a long French bread will do. Cut the rolls in half horizontally and scoop out most of the inside crumb. Rub the inside with a cut clove of garlic. Trickle in some olive oil, a few drops of vinegar, salt, and pepper. Fill the hollows with *salade niçoise* or a few slices of tomato and sweet onion, and sandwich the bread together again. Put a cloth on top with a board over it, and leave it weighted for an hour or so for the flavors to mingle. It makes a splendid picnic lunch.

POTATO SALAD

Salade de pommes de terre (France)

This is an excellent salad from the olive groves of Provence. Potatoes grow well in the sandy soil of the coast, waxy and yellow and perfect for the purpose.

SERVES: 6

TIME: 20 minutes

2 pounds (10) small new waxy potatoes	1 garlic clove, peeled and crushed with a pinch of salt
2 tablespoons mild Dijon mustard	1 small bunch of scallions, trimmed and chopped
4 tablespoons olive oil	
2 tablespoons wine vinegar	1 glass of white wine (or the same quantity of meat stock)
2 slices of day-old bread, in small cubes	
	Pepper

You will need a roomy saucepan and a wide shallow earthenware dish. Bring a pan of salted water to a boil. Scrub the potatoes and then plunge them into the boiling water. Boil them for 15 to 20 minutes, until they are just soft.

Meanwhile, mix the mustard, oil, and vinegar with the bread and the garlic. Add the scallions. Put this dressing into a wide shallow earthenware dish.

Drain the potatoes when they are ready. Slice them roughly, skin and all, into the sauce. Pour in the wine and freshly milled pepper, and mix everything together. The potatoes will drink all the liquid as they cool. Serve with a plate of *charcuterie*—sliced dried sausages and raw dried ham, *jambón de bayonne*, or *Parma*, with a pat of sweet butter and plenty of crusty French bread.

◆

DEVILED PEPPERS

Piments à la diable (France)

Part of the Provençal table, this is a simple and delicious salad. Red peppers grow plump and sweet in the Mediterranean sun.

SERVES: 4

TIME: Start the day before; 20 to 25 minutes

6 large red peppers
3 tablespoons olive oil
1 small bunch of fresh basil

Grill the peppers until their skins turn black. This can be done either under a very hot broiler, or by turning them, speared on a knife, over a direct flame. You can let them rest in a paper bag for 10 minutes or so to loosen the skins.

The blackened skins will then peel cleanly back to their soft scarlet flesh. Hull and seed them, and cut them lengthwise into strips. Put them on a plate and film them over with the oil. Leave them overnight in a cool place—not in the refrigerator. The next day sprinkle with the basil, well chopped. They will provide a delicious little hors d'oeuvre.

◆

SERBIAN SALAD

Ajvar (Yugoslavia)

An important member of the salad-purée family, this popular dish is served as an appetizer with olives and bread.

SERVES: 4 to 6

TIME: 20 to 30 minutes plus 10 minutes cooking

2 *sweet red peppers*	1 *cup olive oil*
2 to 3 *large eggplants*	*Salt and pepper*
6 to 8 *garlic cloves*	
1 to 2 *tablespoons wine vinegar or*	
fresh lemon juice	

Preheat the oven to 325°F. You will need a bowl and a wooden spoon. A food processor would do the work in half the time.

Broil or bake the peppers and eggplants in the oven for 20 to 30 minutes, until the skins blister and the vegetables soften. Skin the peppers; then halve and seed them. Peel the eggplants. Peel and chop the garlic. Chop thoroughly together and beat thoroughly until you have a heavy purée; then add the vinegar or lemon juice. Beat in the oil—as much as the mixture will absorb. Add salt and pepper to taste. This can be kept in the refrigerator for 2 to 3 days. Bring it up to room temperature before you serve it.

If you are using a food processor, put all the ingredients except the oil, into the chopping bowl and blend thoroughly. Add the oil in a steady stream until the mixture will absorb no more (it will start pooling).

Serve with bread and olives and quartered lemons, and follow with a grilled fish or kabob.

◆

SAUERKRAUT SALAD

Kisel Zelje (Balkans)

The town of Riesling in northern Yugoslavia makes no concessions to the waves of capitalist tourists who bake themselves on the beaches of the Aegean coast a few miles to the west. The single restaurant in the little town caters to more serious and purposeful travelers; People's plastic and stainless steel accommodated the gray-suited travelers and the single black-clad grandmother which made up the clientele on the day of my visit. The catering and service were strictly institutional, but the salad was excellent. This is the classic Slav salad combination, to be found on every dining table from Belgrade to Budapest. Fresh cabbage would replace sauerkraut in summer.

SERVES: 6

TIME: Start an hour or two ahead; 15 minutes

1 pound sauerkraut or fresh cabbage, shredded and then salted for an hour	1 onion
	6 tablespoons sunflower or olive oil
1 pound carrots	Pepper
1 green pepper	

You will need a salad bowl and a grater. Rinse the salty brine off the sauerkraut if using. Scrape, rinse, and grate the carrots. Seed and slice the pepper. Chop the onion. Toss it all together with the oil and freshly milled pepper to taste. Leave the salad to infuse for an hour or two before you serve it (because of the sauerkraut or presalted cabbage, you should need no extra salt.)

A dish of sliced tomatoes dressed with a sprinkling of sugar and a trickle of oil, a few pickled cucumbers, and black olives makes a perfect starter to a Balkan meal, whether it is a grill or a bean stew like the *pasulj* on p. 120.

◆

SALAD ŠOPSKA

(Yugoslavia)

The salad usually served with grilled meat, this is a favorite throughout the Balkans. The amount of cheese used varies according to the means of the cook.

SERVES: 4 to 6

TIME: 10 minutes

1 pound tomatoes	1 to 2 tablespoons wine vinegar
½ pound peppers (red or green or both)	Salt and pepper to taste
1 large sweet onion	4 to 6 ounces crumbly white cheese, such as feta
5 to 6 tablespoons olive or sunflower oil	1 to 2 small green chilies (optional)

You will need a large bowl. Thinly slice the tomatoes horizontally. Hull and seed the peppers, and cut them into strips. Peel and slice the onion finely. Mix everything together well in the bowl with the oil, vinegar, and seasoning. Grate the cheese over the top and scatter a few rings of sliced chili over all if you like your salad piquant.

Serve the salad either as an appetizer or as a side dish with barbecued meat.

◆

MUSHROOMS

These recipes are mostly interchangeable among the wild mushrooms that are collected all over Europe. Fungi are the most treasured and freely available wild crop of all. Curiously, though, different nations collect different edible fungi and often have strong prejudices against varieties which others collect with enthusiasm. All the recipes can be prepared with ordinary cultivated mushrooms—button are suitable for some, big flat ones for others. Use your discretion.

MUSHROOM RICE

Orez cu ciupera (Rumania)

Wild mushrooms are used in Rumania to flavor soups and stews, and in particular as an addition to a rice pilaf.

SERVES: 4

TIME: 30 minutes

8 ounces (1 cup) rice	1 pound wild (or failing that,
2 ounces bacon	cultivated) mushrooms
1 onion with its green top (or	2 ounces (4 tablespoons) butter or
without, and with a little	bacon fat
bunch of chives)	Salt and pepper
A scant 2 cups water	

You will need a saucepan and a small frying pan. Pick over the rice. Slice the bacon into small cubes. Peel and chop the onion, putting aside the green top with the mushrooms. Fry the bacon in a hot dry saucepan. If you heat the saucepan first, good bacon (which has not been pumped full of water and saturated with chemicals) will not stick to it. Push the bacon to one side, and turn the onions and the rice in the bacon fat until both are transparent (you may need a little extra fat). Add the water, bring to a boil, and simmer the rice, uncovered, for 20 minutes, until all the moisture is absorbed and the rice is tender.

Meanwhile, pick over and wipe your treasure trove of wild mushrooms—a pleasure which will fully occupy the 20 minutes which it takes the rice to become tender. That is, if you have a mound of beautiful wild fungi piled on your kitchen table—fresh from the woods, the green moss and autumn leaves still lightly pressed into their scented flesh. The inky-dark Horn of Plenty goes particularly well in this dish, or its cousin, the apricot-scented, golden-fleshed chanterelle—don't forget to turn it over and admire the delicate cathedral-vault fluting of its gills. Or make the dish in the spring with the most delicious of all mushrooms, the morel, when its dark wrinkled cap and white stipe share the fields with the first speckled purple orchids of the year—little stubby Beasts among so many Beauties.

Slice your crop of mushrooms and chop the onion leaves which you have saved. Melt the butter or bacon fat in a small frying pan. Fry the mushrooms in the butter until they are tender. At the last moment, stir in the onion tops or the chives, well chopped. Add salt and pepper in moderation.

Mix the mushroom ragout into the warm rice. Heaven will have nothing more to offer.

◆

MUSHROOMS IN OIL AND GARLIC

Champignons à la bordelaise (France)

Use, if you can, the big, flat, black-gilled field mushrooms. Penny buns—cèpes or *Boletus edulis*—are even better. Baskets of cèpes are on sale in the markets of Bordeaux from July onwards, and this is the most delicious way of preparing them.

SERVES: 4

TIME: 30 minutes

1 *pound cèpes or flat mushrooms*	*Salt and pepper*
4 to 5 *tablespoons olive oil*	2 *ounces (¼ cup) fresh bread*
1 *handful of parsley, chopped*	*crumbs*
2 *garlic cloves*	

You will need a frying pan. Wipe and slice the mushrooms—remove, if you prefer, the spongy underneaths if you are using cèpes (I don't bother unless I have a glut—but then I like the gluey texture). Sprinkle the fungi with a tablespoon of the olive oil and put them aside. Mince the parsley and crush the garlic. You need plenty of parsley—4 heaping tablespoons is not too much.

Put the rest of the oil to heat in a frying pan. When the oil is warm but not smoking, add the mushrooms. Cook them gently for a few minutes. Add the garlic and parsley, and allow it all to cook together gently for 5 minutes. Season with salt and pepper, and then throw in the bread crumbs—enough to absorb all the juices. Turn the heat up for a moment. They are done.

Serve the mushrooms piping hot with bread and a red wine from the Loire. Follow with a plain-grilled steak flanked by thick-cut french fries (fried golden in half olive oil, half seed oil; fried twice and drained in between—once to cook the potatoes, once to fry them crisp) and a green salad—a delicate one of *mesclun* leaves or tender chicory.

◆

HORN OF PLENTY MUSHROOMS ON TOAST

Croûte aux trompettes de la mort (Switzerland)

The mountains and forests of Switzerland provide fertile territory for fungi, and Swiss mushroom markets are in full swing throughout the autumn. Most farmers have dairy herds to provide the rest of the ingredients. The sinisterly named *trompettes de la mort* are among the most prized of the crop. The same recipe is equally good with their cousin, the chanterelle—and in fact with any of the edible mushrooms, including the fresh morels of springtime.

SERVES: 4

TIME: 30 minutes

1 pound Horn of Plenty (chanterelles or any wild or cultivated mushroom can substitute)	Salt and pepper
	1 cup heavy cream
	4 slices of day-old bread (not the sliced kind—but good, honest country bread, black or white)
3 ounces (6 tablespoons) sweet butter	

You will need a frying pan. Wipe the mushrooms and slice off the hard-earth tip of the stalk. If they are very large, slice them into strips. Heat the butter in a frying pan. When it is frothing (do not allow it to brown), add the mushrooms. Season with salt and pepper.

Horn of Plenty and chanterelles need a little longer to cook than the cultivated variety of mushroom. Let them stew gently in their own juices for 10 minutes. Stir in the cream. Let it all bubble up while you make a large slice of toast for each person.

Put the toast on a warm large dish. Pour the bubbling mushrooms and sauce over them and serve immediately. You can sprinkle parsley over the top, but a good twist of the pepper grinder is more than enough embellishment.

SUGGESTIONS

Next time, serve the mushrooms with scrambled eggs. Or stir in a few ounces of smoked salmon.

CHANTERELLES WITH BACON

Girolles au lard (France)

This dish comes from the wooded hills below Provence's Mount Ventoux, whose cold peak broods over the fertile Rhône basin and is still covered in snow in high summer. The woods provide plenty of the leaf mold needed by these beautiful apricot-yellow fungi.

SERVES: 4

TIME: 30 minutes

1	pound fresh chanterelles (any wild or cultivated mushroom can substitute)	1	small onion or shallot, peeled and chopped fine
4	ounces bacon	1	small handful of chopped parsley
2	ounces (4 tablespoons) butter	Salt and pepper
		1	glass of white wine

You will need a frying pan. Trim and wipe the chanterelles, and slice them if they are large. Slice the bacon into small cubes, and put it to melt gently with the butter in a frying pan over low heat.

Add the chanterelles to the pan when the bacon has taken color and its fat has run. Stir over a gentle heat for a moment. Add the onion, or shallot, and the parsley, salt, pepper, and wine. Raise the heat and cook fast for 5 minutes. Then turn the heat down and continue the cooking for another 20 minutes, shaking the pan occasionally and checking that it does not boil dry.

Serve with fresh crusty bread and a green salad.

◆

STUFFED MILK CAPS

Lactaires delicieux farcis (France)

Good mushrooms for stuffing, milk caps have a rather alarming habit of crying orange tears. The stuffing puts an end to all that. A recipe from the wooded slopes of the hills behind the Roman town of Vaison-la-Romaine.

SERVES: 4

TIME: 30 minutes

12	saffron milk cap mushrooms or cultivated mushrooms	1	tablespoon chopped parsley
½	cup olive oil	1	garlic clove
2	ounces (¼ cup) fresh bread crumbs	Salt	
		½	teaspoon black peppercorns
4	ounces minced pork or ham	1	teaspoon juniper berries
1	egg	4	thin slices of bacon

You will need a pestle and mortar and a shallow baking dish. Wipe the milk caps well and remove the stalks. Leave them to soak in the olive oil while you prepare the stuffing.

Soak the bread crumbs in a little water and then squeeze them dry. Mash them up with the minced pork or ham, the egg, and the parsley. Crush the peeled garlic with salt, peppercorns, and the juniper berries in a mortar, and then add them to the stuffing. Sprinkle with pepper and mix it all well together. Cut each bacon strip into 3 pieces.

Arrange the milk caps, gills upward, in a shallow baking dish. Divide the stuffing among them. Lay a square of bacon on each mound of stuffing. Pour the remaining oil over the mushrooms.

Either cook them under the broiler or bake in a preheated 425°F oven for 20 minutes. They're best of all grilled over a fire of juniper twigs in the open air.

◆

MUSHROOMS IN EGG AND BREAD CRUMBS WITH TARTAR SAUCE

Bundas csiperkegomba (Hungary)

Egg-dipping and bread-crumbing is a favorite Hungarian way with specially prized tidbits. The method preserves flavor and makes the star ingredients go further. Home-grown *foie gras* and small game birds split in half are also treated like this.

SERVES: 4

TIME: Allow an hour—this dish takes patience

1 *pound mushrooms (either large cultivated, or slices of giant puffball or beefsteak fungus)*	2 *eggs*
	1 *tablespoon milk*
	4 *ounces (½ cup) fresh bread crumbs*
1 *tablespoon flour*	
Salt and pepper	*Oil for frying*

TARTAR SAUCE:

2 *egg yolks*	1 *tablespoon sunflower or saf-flower oil*
½ *cup sour cream*	
½ *teaspoon salt*	1 *small glass of white wine*
1 *level teaspoon sugar*	1 *tablespoon chopped fresh dill (optional)*
1 *teaspoon mild mustard*	
2 *tablespoons fresh lemon juice*	

You will need three plates, a frying pan, a draining spoon, a bowl, and a saucepan for the sauce.

Wipe the mushrooms and slice them if they are large ones. Lay out three plates in a line: on the first, spread out the flour seasoned with salt and pepper; put the eggs, lightly mixed together with the milk, in the second; on the third, spread out the bread crumbs.

Make the sauce before you start the frying. Beat the egg yolks together in a bowl. Balance the bowl over a pan of boiling water. Whisk in the sour cream, salt, sugar, mustard, and lemon juice. As the sauce starts to thicken, whisk in the oil gradually, followed by enough of the white wine to give the consistency of a pouring custard. Whisk until smooth. Do not allow the sauce to boil. If it does, add an extra egg yolk and pour the sauce in a blender and blend until the sauce amalgamates. Stir in the dill if you are using it in season—it would be omitted in the winter.

Put a frying pan of deep oil—about 2 inches—on to heat.

Dip each slice of mushroom in the seasoned flour, then dip it in the egg, making sure it is all covered. Finish by coating thoroughly in the bread crumbs.

When the oil is hazed with blue smoke, slip in the first batch of mushrooms in their coating. Fry until the fritters are crisp and golden, turning them once. Remove and drain thoroughly on paper towels. Repeat the process with the rest of the mushrooms.

Serve the fritters as a first course, piled on a hot plate, with quartered lemons and the sauce passed separately. A salad, or (for a special occasion) one of the Hungarian paprika stews would perfectly complete the meal.

◆
TRUFFLE SALAD

Salade aux truffes (France)

A windfall of truffles requires the best of ingredients and simplest of treatments. This recipe is from the olive oil country up the Rhône valley behind Avignon, seat in medieval times of the magnificent popes in exile. The olive growers had their own liquid gold from their trees and black gold in their woods.

SERVES: 5 to 6

TIME: 5 minutes

1 *black truffle per person* *(weighing about 1 ounce each)*	*Salt and pepper* *Juice of 1 lemon*
3 *egg yolks*	1 *tablespoon olive oil*

You will need a small bowl. Wash and brush the truffles, and slice them finely. Cut the slices across again into matchsticks. Lightly beat together the egg yolks, salt, freshly milled pepper, lemon juice, and olive oil. Turn the truffle matchsticks in this little sauce. Serve with plenty of fresh bread and the best bottle of wine in the house—perhaps a bottle from the Avignon popes' own summer stronghold, Châteauneuf du Pape—where the vines grow mysteriously, apparently without soil, in fields of golden pebbles.

◆
TRUFFLE-AND-WALNUT SALAD

Truffes et cernaux (France)

The year's crop of walnuts are still fresh and milky when the truffle season begins. This excellent salad takes advantage of the happy coincidence.

SERVES: 1

TIME: 10 minutes

1 *black truffle per person* *(weighing about 1 ounce each)*	*Walnut or hazelnut oil* *White wine vinegar*
1 *lettuce heart per person*	*Salt and white pepper*
	4 *fresh walnuts per person*

Brush, wipe, and finely slice the truffles. Mix with an equal quantity of the palest of lettuce hearts, dressed with a trickle of hazelnut or walnut oil, a few drops of wine vinegar, salt, freshly milled white pepper, and the green walnuts (very fresh, still dripping sweet milk when they are cut), scooped from their shells.

Serve with fresh bread.

◆

TRUFFLES WITH POTATOES

Pommes de terre aux truffes (France)

This is a fine way to make the most of a single truffle.

SERVES: 4

TIME: 30 minutes plus 30 minutes cooking

> 2   *pounds (6 medium-sized) potatoes*
> 1   *small truffle (weighing about 1 ounce)*
> ½   *cup heavy cream*
> *Salt and pepper*
> *Olive oil*

Preheat the oven to 350°F. You will need a saucepan, a frying pan and a casserole.

Scrub and cook the potatoes in their skins in salted water until they are soft, 20 to 25 minutes boiling. Drain them and peel them as soon as they are cool enough to handle. Cut them into thick slices.

Brush and rinse the truffle. Cut it into fine slices.

Put a layer of sliced potatoes in the bottom of an earthenware casserole. Pour in some of the cream, and sprinkle with salt and pepper. Add a layer of truffles, then a layer of potatoes. Continue the layering, finishing with a layer of potatoes. Trickle a little olive oil over the top along with the last of the cream. Put the casserole in the oven and bake for half an hour.

Serve with a light salad and a bottle of white wine from the Rhône valley.

◆

TRUFFLES IN THE ASHES

Truffes sous les cendres (France)

My neighbor in Provence had an easy time-honored way with his private truffle harvest. He would brush the truffles clean, and then wrap each up in a piece of dough made with flour, water, and a little salt. These nuggets he would put in the warm ashes at the edge of the kitchen fire. Little hot embers would be piled on top. There they would roast for 20 to 30 minutes, until the outside was blackened like an overdone chestnut. A quick turn with his countryman's knife would free the truffle, steaming and fragrant and perfectly cooked, to be eaten with its gritty covering. Here is a more sophisticated version of this ancient dish which, although less innocent, does not take the same risks with the precious ingredients.

SERVES: 1

TIME: 20 minutes plus 20 to 25 minutes baking

1 black truffle per person (1 ounce each)	1 ounce pastry (yeast, flaky, short, or puff) per truffle
Salt and pepper	1 egg yolk to gild the top
1 piece of caul fat or 1 thin slice of pork fat per truffle	

Preheat the oven to 400°F. You will need a baking tray and a rolling pin.

Wipe and brush and rinse the truffles as necessary. Sprinkle each with salt and freshly milled pepper. Wrap each one in a jacket of caul or pork fat.

Roll out a round of pastry for each truffle. You can use a plain bread dough if you beat a little butter into it. Place the jacketed truffle on one side of its pastry circle. Moisten the edges of the pastry, and fold the other side over to make a semicircle enclosing the truffle. Arrange on a baking tray and brush beaten egg over the top of each.

Bake for 20 to 25 minutes. Serve hot on a clean white napkin. Paradise calls for champagne.

OLIVES AND OLIVE OIL DISHES

OLIVE SAUCE

Riste (France)

This is a sauce from Vaison-la-Romaine in the hills above the Rhône valley. The town was an elegant spa resort in Roman times, and this preparation dates back to the Romans, who liked it with fried fish. It is a pungent little sauce which goes a long way.

SERVES: 4

TIME: 20 minutes plus 20 minutes cooking

2	ounces black olives	1	tablespoon flour
1	onion	1	glass of water
3	garlic cloves	1	glass of red wine
1	large tomato (or 2 small ones)		Thyme, parsley, and a bay leaf
2	tablespoons olive oil	1	tablespoon capers

You will need one small saucepan. Remove the pits from the olives and chop them roughly. Peel and chop the onion. Peel and crush the garlic. Pour boiling water over the tomato to loosen the skin; then peel and chop the flesh. Put the oil to warm on low heat, and then throw in the onion and garlic. Sprinkle in the flour and fry gently until it takes a little color. Put in the tomato and then the water and the wine. Add the aromatics. Leave it over a gentle heat to simmer until it reduces to half its volume. Stir in the olives and the capers. You should need no extra salt.

Serve with fried fish. It goes well with lightly boiled vegetables, too.

◆

SALAD DRESSING

Vinaigrette (France)

This is the universal classic oil-and-vinegar dressing for salads. Mix 3 table-spoons of olive oil with 1 tablespoon of wine vinegar, and add salt and freshly ground pepper to taste. This proportion can be varied in many ways: Replace the oil with lemon juice; include chopped fresh herbs in the mix; mash in the yolks of two hard-boiled eggs. Add the oil gradually to a tablespoonful of mild French mustard mixed with the vinegar, much as if making a mayonnaise: This will produce a thick emulsified sauce—good for a marinated salad such as the one made with fine strips of celeriac which is to be bought in all French cooked-meat stores.

◆

MAYONNAISE OR MAYONESA

(France and Spain)

The origins of the classic cold sauce of southwestern Europe are shrouded in the usual swirls of mist and controversy. Carême made a strong case for its derivation from the word "*manier,*" to work by hand. Others suggest it may have come from the ancient Languedoc verb *mahonner,* meaning to tire, pre-cisely as in the modern French use of *fatiguer,* to tire a salad. The residents of Mahón, Minorca's chief port, offer the theory that the recipe made its way into the kitchens of France after the Duc de Richelieu captured the strategi-cally important Minorcan port of Mahón from the English. Whatever the origins of the "butter of the south," *mayonnaise* is very simple to make, and the ingredients are immediately to hand in all Mediterranean countries, available to rich and poor alike.

SERVES: 4

TIME: 20 minutes

2   *egg yolks*
2   *cups olive oil*
2   *tablespoons white wine vinegar or the juice of ½ lemon*
Salt

You will need a bowl, a small jug, a fork or a whisk, and a wooden spoon. Make sure both the egg yolks and the olive oil are at room temperature. The mixture will not emulsify if the two major ingredients are not agreeable to each other. Pour the oil in a small jug. Combine the egg yolks, vinegar or lemon, and salt in a bowl. Beat them together thoroughly with a fork or a whisk. Whisking constantly, trickle the oil drop by drop into the egg. The oil is added to the yolk, rather than the other way around, because the yolk is the emulsifier which needs to coat each particle of oil—an easer job if it starts out as the dominant ingredient. Continue thus until a quarter of the oil has been absorbed; then change to a wooden spoon and speed up the rate of flow. At this stage you should not beat too hard, and as the mixture thickens, you may pour the oil in faster. When the mayonnaise is beautifully shiny and stiff enough for your purposes, it is ready. If you keep it in the refrigerator, the oil will leak. The same thing happens if you put it on hot food. Should the emulsion separate and go liquid again, start with a new egg yolk in a fresh bowl, and add the curdled mixture to it as slowly as at the beginning. Make your *mayonnaise* fresh, and do not leave it out at room temperature for more than 3 hours.

This sauce is one of the few which is far better when done by hand. *Mayonnaise* made in a blender will not be the same—it will be good, but it is a different sauce. This is because the action of the blades is too rapid and consistent for the oil to emulsify properly with the egg yolks alone, so the sauce has to be made with whole eggs or it will not stabilize. This inclusion of the whites gives a lighter, paler sauce, without the rich heaviness of the true *mayonnaise*, which can be thickened so solid that it will cut like soft butter.

SUGGESTIONS

Salsa mayonesa is used in Spain to sauce their excellent grilled or baked fish—particularly the larger white-fleshed species such as the Spaniards' favorite *merluza* (hake) which is sold whole or chopped into thick steaks, and a speciality claimed by the fishermen of the Strait of Gibraltar, *urta*, a large and delicious member of the bream family.

Potato salads and salads of chopped vegetables (*picadilla* or *ensalada rusa*), both generously blanketed with *salsa mayonesa*, have their place in every *tapa* bar.

———————◆———————

AÏOLI GARNI

(France)

This dish is really an excuse to eat the *aïoli* sauce (page 79) itself. It is interesting to compare the recipe with the Greek *skordalia*, bearing in mind the early Greek presence on the Mediterranean seaboard of France. The first pressings of the year's olives are available by early December in Provence, when the oil is fresh and strong and green, just in time for the Christmas Eve fasting dish of *aïoli garni*. The dish is also served as a celebration meal at other times. Although not complicated to prepare, it is at its best with a wide selection of ingredients—and it is this which makes it festive.

S E R V E S : 8 to 10

T I M E : Start 48 hours before if you are using salt cod; 1½ to 2 hours

Prepare the *aïoli garni* first. You will then be clear-minded and relaxed for the preparation of the sauce (recipe follows). The *aïoli* mayonnaise is so rich that its background must be as simple as possible. The contrasting colors—pale creamy fish, green, red and gold of the vegetables and eggs—look their best on a handsome white serving dish. Include four elements in the *aïoli* garnish (weights are very approximate, since you can include more or less of each).

All are to be plainly and perfectly cooked. Here's how to prepare them, in descending order of cooking time (if you are using salt cod, see the fish entry and remember you will have to put it to soak at least the day before you need it).

The meat (unless it is to be a fast-day dish): A small shoulder of lamb (the best and sweetest meat for this dish) to be cooked in its own juices. Wipe the roast and sprinkle it with salt, pepper, and a few sprigs of rosemary and thyme. Wrap it thoroughly in foil. Put it to cook in a preheated medium oven, 350°F, for 1 to 1½ hours (allow 20 minutes per pound).

The vegetables: 4 pounds mixed vegetables: Use small *potatoes*, scrubbed but not peeled. They will take 20 minutes in boiling salted water. If you can find only old potatoes, scrub them even more thoroughly and then boil them in their skins in plenty of salted water—start them in cold water, and time the cooking from the moment the water boils. They will take 20 to 30 minutes to be quite soft (depending on the size of the tubers, which should be more or less even in size.) Drain the potatoes as soon as they are soft, and then shake them over the heat for a moment to dry them.

Sweet potatoes, peeled and cut into slices and poached in salted water until soft, about 30 minutes.

Artichokes, trimmed and washed and cooked in boiling salted water acidulated with a squeeze of lemon. They will take 20 to 30 minutes, depending on the size. They are done when a leaf will pull away easily from the base.

Young *carrots and turnips*, topped and tailed and scrubbed. They will take 12 to 15 minutes in boiling salted water. If you can find only old vegetables, peel them and quarter them lengthwise before you put them to cook.

Cauliflower, divided into florets. Cook briefly in boiling salted water for 5 minutes only, so that the stalks stay slightly crisp.

Green beans, topped and tailed and plunged into boiling salted water for 3 to 4 minutes only.

Raw *tomatoes*, cut into quarters.

The fish: 2 pounds fish. Cod is usually included in an *aïoli garni*—if fresh, it is cut into thick steaks or fillets. Poach the fish in a simmering pan of half milk, half water, flavored with a slice of onion, a bay leaf, ½ teaspoon of salt, and some peppercorns. It will need only 5 to 6 minutes to be perfectly cooked. Drain carefully.

You can use well-soaked dried cod if you wish, in which case cut it into neat portions and put it to soak for 48 hours, changing the water frequently. Poach the soaked fish in half milk, half water, perfumed with a bay leaf and a few peppercorns for 10 minutes. Drain.

The sea snails: Put them to soak in clear water with a handful of salt for an hour or two, so that they spit out as much as possible of their sand. Simmer them in boiling water with salt, peppercorns, and a spoonful of vinegar for 20 minutes.

The eggs: Allow 1 egg per person, and an extra one for the unexpected visitor (a Provençal family always expects a stranger on Christmas Eve). Have the eggs at room temperature. Cover them with lukewarm water and bring them to a boil. The moment they boil, cover them and put aside for 6 minutes. Plunge them immediately into cold water. Peel the shell off as soon as the eggs are cool enough to handle. Use the best eggs you can find: The brighter the yolks and the snowier the whites, the better.

AÏOLI

(France)

This is a garlic mayonnaise, the glory of Provence. All the ingredients should be at room temperature to allow them to emulsify properly.

SERVES: 8 to 10

TIME: 15 minutes

2 to 3 cups olive oil	*Juice of 1 lemon*
10 garlic cloves	1 *tablespoon warm water*
½ teaspoon salt	
1 to 2 egg yolks *(depending on the size of the eggs)*	

You will need a pestle and mortar. Pour the oil into a jug. Peel the cloves of garlic and put them into a bowl with the salt. Pound the garlic and salt together with a pestle until you have a thick paste. Stir in the egg yolk. In Provence you would have a small marble mortar for this job.

Never ceasing to work the mixture, drip in the oil quite slowly. When you have added about 4 spoonfuls of oil, stir in the lemon juice and the water. Trickle in the rest of the oil, beat without pause, using the pestle or a wooden spoon. Watch carefully as the sauce thickens, and add a little more water if the emulsion shows signs of separating. The egg and the vegetable matter both act as emulsifiers of the oil: The making of a mayonnaise is a magical process.

Should such a disaster as the sauce's splitting befall you, don't worry. It happens so frequently, the French have a special phrase for its redress: *"Relever l'aïoli."* Empty the split mixture out of the bowl, and put in another egg yolk and a few drops of lemon juice. Slowly add the split mixture to the fresh yolk. As surely as night follows days, it will thicken.

◆

SUGGESTIONS

Of course you can reduce the quantity of garlic if you wish. However, bear in mind that J. B. Reboul, the great French authority on Provençal cooking, suggests 2 cloves per person, which would bring the tally up to 16 for this particular party.

The egg yolk can be replaced or supplemented by a boiled mashed potato or a crust of dry bread. Some authorities suggest replacing one of the yolks in a 1-quart *aïoli* with one hard-boiled egg yolk.

The garlic mayonnaise can be made in a blender—then you will have to use a whole egg, and the mixture will be paler and lighter.

My household has a passion for garlic and will stir this beautiful sauce into any and all broth soups whether of fish, vegetable, or chicken, and eat it in sandwiches or with fresh raw vegetables. All the ingredients should be at room temperature to allow them to emulsify successfully.

The sauce is delicious served with crudités as prepared for the *bagna caouda* which follows.

◆

VEGETABLE FONDUE

Bagna Caouda (Italy)

This is an ancient recipe which has long been popular both in Piedmont and around Nice in Provence, where the Italian influence is strong. It is basically a fondue of vegetables. The combination of ingredients has its roots in a far older tradition of a pocket meal, to be taken out into the fields as a midday break of bread basted with olive oil, a pickled fish, and a few fresh raw vegetables.

SERVES: 6

TIME: 20 to 30 minutes

Raw vegetables	*2 to 3 garlic cloves*
1 small can of salted anchovies (6	*½ teaspoon salt*
to 8 fillets)	*1 quart olive oil*
2 slices of dry bread	
2 tablespoons milk or light cream	
(water will do)	

You will need a small saucepan, a fondue pan, and a pestle and mortar or a food processor.

Allow 12 ounces of vegetables per person for the main dish of a meal. Choose from: *bulb fennel*, washed and separated into bite-sized segments; *celery*, washed and cut into short lengths; *chicory*, quartered just before you put it out; *lettuce*, more or less separated into leaves (I like them cut into eighths if the heart is tight, but then they must be served immediately); *radishes*, scrubbed and quartered; *tiny artichokes*, quartered; *young carrots*, scrubbed and topped (older ones will have to be peeled and quartered lengthwise); *cauliflower and broccoli*, separated into florets; *baby turnips*, rinsed and quartered; very fresh *cultivated mushrooms*.

Drain the anchovies. You can buy them loose from a barrel in the delicatessen, but then they will need a preliminary soaking of half an hour in milk to get rid of excess salt. Crumble the bread and put it to soak in the milk or cream for a few minutes. Squeeze out the excess liquid.

Peel the garlic and crush it with the salt in a mortar. Add the anchovies and the bread, and pound them thoroughly with the garlic. This is easy to do if you use a food processor.

Prepare a large flat plate of the raw vegetables. Arrange them as carefully as you would a bowl of flowers. Set it out on the table. Provide each guest with a plate, a large napkin, and two forks, one to stir the vegetables in the hot oil, and the other to eat with, for fear they will burn their lips with the hot fork used for frying.

Put the paste and the olive oil into the fondue pan. Bring the oil and paste to a boil, stirring thoroughly. When it is hot but not smoking, call your guests and put the fondue pan over its flame on the table. Allow it to heat to boiling. Each guest then spears a piece of vegetable and swirls it around in the hot bath.

Flank the dishes with plenty of fresh bread and perhaps a plate of raw ham or salami and a fine piece of cheese for those who hanker after something more substantial. Make sure there is plenty of wine to cool throats after the hot salty sauce.

◆

BRINED GREEN OLIVES

Aceitunas en escabeche (Spain)

The pale, dry, unfortified sherry wines of Jerez and Montilla are at their best partnered by the roughly cracked garlic-scented green olives prepared in the little *cortijos* of Andalusia, a pleasure to be savored under the silvery leaves of an ancient grove, the twisted roots of the olive trees lapped by the red earth of the Serrania de Ronda. The first fresh olives, freckled bright emerald, begin to appear in the markets in October, ready to be pickled for Christmas. Later in the harvest they ripen and darken to a full soft plum. The first bitter green ones are the most appreciated in sherry country.

YIELD: 6 quarts of olives

TIME: Start 3 to 4 weeks before; 30 to 40 minutes

4	pounds green olives	1	small bunch of dried thyme
8	ounces (1 cup) salt	1	tablespoon fennel stalks
4	quarts water	2	lemons
1	tablespoon dried oregano	2	whole heads of garlic

You will need a deep crock. Spread the olives out on the kitchen table, and pick out any shriveled ones and odd bits of leaf and stalk. Hit each one with a small hammer or a heavy rolling pin, so that the flesh cracks but the olive remains intact. Put all the crushed olives into the crock and cover them with fresh water. Leave them to soak for a week, changing the water every two days. These little green olives are very bitter—if you taste the water, you will find it gets progressively milder as it is changed.

At the end of a week, drain out all the water. Make a brine by dissolving the salt in the 4 quarts water, and pour it over the olives. They should be completely submerged. Add the herbs and the lemons chopped into chunks. Hold the whole heads of garlic over a flame and char them (the scent is wonderfully evocative of Spanish peasant kitchens). Put the garlic in with the olives.

Ready to use in 2 to 3 weeks, the olives become progressively less bitter as the year wears on. If they begin to ferment a little (the olive, after all, is a fruit), change the brine: They will not keep indefinitely.

In Seville, very bitter little oranges, unpeeled but quartered, are used to flavor the olives.

If you cannot obtain fresh olives, drain a can or two of brined green ones and put them to marinate for a few days in a jar with fresh olive oil, a clove of garlic sliced, a few sprigs of thyme, and a chopped whole lemon. But the fresh ones are best: They are much more interesting than the bland commercially prepared variety.

PICKLED BLACK OLIVES

Olives noires piquées (France)

The Farnoux household, millers to the olive growers of Nyons in the Baronnies of Provence, pickle only the largest and most perfect of the fully mature black olives. M. Farnoux's position as proprietor of the most ancient olive press in the Baronnies allows him to be very selective in these matters. The olives are put to soak out the bitterness in a brine made with a handful of salt (about 4 ounces) to each liter of water. Each household in the area had such a brine pot, topped up annually so that it covered the new olives, with a few bay leaves added when needed, but the liquid itself was not changed from year to year. That water, say the locals, was sometimes a hundred years old, dark and oily and rich, and it pickled the olives as sweetly as honey.

There were those who liked their olives green. Such olives would need to be layered first in wood ash to draw the bitterness. In the old days whole families would turn out for the olive harvest, and the women would climb up the trees to pick the ripe fruit, with a basket slung around their necks and a shawl over their heads and backs to protect them from the dark ripe juice. It was always the largest olives, either unripe and green, or ripe and black, which were kept for pickling. The burghers of Nyons offer instructions for the preparation of their treasure in a locally published brochure as follows:

4 *pounds black olives*	3 *garlic cloves*
Salt	3 *bay leaves*
2 *tablespoons olive oil*	

"Olives picked in the fullness of their maturity must be left in a basket on the windowsill to take the frost for 3 to 4 nights. When they have been well-frozen, take them indoors and prick them all over with a fork or with a cork set with pins. Rub them with fine salt and toss them in a basket 3 or 4 times a day for a week. After that, mix them with a little pure olive oil, bay leaves and some peeled cloves of garlic roughly chopped. Pack them into an earthenware jar for storage."

CAPER-AND-OLIVE PASTE

Tapenade (France)

An olive paste from the kitchens of Provence, today it is made in quantity by millers such as M. Farnoux. J. B. Reboul, writing at the end of the nineteenth century, records *tapenade* as a restaurant invention from the Maison Dorée at Marseilles. It did, however, catch the imagination of the Provencaux, who now use it as their own. Salted capers, anchovies, and tuna were all sold straight from the barrel by weight in M. Reboul's day. The tuna was a far greater luxury than the anchovies. The capers are the principal ingredient: *tapeno* means caper in the patois, although the modern version relies more heavily on the olives than did the original.

YIELD: Will make about 1 pound of *tapenade*

TIME: 20 minutes

8	*ounces black olives*	½	*cup good olive oil*
2	*ounces (1 small can) anchovy fillets*	1	*teaspoon brandy*
2	*ounces (1 small can) brined tuna fish*		*A good powdering of freshly milled pepper*
2	*ounces (2 small jars) capers*	1	*teaspoon strong English mustard*

You will need a pestle and mortar or a food processor and a jar. Drain and pit the olives. Drain the anchovy fillets (salted ones from a barrel will have to be soaked in milk for 30 minutes first). Drain the tuna and the capers.

Pound all the solid ingredients together to a fine paste in a mortar. Trickle in the olive oil, beating with a pestle or a wooden spoon as for a mayonnaise. Stir in the brandy, pepper and mustard. Or conserve your strength and put the whole lot in the food processor. Put in a jar and cover tightly. Store in the refrigerator.

SUGGESTION

Serve the paste as a garnish with hard-cooked eggs cut in half lengthwise, with a little of the *tapenade* mashed into the egg yolks which are then returned to their whites. Trickle olive oil over the top, and serve with a green salad and a tomato salad and plenty of hot fresh bread. This is a light lunch which will leave room for a fruit tart.

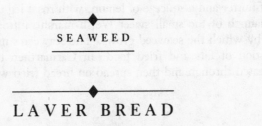

SEAWEED

LAVER BREAD

Bara lawr (Wales)
Sloke (Ireland and Scotland)

Laver bread is not so much a bread as it is a vegetable purée. The vegetable is a seaweed, *Porphyra umbilicalis*, common on the shores of Britain, particularly on the west coast. On the coasts of Europe laver is there for the taking, although most of its devotees, of whom there are many in Wales, buy it in its cooked form as laver bread, since its preparation is somewhat lengthy and laborious. The seaweed itself has thin flat purple leaves and grows, looking rather like strips of wet rubber, on rocks and stones at the edge of the water. Its use is by no means confined to Britain: This family is to be found on the shores of both Atlantic and Pacific oceans, and the Japanese, who know it as *nori*, semicultivate it and use it as a food wrapper, particularly for *sushi*. Look for it, dried, in Oriental supermarkets. If you want to dry it for keeping, wash it well and dry until brittle in a warm turned-off oven—it can be stored in a paper bag in a dry cupboard until you want to soak it (30 minutes in cold water) and use it. Like all seaweeds, laver is rich in minerals and vitamins and tastes mildly metallic.

Wash the laver well. Then stew it gently in water to cover for 5 to 6 hours, until it is like a mush of well-cooked spinach. Drain and serve on fried bread with bacon. Laver bread has little taste of its own—just a slight salty, metallic flavor of the sea.

Laver can be stored in a jar for several days, and it is this purée which is generally sold as laver bread. It refrigerates well and can be deep-frozen successfully.

Let it cool to a stiff jelly and toss spoonfuls into a plateful of fine or medium oatmeal—whole wheat flour can substitute for the oatmeal. Fry the spoonfuls like fritters in bacon fat for a delicious Welsh breakfast. Accompany with a glass of milk.

Laver bread can be bought ready-rolled in oatmeal, but this is inclined to sour it.

◆

Laver bread keeps good company, if used fresh and beaten up with an ounce or two of butter and a squeeze of lemon, with roast leg of lamb or, better still, a roast haunch of the small sweet Welsh marsh mutton, fattened in the salt pastures by which the seaweed grows. The seaweed's minerals are thought to aid digestion of fats and fried food. In Carmarthen the prepared purée is served heated through and then spread on bread fried with bacon.

◆

CARRAGEEN PUDDING

(Ireland)

The brown or green, shading to cream in the sun, fronds of *Chondrus crispus* fringe the Atlantic shores of Britain and Ireland, and the Atlantic Coast of the United States. This seaweed is highly gelatinous and can even be processed into fine sheets for sausage casings. Carrageen or Irish moss is usually used to set jellies, and an ounce or two stewed in a vegetable soup (try it in an herb soup, leaving out the flour) will thicken the soup to perfection. The delicate clumps are best gathered from a clean midtide line during the months of April and May. Wash the seaweed well and remove the dark stems. Then lay it out to dry on the rocks in the salt breeze before you store it. Sun to dry and showers to rinse is the best weather for this. Leave the carrageen out for several days to bleach to a creamy white—if there are no showers, you will have to sprinkle it with water intermittently yourself. Store in paper bags. There are those knowledgeable in the matter who say the bleaching process is unnecessary and removes some of the goodness and flavor. I find it can be dried perfectly satisfactorily, after a thorough washing, in a warm turned-off oven—it will take only an hour or two to evaporate its moisture. Store in a paper bag. Use it fresh, as it is from the shore, well rinsed to remove the sand: 1 ounce dried replaces 4 ounces fresh.

S E R V E S : 4 to 5

T I M E : Start the day before; 10 to 15 minutes

½   ounce dried carrageen (from the health food store)
3¼ cups milk
1   tablespoon sugar
Nutmeg, preferably freshly grated

You will need a saucepan, a strainer, and a jelly mold. Bring all the ingredients to a boil together. Allow to boil until the moss has dissolved and the setting point is reached. This will take only a minute or two, and it will then coat the back of your wooden spoon. Pour the liquid through a strainer into a mold to set. Leave it overnight. Grate a little nutmeg over the top.

Serve the pudding with berries such as blueberries, or in season, strawberries—best of all, a bowl of the tiny sweet strawberries which grow wild in the woods and the heather. It makes a delicious light supper dish with a plate of buttered homemade scones.

SUGGESTIONS

Put in a piece of lemon peel for flavoring.

Stir in an egg yolk as the mixture cools, and then fold in the well-beaten white. Allow to set as usual.

If you would like to use the seaweed fresh from the shore, you will need 2 ounces for this recipe. Wash it thoroughly, and simmer it for 30 minutes, or until the weed has practically dissolved. Add sugar and pour through a sieve into a mold to set.

CHAPTER TWO

Potato Dishes

The potato, a relative newcomer to the European peasant larder, has nonetheless had a prodigious influence on European life. The first potato plants arrived in Spain in the baggage of the conquistadores returning from Peru in 1540. The resourceful Incas had long cultivated the potato to supply their mountain fortresses high in the Andes mountains, where their usual crop of corn could not survive. Just as Amsterdam was built on herrings, so were Machu Picchu and Quito on the potato. The Spanish court failed to see the tuber's culinary potential, but they found the pale mauve blooms very pretty and bedded the plants in flowerpots. The English received their first plants when Sir Francis Drake brought some back from North America. Elizabeth I was not at all sure what to make of them, and she too planted them in her ornamental flower beds.

For the next two centuries the potato as a food source was treated with suspicion. A few brave souls took a chance and planted potatoes on the stony hillsides of Galicia, in the vegetable gardens of Lyons (even then the good burghers of Lyons were in the gastronomic vanguard), and in the flat fields of the Low Countries. Over in England some progress was being made: A dish of potatoes is recorded as appearing on King James' dinner table in 1619. Even with royal patronage the poisonous-looking roots were widely considered untrustworthy, being held responsible for a range of disasters including, in France, an outbreak of leprosy. Nevertheless, the potato patch spread slowly across the fertile fields of Europe throughout the next century. From the sunlit valleys of Spain to the frozen mountains of Scandinavia, the miraculously adaptable food-plant flourished.

Nowhere was it more successful than in the soft climate of Ireland. It was Elizabeth I's favorite sailor, Sir Walter Raleigh, who took the first potato plants to the green hills of the Emerald Isle. A mere century and a half later, virtually all other crops had been abandoned in its favor. A single damp Irish acre planted in potatoes by one Irish peasant, equipped with a spade and a hoe, yielded enough food to fill his family's black iron cooking pot all year—

with some left over for the family pig. The population of Ireland tripled—
from 3 million in 1750 to nearly 9 million a century later. In 1841 the blight
struck the potato. By 1846 a million and a half Irish men, women, and
children had died of starvation. Of those who survived, thousands emigrated
to the New World.

Between 1750 and 1850 not only the Irish but the whole population of
Europe exploded—fed increasingly by the ever-adaptable jack-of-all-foods. An
English traveler in Westphalia in 1780 reports the change in diet:

> Peasants tire of oatbread eaten dry with salt and water. I can
> heartily recommend the potato boiled and then moistened with a little
> milk, roasted in the ashes and eaten with a little butter, or eaten cold
> as a salad. Grated and mixed with eggs, oats and sugar it makes an
> excellent rissole. On this diet the peasants of Sauerland endure hard
> heavy work, and yet live as healthily as fish in the sea.

Whether boiled or baked, eaten as potato bread or in soup, used for
animal fodder or fermented and distilled into alcohol, there was virtually no
culinary need the potato could not supply. Just as the potato had been
essential to the supremacy of the Incas in Peru, so it now dominated the
politics of Europe. Revolution, war, the growth of empires—all were fueled
by the pressures of an expanding population. That curious basket of sprouting
tubers in Francisco Pizzaro's luggage has proved as powerful as any of Alfred
Nobel's explosive mixtures.

The best potatoes are those freshly dug from your own garden—the finest
I have ever tasted grew in the stone-strewn, sheep-manured "tattie" patch
beside a shepherd's farmhouse on the rocky Atlantic coast of a Hebridean
island. They were always freshly dug and scented the kitchen with smells of
peat and bracken. The soft mists seem to make Scottish potatoes particularly
delicious—feathery pillows, plump and sweet. Their skins are pale gold and
translucent, and stretched so tightly over the snowy flesh that they pop when
you bite into them. Hebridean potatoes are scrubbed, never peeled, and
cooked in boiling water with salt. They are eaten scalding hot, straight from
the pot, with, if available, cold sweet butter and salt, washed down with the
Scots' favorite strong tea—better than the finest caviar to an appetite sharpened by a long day's walking the heather in search of a lost newborn lamb.

◆

IRISH POTATOES

An article in *Frazer's Magazine*, dated April 1847, just post-potato blight,
explains the significance of the loss of so important a crop to the Irish peasant:
"Easily boiled in an iron pot, served in a turf-basket or rolled on a table,
peeled with the fingers, and palatable in its own sweet moisture, the Irish
peasant could better spare a far better nutriment."

An Irish working man of the last century would have managed a daily
quota of 10 to 14 pounds of boiled "tatties".

S E R V E S : 4

T I M E : 10 minutes plus 20 to 30 minutes cooking

2 *pounds (4 to 6 large) old floury potatoes*
Salt
Unsalted butter

You will need a heavy pot and a frying pan. Choose evenly sized potatoes and scrub them thoroughly. Put them in a heavy pot and just cover them with fresh cold water. Add a teaspoon of rough salt. Bring the water to a boil quickly, and then turn the heat down to a steady simmer. Potatoes will take 20 minutes (up to 30 if large) to cook. When the potatoes are soft right through, drain them, put them in a dry frying pan, and toss them over the heat to dry them. Their skins should burst a little, like roast chestnuts, to show the snowy flesh inside. Serve with salt and a pat of cold fresh butter. (The Irish turned to dairy farming after the disaster of the Potato Famine—Irish butter and cream are now excellent.)

SUGGESTIONS

Potatoes baked in the oven in an unglazed earthenware pot will be light, floury, and have their vitamins intact. Bake in a preheated 350°F oven for an hour.

Dress boiled, skinned potatoes with bread crumbs fried crisp and golden in butter.

BOXTY

(Ireland)

This is a special potato bread for serving at Halloween, when the restless spirits of witches are abroad. This celebration reaches back into pre-Christian harvest festivals—although the potato did not feature until at least the eighteenth century. Country memories are long, and bonfires are still traditionally lit as part of Halloween festivities, which in turn have their roots in thanksgiving to the Sun God—a custom shared with the Scandinavians, who have more cause than most to be anxious for the god's patronage.

> Boxty on the griddle, Boxty in the pan,
> If you don't eat Boxty, you'll never get a man.

YIELD: 4 large cakes

TIME: 20 minutes plus 40 minutes cooking

2	*pounds (6 medium-sized) potatoes*	2	*teaspoons salt*
1	*pound (3½ cups) flour*	½	*cup milk*
			Butter

Preheat the oven to 350°F. You will need a grater (food processors have a useful attachment for this job), a large bowl, and a baking sheet. Peel the potatoes and grate them raw. Mix in the flour and the salt, and leave the mixture to stand for an hour. Add the milk and knead the mixture well on a floured board.

Divide the dough into four. Roll the pieces out into four cakes, roughly 6 inches in diameter. Put them onto a buttered baking tray. Mark the cakes into quarters with a cross.

Bake the cakes in the oven for 40 minutes, until they are cooked through and lightly browned. Serve hot with plenty of butter. This is not a dish for anyone on a diet.

◆

SUGGESTIONS

A lighter mixture can be made by boiling half the quantity of potatoes and then mashing them with 4 ounces of bacon fat. The mashed potato is then kneaded into the raw mixture.

The Boxty batter can be softened to a dropping consistency with extra milk, and then cooked on a lightly greased griddle or in a heavy frying pan, as for drop scones. These are served with butter, and sometimes with molasses or sugar.

◆

COLCANNON

(Ireland)

A Halloween food like Boxty, there used to be a ritual attached to the supping of Colcannon. Four favors would be hidden in the dish: a gold marriage ring, a piece of money, an old maid's thimble, and a bachelor's button. Those who got one in their portion had their fate decided for the coming year. Peas, beans, spinach, or any green vegetable can be used in this recipe.

SERVES: 6

TIME: 40 minutes

2	pounds (6 medium-sized) potatoes	1	cup light cream (milk will do in a pinch)
2	pounds curly kale or dark green cabbage	6	ounces (¾ cup) butter
2	pounds leeks or scallions		Salt and pepper

You will need three saucepans. Peel and quarter the potatoes, and put them to cook in boiling salted water for 20 minutes until cooked through. Drain well.

Meanwhile, rinse, slice, and cook separately the kale or cabbage in a very little water for 15 to 20 minutes (you need the vegetable soft for this dish). Drain well and chop fine.

Wash and slice the leeks or scallions into thin rings, and put them to stew in yet another pan with the cream or milk until soft—about 6 to 7 minutes should be enough.

Put the butter to melt in a small pan on the side of the stove.

Mash the potatoes with the leeks or scallions and the cream. Then beat in the kale or cabbage. Beat it some more over low heat until it is pale green and fluffy. Salt and pepper to taste.

Put the hot mixture into a well-warmed deep dish. Make a well in the center (and don't forget to bury the favors). Pour the melted butter into the well. Put the dish in the middle of the table. Each person takes a helping with a spoonful of butter. Or serve in individual bowls with a piece of butter to melt into a little pool in the middle of each.

◆

SUGGESTION

Omit the kale or cabbage and you have a dish of *champ*.

Leftovers: Colcannon and *champ* will refry beautifully in the leftover butter. Excellent too with a few slices of good bacon and refried in the bacon fat.

◆

Takes at least 1½ hours — allow 2 hours

FISH-AND-POTATO FRY

Fischlabskaus (Germany)

This is a dish from the seacoast of Schleswig-Holstein, where the fishermen's wives can prepare it with any of the fish in the catch. The same dish is made with meat or fish in all the Atlantic ports of Europe, from Tromsö to Liverpool to Lisbon.

SERVES: 4 to 5

TIME: 40 minutes

2   *pounds (6 medium-sized)*   4   *ounces (4 tablespoons) lard or,*
     potatoes   *better still, bacon fat*
1   *pound skinned and filleted fish*   *Salt and pepper*
1   *pound onions*

You will need a heavy shallow frying pan with a lid. Peel the potatoes and slice them thickly. Check the fish for bones. Peel and slice the onions.

Melt the lard or bacon fat in a frying pan with a lid. Fry the onions golden. Lay the potatoes on top and cover with water. Add a little salt and pepper and put the lid on the pan. Simmer gently until the potatoes are soft and most of the water has evaporated. Lay the filleted fish on top. Continue to cook. The base will dry out and begin to fry again. Continue until there is a golden crust underneath. Do not mix up the ingredients too much—it should not be a mush. Serve with a dish of pickled cucumbers.

◆

SUGGESTIONS

Butter or vegetable oil can substitute for the lard or bacon fat—in which case include a bit of bacon, chopped fine.

Labskaus is also delicious made with salted or smoked fish.

Sometimes salt pork or salt beef replaces the fish to make a good simple hash.

Leftovers: Bind the mixture with a beaten egg and fry spoonfuls to make fish cakes.

◆

POTATO-AND-BACON DUMPLINGS

Kroppkakor (Sweden)

SERVES: 5 to 6

TIME: Start the day before; 40 minutes

8   *large potatoes*   ½   *teaspoon salt*
One 4-ounce slab of bacon   4   *ounces (1 cup) flour*
1   *onion, chopped fine*   1   *large egg*

You will need a large saucepan, a small frying pan, a bowl, and a grater. Scrub the potatoes and put them on to boil in their skins—this will take 20 to 30 minutes, depending on size. Drain them and leave them overnight

The next day dice the bacon. Put the bacon in a small pan to melt gently. As soon as there is enough fat from the bacon to fry it, add the onion. Cook gently until soft.

Peel and then grate the potatoes into a large bowl. Mix in the salt, flour, and egg. Swift fingers make light dumplings. Roll out the dough in a sausage shape, and chop into 20 short lengths. Roll each length into a small ball, and push a nest in it with your finger. Fill the nest with a little of the bacon-and-onion mixture, and then close up the hole. Continue until all the dough and bacon are finished.

Meanwhile, set a pan of salted water to boil on the stove. When all the dumplings are made (there should be 15 to 20), put them to poach in the simmering water until they are light and well risen.

Serve with melted butter or a jug of melted bacon drippings with little pieces of bacon still in it.

◆

SUGGESTION

You can, of course, use yesterday's leftover boiled potatoes.

◆

ANCHOVIES AND POTATOES

Janssons Frestelse (Sweden)

This dish was rechristened "Jansson's Temptation" in the eighteenth century, after a deeply religious Swede, Erik Janson, whose name was apparently misspelt during the long Atlantic crossing. Janson, the tempted one, was forbidden any enjoyment by his devout church. This simple but delicious dish from his native land was his one trangression. The Swedish canned anchovies are usually billed as marinated sprats.

SERVES: 4

TIME: 20 minutes plus 75 minutes cooking

2 pounds (6 medium-sized) potatoes	Pepper
½ pound onions	2 cups light cream
20 (2 small cans) salted fillets of anchovy	

Preheat the oven to 400°F. You will need a gratin dish and some aluminum foil.

Peel and slice the potatoes finely. Peel and slice the onions finely. Open the tins of anchovies. Save the oil—if you buy the anchovies from a barrel, you will need to soak them for 10 minutes in milk to desalt them a little, and you will need an ounce (2 tablespoons) of butter.

Layer the potatoes with the onions and the anchovies into a deep gratin dish. Sprinkle with freshly ground pepper as you go. No salt, there should be enough in the anchovies. Finish with a layer of potatoes. Pour in half the cream. Trickle the anchovy oil over the surface, or dot with butter. Cover with foil.

Bake at 400°F for 15 minutes. Then pour in the rest of the cream and turn the heat down to 300°F. Leave to cook gently. The potatoes will take another hour to soften. They're ready when they yield to a knife. Remove the lid for the last 20 minutes to allow the top to gild.

That's all. Simple perfection. No wonder Erik was tempted. A blueberry pie is a good finish in celebration of the American connection.

◆

BAKED POTATOES
(England)

The embers of a wood fire are the best place to cook the last old potatoes of the year. I remember the bonfire my grandfather would light at dusk on a cold November evening—my grandmother knew it was to burn up the dry leaves and debris of summer, but we children knew differently. When the fire burned down, we were allowed to tuck potatoes into the hot ash at the edge. It was our reward for a day's raking fallen leaves and dead branches in the garden. We would crouch, scarlet faces turned to the flames, icy night wind cold on the back of our necks, until long past suppertime. At last we would poke out our very own "tattie," charred and crisp outside, soft and sweet within. My grandmother looked the other way when we thieved a pat of butter and a little salt from the larder. An unbeatable dish.

TIME: 5 minutes plus 1 hour cooking

1 or 2 large potatoes per person (Idahos are perfect)
Salt

Preheat the oven to 350°F. Scrub large potatoes very thoroughly, and puncture the skins with a fork. You can rub the skins with salt if you like a salty crust. They will take about 60 minutes in a moderate oven. (Don't wrap them up in foil or the skins will be soft). Eat the potatoes as soon as they are ready, when they are at their crispest and most succulent, with cold butter and salt.

The skins are the best part, and the most nutritious.

◆

POTATO NOODLES

Krumpli nudli (Hungary)

Undergraduate Miss Ellen Browning, niece of the poet Robert Browning, traveled through Hungary in 1895. She greatly approved the supper she was offered in a peasant farmhouse:

> Presently the good woman began to set about her preparations for supper. We were to have *krumpli nudli*. I begged permission to assist in preparing them, which was readily granted. A large pot of potatoes had been boiling in their jackets. These were now strained off, skinned, mashed with salt and flour into a paste, and rolled into "worms," then dropped into a pan of boiling lard and thrown into a hot colander to drain as soon as they were cooked, then turned into a big dish, sprinkled with bread crumbs and popped into a hot oven for ten minutes. These are excellent, I can assure you, and Madame Irma made them to perfection. She seemed to be a very capable plain cook. For my dinner she had given me roast chicken with pickled-plum compote, followed by "jam-bags" [dumplings stuffed with jam]. [*A Girl's Wanderings in Hungary*, Ellen Browning, 1896]

◆

HEAVEN AND EARTH

Himmel und Erde (Germany)

The German kitchen has some particularly good potato recipes, including delicious pancakes made with raw grated potatoes and served with apples or stewed fruit; and an excellent dish known as "Heaven and Earth" which mixes boiled potatoes with apples and crisp fried bacon. This mixture of fruit and vegetables, sweet and sour, is characteristic of northern country cooking—Holland, Belgium, Alsace, Czechoslovakia, Poland, and Scandinavia all have similar mixtures. Immigrants to America, particularly the German and Dutch settlers in Pennsylvania, took their sweet-salt dishes with them and adapted the recipes to local ingredients. The resident Indians already used sweet maple syrup to dress their meat. Thence developed those peculiarly American dishes such as pumpkin-and-marshmallow pie to eat with the Thanksgiving turkey. Waffles with maple syrup and bacon, even the peanut butter-and-jelly sandwich, belong to the same tradition.

This makes an excellent supper or light luncheon dish.

SERVES: 4

TIME: 40 minutes

2   pounds (6 medium-sized) potatoes
2   pounds apples
One 8-ounce slab of bacon in thick (¼ inch) slices

You will need a large saucepan and a small frying pan. If the potatoes are new and small, you merely need to wash them. If they are old, peel them closely and quarter them. Put them to boil in plenty of salted water. Peel and cut the apples into chunks the size of the potato pieces. Add them to the potatoes after 10 minutes. Finish cooking both together. By the time the potatoes are cooked, the apples will be soft but still holding their shape.

Meanwhile, dice the bacon and fry it in its own fat. Drain the cooked apples and potatoes. Pile them into a hot dish and scatter the crisp bacon, with its cooking juices, over the top. Serve immediately.

◆

SUGGESTIONS

Cook 1 pound of fresh sausage (bratwurst would be most appropriate) with the bacon. Serve all together.

Fry a handful of fresh bread crumbs in the bacon fat until crisp and golden. Scatter over the potatoes.

◆

POTATO PANCAKES

Kartoffelpuffer (Germany)

One of the most delicious ways of preparing potatoes, this classic peasant recipe is simplicity itself.

SERVES: 4

TIME: 30 minutes

2   pounds (6 medium-sized) potatoes
½   teaspoon salt
1   ounce (2 tablespoons) lard or butter

You will need a grater (a food processor saves trouble) and a frying pan. Wash and peel the potatoes. Grate them through the largest holes of the grater to give noodlelike strips. Do not wash them again—they need the natural starchy juice to hold them together. Mix in the salt.

Heat the lard or butter in a frying pan. If you have only cooking oil, fry a small piece of bacon in it first to scent the oil. Drop spoonfuls of the potato mixture into the hot fat, pressing the mounds flat with the back of a wooden spoon. Fry the patties gently and steadily until they are crisp and golden underneath and soft right through—they will unstick from the pan only when the bottom is cooked. Then turn them over and fry the other side.

This is a delicious innocent dish to be served straight from the pan. It is excellent with fried apple quarters or apple sauce.

◆

SUGGESTIONS

Put the peeled potatoes to soak for 10 minutes in water acidulated with vinegar (1 tablespoon vinegar to 2 cups water). This will help them stay white—grated raw potato quickly turns a foggy gray. Then rinse them and grate as above.

In Franconia a more substantial dish is made by mixing the grated potato with an egg or two at the start, together with a large boiled potato well mashed. It is served with a dish of stewed cranberries instead of the apple.

◆

POTATO SOUP

Kartoffelsuppe (Germany)

Soups are staple fare all over Germany. In the colder climate of the north, the preference is for thick rib-sticking potages—potato, pumpkin, root vegetable, perhaps flavored with a piece of smoked meat or a slice of sausage. There is a repertoire of wine soups and beer soups (particularly around Munich, whose brewers are held in high esteem) which make their appearance at the beginning of the meal. Hamburg specializes in fruit soups. The lowland farmer likes his broth clear and strong, fortified with little dumplings, slices of egg custard, and semolina or noodles.

This is one of those thick soups designed to precede not a meat course, but the housewife's best strudel or fruit pie. It is the favorite Friday soup.

SERVES: 6

TIME: 20 minutes plus 30 minutes cooking

3	pounds (9 medium-sized) potatoes	1	ounce (2 tablespoons) butter or lard
3	pounds root vegetables: carrots, turnips, rutabagas, celeriac, parsnips (any or all of these)		1½ quarts water or stock Salt and pepper Fresh herbs for flavoring: lovage, basil, parsley, marjoram (any
1	pound onions		or all)

You will need a large stew pot. If the potatoes are new, just scrub them and cut them in half. Otherwise, peel and chop the potatoes into 1-inch cubes. Wash and scrape the vegetables and cut them into similar chunks. Peel and slice the onions.

Heat the butter or lard in a large stew pot, and fry the onions gently until transparent. Add the potatoes and vegetables. Pour in the water or stock, bring to a boil, cover the pot, and simmer the soup for half an hour. Mash the vegetables lightly to thicken the broth.

Season with salt and pepper. Chop the herbs finely, and stir them into the soup just before you serve it. If you are using dried herbs, they should be added at the start.

Enjoy your strudel to finish.

SUGGESTIONS

Add 1 ounce of dried mushrooms (cèpes are best—they have a delightful gluey texture). Soak them in a little warm water before adding them, with their liquid, to the soup. A half pound raw cultivated mushrooms can be used, but they are not so well-flavored and robust.

The Franconians would include a crust of dark rye bread to be stewed with the vegetables to give a slightly nutty flavor. Marjoram should be used to flavor this version.

Dice and fry 4 ounces of bacon and sprinkle it on the soup as you serve it. (This would naturally not have been permitted on a fast day such as Friday.) Once again, use only marjoram to flavor this version.

For another non-fast-day meal, cook a few slices of smoked sausage in the soup.

Serve the soup with a bowl of sour cream or grated cheese.

POTATO GRATIN

Pommes de terre au gratin (France)

There are many regional variations of this dish, all floodlit with passionate controversy, raging mainly over the inclusion of eggs, cheese, onions, cream, and nutmeg. I give here one of the simplest Provençal versions. It is just as delicious as the more complicated recipes.

SERVES: 6

TIME: 20 minutes plus 1 hour cooking

3	pounds (9 medium-sized)	Olive oil	
	potatoes	4	ounces grated mature cheese
1	onion		(Cantal, Gruyère, cheddar,
2	cups strong meat or chicken		Parmesan)
	bouillon	Salt and pepper	

Preheat the oven to 350°F. You will need a shallow gratin dish and some foil. A food processor with a slicing attachment would be useful.

Peel, rinse, and slice the potatoes thin. French housewives have an instrument called a *mandoline*—a neat wooden board which has two slanted razor-sharp blades embedded in it—which is perfect for this job. Peel and slice the onion finely. Heat the stock.

Pour 2 tablespoons of olive oil into the bottom of the gratin dish. Put in a layer of potato; then layer in the sliced onion, half the grated cheese, and the rest of the potatoes. Season as you go. Pour in the hot stock. Trickle a little oil over the surface, and cover the dish with foil.

Put the dish to cook gently in the oven for 50 to 60 minutes in all. Keep the dish covered for the first half hour; then take off the cover and sprinkle on the rest of the grated cheese. Allow to finish cooking and gild a rich brown.

Serve the gratin in its own dish, bubbling hot and accompanied by a plain-grilled chop or a chicken roasted with a little olive oil and rosemary or thyme.

In season, follow with a *salade de mesclun* or a beautiful Provençal vegetable dish. A meal for a long leisurely Sunday lunch.

◆

GRATIN DAUPHINOIS
(France)

This most simple and perfect of all potato dishes undergoes many unnecessary embellishments in the course of its travels from the Alps of the Dauphiné. Cheese is added to it, and eggs—all too frequently scrambled slowly to a grainy water; nutmeg is sprinkled in; the potatoes are parboiled before being sliced; flour is added to the cream. This gratin is a mountain dish, as befits the hardy potato. Made carefully and cooked slowly, it will be as you would expect to find it in its home country. The quantity of cream is lavish—but you will serve nothing else rich in the meal, and it will be much more delicious than if you had stuffed the same amount of cream into a cake.

S E R V E S : 4

T I M E : 20 to 30 minutes plus 1½ hours cooking

2   pounds (6 medium-sized) old   2   cups heavy cream
     potatoes   Salt and pepper
1   garlic clove   1   ounce (2 tablespoons) butter

Preheat the oven to 300°F. A round earthenware dish is considered proper for the *gratin dauphinois*. You will need some foil. A *mandoline* or a food processor with a slicing attachment will make the work easier.

Peel and slice the potatoes as fine as gold florins. Peel, crush, and mince the garlic.

Layer the potatoes into the gratin dish, sprinkling with salt, plenty of pepper, and crushed garlic as you go. Pour in the cream. Dot the surface with little bits of butter, and cover loosely with foil.

Put the gratin to bake for 1½ hours. Uncover it and turn the oven up to 350°F for the last 10 minutes to brown the crust.

Accompany with a perfect steak plain-grilled with plenty of pepper, or a pair of plump baby lamb chops, lightly grilled so that they are still pink and juicy within, and served in their innocence garlanded with no more than a small bunch of watercress.

In season, a bowl of fresh strawberries dressed with orange juice, or raspberries sprinkled with sugar, might follow. No cream: Perish the thought.

◆

GRATED POTATO CAKE

Rösti (Switzerland)

This is the favorite Swiss way with potatoes. It is a requirement of those who wish to become Swiss citizens that they "eat Swiss," and government inspectors are liable to arrive unannounced at the back door of those seeking citizenship to check on the dish of the day. Tax exiles would do well to start cooking a dish of *rösti*.

S E R V E S : 5 to 6

T I M E : 20 minutes

3   pounds (9 medium-sized) potatoes
4   ounces (½ cup) butter or lard

You will need a grater or a food processor with a grating attachment, and a frying pan. Grate the potatoes coarsely while you put the butter to melt in the frying pan. When the butter foams, add the grated potatoes. Fork over the mixture constantly for the first 15 to 20 minutes while the flakes soften and take color. When they are brown and cooked, flatten them into a cake and leave it to crisp on the base. Turn out, crisp side up, onto a plate to serve.

This is delicious on a cold night with a mug of mulled wine and a piece of Swiss cheese. Try the Swiss Vacherin: somewhat like a very soft Brie, it has a hard rind and must be eaten with a spoon. It is only made in the autumn for consumption before the spring. It'll satisfy the inspectors, too.

◆

SUGGESTION

In some households the potatoes are cooked in their jackets the day before and then grated. Fry as in the recipe—they will take half the time.

◆

LOBSCOUSE

Labskova (Denmark)

This dish is universal fare around the Atlantic coasts of Europe. On the Baltic coast of Germany, it is made with fish and called *Fischlabskaus* (page 92). In England, Liverpudlians make it with neck of mutton or lamb, and claim it as *lobscouse*—from which comes their sobriquet "scouse." The link appears to be the sea: The dish was a convenient way of making ship's stores palatable. The dish can be made with fresh raw food or leftovers. It can be cooked in the oven, and it used to be cooked in a black iron cauldron slowly over the hearth fire. For the rest of us, a heavy frying pan and a low heat will do well enough.

SERVES: 4

TIME: 20 minutes plus 50 minutes cooking

1 pound beef (a nice cheap cut such as brisket with plenty of golden fat)	2 ounces (4 tablespoons) lard or beef drippings
2 pounds (6 medium-sized) potatoes	2 cups stock or water
	1 bay leaf
	Salt and pepper

You will need a large frying pan with a lid. Cut the beef into 1-inch cubes. Peel and cut the potatoes into similar chunks. Melt the fat in a heavy frying pan. Add the meat and brown gently, turning to gild all sides. Add the potatoes, and then pour in the stock or water. The potatoes should not be submerged, but should just steam above the meat. Tuck in the bay leaf and add salt and pepper. Cover tightly and simmer on the top of the stove very gently for 50 to 60 minutes. Take the lid off and stir all together. Turn up the heat to allow the remaining liquid to evaporate and the base to brown. Reverse it when you turn it out. Serve with a knob of cold butter on each helping.

SUGGESTIONS

The dish can be made with leftovers of both meat and potatoes, and it will then need less cooking. If made with green cabbage or spinach instead of the meat, it will become "bubble and squeak" (particularly delicious if cooked in bacon fat, with a runny-yolked fried egg on top).

OLD CLOTHES WITH HOT SAUCE

Roupa velha con salsa piripiri (Portugal)

Roupa velha is the Portuguese version of *lobscouse*, and like that versatile and much-traveled dish, the basic hash can be made with fresh ingredients or with leftovers. Sailors everywhere love it. The Portuguese have a taste for hot chilies, acquired courtesy of the fiery palates of the natives of their former colony Brazil. *Piripiri* sauce is often used for flavoring or sparking up soups and dishes such as this one, whose taste is essentially bland. Addicts like the sauce on plain-grilled fish as well.

SERVES: 4 to 5

TIME: Make the sauce a few days before; 30 minutes

THE *PIRIPIRI* SAUCE:
12 tiny chili peppers
About ½ cup olive oil

THE FISH:

1	*pound filleted fresh fish (or cooked)*	*2*	*garlic cloves*
2	*pounds (6 medium-sized) potatoes (cooked, if the fish is already cooked)*	*6*	*tablespoons olive oil*
		2	*bay leaves*
		1	*cup water*
1	*large onion*	*½*	*teaspoon salt*
		2	*tablespoons vinegar*

You will need a glass jar and a heavy saucepan. The tiny fierce Brazilian *malagueta* chili pepper is the best one for this wicked little sauce. Any small hot green or red chili will do—although I find the red ones sweeter. Pack the peppers, whole and still with their stalks, into the jar. Cover with the olive oil and seal. Ready in a day or two, *piripiri* will keep for a long time. The oil will be well spiked, and the chilies in turn give up some of their fire. Use with discretion.

Skin the fish and remove the bones. Peel the potatoes and slice them. Peel the onion and the garlic, and slice them too.

Heat the olive oil in a heavy saucepan, and put in a layer of onion and garlic. Fry gently for a moment. Add a layer of the sliced potatoes and the bay leaves, and cover with the water. Sprinkle on the salt and the vinegar. Cover the pan and allow the "old clothes" to stew steadily for 15 minutes, when the potatoes should be nearly done. (If the potatoes are already cooked, 5 minutes will be enough to warm them through). Lay the fish on top of the potatoes and put the lid back on. Stew gently for another 5 to 10 minutes, until the fish is done. Take the lid off, and turn the heat up to evaporate any extra liquid and allow the base to brown.

Serve warm with a crisp salad of cos lettuce, dressed with lemon juice and salt and a shake of *piripiri*.

◆

HOT LIGHTNING

Hete bliksem (Holland)

The Dutch were as slow as the rest of Europe to grasp the potential of the potato. Although the tuber had been championed vigorously by the botanist Carolus Clusius at the end of the sixteenth century in Vienna, Frankfurt, and Leiden, it was not until the eighteenth century that it began to be planted widely in northern Europe. By the middle of the century, potatoes were being grown in all the United Provinces, and they rapidly replaced grain products and bread in the diet of the poor, particularly after the disastrous grain shortages of 1770–71. At this time the bourgeoisie sometimes ate potatoes, particularly with haddock, although the aristocrats hardly touched them.

SERVES: 4 to 5

TIME: 20 minutes plus 30 minutes cooking

2　pounds (10) small potatoes	2　pounds apples or pears (dried
8　ounces lean slab bacon	and soaked will do well
2　ounces (4 tablespoons) butter	enough—but halve the weight)
Salt, sugar, and pepper	

You will need an earthenware heatproof casserole or a heavy iron pot with a lid. Scrub the potatoes. Remove the bacon rind. Put both into a casserole or pot with the butter. Salt, sugar, and pepper to taste. Cover tightly and put to cook on top of the stove, shaking the casserole or pot to avoid sticking. Or cook in a preheated moderate oven, 350°F, if you are worried about subjecting the casserole to direct heat.

Meanwhile, peel, quarter, and core the apples or wipe, quarter, and core the pears. Add them to the casserole after 20 minutes, when the potatoes are half-cooked. Continue to cook until everything is soft—about 30 to 40 minutes in all.

Take the bacon out, cut it into slices, and serve on top of the potatoes and apples or pears, which should still hold their shape.

SUGGESTION

Instead of bacon, sausages can be cooked with the potatoes.

HOTCHPOTCH OF CARROTS AND POTATOES

Hochepot (Holland)

The hotchpotch is a traditional old recipe, economical and simple.

SERVES: 4 as a main dish; 6 as a side dish (without the meat.)

TIME: 40 to 60 minutes

2 pounds old carrots	2 ounces (4 tablespoons) butter
2 pounds (6 medium-sized) potatoes	1 onion
	Salt and pepper
1 pound flank steak, fresh or salted (see p. 184) for 2 days (optional)	

You will need two medium saucepans. Scrape the carrots and cut them into chunks. Peel the potatoes and cut them into thick slices. Put the carrots and potatoes to cook in water—salted if you are using fresh flank steak—until nearly done (about 15 minutes). Cut the meat into bite-sized squares and lay it over the top of the vegetables.

Meanwhile, peel and chop up the onion, and fry it in the butter in another pan until lightly golden. Lift out the the nearly-cooked vegetables and add them to the pan containing the onion, leaving the meat to continue to simmer in the water. Leave the two pans to cook gently until everything is done. Taste, and adjust the seasoning. Serve the meat on a separate plate.

◆

OYSTER-SHELL POTATOES

Pommes de terre en coquille (Holland)

These potatoes were baked, in the days before the installation of kitchen ovens, in a copper kettle on a tripod with the lid reversed to hold hot coals. The heat above had to be very strong to give a crisp brown top, and underneath the pot, the fire was just enough to keep the dish warm.

S E R V E S : 6

T I M E : 15 minutes plus 20 to 25 minutes cooking

2   *pounds (6 medium-sized) potatoes*
4   *ounces (½ cup) butter*
Salt
12   *oyster shells*

You will need a saucepan and a broiler. Scrub and then boil the potatoes with salt until they are soft—about 20 to 25 minutes. Peel them while still hot. Mash them thoroughly with the butter. Taste, and adjust the seasoning with salt if necessary. Fill the oyster shells with the mixture, dot with butter, and then brown them well under the broiler. Serve the oysters themselves, each wrapped in a fine slice of bacon and flashed under the broiler just long enough to sizzle the bacon and warm the oyster through.

As Sam Weller said in Dickens' *Pickwick Papers:* "Poverty and oysters always seem to go together."

◆

KILL-HUNGER

Matafaim or *Crique* (France)

Exactly as its name implies, this is fast food in Provence. In early September there are many fields to harvest all at once, and for those who share machinery, as do many in the village cooperatives of farmers, the harvesting goes on through the night in the light from the headlamps of the combine harvesters, until the morning dew makes reaping impossible. A dish of *matafaim* will be waiting on the farmhouse table as the workers return home in the autumn dawn.

SERVES: 2

TIME: 10 minutes plus 20 minutes cooking

2 pounds (6 medium-sized) potatoes	Salt and pepper
	1 garlic clove
2 eggs	3 tablespoons olive oil

You will need a heavy frying pan and a grater. Peel and grate the potatoes. Beat the eggs with the salt, pepper, and the garlic clove crushed with a little salt under the flat side of a heavy knife. Stir in the grated potatoes and mix well.

Heat the frying pan before you add the oil—this stops anything from sticking to the pan. When the oil is smoking, pour in the potato-and-egg mixture, and spread it well over the pan, patting it down with a wooden spoon to make a thin pancake. Leave it to cook gently for 15 minutes—shaking the pan every now and again to discourage sticking. Turn the pancake, and cook it for another 5 minutes to brown the other side. While it is cooking, make a salad to serve with it. Turn it out onto a hot plate and serve the "kill-hunger" immediately.

◆

SPANISH POTATO STEW

Patatas a la riojana (Spain)

The gardeners of Spain were among the first to appreciate the possibilities of the potato. Rioja, the most famous wine-growing district of Spain, skirts the river Ebro about halfway between Pamplona and Burgos, a lush countryside where vegetables grow fat and sweet among the vines.

SERVES: 4

TIME: 20 minutes plus 20 minutes cooking

1 large Spanish onion	4 tablespoons olive oil
3 garlic cloves	2 pounds (6 medium-sized) old waxy potatoes
One 2-ounce slab of bacon or serrano *ham*	
	1 to 2 bay leaves
1 pound tomatoes (or a 1-pound can of tomatoes)	1 glass of water
	Salt and pepper

You will need a wide shallow pan with a lid, a heavy frying pan will do. Peel and slice the onion and garlic cloves. Chop the bacon or ham into small cubes. Pour boiling water over the fresh tomatoes to loosen the skins, peel, and then chop them roughly.

Put the olive oil to warm in the pan. Add the onion and garlic and fry it lightly. Add the bacon or ham. Add the tomatoes and allow them to simmer uncovered for 10 minutes while you peel and slice the potatoes into thick rounds.

Lay the potato rounds on top of the tomato mixture, add the bay leaves, and pour in the glass of water. Cover and leave to simmer for 20 minutes or so, until the potatoes are soft.

Taste, and adjust the seasoning with salt and pepper. Serve the potato stew on its own, or with a fried egg for each diner, or with baby lamb chops broiled over vine twigs. To finish the meal, Burgos is famous for its delicious thick yogurt served with honey. Accompany, naturally, with the good red wine of Rioja.

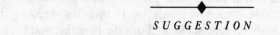

SUGGESTION

Artichoke hearts, beans, leeks, zucchini, and red and green peppers can all be added to make a *pisto manchego*.

CHAPTER THREE

Corner Cupboard Dishes

Beans-and-bones dishes are classic and staple peasant food in all Mediterranean countries. Recipes range from the simple *cocidos* and *ollas* of Spain to the stupendous *cassoulet* of southern France. Small farmers grew, and in many countries still grow, their own preferred variety of beans and chick-peas, which would be dried and stored for the winter. A peasant family in Spain rarely has a meal which does not include these vegetables in one form or another. The flavoring bones and bacon often came from home-cured pork. All but the most perishable parts of the family pig were conserved for the larder.

Ritual surrounded the planting of all such important staples, as an Andalusian smallholder, Jesús Peinado, pointed out to Ronald Fraser in 1958:

> There are plenty of crops you can't plant when the moon is waning. The May moon is bad, for example; if you plant beans then, they make a mass of stalks and no fruit. You have to plant seedbeds of onions, lettuce, melon and pumpkins with the waning moon as you do vetch and alfalfa. If the latter is planted at any other time, the livestock swell up and die when they eat it. That's the truth. I don't know why it is, but everyone here knows it. [*The Pueblo*, Ronald Fraser, 1973]

◆

BEAN STEW

Cocido (Spain)

A *cocido* is an everything-in-the-pot boiled dinner, Spanish style. Before the arrival of New World haricot beans, such dishes were made with chick-peas or dried fava beans, the *ful* of the Middle East. These pot stews are the most popular everyday dish to be found on the Iberian peninsula. Each region has its variations, dictated by available local ingredients and preferences: in Andalusia, vegetables are usually included, particularly greens such as Swiss chard, spinach, small artichokes, and carrots. The Madrid version is the grandest, and includes a large piece of beef and a good selection of everyone else's ingredients as well. It is served in two parts: first the broth, with a handful of bread crumbs or fine noodles poached in it, and then the meats. Meatballs (page 353) are stewed in the Galician *pote gallego*. Catalonia calls it an *escudella* and incorporates the region's favorite white sausage.

The simplest peasant recipe uses the widely available products of the pig *matanza* (butchering) together with a few vegetables. The beans can be chick-peas or white beans—this is essentially a pale stew. Many rural communities cultivate and dry their own beans. The dish is so widespread that it has a variety of names, which makes its true identity somewhat confusing to determine. It often appears as *olla podrida*, meaning a "rotting" or "powerful" dish—a name which occurs in early English cookbooks influenced, no doubt, by the Spanish princesses imported as royal wives at the time. In Andalusia it is sometimes called a *pringa* or *puchero*.

The list of designations, and variations in its making, could be extended almost indefinitely. What follows is the *cocido* as prepared in the tiny *venta*, or inn, of the Guadalmesi, the little village at the foot of the Andalusian valley, which was my home for many years. The few dozen inhabitants of the Guadalmesi settlement managed to make a living out of the fertile alluvial flat which had formed at the mouth of the river where it flowed into the sea. All the ingredients were home grown and the recipe is, I think, as old and true as any in the patchwork quilt of ancient kingdoms which make up modern Spain.

The ancestors of my friends and neighbors in the Guadalmesi had, after all, been eating their *cocidos* there long before Homer wrote of the Pillars of Hercules above which the valley stands sentinel.

SERVES: 8

TIME: Start 3 to 4 hours ahead; 30 minutes plus 1½ to 3 hours cooking

1 *pound chick-peas or white beans*
4 *ounces* morcilla *(black pudding)*
   (optional)
4 *ounces salted pork belly or bacon*
2 *dried red peppers (not the hot*
   variety) or 1 tablespoon sweet
   paprika or 1 fresh red pepper)
1 *head of garlic*
4 to 5 *tablespoons olive oil*
About 2 quarts water (excluding
   soaking water)
1 or 2 *short lengths of ham bone*
   (optional)

2 *small* chorizos *(Spanish pork*
   sausage) or 4 ounces dried
   spicy sausage
½ *pound cubed meat (pork,*
   chicken, beef, rabbit)
A choice of optional ingredients, no
   more than 1 pound altogether,
   from: green peppers, onions,
   leeks, tomatoes, potatoes, or
   any of the regional variations
   mentioned in the recipe
   introduction
Salt

You will need a large, heavy cooking pot with a lid. Put the chick-peas or beans to soak in fresh water for 3 to 4 hours.

Slice the *morcilla* into short lengths, cut off the rind from the pork belly, and cut the rind into squares. Seed the red peppers. Do not peel the garlic, but hold it in a flame to char the covering and roast the cloves a little. This releases and enhances its flavor.

Heat the oil in the pot. Fry the salt pork gently in the oil for a few minutes. Add the water, chick-peas or beans (the beans should be well submerged), ham bone, whole garlic head, and peppers or paprika (or fresh red pepper, seeded and sliced). Bring to a boil, and then turn it down to simmer. You may need to add extra boiling water during the course of the cooking.

Beans are variable in the length of time they take to soften—they can take anywhere from 1½ to 3 hours to cook. When they are soft but still firm—this should take about an hour—put in the *chorizos* or dried sausage, well pricked, along with the cubed meat. Add the black pudding and the optional vegetable ingredients toward the end of the cooking time: *Morcilla* and peeled chopped potatoes should go in 30 minutes before the end, and the green vegetables about 20 minutes before.

To finish, taste and add salt (the pork will have contributed to the saltiness), and stir in a spoonful of olive oil and a crushed clove of garlic.

Serve the *cocido* in deep plates with plenty of fresh bread. Accompany with sliced tomatoes or a salad of crisp green lettuce dressed with olive oil, wine vinegar, and salt.

SUGGESTION

Sometimes the good lady of the *venta* would stir in, at the end, a Guadalmesi ladleful of ready-boiled cabbage fried with garlic.

Leftovers: Fry steadily in a little oil until all the liquid evaporates and the base forms a hard crisp crust. Stir the crust several times and continue to fry until the mixture is dry and crumbly. This trick works with all bean stews (the Mexicans call it a *refrito,* and the result is quite delicious, particularly if served with a fried egg for each person and a simple fresh tomato sauce spiked with a little chili).

◆

LENTIL SOUP-STEW

Sopa de lentejas (Spain)

Daily life in the little hill villages of Andalusia has changed remarkably little from the centuries-old pattern. On a fine cold, clear October evening in the mountains above Ronda, black cliffs soar over white villages, eagles patrol the crags, and the last blooms of the rock roses and late scillas glow in the pearl-gray boulders under the olive trees. In the narrow main street of the village of El Gastór, the women set up their cooking braziers, shallow metal bowls balanced on slender tripods.

They cook the evening meal in the scrubbed street outside their shadowed doorways. The fuel is walnut or olive shells, fired with olive pits and ground to a mush between the millstones—debris of the harvest. Such fuel burns with a clean strong glow and keeps its heat like charcoal. The cooking pots are copper pans—tarred black as pitch outside, mirror-bright within. Their handles are long, made of beaten iron welded on with iron rivets— identical to the pots the Romans used 2,000 years ago. The scent of cooking drifts down the narrow street, past the scrubbed doorsteps and iron balconies strung around with pots of scarlet geraniums. The stews begin to bubble with lentils, garlic, dried mountain ham, wild greens, peppers, and olive oil. To ward off the chill of autumn in the hills of the Spanish sierras, it will be a *sopa de lentejas* for supper.

SERVES: 6

TIME: 20 minutes plus 70 minutes cooking

1 *pound brown lentils*	2 *short lengths of raw ham bone*
4 *garlic cloves*	*with meat still on it or a*
4 *ounces pork (belly or lean)*	*4-ounce piece of slab bacon*
1 *pound greens: Swiss chard,*	*(optional)*
spinach, spring greens,	4 *ounces morcilla (black pudding)*
cabbage	*or chorizo (optional)*
½ *pound (2 small) potatoes*	1 *dried or fresh red pepper (seeded*
4 *tablespoons olive oil*	*and torn into pieces)*
2¾ *quarts water*	*Salt*

Lentils happily do not need soaking—they are the fast food of the bean tribe and only take an hour to cook. Pick them over and remove any tiny tooth-breaking stones (which look exactly like lentils).

Peel the garlic and leave the cloves whole. Cube the pork and chop the greens. Peel the potatoes and cut them into bite-sized chunks.

Fry the garlic and pork gently in the olive oil. Add the lentils and cover with the water. Add the ham bone, *morcilla*, and dried red peppers.

Stew gently for 40 minutes. Add the potatoes to the stew, and continue to cook for 20 minutes. Add the vegetables, and cook for 10 minutes more. When the vegetables are ready, add salt and stir in an extra spoonful of oil before serving.

SUGGESTIONS

This is a very variable recipe, depending largely on the products and fortune of those preparing it. Green peppers can be included. Tomatoes are sometimes added, as are onions, carrots, or young tender artichokes. There are several wild greens—in particular the leaf stems of a thistle *Scolymus hispanicus (tagarnina)* —which are particularly appreciated in this sturdy soup.

One fresh red pepper or 1 teaspoon of paprika can substitute for the dried red peppers so easily available in Spain, where strings of them hang beside the garlic braid from the beam in every country kitchen.

YELLOW PEA SOUP

Ertesuppe (Norway)

A meal in itself, this is a delicately flavored thick golden soup. If you feel those at the table may still be hungry afterwards, serve a filling dessert such as jam-filled pancakes.

SERVES: 6

TIME: 15 minutes plus 90 minutes cooking

1   pound dried yellow split peas
1½   quarts water
1   length of salt lamb bone or ham bone (soak it for a few hours if it is very
     salty) or ½ pound breast of lamb or slab bacon
Fresh herbs: Leek top, celery top, parsley

You will need a large saucepan. Put the peas into a saucepan with the water. Add the bone, or the meat, and the flavoring herbs, well chopped, and bring to a boil. Turn down the heat and simmer the soup gently until the peas are soft, which will take about 1½ hours, depending on the peas. Add more boiling water if necessary.

Serve piping hot, with *flatbrød* (page 419)

SUGGESTIONS

The bone from a roast shoulder or leg of lamb gives good results. The dish can be made with the addition of root vegetables (carrots, turnips, leeks, potatoes). Each household has its preferred recipe.

The Danes and the Swedes also love this soup. In Denmark it is called *gule aerter* and the pork is likely to be simmered separately, with the same herbs, until tender—then the stock is used to cook the peas.

PEASE PUDDING

(England)

This is one of the oldest dishes in the English culinary repertoire. The dish was made from dried peas with their skins still on, rather than split peas or old fresh peas. A double handful of these was tied in a clean floured cloth and hung in the pot in which the ham or bacon was boiling. They would swell into a green floury ball, which would be served at the same time as the meat.

SERVES: 6

TIME: Start the day before; 15 minutes plus 2 hours cooking

1   *pound dried peas or split peas or 2 pounds old fresh peas, weighed without
    the shell (fresh peas will not need soaking)*
1   *bunch of herbs: mint, thyme, marjoram, parsley*
2   *ounces (4 tablespoons) butter*
Salt and pepper

You will need a saucepan, a 6-cup pudding basin, and foil. A blender would be useful. Soak the peas in cold water overnight. Drain off the surplus soaking water; put the peas in a saucepan, and cover them either with ham stock (if not too salty) or with fresh water. Add the herbs tied together in a bunch.

Cook gently until the peas are soft and the skins loosen—about an hour. Remove the herbs, drain the peas thoroughly, and then mash or blend them with the butter. Add salt and pepper, and put the mixture into a pudding basin and cover with buttered foil. Either steam it steadily for an hour in a saucepan full of water to come two thirds of the way up the basin, or bake the pudding in a preheated 325°F oven for an hour.

Serve with sausages or with ham done any way you please. It is also good with roast pork. Or serve it on its own with a jug of melted butter.

SUGGESTION

To make a richer pudding, beat an egg and ½ cup of heavy cream into the mixture before you bake it.

BEAN SOUP

Ciorba de fasole (Rumania)

This is a favorite Rumanian one-pot meal, thick and nourishing in the cold winter months. Vegetable and herb flavorings such as carrot, tomato, garlic, savory, tarragon, and thyme can replace the bacon. It is really a matter of making the best use of what you have.

SERVES: 6 to 8

TIME: Start 3 to 4 hours or a day ahead; 10 minutes plus 1½ to 3 hours cooking

6 ounces navy or butter beans (white)	2 egg yolks
6 ounces pinto beans (the speckled red ones)	½ cup sour cream
	1 tablespoon vinegar
One 4-ounce slab of bacon	Salt and pepper
2 quarts water	1 small bunch of dill
1 lettuce (cos is best; green beans or chard can substitute—in winter, a cup of sauerkraut might be used)	

You will need a roomy saucepan. Put the beans to soak in cold water for 3 to 4 hours or overnight.

The next day cube the bacon. Drain the beans and put them into a roomy saucepan with the bacon: Beans need plenty of room to expand. Add the 2 quarts water. Bring to a boil, skim, and then turn the heat down. Simmer the beans for 1½ to 3 hours, until they are soft. You may need a little more water—it depends on the beans.

Shred the lettuce and stir it into the soup when the beans are soft. Cook for 10 to 15 minutes.

Mash the beans a little to thicken the soup. Mix the egg yolks, sour cream, and vinegar together, and stir the mixture into the boiling-hot soup. Season with salt and pepper. Chop the dill finely and scatter it over the surface.

Serve the soup with good dark bread and a bottle of two of Rumanian red wine. Fresh fruit should follow—plums, apples, or pears, or a dish of apricots—or, if you and your diners are still hungry, a plate of *papanasi* (page 472).

◆

BAKED BEAN STEW

Cassoulet de Castelnaudary (France)

Mme. Escrieu, sturdy mother of four strapping sons, lived with her family, two pigs, a dozen rabbits, a cow, three bird dogs, a yardful of chickens and guinea fowl, and a loftful of plump pigeons, in one of the farmhouses near my cottage in the Languedoc. Madame, a massively built matriarch, told me she made a *cassoulet* every two weeks in the winter months for her family's Sunday luncheon—never for the evening dinner, as at least six hours were needed to digest it. More often would have been too much even for their gargantuan appetites. Her method began with the preparation of her own *confit d'oie* made from goose or duck fattened for *foie gras*, but from which the precious liver had been removed and potted. The down from the birds had already been sterilized in the oven and used to restuff the matrimonial featherbed. I watched her construct her mighty masterpiece.

The *cassoulet*, the archetypical peasant meal, is a controversial dish. Food writers, culinary scholars, and restaurant chefs have been plucking and worrying at it for years. The *cassoulet*, quite simply, is the creature of its maker: a balance of habit, necessity, availability, and as with all the best peasant cooking, the special genius of the cook. The *cassoulet* is unusual in that most of its ingredients are home prepared pantry items which demonstrate the cook's abilities in depth. The perfect *cassoulet* can only spring from the perfect larder. Even the cook's good night's sleep on her well-stuffed goose-feather bed can make all the difference.

Toulouse, where the subject has entered the more rarified air of *gastronomie*, insists on the addition of a length of fresh Toulouse sausage and leg of mutton to the stew. Carcassonne adds both mutton and partridges—and brooks no deviation. Others add what they judge to be their essentials. I put my money on Mme. Escrieu.

SERVES: 10

TIME: Start a day ahead; 30 to 40 minutes plus 4 hours cooking

FIRST COOKING:

1½ *pounds white beans (those
    from Soissons are held to be best)*
4   *ounces fresh pork skin rolled up
    and tied*
½   *pound cubed salt pork belly*
2   *carrots, scraped and sliced*

1   *onion, peeled and stuck with 6
    cloves*
3   *garlic cloves, peeled*
1   *bunch of fresh herbs: parsley,
    thyme, rosemary, fennel, bay
    leaf, tied together*
6   *black peppercorns, crushed*

SECOND COOKING:

1   *leg of preserved goose or duck
    (confit), with its dripping (¼
    of a fresh bird can substitute)*
1   *pound boned, rolled, and tied
    shoulder of lamb (optional, but
    it may substitute for the goose)*
½   *pound lean pork cut into large
    pieces*

½   *pound fresh pork sausage
    (saucisse de Toulouse or any
    garlic-flavored fresh pork sausage)*
3   *garlic cloves, crushed*
2   *onions, chopped*
2   *large tomatoes, skinned and
    chopped (or an 8-ounce can
    of tomatoes)*
½   *pound dried spicy garlic sausage*
    Salt and pepper

You will need a heavy saucepan, a frying pan, and a *cassole* or *toupin*, or your favorite large earthenware pot with a lid. Check the beans for little bits of gravel, and then put them to soak overnight in cold water.

The next day, drain the beans and put them into a saucepan with the rest of the "first cooking" ingredients. Cover everything with fresh water, bring to a boil, and skim off the gray foam which rises. Turn down the heat and simmer the beans for an hour, until they are soft but still whole, adding more boiling water if necessary.

Meanwhile, prepare the meats in the "second cooking" group. Put the preserved leg of goose or duck into a frying pan and melt off the drippings. Take out and reserve the leg itself. Or prepare the piece of fresh bird by broiling it gently for 10 minutes on each side until the fat runs (put these drippings into the frying pan). If you're using lamb, fry it until the outside is caramelized. Fry the pork with the garlic in the goose drippings, until browned. Remove and reserve them. Fry the onions. Drain off the fat which remains and save it for the finishing.

When the beans are ready, take out the onion and the bunch of herbs. Untie and lay the pork skin (with the fat side down) in the base of the earthenware casserole.

Layer the beans with the meats, onions, tomatoes, and garlic sausage into the casserole, finishing with a layer of beans. From now on it is only a matter of oven time: Long, slow cooking is the trick. Cover the pot and put it in a preheated 250°F oven for 2 hours (if the beans get too dry, pour in a little *boiling* water—the beans will harden if you use cold water).

At the end of this time, take the lid off the casserole for the final stage, which will take another hour (completing the 4 hours).

Pour a tablespoonful of the melted goose fat over the surface of the casserole. Increase the oven heat to 325°F and return the dish uncovered to the oven. It will take half an hour to form a beautiful crust. Break this with a spoon and stir it into the beans. Mme. Escrieu maintained it is this operation which gives the *cassoulet* authenticity. On the final stirring, taste, and adjust the seasoning with salt and pepper. Leave for the final half hour. Now you reap the reward of your patience: Beneath the golden crust the meats will be tender and fragrant and the beans melted into a delicious creamy mass.

Serve the *cassoulet* with a strong red wine—perhaps that of Cahors. M. Escrieu still held the license, from his father and his father before him, to distill his own walnut-leaf-flavored *eau-de-vie*—which made a fine *digestif* after his good lady's masterpiece.

A green salad completes the meal, together with a small piece of a pungent goat's cheese such as that supplied to the Escrieux from a cousin in the nearby Montagne Noire.

◆

SUGGESTIONS

The *cassoulet* can be made the day before, but give it an hour and a half in a gentle (250°F) oven to reheat and crisp the crust.

If you have no preserved goose, omit it. Mme. Escrieu did not always include it either. Use good lard instead of the goose drippings.

If you would like a particularly crackly crust, scatter freshly made white bread crumbs over the surface of the beans for the final crisping.

Stir 1 tablespoon of chopped fresh herbs (parsley, chives, tarragon) into the stew when you stir in the crust for the last time.

Pork can replace lamb, or both fresh meats can be omitted, or replaced by fresh all-meat pork sausage. Mme. Escrieu would only add (and indeed only had) the fresh sausage just after the annual pig killing.

Mme. Escrieu would sometimes replace the fresh meat with a scrag end of one of her home-dried hams, particularly toward the end of the winter when supplies were running down.

◆

BROWN BEANS AND BACON

Bruine bonen (Holland)

This is a good sturdy meal for hungry countrymen, sometimes served with honey or golden syrup. The Dutch, long a maritime and colonial nation, had early access to Eastern spices and plentiful sugar. They reexported these valuable goods to Norway, and for many years a profitable triangular trade in Scandinavian berries and fish, English wool, and Dutch sugar and spices operated.

SERVES: 6

TIME: Start a day ahead; 15 to 20 minutes plus 1½ to 2 hours cooking

1 pound dried brown beans	2 large old potatoes
One ½-pound slab of bacon	½ pound onions, peeled and chopped
1 pound leeks	Pepper

You will need a large saucepan and a frying pan. Put the beans in cold water to cover. Leave them overnight to soak.

The following day drain the beans, and cook them in enough water to cover them to a depth of two fingers, for 1½ to 2 hours, until soft. The water should be mostly absorbed. Drain the beans and rinse them under cold running water.

Meanwhile, dice the bacon, wash and slice the leeks, and peel and slice the potatoes. Put the bacon to sweat in a hot frying pan until its fat runs. When the bacon is golden, add the onions and fry them gently. Then add the leeks and fry them too. You may need a little extra lard—it depends on the fattiness of the bacon. Finally add the drained beans. Turn everything together until well mixed. Fry gently until the beans have absorbed all the bacon drippings and are well flavored. Taste, and add pepper (the bacon should have added enough salt already). This is delicious served with a jug of warm syrup or honey.

SUGGESTIONS

Brown bean soup: The same mixture makes an excellent soup. Cube the bacon, slice the leeks and onions, and cook all the ingredients together with 3 pints of water for 1½ to 2 hours, until the beans are tender. Mash together to thicken the soup.

Leftovers: Refry the beans, and serve with fried eggs and a bowl of fresh tomato sauce with chili, for a wonderful lunch dish—or, best of all, late breakfast.

◆

CHICK-PEA PORRIDGE

Socca (France)

A preparation much like *mamaliga* and *polenta*, this was the staple of many a peasant diet in poor districts of southeastern France. Chick-peas grow easily and need little room. They are harvested in the late summer and dried on trays for storage throughout the winter. Today *socca* is most often found on market day. A wood-fired oven and copper dishes are the required instruments.

SERVES: 4

TIME: 15 minutes plus 20 minutes baking

6	ounces (1½ cups) chick-pea flour
2	cups cold water
2	tablespoons olive oil
1	tablespoon salt

Preheat the oven to 475°F. You will need a bowl and a large baking tray.

Mix the chick-pea flour with the water in a bowl. Stir in the oil and the salt, beating well to eliminate lumps. Pour the mixture into an oiled baking tray so that it lies in a layer no more than 1 inch thick.

Bake for 20 minutes. You are aiming to achieve the black blisters on the surface which would be produced by a charcoal-fired oven working at full temperature. Cut into squares and serve hot. A dish of stewed tomatoes and a fried egg could accompany this, although *socca* is usually appreciated on its own.

◆

SUGGESTION

Beat a big lump of butter into the *socca*, and plenty of black pepper. Your neighbors would certainly not approve of such deviations.

◆

SERBIAN BEAN SOUP

Pasulj (Yugoslavia)

Pasulj (pronounced poss-ool-ya) means "very small." This dish is a good winter standby, a classic peasant one-pot meal to be eaten with a spoon. It originates in the mountains of eastern Yugoslavia and its capital, Belgrade. The cold winds which sweep from the high plain down the valleys would certainly be kept at bay with such a supper.

SERVES: 5 to 6

TIME: 2 to 2½ hours

1	pound dried white beans (navy or cannellini)	5 to 6	whole peppercorns
2	onions, chopped	1	pound kielbasa, thickly sliced
3	garlic cloves, minced	½	tablespoon salt
3	bay leaves	2	tablespoons olive oil
2	tablespoons chopped parsley	1	teaspoon paprika
2	tablespoons tomato paste	2	tablespoons flour
1	large carrot, scraped and sliced		

You will need a large saucepan. Pick over the beans for bits of grit and chaff, and rinse them twice in cold water. Put the beans in a large saucepan and cover them with water to a depth of 1 to 2 inches. Bring the water to a boil and then turn down the heat. Leave to simmer gently for half an hour.

Remove the pan from the heat and pour in enough cold water to cover the beans to a depth of 3 inches. The beans will settle on the bottom. Leave them for a minute or two; then pour off the water and replace with fresh water. Bring the water to a boil and then turn down the heat to simmer.

Add the onions, garlic, bay leaves, parsley, tomato paste, carrot, and peppercorns to the beans. Cook gently over very low heat for 1½ to 2 hours, until the beans are soft. After 45 minutes of the cooking, add the *kielbasa*.

Fifteen minutes before you are ready to serve, add the salt and prepare a *liaison* for the soup. Heat the oil until it is smoking lightly; then quickly stir in the paprika, followed by the flour. Mix to a thin paste. Add this to the soup, stirring well. Simmer for 5 minutes, until the soup is thick and rich.

Serve with plenty of bread and good red wine.

SUGGESTION

Leftovers: Pasulj tastes very good reheated on the second day.

◆

WHITE BEAN SALAD

Fasoul jahnia (Bulgaria)

The Turkish and Greek influence is so strong in Bulgaria, after five centuries of conquest and domination, that it is difficult to untangle the threads of the national origins of this dish. Culinary variations often depend on preferred and local ingredients. In Bulgaria sunflower is the favored oil and the favorite herbs are mint, dill, savory, thyme, and tarragon. Lentils, peas, and haricot beans were all listed by the Ottoman tax collectors in fifteenth-century Bulgarian markets. Lemon is preferred to vinegar as a sour flavoring.

SERVES: 6

TIME: Start 3 to 4 hours ahead; 20 minutes plus 2 hours cooking

1 *pound dried white beans (navy or cannellini)*	*Salt and pepper*
4 *garlic cloves*	*Mint, dill, thyme, tarragon, savory (any or a mixture)*
2 *onions*	1 *hard-cooked egg (optional, for garnish)*
2 to 3 *carrots*	
½ *cup sunflower or sesame oil*	*A few black olives (optional, for garnish)*
2 *tablespoons lemon juice*	

You will need a roomy saucepan. Pick over the beans and remove any little bits of grit. Put them to soak in cold water to cover for 3 to 4 hours.

Drain the beans and put them in a roomy saucepan. Cover them to a depth of two fingers with fresh water. Bring them to a boil and cook them for an hour. Add the peeled crushed garlic and the peeled diced vegetables. Bring it all back to a boil, and cook for another hour. Stir in the oil, lemon juice, salt, and plenty of freshly ground black pepper, and allow to cool.

Serve in a shallow dish, sprinkled with chopped mint and herbs. Garnish if you please with a few slices of hard-cooked egg and a scattering of black olives. Follow this little salad with some freshly caught grilled fish, served with bread and quartered lemons, for a perfect light lunch.

◆

FLAGEOLET SALAD

Salade de flageolets (France)

This is a little salad to be served as an entrée. Flageolets are the most delicate of the dried bean tribe. Pale green in color, they are the dried seeds of a variety of dwarf green bean.

S E R V E S : 6

T I M E : Start 2 to 3 hours before; 10 to 15 minutes plus 2 hours cooking

1 pound flageolets (small green dried beans—the best are imported from France)	*6 tablespoons olive oil*
	1 tablespoon wine vinegar
	2 garlic cloves
1 teaspoon salt	*1 small bunch of parsley*
6 to 8 peppercorns	*Pepper*

You will need a roomy saucepan. Put the beans to soak in water for 2 to 3 hours. Drain them, put them in a saucepan, and cover them to a depth of one finger with fresh water—in France, preferably soft rainwater. Cook them with salt and peppercorns for 1 hour, until they are soft. Don't let the water stop boiling gently, and add boiling water if necessary.

Drain the beans. Mix them with the oil and vinegar. Toss in the peeled and finely chopped garlic and the parsley—at least a tablespoon. Sprinkle with freshly ground pepper and additional salt. Leave for half an hour to cool.

SUGGESTION

This salad can be made with chick-peas, white beans, or any other dried beans.

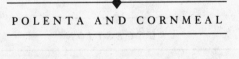

POLENTA AND CORNMEAL

CORNMEAL MUSH

Polenta (Italy)

The original *polenta* was made of chestnut flour, a product of the ancient plantations of chestnut trees which flourish in the hills of Italy. When the corn of the New World was introduced into Europe, it took so well to the climate of northern Italy and the Balkans—and it was so easy to harvest and store—that it quickly replaced the chestnut as a staple of the poor, in particular among sharecropping peasants.

The new miracle-food did, however, have its drawbacks: When it became the single item of diet, its dependents were liable to pellagra, a protein-deficiency disease. In the Americas corn has been under cultivation since

3,500 B.C. Needing on average only a day's work a week per man, cornmeal provided the dietary powerhouse behind the cultural explosions of the Mayan, Inca, and Aztec civilizations. Recipes for cornmeal porridges are to be found all over Eastern Europe. Cornmeal for *polenta* is best when freshly ground. The coarse-ground is suitable for a porridge or mush; the fine-ground will give a harder paste better suited to cakes for grilling.

SERVES: 4

TIME: 40 minutes

> 3   *cups water*
> ½   *pound (1½ cups) coarse-ground yellow cornmeal*
> 1   *tablespoon salt*

You will need a heavy saucepan. Bring the water to a boil in a saucepan. Trickle in the cornmeal from your hand, stirring constantly with a wooden spoon with the other hand. Make sure the mixture is smooth, and press out any lumps with the back of the spoon. The process is much like making oatmeal. Add the salt.

Bring to a boil and then simmer on low heat for 30 minutes or so, stirring throughout the cooking process to avoid sticking. When the mixture is well thickened and comes away from the sides of the pan, it is done. The *polenta* may need a little more or less water.

Serve with your favorite well-flavored sauce for pasta (one with a mushroom base is particularly suitable). Pass a bowl of grated Parmesan or Pecorino separately.

SUGGESTION

Serve with grilled meat or a rich game stew.

POLENTA CAKES

(Italy)

Make the *polenta* as in the preceding recipe, but using fine-ground meal instead of the coarse-ground. When the mush is cooked, pour it out into a shallow dish to a depth of about ½ inch and allow it to cool.

When cold, this paste can be cut with a wet knife or molded with floured fingers into any shape you wish. Proceed in one of the following ways:

Cut the cold mush into squares, top each square with a slice of mozzarella, or Bel Paese, and a sprinkle of oil; then arrange the pieces in a lightly oiled flat ovenproof dish. Bake in a preheated 400°F oven until the cheese is melted and golden. This can be done very effectively under a broiler, but you will need to heat the *polenta* through in the oven first. Serve on its own or with a tomato sauce, or with grilled meat and a salad.

To make *polenta al sugo* for four, you will need 1 cup of *ragù* (page 144), or tomato sauce, and ¼ pound of grated Parmesan or pecorino. Roll the *polenta* into small balls with well-floured hands, or slice it into squares with a wet knife. Pour a tablespoon of oil into the bottom of an ovenproof dish, and arrange half the *polenta* balls in a single layer. Cover with half the *râgú* sauce and half the grated cheese. Repeat with the rest of the *polenta*, sauce, and cheese. Bake in a preheated 425°F oven for 20 minutes, until it is hot and bubbling and the cheese is gilded.

The Basque make a dish called *broyo*, which is cornmeal mush served with *boeuf en daube* (page 378).

◆

CORNMEAL MUSH

Mamaliga (Rumania)

Theresa Stratilesco appreciated the niceties of *mamaliga* preparation in her travels, as recorded in *From Carpathian to Pindus*, around the year 1900:

Roumanian cookery is very elaborate, and there is a number of dishes a Roumanian peasant woman can cook if she only can afford it, but as a matter of fact, want will come to the rescue and make things ever so much easier. The plainest kind of food, the real national dish, is the mamaliga with branza (sheep cheese). The mamaliga takes the place of bread, which is considered a luxury in a peasant's house; cold mamaliga can be eaten too, but if a fire is at hand, it is cut into slices and fried on the embers. Also a baked bread can be made of Indian meal, called malai, very tasty and sweet. Dishes of herbs and vegetables, and of fowl and fish, are very numerous; meat is rarely used.

No table cloth except on festive occasions. The table is scrubbed till it shines milk-white. The mamaliga is turned out into the middle of it from the ciaun (iron round kettle) and stands like a golden cupola smoking there until everybody has sat down round the bale. In the meantime the wife is careful to take off the fire the prostii—iron tripod—or she might burn in hell's flames. If the mamaliga is furrowed with cracks, this means an unexpected journey is at hand for some one of the household. They all make the sign of the cross. Then the mamaliga is cut into slices, with a thread, carefully from upside down, and not the other way, as then the maize grows ear, and divided among the members of the family. [*From Carpathian to Pindus*, Theresa Stratilesco, 1906]

SERVES: 4

TIME: 40 minutes

3   *cups water*
1   *tablespoon salt*
½   *pound (1½ cups) coarse-ground yellow cornmeal*
2   *ounces (4 tablespoons) butter*

You will need a large saucepan. Bring the water to a boil with the salt. If you wish to be authentic, sprinkle the cornmeal over the boiling water in handfuls, beating constantly to avoid lumps. Stir vigorously until the mush thickens. It is, however, more easily made if you mix the meal with a little cold water first, and then stir the liquid into the rest of the cold water in a roomy saucepan. Proceed as before.

Beat in the butter. Bubble the mixture for a few moments, and then turn the heat down. Stir over low heat for 30 minutes, until the cornmeal is well cooked.

Serve it on its own or with sour cream. Or like a sorbet, between courses. Or like a Yorkshire pudding, to fill up before the meat course. Served authentically, it is always a dish on its own.

◆

SUGGESTIONS

To make the *mamaliga* special, pour a shallow layer into a buttered gratin dish, dot with more butter, and bake in a preheated 425°F oven for 10 minutes. Spoon sour cream over it when it is brown and bubbling. Cut the *mamaliga* into squares while it is still hot.

Serve it with fresh cream, cinnamon, and sugar, as a sweet dish after a thick soup.

Or turn spoonfuls of *mamaliga* in poppy seeds and honey, and eat with cream.

Or serve the hot *mamaliga* squares accompanied by a dish of stewed plums or apples.

Or fry bread crumbs in butter and drop spoonfuls of the *mamaliga* in, shaking them around to coat them in the fragrant crisp crumbs.

Spread a third of the *mamaliga* into a buttered casserole. Cover with a layer of grated cheese. Continue alternate layers until it is all used up, finishing with cornmeal. Dot with butter and put into a preheated 350°F oven for 20 to 25 minutes, until the dish is piping hot and the crust is golden.

Leftovers: Allow the *mamaliga* to cool down; then cut into slices, dip into a beaten egg, and roll in grated cheese. Fry quickly on both sides in hot butter. This is wonderful as a light lunch with a bowl of sour cream or yogurt and a fresh little salad.

◆

SWEET CORNMEAL PUDDING

Milhassou (Spain and France)

This cake was originally made with millet flour and is a great favorite on both sides of the Pyrenees.

SERVES: 6

TIME: 30 minutes plus 20 minutes cooking

2	cups milk		Grated rind of 1 lemon
3	ounces coarse-ground cornmeal	4	whole eggs
½	pound honey	1	ounce (2 tablespoons) butter

Preheat the oven to 425°F. You will need a heavy saucepan, a mixing bowl, and a Bundt pan.

Bring the milk to a boil in a saucepan (milk burns easily—if you rinse the pan out with cold water first, the milk is less likely to stick).

Mix the cornmeal, honey, and grated lemon rind together. Beat in the eggs. Add the hot milk slowly, beating to prevent lumps from forming. Butter the Bundt pan—or choose little molds to make small cakes for children, or more delicate cakes for grown-ups. Pour the mixture into the pan.

Bake for 30 minutes for a large cake, or half the time for the little ones. This is delicious on a wintry evening, with a glass of sweet white wine made from grapes which have been left on the vine so long they have shriveled in the frost.

◆

POOR MAN'S POLENTA

Polenta povera (Italy)

This is a delicious and simple dish from Italy which takes advantage of those ingredients most easily available to the peasant household. The flavor is best if the pits are left in the olives—but beware not to crack your teeth on them.

SERVES: 4

TIME: Start a few hours before; 30 minutes

2   *ounces black olives*   3   *cups water*
2   *ounces green olives*   1   *tablespoon olive oil*
½   *pound (1½ cups) coarse-ground*
    cornmeal

You will need a saucepan, a wooden spoon, a deep mold—a bread pan will do—and a frying pan if you wish to fry the *polenta* at the end. Rinse the excess salt off the olives and set them aside. Put the cornmeal in a saucepan with the water. Bring to a boil and then turn down the heat. Simmer gently for 20 minutes, stirring all the while with a wooden spoon. *Polenta* is a terrible sticker. At the end of the cooking time, stir in the olives. Mix well, taste, and add salt only if necessary.

Oil the mold and pour in the *polenta*. Allow it to cool completely before turning it out. Serve either as it is, cut in slices, with a tomato and fennel salad, or fry the slices in a little hot olive oil and serve with a green salad. It is also delicious with a little tomato sauce spiked with chili pepper in place of the olive sauce.

PORRIDGE

Porridge, a thick gruel which could be made with barley or rye as well as oats, was always the great staple dish of the northern peasantry, particularly in Scandinavia and Scotland, which share many culinary preferences as well as climate. During their military scurries with the Scots, the English sometimes attributed their opponents' success to their excessively simple and easily prepared diet. Porridge needs minimum preparation in exchange for maximum food value.

OATMEAL PORRIDGE

(Scotland)

The shepherds of Glen Feshie lived on porridge, reported Elizabeth Grant in 1898:

> The shepherds lived in bothies on the hill, miles from any other habitation, often quite alone, their collie dog their only companion, and with no provisions beyond a bag of meal. This they generally ate

uncooked, mixed with either milk or water as happened to suit, the milk or water being mostly cold, few of these hardy mountaineers troubling themselves to keep a fire lighted in fine weather. This simple food, called *brose*, is rather relished by the Highlanders; made with but water or with good milk they think it excellent fare; made with beef *broo*—the fat skimmings of the broth pot—it is considered quite a treat. Beef brose is entertainment for any one. The water brose must be wholesome; no men looked better in health than the masons, who ate it regularly, and the shepherds. These last came down from their high ground to attend the kirk sometimes, in such looks as put to shame the luxurious dwellers in the smoky huts with their hot porridge and other delicacies. [*Memoirs of a Highland Lady*, Elizabeth Grant of Rothiemurchus, 1830]

Midlothian oats are reputedly the best, but some reckon the small Highland ones are better.

SERVES: 1

TIME: 5 minutes plus 20 to 30 minutes cooking

1   breakfast bowlful water (*just under a half pint*) per person
1   handful coarsely milled oatmeal (*a little over 1 ounce*) per person
½   teaspoon salt

You will need a saucepan. Bring the water to a boil in a saucepan—preferably one kept just for porridge, which picks up alien scents very easily. Sprinkle the oats in loose handfuls over the surface of the boiling water, stirring constantly with a flat wooden stick (a spurtle). When the porridge is boiling well, turn the heat down and cover the saucepan. Simmer very gently, stirring regularly (porridge is terrible for sticking) for 20 to 30 minutes, until the porridge is cooked. Add the salt halfway through the cooking—it is thought (and my Scots grandmother agreed) that the oats will not soften properly if salt is added at the beginning. Well-cooked porridge should be so stiff that the wooden stick will stand up in it.

The Scots like their porridge sprinkled with salt. Pour the porridge into a cold plate and trickle plenty of cold fresh milk around the edge to make a moat. The milk should remain cold, next to the plate, and each spoonful of hot porridge may then be dipped into the cold liquid. Southerners and some northerners like their porridge with molasses or brown sugar.

◆

Some Scots add pinches of dry meal throughout the cooking process, thereby achieving a much more grainy and variable texture. You must find your own preferences. There are even those (particularly children) who love their porridge lumpy. Others like a piece of sweet butter melted into a creamy pool in the middle of their bowl of porridge.

Today porridge is usually made from prepared rolled oats and can be ready in a few minutes. But the old way gives a rich hay-sweet dish that's a different kettle altogether. Either way, it makes the best winter breakfast a northerner could wish for.

◆

BROSE

(Scotland)

This is a version of porridge which is not boiled, but mixed with hot water or boiling milk. Proportions are a little different, as the oatmeal is not given time to swell: Allow 2 handfuls of oats to 1 cup of liquid (measurements to be translated as for the preceding porridge recipe). A little salt should be sprinkled in. Pour the scalding liquid straight onto the oatmeal in the bowl. Stir, preferably with a horn spoon, allowing the mixture to form lumps, called "knots." The lumps should be raw and powdery inside. Eat with butter melted into it, or cold milk.

◆

OATMEAL JELLY

Sughan or *Sowans*
(Wales and Scotland)

In the days of local mills, when the oats that had been winnowed and threshed had been returned as meal, the miller always sent it with a bag of "sids"—the inner husks of the oat grain—to which adheres some of the finest and most nutritive substances of the meal. This was made into a kind of smooth pudding or gruel called sowans (Gaelic *sughan*), an ancient dish of Celtic origin. It has a slightly sour taste which some find unpalatable at first, but which usually "grows on" one. It is a very wholesome and sustaining food, and is said to be an ideal diet for invalids, especially dyspeptics. [*The Scots Kitchen*, F. Marian McNeill, 1929]

The "sids" must be steeped in cold water for 4 to 5 days. The resulting liquid is then pressed through a sieve and allowed to stand for another 2 days so that the sediment can sink to the bottom. The clear liquid at the top (the "swats") is then poured off, and the residue cooked like porridge. Serve like porridge, with plenty of thin cream.

OATMEAL SOUP

Potage à l'avoine (France)

Oats are much favored as feed for domestic animals, including poultry and cattle. A storehouse staple among the peasantry of France, oats could also be turned to good account for a farmhouse supper.

SERVES: 4

TIME: 5 minutes plus 30 minutes cooking

> 1   *quart good chicken or meat stock*
> 4   *heaped tablespoons oatmeal*
> Salt
> 2   *ounces (4 tablespoons) butter*

You will need a large saucepan with a lid. Put the stock in a saucepan and stir in the oatmeal. Bring to a boil, and then turn the heat down to simmer. Cook gently for half an hour, until the soup is thick and rich. Taste, and add salt if necessary. Stir in the butter just before serving.

WHITE PUDDING

(Ireland)

A useful little dish for those who like haggis-type mixtures, it can be baked in a covered pudding basin standing in a bain-marie in a low oven, or steamed over boiling water, like suet pudding. With the addition of half a pound of boiled and grated liver, it makes an excellent simple haggis—the oatmeal equivalent of the dumpling.

SERVES: 4

TIME: 30 to 40 minutes plus 40 minutes

½ pound (2¾ cups) coarse oatmeal	2 onions
2 ounces sausage skins (optional)	Thyme, sage, parsley, pennyroyal (or mint)
¼ pound suet or lard	Salt and papper

Preheat the oven to 300°F. You will need a baking tray and a medium saucepan.

Spread the oatmeal out on a baking tray, and put it to roast in the oven until it is lightly toasted.

Meanwhile, put the sausage skins to soak if they have been in salt. Peel and chop the onions finely. Chop the herbs.

Mix everything well with the toasted oatmeal and suet, add salt and pepper, and then stuff the mixture into the sausage skins, tying the skins with thread at 3-inch intervals, but leaving at least one third of the space empty for the sausages to swell. Two knots spaced a half inch apart is best of all—the sausages will then not burst when you divide them. Pierce the sausages with a needle, then poach them in simmering water for an hour.

If you have no sausage skins, cook the mixture in a saucepan with enough water to wet it—start with a cup of water and add more as it is absorbed. This method of cooking will take about 40 to 50 minutes. You will have to keep stirring to avoid sticking. Or the mixture can be put in a scalded greased-and-floured cloth and cooked like a pease pudding. Two hours will see it well cooked. Either way, it is delicious with a piece of boiled ham.

RICE

UN ARROZ

(Spain)

Valencia is the home of Spanish rice. Ernest Hemingway, on his way to a bullfight in 1960, made a fine meal of it:

> Dinner at Pepica's was wonderful. It was a big, clean, open-air place and everything was cooked in plain sight. You could pick out what you wanted to have grilled or broiled and the seafood and the Valencian rice dishes were the best on the beach. Everyone felt good after the fight and we were all hungry and ate well. The place was run by a family and everyone knew everyone else. You could hear the sea breaking on the beach and the light shone on the wet sand. We drank sangría, red wine with fresh orange and lemon juice in it, served in big pitchers and ate local sausages to start with, fresh tuna, fresh prawns, and crisp fried octopus tentacles that tasted like lobster.

Then some ate steaks and others roasted or grilled chicken with saffron yellow rice with pimento. [*Dangerous Summer*, Ernest Hemingway, 1985]

Spain loves its rice dishes and has grown its own supplies since Roman times. *Un arroz*, "a rice," is an essential dish in rural celebrations, and for those who can afford it, for the midday meal. It appears as a course on its own after the soup and before the main meat dish. It is not always flavored and colored with saffron, but it *is* always turned in oil before the cooking liquid is added.

SERVES: 6

TIME: 15 minutes plus 30 to 35 minutes cooking

6	threads of saffron	1	quart well-flavored stock (water will do, but then a little extra flavoring such as some chopped dried ham or chorizo should be added)
1	pound (½ cup) round rice (not long-grain)		
2	tablespoons olive oil		
2	garlic cloves	Salt	
1	onion		
1	green pepper		

You will need a heavy, wide frying pan. Put the saffron threads to soak in a little boiling water. Pick over the rice for tiny pebbles and errant seeds.

Warm the oil in a frying pan. Fry the garlic, peeled and crushed, the onion, peeled and chopped, and the green pepper, seeded and sliced (plus any extra bits and pieces—even a bit of chopped smoked bacon helps the flavor). Add the rice and turn it in the oil until it turns transparent. Pour in the stock or water, and strain in the saffron water, pressing well to extract all the color and flavor. Cook uncovered for 20 minutes. Rice cooked in the Spanish fashion should always be taken off the heat before it is quite soft. Leave loosely covered for 10 to 15 minutes to rest so the rice can finish swelling.

Serve with a crisp fried egg or two (page 192) for each diner, and a sauce made with a few fresh tomatoes stewed quickly with a little olive oil and garlic. In Valencia, the rice is sometimes deliberately left to stick and fry lightly on the base, giving a lovely crisp crust.

◆

SUGGESTIONS

This basic rice is the vehicle for a great many regional variations:

Moros y cristianos is white rice (omit the saffron) served in the company of a dish of stewed black beans—a combination whose name records the Moorish occupation.

Arroz negro, black rice, is dyed with squid ink: Buy 1 pound of squid and carefully remove the ink sacks—break them open into a glass of red wine. Make the rice according to the recipe, including the cleaned chopped body and tentacles of the squid with the rest of the ingredients. Strain the inky black wine into the rice 10 minutes before the end of the cooking time (you will need less of the other liquids).

Make a seafood rice, *arroz a la marinera*, with raw shrimps, prawns, shellfish, and clams thrown on top of the rice to cook in the steam for the last 5 minutes of cooking—anything small your fisherman's net hauls in that is fresh and edible.

Colonial-period Spain transplanted the banana from the Canaries to their New World possessions in Mexico and Central America. Today one of the most popular dishes in the mother country is Cuban Rice—*arroz a la cubana*—which flanks each portion of rice with a fried banana, a fried egg, and a chili sauce made with a few fresh or canned tomatoes stewed until thick and smooth with 2 to 3 seeded and chopped chilis, a chopped onion, and a tablespoon of olive oil—delicious. The Cubans like it hot.

Leftovers: Leftover rice or *paella* makes excellent little *croquetas*, one of the favorites of the *tapa* table. Bind the leftover rice with beaten egg, shape into little cylinders, roll in flour, coat with more beaten egg and bread crumbs, and deep-fry until golden and crisp.

◆

SPANISH RICE

Paella (Spain)

Paella has its origin in the Roman word for pan: *patella*—perfectly proper naming, since it was the Romans who first imported rice for cultivation in the wetlands around Valencia, from whose rice fields and shores springs the great seafood rice dish *paella valenciana*. Snails, eels, green vegetables, and all manner of *mariscos*—seafood—brought in by Valencia's fishing boats will make their way into the local *paella*.

A rural *paella*—a *paella de campo*—is best cooked in one of those shallow, double-handled iron pans, about 15 to 17 inches in diameter, in the open air over a wood fire. A wide shallow pan allows the proper degree of evaporation of liquid; the wood fire, when reduced to a wide circle of charcoal, gives a steady heat all over the base of the pan. The key ingredient is the round absorbent pudding variety of rice and its preliminary turning in good olive oil: The rest of the ingredients are as variable as the produce of the neighborhood can make them. This is a dish which those who do not normally cook rather enjoy preparing. It is both dramatic and very easy.

SERVES: 8 to 10

TIME: 30 minutes plus 30 minutes cooking

2 dozen water crayfish or precooked large snails (see page 265)	1 small wild rabbit, cut into 16 pieces (optional)
5 to 6 threads of saffron	1½ pounds (3 cups) round rice (not long-grain)
1 pound peppers, both red and green	1 pound tomatoes
4 garlic cloves	A handful of peas and a few small clams or mussels, put to open in the steam on top of the rice for the last 5 minutes of cooking (optional)
6 tablespoons olive oil	
1 chicken, cut into 16 pieces (see page 275)	

You will need a wide shallow iron pan—a Spanish *paellera* if you have one. A flat-bottomed wok makes an acceptable substitute. You will also need a saucepan. Bring the crayfish to a boil in a panful of lightly salted water. (The snails will of course take longer if they have not been prepared in advance). The crayfish will immediately turn a wonderful scarlet. Boil them for two minutes only. Save the water, using a cupful to soak the saffron. Seed the peppers and slice them into strips. Peel and chop the garlic. Have the pieces of meat within easy reach.

Heat the *paella* pan on the fire and pour in the oil. When it is lightly smoke-hazed, put in the chicken and rabbit pieces, turning and frying them on all sides. Then add the garlic and the peppers, and fry them until soft. Add the rice, and turn it in the oil until all the grains are coated and transparent. Finally, add the tomatoes, and pour on the cupful of saffron water and as much crayfish liquor as will cover the layer of rice and meats.

The circle of charcoal should provide a gentle, even heat, which will allow the rice to cook without being disturbed. Add more hot liquid as the moisture evaporates. Leave to cook for 20 minutes. Five minutes before the end, arrange the cooked crayfish over the top, and also the optional ingredients—clams, mussels, peas. The *paella* should still be moist when you take it off the fire. Let it rest (covered in newspaper or a cloth) for at least 10 minutes—this gives the rice time to finish swelling and the grains time to separate. The rice should never be dry, but should stay moist and succulent.

The traditional way to eat a *paella de campo*, usually a Sunday-outing family affair, with the father in charge of hunting the rabbit and the children taking care of the crayfish, is out of the communal cooking pan itself. When you are ready to serve, see that everyone has a fork and a large hunk of fresh bread, and is sitting around the *paellera* in a circle. Put an inverted plate in the middle, and balance a dish of salad on top (chopped crisp cos lettuce, with sliced tomatoes and onions, salted and dressed with wine vinegar and olive oil). Everyone then eats the section nearest to them. The *paella* under the plate keeps hot for second helpings.

If you must cook on a gas or electric stove, you will have to keep the rice moving as it cooks, since the area of heat under the pan is too small to cook the rice evenly. Then you do not need to give it the resting period at the end.

In the absence of a *paellera* or a wok, a large frying pan can be used instead, and almost any combination of shellfish and meat will be good. I have had *paellas* made with prawns, squid, mussels, pork, smoked ham, even black pudding and *chorizo* sausage, all of them delicious.

Leftovers: Use leftover *paella* to make *croquetas* as for *un arroz* (page 134), or simply mix with a beaten egg or two, drop into hot oil, and fry crisp—this makes excellent fritters, particularly when served with a fresh tomato sauce or *a la cubana*, with fried bananas, fried eggs, and fresh tomato sauce spiced up with a chili.

RISOTTO
(Italy)

The rice recipes of Spain, Portugal, and Italy are all Arabian in inspiration. The grain was probably introduced to Europe by Alexander the Great before 300 B.C. It was not cultivated in Europe in any quantity until the Moors brought it to the wetlands of southern Spain. European rice recipes are characterized by a preliminary turning in hot oil, often with relatively small quantities of meat, fish, and/or vegetables for added flavoring, and then a cooking in good broth. The rice is not white-cooked in plain water or until dry, as is customary in India and China. The Italians like their rice as chewy and *al dente* as their pasta.

SERVES: 6

TIME: 15 minutes plus 20 minutes cooking

1 *pound (2 cups) round rice (preferably Arborio)*	1 *teaspoon salt*
	Butter
1 *onion*	*Pepper*
2 *tablespoons olive oil*	*Parmesan or pecorino cheese*
Water or stock (or well-flavored zamponi broth) to cover	

You will need a heavy wide saucepan. Pick over the rice, removing any alien grains. Mince the onion finely. Put the oil to heat in a large saucepan. Fry the onion in the hot oil until it turns golden—do not overheat the oil or it will turn bitter. Add the rice and fry it gently until it becomes transparent. Add enough water (or a good homemade stock, page 241) to cover it to the depth of one finger. Sprinkle in the salt. Cover the pot tightly and leave to simmer for 20 minutes. Take it off the heat. The Italians like their rice well moistened and soupy, with the grains separate but still slightly nutty in the center.

Meanwhile, put a large flat serving dish to warm. Turn the *risotto* out onto the hot dish. Scatter with small pieces of butter, freshly milled black pepper, and a generous grating of hard strong cheese.

The only stew with which the Italians serve rice is *osso buco* (page 369). Otherwise it is always served on its own, prepared in any one of hundreds of regional variations of added ingredients.

SUGGESTIONS

Pass a fresh meat or tomato sauce separately along with extra cheese.

Risotto can be cooked with chopped chicken livers, little cubes of *prosciutto* ham or *pancetta*, fresh green peas (a popular dish called *risi e bisi*) or fava beans, diced wild mushrooms, baby artichokes, snails, or, perhaps most delicious of all, the prawns, shrimps, or small clams available to those who live close to the sea.

A *risotto* is also sometimes cooked with saffron threads to color and flavor it—particularly around Milan, where white wine or Marsala may be included with the stock.

Leftovers: Make *Suppli al telefono*, fried croquettes of left-over risotto, each with a small square of ham and mozzarella buried in the middle. The cheese pulls into "telephone lines" when you bite into a hot croquette.

RICE PILAF

Pilāu (Turkey and the Balkans)

Rice has been cultivated around the Mediterranean for at least 3,000 years. The water-loving grain was apparently first planted by Indo-Iranian tribes who had migrated from further east. The basic rice dish of the Middle East is never served plain-boiled. The variety used for pilaf is long-grain—the aromatic Basmati or Patna is best. None of the cooking liquid is thrown away as in some Indian and Chinese methods; all is absorbed by the rice, which makes it the perfect vehicle for a wide variety of flavorings and embellishments. It can be colored with saffron or scented with spices. A pilaf can be cooked with virtually any meat, chicken, vegetables, or fish. Half a pound of rice will need just under 2 cups of liquid to cook it soft. The second half pound of rice will only need 1½ cups of water added.

Turkish rice is not served as wet as the Italian *risotto* and the Spanish *paella* (both of which are made with the round rather than the long grains used in the Balkans). Rice pilaf is a wedding- and circumcision-feast dish. The most common filler in Asian-Turkish food is wheat, not rice. Bulgur (cracked wheat) is the usual pilaf grain.

S E R V E S : 4

T I M E : 10 minutes plus 30 minutes cooking

2	ounces (4 tablespoons) clarified butter or 3 tablespoons olive oil
½	pound (1 cup) long-grain or Basmati rice
2	cups water
1	teaspoon salt

You will need a large shallow pan with a lid. Heat the butter or oil in a pan. Add the rice and stir it around until it is transparent. Add the water and the salt, bring to a boil, and allow it to bubble fiercely for a couple of minutes. Turn down the heat, cover the pan, and simmer gently for 20 minutes, until all the liquid has been absorbed and the surface is pitted with little craters.

When the rice is soft, turn off the heat and draw the pan to the side of the stove. Replace the lid with a cloth, and leave the rice to stand for 10 minutes to steam itself dry.

This is a plain pilaf, to be served with a skewer of grilled fish or meat—or with a meat, fish, or game stew made with plenty of sauce.

SUGGESTIONS

Fry a chopped onion in the oil before you stir in the rice.

Or infuse some of the cooking liquid with a few strands of saffron before adding it to the rest of the cooking liquid. Turkey is the home-territory of the saffron crocus.

Leftovers: Use to make *dolmades* (page 46) or in a stuffing for vegetables (page 37).

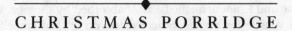

CHRISTMAS PORRIDGE
Risgrynsgröt (Sweden)

Scandinavians love imported rice as much as they love the teas which were trekked from China over the trans-Asian trade routes. *Risgrynsgröt* is a special

Christmas treat, served before the goose on Christmas Eve. There is always an almond hidden it, for the children to find for luck.

SERVES: 6 to 8

TIME: 1 hour

1   *cup water*
½   *pound (1 cup) round rice (not long-grain)*
2   *tablespoons butter*
1   *quart milk*

You will need a roomy, heavy-bottomed saucepan. Bring the water to a boil and add the rice. Cook at a gentle simmer for 15 minutes or so, until the water is absorbed. Beat in half the butter. Add the milk and heat again until boiling. Turn down the heat, and simmer gently (stirring every now and then) for another 45 minutes, until the rice is tender and the liquid virtually absorbed. Stir in the rest of the butter.

Serve the porridge with cold thin cream and a sprinkling of powdered cinnamon—the spice chest may be unlocked for Christmas.

◆

SUGGESTIONS

Leftovers: Beat an egg or two into the leftover porridge and pour it into a baking dish. Smooth down the top and dot with butter. Bake for 30 minutes in a preheated 350°F oven. Serve with a bowl of sweet thick or sour cream.

Risgrynoläter or rice fritters: Beat 1 egg (for each quarter pound dry weight of rice) into the leftover porridge. Melt 2 tablespoons of butter in a frying pan, and drop in spoonfuls of the mixture. Fry the fritters on each side until golden brown. Sprinkle with sugar and serve with a spoonful of jam.

CHAPTER FOUR

Pasta, Noodles, and Other Dough-Based Dishes

◆

PASTA

Wherever its birthplace may have been, noodle paste is a primitive unleavened dough and a natural way to prepare grains for cooking. The manufacture of pasta is an even simpler process than bread making, so it seems likely that the technique evolved simultaneously in several different places, including India, China, the Middle East, and central Europe. The earliest European pastas were probably variations on *trahana* (page 163), a very simple grated- or rolled-dough noodle, which looks and cooks like rice.

Today the pasta dishes of Italy are the most sophisticated and highly developed of this most ancient group of grain-food recipes. Popular mythology credits that energetic traveler, Marco Polo, who visited the noodle-making Chinese in 1271, with the introduction of pasta to Italy. However, Italian literature of the time seems to indicate that macaroni and *ravioli* were already well-established by then in the Italian kitchen. The poet Iacopone da Todi, a contemporary of Marco Polo's, has a reference to *lasagna* in one of his moral tales. In the *Decameron*, Boccaccio, born in 1313, spins an image of peasant gluttons dreaming of limitless macaroni and *ravioli* cooked in capon broth. The early forms of Italian pasta were probably rather dumplinglike, closer to *gnocchi*, and only began to assume their recognizable modern shapes during the eighteenth century, when machines for molding and cutting the pasta appeared in Naples. The bourgeoisie took to the new machine-extruded pastas with enthusiasm. The peasantry continued to roll its own, and it was not until the 1930s that country people began to accept the change. Today the average Italian eats about sixty-five pounds of pasta a year.

As for Marco Polo, he might even have reversed the accepted theory and been teacher rather than pupil in fourteenth-century China's kitchens. Certainly the Chinese were kneading noodles with their customary skill by the first century A.D. But one of their early writers on food suggests that after the Chinese peasants invented noodles, they learned how to make them delicious from foreigners.

The basic Italian pasta dough is best made with fine-milled durum semolina (the *semola*, the hard seed at the center of the wheat grain) or, in a pinch, high-gluten bread flour. Soft-wheat flours, which are used in cake and bread making, have a weaker gluten content in order to allow the dough to stretch and rise when leavened.

Pasta is a comparatively stiff dough, made with only 25 percent liquid, whereas bread has a water content of about 35 percent. The machine-extruded varieties of pasta usually sold dried, such as spaghetti, macaroni, and a multitude of bows and shells and shapes, are molded from a semolina dough made with hard durum wheat—the Mediterranean strain is an appetizing natural yellow. Semolina absorbs less water in the making, is very strong so that it can stand up to machine pressure, and dries out without cracking. Eggs are sometimes included for flavoring and color in these commercial mixes— country cooks, concerned with providing the family with a healthy diet, make all-egg pastas if the hens are laying well. These rolled pastas, such as the many varieties of *tagliatelle, lasagne, cannelloni*, and the rest, are at their best and most nutritious when you make them yourself and prepare them fresh.

You will have to experiment to find your own preferred mix if you are making your own pasta. You may need less liquid if the weather is damp, the flour is very rough-ground, or the eggs are very large. Homemade dough which can be rolled on a little hand machine needs to be wetter than that rolled out in the heavy commercial rollers.

The Italian courtiers who accompanied their mistress Catherine de Médicis, bride of Henri II, to Paris in 1553, gave the French court chefs their grounding in the sophisticated art of saucing. A taste for sauces which are independent of that which they are saucing—that is, those mixtures which are not based on the juices of the food they accompany (such as a *jus* or a gravy), but rather serve to alter and mask its flavor—was fully developed in Italy many centuries earlier by those archpriests of the kitchen, the Romans. The first century author Apicius details a large repertoire of fragrant sauces common in the Roman kitchen of the day—milky baths of pounded nuts, pungent garnishes based on fermented salted fish, herb sauces, reductions of wine, and delicate honey and herb-scented relishes for anything and everything.

Italian country cooks make their sauces with fresh ingredients from their vegetable gardens and the herbs available on the hillside, as well as their own good sausages and hams, cheeses, and oils, to embellish their pasta dishes. Perhaps it was a natural skill as sauce makers which led Italian cooks to develop so perfect a vehicle as pasta for their talents. No other substance can provide such a magnificent foil for a sauce.

1 Spaghetti   2 Conchiglie   3 Fiochetti   4 Fusilli   5 Diamanti   6 Capellitti
7 Farfalle/Farfalline   8 Ruoti   9 Vermicelli   10 Maccheroni   11 Tubetti Lunghi
12 Ditali   13 Rigatoni   14 Elicoidali   15 Penne   16 Lasagne   17 Tagliatelle
18 Linguine   19 Fettucine   20 Tortellini   21 Ravioli   22 Gnocchi   23 Cannelloni

BAKED STUFFED PASTA

Lasagna al forno (Italy)

The little village of Fiesole winds up one side of a narrow olive-tree-clad ravine in the hills above Florence in northern Italy. Twenty-five years ago, vines and lettuces, spinach and onions, tomatoes and carrots grew in all the little gardens. Clay pots cascaded geraniums and sweet basil around the village porches. The roofs and tiles of the houses were of baked terra-cotta, golden as apricots, nestling among rosemary-scented rocks. Here lived Michaela, the cook who worked for the family in whose little *pensione* I was staying.

Michaela cooked for all of us every evening—wonderful broths, thick *minestrone*, and clear beef soups with noodles. Her real specialty was the pasta she would always make herself, piling the kitchen table with elegant pyramids of the yellow and green strings. How she sauced her beautiful dishes would depend on what was fresh in the market that day. I would help her in the kitchen whenever I could, chopping the garlic and herbs, slicing purple eggplants into creamy rings for her to fry and layer into a dish with meat sauce and white sauce to be baked much as she made her *lasagne*, and almost exactly like a *moussaka*.

Michaela would sometimes take me, on her one day off a week, back to her little house in Fiesole to spend Sunday with her family. There I would be allowed to help her make the best *lasagne* in the village. Her children were grown and had babies of their own, but it was always Michaela who cooked the family's Sunday lunch, to be laid out on the wooden table under the back porch, a vine shading it from the early afternoon sun. The *lasagne* was preceded, since it was the feast day, by an antipasto—sometimes a few slices of raw Parma ham and salami sliced and served with a pat of butter, sometimes a few chicken livers fried and then spread on slices of crisp toasted bread. There was always a bowl of olives, a big basket of fresh bread, and plenty of wine for the adults. The children came and went from the table at will and ate as they pleased.

The meat sauce or *ragù* Michaela made for the dish is one of the basic sauces of Italy. Down in the pensione's kitchen, she made a large pan of it once a week, and then kept it on the back of the stove, conveniently at hand with a ladle in it ready to add its richness to a sauce or stew.

The Italians rarely put water into a sauce—they appreciate strong, concentrated flavors which give character and piquancy to their simple background dishes of pasta, *polenta*, and rice. It is this pleasure in surprise and balance—bland and spiced, cold and hot, sweet and sour, cooked and raw—which makes ordinary Italian cooking so sophisticated. Add to this a natural understanding of texture and form, such as that seen in the dozens of different shapes into which pasta is cut, the better to absorb its sauces, and it is no wonder that the Italians taught the rest of Europe how to cook.

SERVES: 8

TIME: 1½ to 2 hours plus 20 to 25 minutes cooking

THE PASTA:

1	*pound (4 cups) hard durum wheat flour or high-gluten flour*	1	*tablespoon olive oil*
1	*teaspoon salt*		Cornmeal or semolina flour for sprinkling (ordinary flour
5 to 6	*eggs*		*will do)*

THE TOMATO SAUCE:

1	*stick of celery*	¼	*pound minced meat (optional)*
1	*carrot*	1½	*pounds ripe tomatoes (or three*
1	*large onion*		*8-ounce cans of tomatoes)*
2	*garlic cloves*	1	*tablespoon concentrated tomato*
¼	*pound* prosciutto *or* pancetta		*paste*
1	*small bunch of oregano, marjoram, or parsley*	1	*cup stock or wine*
			Salt and pepper
4	*tablespoons olive oil*		

THE WHITE SAUCE:

3	*ounces (6 tablespoons) butter*	¼	*pound grated Pecorino, or Italian*
3	*ounces (¾ cup) flour*		*Fontina and Parmesan mixed*
3	*cups milk*		Butter
2	*tablespoons of fresh cream cheese (mascarpone) or heavy cream*		Salt and pepper and grated nutmeg, to taste

You will need a rolling pin or a pasta roller, two small saucepans, one large saucepan, a large bowl, and a big shallow gratin dish. Pour the flour and salt together directly onto the clean scrubbed surface of the kitchen table, or in a large bowl. You will need plenty of elbow room. Mix the eggs together. Make a dip in the flour, and pour in the eggs and the oil. Work them into the dough with your hand, using a circular motion to draw in the flour at the edges. Add a tablespoon of water if you need it to make a soft, pliable dough. This process can be started in your mixer and finished by hand, but you should knead steadily for 10 minutes.

You will soon develop your own method: Michaela used the flat of one hand to turn the ball of dough, while she knuckled the edges into the middle with the other (an action she also used to knead her bread dough for pizza). When the dough is smooth and elastic, oil the outside lightly, cover it with a cloth or plastic wrap, and leave it to rest for 20 to 30 minutes while you make the first sauce.

Wash and chop the celery and carrot finely. Peel and chop the onion.

Peel and crush the garlic. Chop very finely the ham or bacon. Chop the herbs.

Heat the oil gently in a saucepan. Fry the onion and the garlic first until transparent—they should not be allowed to caramelize or the sauce will taste bitter. Add the celery, carrot, ham or bacon, and minced meat, if using, and fry for a moment, until the meat stiffens and loses its pink color.

Meanwhile, pour boiling water over the tomatoes to loosen the skins if you are using fresh ones. Peel, seed, and chop them. Add the tomatoes and the tomato paste (and a teaspoon of sugar if you are using the non-Mediterranean variety of tomato). Stir in the stock or wine. Cover the pot and simmer until you are ready to use the sauce—an hour is not too long. Adjust the seasoning with salt and pepper at the very end.

Turn your attention back to the pasta. Divide the dough into 6 pieces. Flour the board or table, and roll each piece out so fine you can nearly see the work surface through it. Sprinkle the rolled-out dough with a handful of cornmeal or semolina flour and leave it for another 11 to 15 minutes to rest in an oiled bowl, covered.

The easiest method of rolling the pasta is with a pasta roller. If you like fresh pasta, it is well worth acquiring one. The roller bolts onto the kitchen table like a tiny mangle and operates on the same principle. Make 6 long sausages of dough and feed them through the mangle. Roll the dough thin enough by progressively decreasing the gaps between the rollers. (You will not need the cutter slots for *lasagne*.)

While the pasta rests, make the second sauce. Melt the butter in a small pan. Stir in the flour and cook it gently until it is sandy, but has not taken color. Gradually whisk in the milk, beating to avoid any lumps. Simmer the sauce for 5 minutes. Beat in the cream cheese or heavy cream. Taste for salt, pepper and nutmeg.

Pre-heat the oven to 375°F. Fill your largest pot with water, cover, and set to boil. Have ready a bowl of cold water and a clean tea towel for draining the pasta.

Back to the rested pasta: Cut the sheets into 4-inch squares. When the water is boiling, add a spoonful of salt. Throw the pasta squares into the boiling water in small batches. Give the water a stir to keep the squares separate. Make sure the water reboils fast, and cook the pasta for 1 minute only. Lift each piece out with a draining spoon, and pass it through the bowl of cold water as it comes out; then transfer it to the cloth to wait for the next step. The cold water stops the pieces from sticking together.

To assemble the *lasagne:* Spread a ladleful of the white sauce over the base of your gratin dish. Lay a single layer of *lasagna* over it. Ladle a generous layer of tomato sauce on top, then another layer of *lasagne*, then a layer of white sauce plus a tablespoon of the grated cheese. Layer until everything is used up. Finish with white sauce and top with cheese. You can make as many layers as the shape of your dish dictates, but always start and finish with white sauce. Sprinkle a few flakes of butter over the top. You can now leave the assembled *lasagne* to be baked later.

Bake the *lasagne* in a preheated 375°F oven, for 20 to 25 minutes, until the top is brown and bubbling.

Serve a salad after the dish—perhaps fennel dressed with lemon juice and the fresh thick first-pressing olive oil of Tuscany, or a crisp salad of curly endive. Red wine should accompany. Michaela would be proud of you.

◆

This recipe makes plenty of pasta. If you think you have too much (and it is up to you how many layers you use), cut the rest into noodles for another meal: Slice the leftover raw sheets of pasta into strips (see the *tagliatelle* recipe which follows) or feed them through the cutter of the pasta roller. Drop them in handfuls from a height onto a floured board. Bag after 15 to 20 minutes. They will keep refrigerated in a plastic bag for a week; for over a month in the freezer. Or they can be dried for storage—try looping them over a string hung in a current of air and leaving them to dry out for a day or two. Or turn them occasionally as they lie in their handfuls on the board and let them dry out in hanks.

Add half a pound of spinach, cooked and drained and well chopped, to the white sauce.

Or replace the meat in the *ragù* with ¼ pound chopped mushrooms. Or use both.

To make a dish of *canelloni al forno*, follow the same recipe as the *lasagne*, but roll the squares of cooked pasta around a heaping tablespoon of *ragù* filling, pack the rolls into an oiled gratin dish, and cover with the white sauce. Sprinkle with grated Parmesan and bake as for the *lasagne*.

Make the *lasagne* recipe using layers of fine pancakes (page 468), without the sugar) rather than pasta.

◆

SPINACH PASTA WITH ANCHOVY SAUCE

Tagliatelle verde (Italy)

Ribbon pasta, or *tagliatelle*, are the most usual homemade type of pasta. They are good sauced simply with fresh butter and black pepper, with cream simmered with mushrooms, with a *pesto*, with a tomato-based *ragù*. Michaela, my friend the cook at the pensione in Florence, would make this instant sauce on the days she had made a big batch of pasta for drying and was late with the rest of the cooking. It takes no time at all.

SERVES: 6

TIME: 65 minutes

THE PASTA:

½	*pound spinach (fresh or frozen)*
1	*pound (3½ cups) durum wheat flour or high-gluten bread flour*
1	*teaspoon salt*
5	*eggs*

1	*tablespoon olive oil*
1 to 2	*tablespoons reserved spinach water*
	Cornmeal or semolina flour for sprinkling

THE SAUCE:

1	*small can of anchovies (8 to 10 fillets)*
2	*garlic cloves*

1	*large handful of parsley*
½	*cup olive oil*
	Pepper

You will need a rolling pin or a pasta roller, a pestle and mortar, one or two roomy saucepans, and a large bowl for serving. A blender would be useful. Strip out and discard the tough stalks of the spinach and wash the leaves thoroughly if you are using fresh spinach. Cook the spinach in a covered saucepan, in the water which clings to its leaves after washing, for 10 minutes if fresh, less if frozen. Drain the spinach well, reserving the water, and then chop it very finely—the blender will do the job well.

Pour the flour and the salt into a pile on a clean table—one with a marble top is best of all, as it keeps the dough cool. Make a well in the middle of the flour. Mix the eggs together with the oil and the spinach water, and pour the mixture into the well. Work the flour and the liquid together with your hands. You may need a little more flour—it depends on the flour and the size of the eggs. Knead thoroughly for 10 minutes to develop and stretch the flour. At the end of this pummeling, the dough will be smooth and elastic. Put it aside to rest, lightly oiled and covered with a cloth or plastic wrap, for 15 to 20 minutes while you make the sauce.

Put the anchovies to soak in a little milk for 30 minutes if they are from the barrel. Peel the garlic. [Don't ever use a garlic press—it does horrible metallic things to the taste of the garlic.] Wash and chop the parsley. Put the anchovies, garlic, and parsley into a little mortar, and pound them to a paste. Trickle in the oil. This is very easy to do in the blender. Finish with plenty of milled black pepper.

Back to the pasta: Cut the dough into 6 pieces and roll each piece out on a floured board with a floured rolling pin, until the paste is nearly thin enough to read a newspaper through it. Sprinkle the rolled-out dough with a handful of cornmeal or semolina flour, and then leave it to rest again, oiled and covered, for another 15 to 20 minutes.

Roll each piece of pasta up loosely, as you would a carpet for storage, and slice across into strips of the width you require—about ¼ inch is right for *tagliatelle*, narrower for *linguine*. Loosen the strips and drop them in handfuls onto a board well dusted with cornmeal or semolina. The pasta is now ready for cooking.

Or use a pasta-rolling machine (see page 145). Since you are making ribbon noodles, roll the flattened dough through one of the slots equipped with cutters. There is a choice of two ribbon widths: Use the wider one for *tagliatelle* and the narrow one for *linguine*. Dust the pasta regularly with plenty of cornmeal or semolina flour to stop it from sticking to itself. After you cut it, it is wise to hang the long ribbons over a clothesline or the back of a chair to dry the surface a little so the strings do not stick. The pasta is now ready to be cooked.

Put the serving dish in a preheated 300°F oven to warm.

Put on a big pan of water to boil. You will need at least 5 quarts to cook this quantity of *tagliatelle*, so you may need to do it in two batches.

When the water reaches a rolling boil, add a spoonful of salt and drop in the *tagliatelle* by the loose handful. Try not to let the water go off the boil. Give the pasta a quick stir with a wooden fork to make sure it has not stuck together. Cook the pasta for 1 to 2 minutes—test by nibbling it before you take it out. Drain it well.

Transfer it to the warmed bowl and dress with the anchovy sauce. Toss it and take it to the table. Make sure there's a pepper grinder and a bowl of grated Parmesan cheese to accompany.

Follow the pasta, if you are hungry, with a lamb steak cut straight across the leg bone, or a pair of lamb chops, grilled over charcoal if possible, basted with olive oil, garlic, and rosemary, served with young green beans or a fennel salad. The Italians like their grilled lamb crusty on the outside and succulent inside, but not pink as the French prefer it. Serve with plenty of bread.

◆

SUGGESTIONS

Made fresh, egg pasta will keep refrigerated in a sealed bag for a week. Pasta freezes very well for at least three months and can be cooked straight from the freezer.

If you want to dry the *tagliatelle* for keeping, drop it in handfuls onto a clean cloth so that it settles loosely. Leave to dry, and then store in an airtight tin.

Leftovers: Toss the cold pasta in more olive oil, freshly crushed garlic, and plenty of chopped parsley. It will make a delicious little salad.

◆

STUFFED PASTA WITH BUTTER

Tortellini al burro (Italy)

These are plump crescents of fresh pasta, filled with a very delicate stuffing. The stuffing can be used to fill other shapes as well, but is at its best in these seductively curved envelopes—the romantic Italians declare them to have been inspired by the navel of Venus. There are many regional and household variations on the filling, but the principle is the same: The stuffing is precooked and the envelopes are poached in hot liquid for 4 to 5 minutes. Most Italian country cooks make their own *tortellini*, taking great pride in the dish and serving it for very special celebration meals. These are sophisticated little morsels, depending for their excellence on a fresh-tasting well-flavored stuffing; they do not need heavy saucing.

SERVES: 6

TIME: 1 hour and 15 minutes

THE PASTA:
1   pound (4 cups) hard durum wheat flour or high-gluten bread flour
5 to 6 eggs
1   tablespoon oil
1   teaspoon salt

THE FILLING:

2 boneless chicken breasts	1 egg
1 bay leaf	Salt and pepper and grated nutmeg
A few peppercorns	Butter and chopped fresh herbs to
Salt	finish: basil, or a bunch of
2 ounces grated Parmesan or	parsley and a leaf or two of sage
pecorino cheese	(no more: sage is a very
1 garlic clove	strong herb)
1 teaspoon fresh herbs	

You will need a rolling pin or a pasta roller, one small and one large saucepan. Make the pasta dough as for the *tagliatelle* (page 152). While the dough is resting, make the stuffing.

Poach the chicken breasts very gently for 5 minutes in a very little water flavored with a bay leaf, some peppercorns, and a little salt. Drain (strain and save the liquid), and mince the chicken very finely with the cheese, the peeled garlic, and the herbs. Bind into a stiff paste with the egg. Add a spoonful or two of the chicken broth to moisten the mixture. Salt and pepper and nutmeg to taste. Simple. Put the stuffing aside while you finish the pasta making.

Cut the dough in half and roll it out on a well-floured board with a well-floured rolling pin. The rolled-out dough should be fine enough for you to see the wood grain through it. Cut out circles of the dough with a wine glass. Put a little pile of filling on one side of each circle, wet the edge, and then double the semicircle over it. Join the two little wings to make a ring, pinching them lightly together with damp fingers. Now you can see what they mean about Venus' navel.

Put a very large pan of well-salted water on to boil. Stuffed pastas are as perishable as their contents and are at their best cooked on the day they are made. Put the serving dish in a preheated 300°F oven to warm. Chop the herbs.

When the water boils, add a spoonful of salt. Poach the *tortellini*, in two or three batches, for 5 minutes—timed after the water comes back to a rolling boil. Drain them thoroughly—they must not be soggy. Put them in the warm bowl and scatter small pieces of butter over them. Toss them gently. Sprinkle with the chopped herbs. Serve with extra butter and a bowl of grated Parmesan.

Follow with a vegetable dish or a grilled veal cutlet—and don't forget to drink a toast to the Goddess of Beauty whose navel inspired the dish.

SUGGESTION

Leftovers: Heat gently in a little cream.

SPINACH-RICOTTA RAVIOLI

Ravioli alla fiorentina (Italy)

The classic and favorite stuffing for fresh pasta, this can be used to stuff other shapes as well. *Canelloni* are delicious filled with this mixture.

SERVES: 6

TIME: 1 hour

THE PASTA:

½	pound fresh or frozen spinach	1	tablespoon olive oil
1	pound (3½ cups) durum wheat flour or high-gluten bread flour	1 to 2	tablespoons reserved spinach water
5	eggs	1	teaspoon salt

THE FILLING:

6	ounces ricotta (or any fresh soft white cheese)	Salt and pepper
2	tablespoons grated Parmesan	Butter to finish
1	pound spinach (fresh or frozen), precooked	

You will need a rolling pin, one medium and one large saucepan, and a dish for serving (a beautiful white one would complement the green pasta). A zigzag pastry cutter makes neat *ravioli*. Make the spinach pasta as in the *lasagne* recipe (page 144). Don't forget to cook the spinach for the stuffing at the same time you prepare the spinach for the pasta. While the dough is resting, make the stuffing.

Mix the cheese and chopped cooked spinach together very thoroughly. Season with salt and pepper (ricotta will not need much salt).

To make *ravioli*, mark one half of the pasta sheet into squares without cutting through. Divide the filling between the squares, piling little heaps in the center of each. Dampen the pastry between the piles, and then fold the other side of the dough over the top. Cut through both layers with a knife, or a zigzag pastry cutter if you have one, to give you little sealed square envelopes.

Put the serving dish to warm in a preheated 300°F oven, and put a large pan of salted water on to boil.

When the water comes to a rolling boil, throw in the *ravioli* and cook them for 4 to 5 minutes, until the pasta is tender. The stuffing is already cooked, so it needs only to be heated. Take the *ravioli* out with a draining spoon and drop them onto a clean cloth; then transfer them to the warm serving dish. Scatter the *ravioli* with slivers of butter and perhaps a few torn leaves of basil. (Michaela, who taught me to make these, would never chop a basil leaf—she said it brought bad luck, and she would always tear them with her fingers.) Serve with a bowl of grated Parmesan.

Follow with a roasted chicken, or, for a light supper, a salad of curly endive or slices of fennel dressed with the fresh thick olive oil of Tuscany.

SUGGESTION

Leftovers: Heat gently with a little cream. Sprinkle with chopped fresh basil or parsley.

RAVIOLI WITH MEAT

Ravioli alla calabrese (Italy)

This stuffing is from the harsh mountain landscape south of Rome. Calabria is one of the most isolated provinces of Italy. If fresh meat is not available, it is omitted and the weight of sausage doubled.

SERVES: 6

TIME: 1 hour and 15 minutes

THE PASTA:

1   *pound (3½ cups) hard durum wheat flour or high-gluten bread flour*
5 *to 6 eggs*
1   *tablespoon olive oil*
1   *teaspoon salt*

THE FILLING:

¼   *pound finely minced veal or pork*

¼   *pound Italian sausage (or mortadella or bologna)*

2   *ounces grated Parmesan or other strong cheese*

1   *teaspoon finely chopped fresh herbs: parsley, oregano, marjoram*

1   *egg*

Salt and pepper

You will need a rolling pin, one medium and one large saucepan, and a serving dish. The *ravioli* are made as in the previous recipe.

Simmer the minced meat in a little water or stock until it loses its pink color. Empty the sausage meat out of its skin and pound it up with the cooked minced meat, still immersed in the water or stock. Mix in the cheese and the herbs. Bind with the egg. Add salt and pepper—in moderation if the sausage is spicy.

Put a serving dish in a preheated 300°F oven to warm and a large pot of water on to boil. When it boils, add salt and throw in the *ravioli*—they will take no more than 4 to 5 minutes. Serve with a cream sauce (1 cup heavy cream simmered until thick with 1 teaspoon flour), or the tomato sauce from the recipe which follows. Put plenty of grated cheese and black pepper on the table. You will need no more than a plain-grilled chop or a dish of vegetables to follow.

◆

SUGGESTION

Leftovers: Heat the leftovers gently in a fresh tomato sauce.

◆

TAGLIATELLE WITH TOMATO SAUCE

Tagliatelle al pomodoro (Italy)

Mediterranean tomatoes, golden apples, are inevitably sweeter and meatier than the northern-grown varieties. Their arrival in the Italian kitchen-garden during the course of the sixteenth century—they are a New World vegetable—had a dramatic effect on the Italian culinary repertoire. Italian food today without the tomato would be a shadow of itself. This very basic tomato sauce is best made with the large sweet Mediterranean-type tomatoes.

SERVES: 5 to 6

TIME: 1 hour and 15 minutes

THE PASTA:
1   pound (3½ cups) *hard durum wheat flour or high-gluten bread flour*
5 to 6 eggs
1   *tablespoon olive oil*
1   *teaspoon salt*

THE SAUCE:

1½ *pounds tomatoes (or three*   4   *tablespoons olive oil*
    8-ounce cans of tomatoes)   1   *teaspoon sugar*
2   *garlic cloves*   1   *tablespoon tomato paste*
½   *teaspoon salt*   *Pepper*

You will need a rolling pin or a pasta roller, a large saucepan, and a deep serving dish. Make the fresh pasta as in the *tagliatelle verde* (page 146) but without the spinach. The scarlet sauce is prettiest on plain pasta.

Scald the tomatoes with boiling water to loosen the skins. Peel them and chop very thoroughly—this is easily done in a blender. If you have to use canned tomatoes, stew the sauce a little longer. Peel and crush the garlic with the salt (a single blow with the flat side of your heaviest kitchen knife will do the trick nicely).

Warm the olive oil in a saucepan and add the garlic. Stew gently for a moment without allowing it to take color. Add the tomato purée, sugar, and tomato paste. Simmer the sauce for 20 minutes or so, uncovered so that the flavors are concentrated. Adjust the seasoning with salt and pepper.

Put the serving dish to warm in a preheated 300°F oven and a large pot of water on to boil.

When the water comes to a rolling boil, add a spoonful of salt and throw in the fresh pasta. Cook it for no more than a minute or two. Rub the warm serving bowl with garlic and trickle in a little oil. Drain the *tagliatelle* thoroughly and tip it into the warm bowl. Pour the sauce onto the hot pasta, turning it over gently once or twice to mix it in. Serve with a bowl of grated Parmesan cheese.

Follow with something simple—fresh fish grilled with herbs, or perhaps a plain-roasted chicken. Or serve with an antipasto, a plate of sliced Parma ham and dried sausage with a pat of butter and plenty of bread, and to follow the scarlet sauce, a green salad or a dish of fresh green vegetables, lightly cooked and tossed in butter and chopped herbs.

◆

SUGGESTIONS

In hot weather and with sweet juicy tomatoes still warm from the sun, such as you might expect to find in Tuscany in July, the sauce does not need to be cooked—and it doesn't need sugar and tomato paste. Just let the sauce stand on the kitchen table for an hour or so to infuse. The tomato sauce is delicious spooned over an egg fried crisp in olive oil and set on a slice of homemade bread rubbed with garlic. It is also good served as a sauce for boiled meat.

Leftovers: Put the *tagliatelle* mixed with the sauce into a shallow ovenproof dish. Cover with a well-flavored cheese sauce as for the *lasagne* recipe (page 144). Sprinkle with plenty of grated cheese and reheat in a preheated 350°F oven for 15 minutes.

◆

FETTUCINE WITH BASIL SAUCE

Fettucine al pesto (Italy)

Genoa claims the miraculous *pesto* for its own, although the mixture is known and appreciated throughout Italy. The paste will keep all winter if sealed and kept in the refrigerator. It also freezes beautifully. It is delicious stirred into a pasta dish, a soup, or a sauce for grilled fish. It is an invaluable "secret ingredient" for winter dishes. Make a supply for your pantry at the end of the autumn, stripping the summer's crop of basil plants before the first frosts nip the tender leaves.

SERVES: 5 to 6

TIME: 1 hour and 15 minutes

THE PASTA:
1   pound (3½ cups) *hard durum wheat flour or high-gluten bread flour*
5 to 6 *eggs*
1   *tablespoon olive oil*
1   *teaspoon salt*

THE SAUCE:

2 *garlic cloves, chopped*	4 *ounces grated Parmesan or*
1 *handful of basil leaves stripped*	*pecorino cheese, or the*
from their stalks and shredded	*Sardinian Sardo*
1 *ounce pine nuts or walnuts*	6 *tablespoons olive oil*
½ *teaspoon salt*	

You will need a rolling pin or a pasta roller, a pestle and mortar, a large pot, and a serving dish. Make the pasta as in the *tagliatelle verde* recipe (page 146) making the ribbons finer but rolling the dough a little thicker to give you fettucine. The sauce is particularly suited to these fine strings.

Pound the garlic, basil leaves, nuts, and salt together in a mortar.

Add the cheese and the oil gradually until you have a thick creamy paste. This job can be done in a food processor or a blender if you prefer. There is a superstition in Italy about cutting basil leaves with knives, and many of those Italian households equipped with modern gadgets continue to use the old pestle-and-mortar method to make their *pesto*.

Bring a large pot of water to a boil, add a spoonful of salt, and throw the fresh noodles in. Try not to let the water go off the boil, and cook the noodles for 1 minute only. Drain the noodles and toss them with the basil sauce in a warm bowl. This is a very light and delicious dish. Serve a rich stew afterwards.

◆

SUGGESTION

If you want to store the *pesto*, use less oil so it will be thicker, and pack it into small sterilized jars. Cover with a layer of pure oil before you seal the lids. Store at the back of the refrigerator or in the freezer.

◆

DRIED PASTA

Pasta asciutta (Italy)

There are almost as many shapes of dried pasta as there are varieties of fish in the Mediterranean. The basic dough is the same—the pastas differ from one another only in the variety of their lengths and widths, their curves and folds, all of which accept and adapt in different ways to the sauces in which they are bathed.

You will certainly be spoiled for choices in any good pasta shop. There you will find the familiar bundles of *spaghetti* (little strings); the dried versions of the pasta which is available fresh; and a multitude of little shapes, each of which is perfect for someone's special sauce. *Conchiglie* are graceful shells; *fiochetti* are elegant little bows and knots; *fusilli* come in the shape of corkscrews; *diamanti* explain themselves; *capellitti* are shaped like tiny hard hats with zigzag edges (very useful for cupping a cream-and-mushroom sauce); *farfalle* and *farfalline* are, as their names suggest, butterflies both great and small; *ruoti* are shaped like old-fashioned cartwheels.

Vermicelli ("little worms") are used in soup or sometimes as an ordinary pasta. They take very little time to cook—2 to 3 minutes is usually quite enough from dry to *al dente*.

Then there are the various *maccheroni*, macaroni (not to be confused with *maccarone*, which in Italy are potato dumplings), sometimes used as a generic name for ribbon pasta, sometimes for those hollow tube shapes which are perfect for fresh tomato and cream sauces: the *tubetti lunghi* look like little bent elbows; *ditali* and *ditalini*, thimbles for the old grandmother at her darning and mouse-sized thimbles for soup; striped *rigatoni* and spiraled-striped *elicoidali*;

and a variety of *penne*, quill-pen nibs cut on the cross to give a sharp point. Here are all the images of domestic life.

Allow 1 pound of dried pasta for 4 to 5 healthy appetites. Short dried pasta of good quality will be *al dente* in 5 minutes. Long pasta such as *spaghetti* will take a little longer, as indeed will old pasta, or pasta of an inferior quality. Bite a piece (it should be slightly tooth-resistant) to see if it is ready—it needs to be firm, since it will continue to swell as it cools. Imported Italian pasta is usually the best quality, especially Martelli. Accompany all pasta—except for pasta sauced with fish—with a bowl of grated Parmesan or pecorino cheese. It is very important to serve any pasta dish piping hot and as soon as it is ready. Toss the pasta with its sauce before you serve it—don't drown it. The Italians like their pasta lightly coated, not soupy.

◆

SPAGHETTI WITH HAM AND EGGS

Spaghetti alla carbonara (Italy)

This dish is known as the "charcoal-burner's pasta"—perhaps since most of the ingredients can very easily be transported in a satchel. Charcoal burners were accustomed to living rough in the woods for a week or two at a time.

S E R V E S : 4 to 5

T I M E : 20 minutes

2	*garlic cloves*	3	*egg yolks and 1 egg white*
4	*tablespoons olive oil*		Salt and pepper
1	*lemon*	1	*pound spaghetti*
4	*ounces Parma ham, Italian*		
	pancetta, *or any dried ham*		

You will need a large and a small saucepan. Fill a large pot with plenty of water, and put it on to boil while you prepare the rest of the ingredients.

Peel and chop the garlic, put it in a little saucepan with the oil, and leave it to infuse by the fire. If you like your flavors tamed, stew it on low heat. Grate the rind of the lemon. Chop the ham small. Beat the egg yolks and the white together in the serving bowl. Grind in some pepper and a pinch of salt.

When the water comes to a rolling boil, add a spoonful of salt, and lower in the *spaghetti* all in a bunch, pushing it down as it softens. Give it a turn with a wooden fork to keep the strands separate. Bring the water back to a boil as quickly as possible. Wait for the water to return to a boil before timing the cooking—5 to 7 minutes should be enough. Keep tasting for the right moment to take it off. *Spaghetti* is as variable as vegetables—it depends on grain and age. *Al dente* is the Italian way to serve pasta, as with their rice dishes, and requires that pasta in general and *spaghetti* in particular still retain a slight chewiness, a resistance to the teeth, at the center.

Drain the *spaghetti* thoroughly and tip it into the bowl with the eggs. Turn the strands to coat them with sauce. The eggs will cook in the heat from the pasta. Sprinkle with the grated lemon rind and the chopped ham, and pour the infused oil and garlic over everything. Fold it all together.

Make sure that your diners are ready so that you may serve the dish immediately. Pass around a bowl of grated Parmesan and the pepper grinder. Add a dish of sliced tomatoes dressed with a sprinkle of salt and a few slices of sweet raw onion. Fruit and a piece of good Italian cheese should follow—a slice of the delicious smoked Provolone to give you a breath of the charcoal-burners' habitat.

SUGGESTIONS

Leftovers: Put in a baking dish and cover with a nutmeg-flavored white sauce. Sprinkle with grated cheese and heat in a preheated 375°F. oven for 15 to 20 minutes to heat the dish through and gild the top.

FARFALLE WITH CHICKEN LIVERS

Farfalle con fegatini (Italy)

This is a dish of butterfly bows tossed with sliced lightly cooked chicken livers: The shapes complement each other perfectly.

SERVES: 4 to 5

TIME: 25 to 30 minutes

½ pound chicken livers	Salt and pepper
2 garlic cloves	1 pound farfalle
2 ounces (4 tablespoons) butter (Tuscan cooking) or 4 tablespoons olive oil	1 tablespoon chopped herbs: thyme, marjoram, oregano

You will need a large saucepan and a small frying pan. Put a large pot of water on to boil. Put a serving dish in a preheated 300°F oven to warm.

Pick over the chicken livers, remove any strings and bitter green bits, and then slice them. Peel and chop the garlic. Put the butter or oil to warm in a frying pan. Add the garlic and then the chicken livers. Cook gently until the livers are stiff but still pink. Mash them a little. Season with salt and pepper.

When the water is boiling, add a spoonful of salt and throw in the pasta. Cook at a rapid boil for 5 minutes; then nibble one to test. It should retain a slight bite. Drain the pasta and transfer it to the warm dish.

Toss in the livers, garlic, cooking juices, herbs, and plenty of pepper to season. Accompany with a bowl of grated Parmesan. Serve as a main dish for a light luncheon, with a green salad and a tomato salad dressed with sliced scallions and a handful of black olives.

◆

SUGGESTIONS

Leftovers: Moisten the *farfalle* with a little cream, put them back in the saucepan, and reheat for a moment on top of the stove with a little chopped ham. Sprinkle with more chopped fresh herbs. Serve small portions (this will be enough for 8) as a light first course.

◆

PENNE WITH HAM AND MUSHROOMS

Penne alla paesana (Italy)

This is an everyday pasta dish made with ingredients always on hand in the Italian peasant larder—a ham from the autumn pig slaughter, and mushrooms fresh or dried from the woods and fields. The shape of the little quill-pen spaghetti accepts the garnish well; it's particularly good with dried *Boletus porcini*, which are sold in many Italian delicatessens. They will need to be soaked in warm water for 20 to 30 minutes first. Save the strained soaking water to use in a soup or stew.

SERVES: 4 to 5

TIME: 20 to 25 minutes

4 ounces raw Parma ham or lean bacon	4 tablespoons olive oil
4 ounces mushrooms	1 pound penne
2 garlic cloves	Salt and pepper

You will need a large saucepan and a small frying pan. Put a large pot of water on to boil and put the serving dish to warm in a preheated 300°F oven.

Chop the ham or bacon. Wipe and chop the mushrooms. Peel and slice the garlic. Put the oil to warm in a frying pan, and add the garlic and the mushrooms. Fry for a moment.

When the water is boiling, throw in the *penne*. Cook them for 5 minutes and test to see if they are ready. They should still have a slight bite to them.

Drain and transfer them to the serving dish. Toss in the garlic and mushrooms and their oil, and then add the chopped ham or bacon. Mix well. Sprinkle with salt and pepper. Pass a bowl of grated Parmesan separately. Follow with a tomato-and-fennel salad if you are eating lightly or a rich stew or a broiled chop if this is your main meal of the day.

SUGGESTIONS

Leftovers: Toss with oil and vinegar and more pepper. Mix in an equal quantity of chopped fennel bulb and chopped scallion. It makes a delicious little salad.

FUSILLI WITH CHILI

Fusilli alla molisana (Italy)

This is a spiral pasta to hold the tomato sauce in its curves. The southern Italians like hot chili in their food.

SERVES: 4 to 5

TIME: 25 minutes

1 pound tomatoes (or two 8-ounce cans of tomatoes)	2 garlic cloves
	4 tablespoons olive oil
1 small fresh chili (2 to 3 of the tiny dried ones or more to taste)	1 tablespoon tomato paste
	Salt and pepper
	1 pound fusilli pasta

You will need a large and a small saucepan. A blender would be useful. Put a large pot of water on to boil, and the serving dish in a preheated 300°F oven to warm.

Scald the tomatoes with boiling water to loosen the skins. Peel them and chop them finely (use the blender if you like). If using canned tomatoes, they may be blended. Seed the chili and chop finely (don't rub your eyes afterwards— chili gets in everywhere). Peel and chop the garlic. Warm the olive oil in a small saucepan, and add the garlic and the chili. Stew it all gently for a moment without allowing the vegetables to take color. Add the tomatoes, the tomato paste, and salt and pepper. Simmer gently for 15 to 20 minutes.

When the water comes to a boil, add salt and throw in the *fusilli*. Cook them for 5 minutes at a rolling boil. Test to see if they are done—they should still offer a slight resistance to the teeth.

Drain the pasta spirals, and toss them with the sauce. Pass around a bowl of grated Parmesan separately. Follow with a dish of eggplant, cut into rounds, dipped in milk and seasoned flour, and then fried crisp in smoking hot oil. Eggplant is a great favorite in the south of Italy.

◆

SUGGESTIONS

Leftovers: Add a little more tomato sauce—a tablespoon of tomato paste diluted in half a cup of water is fine—and spread the leftovers in a gratin dish. Sprinkle with plenty of cheese, and put the dish in a preheated oven to reheat the pasta and melt the cheese. Fifteen minutes at 375°F should be enough.

◆

CONCHIGLIE WITH MUSHROOMS

Conchiglie con funghi (Italy)

The delicate shell shape of this pasta complements wild mushrooms perfectly. The *boletus* species the Italians call *porcini*, "little pigs," have the right nutty flavor and gluey texture. They can be bought dried from Italian delicatessens; they need soaking to plump them out—20 to 30 minutes in warm water should be sufficient. Two ounces of dried fungi substitutes for 1 pound of fresh. Strain the soaking water and save it for a soup or stew. If using fresh wild or cultivated mushrooms, then wipe them and chop them. Put them to stew gently in a few tablespoons of sweet green olive oil, spiked with a crushed clove of garlic and a handful of chopped parsley. Toss the contents of the pan with the fresh-cooked pasta. Pasta is the perfect vehicle for fresh fungi. Try it with slices of raw truffle scattered over a dish of buttered homemade egg tagliatelle or sauced with a few of the curly-patterned dark morels of spring-time, stewed in fresh cream with plenty of fresh-ground pepper to bring out their subtle flavor.

◆

MACARONI WITH CHEESE AND HAM

Maccheroni alla pastora (Italy)

Eliza Putnam Heaton reports on primitive macaroni—making in Sicily in 1908:

> Let those criticise Vanna's housekeeping who have themselves
> kept house and reared live stock in one room. Beside the cold fireplace
> were heaped brambles and roots of cactus fig for the cooking fire . . .
> While she talked Vanna (the local witch-/wise woman, elf locks hang-
> ing to the floor) did not neglect the macaroni. Rocca held on her knees
> a board carrying a lump of dough, from which from minute to minute
> she pinched off bits. Rolling these between her hands, she passed the
> rolls one by one to Vanna, who sank into each a knitting needle and
> re-rolled the paste on the board to form the hole. Each short piece as
> she slipped it off the needle she hung to dry over the edge of a sieve
> that balanced the rolled up mattress at the foot of the bed. When
> enough for supper was ready she tied the rest of the dough in a
> kerchief and shut it in the chest, throwing the crumbs to the cock with
> a "chi-chi! cu-cu-rucu!" [*By-Paths in Sicily*, Eliza Putnam Heaton, 1920]

SERVES: 4 to 5

TIME: 15 to 20 minutes

6 ounces *fresh riccota cheese*	4 tablespoons *olive oil*
1 pound *dried macaroni*	*Pepper*
4 ounces prosciutto *or* pancetta *or* bacon, *chopped and lightly fried*	

You will need a large saucepan. Put a large pot with plenty of water on the stove to boil. Put a serving dish in a preheated 300°F oven to warm.

Crumble the cheese. As soon as the water boils, add a spoonful of salt and throw in the pasta. Cook at a rolling boil for 5 minutes and then test it by biting a piece. It should be slightly firm to the teeth: *al dente*. Drain and transfer to the warm dish. Toss with the rest of the ingredients, and sprinkle with plenty of pepper. Pass a bowl of grated cheese separately.

◆

Leftovers: Dress with oil and vinegar, and mix with chopped fennel and plenty of freshly milled pepper. Serve at room temperature with a dish of ripe tomatoes, sliced and dressed with finely chopped garlic and a trickle of olive oil.

◆

NOODLE BARLEY

Tarhonya (Hungary)

This is probably the most primitive noodle dough in the world, the ancient solution to the problem of how to make milled grain palatable, storable, and portable. Recipes for the dough, sometimes mixed with yogurt, plain water, sour milk, or anything which will improve its flavor and nutritional value, are to be found all over Europe and Asia. In Hungary today these barley-shaped noodles are made by kneading flour and eggs into a dough, breaking or grating the dough into little pellets, and then drying the pellets (sometimes in the post-harvest sunshine) until they are quite hard. *Tarhonya* are still popular in modern Hungary. They can be plain-boiled to accompany a *gulyas*, thrown at the last minute into a soup or a stew to add protein and body, or fried with onions and paprika and cooked like a *risotto* to be served on their own. This is a useful little staple and very easy to make. Four ounces of dry weight is enough for 2 to 3.

SERVES: 5 to 6

TIME: 25 to 30 minutes

4	*large eggs*
1	*pound (3½ cups) flour*
1	*teaspoon salt*

You will need a grater. Mix the eggs with your hand slowly into the flour and the salt until you have a few pieces of very stiff dough. Work them well. If you need more liquid, add a little water. If the mixture is too soft, add more flour. Leave the dough, covered with a cloth, to rest and dry out a little. If you want to use the dough right away as tiny dumplings in a soup, grate the pasta straight into the hot liquid. The little grains will take only a moment to cook.

If you want to dry *tarhonya* for storage, spread a clean cloth over a roomy tray. Rub the dough through the large holes of a grater onto the cloth, allowing the gratings to fall loosely in a single layer like grains of barley. Leave them on their cloth—tossing them lightly every now and again to keep the grains separate and to allow them to dry evenly—for 3 days in a warm dry kitchen, by which time they should be as hard as catapult pellets.

Tarhonya noodles can be stored in an airtight tin virtually forever.

To boil: Toss the noodle barley into plenty of boiling salted water. Boil for 1 minute after the water reboils if you are using them fresh. Boil for 5 to 10 minutes if they are dried. When they are cooked, drain; then toss them with chopped bacon frying gently in its own fat, or with butter or sour cream. Or cook the little scraps in a clear soup. They are excellent in a plain chicken soup made with an old hen, past her laying days, boiled with an onion and a carrot for flavor.

To fry: Brown the *tarhonya* in hot lard or butter, tossing frequently, for 3 to 4 minutes, until the grains take a little color. Take the pan off the heat, and stir in a sprinkling of paprika and a little salt. Add enough water to cover the *tarhonya*, and simmer either in a preheated 350°F oven for 40 minutes or so, until all the water is absorbed, or on top of the stove, where they will take less time (about 20 minutes), but you will have to keep checking that the water has not boiled away. Sprinkle with plenty of pepper. You can add cream if you want to serve them as a light supper dish.

Tarhonya can be served instead of rice or potatoes with any Eastern European stew, or with a dish of *letcho* (page 21), the vegetable stew which serves both as a dish in itself and as the basis for other dishes.

◆———————◆

MILK NOODLES

Trahana (Bulgaria)

This is the Bulgarian way with the universal staple of the Balkans.

SERVES: 5 to 6

TIME: 25 minutes plus 10 minutes cooking

2 *cups milk*
2 *cups water*
2 *ounces (4 tablespoons) butter*
4 *ounces grated hard cheese*

You will need a grater for the noodles, a large saucepan, and a gratin dish. Make the little noodles as for the Hungarian *tarhonya* (page 162). Preheat the oven to 450°F and put the gratin dish in to warm.

Bring the milk and water to a boil and add the noodles. Cook them for 3 minutes. They will absorb all the liquid. Toss with butter and put them in the heated gratin dish. Sprinkle with grated *kashkaval* cheese, or any strong cheese such as cheddar or Gruyère.

Bake the noodles for 10 minutes. Pass around more cheese when serving. Follow with one of the excellent Bulgarian vegetable stews (page 20).

PORRIDGE NOODLES

Trahana (Greece)

This is the Greek version of this ancient universal staple. Sweet and sour varieties are sold in most Greek grocers. The sour version is made with yogurt or sour milk. The Balkans, Greece, and Turkey have shared one another's territory and habits for so long, it is not surprising they have so many culinary tricks in common.

S E R V E S : 6

T I M E : 20 minutes

1   pound (3½ cups) flour
2   large eggs
5 to 6 tablespoons of yogurt or sour milk

You will need a grater. Make exactly as the Hungarian *tarhonya* (page 162). This noodle paste is still made by hand in the more isolated communities, particularly on the islands, where it is rolled into egg-sized balls which are turned daily until they dry, and then crumbled into small bits and finished off on cotton sheets in the sun. Greek fishermen much appreciate *trahana* cooked in soup as an instant nourishing breakfast. The result is a sort of southern version of porridge.

SUGGESTION

Double or triple the recipe if you would like to store some as a most useful staple to throw into soups. It cooks in the blinking of an eye. It is very good in *minestrone*.

NOODLE-DOUGH TURNOVERS

Schlick Krapfen (Austria)

Reminiscent of the Italian *ravioli*, these little envelopes are cooked in a clear chicken or beef broth, or served with melted butter and grated strong cheese (in Austria this would be a Gruyère-like cheese from the mountains).

SERVES: 4

TIME: 1 hour

THE DOUGH:
   8   ounces (1²/₃ cups) flour
   ½   teaspoon salt
   2   eggs
   About 2 eggshells of water

THE FILLING:
   6   ounces chopped cooked meat
   2   tablespoons reserved meat gravy
   1   tablespoon chopped parsley
   1   egg

You will need a rolling pin or a pasta roller, and a pastry brush. An electric mixer would be useful. Sift the flour and the salt together directly onto the kitchen table. You need plenty of elbow room. Make a dip in the middle and crack the eggs into it. Work them into the dough with your hand. Add water, measured in an eggshell—a natural measuring cup that will give you a good proportion of water to egg. Knead as you go, until you have a soft, pliable ball of dough. (This can be started in your mixer and finished by hand).

Roll out the noodle dough into a flat sheet. Make a stuffing with minced cooked meat moistened with its gravy; mix in the parsley and the egg lightly beaten.

Drop small teaspoons of the meat mixture on half the dough, leaving a good amount of space between each mound. Brush between the piles with water and then fold over the empty half of dough. Cut into squares. Poach gently in clear soup for 10 to 15 minutes.

◆

SUGGESTIONS

Cut the rolled-out dough into fine noodles and use to make one of the following recipes:

Baked noodles and fruit (Suessen Nudelauf): Butter a deep casserole and layer into it noodles which have been boiled in water rather than stock, alternating with sliced apples and pears, sprinkling each layer with sugar and a few currants. Finish with a layer of apple, and top off with bread crumbs fried in butter. A powdering of cinnamon makes this particularly delicious. Bake at 350°F for 20 to 30 minutes. Serve the noodles hot with thick cream. The same dish can be made with stewed plums.

Mohn Nudeln: Toss cooked broad-cut noodles in melted sweet butter and scatter them with poppyseeds and sugar. Serve piping hot after a nourishing soup.

Or make *Fleckerl*, which is the noodle dough cut into squares. It is used in the same way as thin noodles.

SAVORY PUDDINGS AND DUMPLINGS

The divorce of salt and sweet came late to Europe. For centuries, meat puddings and dumplings were as likely to be flavored with plums and raisins, nuts and honey, as they were with herbs and salt. Roman recipes mixed their flavorings with abandon. In Germany, Austria, and the Balkans the division is less marked than it has become in Britain, and fruit or curd dumplings made with yeast-leavened dough still often actually replace the meat course. The English, as befits their culinary expertise and raw materials, specialized in suet pastry dumplings, from whence grew their acknowledged skill as pastry and cake makers.

STEAK-AND-KIDNEY PUDDING

(England)

Boiled puddings made with a suet crust are of a very ancient date and have fed many generations of Englishmen. The original boiled puddings were solid affairs made with flour-and-suet mixtures—preferably suet from the Englishman's favorite meat animal, beef cattle. The dough was rolled into a ball and tied up in a clean floured cloth. The traditional round Christmas pudding belongs to this group. These "cloutie" dumplings were boiled along with a piece of meat or a bit of bacon, and a net of vegetables, all of which hung suspended in boiling water in a cauldron hanging over the hearth fire. There was no distinction between sweet and savory, and it was this taste for unusual combinations, such as mutton or pork with apples, and game with wild berries, which fathered our modern predilection for sweet sauces with meat.

The cauldron broth provided a nourishing soup as well as a plate of dinner. Later, as cooks became more expert, the puddings were made hollow, the crust being supported by a pudding bowl, and then stuffed with a filling—most often a mixture of savory and sweet. Boiling and roasting remain the techniques best understood in the English kitchen, along with a considerable skill, shared by the rest of the British Isles, in baking pies and cakes. Thickened stews and ragouts took a long time to establish themselves in the British culinary tradition.

SERVES: 6

TIME: 1 hour plus 4 hours cooking

- ½   *pound beef kidney*
- 1   *tablespoon malt vinegar or cider vinegar*

THE SUET PASTRY:
- 6   *ounces suet (beef-kidney fat)*
- 12 *ounces (3 cups) self-rising flour*
- 1   *teaspoon salt*
- ½   *cup cold water*

THE FILLING:
- 1   *pound stewing steak (chuck or*   1   *onion*
  rump is good)   1   *tablespoon chopped fresh herbs:*
- *Salt and pepper*   *parsley, thyme, sage*
- ½   *pound mushrooms (optional)*   ½   *cup water or claret or port wine*

You will need a grater or a food processor, a 2-pint pudding bowl, a rolling pin, wax paper, string, and a clean pudding cloth or aluminum foil. Skin, wash, and cube the kidney into 1-inch squares. Put it in a bowl and cover it with water acidulated with the tablespoon of vinegar. Set aside.

Make the *suet pastry*: Suet is the fat which encases a beef kidney. To be properly prepared, it must be shredded, freed from its fibers, and flaked—this is easiest to do through the large holes of a grater or (with a little flour to keep it from sticking) in a food processor. Whatever the method, the suet must be thoroughly chopped.

The filling: Sift the flour into a bowl with the salt, and then stir in the suet. Add the cold water slowly (you may need more or less liquid) to make a smooth, soft dough which leaves the sides of the bowl clean.

Grease the pudding bowl. Cut off two thirds of the pastry, and roll it out on a well-floured board with a rolling pin, until you have a big enough circle to line the bowl. Line the pudding bowl, easing the pastry well down so that it does not shrink too much in the cooking. Roll out the rest to make a lid, and put it aside.

Put a pan of water, one large enough to accommodate your basin, on to boil. Put a metal ring or heatproof saucer on the base of the pudding bowl to keep it away from direct heat. Let the water come to a boil while you turn your attention to the filling.

Cut the meat into fillets not more than ¼ inch thick. Sprinkle each piece with salt and freshly milled black pepper. Drain and dry the kidney, and roll each piece up in a steak fillet. Wipe and slice the mushrooms, if using, and peel and chop the onion. Pack the meat rolls, chopped onion, and mushrooms into the lined pudding bowl, sprinkling with more pepper and salt and the herbs. Add the water. Claret or port would be even better. Dampen the edges of the pastry and fit on the lid. Mark around the lip of the bowl with a fork to seal the edges. Cut a small hole in the center for the steam to escape.

Traditional recipes give very long cooking times—from 7 to 14 hours. Modern meat does not need such drastic treatment—just as well, since the pastry has little chance of surviving this without getting soggy.

Cover with either a round of wax paper and a clean white cloth or a sheet of aluminum foil, in both cases pleated in the middle to allow room for the pastry to rise. If you use a cloth, tie it on with string below the bowl's lip. Stretch a string handle across the bowl for lifting it in and out of the boiling water, which should reach no more than two thirds of the way up. The water must be boiling when you put the pudding in. Add *boiling* water when necessary and make sure it never boils dry. The pudding must not be allowed to come off the boil at any time, or the pastry will be as heavy and gray as a school dinner. Boil for 4 hours. Test for doneness with a skewer.

Serve still in its basin but with its top wrappings removed, swathed in a clean white napkin. Accompany with finely shredded cabbage cooked lightly in no more than half a glass of water and a generous knob of butter, or finely sliced carrots cooked in the same manner. Serve with beer to wash it down, unless you can lay your hands on the Englishman's favorite, imported claret. A syllabub (page 206) will round off the repast in traditional style.

SUGGESTIONS

This recipe gives you the basic suet pastry. As well as being the traditional pudding crust, it can be baked as a pie crust, or bits can be twisted off for dumplings.

If you would rather make a steak-and-kidney pie, use the same pastry and filling, but flour the meat and fry it with the onion and the mushrooms first; then add enough water to cover, and stew it until tender before you make the pie. Allow it to cool before you cover it with the crust (half the recipe should be enough—use the rest to make a rhubarb dumpling for another day.)

Or put a cover of suet pastry over a top-heat-simmered stew such as Lancashire hot pot, a specialty of the English midlands. Cover it well, using a layer of foil under the lid if it doesn't fit tightly, and then cook as usual.

Stuffings: Cut into even-sized cubes: ham or pork with sharp apples; small game birds such as woodcock, or neatly jointed partridges; pigeons with bacon; a jointed rabbit and a handful of field mushrooms; joints of chicken with cubes of bacon. Rook pies, made with the skinned breasts and legs of young rooks, with bacon to add flavor, were an old country favorite. There is no shortage of the raw materials still: A single rook is always a crow; a flock of crows are always rooks.

◆

POTATO-AND-BACON DUMPLINGS

Kroppkakor (Sweden)

The potatoes must be old and floury—Idahos will do very well. The making of potato dumplings is a skill worth acquiring, and much prized in northern cooks.

SERVES: 5 to 6

TIME: Start the day before if possible; 60 minutes

8	large old potatoes	4	ounces (1 cup) flour
One ¼-pound slab of bacon		½	teaspoon salt
1	medium-sized onion	2	eggs

You will need a large saucepan, a bowl, a small frying pan, and a sieve or a grater. Scrub the potatoes and put them on to boil in their skins—this will take 20 to 30 minutes depending on size, and is best done the day before, as the potatoes must be quite cold.

Dice the bacon. Peel and chop the onion finely. Fry the bacon in a small pan on low heat. As soon as there is enough fat from the bacon to fry it, add the onion. Cook gently until soft. Leave to cool.

Peel the cold potatoes, and push them through a sieve or grater so that they fall into the bowl as light and separate flakes. Toss in the flour and the salt. Beat the eggs and pour them in. With light fingers, mix together into a soft dough. Do not overwork it.

Roll the dough into a sausage shape, and chop off 15 to 20 short lengths, about an inch each. Roll each length into a ball, and push a nest into it with your finger. Fill the nest with a little of the bacon-and-onion mixture, and then close up the hole. Continue until all the potatoes and bacon are finished.

Meanwhile, set a pot of salted water to boil on the stove. When all the dumplings are made, slip them into the boiling water. Turn down the heat and leave them to poach in the simmering water for 15 to 20 minutes, until they are light and well risen

Serve the dumplings immediately, while they are hot, with a jug of melted bacon drippings with little pieces of bacon still in it, or with melted butter.

◆

SEMOLINA GNOCCHI

Gnocchi de semolino (Italy)

These little dumplings are probably the original pasta of Italy. Today there are three main varieties made, using three different starch bases. All are poached and then either grilled with cheese or sauced. Semolina is the coarse-milled grain of a particularly hard species of wheat, *Triticum durum* (distinct from the bread wheat, *Triticum aestivum*). Durum wheat flour is used to make pasta.

SERVES: 4

TIME: Start 1 to 2 hours before; 40 to 50 minutes plus 20 minutes cooking

2	cups stock or milk	2	ounces (4 tablespoons) butter
½	onion	2	eggs
1	bay leaf		Salt and pepper
½	pound semolina		Butter and grated cheese to finish

You will need a saucepan, a shallow dish, and a gratin dish. Bring the stock or milk to a boil with the onion and the bay leaf to flavor it. Just before it boils, remove the onion and the bay leaf, and sprinkle the semolina, stirring constantly, in handfuls into the hot liquid. Cook gently until thick and smooth—about 20 minutes in all. Remove from the heat and beat in the butter. Allow to cool a little and then beat in the eggs. Taste, and add salt and pepper. Pour into a flat dish to a depth of one finger.

When the mixture is cold, cut it into squares, circles, or crescents, or whatever you please.

Preheat the oven to 350°F.

Arrange the *gnocchi* shapes like lines of leaning dominoes in a buttered gratin dish on which you have scattered grated cheese. Dot with butter, and sprinkle more grated cheese over the top. Bake for 20 minutes, until the top is well browned. (Do not underdo it—a gratin should be flecked with little burned bits and nicely crisp).

Serve hot, with a salad of young vegetables, such as green beans, lightly cooked in salted boiling water and then tossed with a vinaigrette.

◆

POTATO GNOCCHI

Gnocchi di patate (Italy)

This is the Italian response to the easily grown import from the New World. Potatoes replace semolina, but the recipe is in all other ways unaltered.

SERVES: 4 to 5

TIME: 1 hour plus 30 minutes cooking

2 pounds (6 medium-sized) old potatoes (the dry, mealy varieties are best)	2 eggs
	Salt and pepper
4 ounces (1 cup) flour	Butter and grated cheese to finish

You will need a saucepan, a grater or a sieve, and a gratin dish. Scrub the potatoes and boil them in their skins until tender—this will take about 20 minutes.

Scrub a corner of the kitchen table and sprinkle it with flour. Put the flour in a pile beside you. Peel the hot potatoes as soon as you can handle them, and then grate them onto the floured table. Knead them lightly together with the flour and the beaten eggs—you may need some water, but the dough should be soft and light and not overworked. Roll the paste into sausages; then cut them into disks—¼ inch thick and 1½ inches across—with a knife. Make a little dent in each disk. Bring a large pan of salted water to a boil and slide in the little disks. Poach in simmering water until they float to the top—about 5 to 6 minutes.

Preheat the oven to 325°F.

Drain the *gnocchi* and prop them like leaning dominoes against one another in a well-buttered gratin dish scattered with grated cheese. Dot the top with butter and sprinkle with more grated cheese. Bake for 25 to 30 minutes. Serve piping hot, with grated cheese and a bowl of fresh tomato sauce, and a salad to accompany.

SUGGESTIONS

Yesterday's cold potatoes can be used. The potatoes should either be very hot or stone cold.

Sauce the *gnocchi* with a *ragù* (page 144) before you bake them. Finish with grated cheese.

CHOUX PASTRY GNOCCHI

Gnocchi di Parigi (Italy)

When Catherine de Médicis, betrothed to Henri II of France, took her retinue of Florentines to Paris, it is likely they instructed the chefs of the French court in the Italian culinary arts. Sixteenth-century Florence had the most accomplished cooks in Europe. The visiting Italians also accepted instruction from their talented pupils. This is one of the recipes which emerged later from the collaboration.

SERVES: 4

TIME: 1 hour plus 30 minutes cooking

THE DUMPLINGS:

1	cup milk or water	Salt and cayenne pepper
2	ounces (4 tablespoons) butter	4 ounces grated Parmesan or
6	ounces (1½ cups) flour	pecorino
3	eggs	2 cups cheese sauce

THE CHEESE SAUCE:

2	ounces (4 tablespoons) butter	4 ounces grated Parmesan or
2	ounces (½ cup) flour	pecorino
2	cups milk	1 ounce (2 tablespoons) butter to
	Salt and a pinch of cayenne pepper	finish
	(black pepper will do)	

You will need two to three saucepans and a gratin dish. A food processor would be helpful to beat in the eggs. Bring the milk to a boil with the butter. When it has boiled and the butter is melted, beat in the flour. Beat the mixture over the heat until the dough comes away from the sides of the pan. Take the pan off the heat to cool for a moment, and then beat in the eggs one by one. This is easy to do in a food processor. The paste goes dull when it has accepted all the egg. If it looks like it's becoming too liquid, stop adding egg—it is merely that the eggs are larger than necessary. Add salt and cayenne, and grate in the cheese. There, you have *choux gnocchi*: much easier than the ones made with potato.

Bring a large pan of salted water to a boil. Using 2 teaspoons dipped in cold water, drop in small dumplings of the *choux* mixture. Poach the *gnocchi* gently for 15 minutes, until they bob to the surface, puffed up and firm. Remove and drain carefully with a perforated spoon.

Meanwhile, make the cheese sauce. Melt the butter in a small saucepan and stir in the flour. When the mixture is sandy, whisk in the milk, beating to avoid lumps. Stir in salt and cayenne pepper, and the grated cheese. Or put all the ingredients into a food processor to blend them. The sauce can then be brought to a boil and simmered for 5 minutes. It still needs to be beaten as it cooks.

Preheat the oven to 325°F.

Spread half the sauce on the base of a shallow ovenproof dish. Add the *choux gnocchi* as they come out of the water. Cover with the rest of the sauce. Dot with butter and sprinkle with cheese. Bake for 20 to 30 minutes. Serve hot: A gratin should be bubbling when it comes to the table. Add a dish of wild mushrooms stewed in butter or oil with garlic and herbs, and a salad to accompany.

BREAD DUMPLINGS

Knockerl (Austria)

This is the favorite dumpling for poaching in soups, stews, or anywhere potatoes might otherwise be used. A great standby if you have more mouths to feed than anticipated. They are the work of a moment.

YIELD: 12 dumplings

TIME: 1 hour

4 *ounces dry bread*	*Salt and pepper*
½ *ounce (1 tablespoon) butter or*	1 *tablespoon chopped fresh herbs:*
lard	*parsley, chervil, marjoram*
1 *egg*	*(optional, but a great*
½ *cup milk*	*improvement)*
3 *ounces (¾ cup) flour*	

You will need a frying pan, a small and a large bowl, and a saucepan of water or soup. Dice the bread and fry it lightly in the fat in a frying pan. Meanwhile, mix the egg and the milk in a small bowl. Tip the contents of the frying pan into a large bowl, and pour the egg and milk over all. Stir in the flour, and season with salt and pepper. Add the herbs, if using. You may need more milk to make a soft dough. Allow it to stand for half an hour.

Dip your hand into cold water and roll the mixture into a dozen small balls. Put a pot of salted water on to boil, if there isn't a simmering soup pot waiting. Drop little balls of dough from a teaspoon into the boiling salted water or the soup. Poach them for 10 to 15 minutes, until they are light and firm and well risen.

SUGGESTIONS

Include chopped fried bacon in the mixture, or cubed pork cracklings.

A lighter dumpling can be made if the flour is left out. Less liquid will then be needed.

The mixture can be used to make a cloth or "cloutie" dumpling, which used to be popular in both Britain and Germany. It is made as follows: Line a colander with a clean floured cloth and put the dumpling mix into it. Tie the corners. Put the handle of a wooden spoon through the handles thus made, and, using the spoon as a crossbar, suspend the dumpling in a pot of boiling water to cook for 30 minutes. It is often simmered in the stewpan alongside a piece of meat, and is very good with a game stew.

S U G G E S T I O N S

Leftovers: Scrambled egg and dumplings: Slice the dumplings and fry them in a little lard or bacon fat. Add beaten egg to the pan, and proceed as for scrambled eggs. This is delicious as a late breakfast, or as a light lunch served with a green salad.

SPINACH DUMPLINGS

Spanak Tonka (Bulgaria)

Dumplings are northern Europe's answer to the pasta dishes of the south. Eastern Europe has a wide repertory of these dumplings: small ones pinched off with the fingers and tossed into a soup, sweet ones, sour ones, stuffed ones, plain ones. Bulgarians, the vegetable experts, favor this simple supper dish, which, complete in itself, needs no accompaniment but a glass of wine. Housewives in dumpling-eating nations can buy a special colander to fit inside the saucepan, which makes the removal of the dumplings from their poaching liquid much easier.

S E R V E S : 4 to 5

T I M E : 20 to 30 minutes plus 20 minutes cooking

6	ounces day-old bread or bread rolls	1	rounded tablespoon flour
			Salt and pepper
1½	cups milk	2	ounces (¼ cup) bread crumbs
1	pound fresh spinach (if you use frozen, defrost it but do not cook it)	2	ounces grated cheese (any hard cheese—Gruyère or cheddar will do fine)
4	ounces (½ cup) butter		

You will need a large saucepan and a small frying pan. Crumble the bread and put it to soak in ½ cup of the milk. Pick over the spinach and remove the tough stalks. Melt 2 tablespoons of the butter and stir in the flour. Add the rest of the milk, bring to a boil, and turn down to simmer for 4 to 5 minutes until thick. Meanwhile, squeeze the liquid out of the bread, and chop up the raw spinach. Mix the thickened sauce with the bread and spinach, work all well together, add salt and pepper to taste, and then put the dough aside to rest for 5 to 10 minutes.

Put a large pot (for 4 quarts) of water on to boil. Add a teaspoon of salt.

Using a spoon dipped into hot water, scoop out dumpling balls and drop them into the simmering water. Don't put too many in at once—the water must not be allowed to stop boiling, or the dumplings will be heavy. Poach one test dumpling first, and taste it to see if the mix is all right. If the dumpling collapses into the water, add a little more prepared bread to the dough. If the dumpling is too heavy and hard, add a little more milk to the dough.

Poach the dumplings for 5 to 6 minutes, and pass them through a bowl of cold water as you take them out—this stops them from sticking to one another.

Melt 2 tablespoons of the butter in a frying pan; keep it on a gentle heat and turn the dumplings in the warm butter as they come out of the cold water. Put them on a plate and keep them warm. When all the dumplings are cooked, fry the bread crumbs in the remaining butter, mix in the grated cheese, and scatter the mixture over the dumplings. Pass more grated cheese separately.

That's all. Serve the dumplings hot, with cold white wine.

SUGGESTION

Serves 6 to 8 with a dish of stewed game, or after a thick soup.

PASTRIES AND PIES

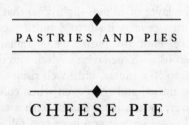

CHEESE PIE

Kolaçod Kajmak (Yugoslavia and the Balkans)

Big trays of this filo-based pie are sold from special kiosks in the marketplaces of Yugoslavia. These little shops also sell *baklava* (page 450) and *kataife*, another honey-and-nut sweet pastry, a very finely shredded pastry made by forcing a noodle paste through pinholes punched through a tin sheet. This cheese pie, when prepared with good ingredients, is one of the most delicious dishes imaginable, not unlike a French *quiche*. The difference is that the crisp filo makes the dish wonderfully light. The filling is fresh, clean, and a perfect match for the delicate pastry.

SERVES: 6

TIME: 30 minutes plus 40 to 50 minutes cooking

½ *pound filo pastry (see page 177)*	4 *eggs*
6 *ounces (¾ cup) clarified butter*	2 *tablespoons heavy cream*
1 *pound* kajmak *cheese (or ½*	*Salt and pepper*
pound feta or other strong	
cheese mixed with ½ pound	
cream cheese or cottage cheese)	

You will need a bowl and a baking sheet. A blender would save time. Take care to keep the filo pastry covered while you work—it dries out and cracks very easily.

Clarified butter is ordinary butter, melted and then allowed to cool so that the whey, salt, and coloring matter settle on the bottom. Pure clarified butter can then be lifted off the top. This butter has a far higher burning point than ordinary butter, so it is very good for frying. It will also keep sweet for a very long time.

Beat the cheese, eggs, and cream together in a bowl. Add salt in accordance with the saltiness of the cheese you are using. Be generous with the pepper. This whole operation can be done to perfection in a blender.

Preheat the oven to 350°F.

Line a buttered 12 by 1 by 8-inch deep-sided baking tray with two thicknesses of filo pastry, leaving an edge which can be tucked up and over the filling. Sprinkle the top sheet with butter; then put on another 2 sheets and sprinkle the top one generously with butter, and so on, until you have 8 thicknesses of filo.

Then spread on the layer of filling—lightly so that you do not press the air out of the layers; then cover with 6 to 8 more sheets of filo pastry and butter, layered as before. Pour any butter which remains (if you have a lot, next time be more generous with the layers). Mark into diamonds and sprinkle with water. Bake for 40 to 50 minutes, until well risen and golden. It puffs up like magic and will stay puffed and crisp even when cold.

Serve as an appetizer, or as a main course with a salad of sliced peppers, tomatoes, and onions dressed with lemon juice and salt.

◆

SUGGESTION

Chop a handful of parsley finely and add at least 2 tablespoons of it to the cheese filling.

◆

FRIED PASTRIES

Borek (Turkey, Greece, and the Balkans)

Borek are a great treat: These small stuffed triangular pastries are made with strips of filo, neatly folded zigzag fashion to keep the filling in. The Turks have brought the preparation and the fillings to a fine art. In the Middle East, where these little pastries are very popular, the filo dough is sometimes made with lemon juice or yogurt—its composition is a matter of passionate debate and each region and even family has its own theories. Find a mix which suits you and form an equally passionate break-away group. The filling is very variable, but should be delicately well minced, and can range from a simple handful of chopped spinach to the most complicated and intricately spiced palace mixtures. Here are few on which to get started.

Y I E L D : 40 to 50 *borek*

T I M E : 1 to 1½ hours

T H E   P A S T R Y :

1 pound (3½ cups) bread flour (high-gluten)	3 eggs
	About ¼ cup water
½ teaspoon salt	1 tablespoon melted butter

(Or use ready-made filo pastry. One package of bought filo pastry usually yields 24 to 30 sheets.)

Pour the flour directly onto a clean tabletop. Make a well in the flour, and put in the salt and the eggs. Work all together thoroughly, adding enough water to give a soft, pliable dough. Work in the butter. Cut the dough into 40 walnut-sized pieces, and roll each out until it is as fine as paper. Or stretch it on your fists as in the strudel recipe on page 441.

Fillings for dough made with 1 pound (3½ cups) of flour: These fillings are given in quantities to stuff pastries made from a dozen 12-inch sheets, yielding 40 to 50 little *borek*. If you want a choice of fillings, adjust the quantities. Keep the filo pastry rolled up and covered with plastic wrap while you work—it dries out in no time and becomes too brittle to roll. You will also need oil or clarified butter to brush the pastry.

Cheese filling: 1 pound grated cheese beaten with 2 eggs. Use Greek *halumi*, or substitute cheddar, Gruyère, or mozzarella plus a spoonful of grated Parmesan. Salt and pepper.

Curd cheese filling: 1 pound soft white cheese mashed with chopped mint, dill, or parsley. Use Greek feta, or any soft white cheese plus plenty of salt and pepper and a spoonful of grated Parmesan.

Spinach filling: 1 pound fresh spinach or other greens and 4 ounces grated hard cheese (*halumi* or Cheddar). Cook the spinach in the water which clings to its leaves after washing—5 to 10 minutes will be enough. Mince it very finely and put it back into the pan with 1 ounce butter, and sweat until it is as soft and dry as possible. Allow the mixture to cool. Beat in 1 egg and the grated cheese and freshly milled pepper—add salt only if the cheese is not already salty enough. Freshly grated nutmeg is a good spice for this mixture.

Eggplant filling: 1 pound eggplant, cubed and fried gently in 2 tablespoons oil, with 1 finely chopped onion. When the vegetables are well browned, add 2 chopped, peeled and seeded tomatoes. Simmer until soft. A minced clove of garlic or a tablespoon of lightly fried pine nuts makes a good addition. Mash well before using.

Meat filling: 1 pound lean minced meat stiffened in a spoonful of olive oil with 1 finely chopped onion. Moisten with ½ cup water; add salt and pepper and any seasonings you like. Cook gently for 10 to 15 minutes. Lamb is the best meat for this, and a tablespoonful of pine nuts, fried with the meat, is a good addition. Allow the mixture to cool before using. Cinnamon is a good spice to include, or allspice.

Sweetbread filling: 1 pound brains or sweetbreads (calf's or lamb's). Prepare the meat by soaking it first for an hour in water with a tablespoonful of lemon juice. Drain it, peel off the outer membrane, and clean away any traces of blood. Simmer the meat in water with a little salt and tablespoonful of lemon juice for 10 to 15 minutes. Drain carefully and then mash it up with a tablespoon of chopped herbs (dill, parsley, chervil, fresh oregano) and salt and pepper. This is a particularly good stuffing. This was a dish for the urban poor, who could, in times of plenty, buy quite cheaply the offal which the rich man foolishly rejected.

To assemble the *borek*, lay out the filo pastry and cut it into strips 2½ inches wide by the full length of the pastry. Put a teaspoon of your chosen filling on the near corner of the strip. Fold it over to make a triangle, and then fold again to make another triangle, and so on up the strip, always rolling away from you, until you have a well-wrapped little *borek* covered in half a dozen thicknesses of pastry.

Put a deep pan of oil on to heat. Deep fry the *borek* in hot oil for 5 minutes, until the pastry is well puffed and golden. Drain the *borek* on paper towels.

They should be served warm—particularly delicious with a tiny glass of raki or ouzo, the anise-flavored liquor of Turkey and Greece. You will not regret making the necessary effort.

◆

SPINACH PASTRIES

Banitsa (Bulgaria)

Banitsa are the Bulgarian filo pastries. The Ottoman Turks occupied Bulgaria for five centuries, until the end of the nineteenth century, and these pastries are one of the more useful legacies of their rule. As with the Turkish *borek*, fillings are variable, ranging from minced meat to walnuts and sugar.

SERVES: 4

TIME: 30 minutes plus 25 to 30 minutes cooking

THE PASTRY:

1   pound (3½ cups) flour
1   teaspoon salt
½   cup oil or melted butter
1   tablespoon wine vinegar

THE FILLING:

1   pound cooked spinach
4   ounces farmer cheese
2   hard-cooked eggs
¼   cup oil or melted butter

You will need a bowl, a rolling pin, and a baking sheet. Sift the flour into a bowl with the salt. Make a well in the middle and pour in the ½ cup oil or melted butter and the vinegar. Knead together until you have a soft, elastic dough—you may need a little water as well. Roll the dough into a long sausage and cut it into 10 equal pieces. Roll each piece out into a fine sheet as thin as paper.

Chop the spinach and beat it into the cheese. Chop the eggs and stir them in.

Preheat the oven to 350°F.

Oil a baking sheet. Lay a sheet of pastry on it, and then brush it over with the oil or butter. Lay on the next sheet, brush on the oil or butter, and so on, until you have 5 layers. Spread the filling on. Finish with the last 5 sheets, brushing each layer with oil or butter as it is laid on.

Bake the pastry until it is crisp and golden, 25 to 30 minutes.

SUGGESTION

Make 10 small pastries by rolling each disk of pastry around a line of the spinach-and-cheese mix, in the fashion of a strudel. They will take less time to bake—20 minutes should be enough.

LEEK TART

Flamiche (France)

The most primitive form of this northern baker's treat was a thinly rolled piece of bread dough, put to cook in the oven for the baker's breakfast just after he had lit the wood fire and the flame was still high. It was left for a moment—all it needed to cook—taken out, spread with butter, and then eaten immediately, perhaps with a slice of raw onion or leek on top.

SERVES: 4

TIME: 25 to 30 minutes plus 40 to 50 minutes cooking

THE PASTRY:
- ½   *pound (1¾ cups) all-purpose flour*
- 1   *teaspoon salt*
- 4   *ounces (½ cup) butter*
- 1   *egg*

THE FILLING:
- 2   *pounds leeks or onions*
- 2   *ounces (4 tablespoons) butter*
- 3   *eggs*
- ¼   *cup heavy cream*
- *Salt and pepper*

You will need a bowl, a small saucepan with a lid, and an 8-inch pie tin. Put the flour and the salt into a bowl and cut in the butter. Work in the egg, beaten with 2 tablespoons water, until you have a soft, elastic dough—you may need to add a little more water.

Roll the dough out and use it to line an 8-inch pie tin; cover with a damp cloth and put aside to rest while you make the filling.

Slice the leeks or onions and wash them well. Put them to sweat in a tightly lidded pan in the butter with no moisture but the water which clings to their leaves. It will take 15 to 20 minutes for them to soften. Leave them to cool while you beat the 3 eggs with the cream. Stir in the leeks. Season with salt and freshly milled pepper.

Bake for 40 to 50 minutes in a preheated 375°F oven. Serve with cold cider or beer and a lightly dressed salad.

My sister-in-law comes from Normandy, and her mother made small cheese *flamiches* for her wedding. She used a basic dough made with a pound of flour and 1 cup water. Work with ½ pound Brie or Camembert with ½ pound softened sweet butter, and spread the mixture over two thirds of the pastry. Fold the pastry in three, as if for puff pastry. Roll it out again to a thickness of ¼ inch, cut the pastry into narrow cheese-straw strips, and twist them twice. Bake these small *flamiches* in a preheated 400°F oven for 10 to 12 minutes until golden.

In some neighborhoods the *flamiche* is made with a sweet, fruited butter and egg-enriched dough, rolled into a flat *galette* and baked in a hot oven. (Make one with leftovers from Marie Antoinette's *Kugelhupf* on page 321.)

Falculella is a similar kind of cheese brioche found in Corsica. It is made with *brocciu*, the mild fresh sheep's cheese of the area.

◆

VENISON PASTY

(England)

This was the fabled picnic of Robin Hood's jolly companion, Friar Tuck. The pies and pasties of England developed from the bag puddings of pre-oven days. With the advent of bread ovens, the same mixtures were often stewed first, then put into a pie dish and lidded with pastry, which then could be baked to a crisp savory perfection while the oven was lit for the bread baking. Local peasantry had access to the village or manorial oven. A complicated system of rights and duties governed this privilege, usually to the disadvantage of the peasant.

SERVES: 6

TIME: Start the day before if possible; 1½ hours plus 30 to 35 minutes cooking

THE FILLING:

2	pounds venison off the bone or the same amount of stewing beef (you will then have a beef pasty, of course)	1	onion
		6	peppercorns
		1	teaspoon juniper and allspice berries
4	ounces bacon	1	ounce (2 tablespoons) lard
½	pound mushrooms (the large dark ones are best)	1	cup water
			Salt and pepper

THE ROUGH PUFF PASTRY:

6	ounces (¾ cup) cold butter	1	teaspoon salt
6	ounces (¾ cup) cold lard	6 to 7	tablespoons cold water
1	pound (3½ cups) plain flour		

You will need a large bowl, a baking sheet, a saucepan, and a rolling pin. Trim and cube the venison into 1-inch squares. (It will do no harm to do this the day before and marinate the meat overnight in a glass of wine, or half vinegar and half water, with 2 bay leaves.) Cube the bacon, slice the mushrooms, peel and chop the onion. Crush the peppercorns with the juniper and allspice berries.

Put the bacon to melt gently in a saucepan. When enough fat has run to grease the pan thoroughly, add the onion and sauté it lightly. Push it aside and add the lard and then the venison. Fry to allow the venison to take color. Push the meat aside and add the mushrooms and the spices, and fry them for a moment. Pour in the water. Stew gently until the meat is soft—an hour should be sufficient, unless the meat is very tough. Keep an eye on the pan so that it does not cook dry. There should be only enough well-flavored gravy left at the end to moisten the stew. Leave it to cool. Taste, and adjust the seasoning with salt and pepper.

Meanwhile, make the pastry. Chop the butter and the lard together. Put the flour and the salt in a roomy bowl, and rub in half the fat, crumbling lightly with your fingers until the mixture looks like fine bread crumbs. Sprinkle in the water and press the dough together. Knead the dough lightly into a soft ball of pastry.

Roll out the pastry into a long rectangle, and spread the rest of the butter and lard over two thirds of it. Fold the unbuttered third into the middle, and then the last third over that, to give you a triple-decker layered with fat. Roll the pastry out. Fold the pastry into a quarter circle and roll it out again. Refold in three. Turn and give it another roll. Refold. Put the pastry to rest in a cool place until you are ready for it.

When the stew is cooked and cooled, preheat the oven to 400°F.

Cut the pastry in half and roll out two large circles. One should be slightly bigger than the other. Put the smaller circle on the baking tray and pile the cooled venison stew onto it. Wet the edges of the pastry and cover with the other circle. Press the edges together lightly with a fork. Rough up the cut sides with a knife so that it looks like horizontal flaking. Cut a hole in the top for the steam to escape.

Bake for 30 to 40 minutes, until the pastry is golden and well risen.

Serve with new peas or beans and English mustard.

◆

SUGGESTIONS

Steak-and-kidney, steak-and-onion, chicken-and-mushroom, all manner of furred and feathered game, fish—haddock in particular—in white sauce with hard-boiled eggs, all make good pie fillings. There are many purely regional pies which make use of local specialties.

The pasty can be baked as a pie, but you will need only half the pastry recipe to make the lid.

◆

CORNISH PASTY

(England)

The best of lunch-pail food, versions of this pasty are to be found all over Europe, although nowhere was it taken to its logical perfection as it was in Cornwall. The Cornish pasty is as easily transportable down the mine as it is into the fishing boat or out into the fields at harvesttime. It is a satisfying, well-balanced meal contained in a pastry crust. The pasty was sometimes stuffed with a sweet filling (jam or apple sauce) at one end, a savory one at the other, with a solid disposable "handle" at one extremity of the half moon to accommodate the miner's or field-worker's blackened thumb. When it emigrated with the Cornish miners to the New World, the immigrant Finns adopted and adapted it, and washed it down with their favorite sour milk. The immigrant Italians spiced it with peppers, tomatoes, and a chopped chili or two, and also claimed it as their own.

SERVES: 4

TIME: 1 hour plus 50 to 60 minutes cooking

THE FILLING:
1   *pound beef or lamb*
1   *pound (3 medium-sized) potatoes*
1   *small onion*
Salt and pepper

THE PASTRY:
1   *pound (3½ cups) flour*
½   *teaspoon salt*
½   *cup water*
½   *pound prepared grated suet (see page 167) or 1 cup butter or lard*

You will need a small bowl, a rolling pin, a large saucepan, and a baking sheet. Slice the meat, and then chop it into small squares; peel and dice the potatoes small; peel and chop the onion. Mix all together in a bowl and season with salt and pepper.

Sift the flour with the salt. Bring the water to a boil in a large pan with the suet, butter, or lard, and boil until the suet melts (if you are using butter or lard, this will happen much quicker). Beat in the flour and salt and cook until the paste comes away from the sides of the pan. It is a hot-water paste and at this point it will look slightly transparent. Tip it out onto a well-floured board, knead into a ball, and cut into quarters. Work quickly because the pastry will crack if it is allowed to cool. Roll each quarter into a circle ¼ inch thick.

Preheat the oven to 350°F.

Divide the meat mixture among the circles, piling the mixture in the middle of each. Dampen the edges of the pastry and pull them over the filling to meet in the middle. Pinch the edges together to make a wavy line, known as the Cornish crimp. Leave a little hole in the middle for escaping steam. Glaze with egg if you like a shiny crust. Bake for 50 to 60 minutes.

--------------◆--------------

SUGGESTIONS

Variations in Cornwall are many, including mutton-and-leek (sometimes raisin), chopped egg-and-bacon, lamb-and-parsley, fish-and-potato, pork-and-apple, turnip-and-carrot, and fruit-and-jam pasties. Mark with the recipient's initials, and stuff and season the pasty to his or her particular taste.

Shortcrust pastry (page 440) can be used instead of the hot-water crust.

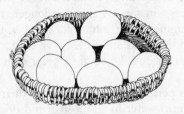

CHAPTER FIVE

EGGS

Barnyard and Dairy

The barnyard has always played an important part in the rural peasant kitchen. The hen is the most useful barnyard animal of all, and only the young cockerels would ever disappear into the pot before their time. A dozen good laying hens can keep a family well supplied with eggs all year and leave a good handful in times of glut for the housewife to trade for her "corner-of-the-apron" money. Eggs are a useful little cash crop. In Spain, eggs were, until recent times, negotiable currency, and an egg-woman would be able to make a living by traveling from farm to farm collecting the surplus eggs to be sold in the local markets, paying for them with pepper, salt, coffee, needles and thread—anything not homegrown. Gerald Brenan reported in *South from Granada* that, in the 1920s, the local "lady of easy virtue" in his village would often accept payment in eggs.

SOFT-COOKED EGGS

Oeufs à la coque and *Oeufs mollets* (France)

This is the preferred French way to boil eggs. Use eggs from your own hens, or the best free-range eggs from the most reliable source you can find. If the eggs have been refrigerated, allow them to come up to room temperature before you start. A perfectly soft-cooked egg is a fine-judged thing.

YIELD: Allow 2 eggs per person

Bring a large saucepan of water to a boil. When it is boiling, slip in the eggs. Cover the pan and leave the eggs to simmer for 3 to 3½ minutes, depending on the size of the eggs. This will give you a soft-set white and a runny yolk.

If you leave the eggs in for 1½ minutes longer, this will give you *oeufs mollets:* Plunge them immediately into cold water and then peel them; the whites will be firm and the yolks still soft. Serve with a cheese sauce, creamed vegetables, or a vegetable stew. There are a great many dishes which require *oeufs mollets*.

To hard-cook eggs perfectly every time, have them at room temperature. Cover the eggs with warm water in a saucepan and bring it to a boil. Remove from the heat and cover as soon as the water boils. Leave them for 6 minutes. Take the eggs out and plunge them into cold water. They will peel easily and are never gray at the edges or tough.

Successful truffle hunters in France sometimes leave a black Périgord truffle in a basket of fresh eggs overnight. The scent of the fresh truffle is pungent enough to perfume the eggs. These are then soft-boiled or scrambled the following day, allowing the frugal folk to eat their truffle and sell it in the market too.

◆

HOLLANDAISE SAUCE

Sauce hollandaise (Huguenot Dutch)

Sauce hollandaise, or Dutch sauce, appears first in the household books of Huguenot refugees who fled to Holland in 1685 to escape religious persecution in the wake of the revocation of the Edict of Nantes. Many of the refugee families came from the south of France, from the Protestant strongholds of the Languedoc and Provence, olive oil country, where Huguenot housewives were used to preparing egg-and-oil sauces such as *aïoli* and mayonnaise.

Holland, flat land of fertile pastures and dairy herds, had only good sweet butter to offer in place of the oil. The resourceful Huguenots needed to make but minor adaptions to their recipe to produce the delicious *sauce hollandaise*. A recipe for "Dutch Sauce: An Easy Way," appears in the household book of Charlotte du Cane, who married William Garnham Luard in 1845. The family lived in Essex, within easy access of their relations who had settled in Holland. Contemporary English versions usually begin with a white sauce.

Put two tablespoons of boiling water with pepper and salt into a small saucepan. Stir into it four ounces of fresh butter melted, and whisk in the yolks of two eggs. Place this first saucepan into a second saucepan which is half filled with cold water. Put it on a moderate fire, stirring the contents of the inner saucepan without cease. When the water in the outer saucepan boils, the sauce will be thickened enough. Finish with lemon juice.

Serve with a dish of *oeufs mollets*, or with fresh spring vegetables, or in any other dish which seems to you appropriate. The sauce is as infinitely adaptable as its creators.

◆

SCRAMBLED EGGS

(England)

The earliest cooked eggs were probably simply roasted in the embers of the fire. Perhaps some enterprising ancient Briton one day solved the problem of a cracked shell by mixing up the contents with a twig and cooking the result.

SERVES: 4

TIME: 10 minutes

8   *eggs*
Salt and pepper to taste
2   *tablespoons milk*
2   *ounces (4 tablespoons) butter*

You will need a bowl and a small saucepan. Break the eggs into a bowl and beat them to a froth with salt and freshly milled black pepper. Add the milk and beat the mixture some more.

Melt the butter gently in a small pan—the butter should only melt, not color. Roll it around the pan. Tip in the egg mixture. Stir constantly with a wooden spoon over low heat while the eggs thicken. They will form soft curds on the bottom of the pan, and this is what you must scrape into the rest of the liquid. When they are at the point of setting but still runny, take them off the heat. Give a final stir.

Serve at once, accompanied by hot toast or fresh bread. They are at their best in the company of crisp-fried thin strips of bacon, or smoked haddock cooked in milk (page 519).

◆

OMELETTE

(France)

The French omelet is served *baveuse*—a wonderfully onomatopoeic adjective to describe the juicy froth which remains enfolded at its tender heart. Make each omelet individually.

SERVES: 1

TIME: 10 minutes

> 2 *eggs*
> *Salt and pepper*
> *Butter*

You will need a small iron omelet pan—the cheap thin ones are the best. If it is made of raw iron such as those available in the marketplaces of the Mediterranean, it will need to be seasoned first. Do this by overheating a tablespoonful of oil in the new pan until it is smoking. Throw in a handful of salt, and when it is smoking again, take a sheet of newspaper and polish the surface well with the hot salt. Wipe out the salt and polish the pan with a fresh sheet of paper.

Put the plate to warm in a preheated 300°F oven before you begin. It should not be too hot, or the omelet will start to cook again.

Whisk the eggs together vigorously with a pinch of salt and a few turns of the pepper mill. When they are well mixed and frothy, put a small nugget of butter in the omelet pan to melt. Move it around the pan; when the butter is good and hot and foamy but has not yet changed color, pour the eggs into the pan. Hold the handle with one hand and a fork with the other. Move the eggs as they cook, pulling them away from the base of the pan in soft creamy curds, much as if you were scrambling them.

When the curds are forming but still frothy, stop moving the pan so that a skin can form on the base. Drop an extra piece of cold butter onto the froth. Fold one third of the omelet over the middle third. Tip the omelet onto the waiting warm plate, folding it over the open third as you do so, to give a plump oblong bolster, set and slightly browned on the outside, and *baveuse* within. The cooking should take no more than 2 to 3 minutes.

◆

SUGGESTIONS

Mix some chopped fresh herbs with the eggs before you start the cooking for an *omelette fines herbes*.

Or sprinkle the soft surface of a plain omelet with chopped ham or grated cheese just before you fold it.

Or fill it with a tablespoonful of something delicious in a creamy sauce. Mushrooms in cream are particularly good.

A plain mushroom omelet can be made by stirring into the beaten eggs a few chopped mushrooms which have been sautéed first in butter. The fillings in a French omelet are always cooked before they are folded in.

Try a spoonful of fresh tomato sauce laid onto the *baveuse* center before you fold the omelet over and serve it.

◆

ITALIAN CHEESE OMELET

Frittata con pecorino (Italy)

The Italians make their omelets flat, cooked through, not juicy, or *baveuse*, as the French omelet should be. The filling is usually fried in the pan first, and then the egg is poured around it into the hot oil. This version, made with cheese, is particularly delicious.

S E R V E S : 2

T I M E : 20 minutes

2   tablespoons olive oil
4   slices of fresh pecorino cheese
4   eggs
Salt and pepper to taste

You will need a small frying pan—one used just for omelets is best. Heat the olive oil in the pan. Lay the slices of cheese in the oil when it is smoking lightly. Fry them swiftly to melt them, turning once.

Meanwhile, beat the eggs with the salt and pepper. When the cheese is melted and beginning to crisp at the edges, pour the eggs around the slices. Turn up the heat and cook until set on top. Either serve it like this, or slide the *frittata* out onto a plate and reverse it back into the hot pan and cook the other side for a moment or two. Serve immediately, with fresh bread and cold white wine. Accompany with a green salad, dressed with olive oil and a squeeze of lemon.

◆

SUGGESTIONS

A strong cheese which melts well—such as Gruyère or a mature cheddar—can be used instead of the pecorino.

Make the *frittata* with tiny green artichokes, sliced vertically across the choke in thin slivers. Cook them quickly in the hot oil before the eggs are poured around.

Make the *frittata* with sliced rings of salami, or *prosciutto*, or black pudding, all fried until crisp in the oil before you add the eggs. Or make it with slices of onion or fresh garlic.

Any *frittata* is very good served with a fresh tomato sauce.

◆

PEASANT OMELET

Bauernomlette (Germany)

This is a particularly good breakfast or light supper dish.

SERVES: 4 to 6

TIME: 20 minutes plus 20 to 30 minutes cooking

2 *pounds (6 medium-sized) old potatoes*	6 *eggs*
1 *pound onions*	*Salt and pepper to taste*
One 4-ounce slab of bacon	*Chives*

You will need a saucepan for the potatoes and a frying pan. Boil the potatoes in their skins in plenty of boiling salted water. This will take 20 to 30 minutes, depending on size. Peel them as soon as they are cool enough to handle, and slice them. Slice the onions and chop the bacon.

Fry the bacon gently in its own fat (you may need a little extra lard). Add the onions and potatoes, and fry until golden.

Meanwhile, lightly beat the eggs with the salt and pepper. When the potatoes are ready, pour the eggs over and around them. Cook until set.

Serve the omelet in its pan, sprinkled with chives. Complete a light supper with a salad of lettuce and a glass of milk curds.

◆

SPANISH POTATO OMELET

Tortilla española (Spain)

Eggs are the great standby of the Spanish kitchen. Hard-boiled eggs with mayonnaise (a Spanish invention, it appears, from the island of Minorca) are nearly always on the *tapa* counter, but the Spaniard loves his potato omelet, a thick, juicy, fragrant egg-cake, best of all. Other folded omelets are designated "French." Whatever other culinary skills she may lack, every Spanish country girl makes a beautiful *tortilla*. It is served hot, cold, or just warm (the best temperature), at any meal. It is good provender for the field-worker; schoolchildren take a portion, wrapped carefully in a square of thick brown paper, for their lunch; toothless old grannies live on it; it is served, cut into small neat squares speared with a toothpick, as a *tapa* in every bar from Cádiz to Bilbao.

SERVES: 4

TIME: 30 minutes

2	*pounds (6 medium-sized)*	*½*	*cup olive oil*
	potatoes	*6*	*eggs*
1	*large Spanish onion (or 2*	*Salt*	
	smaller ones)		

You will need an 8-inch frying pan (in Spain, a thin iron pan is kept well oiled for this job), two bowls, a draining spoon, and a metal spatula. Peel and cut the potatoes into slices or fat chips ¼ to ½ inch thick. Peel and chop the onion. Put the oil to heat in the pan. Stew the potatoes and the onion gently in the oil. They should be absolutely soft, but not take color. Transfer the potatoes and onion to a bowl.

In another bowl, beat the eggs lightly with a little salt, and add them to the potato mixture. Pour most of the oil out of the pan, leaving only a tablespoon or two; heat it again and tip in the egg mixture. Fry gently until the eggs begin to look set. The heat should be low, or the base will burn before the eggs are ready. As it cooks, neaten the sides with a metal spatula to build up a deep straight edge to the *tortilla*. When it looks firm, slide it out onto a plate; then invert it back into the pan to cook the other side. A little more oil in the pan may be necessary. Drain well.

Serve warm, cut into wedges for a main meal, or into squares for *tapas*. If it is to be for a light supper, accompany it with a salad of chopped cos lettuce, chunks of tomato and cucumber, and slices of mild purple Spanish onions, all dressed with olive oil, wine vinegar, and salt.

SUGGESTION

Add chopped raw Spanish ham, *jamón serrano*, a little chopped *chorizo* or dried sausage, and a handful of cooked green beans, peas, and chopped green peppers to the mixture (leave out one of the potatoes) to make a juicy *tortilla paisana* or peasant omelet.

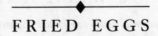

FRIED EGGS

Huevos fritos (Spain)

This very simple meal is excellent when made with fresh free-range eggs and pure olive oil. The better the ingredients, the better the dish.

YIELD: Allow 2 eggs per person

TIME: 10 minutes

Eggs
Olive oil
Rough salt

You will need a small shallow frying pan and a draining spoon. Crack the eggs into a cup. Poor enough oil into the frying pan to give a depth of one finger. Heat the oil until a faint blue smoke rises. Tip the pan to one side on the heat, so that you have a deep pool of oil. Slide the egg into the hot oil and fry swiftly, spooning hot oil over the top and tucking the edges over to make a little round cake. The edges should crisp into a light golden frill, the white set just firm, and the yolk remain runny. Sprinkle with rough salt and serve immediately.

Accompany with a dish of the large sweet Spanish tomatoes (imported as "beefsteak tomatoes"), fried with a little garlic, and a plate of fried green peppers. The green peppers sold in Spain for the purpose are a long slender variety with thin flesh—they cook quickly and are best when slightly charred.

◆
SUGGESTIONS

Fried eggs are delicious served with *migas*, diced dry bread soaked and fried with or without bacon.

Serve with rice (cooked in the Spanish manner: the rice grains are first lightly fried in oil before liquid is added) and a sauce made of fresh tomatoes stewed with a little oil and garlic and then puréed. A little sugar helps imported tomatoes, which have been picked before their time.

The Italians use double quantities of oil to deep-fry their eggs, turning them over halfway through to produce a neat crisp patty.

◆
EGGS WITH HAM

Huevos al plato con jamón (Spain)

This is a favorite instant meal or a first course for the heavy midday meal, which is usually taken around 2 P.M. and is followed by the famous *siesta*. Spaniards lunch prodigiously well if they can, and have a relatively light supper.

SERVES: 4

TIME: 10 minutes

Olive oil
4   *slices of* jamón serrano *or slab bacon*
8   *eggs*
Pepper

You will need four small earthenware heatproof dishes. Pour a film of olive oil into each dish and put it onto direct heat. When the oil is smoking hot, lay a slice of ham in each dish and top each slice with 2 eggs. Fry 3 to 4 minutes to set the whites. Give each dish a turn of the pepper mill and then serve. The eggs will continue to cook in their dishes.

Serve with fresh bread, and a mixed green salad if you are serving this as a light supper.

SUGGESTION

Two or three slices of *chorizo, morcilla,* or any spiced dry sausage can replace the ham. A few peas, green beans, and chopped peppers can be added.

SWISS CHARD OMELET

Trouchia (France)

Equally good cold as hot, this is food for the picnic pocket in the area around Nice, where the Italian influence is very strong. The Niçois have such a passion for *blea,* or Swiss chard, that they have earned the rude nickname of *caga-blea,* or cack-chard. For the *trouchia,* use only the tops of the chard—the stalks are too juicy and make the omelet gray and damp if it is to be eaten cold.

SERVES: 4

TIME: 30 to 40 minutes

1 pound Swiss chard leaves (save the stalks to cook like asparagus)	6 eggs
	Salt and pepper
4 ounces strong cheese (Parmesan is often used; Cantal, Gruyère, Emmenthaler, or cheddar will do)	1 bunch of chervil (basil can be included; Italian parsley can substitute)
	4 tablespoons olive oil

You will need a bowl and a frying pan. Wash and dry the chard leaves. Slice them into strips. Grate the cheese and beat it into the eggs in a bowl. Season with salt and pepper. Chop the herbs—you will need plenty, 3 to 4 heaped tablespoons is about right—and then mix them in with the eggs.

Put 3 tablespoons of the oil to warm in a roomy frying pan. Add the chard. Turn the strips of leaf quickly in the oil until they wilt (don't allow the chard to burn, or it will taste bitter). Tip the contents of the pan into the eggs and stir all together.

Put the last tablespoon of oil into the frying pan. When it is quite hot but not burning, pour in the egg-chard mixture. Cover the pan and cook over a gentle heat until the eggs are set—15 to 20 minutes should do the trick. The method is then the same as for the Spanish *tortilla:* Turn the now-firm pancake onto a plate, reversing it as you do so, so that the cooked side is uppermost. Slide it gently back into the hot pan (add a trickle more oil if necessary) and finish cooking it, uncovered now, on the other side. The *trouchia* will be ready in about another 15 minutes. Notice that the cooking is very gentle—this is the southern way with eggs, and has little in common with the fast butter-cooked French omelet, which is soft inside and rolled onto itself before serving.

For a main meal, serve the *trouchia* as an entrée to a dish of grilled sardines or some other simply prepared fresh fish, or after a plate of *charcuterie* accompanied by radishes and fresh butter.

◆

SUGGESTION

This mixture can also be baked in the oven as a *tian* (page 34).

◆

EGGS AND VEGETABLES

Piperade (Basque)

The Basque nation is highly individual. Their language owes nothing at all to their Latin neighbors and has no readily identifiable relatives. Recent research has come up with a possible link with the Finnish and Hungarian languages— themselves both orphans in the linguistic storm. It is a lovely onomatopoeic tongue which is a delight to the ears—how could the dancing butterfly be better served than with *papalanpausa* for a given name? The Basques share at least one culinary passion with the Hungarians, of rather more recent date than the language: The cooks of both nations took enthusiastically to the New World import, the capsicum pepper. The Hungarians refined the vegetable into their universal seasoning, paprika. The Basques' national egg dish, the delectable *piperade*, is named for the same vegetable.

SERVES: 4

TIME: 30 minutes

	6 to 8 eggs	1	red and 1 green pepper
	Salt and pepper	1	pound ripe tomatoes
1	large sweet onion	2	tablespoons olive oil or goose fat
2	garlic cloves		

You will need a bowl or two and a frying pan or shallow casserole. Beat the eggs lightly with a little salt and pepper. Peel and chop the onion and the garlic. Seed the peppers and slice them into short strips. Peel the tomatoes— the skins will slip off easily enough if you pour boiling water over them first—then chop them well. Sprinkle with a little sugar if they have had no Mediterranean sun to sweeten their flesh.

Put the oil or goose fat to melt in a frying pan or a shallow casserole. The Basques share their neighbors' fondness for beautiful glazed earthenware dishes which can withstand direct flame. Add the chopped onions and garlic to the hot fat, and fry them gently until they turn golden. Push them to one side and add the peppers. Fry them for a moment or two, and then add the tomatoes. Stew together gently so that the tomatoes reduce to a thick sauce. This should take about 10 minutes. The peppers must remain in visibly whole chunks.

Meanwhile, cut some slices of country bread to be served either fresh or fried in a little olive oil or goose drippings. Put four plates to warm in a preheated 300°F oven.

Now that the tomato-and-pepper mixture is thick and rich and its water has evaporated, tell your diners to take their places.

Stir in the eggs over the heat, turning the mixture as it thickens. As soon as it is creamy, take the dish off the heat. You want to avoid a watery, grainy mess and aim for a soft, smooth scramble—and there is only a minute or two of difference between the two. Spoon the *piperade* onto the warm plates, accompanied by the bread you have already prepared. A light red wine from the slopes of the Pyrenees can be served with it.

Add a slice of raw ham per person (the delectable *jambon de bayonne*), or lean bacon, fried and served atop each portion of *piperade*.

Or chop 4 ounces of raw ham or bacon and fry it with the onion at the beginning. Every Basque farmhouse has hams and good bacon: The pig is a versatile and much-traveled beast.

◆

EGGS WITH YOGURT

Yaycha cu Kisselo Mleko (Bulgaria)

This is a delicious sharp-flavored main-dish meal prepared with Bulgaria's favorite product.

SERVES: 2

TIME: 10 minutes plus 30 to 35 minutes cooking

1 cup thick yogurt	2 ounces (¼ cup) fresh bread
4 eggs	crumbs
¼ pound fresh white cheese (labna,	Salt and pepper
perhaps, page 199)	Butter

Preheat the oven to 350°F. You will need a shallow baking dish, plus a blender or a whisk and a bowl. Beat all the ingredients except the butter together until creamy—in the blender if you have one.

Butter the baking dish and pour the mixture in. Put it to bake for 30 to 35 minutes, until firm and gilded.

Serve with thick slices of brown bread and a Bulgarian salad (page 57).

To make a more substantial dish, line the pie dish first with 6 layers of buttered filo pastry.

MILK AND DAIRY PRODUCE

FRESH MILK CURDS

Quark (Germany and Northern Neighbors)

Specially soured milk has always been much appreciated in the dairy-producing regions of northern Europe. It is credited as very healthy fare. The idea is to spoon it from small bowls, accompanied by fresh berries or sugar and cinnamon, or eat it plain with a slice of black bread.

SERVES: 2

2   *cups fresh raw milk*
2   *tablespoons buttermilk or soured milk*

Mix the two ingredients together and set in a warm (not hot) place for a few hours. It will be best if it sets rapidly. Serve cool.

YOGURT

Kisselo mleka (Bulgaria)

Yogurt is eaten with meals or as a snack and praised as the "milk of eternal life." Bulgarian yogurt is the original and only begetter of *Lactobacillus bulgaricus*, the little organism now used worldwide, in company with *Streptococcus thermophilus*, to turn milk into the delicious healthy curds which appear on so many modern breakfast tables.

    Yogurt is very easy to make and needs no complicated apparatus. You will need a tablespoon of "starter" yogurt per pint of milk—any plain unsweetened yogurt will do, but Bulgarian is best. There are those devotees who insist on bringing their very own "starter" from its home territory. Once you have made the first batch, a spoonful of the homemade yogurt can be used in the next batch. The Bulgars have lost none of their ancient enthusiasm for their national delicacy: Refillable glass jars of yogurt are on sale in the State distribution centers all over modern Bulgaria. Sheep's milk makes the best yogurt, but whatever you do, native Bulgarian bacillus notwithstanding, there will still be a few unidentified and elusive organisms native to Balkan wooden troughs, pails, and spoons that produce the perfect sweet-sour thick curd only on home territory. However, your own homemade yogurt will undoubtedly be an excellent runner-up.

The very best Bulgarian yogurt is to be bought at the top of the Shipka pass, where the Russians fought with the Turks to throw off the Ottoman yoke. This is the pass which stands at the head of the Valley of the Roses—where the flowers are harvested to provide most of the world's attar.

YIELD: 4 cups

TIME: Overnight

1   *quart milk (homogenized milk makes a thick rich yogurt)*
1   *tablespoon fresh yogurt*

You will need a saucepan and a thermos, or a large glass bowl plus a small blanket to keep the culture coddled.

Bring the milk to a boil in a heavy saucepan. If you do not boil the milk first, it will not make a smooth yogurt. Turn down the heat as soon as the milk froths up, and simmer it for a minute or two. Remove from the heat. Leave it to cool down to 110 F. The traditional indicator of this temperature is when you can manage to hold your index finger in the liquid while counting to ten. Skim off any skin which has formed on the milk. Beat the spoonful of yogurt "starter" with a little of the warm milk in the bottom of a large bowl, and beat in the rest of the milk.

Pour the mixture into the thermos and seal it. Or cover the bowl with a plate or lid, and then wrap it up tenderly in a blanket and put it in a warm place to set overnight. It will keep well in the refrigerator for a week, but if you want to use a spoonful to start a new batch, do not leave it longer than 3 or 4 days, or the new yogurt will not turn into a thick enough curd.

◆

SUGGESTIONS

Sheep's and goat's milk make excellent thick yogurt by this method. The original yogurt was made of this strong rich milk which, when well salted, does not curdle easily when it is boiled. Cow's milk yogurt *does* curdle, so it must be stabilized first if it is to be used in a hot sauce without separating. For 1 quart of yogurt, beat in a tablespoon of flour mixed with 2 tablespoons of water, or beat an egg into the yogurt before you heat it (in this case do not allow it to boil).

To make a thicker yogurt, such as the Greek strained yogurt used to make *tzatsiki* (page 53), leave ordinary yogurt to drip for a few hours through a jelly cloth.

◆

YOGURT CHEESE

Labna (Eastern Europe)

This is a fresh cheese made by thoroughly draining the whey out of yogurt (as for the Greek strained yogurt in the previous recipe). Fresh white cheese is very popular throughout the Middle East as well as in Greece and the Balkans. Stir in a little salt—a scant teaspoonful per pint of yogurt. Pour the mixture into a clean linen or cotton cloth, which can be tied over an upended stool, as if it were a jelly cloth, or used to line a colander. Allow the whey to drip away overnight, and the following morning you will have a pure-white curd cheese. Roll it into little balls, and sprinkle with fresh herbs or olive oil and paprika. Or use it in any recipe which calls for curd cheese.

If you are able to make the *labna* with goat's milk yogurt, you can prepare the fresh cheese for keeping (it won't work with cow's milk—the curds are too soft and will disintegrate). Dry the little balls of cheese on a clean cloth in a cool pantry for 2 days, and then pack them into a large glass jar. Cover with olive oil. They will keep for months if stored in the refrigerator, and are excellent with fresh bread or used as a stuffing for *borek* (page 177).

◆

BREAD CHEESE

Leipaa Juusto (Finland)

A very unusual preparation, the result is a wheel of creamy yellow curds with a consistency rather like dry cottage cheese—squeaky when you bite into it. It is particularly good with summer berries, although the Finns treat it as a staple storehouse food.

T I M E : 1 to 2 hours to simmer

2½ *quarts fresh milk*
1   *teaspoon rennet (from the health food store)*
1   *teaspoon salt*

You will need a large saucepan and a very large flat baking tin or a wide frying pan. Bring the milk to blood heat and then stir in the rennet. Leave to set into junket—this will take about an hour in a warm place. Heat the junket gently on the fire until the curd separates and you can lift the clots of curd out with your hand. Squeeze out the liquid as you do so.

Pat the curd into a baking pan or a wide frying pan to give a cartwheel of cheese about half an inch thick. Cook either on top of the stove or in a preheated 350 F oven for 1 to 2 hours, until the outside is golden brown. Eat with coffee or milk, or fry slices in butter and sprinkle them with sugar. The Finns treat it as if it were bread.

SUGGESTION

Leftovers: Use the whey to make bread and scones.

CURD CHEESE
Skyr (Iceland)

Skyr is soft white Icelandic cheese made from ewe's milk in the old days, today from cow's milk. It can be eaten on its own, mixed with porridge and served with milk, or served as a luxury (and most delicious of all) with sugar and cream and perhaps a spoonful of bilberries. *Skyr* was a peasant year-round staple and a very important article of a healthy diet. The soft curds, bland and sweet when made by the best cooks, used to be stored in big wooden barrels sealed with tallow—an expertise apparently brought along when the first settlers landed in Iceland during the ninth century. The rennet to turn the milk was made by taking the stomach of the year's last newborn lamb or calf, killed before it took grass. The tiny bag full of strong curd and powerful enzymes was then hung in a corner to dry. The next season, the stomach would be soaked in salted water and the liquid would be used to turn the new year's *skyr*.

This method is common to many cheese-preparing communities, particularly in poor areas, where a small cash crop is needed for items which cannot be homegrown. I have seen goat's cheese made in this fashion in Spain as recently as 1980, although there the little stomach is prepared from the first kid of the year and tiny pieces of the actual curd are used rather than an infusion. In Iceland, chemically made rennet began to replace the old technique during the course of the nineteenth century. Today *skyr* is prepared in large quantities in commercial dairies and is a very popular item in the modern Icelandic diet. Modern methods of refrigeration and pasteurization have also replaced the barrel-and-tallow ritual.

T I M E : 10 minutes plus 4 hours

    3   *quarts skimmed milk*
    1   *tablespoonful previous batch of* skyr, *or soured raw milk*
    1   *drop rennet (from the health food store)*

You will need a large saucepan, a wooden bowl, and a blanket or a large thermos. Commercially prepared skimmed milk will not need boiling to kill the bacteria—the homemade variety will. Bring the skimmed milk to a boil, and then pour it into a big deep bowl—wooden ones are best. Allow the milk to cool down until it feels bearable to the tip of your finger.

Whip up the spoonful of *skyr* (or soured milk or yogurt) until smooth and unctuous. Stir it into the milk very thoroughly. Leave for half an hour. Then stir in the rennet slowly and with care. Cover the bowl with a blanket, or pour it all into a thermos. Put aside in a warm place.

Be warned: Icelanders say it takes a few small experimental batches before the *skyr* will be not too sour but yet well set. When this has been achieved, a spoonful of the perfect batch is used to turn the *skyr* all summer long. The bacteria will then reproduce themselves impeccably every time— wonderful enzymes to help the digestive system, say the Icelanders.

The milk should have curdled within 2 hours. Pour the curds through a linen cloth, as if straining jelly, to allow the whey to drain out. Save the whey—the Icelanders would have put their straining cloth over a wooden barrel in order to catch it. See the entry on whey which follows.

The *skyr* will be ready to eat in 2 hours. Kept in a cool place, it will stay fresh for around a week. After that, it begins to go sour. Serve with sugar, cream, and fresh berries—blueberries are best of all. Sugar has only been in general use in Iceland since the end of the nineteenth century.

SUGGESTIONS

A bowl of *skyr*, plus a bowl of oatmeal porridge, milk, and a slice of blood sausage or liver sausage and a small dish of fresh berries or fruit makes a well-balanced meal for a healthy adult.

For breakfast, take a helping of *skyr*, beat in a raw egg, and top with a spoonful of honey. Accompany with a glass of skimmed milk.

Or mix with chopped onion, chopped herbs, or paprika and salt, and eat as a fresh cream cheese.

WHEY

Mysa (Iceland)

After the making of *skyr* in Iceland, there would be large quantities of whey to be stored in barrels. Sometimes these had a practical nonculinary use, when they were used to extinguish the fires to which wooden houses with no fire-protection devices were always prone. In the old days a broom handle and a barrel of whey were always on hand beside the front door of the wooden dwellings. In the Icelandic sagas a heroic chieftain once hid in a barrelful to escape his enemies. Not only did this provide him with nourishment and shelter in a single container, but it saved him from incineration when the building was burned down around him. A heroic substance indeed.

In a less demanding role, whey provided a healthy drink which was taken by fishermen on long sea voyages. Rich in proteins, salt, and vitamins, no sailor would starve if he had a barrel aboard, and if his catch was inadequate, the whey could be used as a trade item. Whey as a drink was held to be at its best after 2 years' maturing in an oak barrel—not unlike whiskey. It was also valued as a preservative pickle for meat, particularly such vulnerable delicacies as blood sausage and liver sausage, the products of the autumn slaughter of domestic animals which could not be overwintered. The Italian white-curd cheese *ricotta* is still made from whey in the country districts, as is the Norwegians' favorite sweet dark-brown cooked cheese, *mysost*.

In modern times this miracle substance has been redefined as a toxic waste. It was discovered that when the waste whey from modern cheese factories is poured into the local rivers, it acts as a highly efficient fertilizer for algae, whose growth explosion depletes the supply of oxygen in the water with the inevitable catastrophic effect on aquatic life.

The Icelanders are now marketing a fruit-flavored whey drink which they hope will take the place of soft drinks, and will certainly be a great deal healthier for its consumers.

CURDS

Filbunke (Finland)

As she journeyed through Finland in the 1890s, the intrepid Mrs. Ethel Tweedie worked up a fine appetite for her meal in the farmer's kitchen:

> The housewife had two huge soup tureens before her, soup or filbunke, a very favourite summer dish. This is made from fresh milk which has stood in a tureen until it turns sour and forms a sort of curds, when it is eaten with sugar and powdered ginger. It appears at every meal in the summer, and is excellent on a hot day. It must be made of fresh milk left 24 hours in a warm kitchen for the cream to rise, and 24 hours in the cellar to cool afterwards. [*Through Finland in Carts*, Ethel B. Tweedie, 1898]

FRESH BUTTERMILK CHEESE

Hangop (Holland)

Hangop means "hanged"—the name comes from the practice of hanging up a pillowcase on a convenient branch for the buttermilk inside to drip out its whey. The dish is very ancient but still enjoyed today—particularly during the strawberry season.

SERVES: 4

TIME: Start in the morning to be ready for the afternoon; 5 minutes

2   *quarts buttermilk*
½   *pound Dutch rusks (these are usually made with egg—that is a bread
      dough with an egg or two beaten into it, baked in a long thin loaf,
      which is then sliced and dried)*
Brown sugar
Fresh strawberries in season

You will need a colander and two bowls. Take a fresh, clean linen towel and use it to line a large colander. Put the colander in a roomy bowl, big enough to allow the whey to collect beneath. Pour the buttermilk into the lined colander, and leave it for several hours so that the whey drips through. Stir it from time to time. When you have a thick, creamy yogurtlike curd, scrape it into another bowl.

    Serve each person with bowl of the *hangop*. Crumble an egg rusk onto each portion and sprinkle with brown sugar. Pass the strawberries separately.

———————————————◆———————————————

JUNKET AND CURD CHEESE

(Britain and Northern Europe)

Rennet is the curdling medium used for this milk product. It is a very ancient culinary process which makes use of a natural enzyme present in the fourth or "true" stomach of dairy animals.

SERVES: 4 to 6

TIME: Start a few hours before

1   *quart milk*
2   *teaspoons rennet (from the health food store)*
Freshly grated nutmeg (optional)

You will need a large bowl. Warm the milk to blood temperature—test with your finger, as for a baby's bottle. Stir in the rennet. Cover and leave to set—this will take at least 2 hours. Overnight is best. If you would like to serve it as junket, sweeten it with a tablespoon of sugar when it is still warm. Serve with freshly grated nutmeg sprinkled over. This is a very light and delicious pudding, particularly if served with stewed fruit and cream.

If you wish to proceed to make curd cheese, do not add any sugar. When the junket has set, pour the curd into a colander lined with a clean cloth. Leave overnight for the whey to drip through. This quantity will yield only a small amount of cheese.

◆

SOUR CREAM OR CRÈME FRAÎCHE

(Northern Europe)

Take as much fresh milk or cream as you require. To turn it, either use a buttermilk "starter," a tablespoon to a cup of cream stirred in and left to develop for 24 hours in a cool pantry, or stir in a teaspoonful of vinegar or lemon juice, and allow the mixture to stand for an hour or two. If this soured cream is dripped through a scalded jelly cloth as for the junket, it will make good cream cheese. Leave it wrapped in a cloth under a weight in a colander for a day or two.

◆

CLOTTED CREAM

(England)

Pour fresh unhomogenized milk into a shallow pan, and leave it overnight on very low heat: The warm ashes of a fire were the preferred place in the old days. In Devon the pans used to be of earthenware—a material which holds its heat comfortably—although enamel and metal are used today. The following morning you will find a thick, creamy skin has formed. The depth and color of the cream will depend on the pasture, the breed of cow, and the time of year. Spring grass is lusher; summer grass is sweeter. Good hay in winter can be best of all.

Remove the creamy skin and cut it carefully into squares; then roll each up into a little carpet roll. Let the cream rise again—there will be a little more to collect. Clotted cream is wonderful with fresh scones and strawberry jam for tea.

◆

THICK SOURED MILK OR CREAM

Fil-mjolk (Scandinavia)

YIELD: 4 cups

TIME: Overnight or 24 hours

1   *quart milk or light cream (18 percent fat)*
½   *cup sour cream*

You will need a large bowl and a saucepan. Put the soured cream into a roomy bowl. Heat the milk gently to finger temperature (100 F) and then pour it over the soured cream. Stir well. Pour into four 1-cup bowls. Cover with a cloth or paper, and put to stand in a warm place until the milk thickens—about 24 hours.

◆

RICH SOUR CREAM

Crème fraîche (France)

Make as for the previous recipe, but using heavier cream. Commercial *crème fraîche* has 30 percent fat. Half heavy cream (40 percent fat) and half light cream (18 percent fat) will approximate.

◆

CURD CHEESE

Quark (Germany)
Topfen (Austria)

YIELD: ½ pound

TIME: Overnight

4   *tablespoons plain yogurt or wine vinegar, or 5 tablespoons lemon juice*
2   *quarts milk (homogenized gives good results)*

You will need a saucepan, a bowl, and a sieve. If using yogurt, bring the milk to a boil and then leave it to cool to finger temperature (100 F). Mix the milk with the yogurt in a basin. Put it in a warm place for 4 to 5 hours to set as solid as yogurt.

If using vinegar or lemon juice, stir into the milk and bring to a near boil (200 F) in a bowl set in a saucepan of water. Remove and keep in a warm place for 4 to 5 hours.

Pour the mixture into a sieve lined with a scalded clean cloth. After an hour put a plate on top to weight and encourage the whey to drip through. The curds in the cloth are the cheese. Cover and store in a cool pantry, and it will keep for about a week. Drink the whey, flavored with fruit juice, for your health—or use it to make scones. Keep in the refrigerator and eat within 2 days.

BUTTER

(Britain and Central and Northern Europe)

All the farming communities of central and northern Europe made their butter at home until recently.

Dorothy Hartley chronicled butter-making procedures still being used in England during the first half of the twentieth century:

> There is much "traditional" usage involved with the "practical" in dairy work. Wool and cloth must not come into the dairy; old linen for the wood; and scouring sack (hempen) for the floor. White sand from the brook to scour the floor with, and lime "set" with skim milk to whiten the walls . . . A dairywoman's hands should be smooth as butter, white as milk, and cool as spring water. [*Food in England*, Dorothy Hartley, 1934]

SYLLABUB AND HATTED KIT

(England and Scotland)

Syllabub is an ancient recipe for a milk pudding made by milking the cow straight onto a bowl containing "sill," a wine which used to be made in the district of Champagne. Hatted kit is a similar poor-man's version. The following recipe was contributed by a Scottish reader to *Farmer's Weekly* in 1940: She explained it was her grandmother's recipe, and her grandmother's before her.

> Warm slightly over the fire 2 pints of buttermilk. Pour it into a dish and carry it to the side of a cow. Milk into it about 1 pint of milk, having previously put into the dish sufficient rennet for the whole.
>
> After allowing it to stand for a while, lift the curd, place it on a sieve, and press the whey through until the curd is quite stiff. Season with sugar and nutmeg before serving. Whip some thick cream, season it also with a little grated nutmeg and sugar, and mix gently with the curd. This dish can quite well be made without milking the cow into it, although direct milking puts a better "hat" on the Kit.

> Make a modern syllabub with 1 cup heavy cream well whipped and sweetened with a tablespoonful of sugar. Remember that cream whips better when it is cold. Fold into the whipped cream the juice of a lemon, a glass of dry sherry, and a tablespoon of brandy. The old wives will tell you that a syllabub without brandy is like kissing a man without a moustache.

BUFFALO MILK

Bivali Tej (Hungary)

Ellen Browning, a clever young university graduate and kinswoman of Robert Browning, traveled alone through late nineteenth-century Hungary, trying to restore her health while recovering from her father's death. She admitted fear of nothing except mice, and wore long cloth knickers under her gown as an anti-mouse device. She had constant trouble with fleas, but was a very observant traveler:

> If a man is rich enough to keep a buffalo or two, he and his family drink some of the warm milk for breakfast and supper, but cow's milk is considered only as a food for pigs and calves, or to mix with other milk for making cheese. You can't expect human beings to drink such poor stuff as that! they argue gravely. Even the household at "the big house" would have jibbed had they been required to drink cow's milk with their daily coffee. For my palate buffalo milk was too rich in quality *and* flavour, but we used to have it boiled and sent to the table half and half. Even then it tasted like cream. By the way, "brigand's coffee" is a beverage not to be despised. You roast the berries in the wood-ashes of your fire, wrapped in a maize leaf, bruise them whilst hot between two stones, drop them into the iron pot of boiling water, and cover it up for five minutes over the fire; then you pour it off into an earthenware pitcher onto a large lump of wild bees' honey (there are scores of nests about in the forest) and stir it with a wooden spoon. It must be drunk either out of the mug, turn about, or in wooden bowls. We always drank our onion soup with the wooden spoons out of the same bowls, therefore we were never able to indulge ourselves with soup and coffee on the same day. [*A Girl's Wanderings in Hungary*, Ellen Browning, 1896]

CHEESES

Many peasant households managed to keep a cow or a few goats or sheep for milking. Making cheese was part of the household's routine, some to be used fresh, some to be stored, and even some for a small cash crop.

CHEESE DIP

Liptauer (Hungary)

This mixture is made in the northern province of Liptow in Hungary. Earlier versions were made without the paprika, an arrival from the New World. The dip is now popular as a salad purée all over Eastern Europe, from Macedonia to Austria.

YIELD:½ pound

TIME: 5 minutes

½ pound fresh cream cheese	1 tablespoon paprika (as hot or
1 small can anchovies (8 to 10	mild as you please)
fillets)	1 teaspoon caraway seeds
1 tablespoon capers	(optional)
1 tablespoon mild mustard	

Mash up the cream cheese. Pound together the anchovies and the capers. Stir all into the cheese with the mustard, paprika, and caraway seeds, if using. Taste, and adjust the seasoning.

Serve with pickled vegetables (page 522) and rye bread.

SUGGESTION

In olive territory, very finely chopped black olives might replace the capers.

CHEESE AND EGGS

Fonduta (Italy)

The *fonduta*, an Italian fonduelike dish, is at its most sublime in the company of a Piedmont truffle or two. If you can lay your hands on a fresh tuber, ask three of your best friends to share the feast. As with a pound of caviar, four is the maximum number to one good-sized truffle.

SERVES: 4

TIME: 10 minutes plus 1 hour and 15 minutes cooking

½ pound Italian Fontina cheese (Gruyère, Emmenthaler, Cantal, or cheddar
   can substitute)
1 cup rich milk (half and half would be splendid)
4 egg yolks
1 firm, touch-dry, Piedmont truffle (optional)

You will need a basin, a large saucepan, and a food processor. Chop the cheese into tiny pieces with a sharp knife. This is supposed to produce a smoother, less stringy melted cheese than grating. A food processor will do the job in no time.

Put the cheese into a basin with the milk warmed to blood heat. Stand the basin over a saucepanful of boiling water. Cover it with a clean cloth. The milk and cheese must be kept warm on the side of the stove for an hour, so that the cheese melts very gently into the milk.

While you are waiting, make a plain *risotto* (page 136), or prepare thick slices of fresh bread for each of your guests. Put four plates in a preheated 300°F oven to warm.

At the end of the hour, whisk in the egg yolks with the cheese and milk. Put the saucepan on the heat and bring its water to a boil. Turn it down to simmer. Continue whisking while the *fonduta* thickens over the simmering water. Don't hurry it. You want a thick cream, not scrambled eggs.

When the mixture has thickened so that it can comfortably blanket the back of a wooden spoon, take it off the heat.

Make sure your friends are all at the table, each with a warm plate in front of him or her on which you have placed either a thick slice of bread scattered with little pieces of fresh butter, or a mound of *risotto*.

Pour the *fonduta* over the bread or rice.

If you have a truffle, brush and wipe it delicately beforehand. If it's very sandy, you may have to rinse it. Sliver the tuber over each portion in front of your guests, using the cucumber slicer on your grater. You can get special truffle graters for this if you anticipate many such banquets.

◆

MELTED CHEESE

Fondue (Switzerland)

When I lived in the Languedoc in southwestern France, among my acquaintances was a family who kept a small flock of goats on an isolated farm in the hills. The family had a daughter known as La Petite Pascale, "Little Pascale," who went to school with my own children in the neighboring town.

Unusual for the Languedoc, where the dark Catalan Spanish coloring is the norm, Pascale had blond hair and blue eyes. Pascale was soon befriended by my middle daughter, whose coloring matched her own, and the two little blond girls became inseparable. The Languedoc winter was bitter that year, and my own farmhouse was sometimes cut off by snow and floods, but the rough track to Pascale's remote home was even more often blocked. When it happened, Pascale would spend the night with us. On one of those dark and snowbound evenings she offered to make us a real Swiss fondue—revealing, as she did so, the origins of her blond hair and blue eyes.

Pascale, I learned, had a Swiss grandmother, whom she visited each year and from whom she had both her coloring and her skill in the art of fondue making. This is her grandmother's recipe from Neuchâtel, the heart of Switzerland's fondue country.

SERVES: 4

TIME: 30 to 40 minutes

½ *pound Gruyère cheese*	1 *tiny glass of kirsch*
½ *pound Emmenthaler cheese*	1 *loaf of day-old bread*
1 *teaspoon cornmeal or potato*	1 *garlic clove*
starch	*Half bottle of dry white wine*

You will need a chafing dish or a fondue pot. Chop the two cheeses into tiny pieces. Pascale was very particular about this and explained that grating the cheese makes for a tough, stringy fondue. Mix the cornmeal into the kirsch. Cut the bread into bite-sized cubes. Lay the table—you will need a fork and a large napkin for each diner, a plate of bread cubes, and plenty more white wine.

Rub the pan with the garlic to scent it. Pour the wine into the pot, and stir in the cheese. Heat the mixture gently, stirring with a wire whisk, until it bubbles. Stir in the cornmeal-and-kirsch mixture. Cook very gently until the mixture thickens and it no longer smells of alcohol. Take the fondue to those waiting at the table, give it one more stir, and put it on top of the stand over the heat.

Each diner now spears a cube of bread on his fork and stirs it once around the pot to cover it with cheese. Anyone who drops his bread into the fondue has to fetch another bottle of wine. At the end, a beautiful brown crust of toasted cheese is waiting to be discovered on the bottom of the pan. This is the *dentelle* and is the best part of all.

◆

SUGGESTIONS

Many Swiss housewives consider a mixture of at least three cheeses desirable: Jura or Gruyère, Bagues or de Courbier, plus Vacherin fribourgeois. Cider sometimes replaces the wine.

Leftovers: The alternative way to serve a fondue is to pour the melted cheese over a plate of potatoes boiled in their jackets. The leftovers are delicious served like this.

◆

BREAD AND CHEESE

Croûte au fromage (Switzerland)

A very popular dish in Swiss farmhouses, this is easy to prepare and more digestible than the all-cheese fondue. It is very like the Italian *fonduta*.

SERVES: 4

TIME: 15 minutes plus 15 minutes cooking

1	pound hard cheese (Gruyère, Emmenthaler, or cheddar)	8	slices of bread
4	eggs	2	ounces (4 tablespoons) butter
1	glass of dry white wine		Cayenne pepper

You will need a cheese grater and a shallow pan with a lid. Grate the cheese. Beat the eggs lightly, and stir in the cheese and half the wine. Spread this mixture over the slices of bread. Melt half the butter in a pan on medium heat and add half the remaining wine (you will have to cook this in two batches). Lay the cheese-covered bread in the pan and turn up the heat. Cover and let bubble until the cheese melts. Serve immediately. This dish can also be cooked in a preheated 475°F oven.

◆

WELSH RAREBIT—ROASTED CHEESE

Caws pobi (Wales)

Lady Llanover tells the true story of the rarebit from the distance of 1871:

> Welsh toasted cheese and the melted cheese of England are as different in the mode of preparation as the cheese itself; the one being only adapted to strong digestions, and the other being so easily digested that the Hermit frequently gave it to his invalid patients when they were recovering from illness. Cut a slice of the real Welsh cheese, made of sheep and cow's milk; toast it at the fire on both sides, but not so much as to drop; toast a piece of bread less than a quarter of an inch thick, to be quite crisp, and spread it very thinly with fresh cold butter on one side (it must not be saturated with butter); then lay the toasted cheese on the bread, and serve immediately on a very hot plate. The butter on the toast can of course be omitted if not liked, and it is more frequently eaten without butter.
> [*The First Principles of Good Cookery*, Lady Llanover, 1867]

◆

SUGGESTIONS

Use Caerphilly if you can find it, a well-matured cheddar or Cheshire cheese otherwise.

The Swiss serve their special Raclette cheese thus.

The Greeks have a similar trick with ½-inch-thick slabs of Kefalotiri cheese, grilled to a crisp brown crust on a flat iron sheet over the fire. The melted cheese is served immediately, piping hot, with a lemon quarter to squeeze over it. Bread and a couple of the excellent Greek salads should accompany the cheese.

◆

PASTRY MADE WITH CHEESE AND EGG

Gougère (Northern France)

This dish—basically a cheese-flavored choux pastry—provides the perfect partner for the wonderful wines of Burgundy. There are indeed those who say the dish was invented precisely with that purpose in mind. Take the cork out of the best bottle of Burgundy available—there is just time for it to breathe while you cook the *gougère*. You will never have a better excuse for drinking it.

SERVES: 4 to 5

TIME: 30 minutes plus 35 minutes cooking

1 cup water	4 to 5 eggs
4 ounces (½ cup) butter	Salt and pepper
8 ounces (1¾ cups) flour	
8 ounces strong cheese (Comtois or Gruyère is best; cheddar will do)	

You will need a saucepan and a baking tray. An electric mixer will save you trouble. Put the water to boil with the butter chopped up. When it has melted together and come to a rolling boil, take it off the heat and beat in the flour. Put it back on the heat and beat the mixture until it leaves the sides of the pan—which it will swiftly do.

Remove from the heat, and allow the dough to cool for a moment while you chop finely two thirds of the cheese, or grate it through the rough grater. Cut the remaining piece of cheese into fine slivers. The dough will by now have cooled down enough to beat in the eggs one by one. This is easiest to do in a mixer—the dough is at first somewhat reluctant to accept the eggs. Persist: The dough will soon be easier to work, rather as a mayonnaise becomes more malleable. Judge how many eggs you should put in by the appearance of the mixture—when finished, it should be light, shiny, and firm but soft, so that it holds its shape but drops from a spoon. Beat the chopped or grated cheese into the dough. Add a teaspoon of salt and plenty of freshly ground black pepper.

Preheat the oven to 350°F.

Butter a baking tray, and use two tablespoons to drop egg-shaped (and -sized) dollops of the pastry onto it in a circle, each dollop to overlap the other. Smooth the top so that you have a round ring. Sprinkle with the slivers of cheese. Bake for 35 to 40 minutes.

Serve the *gougère* warm. Accompany with a plate of *charcuterie*—a few thick slices of ham, rosy slivers of garlic-flavored sausage, perhaps a slice of a rough pâté—a bowl of well-washed scarlet-skinned radishes, still tied into a bridesmaid's posy, and a salad dressed with walnut oil and salt—no vinegar in the salad to spoil that beautiful bottle of Burgundy.

◆

CHEESE PASTRIES

Tiropiti (Greece)

The Greeks love to use cheese in their cooking. These little fried pastries are often served to favored visitors, accompanied by a tumbler of water, a glass of raki, and a little cup of strong black Turkish coffee.

SERVES: 6 as an appetizer

TIME: 40 minutes

¼ *pound Kefalotiri (or another strong cheese like Parmesan or cheddar)*	2 *eggs*
½ *pound feta cheese (a milder cheese like ricotta can be used instead)*	2 *ounces (4 tablespoons) clarified butter*
	1 *box of filo dough*
	Vegetable oil for frying

You will need a bowl and a deep frying pan. Grate the Kefalotiri. Mash it with the feta and the eggs. Melt the butter.

Lay out a dozen sheets of filo dough—be careful to keep them covered so that they do not dry out and become unmanageably brittle. Cut the dough into long strips, about 3 inches wide and the full length of the pastry. Brush each strip as you come to it with melted butter. Put a little mound of filling in one corner, and fold it over to make a triangle. Fold over and over diagonally until you have a neat little triangular cushion. Continue until you have used up the rest of the filling and the pastry.

Put a deep pan of oil on to heat. When a faint blue haze rises, test it by throwing in a cube of bread: If it turns golden immediately, the oil is hot enough. Slip the pastries a few at a time into the hot oil.

Alternatively, brush them with more melted butter, and then bake them in a preheated 400°F oven for 15 to 20 minutes, until they are puffed up and golden.

These are delicious as a light lunch with a little glass of ouzo and a salad. You might even finish with a bowl of strawberries dressed with a squeeze of lemon, followed by a tiny cup of Turkish coffee and a piece of Turkish delight from the Greek's least-favorite neighbors.

SUGGESTION

The Turks make a similar cheese pastry in the form of a small strudel—just tuck the sides over the stuffing and roll it up. Fry or bake according to the recipe.

CHAPTER SIX

Fish and Food From the Sea

Plentiful, unfenced, and free—fish is the ideal peasant food. Peasant communities with access to fishable waters have long made good use of this superb protein source, and for thousands of years, with one strange and notable exception, fishing has supplemented farming to fill the European family larder. The exception is Ireland, whose inhabitants only began to exploit fish as a resource comparatively recently—an almost inexplicable blindness to the riches of their surrounding waters which cost the Irish dear during the fearsome potato blight of the last century.

Stews, soups, and frying pan cooking are the most common methods of preparation, and shore dwellers throughout Europe all have their favorite recipes. During the Middle Ages, many a prosperous seaside town came into being as a result of the fishing industry. Amsterdam claims to be built, both metaphorically and literally, on herring bones. Ways to preserve what was essentially a seasonal harvest evolved gradually—the methods being dictated by climate and the availability of preserving agents such as salt or wind. The Mediterranean countries pickled with vinegar or brined their glut of fish. The northerly countries salted and smoked or wind-dried theirs. The seagoing Scandinavians, last of the Europeans to be converted to Christianity and the Catholic rules of fast-day fish eating, were the first to turn their ocean treasure into a negotiable asset as they built up their salt-cod trade throughout the Middle Ages. Each to his own.

BASIC PREPARATION

Scale, gut, and wipe, in that order, any fish to be cooked. Wipe the interior with salt to remove the blood. In the case of a large fish, take care to cut around the anus and remove it. Always rinse your hands and implements in *cold* water after preparing the fish, and there will be no trace of fishy smell on either. To cook a whole fish, put it into heavily salted water, bring the water to a boil, and remove from heat, leaving the fish to cool in the water. When the water has cooled to finger temperature, the fish will be perfectly cooked.

FISH SOUP

BOUILLABAISSE WITH SWEET PEPPER SAUCE

Bouillabaisse au rouille (France)

The city of Marseilles claims the *bouillabaisse* for its very own. And if the Greeks founded Marseilles, as its citizens believe, then the origin of the ambrosial soup must, they say again, lie in the kitchens of the gods. Venus herself is credited with the first hand on the soup pot. She is alleged to have brewed up the concoction one merry evening when she had a tryst with Mars and wished to put her blacksmith husband, Vulcan, to sleep during the assignation. A key ingredient in her recipe was saffron, long held to be a soporific about whose powers Alexander complained, somewhat later in the human time scale, when he found his army slumbering on a crocus-carpeted Turkish hillside.

The *bouillabaisse* is the fish soup carried to its ultimate. As prepared today in many restaurants of maritime Provence, it has left the uncertainties of the local fisherman's catch far behind. No longer is the scented broth, a blend of soup and stew, composed of whatever was wriggling in the bottom of the net after the saleable fish and crustaceans had been auctioned off. Nonetheless, *bouillabaisse* in any of its forms remains a superb and authentic Mediterranean coastal dish, as variable as any other and depending for its flavor on the cook's taste and the contents of the larder. It is named for the method of cooking—a *bouillon-abaisse* being broth rapidly boiled to reduce. For those of us dependent on cold-water northern fish as the principal ingredients, *bouillabaisse* cannot be made exactly as Venus prepared it. Yet the soup's ideal composition is not as rigidly circumscribed as the Marseillais would have the rest of us believe.

The dish is ancient, but it was not until Victorian times that the Marseilles version was adopted in more northerly ports such as London, where it was greeted with enthusiasm. William Makepeace Thackeray, the author of *Vanity Fair*, felt the subject worthy of a ballad.

The net to trap the ingredients is cast wide. Out there among the rock pools, the waves and tidal races, the banks and shoals and fishing grounds, who is to say what may swim in to grace the glory of coastal Provence?

Choose among:

- Sea perch (*rascasse*)
- Sea bass (*loup de mer*)
- Angler fish or monkfish (*baudroie*)
- Scorpion fish (*chapon*)—American equivalent: blue mouth, ocean perch, or redfish
- John Dory (*saint-pierre*)—American equivalent: *Zenopsis ocellata*
- Conger eel—American equivalent: *Conger oceanicus*
- Red mullet (*rouget*)—American equivalent: goatfish
- Red gurnard (*galinette*)—American equivalent: sea robin
- Wrasse (*rouquier*)—American equivalent: tautog or blackfish, cunner
- Whiting (*merlan*)—American equivalent: blue whiting, cusk, white and squirrel hake
- Weaver fish (*vive*)—American equivalent: scabbard fish
- Spiny lobster (also known as *langouste*, crawfish, and rock lobster: *Palinurus vulgaris*)—American equivalent: slipper or flat lobster, mantis shrimp
- Little shore crabs: stone crabs, rock, green, blue, oyster or pea crab and red crab.
- All manner of shrimp and prawns (*langoustine*, *squille*, *cigalle*, *crevette*, crayfish)
- Tuna, skate, small turbot, mackerel, bonito, and native crustaceans of a likely hue.

(Note the absence of mussels and clams)

Y I E L D : 7 to 8 participants is the minimum number for which to prepare a proper *bouillabaisse*, according to the great nineteenth-century authority on Provençal cooking, J. B. Reboul. The rule of thumb is to allow ½ to ¾ pound of fish per person, and 2 cups of water plus 1 tablespoon of olive oil per pound of fish. The rest of the ingredients would be on hand, with the exception perhaps of the soporific saffron, in the Provençal vegetable patch.

T I M E : 50 to 60 minutes

THE SOUP:

5   pounds mixed fish (including rascasse *or* sea perch—the one species vital to the dish)

3   medium-sized onions, or 2 onions and 1 leek

3   garlic cloves

2   large tomatoes

Fresh fennel and parsley, thyme (dried or fresh), and a curl of dried orange peel (fresh will do)

½   wine glass (about 6 tablespoons) of olive oil

2½ quarts fresh water (a glass or two of white wine can substitute for an equal amount of water)

6   strands of saffron

Salt and pepper

7 to 8 slices of dry bread (in Marseilles a stick of white bread, marette, *is baked specially for the purpose*)

THE ROUILLE (SWEET PEPPER SAUCE):
3   *garlic cloves*
½   *teaspoon salt*
3   *red peppers (or pimentos, well-drained from a tin)*
2   *slices of white bread (about 3 ounces)*
1   *small chili pepper (optional)*

You will need a large deep cooking pot, several plates, a draining spoon, a strainer, and a blender or a pestle and mortar for the *rouille*. Put the firm fish on one dish: on one side the spiny lobster and crustaceans, on the other the sea perch or *rascasse*, weaver fish, gurnard, eel, angler fish, and anything else that feels hard to the finger. Wash, scale, and gut the fish if necessary. Cut the larger fish into small-fish-sized pieces. Remove such heads and fins as are unaesthetic.

On another dish put the soft fish: sea bass, wrasse, John Dory, whiting, and whatever else you have that looks like a member of the group. Wash, scale, and gut the fish if necessary. Again, cut the larger fish into small-fish-sized pieces.

Peel and chop the onions and crush the garlic with a little salt. Pour boiling water over the tomatoes to loosen the skins. Peel and chop them.

If you have plenty of fish trimmings, simmer them in the cooking water for 20 to 30 minutes to extract their flavor and body. Strain before using.

Make the *rouille* before you start the cooking of the soup: Crush the garlic with the salt. Loosen the skins of the peppers by roasting them in a preheated 400°F oven for 15 minutes, or burning them over a direct flame. Peel. Soak the bread in a little water and then squeeze it dry. Pound all the ingredients together into a smooth paste, in a blender if you like. Transfer the scarlet sauce to a medium-sized bowl to wait for a ladleful or two of the hot fish soup.

Back to the soup. Find a large deep pot and put all the vegetables and the herbs in the base. Lay the crustaceans on this bed, and the firm-fleshed fish (all these from the first plate) over them. Sprinkle the olive oil over all. Cover with the water. Add the saffron, a teaspoon of salt, and a turn or two of the pepper mill. Cover the pot and bring it swiftly to a boil.

Meanwhile, put a soup tureen, deep soup plates, and a large serving dish in the hot oven to warm, and warn your eager guests that you will be ready in exactly 10 minutes.

Allow the broth to boil rapidly for 5 minutes. Then add the soft fish from the second plate. Bring swiftly back to a boil and continue boiling briskly, uncovered, for another 5 minutes.

Take the pot off the heat and gently remove the fish to the serving plate with a perforated spoon. Stir 1 cup of the hot fish broth into the *rouille*. Put the dry bread into the tureen and strain the soup over. Put both broth and fish on the table at the same time. Each diner needs a fork and spoon, a large napkin, and a plate for the little bones.

Pass the bowl of pungent scarlet *rouille* separately, with more bread, fresh this time, to accompany. Each guest eats as he pleases—soup with fish, soup then fish, whatever he wishes, with a glass of the good white wine of the Rhône at his elbow.

SUGGESTIONS

Pass around a bowl of *aïoli* (page 79) as well as the *rouille*. It may be gilding the lily, but it is worth it for the sake of the dramatic contrast between the fiery scarlet of the peppers and the soft gold of the *aïoli*.

Leftovers: Strain and use the soup as a fish stock to make a *bouillabaisse borgne*.

Put the *rouille* in a closed jar in the refrigerator for storage—it will last a week at least. Excellent with fish cakes and fish pie.

FISH SOUP WITH AÏOLI

Bourride (France)

Of all the fish soups, this is my favorite. It seems to embody the rich scents and colors of Provence: camomile meadows and clumps of reed grass hazed with tiny blue flowers; pearly tree trunks and the furry undersides of olive leaves; pink *aïoli*-scented flowering heads of the wild garlic, *Allium roseum*; flocks of goldfinches stripping the dry thistles; lazy swallowtail butterflies hanging on lavender flowers; and, beyond and below, the tumbling dark rocks and bright wavelets of the Mediterranean shore.

SERVES: 6

TIME: 45 to 50 minutes

THE SOUP:

3 pounds of whole fish (choose from: Monkfish, sea bass, whiting, small cod)	2½ quarts warm water (or replace an equal quantity of water with half a bottle of white wine)
1 onion	Salt and pepper
A bouquet of thyme, fennel, bay leaf, and a curl of dried or fresh orange peel	6 slices of dry bread
	4 egg yolks

THE AÏOLI

2 to 3 cups olive oil	Juice of 1 lemon
10 garlic cloves	1 tablespoon warm water
½ teaspoon salt	
1 to 2 egg yolks (depending on the size of the eggs)	

You will need a large cooking pot, a draining spoon, two bowls, a strainer, and a pestle and mortar or a blender. Cut the fish into thick, even-sized steaks, leaving the skin on if it suits you (the monkfish is usually skinned). Peel and chop the onion.

Make the sauce before you embark on the soup cooking. All the sauce ingredients should be at room temperature to allow them to emulsify properly. Pour the oil into a jug. Peel the cloves of garlic and put them into a bowl with the salt. Pound the garlic and salt together with a pestle until you have a thick paste. Pound in the egg yolk. In Provence you would have a small marble mortar for this job. Never ceasing to work the mixture, drip the oil in quite slowly. When you have added about 4 spoonfuls of oil, stir in the lemon juice and the water. Trickle in the rest of the oil, beating without pause. Watch carefully as the sauce thickens, and add a little more water if the emulsion shows signs of separating. The egg and the vegetable matter both act as emulsifiers of the oil: The making of a mayonnaise is a magical process. You can do the whole thing in a blender (use a whole egg)—but the sauce will have a lighter consistency.

Should such a disaster as the sauce splitting befall you, don't worry. It happens so frequently the French have a special phrase for its redress: *Relever l'aïoli.* Empty the split mixture out of the bowl, and put in another egg yolk and a few drops of lemon juice. Slowly add the split mixture to the fresh yolk. As surely as night follows day, it will thicken.

Back to the soup. Put a tureen, a serving dish, and some deep soup plates to heat in a preheated 300 F oven. When you start cooking the soup, it will be ready in no time.

Put the chopped onion and the aromatics in a roomy stewpan. Lay the fish steaks over them. Cover all with the warm water. Add a teaspoon of salt and a grind of the pepper mill. Bring all swiftly to a boil and cook for 10 minutes. Remove from the heat and take out the pieces of fish with a draining spoon. Put them on the warm serving dish and leave them in the turned-off oven while you finish the soup.

Put the slices of dry bread in the bottom of the tureen and sprinkle them with a ladleful of the fish broth. Leave them to soak. Now put half the *aïoli* into a deep bowl and then whisk in the yolks of egg. If the eggs are small, use one per person. Now whisk in a ladleful of the hot soup. Then whisk in another ladleful. Strain the rest of the soup into the bowl and whisk it in well. (This step can be successfully achieved in a blender). Rinse out the saucepan and pour the soup back in. Cook it over a low heat, stirring constantly with a wooden spoon, while it thickens. It is done when it masks the back of the wooden spoon. Take it off the heat. It must not boil, or the soup will become grainy. Pour the beautiful velvet broth over the bread in the tureen. Call your guests to the table.

Serve the soup and the fish at the same time, to be eaten simultaneously or consecutively as you please. Pass the rest of the *aïoli* around with a plentiful supply of fresh bread. Try a *vin gris*, the flinty-dry pinkish wine from the salt flats of the Bouches-du-Rhône, with the soup and complete the meal with a strawberry tart (page 446).

BASQUE FISH SOUP

Ttoro (France and Spain)

A fish stew-soup made with one fish only, this is probably the oldest of all of this family of soups. Basque fishermen were trawling for cod in distant Atlantic waters long before Leif Eriksson girded up his loins to tackle the northern ocean, and certainly centuries before Christopher Columbus acquired his first compass. The original *ttoro* was always made with salted cod heads, cut off when the fish were prepared for salting and kept as the fisherman's portion. The heads had no commercial value to the Basques' southern customers, the Spaniards. Fresh or salted, these heads made a nourishing strong soup, boiled up with onions and garlic and poured over slices of dry bread which had been sprinkled with oil. Cod cheeks are fine and sweet and are the carver's portion of the fish—boiled cod's head and shoulders was considered a great treat on the Victorian dinner table in England.

The Basques finally wearied of the long trek across the dangerous ocean when competition from better-equipped and -backed Portuguese fishermen, who were increasingly encroaching on the ancient fishing grounds, took over their lucrative salt-cod trade. Basque fishermen then turned their attention to home waters and the *ttoro's* cod was replaced by its close relative, the hake. Fresh hake is the fish which is now the one essential to the dish, and a hake-based *ttoro* remains the favorite supper of the Basque mariner home from the sea.

Over the years the soup has evolved and become regionalized. In recent times the Basque-New World connection was reestablished when many Basque woodsmen emigrated to Canada to find employment in the prosperous forestry industry. There they found plenty of Newfoundland cod to provide them with the staple for the original *ttoro*.

SERVES: 6

TIME: 30 minutes plus 1 hour cooking

4 *pounds whole fresh cod or hake, scaled and gutted, but with head and bones*	*Salt and peppercorns*
	½ *loaf of dry white bread*
	4 *tablespoons olive oil*
1 *pound onions*	*A good handful of fresh herbs:*
2½ *quarts water*	*parsley, thyme, chervil*
3 to 4 *bay leaves*	2 *garlic cloves*

You will need a large stewpot, a strainer, and a soup tureen. Wipe the fish inside and out and cut off the heads. Remove the flesh in thick fillets, cut them into bite-sized pieces, and put them aside. Peel and slice the onions. Put the bones and heads into a big saucepan and cover them with the water. Add the bay leaves, a teaspoon of salt, and a dozen peppercorns. Bring all to a boil and then turn down to simmer. Cook for ½ hour, uncovered, by which time the bones will have enriched the soup and the liquid will have reduced by a third. Remove the bones and add the onions. Bring back to the boil and then simmer for another ½ hour.

Cut the bread in cubes into a soup tureen and sprinkle them with the oil. Chop the herbs roughly, and scatter them over the bread. Crush the garlic under the blade of your knife, mash it up with ½ teaspoon salt and then scatter it over the bread. Lay the pieces of fish in the tureen, and add the boiling soup through a strainer. Cover and let the soup develop for 10 minutes while you set the table and call your guests.

Serve the *ttoro* in deep soup plates with more bread, a jug of wine, and a spoon and fork with which to tackle your soup-stew. You will need nothing else tonight, except perhaps a nugget of strong blue-veined Cabrales, a shepherd's goat cheese made in the mountains.

◆

SUGGESTIONS

3 egg yolks and ½ cup of cream may be stirred in at the end to thicken the soup (do not let it boil, or the eggs will curdle).

Fry the bread golden in the oil with the crushed garlic before you put it in the bottom of the soup tureen. But I like the taste of uncooked olive oil myself, on untoasted bread, so you will be on your own.

◆

FISH SOUP

Kakavia (Greece)

The *kakavia* is the pot in which the soup is prepared. The Greeks maintain this is the original *bouillabaisse*—and that it was their adventurous sailors who showed the world how to prepare a fish soup. The recipe, as with all fish soups, is quite rightly as varied as the catch in the fishermen's nets.

SERVES: 6

TIME: 20 minutes plus 40 minutes cooking

3	*pounds small fish—including a few rockfish such as sea perch*	1	*pound tomatoes (or a 1-pound can of tomatoes)*
2½	*quarts water*	6	*tablespoons olive oil*
	Salt and peppercorns	6	*thick-cut slices of bread*
1	*bay leaf*		*Juice of 1 lemon*
1	*pound onions*		

You will need a roomy saucepan, a large soup pot (a *kakavia* if you have it), and a strainer. Scale, gut, and wipe the fish. Remove the heads, and fillet those fish it is convenient to fillet. Put the fillets and larger pieces of fish aside. Put the trimmings and the very small bony fish in a roomy saucepan with the water, a teaspoon of salt, 6 whole peppercorns, and the bay leaf. Bring the water to a boil; then turn it down and simmer for 40 minutes uncovered.

Meanwhile, peel and slice the onions. Scald the tomatoes to loosen the skins; then chop them. Warm the oil in the bottom of the stew pot. Stir in the onions and fry them gently until they are transparent. Add the tomatoes. Leave to melt together until the fish stock is ready. Strain the stock into the soup pot over the tomato mixture. Add the uncooked pieces of fish and bring the soup to a boil. Turn the heat down and leave to simmer for 5 to 10 minutes, until the fish is well cooked but not broken up.

Toast the bread. In Greece this would be slices of dense-textured country bread charred on one of those primitive toasters which can be placed over a flame. Set out six bowls and put a slice of toast in each.

Carefully lift out the fish with a draining spoon. Divide it among the bowls. Stir the lemon juice into the soup and ladle the broth onto the fish and bread in the bowls. Put a plate of quartered lemons, a bowl of little black olives and radishes, and fresh bread on the table.

Drink plenty of retsina with it, followed by fresh fruit and white cheese. Finish with a little cup of strong Turkish coffee.

◆

SUGGESTIONS

This soup is meant to be flexible—embellish and add to it as you please. Try a few potatoes cooked in it before you add the fish.

Leftovers: Make a *psarosoupa avgolemono* (fish soup with egg and lemon). Strain the solids out of 1 quart of soup, and bring it to a boil with a handful of rice (about ⅓ cup). Simmer for 20 minutes until the rice is soft. Then stir a ladleful of the soup into 2 eggs beaten with the juice of a lemon (for 1 quart of soup). Off the heat, stir the soup-egg-lemon mix into the body of the soup. Serve without reboiling. Enough for 4.

◆

FISHERMAN'S STEW

Caldeirada (Portugal)

By the mid-sixteenth century the Portuguese were making inroads in the Far East, particularly in Japan, where they introduced "tempura" cooking—a method of coating small foods (the Portuguese used shrimp) in batter for frying which the Japanese adopted and adapted. Among the flavors with which the travelers returned was a taste for fresh coriander, the herb which not only looks like parsley, but appears in eastern recipes with quite as much frequency as parsley does in the west. It has a very distinctive flavor.

This fisherman's soup is as variable as his catch—which was usually obtained in the cold waters of the Atlantic. The ingredients are easier for Atlantic coastal dwellers to come by than those of its cousin, the Mediterranean *bouillabaisse*. There are no rules, only guidelines. It is the dish which the fishermen would cook for themselves on their long fishing trips. After the first catch, a little charcoal-burning brazier would be set up high in the bows of the vessel where it would be sheltered from the wind and spray. The soup would be cooked over the flame in a heavy iron pot.

S E R V E S : 8 to 10

T I M E : 20 minutes plus 30 to 40 minutes cooking

3	pounds mixed fish (ray, flounder, hake, cod, bass, eel, mullet—whatever is fresh and cheap)	2	garlic cloves
		½	cup olive oil
			Salt and pepper
1	pound squid	1	cup white wine
2	large onions	2	bay leaves
2 to 4	tomatoes, skinned	1	cup water
2	pounds (6 medium-sized) potatoes	1	pound (weighed on the shell) clams or mussels
1	small bunch of fresh coriander or parsley		

You will need a very large stew pot with a lid, and a ladle. Clean the white fish and then cut them into slices if large. Cut the eel into short lengths. Clean the squid: It has a beautiful clear bone, like plastic, which must be pulled out when you separate the tentacle body from the hollow body. Rinse the squid and cut the bunch of tentacles (which you keep) from the head and innards (which you discard). Pull off the freckled mauve outer membrane from the hollow body, and pick out as many as you can of the little sharp "toenails" with which the suckers of the tentacles are equipped. Slice the body into rings and the tentacles into short lengths.

Peel and slice the onions. Chop the tomatoes. Peel and slice the potatoes. Chop the herbs, and peel and chop the garlic. Find your largest and heaviest stewpan, and pour a little oil into the bottom.

Put the ingredients into the stewpan in layers, adding salt and pepper and sprinkling in the oil and wine as you go. Lay half the onion rings on the base, then the potato and the garlic, then half the tomatoes and a bay leaf, then the fish and the squid, then the herbs, then the rest of the tomato and the other bay leaf, finally the remaining onion. Pour the last of the oil over everything, then the wine, and the water. Bring to a boil, then turn it down. Stew very gently for 30 to 40 minutes, either in the oven (350 F) or on top of the stove. Push a knife into the center to see if everything, particularly the potato, is cooked and soft.

Meanwhile, rinse the clams or mussels in fresh running water. Lay them on top of the stew to open in the steam. When they have opened, it is ready.

Serve the stew with a large ladle, keeping the layers separate.

◆

SUGGESTIONS

Red and green peppers can be included. As can shrimps, scallops, or anything fishy and fresh.

The potatoes are not always present—they are sometimes replaced by slices of dry bread.

Crisp-fried anchovies or sardines, or fried-bread croutons, are sometimes served with this dish, laid alongside each portion.

Leftovers: Use to make *roupa velha de peixe*, fish hash—an excellent dish and quite as good as the original stew. Warm a little olive oil in a frying pan over gentle heat, and add the leftover stew. Bubble gently until all the liquid evaporates and the rest begins to fry. Continue frying until the base is dry and golden.

◆

PORTUGUESE FISH SOUP

Sopa de peixe (Portugal)

This soup, as prepared in a fisherman's wife's kitchen in one of the little fishing villages which bead the Algarve coast, has something of that ancient flavor, that concentration of boiled-down essences, which makes a true *pot-au-feu* unique. The basic soup is served from a big cauldron kept, like the *pot-au-feu*, at a constant simmer at the back of the stove. Small fresh fish from the day's catch are added to it as the boats come in. The bones and heads of the fish melt during the course of the long stewing, and a really good stock is so thick and gelatinous, it is almost sticky. The soup might well be as old as the pot in which it cooks.

SERVES: 6 to 8

TIME: 20 minutes plus 2 hours cooking

1 pound small fresh (preferably raw) shrimps	1 tablespoon paprika
3 pounds mixed small fish or pieces of larger ones	2 quarts water
	2 bay leaves
2 large onions	Salt and peppercorns
4 garlic cloves	2 crusts of dry coarse white bread (brown will do)
3 red and/or green peppers	
½ cup olive oil (Portuguese if you can get it)	

You will need a large stewpan and a strainer. Pick over the shrimps. Scale and gut the fish. Leave on their heads and do not bone them. Peel and chop the onions and the garlic very fine. Scorch the skins of the peppers (this makes it possible to peel them) by holding them on a fork over a gas flame or singeing them on an electric stove ring (charred pepper has a spicy pungent aroma with a splendid nostalgia value). Skin the scorched peppers and cut them into small squares.

The Portuguese, unlike all other Mediterranean olive-growing nations, allow their olives to ferment a little before they press them—their olive oil thus has a quite distinctive flavor. Warm the oil in a heavy pot—do not overheat. Add the onions, garlic, peppers, and shrimps. Stew them in the oil for a few minutes. Mash to release the flavors. Add the paprika and then the fish. Cover with the water and add the bay leaves, a little salt, and a few peppercorns. Stew gently, uncovered, on minimal heat for at least 2 hours. More water may be needed, but add sparingly. When the fish is thoroughly pulped, crumble the bread crusts, scatter them over the top, and then stir them in—they will absorb most of the paprika-tinted oil on the surface. Press the soup through a wide-meshed sieve—you aim to achieve an unctuous, dark soup clouded with strands of fish, thick and smooth.

Serve the soup in deep plates, very hot, with plenty of bread and quarters of lemon to be squeezed in by those who wish. Accompany with a salad, a few fried fish, fresh fruit, and a piece of *toucinho do celo* (page 226) to complete your dinner.

BASQUE TUNA-AND-TOMATO STEW

Marmitako (Spain)

Tuna and its smaller cousin the bonito are the prize catch of the Basque fisherman. This stew is considered at its best made aboard the fishing vessel itself, with the well-flavored tail section of the fish. Mackerel is sometimes substituted. The dish takes its name from the iron kettle used for the stew.

SERVES: 5 to 6

TIME: 30 minutes plus 20 to 25 minutes cooking

2	pounds fresh tuna or mackerel	1	dried red pepper, 1 fresh one, or
	Salt		1 teaspoon paprika
1	large Spanish onion	½	wine glass of olive oil
2 to 4	garlic cloves	1	pound old potatoes
1	pound tomatoes (or a 1-pound can of tomatoes)	2	cups water
½	pound green peppers	¼	teaspoon cayenne pepper

You will need a deep soup pot. Skin and bone the fish and cut it into bite-sized chunks; salt lightly and put aside. Peel and chop the onion. Peel and crush the garlic. Pour boiling water over the tomatoes and skin them—or not if you don't mind those little shipwreck-spars of tomato skin. Seed and chop the green and red peppers.

Pour the olive oil into the soup pot and put it on medium heat. Throw in the onion and the garlic, and let them fry for a few moments, until they turn opaque. Add the peppers and let them fry. Add the tomatoes and the paprika if you are using it, and simmer for 15 to 20 minutes, until all is reduced to a thick sauce (if you have a jar of *letcho* (page 21), you can use it instead).

Meanwhile, peel and slice the potatoes. Add them to the tomato stew along with the 2 cups water. Cover and cook until the potatoes are soft—about 15 minutes. Then mash a few of the potatoes into the soup to thicken it, and stir in the cayenne pepper. Lay the fish pieces gently in the stew. Cover the pot again and allow the fish to simmer for 5 to 10 minutes. Taste, and add salt if necessary.

Serve in deep soup plates and make sure there is plenty of bread on the table. A salad and a piece of Manchego cheese or the fresh Queso de Burgos could follow. A strong red wine from Rioja can stand up to this dish with grace.

WHITE FISH

FISH PUDDING

Fiskepudding (Norway)

There are *fiskematbutikks* in most Norwegian seaside towns which sell minced fish. Very often it is all they sell and it is quite excellent too—not ground-up bits and pieces of discards from the catch, but fresh haddock, pike, or young cod. The minced fish is sold either raw as *fiskefarse* or cooked as *fiskeboller*, *fiskepudding*, or *fiskekaker*. In any of its forms it is a delicious and interesting dish—a kind of fish hamburger.

Until recently Norwegian housewives made their own *fiskepudding*, and everyone knew that *their* mother made the best in the country. She served it on feast days and holidays with her own beautiful cream-and-shrimp sauce. The dish is much like those delicate soufflés and quenelles which are the pride of the French kitchen. Simplicity and clarity of flavor are its chief delights. Unlike the French version, no eggs are included: In peasant recipes eggs are rarely used in conjunction with other forms of protein. There is also an interesting similarity of ingredients and method to the French salt-cod dish *brandade de morue*.

The basis of the following three recipes is minced and pounded *fiskefarse*. A Norwegian grandmother would have rolled her sleeves up her brawny arms and pounded her fish in a marble mortar—so large and heavy it stood on the floor and required a waist-high pestle. A food processor provides the perfect modern muscle. The potato or flour are not essential, but they do help the mixture stick together and remain juicy. The fish and the cream, or rich fresh milk, are the only required ingredients—a very simple recipe indeed.

Well-to-do households with access to a merchant would use half a tea-spoonful of powdered mace or nutmeg to spice the mixture. The Scandinavian seafaring nations had better access to such luxuries than most peasant communities through their active involvement in the salt-cod trade. Excellent cream, butter, and milk remain widely available today. Peasant farmers in Scandinavia kept, and still keep, milk cows: Hay to feed the beasts is often the only crop harvested in the more northerly farms above the Arctic Circle.

SERVES: 4

TIME: 30 minutes plus 1 hour cooking

THE PUDDING:

1 pound filleted fish (haddock or pike is best, although cod and salmon are good too; do not use frozen fish as that will result in a watery pudding)	½ teaspoon salt ½ teaspoon pepper ½ teaspoon ground mace or nutmeg (optional) 1 cup light cream
1 tablespoon flour or 1 medium-sized potato, mashed (optional)	Milk 4 ounces (½ cup) unsalted butter

THE SAUCE:
½   teaspoon flour
1   cup fresh or sour cream
¼   pound small peeled shrimps

Preheat the oven to 375 F.

You will need a food processor, or a blender, or a pestle and mortar, a small baking dish or casserole, plus a dish to stand it in, and a small saucepan.

Skin the fillet by gripping the tail end and running a sharp knife held at an angle away from you between the flesh and the skin. Discard the skin. Remove any remaining bones (pike in particular are full of tiny sharp filaments).

Chop the fish flesh roughly and put it in a food processor or blender. (Should you possess neither, you will have to follow the Norwegian grandmother's example.) Mince the fish thoroughly with a fork to make the *fiskefarse*. Stir the flour or mashed potatoe with the salt and a little milk, and continue to process as you add the cream, mace, and pepper, beating until you have a light doughy mixture. You may need a little more liquid. Beat hard, either in the processor or with a wooden spoon. The more air you include, the lighter the mixture. Beat it some more.

Butter a baking dish and pour the mixture in—a *fiskefarse* should be used as fresh as possible. Cover with foil, stand the dish in a baking tray full of hot water, and bake the pudding for 45 to 55 minutes.

Test to see if it is cooked by running a skewer into the center of the pudding. When it comes out clean, the pudding is ready. Run a knife round the sides and turn the pudding onto a hot plate.

Serve with a jug of melted butter and floury boiled potatoes cooked with dill, dried on the heat, and tossed with more chopped dill. Or prepare a sauce made with shrimps and cream: Stir the flour into the cold cream in a small saucepan, bring it to a boil, and simmer for 3 to 4 minutes to cook the flour. Add the shrimps—they will cook immediately.

SUGGESTIONS

Use the mixture to make *fiskekaker*, small fish cakes which are sold hot like doughnuts in Norway's *fiskematbutikks*. Form the mix into little flat cakes (you will need to make it a little more solid), and fry them gently until golden in butter for 6 to 7 minutes a side. Do not flour the cakes. Serve them with a sauce of melted butter. Particularly good if you fry a few chopped slices of bacon in the saucing butter.

Use the mixture to make *fiskeboller*, delicious little morsels of fish, very much like French quenelles. Form the mixture into dumplings with two wet teaspoons and drop them into simmering salted water. They will take about 10 minutes if they are quite small. Sauce them as for the *fiskepudding*. A Norwegian friend of mine remembers being given these to nibble like sweets when, as a small girl, she went shopping with her mother.

Stuff the *fiskefarse* mixture into sausage casings, tie them into lengths, and poach them in simmering water for 20 to 25 minutes. Serve with a cream sauce, perhaps on a bed of spinach.

Mushrooms, particularly dried wild ones, or green peppercorns, can replace the shrimps in the cream sauce.

Prepare a green vegetable to accompany: spinach, peas, or lightly cooked zucchini.

Use any fresh herb or a spoonful of chopped onion instead of dill to dress the potatoes.

Serve with rice instead of potatoes. The Scandinavians are very fond of imported rice, and rice pudding is traditional Christmas fare.

Leftovers: Fish pudding can be sliced and reheated gently in a cream sauce. It will almost be better than the first time round.

Squares of pudding are delicious poached in a clear fish soup made with the trimmings of the fish boiled with herbs and an onion.

COD'S TAIL

Gestoofde kabeljauwstaart (Holland)

This is the most popular way of serving the best part of the cod. The tailmeat on a fresh cod is pure white and firm with an incomparable flavor.

S E R V E S : 4 to 5

T I M E : 10 minutes plus 30 minutes cooking

One 2-pound piece of cod tail	Pepper
Salt	2 ounces (4 tablespoons) butter,
2 pounds (10) small potatoes	diced

You will need a heatproof casserole with a lid. Wipe the fish and sprinkle it with salt. Scrub the potatoes and slice them. Put them in a casserole and pour in enough water to barely cover. Season with salt and pepper, and bring to a boil.

Put the cod tail on top of the potatoes so that it can cook in the steam. Scatter the butter over the fish. Cover tightly and cook the casserole either in a preheated 350°F oven or on top of the stove on gentle heat for 30 minutes. The result is simplicity and perfection, depending on the excellence of the raw materials.

SUGGESTION

Leftovers: Make a fish pie: Mix any leftover fish with a white sauce flavored with parsley and chopped hard-boiled egg, season well, and put in a baking dish. Cover with the remains of the potatoes, well mashed with butter and milk. Dot with butter. Bake in a 350°F oven for 20 minutes, to heat through and gild the top.

COD WITH BEER

Morue à la flamande (Belgium)

This is an excellent combination, and entirely proper to the seaside dwellers of Belgium, as this recipe features two of their prime ingredients.

SERVES: 4 to 5

TIME: 20 minutes plus 25 minutes cooking

2	*pounds cod fillets*	1	*bay leaf*
½	*teaspoon salt*	1	*cup strong lager (pale beer)*
	Pepper	½	*cup fresh bread crumbs*
1	*pound onions*		*Butter to finish*
2	*ounces (4 tablespoons) butter*		

Preheat the oven to 400°F. You will need a frying pan and a casserole.

Skin the cod fillets with a sharp knife, starting from the tail end and gripping the skin firmly with one hand. Season the fillets with the salt and some freshly ground pepper. Peel and slice the onions. Fry them in the butter in a frying pan. Pour in the beer and bay leaf, heat, and boil fiercely for a few minutes to evaporate the alcohol. Your nose will tell you when this is done. Pour into a casserole and lay the fish fillets on top. Scatter a layer of bread crumbs (fresh, not dried—they do not give the same result) over the top. Dot with more butter.

Bake for 20 to 25 minutes, until the fish is cooked and the topping is crisp. This is a delicious dish with its traditional accompaniment of young hop shoots, boiled with salt and served with butter. As a substitute for hop shoots, use baby green beans, blanched in boiling salted water for no more than 2 minutes.

SALT-COD CASSEROLE

Cazuela de bacalao (Spain)

Choose a clean white salt cod (not a yellow-tinged one) and wash it thoroughly. Soak for 24 hours in cold water, changing the water several times. If the fish is particularly large, it may need an extra day. Poke it with your finger and taste to see if it is sufficiently desalted. If so, drain the cod. It is now ready to be cooked. Salt cod is perfect with tomatoes and potatoes. In the peasant kitchen the most usual method of preparation is in a soup-stew—using the salt cod in place of fresh fish or meat to give substance and body.

Variations of this dish are eaten all around the Mediterranean. The soup is flavored with the herbs of the maquis (rosemary, thyme, and fennel, which grows tall and feathery all summer) and enriched with olive oil. It cooks best in an earthenware casserole which has been tempered to withstand direct heat. An enamel pot or roomy saucepan will serve almost as well. It is homely but classic fare which has comforted many an empty-handed fisherman—and indeed a full-handed one too, since the salt cod is often preferred to the fresh.

SERVES: 6

TIME: Start 24 hours before; 30 minutes plus 30 minutes cooking

*1½ pounds salt cod (2 pounds fresh
     fish can be used instead—see
     Suggestions)*
2   large onions
3   garlic cloves
½   cup olive oil
*1   pound tomatoes (or a 1-pound
     can of tomatoes)*

*2   pounds (6 medium-sized)
     potatoes*
*1   sprig of thyme and 1 sprig of
     rosemary*
1   bay leaf
About 1 quart water
*1   pound greens: spinach or Swiss
     chard*

You will need a deep casserole or a large stew pot. Soak the salt cod in several changes of water for 24 hours at least.

Drain and dry the cod and chop it into bite-sized pieces. Do not skin the fish—but do remove all visible bones.

Skin and slice the onions and the garlic. Heat the olive oil gently in a deep casserole or stew pot. Put in the onions and the garlic, and soften them for a few minutes. They should not take color. Add the tomatoes, skinned and roughly chopped. Raise the heat and boil hard for 5 minutes more, uncovered.

Peel the potatoes and cut them into thick slices.

Turn down the heat under the casserole and lay the salt cod on top of the tomato sauce mixture. Chop the herbs and sprinkle them over. Tuck in the bay leaf. Then lay on the potatoes. Add enough water to cover to a depth of two fingers. No salt—the cod has plenty of its own. Bring to a boil and then lower to a simmer. Leave to cook gently for 25 minutes, by which time the cod and the potatoes should be soft. Chop or prepare the green vegetable you have chosen. Add it at the end. Five minutes more will be enough to cook it. Serve the soup-stew in deep bowls and eat with a spoon and fork.

To mop up the soup, you will need good bread, best of all a loaf of your own making. The Spanish *pan de campo* (page 403) or a Greek country bread spiked with olives (page 410) is ideal.

Have on hand a chilled bottle of young red wine to wash the meal down. Fresh fruit and a piece of cheese to finish.

You can use fresh cod. It will be good, but will not give the same gelatinous texture to the stew. Fillet the fish and cut it into squares. Add it last so that it cooks for only 5 minutes. You will need to add salt.

Red or green peppers can be included at the beginning—fry them lightly in the olive oil first.

Leftovers: Reheat and at the last moment stir in a tablespoonful of fresh herbs (parsley, oregano, marjoram, fennel leaves) chopped finely with a clove of garlic.

Or reheat and serve with a bowl of bread-cube croutons fried with a little chopped bacon. They should be so hot that they sizzle when you add them to the soup.

SALT COD AND SCRAMBLED EGGS

Balcalhau e ovos (Portugal)

The Portuguese have been preserving fish since at least the first millennium B.C. Prehistoric fish-salting tanks have been discovered at many sites on Portugal's coast, and the Romans' favorite condiment, *garum*, a strong fermented fish paste, was exported to Rome in enormous quantities during the days of the Empire. Later, these same salting centers provisioned the mariner-explorers, and salt cod became a major trade item—in particular with Brazil, then a Portuguese colony.

The combination of eggs and salt cod is a very popular dish in the home country. Today salt cod has become a rather expensive ingredient—the following recipe makes it go further and produces one of the best and simplest of this range of dishes.

SERVES: 6

TIME: Start the day before; 40 to 50 minutes

1 pound salt cod (or 2 pounds fresh cod, plus 1 teaspoon salt)	¼ pound ripe black olives
	8 eggs
2 pounds (6 medium-sized) potatoes	*Pepper*
1 pound onions	1 cup olive oil
3 garlic cloves	

You will need two to three bowls and a deep frying pan. Soak the *bacalhau* in several changes of water for 24 hours at least.

Peel and slice the potatoes as for french fries. Peel and slice the onions and the garlic. Pit the olives. Beat the eggs together lightly. Season with a turn or two of the pepper mill—you are unlikely to need extra salt since both the *bacalhau* and the olives will have been well brined.

When the *bacalhau* is well soaked (poke it and lick your finger to test for saltiness—some fish need longer than others), drain it and pat it dry. Remove the skin and bones (toss them into your cauldron of fish soup), and flake it into large pieces. If using fresh cod: skin, bone, fillet, and flake it.

Heat the olive oil in a deep frying pan. Fry the chips until soft. Drain and put aside in a roomy bowl. Pour half the oil out of the pan and reserve it. In the remaining oil, fry the onions and the garlic. Drain them and add them to the chipped potatoes. Drop the *bacalhau* into the hot oil and continue to fry for 10 minutes (add some more oil if it looks too dry). Take out the *bacalhau* and put it with the vegetables. Put back 2 tablespoons of the remaining oil and stir in the eggs. Scramble them gently until creamy, and then stir in the fish and potatoes, onions and olives.

Serve in their own pan with plenty of fresh bread and a simple salad—perhaps thinly sliced raw peppers, or tomato and onion. My own favorite is made with the big juicy Mediterranean tomatoes, sliced and dressed with a trickle of olive oil, a little sugar, freshly ground pepper, and a sprinkling of chopped garlic.

SUGGESTIONS

Substitute smoked haddock for the *bacalhau*.

Some cooks prefer to bake this dish in a preheated 350°F oven for 30 minutes, without the eggs, but after the potatoes and onions have been cooked through. The eggs, hard-cooked and quartered, are added at the end as a garnish.

SALT-COD FRITTERS

Bakalarios (Greece)

The much-traveled salt cod, named *bakalarios* in Greece, is often prepared well soaked, drained, boned, and cut into bite-sized pieces which are dipped into batter and then deep-fried until golden. Alternatively, use this more sophisticated recipe which, as in the previous recipe, makes the expensive commodity go further.

SERVES: 5 to 6

TIME: Start the day before; 30 to 40 minutes (with an hour or two rest period)

1	pound salt cod (or 2 pounds fresh cod, plus 1 teaspoon salt)	2	ounces hard cheese
1	pound (3 medium-sized) potatoes	2	tablespoons parsley
½	cup milk		All-purpose flour
2	eggs		Bread crumbs
Pepper			Oil for frying

You will need two saucepans and a frying pan. Soak the cod for 24 hours in several changes of water. Put it in a saucepan and bring it to a boil in fresh water. Simmer it for 10 minutes; then drain it and mash it with a fork. Peel and then boil the potatoes in salted water until soft. Drain and mash them well with the milk.

Separate one of the eggs and reserve the white. Beat the yolk and the other egg into the fish mixture. Beat in the mashed potatoes. Add freshly ground pepper—you are not likely to need extra salt. Grate the cheese and stir it in. Stir in the well-chopped parsley. Leave the mixture to firm up in the refrigerator for an hour or two.

Form the mixture into croquettes and roll them first in flour, then in the egg white, and then in the bread crumbs. Put the oil on to heat. When it is smoking faintly blue, slide in the croquettes and fry them crisp.

Serve with bread and a generous bowl of *skordalia* (page 56). This is a proper food for the wide-ranging Greeks and one of their best-loved dishes.

◆

PURÉE OF SALT COD

Brandade de morue (France)

By the early Middle Ages, salt cod was already one of the main imports of the countries of southern Europe. Much cheaper than dried or smoked meat, it provided winter food for the poor, both urban and rural, and a Lenten diet for the rich. From the seventeenth century onwards, *brandade de morue* became a feast dish for all, particularly at Easter. It seems to have appeared first in the Languedoc—one of the few areas where cows rub shoulders with olive trees. However, the Norwegian cream-and-pounded-fish *fiskefarse* recipes are near enough in spirit to suggest that the Nordic purveyor of the delicacy might have given a few culinary hints to his customers, particularly in the matter of the inclusion of the cream, a Scandinavian staple. *Brandade* is eaten all over France, from Brittany to Nice, although today it is usually commercially prepared. It is basically a rich "dip."

This *brandade* recipe comes from the Farnoux family, who live deep in olive country in the hills of Provence. M. Farnoux inherited his olive mill from his father—who in turn inherited the ancient press from his own father. There has been an olive mill in the same little village for five centuries at least. There may well have been a mill there since the Romans built their amphitheater and spa at neighboring Vaison-la-Romaine.

M. Farnoux' hometown of Nyons is famous for its olives. Groves of the ancient trees, said to take thirty years to grow, thirty years to mature, and thirty years to die, flash silver leaves on every surrounding hillside. The harvest begins in November when the Farnoux' great wooden corkscrew press works far into the night crushing green juice from ripe fruit. Speed is essential—a few hours' delay and the fruit will ferment. Then the oil will not settle into that beautiful golden *huile vierge* which is used in the family recipe for *brandade de morue*. Mme. Farnoux' neighbor makes her *brandade* without the milk—she feels this is the more truly Provençal version of the dish.

SERVES: 6 to 8

TIME: Start the day before; 1 hour

2	pounds salt cod (or 3½ pounds fresh cod, plus 1 teaspoon salt)	1 to 2	garlic cloves
6	peppercorns	1	cup milk or cream
2	bay leaves	½	teaspoon pepper
2	cups extra virgin olive oil (it is worth getting the best for this dish)		

You will need two to three saucepans and a blender or a food processor. Soak the salt cod for 24 hours, changing the water at least four times. The fish will smell unpleasant, but persevere—at least the odor will not be as bad as that of its Scandinavian cousin, the *lutefisk*, which needs 10 days' soaking. Fresh cod needs no such preparation.

Drain the softened fish and cut it into large pieces. Put the fish (if fresh, with the added salt), the peppercorns, and the bay leaves into a pan of cold water, and bring it gently to a boil. Skim the water and then turn down the heat. Poach the cod for 10 minutes only—it must not be allowed to overcook. Drain thoroughly. Remove the bones but leave the skin on. This gives more body to the dish—and a rather pretty peppered appearance from the gray flecks of skin.

Put the oil into one small saucepan with the garlic (crushed), and the milk or cream into another. Warm the two liquids until the heat is only just bearable to your finger.

In the old days you would now have had to *brander*, or crush, the fish with the oil and the milk or cream until they formed a smooth emulsion, a time-consuming activity which would have had the advantage of sharpening your appetite and building your muscles. The electric blender offers a welcome alternative.

Put the pieces of cooked cod, still hot, straight into a blender or food processor. Using the machine on a medium speed, add the warm oil and garlic alternately with the equally warm milk or cream. Do not allow the liquids to cool or overheat—if the mixture is too hot, it will curdle, but can be revived by further beating. A last resort is the addition of a pounded boiled potato. When ready, the *brandade* will be a thick, creamy purée much like mashed potatoes. Season with freshly ground black pepper. More salt should not be necessary.

Serve with slices of bread, rubbed first with garlic and then fried golden in olive oil, and a salad to accompany—perhaps tomatoes dressed with oil and a sprinkling of sugar and black pepper, or a plain green salad tossed with oil and vinegar and little chopped raw onion, or a salad of baby green beans, cooked for 3 minutes only in boiling water and dressed with oil and vinegar while still hot. A bowl of black olives is appropriate on the side.

SUGGESTIONS

Leftovers: Serve the gently reheated *brandade* in deep-fried day-old bread rolls which have had their insides scooped out to make a hollow cup. If it splits and you cannot beat it back to a cream, add the mixture to a hot mashed boiled potato.

Reheat in little precooked pastry cases (with care—do not overheat). Use the savory pastry recipe on page 324. Serve as a first course.

Reheat and serve with crudités—fresh raw vegetables cut into short lengths for dipping. Raw carrots cut into sticks, baby turnips washed and quartered, baby raw beans, sticks of cucumber and celery, raw baby artichokes—any vegetables that are young, crisp, and fresh.

Beat the leftover *brandade* into an equal quantity of mashed potato, add a beaten egg to bind, and fry in hot oil in spoonfuls. Serve with a fresh tomato sauce (page 153).

TROUT AND SALMON

TROUT IN SOUR CREAM
Ørret og Rømme (Norway)

Norway's many lakes and streams are well stocked with little mountain trout and rosy-flanked char. Sweet-fleshed and delicious, they are at their best when fried in fresh butter with the blue water-bloom still on them. Sour cream, pale and thick and brought down, in the old days, from the upland summer farms, should be the basis of the sauce to accompany them.

SERVES: 1

TIME: 10 to 15 minutes

1 *fish weighing at least 10 ounces before cleaning (or, if smaller, 2 for each person)*	2 *tablespoons sour cream*
	2 *tablespoons water*
	Pepper
Salt	
1 *ounce (2 tablespoons) unsalted butter*	

You will need a frying pan large enough to accommodate the trout. The fish is best if prepared as soon as it is caught. Gut it and wipe out the cavity, although not the fish itself, with a little salt.

Melt the butter in a frying pan. When it foams, add the fish. Brown swiftly, turning once. Pour the sour cream and the water around it, add salt and freshly ground pepper, and let the fish simmer for 10 minutes, turning once.

This dish is particularly good served with wild mushrooms, such as apricot-yellow chanterelles, fried in butter and cooked with the fish. Little new potatoes boiled in their jackets, sweet as nuts (and called almond potatoes by the Norwegians), go beautifully with the fish.

◆

OATMEALED TROUT OR HERRINGS

(Scotland)

This dish can be prepared with either of Scotland's two favorite fish. Highland burn trout, in the view of the Scots, are the best in the world. There are still those who practice the old art of tickling or "guddling" to catch them. Rising early, when the first violet light streaks the sky above the moor, the fishermen go down to the stream, spot a trout lying close to the bank in the shallows, and slide their hand into the water behind its tail. With immense care and patience, they move their fingers forward until they are cupping the fish's belly. Then they grip the trout and swiftly lift it out. Only the wiliest old fish knows the tickling fingers are not fronds of weed.

TIME: 15 minutes

1   *trout or 2 herrings per person*
1   *tablespoon fine oatmeal per fish*
½   *teaspoon salt per fish*
1   *tablespoon butter per fish*

You will need a large heavy frying pan. If you are preparing trout, rinse and gut but do not wipe the fish, and then roll it in the oatmeal. If it is herrings, scale, gut, and behead the fish, split them in half down the back, and lift out the backbone. Pat dry and then roll each fish in the oatmeal.

Put a heavy iron frying pan on the heat, and sprinkle in the salt. You will need no extra fat to fry if you put the fish in the pan onto the *hot* salt and keep shaking the pan so that the fish does not stick.

You could also grill the fish, but then you would need to dot it with butter or bacon fat. The oatmeal coating is delicious and filling, particularly when served with mustard and a hot buttered oatcake. This is excellent as a light lunch or supper, or as a sturdy breakfast dish for a frosty morning.

◆

BLUE TROUT

Forelle blau (Germany)

Germany is well served for fish: The mountain streams of the Alps yield fine trout and char, while the clear waters of the Baltic provide a plentiful harvest of herring, mackerel, and flatfish. The technique of "blue-cooking," when the fresh fish is either doused with vinegar just before cooking or is cooked in a vinegar-spiked liquor, is a major contribution to European fish cookery—there is no better way to prepare perfectly fresh trout. Whether the technique is of French or German origin is difficult to judge—across the centuries the boundaries of the two countries have ebbed and flowed as freely as the rivers which cross their modern frontiers.

The trout must be as freshly caught as possible. Best of all, it should be still alive when it reaches the cook's hand. If so, bang its head sharply against the table to stun it. Gut the fish and wipe out the cavity with salt. Do not wash the skin or wipe off its natural bloom; it is this delicate veil which brings a blue blush to the cooked trout.

TIME: 15 to 20 minutes

1   *medium-sized trout per person*
1   *tablespoon wine vinegar or cider vinegar per trout*

You will need a large saucepan. Bring a pan of water to a boil. Douse the fish with vinegar before you slip it into the boiling water. If the fish is very fresh, it will stiffen and curl immediately. Bring the water back to a boil—allow one thumping bubble, and then turn off the heat. Depending on size, leave the fish in the water for 5 to 10 minutes; it will be cooked when the eyes are white and the fin pulls easily from the flesh.

Accompany with a sauceboat of very lightly browned butter—make it with sweet butter. (German butter is not salted.) Serve with plain-boiled potatoes dressed with chopped dill or fennel.

◆

SUGGESTIONS

Any small or medium-sized fresh fish can be cooked in this manner. Cook mackerel "blue" and serve with a fruit sauce—stewed gooseberries, cranberries, or red currants. This is a dish from the Baltic coast of Germany.

To serve the trout cold, allow it to cool in its liquor (do not serve it refrigerated—only sorbets and ice creams are good ice cold). I find trout too rich for a mayonnaise. It is much nicer with a horseradish sauce, made with whipped cream soured with a little vinegar, into which you fold grated horseradish—the proportion being 1 tablespoon of horseradish to ½ cup of heavy cream.

Note: Hatchery trout are often pink because they have been fed paprika which contains carotene, a substance found in shrimps, the natural prey of the sea trout. This turns their flesh the rose hue of salmon. Carotene also provides the pigment which tints flamingos pink—zoo birds quickly turn pale when deprived of their diet of shrimp and have to be fed paprika or carrot.

◆

CURED SALMON

Gravlaks (Norway)

The ancient Scandinavians evolved a variety of ingenious ways to take culinary advantage of a climate where the ground is frozen for half the year. Those who lived on the seashore found wind-drying, supplemented later by salting, the easiest and most satisfactory method of fish preserving. Inland, without the benefit of the sea breezes, the country people took to burying their perishables, particularly their fish—a logical development given a landscape which is one huge potential cold store.

Some of the more northerly groups buried cheese and the crock with the aquavit as well. Today a cured leg of mutton—fenalår—is a favorite standby in the pantry: The mutton is salted and left for some weeks before it is hung up to dry in a cold room. In the old days, as still happens in some country districts, this would have been either in the outside *stabbur* or in the attic.

The most original product of Scandinavia is probably "fermented" fish.

Pike, char, perch, and best of all, trout and salmon have long been subjected to the universal deep freeze. *Gravlaks*—buried or "grave" salmon—is the direct modern descendant, and is now becoming increasingly popular outside Scandinavia. The *gravlaks* method is one of the most ancient and primitive of all, not even requiring a cooking fire. There is a record of its use in a manuscript of 1348, and the technique is almost certainly thousands of years older still. It evolved originally as a way of preserving the catch when the fishermen were far from home. The fish, sandwiched between two layers of birch bark and fir branches weighted down with stones, was buried in a hole dug out of the soft sandy shore. It could either be eaten after 4 to 6 days or allowed to lie for 6 to 12 weeks, during which time the flesh fermented.

Raw fish prepared by the *gravlaks* method rivals any Japanese delicacy. Today most fish is fermented for a relatively short time and mechanical refrigeration has replaced the natural icebox. This recipe comes courtesy of Dr. Astri Riddervold of Oslo. She says the weighing is important because precise measurements allow you to use less salt, and also that the inclusion of a small quantity of good alcohol improves the flavor without toughening the fish.

YIELD: ¼ pound prepared fish serves 1

TIME: Start 3 to 4 days before; 40 minutes

6- to 7-pound (or even bigger) whole fresh or deep-frozen salmon	2 soupspoons (1½ ounces) rock salt
	1 soupspoon (¾ ounce) sugar
	Pepper
1 liquor glass of brandy (optional)	1 good bunch of fresh dill

You will need a large china plate, foil, a board, and a weight. Cut off the head and tail of the fish, and carefully remove the intestines and the blood. Remove the gut string by cutting a circle around the anus. Take care not to press out the contents. Do not wash the fish, but wipe it well with a paper towel.

Cut out the bone, leaving two sides with the skin on. Sprinkle the flesh with the brandy.

Mix the salt and the sugar and a good helping of freshly ground pepper. Scatter the mixture over the fillets. Put one of them skin side down on the china plate. Roughly chop the dill and spread it over. Place the other fillet on top of the first, skin side up, head to tail, sandwiching the dill between them. Cover the salmon with foil and put a weight on top—a 1-pound can on a carving board is about right.

Leave it in a cool place. The temperature is important: It should be about 38° to 40°F. The vegetable compartment of a refrigerator with the thermostat set in the middle range can be used. A clean, dry, and cool storeroom in the cellar with the right temperature is preferable. You aim to achieve ground temperature in the early months of a Scandinavian winter.

Turn the fillets twice a day and pour the pressed-out liquid back between the fillets. Remove the weights after two days. The *gravlaks* will be ready in 3 to 4 days, and no further preparation is needed. Serve it cut in very thin slices, sprinkled with more pepper and chopped dill.

Accompany the *gravlaks* with rye bread and butter, and potato salad dressed with dill. Or serve with that other excellent product of the Scandinavian peasant kitchen, flat bread, today still sometimes home-baked and rolled as fine as brown paper (page 419). Add a bowl of floury boiled potatoes, cubed and tossed with sour cream. Wash it down with good light beer and a swallow of aquavit to sharpen the tastebuds. To finish, if they are in season, a bowl of fresh berries—blueberries, raspberries, wild strawberries or, best of all in Scandinavia, the delicious cloudberries (like plump golden raspberries but with a faint flavor of pine needles) which grow wild on the arctic moors and need the midnight sun to ripen them.

Serve the berries with sour cream or *seter rømme*, a thick cream which used to be home-soured at a *seter*, or summer mountain farm, where the cattle were, and in places still are, pastured in fields of purple cranesbill, egg-yolk yellow vetch, and sweet meadow grasses. No sugar is necessary. That is kept for the delicate syrups and wild berry jams which are stored for the winter. For the rest of us who have no direct access to the heather- and silver birch-clad uplands beyond the Arctic Circle, the Finns make a cloudberry liqueur which is exported widely. It has echoes of the real thing, and a glass of it to follow such a meal would be most appropriate.

SUGGESTIONS

If you do not have a whole salmon, bone a single side and lay the raw sides together to marinate, the thin end of the wedge to lie on the thick.

Serve with lemon wedges and buttered brown bread, as for smoked salmon.

Serve with creamed spinach.

GRAVLAKS SAUCE

(Norway)

Modern Scandinavians often make a dill sauce (basically a mustard vinaigrette) to accompany the *gravlaks*. To visualize the combination, imagine, if you will, a dish for a tall blond Nordic fisherman who has acquired a beautiful dark-haired Mediterranean wife while trading his salt cod for her southern wine and olive oil.

YIELD: Sauces 1 pound of *gravlaks* to serve 4

TIME: 10 minutes

2	tablespoons mild mustard	½	teaspoon pepper
1	tablespoon wine vinegar	6	tablespoons light oil
1	tablespoon brown sugar	1	heaping tablespoon chopped dill

In a shallow bowl, mix the mustard, vinegar, sugar, and freshly ground pepper with a fork. Add the oil in a trickle, as if for a mayonnaise. Be patient and the mixture will thicken. Add the dill. Serve in a bowl alongside the salmon.

MORE CURED OR "BURIED" FISH

Several species of fish are traditionally cured in the same way as the *gravlaks* and eaten raw. It is now considered advisable to freeze for 24 hours all fish to be eaten raw. This kills any parasites living in the muscles of the fish. However, the process does not destroy potentially dangerous microbes, so cleanliness remains essential as a safeguard in preparing any food which is not subject to cooking.

Salt-cured trout: Prepare as for *gravlaks*. Marinate for 2 to 3 days, depending on the size of the trout. Serve with a horseradish-and-cream sauce.

Salt-cured halibut: Prepare as for *gravlaks*. The fish will be ready after 2 to 3 days in its brine. A bowl of sour cream and a pickled cucumber (page 522) will keep it good company.

Salt-cured mackerel: Freeze the fish for 24 hours. Prepare as for *gravlaks*. Mackerel will need 2 to 3 days in the brine. Coat with plenty of pepper, roughly crushed in a mortar.

Salt-cured herrings: Freeze the fish for 24 hours. Prepare pickle as for *gravlaks*. Scale and gut the herrings, and split them by running a sharp knife between the flesh and the backbone. Leave the fish whole, opened out in a butterfly shape, and sandwich them together in pairs. The herrings will need 2 to 3 days to take the salt. Horseradish, mustard and sour cream are good accompaniments. Serve with a bowl of potatoes boiled with salt and dill.

SUGGESTION

Leftovers: Dress for the smørgåsbord table as for salt herrings. They are also excellent for a Scandinavian breakfast.

◆

BRINED SALMON

Lenrimmad lax (Sweden)

This is the simplest method of salting salmon, or any other good fresh fish, and uses a made-up brine instead of dry salting. The salmon is milder in flavor than the *gravlaks* and is nearly transparent when sliced. The whole process of brining is very simple, requiring only good fresh materials and a little patience. Pork, beef, mutton, and lamb can all be brined in the same fashion.

Y I E L D : ¼ pound fish serves 1

T I M E : Start 2 days before; 30 minutes

1   salmon
2   ounces Kosher or rock salt, *(not the dry kitchen variety) for each pound of filleted fish*
2   *cups water for each pound of filleted fish*

You will need a large deep china dish. Prepare and fillet the salmon as for *gravlaks* (page 240). Dissolve the salt in the boiling water. Allow the brine to cool. Put the fish in the china dish. Cover the fish with the brine. Leave in a cold cupboard or the salad compartment of the refrigerator for 2 days.

Drain and dry the fish. Slice finely against the grain, and serve with rye bread and unsalted butter. This is a fine simple dish for a warm summer evening. Follow with a bowl of strawberries, tiny wild ones if you can get them, or fresh raspberries to complete the pleasure—most Swedish kitchen plots boast a raspberry-cane fence and a strawberry patch.

◆

SUGGESTIONS

You do not need a whole salmon. A nice plump tail or middle piece will do very well.

Serve potatoes boiled with a teaspoon of dill seeds, or a whole head of dill.

Serve with a potato salad dressed with sour cream and chopped dill.

Serve with a bowl of thin-sliced cucumber dressed with yogurt and dill.

Leftovers: If you are fortunate enough to have any left, this is a useful addition to the smørgåsbord table, particularly if the salmon is dressed with a *gravlaks* sauce (page 242). It can be treated as for any of the smørgåsbord herring recipes.

Slices fried for a few minutes in butter are delicious. Serve with floury boiled potatoes cooked and tossed with dill.

HERRING AND MACKEREL

Herring and its relations in the *Clupeidai* family are probably the most important food fish in Europe. The behavior of the huge herring shoals has influenced human behavior since Europe was colonized by man. In America, the most prolific member of this group is the shad and its many relations, the alewife and the menhaden, mossbunker or pogy.

STOVED HERRINGS

(Scotland)

The best herrings come from Loch Fyne, and the local Clydeside method of cooking them fresh is excellent.

YIELD: 2 herrings serve 1

TIME: 15 to 20 minutes

2   *herrings per person*
½ *ounce (1 tablespoon) butter per pair of herrings*
Salt

You will need a frying pan. Scale, gut, and wipe the fish inside and out. Split the herrings down the back kipper-fashion, and remove the backbone. This is easily done if you press along the backbone first. Dot the flesh with bits of butter and sprinkle with salt. Sandwich the opened fish together, flesh to flesh. Skewer them in place and then grill or fry them in a lightly greased frying pan (herrings have plenty of their own fat and need no extra in the pan). Serve with more cold butter and floury boiled potatoes, well-drained and shaken over the heat to dry.

MARINATED SALT HERRING

Inlagd sill (Scandinavia)

Visiting Göteburg in 1871, the French traveler Paul du Chaillu appreciated the Scandinavian way of dining:

I was led to a little table, called smorgasbord, around which we all clustered and upon which I saw a display of smoked reindeer meat, cut into small thin slices; smoked salmon with poached eggs, fresh, raw sliced salmon, called graflax, upon which salt had been put about an hour before; hard-boiled eggs; caviare; fried sausage; a sort of anchovy, caught on the western coast; raw salted Norwegian herring, exceedingly fat, cut into small pieces; sillsalat, made of pickled herring, small pieces of boiled meat, potato etc with olive oil and vinegar; smoked goose-breast; cucumbers, soft brown and white bread, cut into small slices; knackebrod, a sort of flat, hard bread made of coarse rye flour and flavored with aniseed; siktadt bread, very thin, and made of the finest bolted flour; butter; gammal ost, the strongest old cheese one can taste, and kummin ost, a cheese seasoned with caraway; three crystal decanters, containing different kinds of branvin (spirits); renadt, made from rye or potatoes; pomerans, made from renadt, with the addition of oil or bitter orange and somewhat sweet, and finkelbranvin, or unpurified spirit. [*Land of the Midnight Sun*, Paul Du Chaillu, 1881]

The Swedish smørgåsbord (the arrangement goes by different names in the other countries of Scandinavia)—literally the "bread-and-butter table"—is a full self-serve meal made up of several different dishes, mostly cold and ranging from smoked meats to raw fish to berry compotes. The composition is a direct descendant of the classic peasant party meal. All guests at such a gathering, perhaps a wedding or a christening, would bring their own contributions. The Danes and Norwegians call the arrangement a *koldt bord*, and have their own variations.

It is a delightful way to eat: Each diner helps him- or herself to the dish that best pleases them. In former times it also gave the family cook an opportunity to taste the neighbor's delicacies without the trouble and expense of full-scale entertaining—a system which adapts well to life today. The dishes can include meat specialities such as salt-cured lamb, potato dishes, ham, meatballs, headcheese and brawn, seafood such as salmon, eel, and shrimp, and all the various breads and cheeses. The one essential ingredient is a varied supply of herring dishes, and these are traditionally the first to be sampled.

Salt herrings can be bought in cans, or straight from the barrel in a delicatessen. They will all need soaking to desalt except for the variety sold as *Matjes herring* (a Dutch cure), which will not need the treatment. Although salt herrings used to be so much a staple of the Scandinavian diet that they would be eaten in simple homes without further embellishment, they are much improved by the addition of a few imported ingredients.

SERVES: 6, as part of a smørgåsbord table

TIME: Start 2 to 3 days before; 20 minutes

6	salted herrings	2	bay leaves
1	cup vinegar	½	teaspoon peppercorns
1	cup water	1	medium onion
4	ounces (½ cup) sugar		

You will need a medium saucepan and a large jar for the herrings. Skin and fillet the salted herrings if this has not already been done. Soak the fillets in water, or water and milk, for an hour, if they are commercially prepared and already soaked, to remove excess saltiness. If they are home-cured or cured in an equivalent manner, they will need several hours (say overnight).

Meanwhile, bring the vinegar, water, and sugar to a boil with the bay leaves and the peppercorns. Allow to cool. Peel and slice the onion.

Put the filleted herrings into a large jar, tucking the rings of raw onion in the space. Add the marinade. The herrings will be ready to eat in 2 days but will keep for 2 weeks in the refrigerator, or longer if sealed. Drain and eat the herrings with boiled potatoes, sour cream, and a sprinkling of chopped chives.

With their smørgåsbord the Danes like to serve *rye bread* (page 407), the Norwegians *flatbrød* (page 408), and the Swedes their thicker *knäckebröd* (page 408), plus the various Scandinavian soft breads and black breads. A Swede would serve beer and schnapps with the meal. The Danes make very good beer and the Finns particularly good aquavit—both drinks are excellent all over Scandinavia.

◆

SUGGESTIONS

Concoct your own delicious marinated herring dishes by mixing the fish with suitable vegetables. The mixer should equal the fish in volume. Allow a dressed salad to stand for half an hour before serving. Serve cool but not ice-cold. For a simple main meal, serve three or four different salads together with a pile of potato pancakes, *lompe* (page 420), so that each person can roll and fill his or her own. The do-it-yourself element is an integral part of an independent and servantless community. Aquavit in Denmark and the same liquor by a different name, *brannvinn*, in Sweden and Norway would accompany.

Salt herring with cucumber: Mix equal quantities of marinated herring, drained and chopped into bite-sized pieces, and cubed cucumber. Dress with sour cream or yogurt and dill.

Salt herring with cooked carrots: Chop the herrings and sliced cooked carrots—equal quantities of vegetable to fish. Dress with some of the marinade and a little extra sugar.

Salt herring with potatoes: Mix equal quantities of cold boiled potatoes with chopped marinated herring. Dress with the marinade thickened with a little mild mustard. Sprinkle with chopped dill or chives.

Salt herring with dill and beets: Mix equal quantities of chopped marinated herring and cubed baked beets with lots of chopped dill. Dress with a few spoonfuls of the marinade.

Salt herring with potatoes and pickled cucumbers: Mix equal quantities of drained chopped marinated herring with diced cold potatoes and slices of pickled cucumber (page 522). Dress with sour cream or yogurt. Sprinkle with plenty of chopped dill or chives.

◆

SUGGESTIONS

Leftovers: The Scandinavians love to eat their leftover smørgåsbord dishes for breakfast.

Otherwise, arrange the dressed fish on a slice of buttered bread as a smørrebrød or open sandwich, the Danes' favorite lunch.

◆

MACKEREL WITH BACON

Makrelen mit Speck (Germany)

Fish dishes which include bacon and pork appear up and down the Atlantic Littoral, from Scandinavia to Wales, Germany to Portugal. The fisherman's wife kept a pig and salted her flitches of bacon each autumn, so the main ingredients were always on hand to complement her husband's catch.

YIELD: 1 fish serves 1

TIME: 5 minutes per fish plus 20 to 30 minutes cooking

1   *mackerel per person*
4   *thin slices of bacon per mackerel*
Pepper

You will need a baking dish and foil or a lidded frying pan. Preheat the oven to 350°F.

Fillet your fine fresh mackerel to give 4 fillets from each fish. Place each fillet on its own slice of bacon (remove the rind first). Roll up in a tight little parcel like a swiss roll. Continue until all the fish are done. Pack the rolls into a baking dish which will fit them exactly. Pepper them well—the bacon should provide enough salt. Cover the dish with foil. Bake for 20 to 30 minutes, or cook on top of the stove in a covered frying pan for a bit less time, turning the fish once.

SMALL FISH

GRILLED SKEWERED FISH

Souvlakia apo Psari (Greece)

The Greeks love everything from the sea—a natural taste in one of the world's great seafaring nations. If it comes from the waves, they believe, it must be good: eels, cuttlefish, squid, octopus, sea urchins, devil fish, giant mussels as long as a man's arm—as fish eaters, the Greeks have the most catholic of tastes.

Cut the fish you have chosen into walnut-sized pieces. Thread the pieces onto fine wooden skewers. Trickle olive oil and lemon juice over them, sprinkle with salt and pepper, and leave to marinate for half an hour. Sprinkle the fish with a little marjoram or oregano or thyme to remind you of the herbs crushed underfoot among the dry gray rocks of the Greek hillside. Make a basting liquid with 1 part lemon juice to 4 parts olive oil, and put a cut garlic clove to infuse in it while the fish is marinating.

Cook the skewered fish over charcoal or under a hot broiler. Baste with the mixture throughout. Serve with a sauce passed separately, either a simple oil-and-lemon mixture with the addition of a handful of fine-chopped parsley, or with a bowl of *skordalia* (page 56).

FRIED FISH IN BATTER

Psari tiganito (Greece)

SERVES: 3 to 4

TIME: Start about an hour before; 20 minutes

4 *ounces (¾ cup) all-purpose flour*	1 *pound fish*
Salt	*Vegetable oil for frying*
1 *egg*	

You will need a bowl, a deep frying pan, a draining spoon, and kitchen paper. Make a frying batter with the flour and enough slightly warm water to produce a liquid like pouring cream. Beat it well and add a little salt. Beat it some more. Leave for half an hour or so. When you are ready to fry, beat in the yolk of the egg, and then fold in the well beaten white just before you use it.

Use this as a frying batter for fish steaks or vegetable fritters. Particularly good as used in Turkey, where street vendors in the villages on the Bosporus make a summer living selling roasted sweet corn and deep-fried mussels. All morning the fishermen sit out on the decks of the fishing boats shucking gunmetal-dark mussel shells 3 or 4 inches long. They yield bucketfuls of sweet, plump, orange mollusks. All afternoon and into the night the vendors thread the fat little fish on skewers, dip them in a bucketful of the batter, and fry them—waterfront street food. Each skewerful comes with a lemon quarter and a slice of bread. This is wonderful with a garlicky *skordalia* (page 56).

◆

LITTLE FRIED FISH

Boquerones fritos (Spain)

It is hard to know quite why the coastal dwellers of Spain fry fish so perfectly, but they do. Certainly the excellence has something to do with the superb raw materials available, and the beautiful olive oil (now sadly becoming so expensive that cheaper vegetable oils are often used instead), the good rough salt, and the well-tempered iron pans. But it also owes much to the housewife's unsurpassed sleight of hand in the flouring and handling of the most fragile sea creatures—a talent which echoes her skill with the crochet hook and the embroidery needle when making tiny garments for her children. Babies, fish, and donkeys are always well dressed in Spain, whatever else is not.

SERVES: 3 to 4

TIME: 20 minutes

1   *pound fresh anchovies (smelts or any fish no longer than 4 inches will do)*
3   *ounces (⅔ cup) all-purpose flour*
1   *teaspoon coarse salt*
*Olive oil or vegetable oil for frying (a mixture of olive and sunflower oils is
    good)*

You will need a plate, a deep frying pan, a draining spoon, and kitchen paper. Gut the fish and nip their heads off. Rinse them in fresh water and drain well. Mix the flour with the salt and spread it on a flat plate. Dip the damp fish in the flour and pinch the tails together to make fan-shaped groups of 3 to 5 fish. The tails fry together deliciously crisp and make the fish much easier to handle.

Heat the oil in a frying pan. When it is hazed with blue, test it by putting in a small piece of bread. If it bubbles and turns golden immediately, you may start frying.

Fry the fish in their groups quickly until golden, turning once. Put them on paper to drain. Serve piping hot with quartered lemons, a plate of chips, and a salad of romaine lettuce and onion rings dressed with lemon juice, olive oil, and salt.

◆

SUGGESTIONS

The tiniest fish of all, *chunquetes*, no longer than a pin, are at this writing an illegal catch in order to conserve stocks, but they may reappear in the markets at some stage in the future. They are delectable and need perfect skill. They are tossed, a handful at a time, into a sieve full of salted flour; then thrown into hot oil for no more than a moment, during which they have to be constantly moved to keep them separate. They are removed just as they crisp but before they have taken color, drained immediately, and served piping hot. Wonderful.

Squid or *calamares*—both the large ones, which have to be sliced into rings, and the tiny *chocos*, baby cuttlefish, which are fried whole—are also prepared thus, and can be dipped in milk before being fried. Do not salt squid, octopus, or cuttlefish before frying, as this makes them tough. Other fish which take kindly to the treatment include small sole, little whiting, and any larger fish which can be cut into steaks. Very often a whole plate of mixed fish will be presented, the freshest and cheapest the market can offer.

◆

PICKLED ANCHOVIES

Boquerones en vinagre (Spain)

Until the middle of the twentieth century, the peasants of the hill villages of the Alpujarras below Granada had fresh fish every day. The two-way trade between the coast and the hills bartered anchovies and sardines for silkworm cocoons, a cash crop common to the peasantry of the southeastern Mediterranean. The donkey boys would set out from the coast before dawn, as soon as the first fishing boats returned to harbor. Boy and donkey would swiftly climb the herb-scented hills, racing the competition—the first salesman makes the best sales. They would reach the top villages on the ridge, five or six miles up the steep oleander-tangled ravines, by midday at the latest. In twin panniers woven from tough esparto grass slung over the gray flanks of the tough little beasts of burden, their wares glistened emerald and silver.

On the return journey the donkey panniers would be piled high with silkworm cocoons—huge pale pyramids as light as thistledown—on their way to the silk merchants in the town far below. Those were the days before nylon put the silkworm breeders out of business, and did many a poor housewife out of her pin money. Mulberry trees, on whose leaves the silkworms fattened, still shade many a village patio, but the fisherboys' donkeys have been replaced by vans and motorbicycles. The fish vendor only visits once or twice a week now, and only the rich can afford to have their cloth spun by the diligent little caterpillars.

Pickled anchovies are a legacy from the silk-fish trade. Thus prepared, the highly perishable little fish would keep sweet and fresh in a cool place for a week. They are still much appreciated even today, when refrigeration makes preservation unnecessary, as a favorite *tapa* dish served in little bars all over Spain.

Reminiscing about the trade, Miguel Moreno, an Andalusian fish vendor, said in 1958: "In the villages the demand was only for the cheaper sorts of fish: sardines, *jureles* (scad or horse mackerel), whitebait (anchovies), sea-bream." (*The Pueblo*, Ronald Fraser, 1973) Miguel's record load was 107 kilos, carried on his own back.

SERVES: 4

TIME: Start 1 to 2 days before; 20 minutes

1 *pound fresh anchovies (or small smelts, sardines, or any other small fresh fish)*	1 *cup white wine vinegar or sherry vinegar*
½ *teaspoon salt*	4 *garlic cloves*
	1 *small bunch of Italian parsley*

You will need a shallow china dish and aluminum foil. European anchovies, *Engraulis encrasicolus*, and smelts, *Osmerus eperlanus*, do not have to be scaled (the American striped anchovy, *Anchoa hepsetus*, and most other little fish need this attention).

Clean, gut, and slit the little fish down the backbone. Butterfly them without cutting them in two. The backbone will pull out easily—sever it neatly just before the tail. Lay the fish, opened out, skin side up in a large shallow dish, sprinkle with salt, and pour most of the vinegar over them. Cover with foil and leave to marinate for a day or two in a cool place.

Drain the anchovies and turn them over, so that they are flesh side up. Pour some more fresh vinegar over them. Peel and slice the garlic finely and scatter it over the little fish. Chop the parsley and sprinkle it over the top. Serve with chunks of fresh bread and a glass of dry sherry, or the wine of Montilla, which lays claim to be the original sherry.

Pickled anchovies will keep in a cool place for at least a week.

◆

PICKLED FISH

Peixe frita de escabeche (Portugal)

A very common way of preserving fish, similar preparations are found in Spain and, under the Iberian influence, all over Latin America including

Mexico where, as *seviche*, the dish is prepared with raw fish marinated in lemon juice. *The Lady's Companion* of 1733 has an almost identical recipe for pickling mackerel.

SERVES: 4

TIME: Start the day before; 30 minutes

1 pound fresh fish (sardines, anchovies, mackerel, whatever is fresh)	4 tablespoons olive oil
	Juice of 1 lemon
2 garlic cloves	4 tablespoons all-purpose flour, seasoned with salt and pepper
Several sprigs of marjoram and/or parsley	1 large glass of white wine or 1 cup in all of white wine vinegar mixed with one third water
1 tablespoon salt	
½ tablespoon ground peppercorns	
2 bay leaves	

You will need a small pestle and mortar or a blender, a frying pan, and a deep china dish. Behead, clean, scale, and gut the fish. Cut them into chunks if they are too large for one bite. Peel and chop the garlic and the herbs. Make a marinade by pounding together the garlic, salt, pepper, bay leaves, and herbs and then mixing the paste with 2 tablespoons of the olive oil and the lemon juice. Or mix all in a blender. Rub it well into the fish and leave to stand for an hour or two.

Scrape off the marinade and save it. Roll the pieces of fish in the seasoned flour. Heat the rest of the oil in a frying pan until a faint blue haze rises. Fry the chunks of fish in shallow oil until cooked through and golden. Put them in a deep dish. Pour the white wine or vinegar-and-water mixture into the frying pan juices and allow them to bubble for a moment. Stir in the reserved marinade and bubble that up. Pour it over the fish while it is still hot. Ready to eat in a day, it will keep in the refrigerator for a week.

EEL

Although the moray and conger are both fished in European waters, the species most often found in the European cooking pot is *Anguilla anguilla*—the common eel. The common eel is born and dies in the sea, but spends most of its life in freshwater. Eels can survive out of their native element for a comparatively long time, and their flesh remains sweet and fresh for a considerable while after death. American and European common eels use adjacent spawning grounds in the Sargasso sea. The tiny, transparent, pin-eyed American elvers take a year to reach their destination in the estuaries and rivers, but the Europeans must journey all of three years before they reach their feeding grounds.

If they are not caught for the Spanish and Italian tables, where they are much appreciated as elvers, the eels swim upriver, turning dark and opaque as they go, where they live for an average of nine to twelve years. The delta of the great river Rhône, which flows into the Mediterranean to the west of Marseilles, has been a rich hunting ground for eel fishermen for thousands of years—so much so that the Camargue is now a largely manmade landscape dominated by *digues*, great earthworks thrown up over the centuries to accommodate and trap the river's large eel population. Rosy flamingos and millions of seabirds have long since learned to take full advantage of the arrangement.

◆

GRILLED EEL

Anguille grillé (France)

Eel flesh is very rich. Although the eel fishermen of the Camargue treat their catch as a cash crop for export, they will sometimes eat the delicacy themselves. I have eaten this dish on a bright spring day in a patio on the Marais, watched with interest by a migrating flock of bee eaters, their blue and gold feathers dazzling in the sunlight.

The Camargais are as dark as gypsies and their food has a strong Spanish flavor. Old Sara, owner of a *mas*, or marshy farmstead, on the crossroads near Les Saintes Maries de la Mer (and herself named for the black servant of the two Maries of blessed memory), serves a midday meal to the herdsmen of the half-wild cattle which pasture the reed beds. The Camargais are somewhat suspicious of outsiders, but Sara can sometimes be persuaded to cook for passing strangers as well as her regulars. Her barbecue fire in the chicken-scratched backyard, fueled by the trimmings from the vineyards which surround the *mas*, never seems to go out. Presented with an eel, Sarah has no time for niceties. She stuns it with a blow to its head on the table, hangs it from a hook on a wooden post, and unceremoniously skins it.

Have your fishmonger perform this service for you.

SERVES: 4

TIME: 20 to 30 minutes

1   *pound eel, cut into slices*
1   *teaspoon dried thyme*
Pepper
Olive oil

You will need a barbecue or a very hot grill. Sprinkle the slices of eel with the thyme and pepper, and brush them with olive oil. Leave them to marinate while the grill heats.

Put the slices of eel to grill. They will take 10 to 15 minutes if they are thick. Serve them with quartered lemons and salt. Sara accompanies the dish with a bottle of *vin gris*, dry, pale pink, and slightly salty; plenty of home-baked bread, dense-textured and sweet; a generous plate of crisp-fried potatoes; and a salad of roughly chopped lettuce, tomatoes, and mild purple onions. Before the meal, serve Provençal olives to take away the first pangs of hunger.

◆

GREEN EEL STEW

Paling in't groen (Belgium)

As before, if possible buy your eel alive and have your fishmonger kill, bleed, clean, skin, gut, and cut it into lengths for you on the spot. The other main ingredient, sorrel, is rumored, via its content of oxalic acid, to dissolve small bones when it is cooked with bony fish—however, in practice it is the sharpness of the flavor which makes the special relationship. Hence springs sorrel's traditional affinity with shad in France and eel in Belgium.

SERVES: 6 to 8

TIME: 40 to 50 minutes

> *2 to 3 pounds eel cut into 2-inch lengths*
> *1½ pounds fresh green herbs: sorrel is almost essential (watercress the only*
> *possible substitute), plus a selection from parsley, celery tops, mint, sage,*
> *chervil, and summer savory*
> *1   medium onion*
> *3 to 4 ounces (6 to 8 tablespoons) butter*

You will need two saucepans. Wipe the pieces of eel and put them in a saucepan with salted water to cover. Bring quickly to a boil and cook for 5 minutes. Take them off the heat and leave them in the water while you prepare the greens.

Pick over the leaves and remove any thick stalks; then shred them finely. Peel and chop the onion. Rinse the greens, leaving water clinging to them. Put them with the minced onion into a heavy pan with half the butter. Cover tightly. Stew the greens gently, shaking the pan occasionally so that they do not stick, for 10 minutes. Then add the pieces of eel and a cupful of the cooking liquid. Cover again and continue to cook for another 10 minutes.

Remove the pieces of eel and transfer them to a hot plate. Stir the remaining butter into the green sauce. Adjust the seasoning, adding pepper if you like. Pour the sauce over the eel pieces and serve with thick slices of well-buttered bread.

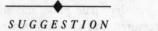

SUGGESTION

If you cannot find any sorrel, use watercress with the juice of half a lemon or a tablespoon of vinegar.

SMOKED EEL

Anguille fumé (Belgium)

Do not skin a fine fat eel, but clean it and chop its body into 6-inch lengths. Sprinkle with salt and then hot-smoke it for 30 to 40 minutes in a small home smoker.

Fillet into its convenient square fillets. Serve with grated horseradish mixed with thick cream beaten with a little mustard, and accompanied by thick slices of buttered brown bread. This is quite the best way to eat eel.

SHELLFISH

Europe's generous larder of shore-based shellfish provided her earliest hunter-gathering inhabitants with one of their most easily obtained suppers. Excavation of prehistoric sites, such as those in Portugal's Tagus valley, have yielded quantities of emptied mollusk shells alongside the wild pig and cattle bones. Dishes which include cockles in sauces for pork still survive in Portugal and Wales.

The smaller mollusks are usually full of mud and sand, and should be left overnight (if possible) in fresh running water to spit out their grit. Check that each shell contains a live fish and discard those which are heavy with sand.

Oysters: Since prehistoric times these most succulent of shellfish have been gathered around the shores of Europe. Until the oyster beds succumbed suddenly to overfishing and pollution in the middle of the nineteenth century, they were a staple of the poor. Wild oysters of the species *Ostrea edulis* are the best. They have a stronger sea flavor than cultivated oysters, which are fattened in river mouths where they are washed with alternate tides of sea and freshwater. Otherwise, differences depend on size and source. Portuguese oysters are the long and narrow ones. Cheaper and not as finely flavored, they are a different species, *Crassostrea angulata*. Oysters out of season (the months without an "r") are perfectly edible, but will be breeding—this gives them a milky appearance which the French call *laiteuse*. They are at their most delicious eaten raw, sauced only with a squeeze of lemon, or a shake of chili vinegar, a turn of the pepper grinder, and their own sweet liquor.

Scallops: The *Pecten maximus* has been known as the pilgrim shell since the Middle Ages, when religious travelers adopted it as their emblem. The scallop, as the pilgrims had observed, is no mean traveler itself, propelling its shell great distances through the water by means of a kind of squirting action achieved with its large white adductor muscle (the white meat of the creature). Scallops do not burrow in the sandy shore. If your scallops are not opened (they are much better and will taste of the sea if they are still in the shell), leave them in a pan of cold water after you have scrubbed them. They will then open and allow you to get your knife in.

Clams: A catholic selection of the *Veneridae* family is collected and eaten all around the shores of Europe. They can be cooked like mussels or scallops. These bivalves' shells can have rough or smooth ribbing. Clams burrow in the sandy shore—hence their large "feet." Carpet shells and venus shells are the *palourdes* of France.

◆

OYSTERS IN THE SHELL

Huitres en coquille (France)

SERVES: 2

TIME: 20 minutes

12 oysters	1 small glass Pernod (optional)
2 ounces (¼ cup) fresh bread crumbs	2 ounces (4 tablespoons) butter or 3 slices thin-cut bacon cut into 2-inch pieces
1 small bunch of parsley	
2 garlic cloves or 1 small onion	

You will need a frying pan and a large shallow ovenproof dish. Open the oysters by levering the shells apart. There are daggerlike instruments for the task on sale in French markets. A short strong knife should be up to the job if you lack the right tool. Grip the rough shell firmly in a cloth while you work.

When the oysters are opened, leave the fish on the deepest of its two shells. Sprinkle it with the fresh bread crumbs, chopped parsley, and either finely chopped garlic or finely chopped onion. Add a few drops of Pernod if you have it. Dot the oysters with the butter, arrange them in a wide shallow dish, and cook them under the broiler for 5 minutes or in a preheated 400°F oven for 7 to 8 minutes. If you prefer, instead of the butter, lay a piece of bacon over each oyster, and broil. Don't try to move them from their natural-born dish, but serve them as they are with bread to mop up the juices.

◆

BAKED OYSTERS

Huitres au four (France)

This is the way the oystermen of Brittany themselves like their oysters cooked. Usually, of course, they are eaten raw.

SERVES: 2

TIME: 20 minutes

12 oysters	2 to 3 chopped shallots or 1 small
2 ounces (¼ cup) fresh bread	onion
crumbs	Salt and pepper
2 tablespoons milk	¼ pound grated cheese

You will need a shallow gratin dish and a bowl. Open the oysters and leave each fish on the deepest shell of the two. Arrange them in a shallow gratin dish in a single layer. Soak the bread crumbs in the milk while you chop the shallots or onion finely. Top the oysters—do not stuff them, this is a crisp little hat, not a blanket—with the soaked bread crumbs, the chopped shallots, salt and freshly ground pepper, and a sprinkle of the grated cheese.

Bake the oysters in a preheated 400°F oven or under a grill for 6 to 7 minutes—just long enough to melt the cheese. Serve on the instant with plenty of bread to accompany and a glass of cold Muscadet to sip when you have burned your tongue on the cheese.

◆

CLAMS

Almejas (Spain)

There are at least half a dozen different varieties of *conchas* or shells which are collected and enjoyed around the coastline of Spain. The smallest and sweetest, *conchas finas*, or "delicate clams," have a pale, fine, near-translucent shell with a mauve blush inside. These clams are sold raw and on the shell. They are sometimes cooked *a la plancha*, on the plank—a metal sheet laid over a fire which acts as a simple grill. Otherwise they are cooked in a wide frying pan—in my view the best way for these little mollusks to be treated. They are eaten immediately, before they have time to toughen.

SERVES: 4 to 6

TIME: 15 to 20 minutes

2	pounds clams or any small shellfish (fresh and in their shells)	1	small bunch of parsley
		2	tablespoons olive oil
2	garlic cloves	1	wine glass of dry white wine or sherry

You will need a large shallow pan. Rinse the shellfish, checking over and discarding any which are broken or filled with sand. Peel and slice the garlic. Chop the parsley.

Heat the oil in your widest frying pan (a wok comes into its own here). When it is lightly hazed with blue smoke, toss in the garlic and fry for a moment. Add the parsley, quickly followed by the shellfish. Pour in the wine or sherry. Turn up the heat.

Cover with a lid, shaking the pan to redistribute the shells so that all have a chance to cook. If you have no lid, keep moving the clams with a metal drainer. They will take 3 to 4 minutes for all the shells to open. Do not cook them any longer but serve immediately. They should not be reheated, and are delicious even when cold.

◆

SUGGESTIONS

In Portugal these little shellfish are often cooked with diced bacon or cubed fresh pork, plus a chopped onion and chopped tomato. All the ingredients, with ½ glass olive oil and the well-rinsed clams and perhaps a few slices of *chorizo*, are then put into a woklike covered frying pan and given 20 minutes over a moderate heat.

Leftovers: Serve with a dish of rice—using the liquor in the cooking of the grains and putting the fish, in or out of their shells, on the top to warm quickly in the steam, but without allowing them time to get rubbery.

◆

MUSSEL STEW

Moules marinières (France)

Collecting mussels from the seashore is one of the most satisfying of seaside holiday amusements. There is the pleasure of spotting the beds at low tide: rockscapes clustered thickly with indigo colonies, flashing gunmetal and ink, stacked in tide pools thick as tenants in tenements, baby shells no bigger than a finger nail, small and sweet and pale-fleshed, together with plump old monsters sheltering at the base of wooden breakwaters.

Cold-water mussels are the best. Mussels thrive in mud and sand, and by the time they arrive in the kitchen, they are in need of a good wash. Give it to them, overnight if possible, in a large bucket of cold water with a handful of salt sprinkled into it. The following day, rinse them again. The simplest way to prepare them then, and one of the best, is as follows. Those who gather them often prefer to eat them raw like oysters, with a squeeze of lemon. They pick up waste and toxins very easily, so be careful where you collect your own.

SERVES: 4 to 5

TIME: 15 to 20 minutes

> 3   *quarts mussels*
> *Plenty of parsley*
> 1   *cup dry white wine or dry cider or water*
> 1   *onion*

You will need a very large shallow pan with a lid, a draining spoon, a strainer, and a small saucepan. Pick over the mussels carefully. Discard any which are broken, or whose shells do not close when you stir them in the bucket. Any shells which are particularly heavy are probably full of sand—throw them out, they will do the broth no good at all. Scrape the barnacles and seaweed off the shells, and pull out the little black seaweedlike beards.

Put four to five deep soup plates in a preheated 300°F oven to warm. Chop the parsley. You will need plenty—4 to 5 tablespoons is not too much.

Put the water or wine or cider in a large shallow pan and bring it to a boil (I find a wok with a lid very useful for this dish). Throw in the mussels, turn up the heat, and let them open in their own juices. Cover the pan and shake it to distribute the heat. As soon as all the mussels are open—which will take only a few minutes—lift them out with a draining spoon and distribute them between the hot soup plates. Mussels should be eaten as soon as they are cooked. Prolonged cooking makes them like little pieces of orange rubber. Strain the broth into a smaller pan, and throw in plenty of chopped parsley and the onion finely chopped. Reheat and serve this separately in a pitcher.

Accompany with plenty of bread, radishes, sweet butter, and a good cheese. The Atlantic coast of France, where this recipe comes from, has rich pickings: Serve a Port Salut, a Camembert, or a quarter of a wheel of Brie (from a little further inland, on the outskirts of Paris, as befits the favorite cheese of that elegant diplomat M. Talleyrand). Accompany the dish, too, with dry white wine or good Normandy cider. Follow with a big round wheel of deep-dish apple pie (page 443) with *crème fraîche* (page 204) on the side.

When the mussels have been cooked to this stage, they can be picked out of their shells and cooked in a sauce. Try them with ½ cup of cream stirred into the strained cooking liquor. Bring to a boil and pour it over the mussels.

Try them as a substitute for the snails in the recipes on page 314. They are particularly good heated with garlic butter—the French sell flat earthenware dishes with dimples for holding snails, with or without their shells, which are perfect for this substitution.

Leftovers: Arrange the cooked mussels, each on a single shell, in a large dish which will accommodate them in one layer. Finely chop tomatoes, peppers, and sweet onions, mix together, and dress them with oil and vinegar. Top the mussels with this mixture, so that each little shell has its share. Leave overnight to marinate. This is an excellent Spanish *tapa*.

◆

SCALLOPS IN THEIR SHELLS

St. Jacques en coquille (France)

I have often eaten these fine shellfish, prepared in this way, beside the salt marshes beneath Mont-Saint-Michel. There, where the ancient island fortress marks the border between Brittany and Normandy, the products of orchard, dairy, and ocean are all at their finest.

SERVES: 4

TIME: 20 to 25 minutes

6 to 10 scallops (they vary greatly in size)	*1 ounce (2 tablespoons) butter*
	1 tablespoon oil
1 large glass of cider	*1 small bunch of parsley*
½ cup cream	*1 ounce fresh bread crumbs*
Salt and pepper	

You will need a shallow pan, a small saucepan, and a frying pan. Put the scallops in their shells, well scrubbed and round side down to cup the juices, in a shallow pan of boiling water or into a low oven. After a few moments they will open. Remove the frills and the little sandy sack of intestine. Slice the white adductor muscle horizontally into 3 or 4 medallions and put them aside with the coral, or scallop roe, if you can get it. Scrub the four largest of the curved shells and put them aside.

Preheat the oven to 350°F.

Put the cider into a small pan and bring it to a boil. Slide in the scallop pieces and poach them for 6 to 7 minutes. Remove and divide them among the 4 curved shells. Boil the cooking juices until they are reduced by half. Stir in the cream. Bubble it all up again. Taste, and adjust the seasoning with salt and pepper.

Heat the butter and the oil in a frying pan until it foams, and then throw in the chopped parsley and the bread crumbs. Fry until golden; then scatter them over the scallops. Put the dish in the oven for a moment to heat through. Serve very hot.

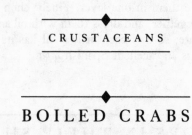

CRUSTACEANS

BOILED CRABS

(Scotland)

The sweetest crabs I know are caught in creels off the rocky coast of the Hebrides, in the strait which isolates Iona, sacred haunt of Saint Columba and one of the most ancient of the Christian holy places. This is how the local fishermen advise the preparation of their catch.

YIELD: 1 large crab (*Cancer pagarus* is the likely lad) weighing 2½ pounds will give 1 pound of meat, enough for 4 moderate appetites.

TIME: 40 to 50 minutes

    1   live crab
    3   quarts water
    8   ounces (1 cup) salt

You will need a large saucepan. Fill a large saucepan with the heavily salted water or ordinary seawater with (½ cup) added salt. Put in the crab with its claws tied while the water is still cold, and then bring it gently to a boil. Hold it under for two minutes so that the poor creature has an easy demise—the nearest thing to Davy Jones's locker. Keep the water just boiling for 15 minutes for the first 1 pound, and 10 minutes for each subsequent pound.

Female crabs are considered the sweeter. You can tell the sex by looking at the tail flap which is tucked under the body: The male's is much narrower than the female's, which needs the extra width to protect her eggs. When cooked, the crab should feel heavy for its size. Let it cool. To prepare, pull the body from the shell, remove the ring of feathery gray "dead-man's-fingers," and snap off the mouthpart. Everything else is edible. Hit the claws with a hammer to crack them.

Eat with your fingers and let the "de'il tak' the hindmost." A sharp instrument can be provided for picking meat out of the claws. Put a bowl of plain-boiled potatoes and a dish of fresh butter on the table for those who still have a corner unfilled. In season, finish with fresh raspberries to remind you of the heather and hills of Scotland, and a dram of whiskey. The fasting Saint Columba himself could not turn down such a meal.

SUGGESTIONS

Serve the cooled crab with a homemade mayonnaise, quartered lemons, lettuce hearts with no dressing, and thin slices of brown bread and butter.

BOILED LOBSTER

Kokt hummer (Sweden)

The Scandinavians and the Scots have the best crustaceans in Europe. There is something about the cold waters of the North Atlantic which firms and sweetens the flesh of lobsters and crabs like no other.

Helgoland, a tiny island in the North Sea between Denmark and the northwest coast of Germany, used to be, before the gastronomes of Europe outate its capacities, the most famous North Atlantic lobster fishing ground. The British bartered the island with Germany at the end of the nineteenth century, in exchange for the then more strategically useful clove island of Zanzibar. The Scandinavians are very knowledgeable about their seafood. Providing it is fresh, they feel the lily needs no gilding.

YIELD: 1 medium-sized lobster serves 2

TIME: 20 to 55 minutes

3   *quarts seawater or 3 quarts freshwater and 4 ounces (½ cup) salt*
1   *crown of dill (the flowering head with its seed) or 1 teaspoon dill seeds*
1   *live lobster*

You will need a large saucepan. Bring the water to a rapid boil with the dill, and plunge the lobster in headfirst. Hold it under while you count to a hundred. Cover and simmer for 12 minutes for a ½-pound lobster, 15 minutes for a 1-pound lobster, 25 minutes for a 2-pound lobster, and so on in 10-minute increases per pound.

Allow the creature to cool in the water; then drain it. Split the body and remove the dark intestinal vein. Crack the claws. Give each diner a large napkin and a bowl of warm water to rinse his or her fingers. The sweet flesh needs no embellishment except sea salt and a slice of dark rye bread spread with pale unsalted butter.

◆

GRILLED PRAWNS

Gambas a la plancha (Spain)

This is the Cádiz fisherman's way with his inshore catch. The grill he uses is a simple metal sheet with a charcoal fire beneath. Larger specimens of *Palaemon serratus*, so fresh they are still gray-blue and stiff, are simply salted with the grainy bay salt which has been dried since Roman times in the salt flats around Cádiz bay. The metal sheet is then wiped over with a rag dipped in olive oil, and the prawns are ready in a few minutes.

SERVES: 4; allow 6 large prawns per person

TIME: 5 minutes

2   pounds fresh prawns (the largest possible)
Rough salt
Olive oil

You will need a metal *plancha* or a very heavy iron frying pan or griddle. Salt the prawns. Put the frying pan or griddle to heat. When it is good and hot—a drop of water should bounce off it immediately—wipe the surface with oil and add the prawns. They will be done in 2 minutes a side—depending on the thickness of the creatures.

Serve with plenty of thick-cut *pan de campo* (page 403) and quartered lemons. Accompany with a dry manzanilla sherry (well chilled) from Sanlúcar de Barrameda, the little port at the mouth of the Guadalquivir River from where Columbus set sail on his first and most momentous voyage. The prawns caught by the fishermen off its pine-clad dunes are the most prized in Spain, and its wines rival those of Jerez.

CRAYFISH

Kraftor (Sweden)

On the stroke of midnight on August 7 every year, freshwater crayfish can legally be netted in Scandinavia. The season only lasts until mid-September. Traditionally, crayfish parties are held at night when the creatures can be caught by torchlight in the chalk streams. A piece of rotten meat trailed in a net in the water will bring them scuttling to the bait.

Plunge your crayfish live into plenty of boiling salted water, in which you have included a crown or two of dill or a teaspoon of dill seeds. Bring the water back to a boil and simmer for 5 to 6 minutes. Cooked crayfish blush a deep carmine—brighter than any other shellfish. Leave them in their liquid until they are quite cool. Drain and serve these exquisite little morsels piled up on your best dish. Crack the claws in your teeth and suck out the juices.

Accompany the feast with rye bread, sweet butter, and rough salt—and perhaps a little bowl of chopped dill. Afterwards a generous piece of cheese will fill the gaps—crayfish are delicious, but not very substantial. Serve with light beer and ice-cold *brannvinn* to drink under the midnight sun.

CRAYFISH IN WHITE WINE

Ecrevisse à la nage (France)

Catch your own crayfish if you can. They are to be found in swift-running mountain streams. Like all their tribe, they are scavengers and can easily be tempted with a piece of meat (rotten is best) on the end of a string or in a net. Being creatures of little brain, once they have found it, they will hang on to the bitter end. They hide under stones and give an unwary toe a nasty nip.

SERVES: 4

TIME: 45 minutes

3	pounds live crayfish—they survive for a long time out of water	1	onion, sliced
		6	peppercorns
		1	teaspoon salt
2	cups water	1	bottle of white wine (a
1	handful of fresh herbs: thyme, parsley, fennel stalks, bay leaves		Muscadet, dry and pale, is excellent)

You will need a large stewpan. Rinse the crayfish. Put the water with the herbs, onion, peppercorns, and salt into a roomy pan. Bring to a boil and then turn down to simmer for 20 minutes.

Add the wine and bring it back to a boil. Throw in the crayfish. They will jump for a moment and then all will be peaceful—humanity dictates that once again you bring the pan swiftly back to a boil. Turn the heat down a little and cook for 10 minutes. The crayfish will turn a brilliant scarlet. Serve them as they are in a deep dish with their liquor. Don't worry about the dark stripe of intestine down the back that some advise removing. It makes no difference to the flavor.

Accompany with plenty of bread and a salad of green leaves—corn salad and dandelion, watercress and lettuce, dressed with a vinaigrette. Afterwards serve a fruit tart with cream. Finally, as your guests may still be hungry, you have an excellent opportunity to serve a selection of really good cheeses.

SUGGESTIONS

Leftovers: Make a crayfish salad. Pound up the shells and heads—an easy job in a blender—and press out all the delicious well-flavored juice through a sieve. Stir this into a homemade mayonnaise (page 76). Compose a salad with the leftover crayfish meat, fresh crisp lettuce hearts, and perhaps some baby green or fava beans—blanched for no more than 2 to 3 minutes in boiling salted water and drained immediately. Don't douse them in cold water; it does them no good. Sauce with the crayfish-flavored mayonnaise and sprinkle with chopped dill, chives, or parsley.

BOILED SHRIMPS AND POTTED SHRIMPS

(England)

The best way to cook tiny brown shrimps, *Crangon crangon,* is to plunge them live into boiling salted water (seawater is best) as soon as they are caught. Bring the water back to a boil as fast as you can. The shrimps will turn pinky-brown and opaque immediately. Drain them at once. Eat with brown bread and butter. It is a matter of individual choice whether you peel them or eat them whole. Morecambe Bay potted shrimps can be made with these little scavengers whose European range stretches from the Dardanelles to the North Cape. To pot, peel the shrimps and warm them in enough melted butter to cover. When the butter has frothed up, pack all into pots with plenty of pepper.

If they are too small to peel, put them whole in the blender with melted butter and pepper. They grind up into a superb paste for spreading on toast.

GARLIC SHRIMPS

Gambas al ajillo (Spain)

This dish is known as *gambas pil-pil* in what was for several years my local Andalusian port of Tarifa, guardian of the Pillars of Hercules and ancient haunt of Phoenician, Greek, and Roman mariners. The legendary Spanish hero, Guzmán the Good, held Tarifa's fortress against the invading Moors. His most glorious moment came when, faced with the threatened death of his hostage son, he hurled his own sword from the battlements to the invaders below as an instrument of execution.

The men of Tarifa have always been sailors and fishermen. Their little bars and waterfront cafés make the best of the local catch. The best time of year for a Tarifan feast is February and March, when the big scarlet spider crabs scuttle for cover from the storms and are caught inshore in the hundreds. The nets also yield black and yellow eels, octopus and cuttlefish, and shrimp and prawns, all driven to take shelter from the rough Atlantic storms. Then the market brims over and the fish trucks trail their watery loads up into the hills, along the same roads and tracks which for centuries were used by donkey-borne vendors of the sea's harvest.

SERVES: 4

TIME: 15 minutes

4 garlic cloves	½ cup olive oil
4 small dried chilies or one fresh green chili, seeded	Salt
1 pound raw shrimps (frozen ones should be defrosted and drained first)	

You will need, if you have them, four small shallow earthenware dishes. If not, a shallow *gratin* dish will do. Peel and slice the garlic. Chop the chilies. Peel the raw shrimps. Divide all three ingredients between 4 individual flat earthenware dishes, or cocotte dishes. Divide the olive oil equally among the dishes. Sprinkle with salt. Put the dishes onto the heat if they are flameproof, or under a very hot broiler, until they bubble fiercely. Remove immediately—the shrimps toughen and lose their delicacy if overcooked.

Serve very hot with bread to sop up the juices.

◆

SUGGESTIONS

The recipe is also very good made with cooked crabmeat.

Angulas, tiny eel fry, now largely caught in Great Britain's Severn estuary and exported to Spain, are cooked in this way and served, looking like a pile of little noodles, to be eaten with wooden forks while still sizzling hot.

Leftovers: Use the shells and heads of the shrimps to make a fish broth—add a pinch of paprika and a few strands of saffron for the color and scent, and a chopped carrot, onion, and bay leaf for flavor. Simmer for half an hour. Then strain the broth, mashing the debris well and forcing as much as possible through a sieve. Reheat the broth and poach some slices of potato or rice in it. When they are soft, drop in any leftover shrimps or a few squares of fresh fish. Serve with little piping hot croutons fried in oil. All the better if you have some leftover *rouille* or *aïoli* to stir in too.

◆

SHRIMP FRITTERS

Camarones fritos eu massa (Portugal)

A most interesting recipe, not only because the dish is delicious but because it is the mother of the now universally popular Japanese dish *tempura*. The recipe was exported by Portuguese sailors and traders on their highly successful sixteenth-century travels, when their Japanese hosts, eager to flatter the unaesthetic but powerful Europeans, had the dish prepared to please their guests. The resourceful cooks of Japan adopted the technique and expanded and refined the dish to include meats other than shrimp.

In Portugal these excellent fritters are still the shore dweller's standard way of preparing small shrimp. They are particularly good made with the tiny krill-like creatures which jump like fleas and are sold out of salt-streaked buckets by small boys in the southern fishing villages. The shrimps are plunged into the batter live and unpeeled, and their crunchy carapaces add to the crispness of the fritter. It is, however, necessary to peel the shrimps if they are the fishmonger's larger variety.

SERVES: 4

TIME: 25 to 30 minutes

1 egg	Oil for frying
4 ounces (1 cup) flour	1 pound raw shrimps (frozen ones
½ teaspoon salt	should be defrosted and
2 tablespoons olive oil	drained first)
½ cup water	

You will need a sieve, two bowls, and a frying pan. Separate the white from the yolk of the egg. Sieve the flour, and put the yolk and the salt into a hole in the middle. Add the oil and most of the water, and stir until you have a smooth cream. Beat it a little. Leave it to rest for at least half an hour—or long enough for you to catch a pailful of little jumping shrimps.

Beat the egg white stiff and fold it in just before you are ready to fry. Heat a pan of oil until you can see a faint blue haze rising from it.

Stir the shrimps into the batter. Drop spoonfuls of the mixture into the hot oil. Each fritter will puff up crisp and golden within a few minutes. Drain and serve without delay, with quarters of lemon.

◆

SUGGESTIONS

Leftovers: Use any leftover batter to coat thin slices of zucchini; sliced, salted, and drained eggplant; onions cut into rings; or thin slices of baby artichokes. In fact, make extra batter for the pleasure of these delicious fritters. Serve piled up together, shrimps and vegetables, in a large hot dish with plenty of lemon quarters to squeeze over and a little bottle of chili oil (page 103), in case someone likes their food hot.

◆

SHRIMP CROQUETTES

Croquetas (Spain)

Spanish cooking came under the Dutch influence during the sixteenth century, when Charles V, the Holy Roman Emperor, managed to unite most of Europe. Today these Flemish-style *croquetas* are nearly as popular a dish in Spain as the *tortilla*. A certain dexterity is needed to roll the soft shapes, but it is a skill which many otherwise simple peasant cooks have mastered. Much as all Spanish women can turn out a good *tortilla*, so can most of them make a *croqueta*.

Croquetas are often served as a *tapa*, as the tidbits served with wine in Spanish bars are named. *Tapas* can range from a simple dish of green olives to tiny portions of complicated *cocidos* or stews. The name seems to have come from the Spanish word *tapar*, meaning "to cover." Little dishes of delicacies used to be balanced on top of the bar's specialty—a glass of the local red wine or the light dry sherries of Jerez and Montilla. There is usually one house in even the tiniest of rural communities which serves as a bar, and everyone who can afford the price of a drink will take an evening glass or two, accompanied by its "cover."

SERVES: 4 to 6 (25 to 30 *croquetas*)

TIME: Start the day before if possible; 50 to 60 minutes plus a half hour rest period

¼ *pound cooked shelled shrimps or prawns*	1 *small glass dry sherry*
6 *ounces (¾ cup) butter or 6 tablespoons oil*	*Salt and pepper*
	Flour for coating
6 *ounces (1½ cups) flour*	2 *eggs*
2 *cups milk or stock (or a mixture of both)*	*Bread crumbs for coating (homemade are best, page 405)*
	Oil for frying

You will need a small saucepan, several flat plates, and a frying pan. Chop the shrimps or prawns finely. Warm the butter or oil in a small saucepan. Stir in the flour and cook gently until the mixture looks sandy. Stir in the liquids, beating to avoid lumps—if you are nervous, heat the liquid before you add it, and then there will be no question of anything but a beautifully smooth sauce. Cook gently over low heat, stirring until the mixture is thick. This will take about 10 minutes. Add the shrimps, a teaspoon of salt, and plenty of black pepper, and boil it up again. Pour it onto a large flat dish, and leave it to cool and solidify for an hour or two.

When you are ready to proceed, set out in a line in front of you first the now-solid *croqueta* mixture in its dish, then a plate with seasoned flour, then a plate with the eggs beaten with a little milk, then a plate with bread crumbs, then an empty plate. You now have a conveyor-belt arrangement. Drop spoonfuls of the mixture into the seasoned flour and roll each spoonful into small bolsters with well-floured hands. Roll the bolsters in the egg and then in the bread crumbs, and transfer them to the empty plate. Continue until all the mixture is used up. When you are skilled at this, you'll use less flour and produce more delicate *croquetas*.

Put the *croquetas* in the refrigerator to rest for half an hour if there is time. Put on a deep pan of oil to heat. When a fine blue haze rises and a cube of bread turns golden in a moment, drop in the *croquetas* and fry them until golden—5 to 6 minutes should be enough. Do not do too many at a time, or the temperature of the oil will drop too low. Continue frying until all are ready.

Best served hot from the pan, accompany the *croquetas* with a cos lettuce, tomato, cucumber, and onion salad, chopped roughly in the Spanish manner and dressed with olive oil, vinegar, and salt. Add a plate of thin-fleshed green peppers fried (whole but seeded) in olive oil with a few slices of garlic (the imported variety of pepper will have to be stalked, seeded, and sliced length-wise first). Serve with some cold light beer or a bottle of chilled dry sherry, and your meal will have been well worth the effort.

SUGGESTIONS

Sometimes the white sauce is flavored with chopped *serrano* ham, sometimes with cheese (Dutch Gouda, called *Bolla* in Spain, is the favorite), sometimes with chopped hard-cooked egg. Any little bit of cooked ham, chicken, or fish flavors the mix, although it is often made innocent of any complications.

The men of Oostduinkerke on the Belgian coast, where the last of the equestrian shrimp fishermen ride their cart horses through the surf, prefer their catch cooked in a similar manner. The peeled shrimps are bathed in a thickened sauce made not with stock or milk, but with dark beer. The mixture is then piled into scallop shells, and the bread crumbs are sprinkled over and dotted with butter before being put under a hot grill to brown.

SEA URCHINS

Oursins (France and the Mediterranean)

These hedgehog-prickled sea creatures are sold in every Mediterranean harbor market as a mid-morning snack. They are clipped around the middle by the deft salesman, with a special *coupe-oursins*. The customer consumes the sweet orange flesh then and there without embellishment save a squeeze of lemon. Eliza Puttnam Heaton went fishing for sea urchins in Sicily, in 1908:

> He [the fisherman] dipped a reed into his oil-jar and let fall on the choppy water a drop or two of oil. Then he put overboard a tangle of net, dragging it across the bottom by the hook on his cane rod, keeping within the circle of the oil mirror. After a little he lifted the net and took out of it, enmeshed by their spines, half a dozen big brown sea urchins. "Shall we eat?" he suggested, bringing out the basket with bread and cutting the "fruit of the sea" as one might slice off the top of a lemon. [*By-Paths in Sicily*, Eliza Putnam Heaton, 1920]

CAVIAR

KEEPING CAVIAR

Kaviaari (Finland and Scandinavia)

Fish eggs are the fisherman's portion. Fresh caviar is a highly perishable delicacy and was, before the advent of refrigerated transport, consumed on the spot. The mighty sturgeon, whose roe has long been the food of the emperor as well as his peasantry, and the lumpfish (or sucker-fish or paddle-cock, provider of those salty little black or red-dyed fish eggs familiar from delicatessen shelves) are not the only fish which bear good caviar. Excellent eating, too, are the eggs of salmon, trout, capelin (an inhabitant of the Arctic seas chiefly famous as the cod's lunch), and the two whitefish—powan and vendace—which migrate between fresh and salt northern waters. Mullet, shad, turbot, and pike can also be added to the list. All caviar is at its best eaten fresh without further fuss. Simply spoon it onto buttered dark bread (page 407) with a little chopped onion or a squeeze of fresh lemon.

If you need to store your caviar, prepare it as follows.

SERVES: 4

TIME: 10 minutes

½ pound fish eggs
1 tablespoon salt
½ tablespoon plain aquavit, vodka, or eau-de-vie
1 tablespoon light seed oil (sunflower or rapeseed)

You will need a bowl and 2 to 3 small jars. Leaving the roe whole, salt the covering membrane thoroughly. Leave in the refrigerator overnight to firm up.

The following morning split the membrane and empty the contents into a bowl. Sprinkle with the alcohol. Pot the caviar and trickle a thin film of oil over. Seal and keep in the refrigerator. Thus prepared, the caviar will be good for a week.

Serve with rye bread and sweet butter, pepper, quartered lemons, and a bowl of chopped onion on the side. Or serve with potato *lompe* (page 420), in which to roll up each spoonful of caviar with some sour cream. A glass of Finnish vodka will complete the pleasure.

COD'S ROE SALAD-PURÉE

Taramasalata (Greece)

The roe of the gray mullet, *tarama*, which is still salted, dried, and preserved in wax all around the Mediterranean, was the original ingredient for this ancient preparation. It is now so expensive that even the Greeks use cod's roe as a substitute. This is the most famous of all the Greek salad-purées.

SERVES: 6 to 8

TIME: 20 minutes

12	ounces tarama *or salted smoked cod's roe*	2	*slices of day-old bread*
		1	*cup olive oil*
1	*small onion*	2	*tablespoons lemon juice*

You will need a pestle and mortar or a blender, and a bowl. Remove the hard bits of skin from the roe. Peel and then mince the onion very fine. If the onion's flavor is strong, sprinkle it with salt and leave it to drain for 15 to 20 minutes. Rinse off the salt before using. Put the bread to soak in a little water. When it is soggy, squeeze it dry. Pound the roe with the bread, and then slowly beat in the oil and the lemon juice until you have a smooth light paste.

Alternatively, all the ingredients can be put into a blender—in which case, the oil should be added in a steady stream as for a mayonnaise. This method produces a creamier mixture than the handmade version—very good, but slightly different. Serve cool. It will keep for at least a week stored in a tightly covered jar in the refrigerator.

Decorate with a few black olives and serve with a dish of radishes and hot pita bread. Sit in the sun and scoop the *taramasalata* up on your bread. Have a little glass of *raki* and a tumbler of fresh spring water at your elbow—the fish paste is salty. To follow, serve a dish of Greek salad topped with a slice or two of well-flavored feta cheese, and a plate of french fries, fried twice (once to soften them and once to crisp them) in good olive oil.

SUGGESTIONS

You can include garlic in the *taramasalata* if you must, but this is often done only to add taste if the mixture has not sufficient fish roe and has been bulked out with bread. Save the extra stale bread for a *skordalia* (page 56) to accompany this salad.

CHAPTER SEVEN

Poultry

Even the poorest European peasant households could usually support a few barnyard fowl, particularly since good egg layers often provided the wife's cash crop. Although farm hens were primarily kept for eggs rather than meat, a few young cockerels were often fattened up for high days and holidays. Most peasant recipes concentrate on ways of dealing with elderly birds—plenty of soups and stews, and slow-cooking are the norm.

The actual killing of poultry was almost invariably woman's work. Gray-haired María, the baker's sturdy wife at my nearby village of Pelayo in southern Spain, was the local expert. María kept hens herself and sold the eggs. Sometimes at Christmas she would act as agent for the farmers who lived in the hills behind, and they would walk their turkeys and geese down to the little bakery beside the main road for her to sell on their behalf. The unwary purchaser, perhaps a motorist on his way home to the town below, was likely to find his Christmas dinner fully feathered and squawking on the seat beside him unless he specified in advance that he did not wish to receive it on the hoof—or, more accurately, on the claw.

When María consented to act as executioner, the good lady would make her customer secure the bird's legs and then with one swift sure movement, double over the chicken's head and sever the spine at the base of the skull. She preferred to pluck her chickens dry, sitting out on the back stoop in the sun and working from the head to the tail. It never took her more than 3 minutes a bird. Head, feet, gizzards, and neck all went into the stew pot. Any of the little golden unlaid eggs she found inside would go to enrich the *puchero*. Nothing was ever wasted.

CHICKEN

GARLIC CHICKEN

Pollo al ajillo (Spain)

This is a favorite way with both chicken and rabbit, the meats most likely to be found, along with the products of the family porker, in the Spanish peasant kitchen. A peasant neighbor in Spain, who lived with his goat-herding and cheese-making family down the valley from my house, used to be sent out as a child during Spain's civil war on an unusual, but typically ingenious, form of rabbit hunt when there was no young cockerel to be spared for the pot. He had to watch from below a cliff where a pair of huge eagle owls nested until one of the birds returned to its young with a rabbit. He would then run to alert his father, who climbed the cliff and robbed the owlets of their supper. This is how the family liked its young chickens or pirated rabbits cooked.

SERVES: 4

TIME: Start the day before if you are using rabbit; 20 minutes plus 25 minutes cooking

1 free-range chicken or rabbit	5 to 6 tablespoons olive oil
1 tablespoon flour	1 large glass of dry sherry or
Salt and pepper	white wine
1 large head of garlic	

You will need a wide shallow frying pan. Chop the bird into 16 pieces: drumsticks and thighs (4), wings (2), neck (1); chop the back into three sections (3), and each side of breast into 3 (6). Peasant cooks use all of their valuable chicken, including the bony back piece, to be nibbled and sucked of all its little corners of meat. This allows one chicken to feed many.

If you are using a rabbit, it will be best if you marinate it overnight in 2 to 3 tablespoons of white wine vinegar. The next day dry it and cut it into pieces, and proceed as for the chicken.

Roll the pieces of chicken or rabbit lightly in the flour seasoned with salt and freshly milled pepper. Peel the garlic—there should be 10 to 12 good fat cloves—and chop it roughly.

Heat the oil gently in a wide shallow pan. Hold the chicken or rabbit pieces and allow them to take color. Add the garlic and fry together for a moment. Add the sherry or wine, and allow it to bubble up and evaporate the alcohol. Cover the pan and let stew on low heat for 30 to 40 minutes, until the meat is tender and the liquid nearly evaporated.

Serve in its own garlic-scented oil with plenty of bread to mop up the juices, and a plate of thick-cut french fries fried golden in olive oil—the more to dinner, the more french fries. Accompany with a salad of fresh tomatoes sliced and sprinkled with a little chopped garlic, a teaspoon of sugar, and plenty of freshly milled pepper. Finish with a summer fruit—custard apples, ivory flesh starred with ebony pips, to be cut in half and eaten with a spoon, or sweet orange-fleshed medlars are perfect.

◆

GARLIC CHICKEN

Poulet à l'ail (France)

This is a dish to be eaten in the evening. The Gallic gentleman who recommends the recipe follows it with this advice:

> Enjoy your garlic at home parties only, maybe for lunch in the country; but in town, only for supper, so that everybody has a good night's sleep ahead to eliminate the fragrance which could be unbearable to others. Garlic has to be restrained to private pleasure.

SERVES: 4

TIME: 20 minutes plus 1 hour and 15 minutes cooking

1 *wine glass of olive oil*	*Sprigs of thyme, rosemary, and*
40 *garlic cloves, unpeeled (more if*	*mixed herbs: bay, wild*
the chicken is large)	*thyme, savory, marjoram,*
1 *roasting chicken*	*chives, hyssop, chervil*
Salt and pepper	

Preheat the oven to 350°F. You will need a casserole which will accommodate the whole chicken.

Pour half the oil into the casserole and then add the unpeeled garlic cloves. Settle the neatly trussed roasting chicken on this pearly bed. Sprinkle with salt and pepper, and pour on the rest of the oil. Tuck the branches of herbs all around and above. Cover tightly, sealing the lid with a flour-and-water paste if it does not fit absolutely snugly.

Bake the casserole for 1 hour and 15 minutes. Use the last 15 minutes' waiting time to make a green salad and to cut 2 or 3 thick slices of bread for each diner. Toast the bread under a very hot broiler—there are wire-grid contraptions sold in Mediterranean countries for toasting bread over a top flame; this gives a delicious singed flavor to the toast. Large napkins and water bowls for the fingers may be necessary. Call your guests to the table and carry in the still-sealed casserole.

When everyone is seated, remove the lid. The scent will be heavenly—and the chicken perfectly cooked and deliciously succulent. Each diner helps himself to bread, a piece of chicken, and a few of the whole cloves of garlic which are still sealed in their papery jackets. The garlic cloves are to be squeezed out onto a piece of hot toasted bread—you will find baked garlic tender and remarkably mild and sweet—and topped with a little piece of chicken. There are those who put the cloves of garlic straight into the mouth and then pop the skins with their teeth. Then you have only to solve the delicate problem of transferring the empty shell to the rim of your plate. Rinse your fingers and take a big swallow of cold white wine. A perfect cheese and a tender green salad complete the pleasure.

◆

PAN-FRIED CHICKEN

Pollo in padella (Italy)

Conchetta, my neighbor near Siena in Tuscany, would serve one of her young cockerels as the main dish for Sunday lunch. A meat dish such as this is put on the table after the pasta, which, on the day I shared the family's midday meal, was spaghetti turned in a ladle or two of tomato-and-meat sauce.

SERVES: 4 as a main dish; 6 to 8 after a filling pasta dish

TIME: 20 minutes plus 30 minutes cooking

1	chicken, jointed into 12 to 14 pieces	2 to 3 sage leaves and/or a branch of rosemary
3	garlic cloves	Salt and pepper
4	tablespoons olive oil	1 glass of white wine

You will need a large heavy frying pan. Wipe the chicken. Peel and crush the garlic. Heat the oil gently in a wide frying pan. Add the herbs and the garlic and let them fry for a moment to scent the oil. Add the chicken and turn it in the oil until it has taken a little color. Sprinkle with a little salt and freshly milled pepper, and throw in the white wine. Turn the heat down and leave the chicken pieces to simmer uncovered for 20 to 30 minutes, until the wine has evaporated and the chicken is tender and just moist.

Serve as a main dish with a side dish of spinach finished with oil and lemon, or young artichokes stewed with olive oil and just enough water to keep them moist.

Follow with a salad—perhaps tomatoes dressed with olive oil and a few leaves of fresh basil. In Italian rural households a bowl of whole tomatoes plus small bottles of oil and vinegar might be offered—salads are often served without dressing to be finished to your own taste.

A piece of cheese and some fresh fruit, followed by a tiny cup of bitter black coffee, is the Italians' preferred way to round off a meal. Pecorino and Grana are the favorites of rural Tuscany: Italian cheeses, except for the local ones eaten absolutely fresh, are usually matured, well-flavored, salty, and strong. The repertoire lacks the wide variety and sophistication of the French cheese board, but makes up for it in honesty and vigor.

◆

CHICKEN STUFFED WITH PINE NUTS

Kotopoulo Yemisto (Greece)

The Turkish culinary influence was so strong in the days of the Ottoman Empire that this stuffing is universal throughout Greece and the Balkans, and can often be found in Italy and Spain (probably via the Moors) as well.

SERVES: 6 to 7

TIME: 30 to 40 minutes plus 1 hour cooking

1 chicken	4 ounces (½ cup) rice
4 tablespoons olive oil	1 cup water
Salt and pepper	2 tablespoons raisins or currants
2 tablespoons pine nuts	

You will need a medium-size frying pan and an ovenproof dish. Wipe the chicken and trim off any stray feathers. Rub the skin with a little of the oil, salt, and freshly milled pepper. Put the rest of the oil to warm in a frying pan. Add the pine nuts and turn them in the oil until they toast golden. Push them to one side and add the rice, turning it until it looks transparent. Pour in the water and let it bubble up. Add the raisins or currants. Simmer uncovered for 20 minutes until the water has evaporated, the raisins or currants are plump, and the rice is soft.

Preheat the oven to 350°F.

Stuff the chicken with this mixture and put it in an ovenproof dish. Trickle a little more oil over. Broil or roast the chicken for at least an hour, until the juices from the leg run clear when pierced with a skewer. Let it cool a little before you serve it—the Greeks don't approve of very hot food. Cut the chicken into convenient pieces and serve each piece with a spoonful of rice stuffing. Precede with one of the Greek salad-purées, and accompany with a Greek salad of roughly chunked tomatoes, green peppers, back olives, and purple onion, dressed with olive oil, salt, and a squeeze of lemon. French fries sprinkled with a little grated strong white cheese can be served as well if you have many people to feed.

Use the rice mixture to stuff vegetables—tomatoes, eggplant, zucchini. Left-over stuffing mixed with any odd bits of chicken, well chopped, makes a good stuffing for hollowed-out parboiled potatoes. See stuffed vegetables on page 37 for further instructions.

BOILED CHICKEN AND NOODLES

Suppenhuhn mit Nudeln (Austria)

This is an innkeeper's dish, very popular as a second breakfast. An elderly boiler past its egg-laying days will do as well as a spring chicken—the flavor of an old barnyard fowl is far superior to that of a young battery hen. Serve with noodles cooked in the broth—either noodles you have bought or, preferably, your own.

SERVES: 6 to 8

TIME: 1 hour (if you make your own noodles) plus 1 to 2 hours cooking

THE SOUP:

1 large chicken	2 *leeks, scrubbed but not peeled,*
1 *bunch of Italian parsley or a*	*or 2 onions*
parsley root	3 *quarts water*
A few sprigs of lovage or celery	1 *teasploon salt*
leaves	*Peppercorns*
1 *pound carrots, scrubbed but not*	
peeled	

THE EGG NOODLES:

½   *pound (1¾ cups) all-purpose flour*
½   *teaspoon salt*
2   *eggs*
About 2 eggcups of water

You will need a large stew pot and a rolling pin or a pasta maker. Wipe the chicken and put it in a big stew pot with the parsley, lovage or celery leaves, carrots, leeks or onions, and water. Bring to a boil and then skim off the gray foam. Turn down to simmer, and add the salt and half a dozen whole peppercorns.

Simmer gently for 1 to 2 hours, depending on the age of the bird. When it is soft and the soup well-flavored, take out the bird and put it aside to keep warm. Strain the soup, return it to the pan, and heat it again, ready for the noodles to be cooked in it.

Sift the flour and the salt together directly onto the kitchen table. You need plenty of elbow room. Make a dip in the middle and crack the eggs into it. Work them into the dough with your hand. Add the water, kneading as you go, until you have a soft, pliable dough. (This can be started in your mixer and finished by hand).

If you have a pasta roller, so much the better. It is the easiest way to make noodles, and if you like both them and the various pastas, it is well worth acquiring one. A pasta roller is an implement which bolts onto the kitchen table like a little mangle, and operates on the same principle. When you have rolled the dough thin enough by progressively decreasing the gaps between the rollers, you then roll it through a slot equipped with cutters—there is normally a choice of two or three ribbon widths.

If you have no roller, flour the table and roll out the dough until it is very thin. It will spring back, but persevere—there is a trick for rolling it out loosely, curling it back over the rolling pin as you go, so that the rolling pin becomes the center of a several-layered bolster. Leave the flat sheet to dry out for 15 minutes. Then sprinkle it generously with flour, roll it up into a jelly-roll cylinder, and slice it into rings—fine-cut for soup, thicker if they are to be served plain with butter or with a cream sauce spiked with chopped ham or dried mushrooms. Leave the noodles piled loosely to dry out for another half hour.

The noodles should be poached in boiling soup, or boiling water, for 2 to 4 minutes, depending on size and freshness.

Serve the soup in deep soup plates. It is very comforting on a cold day.

◆

SUGGESTIONS

Egg noodles store well—make a double recipe and allow one portion to dry until brittle; then keep it in an airtight jar in the cupboard.

Serve either in the soup or as a sweet—tossed in melted butter, pounded walnuts and sugar—after a thick vegetable soup. No German or Austrian farmhouse cook would dream of producing a main meal that did not include a noodle, dumpling, or strudel dish.

◆

SOUR SOUP MADE FROM CHICKEN

Ciorba de pui (Rumania)

This is a much-loved peasant staple, made usually, naturally enough, with an old hen past her useful egg-laying age. It was appreciated in 1939 by the traveler D. J. Hall, taking a welcome meal with the village doctor:

I have never eaten such a meal as I did the next day; and that is saying a good deal of a meal in a country whose people are the most prodigious eaters perhaps in the world. Though capacities might increase everywhere if food became as plentiful and cheap as it is in Romania. We had first *ciorba de pui*, a sour soup made from chicken, rich with butter and filled with vegetables. This was followed by a sucking pig. It came on to the table whole, half an apple in its mouth, a blue bow on its forehead. I felt sad till I began to eat it, and then my sorrow passed. That seemed to me to be enough. But then came slices of roast goose with peppers, and afterwards a cheese pancake. The wine was good too. [*Romanian Furrow*, D. J. Hall, 1939]

SERVES: 6

TIME: 20 minutes plus 1½ to 2½ hours cooking

1 chicken (weighing 2 to 3 pounds)	6 peppercorns
	1 teaspoon salt
Bay leaf and allspice	½ cabbage (optional)
3 medium-sized onions	2 slices of old bread
3 carrots	1 tablespoon vinegar
1 celery root	3 egg yolks
Parsley root (if you can find it)	Dill and savory

You will need a large stew pot. Wipe the chicken and trim off any stray feathers. If it is an old boiler, it will take twice as long to cook as a roaster, so put it on to boil in enough water to cover, with the bay leaves and allspice, for an hour before you add the vegetables, trimmed, peeled, and left more or less whole.

If you have a roasting chicken, put it in a roomy pot and immediately add the mixed vegetables, bay leaf, allspice, peppercorns, and a little salt. Cover with cold water. Bring to a boil 3 times; skim and add a little cold water each time to send the cloudy bits to the bottom. Simmer for 1¼ to 1½ hours, until the chicken is tender.

Fifteen minutes before the end of the cooking time, add the sliced cabbage if you wish. Mash the bread (you can upgrade the soup by replacing the bread with a small carton of cream) with the vinegar. Beat it into the egg yolks and add a ladleful of the hot chicken broth to the mixture. Beat it well in. Take the pot off the fire and stir the egg-yolk mixture into the soup. Do not boil it again. Cut the chicken into serving pieces.

Chop up the herbs and scatter them over the top. Serve the soup with bread and wine. A handful of sweet grapes or plums, and a glass of *tuica* plum brandy (page 477) will finish the meal.

Save the chicken itself for the recipe which follows, and you will have two dishes for the price of one.

CHICKEN POT ROAST

Tocana de pui (Rumania)

The young woman who gave me this recipe, a shepherd's wife in the Carpathians, had just bought in the market at Sibiu a special dish in which to cook it. She showed me a chicken-shaped earthenware casserole, oval and unlidded. Carpathian shepherds are exempt from modern Rumanian state collectivization, and their pantries are well stocked—there is no shortage of cheese from the sheep, butter and cream from the family cow, or eggs and poultry from the yard, as there is in the rest of the country.

SERVES: 4

TIME: 10 minutes plus 30 minutes cooking

15 to 20 *garlic cloves*
1   *boiled chicken or any piece of boiled meat*
2   *ounces (4 tablespoons) butter*
½   *cup fresh or sour cream*

Preheat the oven to 350°F. You will need a small baking dish.
   Peel the garlic, slice it, and scatter it over and in the chicken. Put the bird in a close-fitting casserole, tuck the butter inside it, and pour the cream over it. Cover with wax paper or foil, and roast or broil in the oven for half an hour. Serve with noodles, a salad, and cold white wine. Mme. Frunzete, the shepherd's wife, grew beautiful grapes in her courtyard, and would serve them to finish the meal.
   This treatment of a soup meat as a roast after its preliminary boiling is characteristic of the Transylvanian kitchen. The method is effective with any tough piece of meat. The roots of the technique can be found (appropriately enough to the Roman colony of Dacia) in ancient Rome: Apicius gives similar recipes in his fifth-century work, *De Re Coquinaria*—ancient lessons well learned.

CHICKEN PORKOLT POT ROAST

Porkolt csirke (Hungary)

Porkolt means "singed," which indicates the culinary method that distinguishes this dish from a *gulyas:* The meat is boiled so dry it fries for the last few moments of cooking. *Porkolt* can be made with any kind of meat or game or even fish. This is the dish served in Austria as a goulash. Like the *gulyas,* it has no cream and no flour. See the Austro-Hungarian *gulyas* recipe (page 375) for the version made with veal. As for the chicken, there is an old Hungarian town dwellers' joke that when peasant kills a chicken, either the peasant is sick—or the chicken. In this case, assume it's a dish to fortify a poorly peasant.

S E R V E S : 4 to 5

T I M E : 25 to 30 minutes plus 50 to 90 minutes cooking

One 2 to 3 pound chicken, young or old	2 ounces (4 tablespoons) lard
1½ pounds onions	2 tablespoons Noble Rose or sweet paprika
2 garlic cloves	Pepper to taste
1 teaspoon salt	1 wine glass of water

You will need a large stew pot. Cut the chicken into a dozen pieces—using the whole carcass. Peel the onions and slice finely. Peel the garlic and crush it with the salt. Melt the lard in a heavy stew pot.

When the fat is well melted, add the onions and the garlic. Fry them gently until golden. Add the pieces of chicken. Fry them gently too. The whole operation will take 10 minutes and is more like stewing than frying.

Take the pot off the heat and stir in the paprika and a good sprinkling of freshly milled pepper. Put the pot back on the heat and add the water. Bring it to a boil; then cover the pot tightly and stew very gently for 50 to 60 minutes if you have a young bird, and for an hour and a half if the bird is an old boiler. Check regularly that the pot has not boiled dry—adding the minimum of liquid necessary.

Turn up the heat and take the lid off the pot at the end. Watch carefully as the liquid boils nearly clean away. Take it off just before anything burns. Paprika is a vegetable and the flavor is fugitive.

Serve the chicken *porkolt* immediately with its own minimal but wonderfully aromatic juices. There won't be any leftovers—just as well, since chicken *porkolt* is at its best on the day it is made. Accompany with flat or "barley" noodles (see *tahonya* on page 162). Take a glass of *palinka*, the excellent Hungarian fruit brandy which is drunk both before and after the meal. Best of all is the delicious *barakpalinka*, a dry apricot brandy so strongly flavored with the ripe fruit it is traditionally likened to drinking sunshine.

SUGGESTIONS

Optional, in deference to Hungarian gardening skills, include 2 to 3 cloves of garlic crushed with salt, and 1 green pepper, seeded and cubed.

Fish porkolt: Make a *porkolt* with a large fish cut into pieces. A carp is particularly good: Eighteenth-century French monks originally selectively bred this naturally rather muddy-flavored and tough-scaled fish into its present domestic excellence. The variety called mirror carp is now found all over Eastern Europe, fed in ponds for a year or two until it reaches a weight of 3 to 4 pounds. The fish are then kept alive in tanks in the fish markets, to be individually chosen and scooped out in a net on demand by housewives from the Bosporus to the Baltic. To a northern visitor, enormous fish tanks, crammed with slow-moving bodies and unwinking eyes, are one of the more exotic sights in the markets of the Balkans.

Prepare the sauce first, as for the chicken *porkolt*. The fish will take only 5 to 10 minutes to cook, depending on the size of the pieces. If you do not fry the onions first, but only lay the pieces of fish on top and add more water, you will have the famous *szeged* fish soup. A 4-pound fish will feed 6 people.

CHICKEN-AND-VEGETABLE STEW

Jachnia (Bulgaria)

This is a recipe midway between the southern and the northern kitchen. The practice of frying food before stewing liquid is added was introduced into the European kitchen from the Middle East. Its purpose is usually explained as "sealing in the juices of the meat." In reality it does no such thing: It is the function of the stewing process to break down such barriers. However, the browning of meat or sugar-rich vegetables like onions gives the dish an appetizing color and a lovely roasted flavor.

SERVES : 6

T I M E : 25 to 30 minutes plus 1 hour cooking

1	chicken	½	cup sunflower oil
1	pound scallions with their leaves		Salt and pepper
2	fresh spring garlics with leaves		Fresh herbs, 1 tablespoon each:
	or 4 dried garlic cloves		savory, mint, Italian parsley
1	pound eggplant		
1	pound tomatoes, skinned (or a		
	1-pound can of tomatoes)		

You will need a casserole or a medium-sized stew pot. Wipe dry and then joint the chicken into 12 pieces. Top and tail the scallions—leaving the green leaves on. Do the same for the fresh garlic, or peel and chop the dried garlic. Cut off the stalk, wipe, and cube the eggplant. Chop the tomatoes.

Heat 2 tablespoons of the oil in a casserole or stewpan with a lid, and add the chicken pieces. Fry the joints gently until they brown. Push them to one side, and add the onions and the garlic. Fry them until they soften. Add the rest of the oil and lightly fry the eggplant in it. Season with salt and pepper. Add the tomatoes. Cover and simmer gently for an hour.

Chop the herbs finely and add them 5 minutes before the end of cooking time.

Serve with rice or bread. There are some good light Bulgarian red wines which would pleasantly accompany the dish.

◆

COCK-A-LEEKIE

(Scotland)

Kissing cousin to the ancient English dishes of Malachi and Gallimawfrey, Cock-a-leekie is the only version of this soup-stew which has survived into the modern British kitchen. The dish can be prepared with a good bone stock and the leeks on their own. The chicken is a luxury addition, a special-occasion food: The loser in a cockfight used to be recommended, since its sinews would be firm and give body to the soup. Today an ordinary roasting chicken normally has to serve instead.

SERVES: 6

TIME: 10 minutes plus 2½ hours cooking

1	large boiling fowl (weighing 2	1	teaspoon salt
	to 3 pounds)	1	teaspoon peppercorns
3	quarts water	5	pounds leeks

You will need a large stewpan. Wipe the chicken and put it in a roomy saucepan. Cover it with the water, salted, and with the crushed peppercorns sprinkled in. Boil gently, skimming regularly, for half an hour.

Wash and cut the leeks into short lengths. After half an hour, add half of the leeks to the soup. Continue simmering for another 1½ hours. Add the rest of the leeks and continue to cook for another half hour. The soup must be very thick with leeks, and the first part of them must be boiled down into the soup until they become almost liquid themselves.

Sometimes the capon is served in the tureen with the soup. Sometimes it is served afterwards, cut in pieces and accompanied with potatoes, peeled and sliced and simmered in a little of the soup.

This makes a pleasant leek soup without the chicken, just using good bone stock.

◆

SUGGESTIONS

The inclusion of prunes or raisins in the soup is a matter of contentious debate among experts on this famous dish. If you wish to do so, add a handful, well soaked, half an hour before the end of the cooking period. Talleyrand, diplomatic as always, suggested that the prunes be cooked in the broth but not served in the soup. This would serve to lightly color and sweeten the soup—a logical notion since all the onion tribe, to which the leek belongs, have a high sugar content. Some traditional recipes advocate a teaspoon of molasses should be included.

The soup is sometimes thickened with a handful of fine-ground oatmeal.

A pound of chopped spinach or chard can be added half an hour before the end of the cooking time.

◆

GRAPE-PICKERS' SOUP

Soupe des vendanges (France)

This is the *soupe* on which the grape harvesters of southwestern France sup after a hard day in the fields. The scent will have been curling out of the farmhouse kitchen window all afternoon, perfuming the soft autumn air in the vineyards below. The supper-soup is eaten in three courses out of a large deep-rimmed soup plate: first as a soup, then as *chabrot*, finally as a boiled dinner of the meat and vegetables. It is a magnificent feast which has its own rhythm and ritual.

Find a huge earthenware pot or saucepan to hold all the meats. In France special marmites are sold for just these soup-stews. There is always a pottery merchant in the market who sets up his wares alongside the vegetable stalls. He lines up his stock of marmites along the pavement in regiments of descending size, like an army of squat brown-lipped chimney pots on a palace roof. Beside them, still half-swaddled in their skins of brown tissue paper, is his range of speckled enameled saucepans. Behind them looms a forest of wooden spoons and ladles, peeled-twig whisks, wooden pastry wheels, round wooden boards for cheese, and all manner of odd little kitchen instruments: wire grills for making toast over flame, olive pitters, cocotte dishes, larding needles, snail tongs, skewers, pestles, mortars, mousetraps to supplement the farmyard cats' vigilance—in short, all the equipment deemed essential by the French country wife.

SERVES: 12

TIME: 4 hours

1 *boiling fowl with its own*	1 *bunch of parsley*
liver—plus any unlaid eggs	2 *onions plus 6 cloves*
inside or 1 whole egg	4 *garlic cloves*
3 *ounces fresh bread crumbs*	*Peppercorns*
Parsley, chervil, chives, tarragon	*Salt*
3 *pounds shin beef on the bone*	2 *pounds knuckle of veal*
plus a few extra bones	2 *pounds turnips*
6 *fat leeks*	2 *pounds carrots*
2 *heads of celery*	

TO ACCOMPANY THE MEAL:

2 *pounds ripe tomatoes*	1 *large jar of pickled gherkins*
1 *loaf of dry bread*	*Several bottles of strong red wine*
1 *pound grated Gruyère*	*such as St. Emilion*
1 *jar of capers*	

You will need a mammoth stewing pot—a 12-quart monster—and a large and a small saucepan. Put the chicken, bread crumbs, and herbs aside while you prepare the broth, which will take far longer to cook than the rest.

Put the beef and bones into the marmite or stewpan and add 5 quarts of cold water. Bring to a boil, allow it one big belch, and then turn it down to simmer. Skim off the gray froth which rises. Trim off and add to the pot the tops of the leeks, the leaves of the celery, and the stalks of the parsley. Turn off the heat every time you add fresh meats to the broth, to allow the sediment to settle so that the broth is as clear as you could wish. Add the onions (unpeeled so that their skins can add a little color to the soup) stuck with the cloves. Add the garlic cloves, also unpeeled, a dozen peppercorns, and a teaspoon of salt.

Allow it all to simmer for half an hour. Then add the knuckle of veal. Bring the soup back to a boil. Then skim off the foam and turn the broth down to simmer. You will be adding the chicken in half an hour's time.

Skim the fat off, roughly enough, soup and all, from time to time—and put in a separate saucepan on the side of the stove.

Meanwhile, prepare the chicken. Put the bread crumbs to soak in 2 tablespoons milk for a moment or two, and then squeeze them dry. Chop the chicken liver. Mix the chopped liver with the bread crumbs, and add just a pinch of salt and freshly milled pepper. Wipe the chicken and pluck out any little feather stumps which have escaped attention. Feel around inside and pull out any unlaid eggs there may be in the cavity of the chicken—they can be added to the stuffing. Chop the herbs and add 2 tablespoonfuls of them to the mix. Stuff the bird and sew it up. Turn off the heat and lower the stuffed chicken into the broth. Bring it back to a boil, allow it one big belch, skim it, and turn it down to simmer. If you are using a young bird which has not yet started laying, add an egg to the stuffing and do not put the bird in to cook until an hour before you are ready to dish up.

Simmer the meats for another hour. The soup has now been cooking for 2 hours and you are ready to add the vegetables, rinsed and chopped into short lengths. But first take the pot off the heat, and remove the bones and vegetable debris with a strainer spoon. These leftovers will now be appreciated only by the household pig.

Bring the soup back to a boil with all its meats and vegetables. Then turn it down and simmer for another 40 minutes.

Meanwhile, prepare the accompaniments. Pour boiling water over the tomatoes to loosen the skins, and then peel them and chop them. Put them into a small pan on low heat to melt into a sweet fresh sauce (you can put this through the blender if you wish). Cut the stale loaf of bread into thin slices. Grate the cheese. Open the jars of capers and pickled gherkins, and decant them into separate bowls.

Turn your attention back to the stove. Take out all the meats, which should now be soft, and the vegetables, which should now be cooked. Put them to keep warm in your second pot, which is by now half-full of the oily stock skimmings.

Turn the heat up under the soup, and boil it uncovered for 20 minutes to allow it to reduce and strengthen.

Put twelve deep plates and a large serving dish in a preheated 300°F oven to warm. When the diners are seated, remove the soup from the heat and stir in half a ladleful of cold water to send any cloudiness to the bottom. Put a slice of dry bread into each plate, and cover it with a ladleful of the broth. Allow the bread to swell for a moment before handing the plates around. Pass around the grated cheese.

While the soup is being eaten, you can prepare the meats. Take them out of the stock and put them on the serving dish. Put the fat stock back onto the heat. Slice up the beef, veal, and chicken, and its stuffing. Arrange the vegetables around.

By now the first course has been finished. Put the two bottles of red wine on the table. Fill each plate half-full with very hot fat stock. Each person now adds as much red wine to his plate as he wishes, stirs it around, and then, to be strictly correct, drinks it straight out of the plate. This process is called *faire chabrot*. No southern-born French countryman would miss it for the world.

Either pass around fresh deep plates, or give each person a chunk of fresh bread to wipe the old one clean.

It is time for the third course, the boiled dinner. Bathe the meats with a ladleful of hot fat stock, and set the steaming dish on the table for each person to help himself. Accompany the meats with a bowl of the tomato sauce, lightly seasoned and diluted with a little of the fat stock, the bowl of capers, and the bowl of pickled gherkins.

Peace descends on the company, and you can at last eat your own dinner. Set out a bowl of the year's new walnuts for those who still have a corner to fill.

You will not have to cook again tomorrow: The leftover bouillon will reheat to perfection with a handful of new vegetables. Perhaps the next day you might serve such of the meat as remains (tossed with a few capers and gherkins) in a sharp little vinaigrette, well spiked with mustard—but that is tomorrow's task.

ROAST CHICKEN AND BREAD SAUCE

(England)

The classic English way with a bird, the same method can be used for game birds—pheasant, grouse, and partridges. Today's battery farmers produce table birds so cheaply that roast chicken has overtaken beef in popularity as the British Sunday dinner. The frugal barnyard-tending housewife would not have wasted her future laying-hens on such a dish, and only the young roosters would be taken at a tender enough age for roasting. A dish this pure and simple is really only good prepared with a free-range bird. Try and buy the best you can find. The sauce is a recipe which dates back to the bread-thickened sauces of the Middle Ages. It has the peasant virtue of making the meat go further, as well as being an excellent complement to all roast birds.

YIELD: A 3-pound bird serves 5 to 6

TIME: 40 minutes plus 1 hour cooking

THE CHICKEN:
1 roasting chicken
2 ounces (4 tablespoons) butter
3 to 4 thin slices of smoked bacon

½ onion and a few fresh herbs: thyme, rosemary, and Italian parsley
Peppercorns

THE SAUCE:

3   cloves (a luxury for those who
    could afford this expensive spice,
    wartime recipes usually
    instruct readers to rinse them off
    and reuse them)
1   onion (or the other half of the
    one that went into the bird)

1   cup milk
2   ounces (¼ cup) fresh bread
    crumbs
Salt and pepper
1   ounce (2 tablespoons) butter and
    a little cream

You will need a roasting pan for the chicken and a small saucepan for the bread sauce. Preheat the oven to 375°F.

Truss the chicken if this has not already been done for you. Spread half the butter over the bird and cover it with the bacon. Put the onion, herbs, and the rest of the butter inside with the liver (well wiped and with any bitter green bits trimmed off). A hollow bird must be stuffed, or it will dry out in the roasting oven.

Put the chicken into a roasting pan. Roast it for 1 hour and 15 minutes, allowing 25 minutes to the pound at 375°F. Start the cooking with the bird lying first on one side and then on the other—leaving it breast side up for the last half hour. Baste frequently. Remove the bacon fat from the breast 10 minutes before the end of the cooking time to allow the skin to crisp. Test by piercing the leg with a skewer—the juices should run clear. If they run pink, it is not yet done, and chickens, particularly battery chickens, must be well cooked. If no juice runs at all, the chicken is still raw.

While the chicken cooks, put the gizzard, neck and heart, and some peppercorns to simmer in a little water so that you have a stock for the gravy.

Meanwhile, prepare the sauce. Stick the cloves into the onion, and put it with the milk and the bread crumbs into a small saucepan to infuse while the bird is roasting.

Ten minutes before you are ready to serve, heat the sauce gently. Allow it one big belch and then turn down the heat. Simmer gently for 10 minutes. Stir in a few more bread crumbs if it is not thick enough—bread sauce should not be too runny. Add salt and plenty of pepper, and stir in the butter and cream. Pass separately and very hot, with the roast bird.

When the bird is cooked to a turn, transfer it to a serving dish and put it to rest in the barely warm oven while you make a gravy. Strain 1 cup of giblet stock into the brown juices in the roasting pan. Boil together fiercely, scraping all the sticky little well-flavored bits into the gravy. Tip in the juices which have meanwhile run from the chicken. Taste, and adjust the seasoning. Serve in a separate gravy boat.

Accompany the roast chicken with the bread sauce, roast potatoes (page 32), and a dish of young peas or little fava beans, or green beans or carrots lightly boiled and tossed with butter.

Instead of the onion and herbs, stuff the chicken with a delicate forcemeat made with 2 ounces (¼ cup) of bread crumbs mixed with 1 ounce (2 table-spoons) of melted butter, plenty of chopped herbs—shallot, parsley, thyme—and the chopped chicken liver, salt, and pepper.

Feathered game such as pheasant, partridge, and grouse can be cooked in the same way and with the same accompaniments, but with the addition of fried bread crumbs and a sharp clear fruit jelly—rowan jelly is particularly good with grouse.

◆

CHICKEN STEW

Waterzootsje (Belguim)

This is the Belgian boiled chicken dish. All regional cooks have their own version, and this soup-stew was also made with fish. In the days of furnaces and steam power, hungry deep-sea fishermen would cook the stew in a great iron cauldron hanging over the furnaces of the fishing boat.

SERVES: 5 to 6

TIME: 20 minutes plus 25 to 30 minutes cooking

1	boiling fowl or a large roasting chicken		Italian parsley and sage
			Salt
3	celery stalks	1	quart water
3	ounces (6 tablespoons) butter	1	cup lager beer

You will need a large stewpan. Cut the chicken into 10 to 12 pieces. Rinse and slice the celery. Melt half the butter in a heavy stewpan and lightly cook the celery in it for a few moments. Lay the chicken pieces on top, and sprinkle in the herbs and salt. Cover with the water and the beer.

Bring to a boil and dot the surface with the rest of the butter. Turn the heat down, cover, and simmer for an hour (depending on the youth of the bird), until the meat is tender and the water has reduced to a well-flavored sauce. Serve with slices of buttered bread and a glass of Belgian beer.

If you want to make the fish version, use the bones and trimmings to make a strong stock first (3 cups of water and 30 minutes' simmering will be enough to extract the juices). Strain and reboil for another 20 minutes with the vegetables. Add the fish, cut into slices, dot with butter, and cook for 15 to 20 minutes, half uncovered so that the liquid reduces and strengthens.

TURKEY OR CHICKEN WITH YOGURT

Pile Kisselo Mleko (Bulgaria)

The Bulgarians have two specialties: yogurt and vegetables. Turkeys were supplied from The New World by their Ottoman ancestors.

SERVES: 4

TIME: 30 to 35 minutes plus 30 minutes cooking

1 pound turkey or chicken meat, off the bone	2 green peppers
1 garlic clove	½ pound tomatoes (or an 8-ounce can of tomatoes)
½ teaspoon salt	1 small cucumber
6 tablespoons oil	1 handful of Italian parsley
1 teaspoon paprika	½ cup thick yogurt (see note below)
Pepper	
2 leeks	

Note: Yogurt can be thickened by leaving it to drip for a few hours in a sieve or colander lined with a clean, scalded cloth. The longer you leave it, the thicker it will become, until eventually you have a fresh curd cheese.

You will need a heavy casserole. Chop the turkey or chicken meat. Crush the garlic with the salt, and work it into the meat along with a tablespoon of the oil and the paprika. Season with pepper and leave aside to marinate while you prepare the vegetables.

Wash and slice the leeks. Hull and seed the peppers, and cut them into chunks. Plunge the tomatoes into boiling water to loosen the skins; then peel and chop them. Peel and chunk the cucumber. Wash the parsley and chop it finely. All the solid ingredients should be more or less the same size.

Put the oil to warm in a heavy casserole. Sauté the leeks in the hot oil, and then add the peppers. Fry for a moment. Push them to one side and add the marinated meat. Fry for a moment. Add the tomatoes and a tablespoon of water. Cover tightly and simmer for 15 minutes. Add the cucumber pieces. Simmer for 15 minutes more. Stir in the parsley.

Serve in its own casserole, or in a shallow earthenware dish, with the yogurt poured over it. Accompany with plenty of bread, and you will be well content. Finish your meal with black Turkish coffee and a glass of *slivova*.

DUCK AND GOOSE

DUCK WITH CUCUMBERS

Rata cu castravete (Rumania)

Rural Rumanians wove strong fences to keep marauding wild animals at bay—there are still wolves and bears roaming the uplands of the Carpathians today. The poultry would wander free in the yard during the day, protected by the basketwork walls which circled the smallholding. Rumanian farm wives found the duck feathers and down useful for stuffing the household's bedding. Duck and geese bones weigh heavy, so there is always comparatively little meat on the birds. This is a light and delicious way with the rich flesh.

SERVES: 4

TIME: 30 minutes plus 40 minutes cooking

1 duck for roasting	1 glass of water
Salt and pepper	1 pound small pickling cucumbers
1 tablespoon chopped marjoram	or 1 large cucumber
4 tablespoons sunflower oil	2 medium-sized onions

You will need a heavy casserole, a colander, and a frying pan. Wipe and then quarter the bird. Rub it well with salt, pepper, and the marjoram. Heat a tablespoon of the oil in a shallow casserole. When it is lightly smoking, add the duck pieces and turn them until they take color. Add the glass of water and cover the casserole. Leave the duck to simmer for 30 to 40 minutes until it is tender.

Meanwhile, grate the cucumbers and put them in a colander to drain. Peel and slice the onions, and sauté them gently in a frying pan with the rest of the oil. Ten minutes before the end of the duck's cooking time, add the onions and the cucumbers to the casserole.

Serve after a dish of *mamaliga* baked with sour cream (page 125). Cool white wine should accompany the meal.

POTTED GOOSE OR DUCK

Confit d'oie ou de canard (France)

Anser segetum, the wild goose, is the begetter of all geese used for food in Europe. For roasting, there is a breed known as the gray, or farmyard, goose, which attains a weight of between 8 and 10 pounds before being ready for the table. The Toulouse goose is fattened for the sake of its liver and for potting; it can grow to a net weight of 20 to 24 pounds, of which up to 4 pounds can be liver. This larger bird is really best suited to the *confit* pot—it is too rich and fatty to be roasted in the normal way.

The *confit* pot is one of the most useful storage items in the French farmhouse kitchen. The meat is succulent and wonderfully well-flavored, while the goose butter in which it is preserved can be used to make the simplest of dishes, such as plain sautéed potatoes, into food for the gods. It is used in many of the beans-and-bones dishes and the *garbures*, healthy soups which defy the icy winds that sweep the Languedoc plain in winter.

The household *confit* is prepared sometime between mid-October and early January, when the geese which have been fattened for the Christmas *foie gras* are sent to market. Mme. Escrieu, my Languedoc neighbor, fattened her own geese: two for her family storecupboard, and perhaps three or four more birds as her small cash crop. Acorns and walnuts collected by the children, corn from a corner of the vegetable patch, and greens gathered from the neighboring hedgerows all went to fatten her flock. By early September the great white-and-gray birds had disappeared from the yard, and *la mère* Escrieu was to be seen disappearing into one of her steadings with a basket of chestnuts and acorns with which to force-feed them.

Preparing the geese for market is women's work, as the care of the barnyard always has been, whether it involves the plump doves in the loft or the rooster outside the kitchen door. Any financial return from the sale of eggs or *foie gras* goes into a corner of the housewife's apron. Mme. Escrieu took her crop to the Saturday market in the local town of Revel, the wicker baskets bulging inside her son's battered pickup truck. Once there, she would lay out the carcasses, plucked clean to the polished ivory skin, on white cloths spread over testle tables in the square. The women of the town prodded her wares and interrogated her carefully about their diet and habitat: the size of the unseen liver, the *foie gras*, is at the purchaser's own risk. Then, her sales made, Mme. Escrieu would replace the birds from the box of new-hatched goslings under the poultry man's conveniently adjacent stall.

The cycle began again when she returned home and the fluffy little creatures were installed in the farmhouse kitchen, warm in a corner by the stove inside a shoebox lined with a piece of an old winter coat. There they were cosseted like newborn babies all through the first cold weeks of spring.

YIELD: Makes enough for a small family's winter supply

TIME: Start the day before; 1 to 2 hours

2 plump geese or domestic ducks *(preferably those which have been fattened for* foie gras*)*	5 garlic cloves
	1 small bunch of thyme
	6 cloves
Salt	1 teaspoon peppercorns
Additional pure white lard (the exact quantity being dependent on the fatness of the birds)	

You will need a very heavy iron pot and a large pottery storage jar with a 10-inch diameter. Quarter the birds and remove all their interior fat. The livers you will, of course, have potted for another purpose. The rest of the giblets will do very well for a giblet soup (page 349).

Put the golden fat to render slowly in a heavy pan until it has completely liquefied. Save the little crisp golden nuggets which are all that remain of the solids, and salt them for the children to nibble, or make crackling bread.

Meanwhile, rub the goose or duck joints with rough salt. Leave them to cure in their own brine for at least 24 hours. Then brush off the excess salt and pat dry. Warm the rendered fat—add extra lard as you think you need it—with the peeled garlic cloves, a few sprigs of thyme, the cloves, and the peppercorns, and when hot, but not smoking, add the goose joints. Cook gently for an hour. The meat must be thoroughly cooked: Test it with a skewer, and when the juice runs clear rather than pink, it is done. Lay the pieces in an earthenware crock and pour the fat over them, making sure the pieces are completely submerged. Next day, pour another layer of pure lard over to seal. Press a circle of wax paper directly onto the solidified lard, and tie more paper over the top.

Confit can be kept for months in a cool, dry place. Whenever you take a piece of goose out, make sure the remaining pieces are completely covered with fat.

◆

SUGGESTIONS

Apart from its use in the *cassoulet* (page 116) and the *garbure* (page 29), there are many delicious dishes in which the *confit* stars. These are my favorites.

Confit with potatoes: Take out a piece of *confit* and warm it in its own fat. Meanwhile, peel and boil a sufficiency of potatoes—remembering that a sufficiency of this dish is never quite enough. When the potatoes are soft, slice them while they are still hot, and put them to sauté in the goose fat. They are ready when they are golden brown and flecked with little crisp bits. For absolute perfection, include a few slivers of black Périgord truffle (page 494). Even the medieval Albigensians, whose famous Heresy held the world to be the domain of the devil, might be moved to call the dish heavenly.

Confit with cèpes: Take out a piece of *confit* and warm it in its own fat. Slice the *cèpes*—or any available wild mushrooms—and sauté them in the goose fat.

As you finish the cooking, toss in a handful of chopped parsley and garlic crushed in a very little salt. There is something very compatible about geese and mushrooms.

Confit with cabbage: Geese are grazing beasts. In Hungary they crop the roadside meadows like cattle, so perhaps their affinity with green cabbage is unsurprising. Slice, wash, and cook a small cabbage in the water which dews the leaves after rinsing. Take out a piece of *confit* and warm it in its own fat in a heavy casserole. Remove the piece of goose and replace it with the lightly cooked cabbage. Braise for 20 minutes, and serve all together.

◆

POTTED GOOSELIVER

Confit de foie gras (France)

Selecting your *foie gras* is much easier if it has already been removed from its original owner. If it is still in the bird, as is normally the case in French country markets, feel the tautness of the surrounding skin and the swell of its curves. A plump skin, pearly with fat, is a good indication that the liver will be a good one. If you can examine the liver itself, you are looking for an object which is firm to the finger, pale as ivory, and only lightly tinged with pink. There should be as few dark veins as possible. Toulouse and Strasbourg are the two main centers in France. Austria, Hungary, and Czechoslovakia also produce good *foie gras*, although it never seems to achieve the creamy perfection of the farm wife's hand-reared goose of Toulouse.

SERVES: 6 to 8

TIME: Start the day before; 10 minutes plus 1 to 1½ hours cooking

1　*fresh* foie gras
1　*tablespoonful of salt*

You will need preserving jars and a large saucepan or a roasting tin. Detach the *foie* from the cavity of the bird with care. Check the surface for dark blood vessels or veins, and gently remove them. Look also for the dark streak of green which betrays a bitter gall bladder stain. Sprinkle the *foie* with salt and leave overnight under a weighted plate. There are those who also sprinkle on a small glass of brandy. Mme. Escrieu, whose instructions these are, preferred to drink the brandy as she contemplated the pleasure to come. The following morning, drain, pat dry, and wipe off any excess salt.

Sterilize the jars. For convenience, divide the *foie* into 1-pound pieces and pack them into jars suitable for this size. Clip down the lids to seal, and place the jars in a pan of water. Boil steadily for an hour if the *foie* weighs 1 pound,

1½ hours for a 2-pound *foie*, or bake the jars, standing in a pan of water, in a fairly hot oven, 350°F, for 10 minutes longer than you need for the top heat.

The *foie gras* will keep, unopened and kept cool, for several months if need be and if you can withstand the temptation. The French enjoy their *foie gras* in the company of the best sweet wine the neighborhood can offer. Those who live near Château Yquem are doubly blessed.

STEW OF GOOSE OR DUCK GIBLETS

Alicot (Central France)

The goose is a versatile bird: There is barely one part of the creature which cannot be made into an excellent dish. It is a very efficient converter of grain to meat and is a popular barnyard bird particularly among the poor—so much so that the presence of geese is an indicator of a peasant-farming community. This stew is designed to be made with the fresh giblets (excluding the liver, of course) of a fine fat *foie gras* goose on the evening of market day, after you have potted the *foie gras* and put up your *confit*. The dish can also be prepared from the giblets of an ordinary roasting goose, or indeed from those of turkeys or chickens. However, you will miss the pale sweet goose fat, which the Romans, who prized it more highly than butter, considered an aphrodisiac. It should be remembered the Romans considered many curious things to be aphrodisiac—and on the flimsiest of evidence. The true aphrodisiac nature of goose fat may have been better recognized by the beauties of medieval times, who used it as the basis for complexion creams and body lotions.

SERVES: 6 to 8

TIME: 25 to 30 minutes plus 2 to 3 hours cooking

1 pound onions	1 pound tomatoes (or a 1-pound can of tomatoes)
4 garlic cloves	
1 tablespoon goose drippings or lard	1 cup stock or white wine and water
½ pound salt pork or bacon	Peppercorns
2 pounds giblets (hearts, gizzards, necks, wing tips)	A bouquet of bay leaf, rosemary, thyme, and Italian parsley
3 large carrots	

Preheat the oven to 300°F. You will need a heavy casserole.

Peel and chop the onions and the garlic. Put the drippings or lard to melt in a heavy casserole. Add the onions and the garlic, and leave them to fry gently while you cube the pork or bacon. Wipe and slice the giblets where necessary. Push the onions to one side, and add the meat and the giblets.

Leave them sizzling quietly while you scrape and slice the carrots, and peel and chop the tomatoes. (Cover the tomatoes with boiling water first to loosen the skins. Tomato skins never seem to break down however long you cook them, and end up, after 3 or 4 hours' stewing, marooned in the sauce like spars from a shipwreck.)

Add the vegetables and stew all together for a moment. Add the liquid, with a few peppercorns and the bouquet of herbs. Cover tightly and put into the oven to simmer slowly for 2 to 3 hours.

This is delicious with a dish of white beans, stewed with a little garlic, herbs, and olive oil, or served quite simply with bread and a green salad.

◆

GIBLETS WITH MUSHROOMS

Dragomiroff (Rumania)

In peasant communities, poultry is chiefly valued for its egg-laying potential. When a chicken is killed for the pot, everything edible has its recipe. Feet and head go into the soup pot. Neck skin envelopes a neck pudding. The giblets, a great delicacy, keep company with that other gastronomic treat of Rumania, her year-round harvest of wild mushrooms. Giblet meats include livers, hearts, well-washed gizzards, neck bones and meat, and wing tips. In Bulgaria sauerkraut and bacon replace the mushrooms and cream in a similar giblet stew, *shchi*.

SERVES: 4

TIME: 1 hour and 15 minutes

1 pound chicken giblets	*½ cup sour cream*
1 cup water	*2 tablespoons bread crumbs*
6 peppercorns	*1 ounce (1 tablespoon) butter*
½ teaspoon salt	*2 ounces grated strong cheese*
½ pound mushrooms (oyster or any wild mushrooms would be best; 1 ounce dried Boletus *is perfect)*	

You will need a heavy medium-sized saucepan, a strainer, and a small frying pan. Wash the giblets carefully, and put them in a saucepan with the water, peppercorns, and salt. Bring to a boil and turn down to simmer for 50 to 60 minutes, until the giblets are tender. Wipe and slice the mushrooms, and add them to the simmering water after half an hour. When the meat is soft, remove and drain it. Pick the meat off the neck bones and wing tips if you have included any. Chop the rest of the meat. Strain out the mushrooms, return the stock to the pan, and boil fiercely to reduce it to half a cup. Put a serving dish to warm in a preheated 350° oven.

Return the meat and the mushrooms to the pan and heat all together. When the stew is piping hot, take the pan off the heat and stir in the sour cream. Transfer the stew to the warm serving dish.

Meanwhile, fry the bread crumbs until golden in the butter. Stir in the grated cheese and sprinkle the mixture over the *dragomiroff*.

Serve with bread and a salad of chopped green peppers, sweet onions, and tomatoes, dressed with salt and a squeeze of lemon.

GUINEAFOWL

All recipes for chicken and feathered game are suitable for this recently domesticated bird. Its flavor is somewhere between pheasant and chicken, and it is very popular in the French barnyard. Recipes which make use of wild mushrooms are particularly compatible. Remember the guineafowl if you come across a few morels in the spring or chanterelles in the autumn.

CHAPTER EIGHT

Small Game

Pigeons, partridges, quail, and all manner of small birds, including larger marauders such as rooks, found their way into the peasant pot. Rabbit and hare were traditionally the poor man's portion. Snails and frogs are available equally to the poor and the rich—to anyone, in fact, with a trained eye for the ways of the countryside.

Country techniques for catching wild prey ranged from liming, when tree branches are smeared with glue to ensnare roosting birds, to minute and intricate twig-and-thread traps for ground game. Some of the ancient methods are remarkably ingenious. Writing of rural life in southern Spain, Nicholas Luard describes one which was still being used in the early 1980s:

> Toni (a peasant boy of twelve) was extraordinarily skilful with his hands. His favourite pastime was to make and fly a baited kite with which he caught darting swifts, among the fastest of all birds, on the wing. The bait was a fragment of dried grass which hung glittering like an insect from a thread below the kite. Attached to the piece of grass was the noose of a draw-string. When the kite was flown, the swifts would swoop to take the bait, the draw-string would pull tight, and Toni would haul the birds down from the clouds like a fisherman reeling in trout. When he'd caught enough, a fire would be built, the birds would be plucked, and the boys would roast and eat them.
> [*Andalucía*, Nicholas Luard, London, 1984]

WILD FOWL

LITTLE STEWED BIRDS

Pajaritos en salsa (Spain)

Today the tiny bird on your plate in a hill *venta*, a little roadside bar, is more likely to be a farmed quail than a plump robin. It was not always so. Robins, sparrows, blue tits, thrushes, blackbirds, goldfinches, anything and every-thing feathered and foolish enough to be netted, limed, or trapped used to be reckoned the most delicate of dishes in the Mediterranean countryside. They were caught by small boys and sold, strung together in garlands, by black-clad old women at the entrance to Andalusian villages.

Happily for the cause of conservation, the increasing number of wildlife programs on television, together with wildlife protection laws, have largely reeducated all but the most recalcitrant of hunters. When the birds are cooked with the powerful aromatics so beloved of the Mediterranean palate, there is not much difference in flavor between the farmed and the wild.

SERVES: 4

TIME: Start the day before; 30 minutes plus 40 minutes cooking

THE BIRDS:
  8   quail
  (Or) 8 *thin-cut scallops of beef (called in France* oiseaux sans têtes) *plus 4 slices of thin-cut bacon plus the 2 fillets of a breast of chicken*

THE MARINADE:
½ *teaspoon juniper berries*	1 *garlic clove*
½ *teaspoon black peppercorns*	1 *glass dry sherry or white wine*
1 *teaspoon salt*	

THE SAUCE:
2 *garlic cloves*	2 *ounces* chorizo *or* jamón
2 *onions*	serrano
2 *green or red peppers*	1 *bay leaf*
½ *pound tomatoes (or an 8-ounce*	*Thyme and rosemary*
can of tomatoes)	1 *small glass of* anis seco *(the*
¼ *cup olive oil*	*Spanish Pernod) or brandy*

You will need a pestle and mortar and a medium-sized casserole or a stewpan with a lid.

If using quail, put them to marinate overnight, well-rubbed with the marinating ingredients.

If making the mock "birds," prepare them the day before. Put the juniper, peppercorns, and salt in a small mortar with the peeled garlic cloves, and pound all these aromatics together. Lay the beef scallops flat on the table. Halve the bacon slices and lay one piece on each scallop. Cut each chicken fillet lengthwise into four pieces, and place a strip of white meat across the middle of each piece of beef, so that it can be rolled up in the middle of it. Sprinkle with the pounded aromatics and a tablespoon of the sherry or wine. Roll them up like little carpets, and tie them with a thread or secure them with toothpicks. Leave the "birds" to marinate—a minimum of half an hour, overnight if possible.

Prepare the sauce ingredients. Peel and chop the 2 garlic cloves and the onions. Seed and chop the peppers. Pour boiling water over the tomatoes if you are using fresh ones, and then peel and chop them; canned ones go in as they are.

Warm the oil in the casserole. Add the garlic and the onions. Fry for a moment until they take color. Then push them to one side and turn the marinated birds, real or mock, in the oil. Chop the *chorizo* or ham finely and add them. Add the tomatoes, the bay leaf, and the herbs. Pour in the rest of the sherry or wine from the marinade ingredients, and bubble for a moment to evaporate the alcohol. Cover tightly and stew gently for 30 to 40 minutes. Stir in the glass of *anis* or brandy, and bubble up the sauce again. It will be at its best if you let the dish cool and then reheat it.

Don't forget to remove the thread if you are serving mock birds. Provide plenty of bread for mopping up. Serve with a generous plate of crisp french fries on the side and a salad of chopped tomatoes, onions, and green peppers dressed with olive oil, salt, and vinegar.

Follow, in season, with a dish of ripe figs, purple or green and sweet as honey. This dish used to be made with plump little fruit-stealing fig peckers. A glass of *anis dulce*, the sweet Spanish anise-flavored liqueur, is a fine finish.

SUGGESTIONS

Make the little "birds" as in the recipe, but stew them with mushrooms and cream, as in the Austrian hare recipe (page 308).

The Italians like their small game stewed in the same manner, but with mushrooms included in the stew, preferably wild ones such as *porcini*, sold dried in Italian delicatessens.

Leftovers: Reheat gently, stir in a tablespoon of garlic chopped up with parsley and fresh herbs such as oregano or marjoram, and serve with a dish of rice.

PARTRIDGES WITH SAUERKRAUT

Rebhuhner mit Sauerkraut (Germany and Neighbors)

SERVES: 4

TIME: 30 minutes plus 40 to 60 minutes cooking (the sauerkraut will take longer)

2	*pounds* sauerkraut	1	*onion*
2	*ounces fatback or 4 tablespoons lard*	1	*teaspoon juniper berries*
½	*teaspoon caraway seeds*	½	*teaspoon peppercorns*
	Water or white wine and water, about 1 pint	2	*ounces bacon*
2	*partridges (old birds are fine for this dish)*	½	*cup sour cream*

You will need a roomy saucepan with a lid, a heatproof lidded casserole, and a colander. Rinse the *sauerkraut* in cold water. Put the fatback, cubed small, or lard into a large saucepan to melt. Add the *sauerkraut* and the caraway seeds, and barely cover with water or wine and water. Cover the saucepan. Bring to a boil and then turn down to simmer gently for 1 to 1½ hours.

Wipe the partridges. Peel the onion and chop it. Crush the juniper berries and the peppercorns. Cube the bacon and put it to melt in the casserole. Sauté the birds gently in the bacon fat until nicely brown. Add the onions, juniper berries, and peppercorns. Add water or water and wine to cover. Cover and stew gently for 40 to 60 minutes, until the birds are tender. Take out the birds and joint them. Raise the heat under the pan to reduce the liquid to 1 cup of well-flavored juice. Stir in the sour cream.

Drain the *sauerkraut* in a colander and put it in a warmed serving dish. Put the partridge joints on top and bathe the dish with the creamy sharp gravy.

PARTRIDGE STEW

Pistach de perdreaux (France)

This rich garlicky stew is claimed equally by the Catalans and their neighbors in the Bas Languedoc. A boned rolled shoulder of mutton or lamb, proper to a shepherding community, is used when the partridges are out of season.

SERVES: 6

TIME: 30 minutes plus 1 hour cooking

3	partridges (old birds are fine) or a boned rolled shoulder of lamb (see note)	1	glass of white wine (not too dry—a sweetish wine complements the garlic)
2	slices of unsmoked ham (see note)	1	glass of water or stock
40	garlic cloves (about 4 whole heads)	1	bundle of fresh herbs: thyme, rosemary, a bay leaf, parsley, with a piece of dried (or fresh) orange peel tied in
2	tablespoons goose fat or 3 tablespoons olive oil		

Pepper

You will need a heavy casserole into which the birds or lamb will fit snugly. Pluck and draw the birds if this has not already been done. Wipe them over and pull out any stray feathers. The birds should not be hung for this dish—the French do not like their birds "high" in the English manner. Cube the ham. Peel the garlic cloves: This is easiest if you swat them with a heavy can first—the skins then come off easily and the cloves remain more or less whole.

Preheat the oven to 350°F.

Put the goose fat or oil in the casserole to warm on top of the stove. Add the ham and the garlic, and fry them gently for a moment. Then push them aside and add the little birds. Turn them in the hot fat. Add the wine, the water or stock, the bundle of herbs, and a turn or two from the pepper grinder.

Cover the dish tightly and put it in the oven. Leave it to cook for an hour, until the birds are tender and the garlic has melted into a thick sweet sauce.

Take the casserole out of the oven. Joint the birds (or slice up the lamb), and transfer the pieces to a warm serving dish. Mash the garlic well into the liquid to thicken it. Serve the birds bathed in their own rich gravy.

Serve with plenty of bread, and follow with a dish of lightly cooked fresh vegetables or a *gratin* of potatoes (page 99) and a green salad. Accompany with the wine you have chosen to use in the *pistache*.

◆

SUGGESTIONS

Pigeons can well replace the partridges in the pot, as can lamb or mutton. Adjust the cooking time and garlic quantity accordingly: A fine fat roast of year-old lamb or mutton takes 50 cloves of garlic as its portion—enough to keep all the somber devils of the Languedoc Cathars at bay. Give the roast, boned and rolled, 1 to 1½ hours depending on its bulk, in a preheated 350°F. oven.

Note: The ham must not be already cooked—a piece of lean bacon will do instead. Spanish *jamón serrano*, Italian Parma ham, and French *jambon de bayonne* and *Toulouse* are all unsmoked and raw—and alas, virtually unavailable in America. *Prosciutto* from Switzerland is a good substitute.

◆

BRAISED QUAIL

Tendzhera otu pudpuduku (Bulgaria)

These elegant little migratory game birds are a favorite huntsman's quarry in Eastern Europe. Quail prefer the wide open spaces, and the Thracian and Hungarian plains suit them admirably. The birds have adapted comfortably to cultivation—fields of winter wheat, early barley, and rye afford them good nesting cover. In spite of this, hunting, particularly when the flocks are in migration, has decreased their numbers in recent decades. Quail farms now supply most of the table birds in the West. Romany gatherers supply the markets of Eastern Europe with a wide variety of wild mushrooms.

S E R V E S : 4

T I M E : 20 minutes plus 30 minutes cooking

8	quails, plucked and drawn, or 4 pigeons or partridges	6	tablespoons sunflower or corn oil
½	pound tomatoes (or an 8-ounce can of tomatoes)	1	glass of light red wine
		1	sprig of thyme and a bay leaf
2	onions	1	teaspoon salt
½	pound mushrooms		Pepper
2	ounces black olives	2	more tablespoons oil
		8	small rounds of bread

You will need a heavy casserole and a frying pan. Pick over and wipe the quail. If you are using pigeons or partridges, split them in half. If using fresh tomatoes, scald them with boiling water to loosen the skins, and then peel and chop them. Peel and chop the onions. Wipe and slice the mushrooms. Pit and roughly chop the olives.

Put the oil into a heavy casserole, heat it gently and add the onions. Fry them for a moment and then add the birds. When they are sizzling, add the mushrooms and fry again. Then add the tomatoes (with a teaspoon of sugar if they are sun-starved northern vegetables) and the olives. Simmer for a few moments before pouring in the wine and the herbs. Sprinkle with the salt and a few turns of the pepper grinder. Cover and stew gently for 40 to 60 minutes, depending on the age and size of the birds, until they are tender. If there is too much juice, remove the lid to allow the liquid to evaporate for the last 10 minutes.

Put the 2 tablespoons oil in a frying pan to heat, and then toss the bread rounds in it: The oil will immediately be soaked up. Continue to dry-fry the pieces of bread in the hot pan. Don't worry if the edges blacken a little—this is how it should be.

Serve each bird on a round of bread with some sauce. Wonderful. Eat them with your fingers and suck the delicious juices from the bones. The bread will be best of all, so leave it until the end.

◆

GRILLED SMALL BIRDS

Oiseaux en brochette (France)

Farmed quail must serve in these days of dwindling wild stock. The marinade will serve to replace the incomparable flavor of a diet of herbs and berries on the maquis.

S E R V E S : 4

T I M E : Start the day before; 20 to 25 minutes

8	quail	1	teaspoon juniper berries
2	tablespoons olive oil	½	teaspoon peppercorns
1	glass of white wine	2	garlic cloves
2	bay leaves	One 2-ounce piece of fatback (petit
1	small bunch of thyme		salé)

You will need a pestle and mortar, a skewer or a toasting fork, and a hot broiler—a barbeque is best. Split the little birds down the back. Spread them out, flattening the breastbones, so that they look like frogs. The French call this *à la crapaudine*. Make a marinade with the olive oil, wine, bay leaves, thyme, juniper berries, peppercorns, and garlic pounded together. Leave the birds in the marinade overnight if possible. Preheat the broiler or barbecue.

Brush the marinade off the birds. Spear the piece of bacon or *petit salé* on the end of a skewer or toasting fork. Hold it under the broiler or over the barbecue until the fat runs. Lay the frog-shaped birds under the broiler or on the barbecue. Baste them as they cook with the melting bacon on its skewer. The birds will take 15 to 20 minutes to cook. Turn them once.

Serve with plenty of fresh bread and a salad. A light red wine from Bordeaux should accompany, with a good cheese to follow.

[handwritten: ✳ Start in this way but remove from broiler and braise Coviod new etc]

◆

SUGGESTIONS

Spanish quail: In southern Spain the birds are split down the back and then marinated in garlic, oil, and lemon juice overnight. The following day they are wiped, dried, and deep-fried in olive oil. They are served sprinkled with rough bay salt from the Cádiz salt flats, and with thick wedges of Spanish country bread. A salad of sliced cos lettuce dressed with oil, vinegar, and salt completes a light meal.

Leftovers: Put any leftover birds to reheat in a well-flavored sauce, as for *pajaritos en salsa* (page 300).

◆

PIGEONS WITH BACON

Pigeonneau en compote (Belgium)

The Belgians are fond of their vegetables, of which they have a goodly repertoire. They have long been excellent gardeners, numbering the brussels sprout and Belgian chicory (specially blanched in heaped-up furrows) among their contributions to the vegetable markets of the world. The battle between the sower of seed and those he sees as seed stealers is very ancient: In this recipe the thieves are stewed with the gardener's vegetables. It is a dish for all seasons.

SERVES: 4

TIME: 30 minutes plus 1 hour cooking

4 *young pigeons or 2 baby chickens*	¼ *pound fatback*
	½ *pound small onions*
2 *ounces (4 tablespoons) butter*	½ *pound carrots*
Salt and pepper	1 *pound (5) small potatoes*
1 *bunch of winter savory (parsley can be substituted)*	1 *small cauliflower*

You will need a small bowl and a deep casserole. Pluck, draw, and wipe the birds. Put a knob of butter in each, worked in a small bowl with salt and pepper and the savory, chopped fine. Cube the fatback and sweat it in a deep casserole until the fat runs.

Meanwhile, peel the onions (tiny ones are best and can be used whole) and quarter them. Peel and slice the carrots. Scrub the little potatoes. Divide the cauliflower into small florets.

Preheat the oven to 375°F.

Turn the birds in the hot fat until they sizzle. Tuck all the vegetables around them and add two tablespoons of water. Sprinkle with salt and pepper and a little more chopped savory. Bring swiftly to a boil. Cover tightly, sealing the lid with a paste of flour and water. No steam must be allowed to escape.

Stew in the oven for an hour. Unseal the lid at the table. The gardener has his revenge. It needs no other accompaniment but good Belgian beer.

SADDLE OF HARE WITH SOURED CREAM

Hasenbraten mit Rahmsauce (Austria and Neighbors)

Hunting is an Austrian passion. Neighboring Germany, Hungary, and Czechoslovakia have equally itchy trigger fingers. All have access to beautiful forests, including the Vienna Woods and the Black Forest, which blaze with color in the autumn hunting season. There can be no more beautiful shelter for deer and boar. Game is one of the major culinary pleasures of the Austrian table, and the recipes of the countryside have usually been tried and tested over many generations. The game and the mushroom seasons coincide, so there are many recipes which include both.

Game which has not been hung, as in Britain, for a relatively long time, is best marinated to develop its flavor. If this is not done, the meat can taste disappointingly ordinary. Marinating also helps break down the fibers in naturally tough meat (it would have to be a very young wild creature indeed which has not developed good muscles for escaping predators).

SERVES: 4 to 8 (hares vary markedly in size)

TIME: Start 2 days before; 20 minutes plus 1 to 1½ hours cooking

1   *hare*

THE MARINADE:
1 *teaspoon peppercorns*	1 *cup red wine*
1 *teaspoon juniper berries*	1 *cup water*
1 *cup wine vinegar*	2 *bay leaves*

TO COOK:
¼ *pound fatback*	1 *cup thick sour cream (more or*
1 *onion*	*less, depending on the size of*
1 *carrot*	*the hare)*
Thyme and marjoram	
Wild mushrooms, dried or fresh	
(optional)	

You will need a deep stewing pot with a lid. Game to be marinated must first be jointed, and then the outer membranes must be stripped off with a sharp knife—particularly so for hare, which has a very tough membrane indeed all over the legs and saddle.

First make the marinade. Crush the peppercorns and the juniper berries. Mix the liquids, spices, and bay leaves together, bring to a boil, and then allow to cool. Pour the marinade over the game to cover. Leave to marinate for 2 days, depending on the size of the joint.

Take the hare out of the marinade and pat it dry. Reserve the marinade. Cube the fatback and sweat it in the stew pot until the fat runs (you may need extra fat). Push it to one side and add the hare to the hot fat. Brown the meat gently.

Meanwhile, peel and slice the onion and the carrot. Add them to the browning meat. Add the herbs, and the mushrooms if you have them. Pour in half a cup of the marinade, including the crushed spices and the bay leaves. Cover tightly. Cook slowly until tender, adding more (but the minimum) marinade when necessary. The dish can also be put to cook in a preheated 350°F oven. It will take between 1 and 1½ hours. When the meat is soft, the dish is ready. Stir in the sour cream.

Serve with stewed cranberries, dumplings or boiled potatoes, and red cabbage.

◆

SUGGESTIONS

A spiced wine-and-vinegar marinade gives good results and, in addition, provides a cooking juice. If you use another method of marinating, then red wine and water will have to be used in the recipe instead of the marinade liquid (don't forget to include the juniper, pepper, and bay leaves). Large joints like a saddle of venison can be marinated by wrapping in a cloth soaked in vinegar for 4 to 5 days. Buttermilk is often used as a marinade—particularly for boar. Five days' soaking will be needed for a large ham.

This recipe can be used for joints of boar and venison. A leg, shoulder, or saddle, boned and weighing about 5 pounds, should be left for 4 to 5 days in double quantities of the marinade—turn it every day and baste it well with its own liquids. Leave for one additional day for each additional pound. The marinade will also do wonderful things for a tough cut of beef (see the *sauerbraten* recipe, page 365). Leg roasts take longer to cook than the saddle, so bear this in mind when preparing all game. Allow 20 minutes to the pound in a moderate oven (350°F) for the saddle. Increase it to 25 minutes per pound for the leg and shoulder.

A spoonful of gin will enhance the juniper flavor.

RABBIT WITH BEER AND PRUNES

Konijn met pruinen (Belgium)

Rabbit is Europe's most widely distributed wild game. Considered a crop-destroying pest since the first pair escaped from the domestic warrens installed in their colonies by the Romans, rabbit meat has long been the fare of the poor. The Belgians carried on the Roman tradition and bred ever-larger rabbits for meat. Their Flemish giant now stocks commercial rabbit farms all over the world. My family's pet buck rabbit, Pila, who must have weighed 12 pounds in his prime, was a powerful and fertile member of the breed. He would thump through his chicken wire run when he pleased, and succeeded in increasing the number and individual weight of the wild rabbit population in our Andalusian valley by at least half. My Belgian neighbor, proud of his garden and fearful for his fine young lettuces, took to patrolling his boundaries with a shotgun. This is what he did with the victims.

SERVES: 6 to 8

TIME: Start a day in advance; 20 minutes plus 1 hour cooking

1	*pound prunes*	1	*pound onions*
2	*cups water*	1	*pound carrots*
2	*small wild rabbits or 1 Flemish giant, or 1 chicken*	2	*ounces (4 tablespoons) butter or lard*
1	*teaspoon salt*	2	*cups lager (gueuze is preferred for the dish in Belgium)*
	Pepper		
1	*teaspoon juniper berries*		

You will need a deep casserole. Put the prunes to soak in the water—overnight if they are very dry, an hour or two otherwise.

Skin the rabbit if this has not already been done for you. It is very simple. Paunch it by slitting the belly fur and pulling out all the insides onto a sheet of newspaper. Save the liver, the heart, and the kidneys, and throw the rest away. Be careful of the little bitter gland near the tail. Slit around the paws and up the back legs to the cut in the belly. Grip the flap of skin where the hind leg skin has been cut, and pull steadily down toward the head (easiest if you hang the back legs from a hook). The rabbit will skin as easily as pulling off a glove. Chop across the saddle to give 4 to 6 joints, depending on the size of the beast; then chop each hind and fore haunch into 2 to 3 sections each. Include the liver, heart, and the little kidneys. A peasant household would certainly include the head, split in two. If you are using a chicken, joint it into 12 to 16 pieces. Season the meat with the salt, pepper, and crushed juniper berries.

Peel and slice the onions and the carrots. Put the butter or lard to melt in a casserole. Add the vegetables and sauté them for a moment. Push them to one side and add the rabbit joints. Fry them until they take a little color. Cover with the lager and bring to a boil. Add the prunes with their soaking liquid and continue to cook, either on top of the stove or in the oven at 350°F, for an hour—keep the lid on for the first half-hour. Before serving, crush the carrots, onions, and loose bits of prune into the stew to thicken the sauce—if you like your sauce smooth, purée some of the vegetables with the juices in a blender.

SUGGESTION

Leftovers: Warm long enough to cook a few thin slices of potato in the sauce, into which you have stirred a small glass of strong, juniper-flavored Dutch gin. It will be even better than the first time around.

COUNTRY DELICACIES

FRIED FROGS' LEGS

Grenouilles sautés au beurre (France)

Unfortunately, the world population of frogs is not able to keep pace with the world population of humans. It is therefore probably time to call a halt to the consumption of the one species by the other, so this recipe is included for nostalgia.

The chef-proprietor of the excellent *hostellerie* in my neighboring village in the Languedoc, Saint-Felix Lauragais, had bought himself a country retreat some twenty miles distant and so far off the beaten track that no anxious diner could winkle him out on his day off. There on a Monday he would busy himself building dams and hollowing banks to establish a line of descending pools along the stream which watered his territory. The sole purpose was to encourage the local population of *Rana esculenta* to move in and multiply. When both he and they were well established, he explained, the arrangement would benefit both parties.

The frogs were caught in the traditional way. A light cane rod is strung with fine line, weighted with a lead pellet and carrying a hook baited with a scrap of red rag. A skilled fisherman can make the bait dance across the reeds in such a way that it proves irresistible to frogs. The prey must be killed immediately to put them out of their misery, the frog fisherman insisted, by tapping their heads against the rod. Only the back legs are snipped off and skinned for use. My gourmet neighbor approved only the simplest of treatments.

SERVES: 4 to 6

TIME: 20 minutes

4 *ounces (8 tablespoons) butter*	1 *lemon*
12 *pairs of frogs' legs*	*Salt and pepper*
1 *large handful of Italian parsley*	

You will need a frying pan and hot plates. Melt a piece of the butter in a frying pan. When it is hot, add the frogs' legs. Cook them gently, shaking the pan occasionally so that they do not stick, for 10 minutes in total. Turn them over once. While they cook, chop the parsley finely. Quarter the lemon. When the frogs' legs are done, add the rest of the butter, season them with salt and pepper, and sprinkle them with the parsley. Serve immediately on the hot plates, each portion with a quarter of lemon, and sauced with their own butter. Accompany with bread and a bottle of dry white wine. Large napkins and finger bowls are useful.

◆

SUGGESTION

Should you have on hand a small glass of Pernod or any anise-flavored liquor, throw it over the frogs' legs at the end of the cooking, flame it, and serve immediately.

◆

LITTLE SNAILS IN THEIR BROTH

Caracolitos en caldo (Spain)

In Spain two varieties of snails are eaten—the usual large Roman snail, *Helix pomata*, and its close relations; and the tiny cream-and-brown species, never bigger than a thumbnail, which estivates on the dry thistles in the summer heat of Andalusia. All the world's land snails are edible, including the giant African snail, which was domesticated by the Romans and mentioned in the dispatches of Apicius. The only problem is that as herbivores snails may feed off plants which man finds toxic. They must therefore be starved before preparation to empty their digestive systems. Snails which have hibernated, and the small summer-hibernating varieties, are self-starved. Care must also be taken not to collect snails from pylons or fences which might have been painted with lead paint.

    In early summer the meadows of southern Spain are brilliant with ten-foot-high yellow-flowered tree thistles, *Carthamus arborescens*, and the more modest but equally beautiful blue *Cynara humilis*, whose spiny stalks are often completely covered by little gastropods. From mid-June onwards, as soon as the spring rains are truly over, parties of women and children make day-long expeditions to favored fields with buckets and stout sticks to gather the snail harvest. It is hard, hot, and prickly work, but the snails are so prized as a summer treat and their soup so valued for its curative powers, that there is never any shortage of helpers. At the same time the harvesters gather bundles of pennyroyal, a spearmint, which is used to brush the foam off the simmering snails and to flavor the soup. The old spice-woman in any Andalusian country market will make up a paper twist of snail spices to order in appropriate quantities.

SERVES: 12

TIME: 4 hours

4	*pounds tiny snails*	1	*whole head of garlic*
1	*pound salt*	1	*teaspoon peppercorns*
1	*small bunch of pennyroyal or*	2	*little dried red chilies*
	mint	1	*teaspoon coriander seeds*
1	*tablespoon vinegar*	1	*tablespoon dried fennel stalks*

You will need a large saucepan. Salt the snails to make them froth. Then wash them thoroughly in five changes of fresh water, salting in between and rubbing off the foam as you do so.

Put the snails into a deep, roomy saucepan. Cover them with cold water. Bring the water gently to a boil. As the bath warms, the snails will be lulled into emerging from their shells. This makes them much easier to pick out later. When the water boils, it will froth up. Brush off the foam with a bundle of pennyroyal. Throw in the vinegar—the foam will subside.

Singe the whole head of garlic by holding it on the point of a knife over a flame. The paper cover burns black and the garlic is lightly roasted; this gives the broth its characteristic flavor. Put the whole head in with the snails.

Now add the spices: The peppercorns stay whole, the chilies should have their seeds removed (with care not to rub your eyes—they are very fiery), and the coriander must be crushed a little to release the seeds and oil. Add the fennel stalks and a few more sprigs of pennyroyal or mint.

Simmer the brew gently for at least an hour. Taste, and add salt if necessary. The pot can be reheated as often as you like and is almost immortal. Serve the snails in their broth in a bowl, with a toothpick or a pin to winkle them out. When you have finished, drink the delicious peppery liquid which remains, or mop it up with fresh bread.

SUGGESTIONS

The pot with the snails is kept on the back of the stove, and ladlefuls are warmed up when required. This is a great treat during the annual fiestas—

carnivals with fairs, bullfights, and dancing until dawn—which are held in every village each year. Beer often accompanies the snails at fiesta time.

The black spicy broth is drunk as a tonic by anyone who feels poorly. I find it an excellent cold cure.

Leftovers: Migrate any leftover snails into the French peasant kitchen. Remove the gastropods from their shells (pinch off the dark length of intestine at the end of the curl) and put them in a small shallow earthenware dish (a *cassolette*). For the amount of snail meat yielded by the original recipe, crush 6 large peeled cloves of garlic into a large knob of butter with 2 tablespoons of chopped parsley. Dot the snails with this butter. Season with pepper and salt, and moisten with a small glass of *marc de bourgogne* or brandy. Sprinkle a handful of fresh bread crumbs over the top. Heat in a preheated 350°F oven for 25 minutes, until all is piping hot and bubbling. Eat with a spoon and plenty of bread. There you have your *cassolette d'escargots*.

◆

SNAILS IN GARLIC BUTTER

Escargots à la bourguinonne (France)

Snails are creatures of regular habit—an ideal target for the pastoral terrorist. If you wish to raid your local natural resources, you will have to study the landscape and take note of the habits of its gastropod population. In the Languedoc in southwest France, just before the dew-laden dawn broke over the remote rib of upland which bore my farmhouse, a small brown army would begin their ascent of the hedgerows. They climbed for no more than twenty minutes, during which time they could be picked off the twigs like crab apples from a branch. Then, as soon as the sun rose over the horizon, down they came. Five minutes later they had all vanished into the long wet grass.

If you cannot find fresh snails in the market, be brave and go out and collect your own. Once again, if you are not sure of their grazing habits, starve them for a week or two before using, to allow them to evacuate whatever they have ingested.

SERVES: 4

TIME: Start a week or two earlier if you pick your own; 30 to 40 minutes plus 2 hours cooking

THE SNAILS:

48	*large snails*	1	*onion*
1	*tablespoon vinegar*	1	*handful of fresh herbs*
½	*bottle of white wine*	1	*teaspoon salt*
2	*cups water*	1	*teaspoon peppercorns*
1	*carrot*	1	*bay leaf*

THE BUTTER:
   6   *ounces (¾ cup) butter or more*
   Handful of parsley
   3   *large garlic cloves*
   Salt and pepper

You will need a large lidded saucepan and, if possible, snail dishes and tongs. Wash the snails very thoroughly in several changes of cold fresh water and salt. Blanch them in boiling water acidulated with the vinegar, for 5 minutes. Drain them, and rinse them with cold water. Pick the snails from their shells. Pinch off the black curl at the end of the intestine. Put the unshelled snails back into the saucepan with the wine, the 2 cups water, the carrot scrubbed and chopped, the onion quartered, and the herbs, salt, peppercorn, and bay leaf. Cover and simmer for 1½ hours.

Meanwhile, wash the shells thoroughly and prepare the butter. Soften the butter and mash it with a fork. Chop the parsley and the garlic together very finely, and then mash them into the butter with plenty of salt and pepper. A dash of *marc de bourgogne* would do no harm.

Preheat the oven to 375°F.

Push a small knob of the garlic butter into the base of each snail shell. Press the snail back into its home. Fill up the entrance with another knob of garlic butter. Continue until all the snails are ready. Arrange the shells in a snail dish if you have one—if not, either prop the shells against each other with the opening pointing up so that the juices do not run down, or cut small holes out of slices of day-old bread and put them in a baking tray. The shells will stay upright and the bread will toast deliciously.

Transfer the dish to the hot oven and give the snails 15 minutes. Serve them piping hot with fresh bread and a good supply of toothpicks to pluck them out of their shells. Serve with a cold white wine, a Muscadet perhaps, followed by salad and cheese and a beautiful wheel of apple tart to finish.

CHAPTER NINE

Pork

The most important domestic animal in the European peasant yard was the pig. The winter larder depended on him, and the autumn pig killing was an occasion for celebration and thanksgiving. Mlle. Louise Morell, born at the turn of the century in Buis-les-Baronnies, in the hills of Provence, remembered for me in 1985 the responsibilities of her childhood:

> While the grandmother was alive, our family always had a pig, or if it had been a good year, two—one to sell in the market. The pig was an important member of the household. He lived in a shed at the back of the house, and it was my special responsibility to feed him, morning, noon, and evening. His morning and evening meals were the peelings and gratings from the day's vegetables. I had to wash them and boil them; and then they had to be mashed. At midday he had grain swollen in water. I was small and a little scared he might bite me, so my father cut a flap into the wooden wall for me to push the dish in and out.
>
> By late October the vegetables were running out and the pig was fully grown. I was always given a new baby pig in the spring, but that October pig was ripe for sausages and hams. The grandmother made wonderful hams. She had a special old wooden drawer for the salting. Her hams always took the salt better than anyone else's. It was the wooden drawer, the grandmother said—it was like an old midwife who knew her business. And she would rub just a little pepper round the bone. That's all. Nothing else. Then when the brine had finished running, when there was no more juice, the hams would be bound in special clean white cloths and hung up from the beam. And there would be ham until Pentecost.
>
> The rest of the meat was made into sausages. The grandmother prepared them with rosemary and thyme, with garlic, with pepper, the meat chopped sometimes large, sometimes small, the finished

sausages, were salted and dried and then rolled in flour to keep them fresh. I would help my grandmother wash and salt the intestines, scrubbing and bleaching them until they were as white and clean as her ham cloths. I had a child's quick little fingers and I was good at stuffing the skins. I would sit on the table pushing the mixture through the funnel into the long white tubes, while my mother made black pudding with the pig's blood. They looked like long snakes, the black pudding coiled into the enamel bucket until it was full. My sausages were salted and hung up to dry in the cold larder, and I had one more duty to perform. The *boudin* had to be cooked in salted water until they were firm—the water could not be allowed to boil or the skins would burst, so I had to watch that the bubbles in the water did not get too large.

The tripes of the pig would be prepared for the evening meal, Mlle. Morell said, stewed slowly with wine and a few carrots, a turnip or two, and a bunch of fresh herbs from the *garrigues*, and the neighbors and perhaps the curé would be invited in.

Mlle. Morell finished:

Let me tell you the best of all. Later in the year the grand-mother would make her own specialty after the pig killing, her spin-ach *boudin*. Sometimes, as it was late in the year, there was not much left in the vegetable patch. Then she would chop cabbage and chard in with the mixture too, together with a handful of minced sweet pork fat, a chopped onion, and a little garlic. She cooked them with a little more pork fat and a glass of wine, in the earthenware casserole which sat on its tripod by the fire. Other people made these sausages—but they all said the grandmother's were a work of art.

◆

SPINACH FAGGOTS

Caillettes aux épinards (France)

SERVES: 6

TIME: 45 to 50 minutes plus 1 hour cooking

3 pounds spinach	3 garlic cloves
A few leaves of sorrel or a small bunch of watercress	Parsley
	Salt and pepper
1/4 pound pork liver	1/2 pound pig's caul (optional)
1/2 pound fatback	1 glass of dry white wine
1 onion	

You will need a gratin dish or pâté dish. A food processor would be useful.

Wash and strip out the leaves of the spinach. Put the spinach and the sorrel or watercress to blanch in boiling water for a few minutes. When the leaves have wilted, drain them and squeeze out all the liquid. Chop up the spinach very thoroughly with the lean and fat pork (a sharp knife or a processor is better for this than a mincer), the peeled onion and garlic, the parsley, and salt and pepper.

Preheat the oven to 325°F.

Make six balls with the stuffing, and enclose each in a caul, if using. Dot with a little extra lard, pour the wine around, and cover and bake for an hour.

If your butcher cannot supply caul, you can bake the mixture as if it were a pâté—in which case include the wine in the mixture, pack it into a pâté dish, and lay thin slices of pork fat over the top. It will need 1½ hours in the oven.

Serve with bread and a glass of chilled sweet white wine. A potato gratin and cheese complete a light meal.

◆

TRIPES À LA MODE

(France)

A simple, fresh-tasting recipe for this delicious and much neglected meat, this is Mlle. Morell's post-pig killing dish. Her mother handed down to her a special tripe pot, a *tripiere*, a glazed earthenware dish with a narrow mouth which kept all the juices sealed in during the long cooking. The dish was taken to the local baker's oven to be left in all day as the oven cooled after the morning's bread baking.

SERVES: 5 to 6

TIME: 20 to 25 minutes plus 3 hours cooking if the tripe has been precooked (if not, the dish will take around 10 hours cooking)

2 pounds well-washed precooked tripe	4 glasses of dry white wine
2 to 3 large carrots	6 peppercorns
4 to 5 small turnips	1 teaspoon salt
2 onions or leeks	Fresh herbs to finish: marjoram,
2 bay leaves, 1 sprig of thyme and rosemary	spring onion top, Italian parsley

Preheat the oven to 275°F. You will need a casserole with a well-fitting lid, or a *tripiere*.

Cut the tripe into 1-inch squares. Scrape and chunk the carrots. Wash and quarter the turnips. Peel and chop the onions, or wash, trim, and chop the leeks. Put all the ingredients in your casserole or *tripiere*—you may need more or less wine to cover, depending on the shape of your casserole. Seal the lid with a flour-and-water paste. Put the casserole in the oven to cook for 3 hours. Chop the fresh herbs and stir them in right at the end of the cooking time. A glass of *marc* (or any white brandy such as Calvados) can be poured in just before you serve it.

Serve the tripe in its own dish, with big white napkins to tuck under each diner's chin. Accompany the tripe with plenty of thick-cut bread to mop up the gelatinous juices, together with a salad of crisp lettuce and chunked tomatoes, dressed with a sharp vinaigrette. Wash it down with more of the white wine you used in the cooking—tripe is thirsty work.

◆

COUNTRY PÂTÉ

Pâté de campagne (France)

Every French *charcuterie* worthy of the name has its own recipe, and every French country housewife has her own secret variation. The basic mix is pork, but other meats can be included, particularly poultry and game. These *pâtés* used to be encased in pastry, as they still are in England to make pork pies.

Y I E L D : Makes a 3-pound pâté

T I M E : Start the day before; 30 to 40 minutes plus 2 to 3 hours cooking

2	*pounds lean pork*	1 to 2	*garlic cloves, peeled*
1	*pound fatback (if you are in*	1	*small glass of brandy*
	France, ask for a ½ pound	½	*pound onions*
	each of panne *and* gras dur*)*	2	*ounces (4 tablespoons) butter*
1	*teaspoon salt*	1	*egg*
½	*teaspoon peppercorns*	2	*glasses of white wine*
1	*teaspoon allspice*	1	*ounce fresh bread crumbs*
1	*teaspoon juniper berries*	6	*ounces thin-sliced bacon, or 6*
	Thyme		*ounces pork belly with salt*
	Parsley		*rubbed into it and left overnight*

You will need a large bowl, a small frying pan, a medium-sized pâté dish, and a roasting tin. A food processor would be helpful. Mince or chop the lean pork and the fatback, and put it in a bowl. Pound the salt, spices, herbs, and garlic together. Work well into the meat with the brandy. Leave to marinate overnight.

Next day, peel and chop the onions finely. Melt the butter in a small frying pan and fry the onions gently until they soften. Add them to the marinated meat; then mix in the egg, lightly beaten with the wine and the bread crumbs.

Preheat the oven to 325°F.

Line a pâté dish with the bacon, or with the salted piece of pork belly sliced as finely as possible. Leave long ends hanging down at the sides to fold over and seal the top. Pack the meat mixture into the middle. Fold over the ends.

Cover with foil and put it in a roasting pan filled with water. Bake for 2 to 3 hours (the depth of your pâté dish is the determining factor). When the sides are pulled away and the juice runs clear, it is done. Leave it to cool under a weight overnight. Eat within three days, with crusty bread, sweet butter, and a bunch of well-washed radishes.

◆

SUGGESTION

Cook the mixture in a sealed preserving jar. It will require the same oven time, but it will keep much longer.

ROAST PORK AND APPLESAUCE

(England)

A favorite roast, pork was always widely available to country households, since a pig could be fattened not only on kitchen scraps, but on windfall apples in the orchards and on the edges of communal woodland. The leg or shoulder or loin are all suitable joints for roasting. The English like to roast their pork with the skin on, to produce a delicious crisp crackling. Your butcher will score it for you with a sharp knife.

SERVES: 5 to 6

TIME: 15 to 20 minutes plus 1 hour and 15 minutes cooking

THE PORK:
*3   pounds fresh pork ham on the bone, with its skin on, scored heavily so that
     the skin can crisp to crackling*
Lard or oil
Salt and pepper
A few sage leaves

THE APPLESAUCE:
1½ pounds sharp apples

THE GRAVY:
½   tablespoon flour
1   glass of cider
1   glass of water

You will need a roasting pan with a rack, and a small ovenproof lidded pot. Preheat the oven to 375°F.

Dry the pork very thoroughly with a clean cloth. It will not crisp properly otherwise. Rub the skin with lard or oil, and sprinkle salt and pepper over the flesh side. Tuck a few sage leaves in near the bone.

Put the roast on the rack with a roasting pan beneath to catch the drippings. Allow 25 minutes to the pound in a moderately hot oven, 375°F; so this roast will need 1 hour and 15 minutes. Baste the meat regularly. Meanwhile, prepare the rest of the accompaniments to the Sunday lunch.

Peel, quarter, and core the apples, and put them in a covered pot in the oven for the last 40 minutes of cooking time. They will melt down into a thick sauce. Pass this around separately.

Turn the oven heat up at the end of the cooking time to crisp the crackling. Take the meat out when it is thoroughly cooked—the juices should run clear when you pierce the roast with a skewer. Transfer the joint to a warm serving dish. Allow the meat to settle for 15 to 20 minutes before you carve it.

To make a gravy, pour off most of the fat from the baking tray and stir in the flour. Fry for a moment and then stir in the cider. Boil fiercely for a few seconds to evaporate the alcohol. Add the water. Boil up the gravy again, stirring to make sure it is not lumpy, and strain it if you would like it elegant. Pass the gravy around separately in a jug or gravy boat.

Plain boiled potatoes are the best accompaniment for the pork—it is a very rich meat. Save the delicious drippings to roast vegetables for another meal (page 31). There are those who reckon Sunday dinner *must* include roast potatoes, so you may have to bow to pressure and cook a few, parboiled first, in the dripping tray along with some stuffing balls.

◆

SUGGESTIONS

Accompany the pork with sage-and-onion stuffing balls. Make some little dumplings with 4 ounces (½ cup) of fresh bread crumbs, soaked in 2 tablespoons of cold water for 5 minutes, and then squeezed dry. Bind with a beaten egg and a tablespoon of melted drippings, flavored with a finely chopped onion and a tablespoon of chopped sage. Do not forget the salt and pepper. Put the balls to roast in the tray under the meat—pour out and save any excess fat for basting the meat. They should be nicely crisp after 30 to 40 minutes.

◆

BRAWN

(England)

Brawn, or headcheese, is made from the meat and skin of a pig's head (or indeed a calf's head or sheep's head), sometimes salted first, sometimes not. It can include any other trimmings: heart, trotters and tail, or even a piece of shin of beef. Whatever the ingredients, they must be well boiled with aromatics until all is soft and gelatinous. It is a most excellent dish.

SERVES: 6

TIME: Start 3 days before; 30 minutes plus 4 hours cooking

1 *pig's head, complete with ears and tongue*	3 to 4 *bay leaves*
1 *bunch of sage*	1 *teaspoon salt*
1 *teaspoon peppercorns*	*Onion skins (the papery brown outside only)*

You will need a large stewpan and a pudding basin or earthenware mold. If you want the brawn to be a pretty pink, put it to pickle rubbed with ¼ pound salt and ½ ounce saltpeter (from the drugstore) for 48 hours before cooking.

Have the butcher split the head in two. Put it in a heavy saucepan just large enough to accommodate the meat, with the aromatics, salt, and onion skins (these serve to tint the jelly a pale gold—the onion itself is not used, as it encourages the jelly to ferment). Cover with cold water. Bring to a boil, and then turn down the heat and skim the froth off the liquid.

Simmer steadily for 4 hours, until the meat virtually drops off the bones. Take out all the solids and strain the stock back into the pan. Leave the stock to boil and reduce uncovered while you pick the meat off the bones. Chop all the pieces and pack them neatly into a pudding basin or earthenware mold.

When the stock is well reduced to about 2 cups, taste and adjust its seasoning and pour it over the meats. Allow it to cool, and then put it in the refrigerator for 24 hours for the jelly to set solid. When you are ready to eat it, unmold by pouring hot water swiftly over the outside. It will unmold instantly and elegantly. Serve on a bed of watercress or parsley.

Brawn will keep in the refrigerator for 2 weeks, but don't store it in the freezer or the jelly is likely to liquefy when you defrost it.

Serve plenty of strong English mustard with the cold brawn, or a jug of white sauce vigorously flavored with strong mustard. Baked potatoes (page 95) are good with brawn.

◆
SUGGESTIONS

If you are going to eat it right away, stir plenty of chopped parsley and a little grated lemon rind into the jelly when it is cool but still liquid, before you pour it over the meat.

For a sharper flavor, add a tablespoon of vinegar to the stock before its final reduction.

Pihti is the very similar Christmas dish of brawn prepared in Greek villages. Carrots and 2 or 3 sliced hard-boiled eggs are set in the jelly with the meat from the pig's head.

Disznokocsonya is the name for the dish as prepared in Hungary. Pig's head, tongue, knuckle, feet, salt, a clove or two of garlic, and a teaspoon of peppercorns are boiled all together for 4 hours. Strip the flesh from the bones and chop the meats into squares. Pack them into a deep basin. Skim all fat from the cooking liquid and boil until reduced to about 1 quart. Clarify by stirring in the beaten whites of 2 eggs, and boil them so that all the impurities are gathered in. Strain the liquid and pour over the meats. Leave to set overnight.

◆

RAISED PORK PIE

(England)

This is the heir to the medieval "coffin" pie—a solid structure in which all manner of game could be cooked and stored. The "coffin" in turn was the heir to the ancient practice of using a flour-and-water paste to protect small meats, such as birds and rabbits, from the fierce heat of the fire when they were being spit-roasted over an open hearth.

The pie was designed to remain good for a long time without refrigeration, so it includes nothing in the recipe which will encourage it to go bad, such as onion or vegetables.

Y I E L D : Makes 2 pies, to serve 8 altogether

T I M E : 1 hour plus 2 hours and 15 minutes cooking

THE FILLING:

3 pounds lean pork (*weighed when off the bone—do not discard the bones, as you will need them for the stock*)	*Herbs according to the district: sage and marjoram are good*
1 pound fatback	2 pigs' trotters, *blanched and split*
Salt	*Peppercorns*
White or black pepper	*Onion skins (the papery brown outside only)*

THE PASTRY:

1	teaspoon salt	6	ounces (¾ cup) butter
2	pounds all-purpose flour	6	ounces (¾ cup) lard
1	cup milk and water mixed		

You will need a large stewpan, a bowl, a small saucepan, and a baking tray or two baking pans, preferably raised pie pans with hinged sides. Strip the meat from its bones and chop roughly. Chop the pork fat very fine and mix it into the meat. Season well with salt and pepper (chopped herbs, particularly sage and thyme, can be included), and leave aside to absorb the flavors.

Put the bones into a large pan with the pigs' trotters, a few peppercorns, salt, and the brown papery skin of a couple of onions to give the stock color (no onion flesh or the keeping qualities of the jelly will be impaired). Cover with cold water, bring to a boil, and skim off any gray foam which rises. Simmer gently for 1 or 2 hours uncovered to reduce to under 2 cups of liquid. If the stock is not clear, pour it, hot, over a beaten egg white, bring nearly back to a boil, and then remove from the heat and allow it to settle. Pour it through a fine sieve: You will find the egg white has collected all the impurities and it will strain out clear.

Leave all to rest while you make the pastry.

Hot-water crust is the pastry used to make a hand-raised pie crust—that is, a crust which holds its shape without being held in position by a mold. Mix the salt into the flour and pour into a warm bowl. Put the milk and water, butter, and lard into a saucepan and bring to a boil. Pour the hot liquid into a well in the flour, mixing hard with a wooden spoon. (You may need a little less or a little more liquid—so have a kettle of boiling water available). This operation is important, and the liquid must be poured and beaten in while still scalding—you may need an assistant to pour. You should now have a ball of slightly translucent dough. As soon as it is cool enough to handle, knead the dough thoroughly by hand. If you have a mixer, it can be beaten with the dough hook immediately. Leave the dough to develop in a warm place for half an hour. Do not allow it to get cold. If your dough is too cool, it will crumble when you work it; too hot, and it will collapse down the sides of the tin. Cut the dough in half and keep the half you are not working warm.

Take one section of the dough and roll it into a ball. If you have a set of the special hinged pie molds which unclip to allow the sides to brown, it will be an easy job to work the pastry over and up the sides. Pack with meat and then put on a lid made with one quarter of the pastry. If not, you will have to set about the task in the old-fashioned way: Slice a quarter off the top and hollow the rest out by pressing and knuckling with your fist. Or mold the crust around the outside of a wooden cylinder (the instrument looks like a short, fat single-handled rolling pin). A glass preserving jar or an earthenware straight-sided pot will do as a mold. It should be floured first and the pastry allowed to cool before the mold is removed. Shape the second pie.

Preheat the oven to 350°F.

When the pastry shapes are cold and unmolded, fill each with half the meat mixture. Pack all in well. There must be no gaps. Pour in as much reduced stock as will reach to within an inch of the top. Press out the lids and lay them over, moisten and mark the edges with a fork to seal. Cut a hole in the middle for the steam. Decorate them as it pleases you—this pastry is an excellent medium for artists. Gild the top with beaten egg.

Bake for 1 hour at 350°F. Then turn the oven down and bake the pies for another hour and a quarter at 325°F. Test by running a skewer into the meat through the steam holes. When the juice runs clear, they are cooked. As soon as the pies are out of the oven, pour in as much as you can of the hot reduced stock. Allow to cool—overnight is best to allow the jelly to set.

SUGGESTIONS

A firm short-crust pastry made with 2 pounds of all-purpose flour and 1 pound of fat will serve instead of the hot crust.

There are many regional variations on the pie: Nottingham likes a pie made with sour gooseberries instead of meat, and glazed when cold with melted apple jelly.

Veal and ham and chopped bacon fat together make a good pie.

Chopped apples or berries can be included in the stuffing.

The lean pork can be replaced by chopped, skinned and boned game, in whatever proportion is liked. Don't omit the pork fat or you will have a very dry pie. Game is good spiced with juniper berries and thyme.

A peeled hard-cooked egg is sometimes included in the pork or veal-and-ham version.

PIG HAGGIS

(Ireland)

The pig's stomach was the gift to the helper at the pig killing. Wash the stomach very thoroughly, and stuff it with potatoes boiled and mashed with onions and bacon fat. Roast for 2 to 3 hours in a 350°F. oven.

SILESIAN PORK

Schlesische Himmelreich (Germany)

This is a typically northern dish which combines rich sweet pork and a sharp fruit compote, served with potato dumplings to mop up their mingled juices. Sweet and sour are very much at home together in the German kitchen.

SERVES: 4

T I M E : Start the day before; 10 minutes plus 35 minutes cooking

> 1   *pound dried fruit (prunes, apricots, apples, pears)*
> 4   *fine pork chops or 1 pound lean pork steaks*
> 2   *ounces (4 tablespoons) lard or butter*

You will need a medium-sized stewpan with a lid. Soak the fruit for a couple of hours—or overnight if possible—in either plain water or cold tea, which will give a darker, richer juice, to cover.

Fry the chops in the fat, turning them once, so that they take color. Add the fruit and the soaking liquid. Cover and simmer all together for 30 to 35 minutes, until the fruit is soft and the chops cooked through.

Meanwhile, make potato dumplings (page 93). Serve them with the pork and fruit stew.

◆

SUGGESTIONS

In autumn, replace the dried fruit with peeled and quartered fresh apples.

Serve plain boiled potatoes instead of the dumplings—although this will not have quite the same Silesian spirit.

◆

PORK-AND-PRUNE SOUP

Ciorba de porc si pruna (Rumania)

This is a recipe from Giurgiu. The pork-and-prune dishes of northern Europe are among the few sweet-and-salt combinations to survive into the modern kitchen. The use of prunes to enrich a gravy or soup has the same visual effect as the addition of caramel to color a gravy. Plums are the raw material of Rumania's favorite liquor, *tuica*, so there is no shortage of dried plums in the local peasant larder.

SERVES : 6

T I M E : 1 hour

One *½-pound piece of lean smoked bacon or ham or fresh pork*
2   *quarts water*
6   *peppercorns*
2   *parsley roots (2 parsnips and a bunch of parsley can be used instead)*
1   *tablespoon lard*

2   *ounces (¼ cup) rice*
½   *pound dried prunes, soaked in water for an hour*
1   *egg*
4   *ounces (1 cup) flour*
½   *teaspoon salt*
½   *cup sour cream*
1   *lemon*

You will need a heavy saucepan and a frying pan. Simmer the bacon or ham (or fresh pork plus a teaspoon of salt) in the water with the peppercorns in a heavy saucepan until the meat is soft. This will take about an hour.

Meanwhile, scrape and chop the parsley roots or parsnips and fry them in the lard. Stir into the soup after the first 40 minutes of cooking. Add the rice and the prunes (pitted or not, as you please).

Make a dough by working the beaten egg with the flour and the salt. Knead it until you have a firm smooth ball. Chop the dough into small dice with a floured sharp knife. Add these little dumplings to the soup 10 minutes before the end of cooking—they will not take long to cook.

Just before serving, stir in the sour cream. Pass lemon wedges separately. A salad and a piece of sharp-flavored goat's cheese would balance the meal. A little glass of plum brandy would round it off perfectly.

◆

LITTLE KABOBS

Pinchitos—"Little Thorns" (Spain)

A relic of the Moorish occupation, when the meat used was usually lamb, this is one of the most popular snacks at the carnival *ferias*, which are held annually in every village and town, rich or poor, large or small, throughout Spain. The *pinchito* specialist travels with the floats and amusements and circus turns, and sets up his tiny open-air kitchen beside the best-patronized local bar in whatever town has booked its *feria* for the week (in small villages it might only be for a day or two). The *pinchito*-man is an expert at spicing and marinating his meat, which he then strings on long, thin skewers. These days very fine stainless steel knitting needles are the preferred instrument, and the purchaser is honor-bound to return the needles. The *pinchitos* are grilled-to-order over a Moorish brazier—a charcoal-fueled oblong metal box—by the vendor himself, who usually sports a Moroccan fez whatever his ethnic origin. A small piece of bread, speared on the end, is included.

SERVES: 4

TIME: Start the day before; 20 minutes

1	pound pork (other meats such as beef, lamb, or liver can be used)
1	teaspoon cumin seeds
½	tablespoon pepper
1	teaspoon coriander seeds (or a small bunch of fresh coriander)

	Paprika (sometimes turmeric is used as well or instead)
½	teaspoon powdered hot chili pepper
4	tablespoons olive oil
	Salt

You will need a pestle and mortar, a bowl, a dozen fine skewers, and a barbecue or a grill. Cut the meat into small cubes no more than half an inch square—this is why the skewers have to be so thin. Pound the spices in a mortar. Marinate the meat in the spices and the oil overnight if possible.

Heat the barbecue or grill.

Thread the meat onto skewers. Grill over charcoal or under the hottest possible grill. As soon as the heat warms the spices, the meat begins to smell wonderful—no wonder the *pinchito* sellers do such a good trade.

When the meat is crisply charred, sprinkle with salt and serve with a chunk of bread skewered on the end so that each piece of meat can be gripped and pulled off in it. Serve with tankards of iced beer to wash it down. There will be plenty of time for more—during *feria*, the night is always young.

◆

BACON PANCAKES

Spekpannekoeken (Holland)

As a pig-keeping and farming community of long standing, all the ingredients for pancakes come easily to hand in Holland.

6	ounces (1½ cups) all-purpose flour
2	eggs
1	cup milk
½	pound thin-sliced smoked bacon

You will need a small frying pan. Make a well in the flour. Stir in the eggs and the milk. Beat vigorously until the mix is smooth and airy. Allow to stand for half an hour or so.

Cut the bacon strips across the middle into fours. Heat a small frying pan and fry 4 small pieces of bacon until crisp. They should yield enough fat for no further greasing of the pan to be necessary. Add, without removing the bacon, enough of the batter to cover the bottom of the pan. Fry the pancake, flipping it over as soon as the edges curl away from the pan and the mixture looks dry on top. Repeat until batter and bacon are all used up.

Serve straight from the pan, with honey or syrup on the side.

◆

The pancake can be made on its own, without the bacon.

There is a substantial "farmhouse" version too: Along with the bacon, fry a few cooked chopped carrots and potatoes and a spoonful of chopped onion or leek.

◆

PORK AND HERRINGS

Kallalaatiko (Finland)

This is a very characteristic northern European dish: The Finns say that pork keeps you warm and warmth keeps you loving.

SERVES: 4

TIME: 25 to 30 minutes plus 1½ hours cooking

2	*fresh herrings*		*Salt and pepper*
4	*medium-sized potatoes*	4	*pork chops*
4	*onions*	2	*eggs*
1	*ounce (2 tablespoons) butter*	2	*cups milk*

Preheat the oven to 350°F. You will need a casserole.

Wipe, gut, split, and bone the herrings. Cut off the heads and tails. Peel and slice the potatoes and the onions.

Butter the casserole and, seasoning with salt and pepper as you go, put in a layer of onions, followed by a layer of potatoes, then the herrings, laid flat, then the pork, then another layer of onions. Finish with potatoes. Put in the oven to cook for 1 hour.

Mix the eggs with the milk. Season with salt and pepper. Pour this custard into the casserole and put it back to cook for another ½ hour. It cooks for 1½ hours in all. There is your warmth. You will have to find your own loving—share a glass of vodka to help you on your way.

◆

SAUSAGES AND MASH

(England)

If you cannot find good sausages, make your own. Well-made, this dish is fit for king as well as peasant. A perfectly prepared sausage-and-mash is one of the chief glories of the English kitchen. It depends on the excellence of its ingredients—old floury potatoes are as essential as good sausages.

Y I E L D : Makes 4 pounds of sausage—2 pounds will feed 6 people as a main dish. Potatoes given are for 5 to 6 people.

T I M E : 1½ hours

THE SAUSAGES:
A hank of sausage casings
2   pounds lean pork
2   pounds fatback
Plenty of pepper
1   teaspoon salt

Fresh chopped herbs of your choice:
   thyme, marjoram, sage,
   pennyroyal
Lard for frying

THE POTATOES:
3   pounds (9 medium-sized) old
   floury potatoes
½   teaspoon salt
4   ounces (½ cup) butter

½   cup creamy milk or half-and-half
Pepper

You will need a bowl, a large saucepan, and a frying pan. A mincer is helpful but not entirely necessary. Soak the sausage casings for an hour or two in cold water to rid them of the salt used to preserve them.

Put the other ingredients once through the mincer. Then, if you have a sausage funnel which will screw over the mincer's opening, loop the casings over the spout—pushing each length well up, like a glove on a finger, and then tie off the end loosely, so that air can escape.

Put the meat back through the mincer and ease it into the casings. Twist into sausage lengths. Tie the ends. If you have no mincer and attachment, get the butcher to mince the meat for you twice; then season it and push it into the sausage casings through a funnel (you may need to saw the end off so that the opening is wide enough). A very satisfying operation.

Let the sausage dry while you prepare the potatoes for the mash. For six people you will only need half the quantity you have made. Freeze the rest if you do not wish to use them immediately.

Put the potatoes into a roomy saucepan, and cover them to a depth of one finger with cold water. No salt yet. Bring the panful to a boil, turn down the heat, and boil them gently for 20 to 25 minutes, until they are soft all through.

Pour off all the water and then put them back on the heat. Sprinkle the salt over them, and shake them over the heat for a moment or two until they are dry and crumbling. Mash them with a wooden spoon or a special mashing instrument. Beat in the butter and then the milk or half-and-half over gentle heat. Add pepper, and taste to see if you need more salt.

Melt a nugget of lard in a frying pan. Prick the sausages with a fork and put them to cook in the hot fat. Let them sizzle slowly for 20 minutes if you have made thick sausages. They will need turning a few times to brown them on all sides. Serve them on your best Blue Willow-pattern dish, prettily arranged around a pile of creamy mashed potatoes. Accompany with fresh young peas, or, in winter, lightly cooked and well-buttered cabbage. Do not forget to put a pot of strong English mustard on the table. Cider or light ale is the right drink.

◆
SUGGESTIONS

Fry a panful of peeled, cored, and quartered apples in the fat which runs from the sausages. Or make an applesauce (page 320), or a rich gravy (page 321) to serve instead.

If you cannot get your butcher to supply you with sausage casings, just roll the mix into sausage shapes, flour them lightly, and cook them as they are. Or make faggots by encasing a patty of the meat in a piece of caul.

◆

BOILED HAM

(England)

If you have plain-salted ham, it cooks perfectly this way. It is even better if the ham has been sweet-cured and smoked.

S E R V E S : 12+

T I M E : Start the day before; 30 minutes plus 5 hours cooking

1	*whole cured ham (around 14 pounds)*	1	*teaspoon peppercorns*
2	*pounds root vegetables (including onions with their skins on)*	1	*cup cider vinegar and 1 cup cider (or 2 cups sour cider)*
1	*small bunch of herbs: thyme, sage, bay leaf, parsley, chervil*	1	*pound black molasses*
		1	*pound whole apples*

You will need a very large stew pot. Wash and scrub the salt-cured ham thoroughly. Put it to soak for 24 hours in at least two changes of water.

Find a pot which is large enough to take the whole ham comfortably. Wash but do not peel the vegetables and then chop them roughly. In fact, vegetable peelings well washed would do as well. Put a bed of the vegetables in the bottom of the pot. Lay the well-soaked ham on top. Add the herbs, peppercorns, vinegar, cider and molasses, and enough water to cover. Put the chopped apples on top (once again, the peelings and cores would be quite enough). Bring to a boil and then turn the heat down. Simmer for 4 to 5 hours.

To eat hot, drain the ham and then let it rest for 20 minutes. Skin it and serve it with applesauce (page 320) fava beans, and a parsley sauce (see white sauce recipe page 37); or with a pease pudding (page 114), sauced with liquor from the cooking if it is not too salty. There should be cider to drink, of course.

To eat cold, allow the ham to cool in the liquid so that it drinks its own juices. This is a very important procedure if the ham is to be succulent when cold. The following day remove the ham and take off its rind. Either dredge it with brown sugar and stick it with cloves, and then glaze it in a hot oven or cover it with dried bread crumbs and roast it in a hot oven at 425°F for 20 minutes to blister and gild the crust.

BAKED HAM

(England)

SERVES: 12+

TIME: Start the day before; 25 to 30 minutes plus 5 hours cooking

1	*whole cured ham (around 14 pounds)*	*Cloves (optional—traditionally for those with money for such*
3	*pounds all-purpose flour*	*luxuries)*
3	*cups water*	*½ pound molasses or honey*

You will need a large pot, a rolling pin, and a large baking tray. Scrub the ham and then soak it for 24 hours, changing the water at least twice.

Make a "huff crust" with the flour and water by working the two ingredients together into a dough. You may well need less water, as this protective paste (which was the beggars' portion at the medieval table) should be quite stiff. Roll out one third of the dough into a circle large enough to accommodate the base of the ham, and then roll out the other portion into a double-sized circle. Put the smaller circle on an ample floured baking tray.

Preheat the oven to 300°F.

Skin the ham and put it flesh side down on the smaller circle of dough on the tray. Stick the fat of the ham with cloves (if you are using them: This is one of the most expensive spices in the world and an early subject of restrictive trade practices). Baste with the molasses or honey. Drape the second circle of dough over the top, arranging it so that the edges of both circles meet. Moisten the edges and pinch them together. Fold over the edges for added security. Cut a steam hole in the top.

Bake for 4 to 5 hours. The crust is not to be eaten, so it does not matter if it gets too dark. Some of this crust would, in medieval times, have been grated and sprinkled over the ham (the origin of bread-crumbing hams today). The rest of the "huff crust," rich with the melted fat and ham juices, was the poor man's portion.

Serve with baked potatoes and leeks in a white sauce (see recipe for carrots, page 36). Cider goes best with ham: The pig himself was very partial to an apple in his time.

Notes: Over the centuries many different breeds of pig evolved from stock which variously fattened in the orchard, on moorland, on wheatland, and by foraging in woodland. In England Gloucestershire and Buckinghamshire pigs were much prized—they foraged and fattened on beechnuts. Diverse curing techniques also developed from dry-salting to brine cures, combined or not in either case with smoking, and including such flavorings as honey, sugar, molasses, and juniper.

Bath chaps are made from the cheek pieces of a pig well favored in the relevant facial characteristic.

Suffolk hams are characteristically cured in a sweet molasses pickle which includes juniper berries—they have a black skin from the cure.

Suffolk flitch is sweet-cured and then smoked.

PICKLED HAM FOR CHRISTMAS

Julskinka (Sweden)

In Sweden Christmas Eve is "Dipping Day." An account of the ceremony was given by the Scandinavian traveler L. Lloyd in 1870:

> The family and guests then assemble at dinner-time in the kitchen, which is swept and garnished for the occasion; when, instead of sitting down to a regular meal, each one dips his "jul-bread" into an immense pan, containing pig in some shape, that is boiling over the fire, considered the more palatable from the quantity of fat floating on the surface. [*Peasant Life in Sweden*, L. Lloyd, 1870]

Mr. Lloyd didn't take to the dish, but it nonetheless continues to be the mainstay of a very popular Christmas family occasion in modern Scandinavia. Light-salting meat is a useful halfway method which develops flavor without the process taking half a year. The result is succulent and well flavored.

SERVES: 12

TIME: Start 10 to 14 days before; 10 to 15 minutes plus 3½ hours cooking

1 leg of pork about 10 pounds in	*1 quart dark beer*
weight	*2 quarts water*
1 pound salt	*8 peppercorns*
½ pound dark brown sugar	*1 bay leaf*
1 quart light beer	

You will need a pickling crock and a large stew pot. Rub the leg of pork all over with 2 tablespoons of the salt and 1 of the sugar. Leave overnight to take the pickle.

Boil the beer, water, and remaining salt and sugar together, and then allow to cool. This is the marinade.

Put the leg into a large crock and pour the marinade over it. Make sure it is submerged by weighting the top. Leave for 10 to 14 days in a cool place. If the leg is larger, leave it longer.

When you are ready to cook it, take it out and put it in a large stew pot. Cover with cold water, bring it to a boil, and then skim. Throw in the peppercorns and the bay leaf, and turn down to simmer. Leave to cook for at least 3 hours—until tender.

Strip off the skin. If you like, you can paint the fat of the ham with egg white mixed with sugar and mustard, and then sprinkle toasted bread crumbs over all. Put the ham in a preheated 350°F oven for 20 minutes to glaze it. Eat the ham hot with sauerkraut on Christmas Eve, or cold at any time.

Strain the soup and serve it on Christmas Eve with thick slices of bread to dip in the fatty juices on the surface—this is called *dopp i grytan*, or dip-in-the-pan. The meal then has a very jolly family atmosphere, rather like a fondue party.

SUGGESTIONS

The ham looks very dramatic with its fat slashed into squares, sprinkled with brown sugar, and glazed in the oven. Stick the golden squares with cloves.

Sometimes the ham is smoked before being cooked.

To bake, wrap the meat securely in foil. Bake it for 20 minutes per pound, plus an extra 20 minutes (10 pounds will take around 3½ hours).

CHAPTER TEN

Shepherd's Meats

LAMB AND MUTTON

Many peasant communities were shepherds: The poorest pastures, not required for any more demanding agricultural use, could often support their flocks well. While pork was favored by sedentary farmers, mutton and lamb became the meat most readily available to nomadic peoples, as shepherding societies often were.

Mutton hams were salted in Scandinavia, Scotland, and Wales. The Scots and the English had their mutton specialties such as "jump-short-pie," made from those animals unable to clear the ravine; and "braxy," Highland mutton from the flock's casualties, which needed to be soaked in water overnight and then well salted. Sheep's head broth, made with the head, split and blanched and simmered with pot herbs and a handful of barley until the meat dropped off the bone, was a staple of many a poor shepherd's diet. It would often be the piece given to an employee by his landlord.

Harvest home in the remote Cairngorm hills of central Scotland, as Elizabeth Grant of Rothiemurchus recorded in the early nineteenth century, featured plenty of mutton on the menu:

> At the Dell . . . there was always broth, mutton broiled and roasted, fowls, muir-fowl [red grouse], three or four pair on a dish—apple-pie and rice pudding, such jugs upon jugs of cream, cheese, oatcakes and butter; thick bannocks of flour instead of wheaten bread . . . In the kitchen was all the remains of the sheep, more broth, haggis, head and feet singed, puddings black and white, a pile of oaten cakes, a kit of butter (a wooden pail), two whole cheeses, one tub of sowans, another of curd, whey and whisky in plenty. [*Memoirs of a Highland Lady*, Elizabeth Grant of Rothiemurchus, 1830]

Lamb was usually the celebration meat of pastoral communities—above all at the important Easter celebrations throughout Greece and the Balkans, a habit which has since spread across Europe.

Mutton is also a preferred meat in southern Italy. The young American, Eliza Putnam Heaton, traveling in Sicily for her health in 1908, stopped for refreshment in a taverna roofed, she recalled, with the flowering branches of oleander and walled with screens of split and plaited cane:

> These tavernas are furnished with rough tables and benches, and the keepers sell little but the necessaries of life—wine, peasant bread, raw onions, garlic, Sicilian cheese; but it is understood that the patrons will for the most part bring roast sheep and will buy only bread and wine to complete the Homeric feast. How they eat meat, these Sicilians, when they do eat it, storing up flesh food for months when they do not see it! [By-Paths in Sicily, Eliza Putnam Heaton, 1920]

◆

LAMB STEW WITH OREGANO

Arni ladorigani (Greece)

This is a simple and adaptable oven-cooked stew. The flavorings of oregano and lemon are the essence of Greek cooking. This dish can also be made with the internal organs of the lamb—the liver, lights, heart, and all the rest. Cut into bite-sized pieces, it will need no more than 30 to 40 minutes cooking. It is also very good made with a jointed rabbit soaked overnight in wine vinegar and water, or rubbed with lemon juice.

SERVES: 6 to 8

TIME: 15 to 20 minutes plus 1½ hours cooking

3 pounds stewing lamb cut into portion-sized pieces with the bone left in (well-trimmed breast of lamb is good for this dish)	Juice of 2 lemons Salt and pepper
	1 glass of warm water
	1 tablespoon chopped oregano and/or rosemary
4 tablespoons olive oil	

You will need a heavy casserole with a lid. Wipe the meat and put it in a casserole with the oil, lemon juice, and salt and pepper. Cover tightly and cook in a preheated 325°F oven, or on a gentle heat on top of the stove, for 20 to 25 minutes. At the end of that time, open the casserole—the meat will be delicately brown and sizzling. Add the warm water and the oregano and/or rosemary, and stir to incorporate the juices. Cover tightly again. Cook for another hour. By the time the lamb is tender, the juices should have been absorbed, and only the oil and a little lemon-flavored liquid remain.

Serve with plenty of bread, a plate of crisp-fried chips, a bowl of black Calamata olives sprinkled with oregano, and a bottle of Greek white wine— not all the Greek wines are resinated. Choose two of the refreshing Greek salads (pages 53–56) to start the meal.

◆

SHEPHERD'S STEW

Tokana (Rumania)

In the Carpathian mountains of Transylvania, shepherds move their thousand-strong flocks between their winter and summer pastures, protecting them against the wolf packs and bears which still patrol the upland forests. During the long treks, they sleep out beside the sheep and the dogs they use to herd them. In the evenings they will make a thick soup-stew over a blazing fire, the embers glowing all night to ward off the fierce cold. Wrapped in heavy fleeces like their charges, the hardy and stubbornly independent shepherds—their lean Mongolian-cheekboned faces betraying their Slav ancestry—lack for little. Unlike the rest of modern Rumania, their larders are always well stocked, and there is no shortage of meat in their pots whether simmering beneath the chill stars or in the warmth of their mountain homes.

S E R V E S : 4 to 6

T I M E : 20 minutes plus 1½ hours cooking

2	pounds lamb off the bone	2 to 3	bay leaves
1	pound onions	2	pounds potatoes
3	cups water	½	cup sour cream
Salt and pepper		1	tablespoon vinegar

You will need a heavy casserole or saucepan. Cube the meat and trim off the fat (save it). Peel and slice the onions. Put the fat trimmings to render in a heavy casserole or saucepan. Take out the scratchings and add the meat and the onions. Fry until well browned. Add the water, salt and pepper, and bay leaves. Bring to a boil and then turn down the heat. Leave to simmer for an hour.

Peel and slice the potatoes and add them to the stew. Simmer the stew for another 30 minutes. Take the lid off toward the end to allow the gravy to thicken by evaporation. When the potatoes are soft, stir in the sour cream and the vinegar, and remove the stew from the stove.

Pass around the *tuica* (plum brandy) bottle—marc or Calvados will do instead. Serve the *tokana* hot, with plenty of good bread.

SUGGESTIONS

This recipe can be found in many different versions in both Hungary and Rumania. Paprika has crept into the recipe recently on the Hungarian side of the Transylvanian border. Garlic, bacon, and the Hungarian vegetable stew, *letcho*, beef and mushrooms, summer savory and red wine, and mustard and beer all have their place in some household recipes.

LAMB STEW

Kapama (Bulgaria)

The spring version of all-purpose Balkan stew uses baby onions and fresh garlic—which is pure white, has a very mild flavor, and has not yet developed its cloves. The autumn version is particularly good made with a selection of wild mushrooms which stand up well to the long cooking: Use cèpes or chanterelles, both of which grow in profusion in the Bulgarian woods in the autumn. Morel mushrooms could be added in the spring, if you were so fortunate as to find some.

SERVES: 4 to 5

TIME: 20 minutes plus 1 hour cooking

SPRING KAPAMA:

2	pounds lamb off the bone (shoulder or neck fillets)	1	cup boiling water
		½	teaspoon salt
1	pound spring onions or scallions with green leaves		Pepper
2	fresh spring garlics (or 3 to 4 mature garlic cloves plus a handful of chopped chives)		

AUTUMN KAPAMA:

2	pounds lamb off the bone	1	cup boiling water
1	pound mature onions	½	teaspoon salt
½	pound mushrooms, if not wild, then the large flat black ones		Pepper

You will need a large shallow pan or medium-sized casserole with a lid. Trim off excess fat from the meat and cut it into fairly large pieces. Peel off the papery outside of the onions or scallions and trim the garlic (do not throw away the green tops—they are one of the chief beauties of this simple dish). Chop the onions or scallions and the garlic roughly into lengths. If you have only mature bulbs without their greenery, include chopped chives. If you are making the autumn version, peel and chop the onions, and wipe and slice the mushrooms. Fry the mushrooms first in a little of the trimmed fat from the meat.

Find a large shallow pan or casserole with a lid. Put in the scallions or onions, garlic or mushrooms, meat, and boiling water. Add the salt and a grinding of pepper. Stew gently on top of the stove or in a preheated 325°F oven for an hour at least, until the onions and garlic have melted into the sauce and the meat is soft. Taste, and add more salt if you need it. Serve in small earthenware bowls, one for each person, with black bread and boiled potatoes.

A glass of *slivova* or vodka starts the meal.

SUGGESTION

Fresh mint or dill fronds finely chopped can be added right at the end of the cooking.

BAKED LAMB, VEGETABLES, AND RICE

Djuvedj (Yugoslavia)

If the six regions which make up Yugoslavia would admit to a national dish, *djuvedj* is probably it. This dish, a recipe shared with the rest of the Balkans, might even reconcile feuding factions from Slovenia, Croatia, Montenegro, Serbia, Bosnia, and Macedonia. Vegetables and meat are variable, but it is particularly good made with a well-trimmed breast of lamb.

SERVES: 6 to 8

TIME: 20 to 25 minutes plus 1½ hours cooking

2 *pounds lamb off the bone*	½ *cup olive oil*
2 *onions*	1 *teaspoon salt*
3 to 4 *garlic cloves*	½ *teaspoon powdered chili*
2 *pounds mixed vegetables:*	½ *cup rice or 1½ pounds (4 large)*
eggplant, zucchini, green	*potatoes, peeled and thickly*
peppers, green beans	*sliced*
½ *pound tomatoes (or an 8-ounce*	
can of tomatoes)	

You will need a frying pan and a shallow earthenware baking dish with a cover. Cube the meat into small pieces. Peel and slice the onions and the garlic. Hull and slice the vegetables. Scald the tomatoes to loosen the skins; then peel them and slice them.

Preheat the oven to 350°F.

Warm 4 tablespoons of the olive oil in a pan. Add the onions and the garlic, and fry them until they turn a pale gold; then push them to one side and add the meat. Fry gently for a moment and then season with the salt and the chili. Transfer the meat-and-onion mixture with its oil to a wide shallow baking dish—earthenware is best. Cover the meat with a layer of the vegetables. Season again. Sprinkle in a layer of rice or potatoes. Finish with a layer of the sliced tomatoes (and sprinkle on a little sugar if the tomatoes are the hothouse variety).

Add water—it should reach the level of the rice or potatoes—and trickle on the rest of the oil. Cover the dish, and put it to bake in the oven for 1½ hours.

Remove the lid for the final 20 minutes. The kitchen will fill with the enticing scent, and the cooking liquid will be concentrated into a rich sauce. Plenty of bread should accompany, and a bottle of the excellent Yugoslavian red wine—just as good as the country's better-known white.

SUGGESTIONS

Make the dish without meat but with some strong white cheese (feta or grated Cheddar) sprinkled on when you take off the lid at the end of the cooking time. Adjust the quantities: 3 people can manage 2 pounds of vegetables as a main dish.

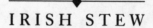

IRISH STEW

(Ireland)

The traditional Irish stew is a white stew of potatoes, mutton (today usually replaced by stewing lamb), and onion. Potatoes are so important an element that they should equal twice the weight of the meat. After the long cooking, the potatoes and the onions will be half reduced to a thick, creamy mash, but Irish stew should never be watery.

SERVES: 6

TIME: 20 to 25 minutes plus 2 hours cooking

2	*pounds neck of mutton or lamb*	3	*cups water or lamb-bone stock*
4	*pounds (12 medium-sized)*		*made with the trimmings*
	potatoes		*Salt and pepper*
1	*pound onions*		

You will need a large casserole with a lid. Have the mutton or lamb cut into chops no more than an inch thick. Peel and slice the potatoes and the onions. Reserve 1 pound of the potatoes (leave them in salted cold water). Arrange in the casserole a layer of potatoes, then meat, then onions, then potatoes, then more meat, then onions, and finally a layer of potatoes, seasoning as you go. Add the water or stock. Cover as tightly as possible.

Bring to a boil. Cook the stew gently on top of the stove or in a preheated 325°F oven for 2 hours. Half an hour before the end of the cooking time, add the remaining slices of potato.

Serve hot in deep soup dishes. A good dark stout should accompany the stew, with a slice of Irish cheese to finish.

◆

SUGGESTION

An Irish stew can be converted into an Irish hot pot by including the lamb's kidneys and removing the lid for the last half hour of cooking to allow the top to brown.

BARLEY OR SCOTCH BROTH

(Scotland)

The great Dr. Samuel Johnson, a demanding gourmet, enjoyed this most traditional of soups on his way to the Hebrides in the 1780s. His biographer, Boswell, recorded the event: "At dinner Dr. Johnson ate several plate-fulls of Scotch broth, with barley and peas in it, and seemed very fond of the dish. I said, 'You never ate it before.' Johnson: 'No, sir; but I don't care how soon I eat it again.' " (*Journal of a Tour to the Hebrides*, James Boswell, 1785.) The soup is simple enough and as variable as your ingredients will allow. Mutton, or lamb, and barley should always be present.

SERVES: 6

TIME: 20 minutes plus 1½ hours cooking

2	*pounds mutton or stewing lamb (neck is excellent)*	*Peppercorns*
4	*ounces (½ cup) barley (pearl or pot)*	2 *teaspoons salt*
		2 *bay leaves*
2	*quarts cold water*	1 *sprig of parsley*
2	*pounds root vegetables: leeks, onions, carrots, turnips*	*Chopped parsley*
		Leek

You will need a large stew pot. Have the meat cut into convenient pieces. Put into a large pot with the barley. Cover with the cold water, bring to a boil, skim, and simmer for half an hour. Meanwhile, peel and chop the vegetables into short lengths. Add them at the end of the half hour, together with a few peppercorns and the salt, bay leaves, and parsley.

Bring the soup back to a boil and simmer for another hour. Sprinkle on a generous handful of chopped parsley and a few fine-sliced circles of raw leek.

Follow with a scone (page 423) and fresh butter and a cup of hot milky tea, or a dram of Scotch whiskey and a slice of rich dark gingerbread.

SUGGESTIONS

Include 2 ounces of dried peas, soaked overnight and added at the beginning of the cooking. If you would like to use freeze-dried peas, add them 20 minutes before the end; fresh ones would be added 5 to 10 minutes before the end. There are households which like to include cabbage or potatoes—there are no strict rules.

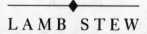

LAMB STEW

Cawl (Wales)

The earliest version of this vegetable-and-meat soup-stew contained a selection of vegetables—pot herbs from the wild as well as from the kitchen patch and a piece of bacon. Sedentary households could manage to rear at least one pig. *Cawl* is still a popular recipe in rural Wales, and even today there remain those who still sup this ancient dish with a special carved spoon from a wooden or pottery bowl.

SERVES: 8 to 10

TIME: 30 minutes plus 2½ hours cooking

3	*pounds neck of lamb or mutton*	12	*peppercorns*
	(Or) 3 pounds well-soaked ham hock	1	*pound root vegetables: rutaba-*
	(Or) a piece of each, or a piece of beef		*gas, carrots, turnips, parsnips*
	as well as if you come from	1	*pound (5) small potatoes*
	South Wales	1	*bunch of pot herbs: parsley,*
2	*quarts cold water*		*chervil, chives*
1	*teaspoon salt*	1	*pound leeks*

You will need a large stew pot. Put the meat on to boil in a large pot with the water (the meat should be in a large piece). If you are using lamb or mutton, add both the salt and the peppercorns. If you use the salted ham hock, only add the peppercorns. Bring to a boil and skim. Turn down the heat and simmer for 1 hour. (If the meat you are using is a tender young roast of lamb, you will not need to cook it for this first hour). Meanwhile, scrub and chop the vegetables into chunks. Scrub the potatoes and cut them in half (leave their skins on).

At the end of the first hour, add the pot herbs (save 1 teaspoon) and the vegetables. Keep back the potatoes and one of the leeks. Simmer for a second hour. Add the potatoes and simmer for another 20 to 30 minutes, until the potatoes are soft. Skim as much of the fat off the top as you can (save it for drippings to fry bread). Chop the reserved leek into fine rings and sprinkle it, and a spoonful of fresh pot herbs chopped fine, over the surface just before you are ready to serve.

Some like to sup the clear broth as a first course, from a wooden bowl with a wooden spoon—the better to drink it piping hot on a cold day. Serve ladlesful of the meat and vegetables afterwards in the same bowl. This is a lovely innocent dish of spoonfood.

◆

SUGGESTIONS

Make a *cawl ffa* or "summer *cawl*" with fava beans, bacon, potatoes, rutabagas and leeks, thickened with a handful of oatmeal.

Harvest *cawl* is celebration *cawl* made with a bit of ham, a whole white cabbage, and new potatoes, all flavored with parsley, savory, leeks, and onion tops.

Leftovers: Should you be but a family of four, make this dish with the leftovers: *cawl ail dwym* or *cawl twymo*. When the broth is cold, lift off the layer of fat on the top (save it for frying or pie making), and add a fresh lot of vegetables to the broth. Boil the soup until the new vegetables are cooked.

◆

ROAST LAMB WITH MINT SAUCE

(England)

The eating of roast lamb with bitter herbs is traditional Easter fare all over Europe. The English have taken the ceremony a stage further and always accompany their roast lamb with mint sauce or mint jelly or rowan jelly. The butcher will break the shank off for you to make stock for the gravy. Saddle, leg, or shoulder are the best joints for roasting. In Wales a small succulent leg of marsh lamb comes ready-wrapped in a net of caul fat, so it needs no basting.

SERVES: 5 to 6

TIME: 20 minutes plus 1 hour and 15 minutes cooking

THE LAMB:

4 pounds roast of lamb plus the shank bone	Flour for dredging
	1 sprig of thyme
Drippings or lard	Salt and pepper

THE SAUCE:

A generous handful of mint leaves
½   cup boiling water
1   tablespoon sugar
½   cup cider vinegar

You will need a roasting pan with a rack, and a small jug. Preheat the oven to 400°F.

If the joint has little fat, spread it well with the drippings or lard and then dredge it with flour mixed with the minced thyme, a little salt, and plenty of ground pepper. Put the lamb on a rack in a roasting pan in a hot oven for a few minutes to let the fat run. Dredge it again to give the tender meat a protective crust. Put it back in the hot oven to seal the crust. After 10 minutes reduce the heat to 375°F and continue roasting. Allowing 20 minutes for the first pound and 15 minutes thereafter; this weight of meat will take 1¼ hours.

Lamb should not be overcooked. Baste it regularly. Turn up the heat again at the end to finish it crisply.

As soon as you have settled the meat in the oven, chop the mint leaves small and cover them with the boiling water. Allow to steep for an hour. Stir in the sugar and the vinegar. Serve in a jug to accompany the roast lamb.

Meanwhile, make a stock with 1½ cups water, the shank bone, and an onion cut in half, but with its skin left on to color the liquid. When the meat is cooked, mix 1 cup of the stock in with the lamb juices in the pan, scraping well to mix in all the little brown bits.

Serve with mint sauce, plain boiled potatoes, and a tender vegetable— young peas or beans or carrots.

SUGGESTION

Serve the roast lamb with oatmealed laver bread (page 85).

Leftovers: Make a shepherd's pie exactly as for the cottage pie (page 363), but using lamb instead of beef. This is a recipe much used by the shepherds' wives of Cumberland and the Lake district, mincing being a particularly good trick for tenderizing tough mutton—they would make the dish starting with raw mutton.

Or make a hot pot with slices of the leftover lamb (as in the recipe which follows).

LANCASHIRE HOT POT

(England)

This hot pot was always made with mutton and cooked in a straight-sided earthenware pot—a small version of the chimney pots which forest the skyline of urban industrial Lancashire.

S E R V E S : 4

T I M E : 20 to 25 minutes plus 2 to 3 hours cooking

2 *pounds neck of lamb on the bone*	1 *pound onions*
or 1 pound leftover lamb	*Salt and pepper*
The lamb's kidneys (optional)	2 *cups water or lamb stock*
2 *pounds (6 medium-sized) potatoes*	*Butter*

You will need a deep casserole with a lid. Slice the meat if it is leftover from the roast. Neck of lamb should be sliced into chops. If you are using kidneys, skin and slice them. Peel and slice the potatoes. Peel and slice the onions.

Preheat the oven to 250°F.

Layer into a deep earthenware casserole, seasoning as you go and finishing with a layer of potatoes. Add the water or stock; then dot with butter and cover tightly. Bring to the boil.

Bake for 2 to 3 hours. Take the lid off for the last hour so that the crust can brown.

Serve with fresh green peas.

◆

BOILED MUTTON OR LAMB WITH CAPER SAUCE

(England)

Modern tastes dictate that this dish be made with lamb—mutton, a well-flavored three-to-four-year-old wether, being a rare visitor to the butcher's slab. This is a shame, for it was an excellent and well-flavored meat, particularly the little Welsh mutton which fed on the sweet marsh grasses and wild thyme and scented herbs of the Cambrian mountains.

SERVES: 6 to 8

TIME: 30 minutes plus 2 to 2½ hours cooking

4 to 5 pounds leg of mutton or lamb	*3 pounds root vegetables: carrots, turnips, leeks, rutabagas, parsnips, onions*
1 teaspoon peppercorns	
1 teaspoon salt	*2 level tablespoons flour*
1 large bunch of herbs: mint, thyme, parsley, bay leaves	*1 small jar of capers*

You will need a large stew pot. Wipe the meat and put it in a large pot. Cover it with cold water and bring to a boil. Skim off the gray foam which rises. Add the peppercorns, salt, and herbs.

Meanwhile, peel the vegetables. Wash all the trimmings and add them to the pot. Simmer the meat for 2 hours if you have mutton, 1 hour for lamb, and then remove the vegetable peelings and herbs. Add the vegetables, cut into chunks. Simmer for another half hour, until the vegetables are soft and the meat tender. Remove as much as you can of the fat which is floating on the top of the stock and put it aside.

Ten minutes before the end, remove 2 cups of stock from the cooking liquor. Fry the flour with 2 tablespoons of the reserved drippings from the stew. Stir in the hot stock, whisking well so there are no lumps, and then add

2 tablespoons of drained capers. Taste, and adjust the seasoning. Stir in a nugget of cold butter just before you pass it around in a jug to accompany the mutton or lamb.

Little fresh peas or beans (green or fava), and boiled potatoes accompany this dish well, with a mild beer to drink.

◆

SUGGESTION

Leftovers: Slice the leftover meat off the bone and layer it with sliced potatoes and the rest of the caper sauce, plenty of parsley, and freshly milled pepper. Cook as for Lancashire Hot-Pot (page 345.)

◆

HAGGIS

(Scotland)

The haggis is a most romantic dish, enjoyed in Scotland by laird and peasant equally. Queen Victoria declared herself pleased by it. It is not open to complication or delicate amendment, being quite simply a large boiling sausage stuffed with oatmeal and a variety of meats flavored with onion. The meats need not be mutton offal: There are recipes which replace it with lean mutton, and others which use venison offal. It can also be made without the stomach bag—cook the mixture very gently in a covered pan for the 3 hours, stirring regularly so that it does not stick. The haggis mix can also be put in a pudding bowl with wax paper tied over it, and then steamed over boiling water for 3 hours. It will be excellent, but not so authentically barbaric.

T. F. Henderson in *Old World Scotland*, published in 1893, explains how the haggis was served in the croft: "In the peasant's home it was set in the center of the table, all gathering round with their horn spoons, and it was 'deil tak' the hindmost."

SERVES: 6

TIME: If you have to do the cleaning and preparing, allow 1 to 2 hours plus 3 hours cooking

1 *sheep's (or lamb's) stomach, well rinsed and fresh*	*1* *sheep's pluck (the liver, heart, and lungs)*
6 *ounces coarse or pinhead oatmeal (not porridge or rolled oats, or you will have a soup mixture and not the light grainy texture of a good haggis)*	*1* *pound suet (the fat which surrounds the kidneys—can be lamb or beef)*
	1 *pound onions*
	Salt and pepper

Preheat the oven to 400°F. You will need plenty of elbow room and a large stewing pan.

Tackle the stomach bag first. Turn it inside out; then scrub and scrape it in several changes of cold water. Scald it and leave it to soak for a few hours in water and salt. Put the oatmeal, well spread out on a baking tray, to toast golden brown in the oven for 10 minutes.

Wash the pluck well. Drain the liver and heart of its blood (your butcher will probably already have done this). If you cannot get the lungs, the kidneys and tongue will do instead. Put the pluck into cold salted water and bring to a boil. Skim and then simmer for at least an hour.

Drain the pluck and check it over, removing the black bits and veins. Grate the liver and chop the rest of the meat. (You may not need all the liver—half is usually enough.) Chop the suet if it is not already prepared, and rub out the membrane scraps with well-floured hands. Mince the onions fine. Mix the meats, suet, and onions together, and spread them out on the table. Sprinkle the oatmeal over the top. Season well with salt and a heavy hand on the pepper mill. Some cooks include lemon juice, cayenne pepper, and a selection of herbs. The secret lies in the proportions, and you will soon establish your own preference. Mix the whole lot together and stuff it into the clean stomach bag—which should be a little over half full to allow room for the oatmeal to swell. Moisten with good stock—enough to make the mixture look juicy. Press out the air and sew up the bag. Put the haggis on an upturned saucer in a pan of boiling water or stock. Heat gently; do not allow to reboil. Prick the bag with a needle when it first swells. Simmer it for 3 hours if the haggis is a large one. When you want to reheat it, simmer it for an extra hour.

Serve the haggis with clapshot—which is a well-seasoned and buttered purée of mashed rutabagas (bashed "neeps") and potatoes ("tatties"). Keep the fire blazing in the hearth. Pour a dram of whiskey on the haggis if you must—I prefer to drink it myself to accompany my efforts.

◆

SUGGESTIONS

You can make a haggis mixture with liver, onions and oatmeal alone, using the pan or bowl method mentioned in the introduction to the recipe. If you cannot get the offal, use mutton or stewing lamb. The suet should not be omitted, but can be replaced with well-minced beef or pork kidney fat if necessary.

Leftovers: Haggis reheats beautifully—just scoop it out of its covering into a saucepan, add a little extra water, and heat it up gently.

LAMB GIBLET SOUP

Mageritsa (Greece)

This is a soup made of lamb's lights, sometimes including the head, split and blanched (although this was more frequently split and roasted on the fire, to be served sprinkled with lemon juice and oregano). This soup is traditionally prepared to be eaten at the beginning of the Easter feast, to break the Lenten fast after midnight on Easter Saturday. The Eastern Church regards Easter celebrations as rather more important than Christmas festivities.

SERVES: 10 to 12

TIME: Put the stock on a few hours before; 40 to 50 minutes plus 1 hour cooking

4	pounds lamb's lights (liver, lungs, and heart)	3	quarts stock made with 2 pounds stewing lamb or bones
1	pound scallions		Salt and pepper
2	garlic cloves	6	ounces (¾ cup) rice
2	tablespoons olive oil	3	eggs
1	big bunch of dill, chopped		Juice of 2 lemons

You will need a large soup pot. Wash the meat thoroughly, cutting out veins and gristle. Chop all the meat into small pieces. Peel and chop the scallions and the garlic. Put the oil to warm in a large pot. Add the scallions and the garlic, and sauté them gently. Add the meat and turn it in the hot oil. Add the dill and pour in the stock. Bring to a boil, skim, and season with salt and pepper; then simmer the pot for half an hour. Sprinkle in the rice and bring back to a boil again. Simmer for another 20 to 30 minutes.

Meanwhile, beat the eggs with the juice of the 2 lemons until thick and white. Just before you are ready to serve, add a ladleful of the hot soup to the egg mixture and whisk it in well. Add another ladleful and whisk again. Draw the soup to the side of the fire, and whisk the egg-and-soup mixture into the rest. It should not need further cooking. Serve warm.

◆

SUGGESTION

Make the soup with breast of lamb and lamb's liver if you cannot get the rest of the meat.

◆

SPIT-ROASTED LAMB

Arni bouti sto furno (Greece)

This is the Easter celebration meal, now prepared in urban Greece by specialist cooks who usually hail from the rural villages. In the villages, each family roasted its own in the open air—the cook having to rise at 4 A.M. to prepare the lamb, the fire, and the spit. One whole lamb takes 6 to 8 hours to cook. The meal was (and still is today), a great community festival banquet, with the whole village visiting their neighbors' barbeque to taste and compare each cook's skill. A more modest roast can still capture the flavor of the celebration.

Y I E L D : A 5-pound leg of lamb serves 6 to 8 people

T I M E : 20 minutes plus 1 hour and 40 minutes cooking

1 *whole roast of lamb (leg, shoulder, or loin weighing about 5 pounds)*	2 *tablespoons olive oil*
	Salt, pepper, and aromatic herbs:
	rosemary, thyme, oregano
4 to 5 *garlic cloves*	

Preheat the oven to 400°F. Wipe the meat and make slits near the bone. Slip the peeled cloves of garlic into the slits. Rub the meat well with the oil, and sprinkle with the salt, pepper, and chopped or powdered herbs. Roast at 400°F for the first 15 minutes; then turn the heat down to 350°F. Roast either in the oven or on a spit. One hour and 40 minutes will finish a 5-pound roast.

Serve a salad of roughly chunked tomatoes, peppers, and onions, dressed with oil, salt, and lemon juice, while you wait patiently for the meat to roast. It always seems to take twice as long as you expect. Serve the meat with a jug of retsina and a basket of country bread. To finish, there might even be a dish of the year's first strawberries, if Easter is late.

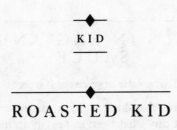

KID

ROASTED KID

Cabrito asado (Spain)

Haunch of kid is the preferred roast meat of rural southern Spain, where the reeducation of the Andalusian population after the departure of the Moors extended to the kitchen: Lamb was the favorite meat of the Muslim Moors, and lamb eating became a sign of pro-Muslim feeling, which led the offender into the arms of the Inquisition and the alternative (somewhat more personalized) barbeque afforded by an auto-da-fé. Kid meat is well flavored and pale in color—it has a rather gluey texture which responds well to barbequing. Insert a clove or two of garlic near the bone, salt the meat well, and baste the roast with a rosemary branch dipped in olive oil while it cooks. A haunch of kid will take about 2 hours on a slow-stoked barbeque and feed 6 to 8, depending on the animal's size. Serve the meat cut into chunks, with thick slices of coarse-textured country bread, quarters of lemon, and young red wine. This is the meal for celebrating the roofing-out of a new dwelling.

SUGGESTION

Stew the rest of the kid meat with olive oil, tomatoes, onions, and garlic, moistened with a glass or two of dry white wine and spiced with bay leaves and pepper. Two pounds of meat, cut into chunks, will take 2 hours' slow stewing—rather longer than the same dish made with lamb.

MINCEMEAT

Mincing (for those with no kitchen gadgets: chopping finely with a sharp knife) remains the favorite way of making tough meat palatable without prolonged cooking. The meat can be beef, lamb, mutton or pork—most peasant communities had all three available to them at different times of year. The commonest ways of preparing mincemeat are as sausages, stuffings for vegetables, or meatballs, and recipes for these, conforming to regional seasonings and methods, are to be found in all the kitchens of Europe. See *ragù* on page 144, stuffed leaves and vegetables on pages 37-52, cottage pie on page 363, sausages on page 499, and recipes in the grilled meats section as well as those which follow.

◆

MEATBALLS IN EGG-AND-LEMON SAUCE

Youvarlakia avgolemono (Greece)

Although the Greeks have the oldest written gastronomic records in Europe, Greek life in postancient times has been so heavily influenced by the Turks to the east and the Bulgarians and Albanians to the north that the country's own culinary identity is almost impossible to disentangle. On the whole, Greek country food is lighter than the Turkish equivalent.

In Turkey *youvarlakia avgolemono* is called *terbiyeli kofta*—*terbiyeli* means "to behave" in Turkish—not something the sauce is naturally inclined to do. Egg-and-lemon sauce is of venerable ancestry: It was made in the kitchens of ancient Egypt, Byzantium, and Rome.

SERVES: 4 to 5

TIME: 25 to 30 minutes plus 30 minutes cooking

1 *pound ground meat (lamb, beef, pork)*	2 *tablespoons chopped Italian parsley, oregano, and mint*
1 *onion*	2 *tablespoons rice*
2 *garlic cloves (optional)*	Salt and pepper
3 *eggs*	3 *tablespoons lemon juice*

You will need a large frying pan with a lid, a bowl, and a ladle. The meat should be well ground—twice is best, or give it a thorough chopping in the food processor. Peel and finely chop the onion and the garlic. Separate the eggs and reserve the yolks. Mix together the minced beef, herbs, onion, garlic, egg whites, rice, and salt and pepper. Knead the mixture into a firm paste with wet hands and form it into walnut-sized balls. This quantity yields about two dozen. Leave the meatballs to rest for 20 to 30 minutes.

Put the meatballs into a shallow pan which just fits the meatballs neatly laid out in a single layer. Pour in enough water to cover them. Cover and simmer for 30 minutes over a low heat until the meatballs are well cooked—25 to 30 minutes, depending on their size. Remove the lid for the last 10 minutes to allow the liquid to reduce to about 2 cups. Shake the pan occasionally to turn the balls over and help them keep their shape.

When the meatballs are ready, beat the egg yolks in a bowl with the lemon juice until frothy and thick. Pour in a couple of tablespoonsful of the hot reduced stock, whisking energetically. Pour the egg mixture into the rest of the stock in the pan. Warm the meatballs gently in the sauce, shaking the pan over a low heat until the sauce thickens. Take off the heat immediately. Serve with bread and quartered lemons. Begin the meal in the Greek manner with a salad-purée or a salad of chunked tomatoes, peppers, and onions, dressed with olive oil and crumbled feta cheese.

SUGGESTIONS

Bread crumbs can be used instead of the rice. Then the meatballs will take only about 20 minutes to cook.

If you make the mixture with bread crumbs, the meatballs can be fried rather than stewed: Hot red wine is then poured over them. Serve bread and a salad.

Or make the mixture (with bread crumbs) into rather larger but slightly flattened balls, oiling your hands well before you roll them. Grill these little hamburgers—preferably over charcoal. Serve with lemon quarters and a Greek salad (page 55).

MEATBALLS

Köttbullar (Sweden)

Made with the basic forcemeat of the Swedish kitchen, these meatballs are a favorite *smørgåsbord* dish. They are served either hot or cold. It is probable that the recipe, very like the Middle Eastern *keftedes*, arrived in Sweden from Turkey, via the offices of the adventuring Swedish King Charles XII, whose exploits are chronicled in the stuffed cabbage recipe on page 48.

YIELD: Makes 12 to 15 meatballs; serves 4

TIME: 30 minutes

1 *pound ground meat*	2 *ounces (4 tablespoons) butter*
4 *ounces (½ cup) fresh bread crumbs*	1 *teaspoon flour*
½ *cup milk or light cream*	1 *cup sour cream*
1 *small onion*	*Salt and pepper*
1 *egg to make a firmer mix (optional)*	

You will need one large and two small bowls and a large frying pan. Put the minced meat into a roomy bowl. Put the bread crumbs in another bowl to soak in the milk or cream.

Peel and chop the onion finely. Add the bread crumbs (and the egg, if using, lightly beaten) and the onion to the meat. Mix all together and knead thoroughly. Shape the mixture into 12 to 15 little balls. This is easiest to do with hands dipped in cold water.

Melt the butter in a frying pan. When it is foaming, put in the meatballs and fry them gently, shaking the pan to keep them a nice round shape, for 5 minutes, until nicely browned. Splash a tablespoon of water into the frying pan and scrape all the well-flavored little brown bits into the liquid. Mix the flour with a little of the sour cream in a small bowl, and then stir in the rest. This will stabilize the sour cream so that it does not split when heated. Pour the sour cream into the pan, and bubble all together for a few minutes, before tasting and adjusting the seasoning with salt and pepper.

Serve as a main dish with boiled potatoes, red cabbage, and a dish of stewed cranberries, or as part of a *smørgåsbord* table.

◆

MEATBALLS IN SAUCE

Albondigas en salsa (Spain)

Any meat will do for this staple of the Spanish kitchen—pork and beef are the most likely. Small meatballs are a popular *tapa* bar snack, and Spanish girls learn to make them at their mother's knee. The proportion of meat to bread and the size of the balls varies according to the means of the cook. Once again, it is probably the Eastern influence which formed the recipe—the Moors were, after all, resident in Spain for nearly 800 years.

SERVES: 4 to 6

TIME: 1 hour

3	slices day-old white bread	1	pound tomatoes (or a 1-pound can of tomatoes)
1	pound ground meat (pork or beef)	1	green pepper (or 3 of the thin-skinned frying variety)
2	garlic cloves, peeled and chopped	1	large Spanish onion
2	tablespoons chopped Italian parsley	2	tablespoons flour
1	egg	4	tablespoons olive oil
1	teaspoon salt	1	glass of white wine, sherry, or water
	Pepper		

You will need a bowl, two plates, and a wide frying pan. A food processor would be helpful. Process or crumble the bread and put it to soak in 2 to 3 tablespoons water while you attend to the rest of the ingredients.

Mix the meat in a bowl with the garlic, parsley, beaten egg, salt, and a few turns of the pepper grinder. Scald, skin, and chop the tomatoes. Seed and chop the pepper. Peel and chop the onion.

Squeeze the bread crumbs dry and add them to the meat. Work the bread crumbs-and-meat mixture together well with your hands. Spread the flour out on a plate. Form the meat mixture into small balls between ½ inch and 1 inch in diameter (the more people to feed, the smaller the meatballs), with wet hands. Roll the meatballs in the flour.

Heat the oil in the frying pan. When it is lightly hazed with blue, add the meatballs. Cook them gently for 10 to 15 minutes, turning them to brown them lightly. Take them out and put them aside. Put in the chopped onion and fry it for a moment; then add the chopped pepper. When that has softened a little, add the tomatoes. Bubble all together for a few moments to make a thick sauce. Return the meatballs to the pan and add the glass of liquid. Simmer uncovered for another 10 minutes, turning the meatballs occasionally.

Serve with Spanish rice or bread or french fries.

◆

MOUSSAKA

Baked meat and vegetables (Greece and Neighbors)

Moussaka is an Arabic name given in Greece to an oven-baked pie made of layers of minced meat and vegetables, or vegetables alone, which can be eggplant, baby squash, zucchini, tomatoes, pumpkin, or potatoes, the whole topped with a white sauce. It is a dish for the family Sunday lunch which is still carried through the streets of country villages to be put into the baker's bread oven to cook. The recipe derives from a medieval Arab dish, *muhklabah*, which is made with rice and sometimes nuts, as well as eggplant and minced meat. It is very popular all over the Middle East, as well as being the dish most usually identified as typical Greek food.

SERVES: 6 to 8

TIME: 45 minutes plus 30 minutes cooking

THE VEGETABLES:

1 *pound eggplant*	1 *pound (3 medium-sized) old*
1 *teaspoon salt*	*potatoes*
½ *pound zucchini*	½ *cup olive oil*
½ *pound peppers*	

THE MEAT:

1	pound ground meat (beef, lamb, pork)	2	tablespoons olive oil
½	pound onions	½	teaspoon chopped sage
2	garlic cloves	1	bay leaf
1	pound tomatoes (or a 1-pound can of tomatoes)		Salt and pepper

THE WHITE SAUCE:

2	ounces (4 tablespoons) butter (clarified butter is used in Greece)	2	ounces grated graviera or Kefalotfiri cheese (Parmesan or any strong cheese can be used instead)
2	heaping tablespoons flour		Salt and pepper
2	cups milk		Freshly grated nutmeg

You will need a wide shallow (preferably earthenware) dish and two sauce-pans. Stalk the eggplant and slice lengthwise. It is customary to salt the slices so that some of the juice drains out before you fry them. This is thought to make them less bitter and less absorbent of oil—anyway, it's a pleasant and time-honored ritual. Stalk and slice the zucchini. Slice the peppers. Peel, rinse, and slice the potatoes.

Heat a little oil in a frying pan and cook the eggplant slices gently in it, turning once, until soft. Drain off excess oil when you take them out. Do the same for the zucchini and the peppers. Fry the potato slices gently until they are soft but have not taken color.

Meanwhile, prepare the meat. A sharp knife is much the best instrument for mincing—then all the juices are not squeezed out by the machinery. A food processor with a chopping attachment is the next best thing. Peel and chop the onions and the garlic. Chop the tomatoes (peel them and seed them, too, if you like).

Heat the oil in a frying pan and turn the onions and the garlic in it until they take color. Push them to one side and add the minced meat. Fry gently until the meat is no longer pink. Add the tomatoes and the herbs, and cook for a moment to reduce to a sauce. Adjust the seasoning with salt and pepper.

Melt the butter in a small saucepan and sprinkle in the flour. Cook until the mixture looks sandy. Beat in the milk gradually, heating and stirring until it thickens. Simmer for 5 minutes to cook the flour. Save the cheese and the nutmeg to sprinkle over the top.

Preheat the oven to 350°F.

To assemble the *moussaka*, line the baking dish with one third of the fried vegetables. Spread half the meat mixture over. Lay on another third of the vegetables, then another layer of meat. Put the rest of the vegetables over all. Pour the white sauce over the top—it should completely cover the surface. Sprinkle with the cheese.

Bake the *moussaka* for 20 to 30 minutes, until the top is golden. Allow to settle and cool, and serve, as with most Greek food, when still warm. Accompany with plenty of bread and retsina, and follow with a dish of fresh fruit. Perhaps a Greek salad (page 55) could whet the appetite first, with a small glass of anise-flavored raki, sipped alternately with a large glass of water.

SUGGESTIONS

There is a Macedonian-Turkish version of *moussaka* which is made with rice [6 ounces (¾ cup) uncooked for 6 people] and baked with a cooked sauce of tomatoes, peppers, onions, garlic, and minced meat (1 pound for 6 people). Bake until the rice is soft and the top golden—about an hour at 350°F. Twenty minutes before the end of the cooking time, cover with a layer of egg custard made with 2 eggs beaten into 2 cups of milk, plus salt and pepper.

CHAPTER ELEVEN

Beef, Reindeer, and Grilled Meats

BEEF

Throughout Europe, whenever there is a choice, beef is the preferred meat. The prejudice seems to lie deeper than a matter of taste: Somehow beef eating seems to confer social status. It is not just that beef is a rich man's meat, it is also the feeling, particularly in relatively primitive peasant societies such as those of Eastern Europe, that the warriors, the overlords, eat beef, and that beef eating reflects favorably on the prowess of the consumer. Even predominantly shepherding communities such as those of Greece will always choose beef in preference to the much more easily available lamb and mutton. Beef eating reaches it apotheosis in England.

Whatever their means, the English have always preferred meat to any other food. Best of all they love roast meat, well seasoned with "the taste of the fire." Necessity brings other victuals, and the laborer frequently had to do without, but the plainest of English cooks could always turn out a beautiful roast, flanked by its traditional accompaniments. Beef was available to the countryman after the annual autumn slaughter of cattle, which were too costly to maintain over winter. The less delicate cuts went to pies and stews, while the roasting meat would be taken to the village baker's oven or to the manor house oven by those who did not have their own. These oven rights were often an important element in the landlord-peasant relationship of the Middle ages.

◆

ROAST BEEF WITH YORKSHIRE PUDDING AND HORSERADISH SAUCE

(England)

Per Kalm, a Swedish diplomat on a visit to England in the 1690s, observed the English at table:

> The Englishmen understand almost better than any other people the art of properly roasting a joint, which also is not to be wondered at; because the art of cooking as practised by most Englishmen does not extend much beyond roast beef and plum pudding. Pudding in the same way is much eaten by Englishmen, yet not so often as butcher's meat, for there are many meals without pudding. I do not believe that any Englishman who is his own master has ever eaten a dinner without meat.

At its best when cooked by the fierce heat of the coal fires of the Black Country, batter pudding is one of the most ancient made-up dishes to be found in the cook's repertoire. In the old manor house kitchen, it was the portion of the spit-boy, a reward for long hours of turning the roasting spit.

SERVES: 8

TIME: 1½ hours

THE BEEF:

5	pounds sirloin or beef on the bone or the same weight standing rib roast		Pepper
		1	tablespoon flour
			Salt

THE YORKSHIRE PUDDING:

8	ounces (2 cups) all-purpose flour	2	cups milk
2	teaspoons salt	2	ounces (4 tablespoons) drippings or lard
2	eggs		

THE HORSERADISH SAUCE:

½	cup heavy cream	1	teaspoon strong English mustard mixed with vinegar
1	freshly grated horseradish root (about 2 ounces)		

You will need one or two roasting pans, a large bowl, a whisk, and a sauceboat. A blender would be useful. Preheat the oven to 425°F.

Wipe and if necessary tie the meat into a neat roast and season with plenty of pepper but no salt until the end of the cooking. To roast beef rare, allow 15 minutes to the pound: 75 minutes in a hot oven at 425°F for the first 20 minutes, then down to 400°F for the rest of the time. If you would like it less rare, add on 15 minutes at the end. Baste the meat throughout with its own juices and drippings, and toward the end of the cooking time dredge it with a sprinkling of flour and salt. This will give the meat a delicious crisp crust and a good basis for a gravy. (If you are serving roast potatoes, start them now—see page 32).

Meanwhile, make the pudding. Put the flour and the salt in a bowl, and make a well in the center. Pour in the eggs beaten with half the milk. Work this in with a wooden spoon and beat it well until it is smooth. Whisk in the rest of the milk. The mixture should be like a pouring custard. Beat it some more. Leave it to rest for half an hour. Then beat it again.

Put the drippings into a roasting pan and heat them in the oven once the roast is removed and resting to settle the juices. When the fat is smoking hot, pour in the batter—it should not be more than ½ inch deep in the pan. Everything should be very hot—the fat, the pan, and the oven. Twenty-five minutes at 450°F should see it well puffed and brown. Don't let it wait around before you serve it.

Whip the cream and fold in the horseradish and the mustard. Add a little more vinegar if you like the sauce a little runny.

Serve the roast beef with mustard, horseradish and cream, roast potatoes, and either roast or plain-boiled vegetables. (No more than two vegetables. The English are overly fond of the loaded plate.) Some like a thickened gravy, although the meat juices deglazed with a little more water in the pan make an excellent gravy without further embellishment.

SUGGESTIONS

Some households serve the Yorkshire pudding first, to take the edge off the appetite for the meat.

Yorkshire pudding does not depend on roast beef to accompany it. It can be enjoyed on its own, with a good gravy.

In Yorkshire it is sometimes served with cream and molasses, or with a couple of cooking apples, sour and sharp flavored, stirred in before the baking.

There are those who always use water instead of milk, and much less of it at that, and swear it makes a far lighter pudding.

Make the pudding into toad-in-the-hole by dropping well-pricked Yorkshire beef sausages or pork sausages at intervals into the batter, after it has been poured into the roasting dish. Serve with gravy.

The bones will make an excellent broth. Fry the bones in a bit of lard, then put them in a stockpot with an onion cut in half, with its papery skin. Add a few parsley stalks, some carrot scrapings, and salt and pepper. Bring to a boil, cover, and simmer slowly for several hours. The stock can be further reduced to produce a lovely meat glaze.

◆

MEAT GRAVY

(England)

This flour-thickened brown sauce based on meat juices is a peculiarly English taste. The word "gravy" comes from the old French *grané*, which in turn derives from the Latin *granatus*, meaning "made with grain," and which was applied to a meat stew with a flour-thickened juice: not so far removed from the modern recipe. The French dropped both the word and the substance, and the only modern gravy in French cookery is the *jus*, or juice of the meat—not the same thing at all. Englishmen like gravy to pour on sausages, with batter pudding, and with plain-boiled potatoes—it acts, it appears, as a kind of meat substitute.

S E R V E S : 4 to 6

T I M E : 10 minutes

1 tablespoon lard or drippings	*Scrapings and juices from the*
1 onion (optional)	*roasting pan*
1 tablespoon flour	
2 cups strong stock (made with bacon rind, ham trimmings, vegetable trimmings, bones, and a few onion skins to give it color)	

You will need a shallow pan. Melt the lard in the shallow pan. Put in the onion, if you are using one, chopped vertically into fine crescents, and sauté it lightly—do not allow it to burn, or the taste will not be pleasant. Add the flour and fry until it turns lightly golden—again, do not allow it to burn. Stir in the stock gradually, beating to avoid lumps. Add the pan scrapings. Bring it all to a boil and add, if you like, a few drops of gravy browning or a splash of port and a nugget of cold butter.

Serve either with a roast of meat, or on its own with Yorkshire pudding, mashed potatoes, and/or sausages.

◆

SUGGESTIONS

Good gravy should be a deep mahogany. Producing the right color is the hardest part of gravy making—in default I sometimes use cold tea (Indian tea gives an undefined faint flavor of herbs—China tea is a bit too distinctive to be used). A useful coloring can be made by melting ½ cup of sugar in a heavy preserving pan on a low fire. Continue to heat gently and stir until it caramelizes to a good rich brown. Throw in a glass of cold water and simmer for a moment to make a rich deep-brown syrup. Bottle and keep on hand if you make gravy often.

MARROWBONES

(England)

This is a delicacy from England's beautiful beef and a treat for high tea, or served as a savory after the meal instead of a pudding. Marrowbones are the femur, or the thighbone, of beef cattle. Marrow was used in medieval cookery in sweet dishes and puddings. One of these, made with barley, oats, or whole wheat soaked in milk and sweetened with honey, was the forerunner of our modern dish of rice pudding.

SERVES: 4

TIME: 5 to 10 minutes plus 1½ hours cooking

2 *marrowbones cut into lengths*	*Bread for toasting*
Flour-and-water paste	

You will need a large saucepan and a clean linen cloth, or a roasting pan. Have the bones sawed into 3-inch lengths, and seal the cut ends with a stiff paste of flour and water. Wrap the bones tightly in a floured cloth and put them to simmer in plenty of salted water for an hour. Or bake them slowly, clothless and waterless, in a preheated 300°F oven for an hour. Serve the bones as they are, with a knife or a long thin spoon to scoop out the delicious marrow onto hot toast.

SUGGESTIONS

Don't throw away the cooking water—it makes good stock.

If you have no marrow, drippings from roast beef—spread on bread or toast and sprinkled with rough salt—is a pleasant alternative.

◆

COTTAGE PIE

(England)

This is a recipe for the tough cuts of meat which were likely to come the way of the cottager or farm laborer. It is equally useful for any bits which might be left over from the Sunday roast. The dish can be made with any meat, cooked or raw, well chopped or minced. Salted meats are not suitable.

SERVES: 4 to 5

TIME: 30 to 40 minutes plus 30 minutes cooking

1 pound beef (leftover or minced fresh)	Worcestershire sauce (optional)
	Parsley
1 large onion	Salt and pepper
1 tablespoon meat drippings or lard	2 pounds (6 medium-sized) old potatoes
1 tablespoon flour	3 ounces (6 tablespoons) butter
1 cup stock or meat gravy	½ cup milk
Gravy browning (page 361) (optional)	

You will need a large and a small saucepan and a gratin dish. Put a pan of salted water on to boil for the potatoes.

Meanwhile, mince or chop the meat thoroughly. Peel and chop the onion. Put the drippings or lard to melt in a small pan. Add the onion and fry until golden. Stir in the flour and the meat if it is raw, and cook until the meat takes a little color. Add the stock and allow it to bubble up. (If you are using leftover, thickened gravy, you will need no flour). Stir in the meat now if it has been precooked. A little gravy browning and a shake from the Worcestershire sauce bottle will help. Chop the parsley and stir a tablespoonful of it in. Bubble all until the gravy is quite thick. Taste, and adjust the seasoning with salt and pepper. Pour the mixture into a shallow ovenproof dish to cool. If you put hot potato on hot gravy, it will sink through the surface and the appearance of your pie will suffer.

Peel the potatoes, cut them into quarters, and plunge them into the water as soon as it boils. Cook them until they are soft, which will take 20 to 25 minutes. Drain them immediately and shake them over the heat to dry. Mash well, beat in the butter and the milk, and season with salt and pepper.

Preheat the oven to 350°F.

Pile the mashed potatoes onto the cooled meat mixture, doming them over it, and mark in plow lines with a fork. Dot with butter, and put to heat and gild the top in the oven for 20 minutes.

Any lightly cooked green vegetable can accompany, but it is nicest of all with a dish of old carrots, well scraped, sliced fine, and cooked in a tightly lidded pan with a tablespoon of water, a knob of salty butter, a ½ teaspoon of sugar, and plenty of freshly milled pepper. There is something about a bunch of fresh-dug, well-grown carrots which is particularly reminiscent of the cottage garden.

SUGGESTION

Chopped mushrooms can be fried in the butter before the flour is added— preferably the delicious field mushrooms which miraculously appear overnight wherever cattle are pastured.

ONE-POT STEW

Pichelsteiner (Germany and Neighbors)

This is the German version of this universal staple.

SERVES: 6 to 8

TIME: 30 minutes plus 1 hour cooking

2 *pounds meat cut from the shoulder of beef, veal, or pork (any or all three)*	1 *quart stock or water* Salt and pepper
2 *onions*	2 *pounds (6 medium-sized) potatoes*
1 *ounce (2 tablespoons) lard*	1 *pound white cabbage or green beans*
1 *pound root vegetables (at least two from carrots, turnips, kohlrabi, celery root, leek)*	3 *tablespoons chopped fresh herbs: lovage, basil, savory (any or all)*
1 *marrowbone chopped into lengths (optional)*	

You will need a large heavy saucepan or a casserole with a lid. Cube the meat and slice the onions. Melt the fat in a deep heavy saucepan or casserole and fry the meat until it loses its redness; then add the onions. Cover and allow to stew gently while you prepare the rest of the vegetables.

Peel and cube the root vegetables. Add these to the meat. Add the marrowbone if you have it, and then the stock or water. Season with salt and pepper. Put the lid on tightly again and bring all to a boil. Turn the heat down to simmer. Total stewing time will be about 1 hour. You may need to add a little more liquid.

Meanwhile, peel and slice the potatoes into thick wedges. Add them 20 minutes before the end of the cooking time (give the stew a stir at the same time). Wash and shred the cabbage, or top-and-tail the beans. Put on top of the stew to cook in the steam for the last 10 minutes.

If you are using a casserole, the dish can be cooked in a preheated oven—give it 375°F for an hour.

When the meat is soft, remove the marrowbones and scrape out the marrow into the sauce. Mash the vegetables in a little to thicken the sauce. Finely chop the fresh herbs and stir them in just before you serve. The dish is complete in itself and needs no accompaniment except a slice of good bread to mop up the gravy.

SUGGESTION

Leftovers: This dish reheats beautifully. The leftovers also make an excellent turnover filling.

BRAISED PICKLED BEEF

Sauerbraten (Germany)

Beef, pork, and poultry provide comfortable farmers' fare all over Europe. In the German kitchen these come supported by dumplings, noodles, or potatoes. Large forest game is normally the bag of the rich landowner. Rabbit, hare, and perhaps a partridge or two from the fields and hedgerows fall to the poor man. Country stews are often soured with vinegar or a sharp young wine. Pickled cabbage and a variety of sturdy cheeses complete the meal. Favorite flavoring herbs include caraway, fennel, lovage, savory, horseradish, and juniper.

Sauerbraten is a farmer's dish for a special treat in the winter—particularly for family gatherings at Christmas. It has a succulent rich flavor, much like venison. In Germany, stewed meat is usually cooked in one whole piece.

S E R V E S : 6 to 8

T I M E : Start 3 to 5 days before; 20 to 30 minutes plus 1½ to 2 hours cooking

2	pounds beef (brisket or shoulder)	½	teaspoon peppercorns
2	cups wine vinegar	One	¼-pound slab of bacon
1	cup red wine	1	ounce (2 tablespoons) lard
1	cup water	1	large onion
1	teaspoon salt	2	pounds vegetables: celeriac,
1	teaspoon juniper berries		celery, carrots, parsnips
2	bay leaves	½	cup sour cream

You will need a deep dish for marinating, and a roomy casserole. Trim the meat and lay it in a deep dish. Add the vinegar, wine, water, salt, juniper berries, bay leaves, and peppercorns. Leave in the refrigerator for at least three days, but not longer than five.

Take the beef out of the marinade, dry it, roll it up, and tie it neatly (save the marinade). Cut the bacon into cubes and sweat it in the lard in a deep casserole until the fat runs. Turn the beef in the hot fat to brown it (this is not done to seal in the juices, but to caramelize the outside, which gives color and a rich roasted flavor to the gravy).

Peel and slice the onion, and add it to the browning meat. Peel or scrape the root vegetables and cut into chunks. Add the vegetables and allow everything to fry together gently for 5 minutes with the lid on. Then add the reserved marinade. Cover tightly.

Either simmer the dish slowly on top of the stove or bake in a preheated 350°F oven for 1½ to 2 hours. Turn the meat every now and again. You may need to add some extra water.

When the meat is tender, stir the sour cream into the gravy. Simmer a few moments longer. Slice the meat, and serve it with its vegetables and juices. Dumplings, noodles, or *spätzle* can accompany, or big floury potatoes boiled in their jackets.

SUGGESTIONS

Make this dish with a tough cut of venison. Put a few dried mushrooms (cèpes or chanterelles) in the stew and serve it with cranberry sauce and *rösti* (page 101).

Leftovers: This dish reheats well—just warm the sliced meat in its gravy. Serve with refried potatoes or dumplings.

BOILED BEEF

Rindsuppe (Austria)

The broth from this dish is the favorite clear soup of Austria. It is traditional innkeeper's fare, served for the second breakfast between nine-thirty and midday.

SERVES: 6 to 8

TIME: 20 to 30 minutes plus 2 hours cooking

2 *pounds beef for boiling (shin, plus a piece of flank or brisket)*	*Peppercorns*
1 *shinbone cut up, with its marrow, plus a chopped rib bone*	*Lovage or celery leaves (optional)*
	½ pound beef liver (optional)
	2 quarts water
1 *large onion*	*Salt*
2 *pounds root vegetables (carrots, celery root, rutabagas, leeks, turnips)*	

You will need a very large stewpan. Tie up the beef neatly with string. If you like your soup well-colored, put the bones to roast in a preheated 350°F oven until they brown before proceeding.

Cut the onion in half, but leave the golden skin on to contribute its color to the soup. Peel and roughly chop the vegetables.

Put all the ingredients into the largest stewpan you can find, and cover them with the cold water. Simmer gently for 2 hours, adding more water if necessary. The meat will be much juicier and more delicious if it is cooked slowly.

When the meat is soft, remove it and keep it warm. Strain out the vegetables—they will be very good for the household pig, but will not have any more to contribute to your own meal. Keep the liver (if used) to make Bavarian liver dumplings.

Serve the rich beef soup first (now you may add salt), with some egg noodles (page 279) poached in it.

Slice the boiled beef and serve with a spoonful of the broth poured over it. Accompany with pickled cucumbers, mild mustard, and grated horseradish (grate the root on the slope so that you get long, thin strips). If you want to serve vegetables with the beef, then poach them plainly in a little of the soup. There will be enough soup left over for a second meal.

◆

Tafelspitz: This is the Viennese version of *Rindsuppe:* slices of boiled beef served in its own juice, with fresh grated horseradish mixed with an equal quantity of grated raw apple (make and serve it when you are ready to eat or the apple will go brown). The usual accompaniments are *rösti* potatoes (page 101) and creamed spinach (page 36, see boiled vegetables) with a little sauce of light oil, mashed egg yolk, and plenty of chopped chives.

Leftovers: Serve any leftovers as a salad, dressed with oil and vinegar and plenty of finely sliced onions. This salad is particularly good made with pumpkin oil, should you be lucky enough to come across it.

◆

LIVER DUMPLINGS

Leberknödel (Austria and Germany)

In Austria liver dumplings are cooked and served in a clear broth. In Germany they are more likely to appear as a main course with a dish of sauerkraut.

YIELD: Makes 8 to 10 dumplings

TIME: 30 minutes

½ pound cooked liver (lamb, pork, or veal)	*A few sprigs of lovage, celery leaves, or Italian parsley*
½ pound fresh bread crumbs	*1 garlic clove*
1 cup milk	*About 1 quart broth (enough broth*
2 eggs	*to poach the dumplings)*

You will need two small and one large bowl, and a roomy shallow pan. Chop the liver very fine. Put the bread crumbs to soak in the milk. Beat the eggs. Chop the herbs, and peel and mince the garlic finely. Mix all together lightly with the tips of your fingers. Form the mixture into dumplings with wet hands—the dumplings should be the size of large marbles and should puff up to the size of Ping-Pong balls. Poach them in simmering broth in a shallow pan for 15 to 20 minutes.

Serve the dumplings hot in the clear broth (you may have to add a beaten egg white and then strain the broth through a muslin cloth if you want it really clear). Or serve the dumplings with a dish of cabbage, sour or fresh, and a bowl of sour cream passed separately.

◆

EGG CUSTARD FOR CLEAR SOUP

Eierstich (Austria)

This is another possibility for the *Rindesuppe*.

2   *eggs*
2   *tablespoons clear soup or water*
Salt and pepper

You will need a casserole and a shallow pan. You should have the same volume of eggs as liquid, beaten together, seasoned with salt and pepper, and cooked in a casserole as a baked custard—standing in a tray of water in the oven or on top of the stove. Allow to cool. Cut into strips or cubes. Add to clear soup when you serve it.

◆

VEAL STEW

Osso buco (Italy)

This is the classic Italian stew. Veal is the favorite celebration meat and expensive, so this is a special dish to be prepared with care. More affluent peasant households of northern Italy did, however, quite often keep a veal calf or two in a pen in the yard, fattening up for special occasions. The method of slow stewing in a *ragù* is also used for game and beef dishes—the long, slow braising tenderizes the toughest of meat cuts and most venerable of wild game.

SERVES: 4 to 6

TIME: 30 minutes plus 2½ to 3 hours cooking

1½ *pounds veal shin with*
   marrowbone left in
2   *garlic cloves*
1   *pound tomatoes (or a 1-pound*
   can of tomatoes)
2   *tablespoons olive oil*

2   *glasses of white wine*
1   *small bunch of fresh herbs:*
   thyme, rosemary, sage,
   parsley
Salt and pepper

You will need a large stewpan or a casserole with a lid. Have the butcher saw through the shinbones so that you have short lengths. If you try chopping them, the fresh bones will splinter. Wipe the bone sawdust off the neat little round joints—three concentric circles of meat, bone, and marrow.

Peel and slice the garlic. Peel and chop the tomatoes. Warm the oil in a heavy stewpan. Add the sliced garlic and fry it for a moment; then add the meat.

Lay the meat in the hot oil and fry it gently on both sides. Add the tomatoes. Stew uncovered for 3 to 4 minutes, long enough to melt the tomatoes into a sauce. Pour in the wine and add the little bunch of herbs. A spoonful of sugar makes a good addition if the wine is dry and the tomatoes have not been ripened in the Mediterranean sun.

Cover the pot tightly and cook for 2½ to 3 hours either on a gentle heat on top of the stove or in a preheated 300°F oven. This may seem a long time, but shin of veal is full of sinews, and if these are allowed to melt through long cooking, they will turn to jelly and the dish will yield a rich thick sauce surrounding a delicious tender meat joint in which the marrow remains. You may need to add a little more wine or tomato juice as the liquid reduces. Taste for salt and pepper.

Serve steaming and perfect in its own dish, with quartered lemons and a *risotto* (page 136)—this is the only stew the Italians serve with a *risotto*—or with a dish of *polenta* (page 123).

◆

SUGGESTIONS

This recipe can be used for any variety of game: partridge, pigeons, hare, rabbit, even a tough cut of venison, or with a mixture of all or any of them. It also very good made with beef. If you have a red meat, it is better to use red rather than white wine.

One cup of the *ragù* (page 144) diluted with a glass of white wine can be used as a stewing liquid after you have fried the garlic and the meat in the oil. It will yield an excellent dish.

Leftovers: Osso buco heats up wonderfully well. It will be even better the second time around. Accompany it with a potato purée or some plain buttered noodles, and a sharp little salad of chicory or watercress.

OXTAIL SOUP

(England)

This recipe comes from the household book of the Luard family, Huguenot refugees who fled to England from France at the end of the seventeenth century to escape the religious persecution which followed the revocation of the Edict of Nantes. The family settled, along with many other refugee families, in the London suburb of Bermondsey, an area which soon became known as "Petty Burgundy."

The locals had long specialized in tanning the ox hides available from the markets which supplied the capital with its beef. The refugees, rich and distinguished citizens in their own country but now impoverished, found they had access to plentiful and cheap meat in the oxtails which were sold to the tanners along with the hides. The fame of the soup that the Huguenot families made with this tough but succulent meat spread throughout the land. The household book of Charlotte du Cane, who married William Garnham Luard in 1845, gives her family's preferred version of the dish. Here is the (adapted) soup.

SERVES: 6 to 8

TIME: Start 1 hour before; 30 minutes plus 3 hours cooking

1	*large oxtail or 2 small ones*		*A bay leaf, parsley, and "sweet*
1½	*quarts cold water*		*herbs" such as marjoram,*
1	*tablespoon salt*		*oregano, mint*
One	*½-pound slab of bacon*	6	*cloves*
3	*large old carrots*	½	*teaspoon peppercorns*
3	*onions*	2	*cups dark beer (porter or*
3	*small turnips*		*Guinness)*
1	*small head of celery*		

You will need a large stewing pot with a lid, and a strainer. A blender would be useful. Have the oxtail cut into joints, and put it to soak in warm water for an hour. Then drain it and put it in the stew pot. Cover it with the cold water and bring to a boil while you prepare the rest of the ingredients. Cube the bacon with its rind. Scrape and chop the carrots into lengths. Peel and slice the onions. Peel and cube the turnips. Wash the celery thoroughly and chop it up. Tie the herbs into a bunch.

Skim off the gray foam which has risen to the surface of the boiling oxtail. Add the vegetables, bay leaf, herbs, bacon, cloves, and peppercorns. Add the beer. Bring to a boil, cover, and turn down to simmer.

Stew slowly for 3 hours. Do not, says Mistress Luard, stew it any longer, or the soup will be ragged and not fit to serve up. Take out the pieces of oxtail, skim off as much of the fat as you can, and push the rest of the soup through a strainer (a blender would do the job more easily). Return the soup to the pot, put back the oxtail, reheat, and serve hot.

◆

SUGGESTION

If you like your oxtail soup darker, stir in a tablespoon of tomato paste or a teaspoon of gravy browning (page 361) as you finish the cooking.

◆

PAPRIKA STEW

Paprikás (Hungary)

Hungarian paprika is the ground spice which is made from the dried ripe fruit of *Capsicum anuum*. The sweet capsicum pepper was one of the vegetables brought back to Europe after Columbus returned from his epic voyage. Plenty of alternative theories on its travel route have been on offer ever since: In Victorian times, the missionary-explorer Dr. Livingstone assured his readers that the plant had long grown wild all over Africa. However, there is no evidence that *Capsicum anuum* appeared on the dinner tables of Europe until fifteenth-century Spain took to the elegant import.

The plant grew well in the sunny Iberian climate and was soon to be found in every stew pot in the land, of lord and peasant alike. Its fame quickly spread, ultimately as far north as the great plain of Hungary. Nowhere was it received with more delight. The seeds of their great culinary passion reached the Hungarians by a circuitous route. The taste for the strange new vegetable traveled from Spain to Italy, which passed the good news on to its trading partners the Turks. The Ottoman Turks in their turn took the seeds to their own colonials, the gifted gardeners of Bulgaria, for cultivation. Those Bulgarians who fled from the Turks planted new gardens in the fertile Danube basin of Hungary—and so it was that the paprika pepper arrived in its spiritual home.

A *paprikás* is made much like other paprika stews, usually with white meat such as chicken or veal or sometimes fish. The recipe for a *paprikás* calls for less onions and less paprika then the *pörkölt*, and the most obvious difference is that sweet or soured cream is stirred into the gravy just before serving. This is the recipe which produces the dish most frequently referred to as a "goulash."

SERVES: 6

TIME: 20 minutes plus 1 hour cooking

2	pounds veal (a glutinous piece	1	heaped teaspoon salt
	from the shoulder or leg is best)	1	wine glass of water
½	pound onions	½	cup sour cream and ½ cup
1	ounce (2 tablespoons) lard		heavy cream mixed
1	level tablespoon paprika (Noble		
	Rose or sweet)		

You will need a heavy stewpan. Cube the veal into bite-sized pieces. Peel and chop the onions. Melt the lard in a heavy pan. Put the onions to fry gently. When they are soft and golden, push them to one side and add the veal. Fry together for 10 minutes. Remove from the heat, and stir in the paprika and the salt.

Replace the pan on the heat and add the water. Not soup, or stock-cube liquid which makes everything taste the same, but pure, clear water.

Bring to a boil, cover tightly, and simmer for an hour. Keep an eye on the pot so that the liquid does not dry out, and only add a splash of water at a time.

When the meat is tender, remove the lid of the pan and boil fiercely to evaporate all but the last of the liquid. Immediately stir in all but 2 tablespoons of the cream.

Serve in a deep dish, with the last of the cream spooned over the top. Flat noodles or *tarhonya* noodles (page 163) go well with this. A light, flowery Hungarian white wine would be perfect with the dish. A handful of apricots and a glass of Hungary's own special apricot brandy, *barakpalinka*, complete the meal.

SUGGESTIONS

Use all sour cream, or all heavy cream and a tablespoon of vinegar.

Leftovers: Stir in an equal quantity of fresh cooked noodles to leftover stew. Spoon more cream, or a white sauce, over all, dot the surface with butter, and sprinkle with cheese. Bake in a preheated 350°F oven for 20 minutes, to heat it through and gild the top. You'll wish you had made double quantities.

BEEF PAPRIKA STEW

Pörkölt (Hungary)

The most popular dish of the old Austro-Hungarian Empire, a *pörkölt* is known as a *goulash* in Austria, not to be confused with the Hungarian *gulyas*, which is a soup. Strings of the essential ingredient of the stew, the brilliant crimson sweet paprika pepper, light up the marketplaces of the elegant towns of the old empire each autumn. This recipe is for veal, but the dish can be made with veal, and in Austria can be served with sauerkraut or sour cream. It can also be served at midday, in the evening, or even for the Austrian "second breakfast" taken around 11 A.M. It is an adaptable and very popular recipe. Buy your paprika in small quantities from a store which has a good turnover—never keep paprika for more than one year to the next, and store it in a screw-top jar away from direct light. Fresh paprika is a bright clear red and clean scented (not dusty and brown).

SERVES: 6

TIME: 30 minutes plus 1 hour cooking

2	*pounds veal*	1	*wine glass of water*
2	*pounds onions*	1	*heaped teaspoon salt*
2	*ounces (4 tablespoons) lard*	1	*teaspoon dried marjoram*
1	*ounce fresh paprika (in Austria*	1	*teaspoon caraway seeds*
	kotanyi edelsvess)	1	*tablespoon wine vinegar*

You will need a stew pot with a lid. Cube the meat. Peel and slice the onions finely. Melt the lard in a deep pot and fry the onions in it until golden. Add the paprika and stir it in the hot fat. Throw in a little water—the paprika burns easily. Add the meat. Stir over the heat until the water has evaporated. Add the salt, spices, and vinegar. Cover tightly and continue to cook over a very low heat (this can be done in a preheated 300°F oven).

Check the progress of the stew occasionally, give it a stir, and add the minimum amount of water necessary. The meat will be soft in an hour or so, depending on the cut chosen. It is this slow dry stewing which gives the *pörkölt* its unique flavor.

Serve with dumplings or boiled potatoes.

SUGGESTIONS

The Austrians have various additions to this stew: Sometimes a spoonful of tomato purée is stirred in to darken the juices, or a crushed clove of garlic, or strips of fresh red or green pepper.

Paprikahendl: This is simply joints of chicken cooked by the goulash method. If you have an old fowl which you have used to make a clear soup, it will be delicious if jointed and finished thus (cut the cooking time in half if the bird has already been cooked.)

Wurstelbraten: The method of cooking is as for the *gulyas*, but instead of cubes of meat, use a whole roast of one of the tougher cuts of meats. For a 2-pound roast to feed 8 people, make four holes the length of the meat with a skewer, and push a frankfurter down each hole. Pot-roast as for the *gulyas*. Serve the meat sliced vertically across the sausages. Very pretty.

Kartoffel gulyas: The same slow pot-roasting method can be adapted for potatoes. For a more substantial meal, slices of frankfurter sausage can be included.

Leftovers: The stew is best of all as a leftover to begin with—that is, made the day before.

Make little pastry strudels filled with the leftovers—for a delicious Viennese meat pie.

♦

PAPRIKA SOUP WITH DUMPLINGS

Bográcsgulyás (Hungary)

There is a wet and dry version of this ancient dish. A *gulyásleves* is a soup and thus made with more liquid, and a *gulyashus* is a stew, so it is drier. The version I give here ranks as a soup. This most famous of all Hungarian dishes has its origin with the Magyar nomads, who cooked and then dried their meat on a sheepskin in the sun, bundling it up and carrying it tied to the saddle. Such habits made the Magyars highly mobile and very successful marauders. The horsemen had but to pitch camp, and reconstitute their dried meat by stewing it in water in a soup kettle, a *bogrács*, until all the liquid evaporated. Small wonder they took over the Danube basin.

Once they had settled down, the Magyars kept their cooking pot, but added those ingredients which only cultivation and settled habits could provide: the domestic pig for the bacon and the kitchen patch for the rest. The primitive stew evolved into a rich aromatic feast whose ingredients always include beef (both meat and innards), paprika, lard or bacon, and onions. There are plenty of optional additions of which caraway seeds is the most usual. Never add any flour: If you want your *gulyás* gravy thicker, take the lid off the pot and let the liquid reduce. Don't add any other spice except caraway. A *gulyás* has no cream, sour or otherwise. If you want a creamy stew, make a *paprikás* or a *tokány*.

SERVES: 6

TIME: 40 minutes plus 1 hour cooking

1½ pounds shin or flank of beef for
    stewing
½ pound onions
2   garlic cloves
2   ounces fatback or 2 tablespoons
    lard
2   tablespoons paprika

1½ quarts water
½ pound root vegetables: carrots,
    turnips, rutabagas, parsnips
Salt and pepper
1½ pounds (4 large) old potatoes

THE DUMPLINGS:
1   egg
4   ounces (1 cup) flour
½   teaspoon salt

You will need a heavy saucepan with a lid. Ideally you need a soup kettle—a *bogrács*. Cut the beef into neat little cubes: This is spoon food to be eaten from a bowl, and you should not need your knife. Peel and chop the onions and the garlic. Cube the fatback if you are using it; then put it or the lard to melt in a heavy stew pot.

Put the onions and the garlic to fry gently in the fat from the fatback or the lard. When they are golden, push to one side and add the beef. Continue frying until the meat takes color. Take the pot off the stove and stir in the paprika. Pour in the water, and add the root vegetables, peeled and chopped. Bring all to a boil, and add salt and pepper; then put on a lid, turn the heat down, and simmer the stew for an hour, by which time the meat should be quite soft.

Meanwhile, peel and chop the potatoes into chunks the same size as your meat cubes. Add them to the stew after the first hour of cooking. Bring to a boil again and simmer for half an hour, until the potatoes are soft. Check the seasoning and adjust if necessary.

Meanwhile, prepare the dumpling dough by mixing the egg into the flour and the salt. Knead into a smooth dough and put aside.

When you are ready to serve the stew, pinch small pea-sized pieces off the dough between your thumb and forefinger, and throw the little dumplings into the simmering stew. They are called *csipetke* and will only need 2 or 3 minutes to be done to perfection.

The wolf will be far from the door tonight. Finish the meal with a cup of coffee topped with thick cream if you wish to keep proper company: Hungarians were particularly fond of buffalo milk with their coffee, in the days when the buffalo was the workhorse of the country. Buffalo milk is rich and delicious. Neighboring Rumania still has some buffalo employed as beasts of burden on the provincial farms.

◆
SUGGESTIONS

Possible extra ingredients are chopped green peppers, chopped tomatoes, and chili peppers—particularly the small fresh green ones, sliced into little rings, and added right at the end of the cooking.

Make a *gulyás* with lamb (or, better still, mutton) and hot paprika. Then it will be an *urugulyás*. All other rules apply.

◆
GREEK STEW

Stifado (Greece)

This is the traditional winter stew of country villagers all over Greece and Macedonia. There are, naturally, as many recipes for this ancient dish as there are cooks. Young beef is the preferred meat when available. The small mountain sheep are for milking, and their flesh is not prized.

SERVES: 5 to 6

TIME: 30 minutes plus 2 hours cooking

1½ pounds boneless beef or pork	Salt and pepper
1 pound scallions	1 small bunch of herbs: bay leaf,
3 garlic cloves	oregano, rosemary
1 pound tomatoes (or a 1-pound can of tomatoes)	1 glass of wine vinegar or young red wine
4 tablespoons olive oil	1 glass of water

You will need a stew pot with a lid. Cut the meat into 1½-inch cubes. Trim and peel the scallions. Peel and chop the garlic. Chop the tomatoes roughly. Put the meat, garlic, oil, tomatoes, seasonings, and herbs into a stew pot. Add the vinegar or wine and the water, bring all to a boil, and then turn down the heat and leave to stew gently for half an hour.

After this time, add the scallions. Cover tightly and do not take the lid off after this addition for at least 1½ hours. Remove the lid to evaporate any remaining liquid. The dish should nearly have boiled dry when you take it off. Let it cool a little before you serve.

Put a dish of Greek salad on the table as a first course, and serve the *stifado* with a plate of crisp, golden french fried potatoes. Wash it down with retsina, the pinesap-scented wine so beloved of the Greeks. Retsina is very strongly flavored and needs a robust dish such as a *stifado* to stand up to it.

◆

SUGGESTIONS

Game birds, hare, or rabbit can be used instead of domestic meat. If you use rabbit, soak it overnight in water acidulated with vinegar.

◆

BEEF STEW

Boeuf en daube (France)

Winter in the Languedoc is long and hard. Month after month the ground is frozen. Flocks of lapwings peck disconsolately at the icy furrows of the farmers' fallow fields, and it seems as if spring will never break through. The days are short and the country people do not leave their stone houses unless there is good reason. Occasionally the wine-rich scent of a slow-cooking *daube* escapes through a gap in the tight-shuttered window of a village house.

The little village of Saint Fereol crouches under the dark cliffs of the Montagne Noire, the aptly named "Black Mountain," near the medieval town of Castres. There each Saturday from early November through March, M. Joinel cooks the best *daube* in the Languedoc for his small but devoted local clientele. He swears it is the near-black wine of Cahors which he uses in the dish which makes the difference. All his clients have good appetites and M. Joinel allows at least ½ pound of meat per man.

SERVES: 6 to 8

TIME: Start the day before; 1 hour plus 4 hours cooking

THE MARINADE:

3 pounds beef (top rump or any piece of lean stewing beef)	½ bottle of strong red wine (the darker the better)
1 sprig of thyme, 2 bay leaves, ½ teaspoon juniper berries	

THE STEW:

2 ounces (4 tablespoons) lard	2 sprigs of thyme and 2 sprigs of savory
3 onions	
3 garlic cloves	2 bay leaves and 6 juniper berries
3 large carrots	4 cloves and a curl of orange peel (dried is best)
3 large tomatoes	
1 medium-sized potato	1 more bottle of strong red wine
4 ounces fatback in small cubes	Salt and pepper
3 tablespoons oil	

You will need a bowl, a frying pan, and an earthenware lidded casserole. If possible, marinate the meat the day before. Otherwise an hour or two will suffice: Cut the meat into 2-inch squares and put it into a bowl with the marinade herbs. Add the red wine, cover, and leave in a cool place overnight. Turn the meat in the marinade a few times.

Next day take the meat out of the marinade and pat it dry (strain the marinade and save it). Rub the casserole with a cut clove of garlic. Put the casserole on gentle heat and melt the lard in it. When it is hot, put in the pieces of meat. Leave the meat to brown gently while you prepare the rest of the ingredients.

Peel and chop the onions. Peel and crush the garlic. Scrape and slice the carrots finely. Scald the tomatoes to loosen the skins, and then peel and chop them. Peel and cube the potato.

Melt the fatback in the oil in the frying pan over a low heat. When the fat is running, add the chopped onions and the crushed garlic. Cook them gently until they soften and gild. Add the carrots and fry them until they soften. Put in the tomatoes and the potato, and add the wine marinade. Bubble fiercely for 5 to 10 minutes, until it is reduced to a thick sauce. Add the sauce to the meat in the casserole with the herbs and the spices. Pour in the second bottle of wine and cover tightly.

Preheat the oven to 250°F.

Put the *daube* to cook long and slowly for at least 4 hours. This can be done on the stove if you wish. The meat will then be so soft, you can eat it with a spoon, which is as it should be, and the sauce rich and thick. Taste, and adjust the seasoning, and mash the sauce a little before you serve the *daube*.

A plain *gratin de pommes de terre* to follow or a creamy purée of potatoes and celeriac would be good with the *daube* and serve to soak up the juices. Complete the meal with a slice of prune tart (the winter specialty of the house—made with soaked prunes, otherwise as for the strawberry tart on page 446) and a piece of salty Roquefort from the chalk uplands behind the Montagne Noire.

M. Joinel would offer his guests a small glass of the local fruit brandy, his special *eau-de-vie de prunelles sauvages de la Montagne Noire*, made from the bitter little plums which grow wild in the copses. The distiller of the brandy, a cheerful old gentleman long past retiring age but who still sported the blue working overalls he had worn all his life, was often to be seen sipping his product in one corner of the bar. He had inherited his right to make it from his father, who in turn had inherited it from his father. But the old man was childless. Once he was put to rest under the blackthorn, he would explain happily, there would be no more firewater from the Black Mountain and the world would be a poorer place.

◆

BOILED DINNER

Pot-au-feu (France)

This dish is known as *bouta-couira* in the patois. The Guilhermat family, parents, grandparents, two daughters and a son, farmed the small acreage beside the little house where I lived in the remote region of the Languedoc in southern France. They looked after us well. French peasant farmers are notoriously individual and independent folk, but my four small children quickly learned there would be an open door and a *pain-au-chocolat*, or a piece of hot bread and honey, waiting for them when the schoolbus dropped them off outside the farmhouse on a cold winter's evening.

The Guilhermats, who spoke to us in French but used a thick Catalan patois among themselves, ran their affairs in true peasant fashion, as their parents and grandparents had done before them. The farm had about fifty acres, thirty of which were given over to a cash crop—often sorghum. The rest was a happy combination of those things that the Guilhermats considered necessary for their comfortable survival.

M. Guilhermat had a long strip planted with vines, whose wine stocked the family's cellar. In spring he would collect a small army of snails from the wild and place them in his vineyard so that the creatures could fatten on the young sweet leaves. Mme. Guilhermat made an excellent *ragoût* with them. At the foot of the vine patch there were two hives whose bees provided honey for the household. The family grew all their own vegetables in a small field near the stream and left clumps of woodland where red-legged partridges could breed. They knew where morel mushrooms grew in the spring, the best places for wild asparagus, and where truffles might be found under the oaks.

As well as its human occupants, the farmhouse sheltered two pigs, a yard full of chickens and guineafowl, several hutches of rabbits, a cow, and a loft with its quota of pigeons. An old mulberry tree and a walnut tree shaded the walls. Mme. Guilhermat's larder was well restocked each autumn with her own hams and sausages.

Each year, when the cash crop was sold, the family would buy good beef for a celebration meal of *pot-au-feu*. This is a classic peasant dish—it is prepared in various forms all over France. The aim is to get a good strong broth, which is eaten first, followed by a well-flavored boiled dinner, plain and wholesome, accompanied by a spicy tomato sauce, capers, and other sharp little pickles, or a glorious garlic mayonnaise, the *aïoli* beloved of all southerners.

The Guilhermat *pot-au-feu* was cooked in an earthenware casserole with a tight-fitting lid. In the grandmother's day, before the family had a kitchen range, this would have been on a tripod by the open fire and fueled by vine trimmings. The ingredients were variable—lamb, bacon, a homemade pork sausage, or a chicken might be used, and the vegetables depended on the season. White beans could replace the potatoes. Sometimes a clove or two went in. Whatever the ingredients, the only hard-and-fast rule was that the cooking must be very gentle and slow. Here is the family recipe for a celebration. Mme. Guilhermat considered that beef, a real luxury, since it had to be acquired with money, made the best dish of all.

SERVES: 6 to 8

TIME: 30 minutes plus 4 hours cooking

2	pounds beef rib roast (on the bone, for flavor)	1	pound carrots
1	pound shin of beef (off the bone, for strength in the broth)	1	small head of unblanched celery
		1	pound of leeks
1	knucklebone or marrowbone, or a length of ham bone	2	small turnips
			Peppercorns, 1 bay leaf, salt
2	quarts cold water	1	pound (3 medium-sized) potatoes
2	onions		Half a small head of green cabbage

You will need a large stewpan or casserole. Put the beef, tied in a bundle with string, and the bones, cut into lengths, into a large stewpan or earthenware casserole. Cover with the cold water. Bring to a boil and skim off the foam.

Cut the onions in half, leaving their skins on (to give a little golden color to the broth). Now wash and peel or trim the carrots, celery, leeks, and turnips. Put all the washed trimmings from these vegetables, with the onions, a few peppercorns, the bay leaf, and a little salt into the pot with the meat.

Bring the soup back to a boil and then simmer (no large bubbles should break the surface) for 3 hours, by which time the meat should be tender. The time might be shorter if the meat is high quality.

Take out the vegetable trimmings. (In the Guilhermat household they would be a treat for the pig.) Leave the meat to cool in its broth. When it is cold, you will be able to lift off the layer of well-flavored fat (Mme. Guilhermat saved it to use for sautéed potatoes or to enrich a bean stew). Alternatively, the *pot-au-feu* can be skimmed of its fat with a spoon while it is still hot. The dish can then be finished when you wish, as it will reheat superbly.

Cut the prepared vegetables into chunks. Any combination of root vegetables is acceptable, but try to use at least three different ones. Peel the potatoes and cut them to match the rest of the vegetables. Slice the cabbage fanshape into the stalk, so that the pieces hold together.

Put all the vegetables, except the potatoes and the cabbage, into the broth with the meat. Bring it back to a boil. Turn down the heat and simmer. After 10 minutes add the potatoes, and 10 minutes later the cabbage. Simmer for 15 minutes more, until the vegetables are ready.

On a cold winter's day Mme. Guilhermat would serve the broth first, with a handful of noodles cooked in it. Then the meat and vegetables would be placed on the table in a wide flat dish, accompanied by a generous bowl of *aïoli* (page 79), deep yellow and so thick it could be cut with a knife. Plenty of good bread, naturally, and young red wine from the family's own vines accompanied the meal.

SUGGESTIONS

The same dish can be made with a chicken and a piece of shin beef or 2 pig's trotters.

BEEF-AND-BEER STEW

Carbonnade à la flamande (Belgium)

There can be no more typically Flemish combination. The Belgians use their excellent lager beer as a cooking medium with the same pleasure and ingenuity as the Mediterranean uses wine. Beer is the national drink and comes in many varieties, including the famous *gueuze*, a spontaneously fermented beer. It is usually flavored with hops—a habit exported to Britain during the early part of the sixteenth century, when Flemish settlers arrived in southern England and planted the Kentish hop fields which are still cultivated today. The hops have a dual function in beer: They both refine it and help to preserve it. In Belgium, and in Kent too, the young hop shoots in season are lightly boiled and served with fried bread and poached eggs.

SERVES: 5 to 6

TIME: 20 to 25 minutes plus 2 hours cooking

2	*pounds chuck steak or skirt steak*	1	*bay leaf*
	Pepper	2	*cups dark beer*
1	*pound onions*	1	*teaspoon sugar*
1	*ounce (2 tablespoons) beef lard*		*Salt*
1	*sprig of thyme*		

You will need a deep casserole with a lid. Cut the beef into 1-inch cubes and pepper it well. Peel and slice the onions.

Put the lard to melt in the casserole. Fry the onions until they soften and turn golden. Push them to one side and add the seasoned meat. Fry until lightly browned. Add the herbs and pour the beer over all. Sprinkle in the sugar and a little salt.

Cook either on a low heat on top of the stove or in a preheated 325°F oven for 2 hours. Mash the onions into the juice to thicken it a little before you serve it. Accompany with plenty of plain-boiled floury potatoes, or a dish of creamy mashed potatoes, and beer to drink, naturally.

SUGGESTIONS

Some households add a chunk or two of ham to the stew. Garlic and vinegar are often included.

◆

BELGIAN HOT POT

Le hoche-pot (Belgium)

Undoubtedly one of the oldest dishes in the Belgian repertoire, even the French class it as *hoche-pot à la flamande*. This is the Belgian boiled dinner and it is served in two courses, first the soup and then the meat. Cook it on top of the stove, preferably in your grandmother's old enamel stew pot. The pig's ears and trotters give a gelatinous richness to the soup, and should not be omitted.

SERVES: 6 to 8

TIME: 30 minutes plus 3 to 4 hours cooking

1	*pound brisket of beef*	1	*teaspoon salt*
1	*pound shoulder of lamb*	2	*pounds mixed vegetables:*
½	*pound breast of lamb*		*carrots, turnips, celery,*
2	*salted pig's ears or ¼ pound salt*		*onions, leeks*
	pork	1	*pound (3 medium-sized) potatoes*
2	*pig's trotters (split and*	1	*small cabbage head*
	blanched)	½	*pound small pork sausages*
2	*quarts water*		*(chipolatas)*

You will need a large stew pot with a lid. Cut the meat into fairly large chunks—2½-inch cubes. Put them with the pig's ears or salt pork and the trotters in a large stew pot. Cover with 2 quarts salted water, bring all to a boil, skim, and then turn down to simmer for 2 to 3 hours, tightly covered, until all the meat is soft and you have a rich, strong soup.

Meanwhile, peel and slice the vegetables. Add them to the hotchpot in succession, starting with the carrots and root vegetables half an hour before the end of cooking, then the onions and leeks, then the potatoes, and last of all the cabbage. Simmer for another hour, until all is cooked. Take out all the solid meat and vegetables, and put them on a large platter. Keep them warm. Bring the soup back to a boil and poach the sausages in it for 5 to 6 minutes. Drain them and put them with the rest of the meat.

Serve the soup and a few vegetables first. Then bring on the steaming hotchpot. Serve with plenty of mild mustard and a dish of fresh horseradish grated into whipped cream.

◆

Instead of the horseradish, serve with a sharp little sauce of chopped pickled vegetables marinated in vinegar, with a handful of chopped parsley and chives stirred in.

Leftovers: You might like to save the pig's trotters for another meal. Let them cool and then remove all their little bones—pig's trotters have as many bones in them as human hands. Brush the trotters with butter, roll them in bread crumbs, and put them on a hot grill to gild. Serve with creamy mashed potatoes and a sharp sauce made with 1 cup of the stock thickened with 1 tablespoon of flour mashed with 1 tablespoon of butter, and flavored with a tablespoon of vinegar, a teaspoon of strong mustard, and a teaspoon of capers.

Any leftover meat makes an excellent salad if dressed with a mustardy vinaigrette and served with lettuce.

Put leftover vegetables into the blender with as much of the broth as you need to make an excellent vegetable soup. Serve with sizzling-hot croutons. Allow 1 cup of soup per person.

◆

BREAST OF VEAL STUFFED WITH BREAD DUMPLING

Befülltes Kalbsbrust (Austria)

Veal from veal calves is not such a luxury in diary-herd country and is often found on the Austrian table. Before the days of refrigeration, veal would be available in the late autumn and early winter, when the young male calves had to be slaughtered before the cold weather covered the ground with snow and deprived them of fodder. Country people would only have had enough hay to feed the stabled milk cows throughout the winter.

SERVES: 6

TIME: 40 minutes plus 1 hour and 15 minutes cooking

1 boned breast of veal (about 2½ pounds in weight)	1 egg
	½ cup milk
Salt and pepper	3 tablespoons flour
4 ounces dry bread	1 tablespoon chopped fresh herbs:
4 ounces (½ cup) butter	parsley, chervil, marjoram

You will need a bowl and a casserole with a tight lid, just large enough to accommodate the rolled veal. Lay the breast of veal flat on the table and sprinkle it with salt and pepper. Dice the bread and fry it lightly in half the butter. Meanwhile, mix the egg and the milk. Tip the contents of the frying pan into a bowl, and pour the egg and milk over all. Stir in the flour and the herbs, and season with salt and pepper. You may need more milk to make the mixture damp enough. Allow it to stand for half an hour.

Preheat the oven to 350°F.

Spread the stuffing mixture over the meat, and then roll it up and tie securely with string. Melt the rest of the butter in a heavy casserole and sear the roll, turning it to brown on all sides. Sprinkle it with salt and pepper, and cover tightly.

Cook for 1 hour and 15 minutes. Remove the lid of the casserole for the last 10 minutes.

Serve with *rösti* (page 101) and creamed spinach and good Austrian white wine.

◆

SUGGESTION

The dish is very good prepared with a roasting chicken—the cooking time is the same for the same weight of bird.

◆

TRIPE AND CHICK-PEAS

Callos con Garbonzos (Spain)

Carne de lidia is the name given to the meat on sale after the bullfight. The morning after the *corrida*, a regular event in my local town of Algeciras, a line would form early in the market for the meat from the *toros bravos*, muscular four-year-olds, six of whom had met their fate in the ring on the previous day. The meat was sold by weight in indiscriminate hacked-off chunks. Since each cut would be on offer at the same knockdown price, early birds caught the best bargains. The liver and lights would go last for a few pesetas to the poorest.

The Spanish way with tripe makes the best of this somewhat awkward, rather slithery meat. Esperanza, one of my neighbors in southern Spain, would walk up the goat track to the main road to catch the bus early on the morning when the *carne de lidia* went on sale. She liked the tripe best, and the local butcher would save a bucket full of the gray honeycomb-patterned stomach meat especially for her. By the early afternoon I would see her with her blue bucket bobbing on her arm, plodding back down the hillside to her little whitewashed house.

Later, as the sun dipped toward the horizon, she would make her way down to the millstream which threaded the valley's floor. There, in the little bay where she always did her washing, she scrubbed the tripe on the stones— rubbing, rinsing, and beating them in the clear running water until they were as white and clean as new linen. Everything else needed for the recipe she grew in her own kitchen *huerta*, the fertile vegetable patch beside her cottage, or stored from the annual pig killing.

SERVES: 5 to 6

TIME: Soak the chick-peas and start unprepared tripe the day before; 30 to 40 minutes if the tripe is ready-cooked plus 40 minutes to 3 or 4 hours depending on the raw materials

1 *pound tripe*	1 *pound tomatoes (or 1-pound can*
1 *salted or fresh pig's trotter or*	*of tomatoes)*
ear	6 *garlic cloves*
½ *pound dried chick-peas (or 2*	*Salt*
cans of cooked chick-peas)	2 *onions*
1 *piece dried ham bone (optional)*	1 *fresh red pepper*
2 *bay leaves*	6 *tablespoons olive oil*
2 *dried pimento peppers or 1*	3 to 4 *links of dried* chorizo *or*
tablespoon sweet paprika	¼ *pound dried spicy sausage*
½ *teaspoon peppercorns*	1 to 2 *tiny red chili peppers*
One ¼-*pound slab of bacon or salted*	1 *glass of white wine*
raw ham with rind (rind	
optional)	

You will need one to three saucepans (if the first three ingredients are un-cooked), a frying pan, and a lidded casserole. In non-Mediterranean countries, tripe is usually sold not only cleaned but ready-cooked—steam-blanched and soft so that it looks like white honeycomb. If it is still in the raw state, then after you have washed it thoroughly, put the tripe to soak overnight in salted water acidulated with vinegar or lemon juice. At the same time split the pig's trotter and, if it is a fresh one, leave it in salted water overnight. If you're using the pig's ear, cut it in four pieces. If you are using dried chick-peas, put them to soak in cold water overnight as well.

If your tripe is ready-cooked and blanched, omit the following prelimi-nary preparations. Unbleached tripe must be blanched. Cover the sheets of tripe with cold water and bring to a boil. Drain and rinse immediately. Cut into 1-inch squares and put it into a heavy pan. Rinse the pig's trotter and put that in, together with the ham bone if you have it. Pour in 2 glasses of water, cover tightly, and leave to simmer for 3 to 4 hours, by which time all the meat should be soft. Take out the trotter and pick out the bones. Return the gelatinous meat, chopped into squares, to the pan.

If your chick-peas are out of a can, omit this paragraph. If not, after the tripe has been on for 2 hours, put the soaked chick-peas in a separate pan and cover them with water to a depth of two fingers. Add the bay leaves, pimento or paprika, peppercorns, and rind of the bacon or ham cut into small squares. Cover the pan and bring the contents to a boil. Cook steadily for 1 to 2 hours, until the chick-peas are soft. Some chick-peas take much longer than others. If you need to add water, let it be boiling. When they are ready, drain the chick-peas and add them to the tripe.

If you have canned chick-peas and pre-cooked tripe, drain the chick-peas and put them in a casserole. Cut the home- or shop-prepared tripe into 1-inch squares and add it to the chick-peas. Your stew will lack most of the characteristic, and to my mind necessary, glueyness imparted by the tripe juices and the bacon rind, but it will be a great deal shorter in the preparation.

Meanwhile, pour boiling water over the tomatoes to loosen the skins. Peel and chop them. Chop the rindless bacon or ham. Peel the garlic cloves and crush them with a little salt. Peel and chop the onions. Stalk, seed, and chop the red pepper. Warm the olive oil in a frying pan, and add the garlic, onions, and red pepper. Fry gently until the vegetables soften. Chop up the *chorizo* or sausage and add it, followed by the chopped tomatoes, the seeded chilis (don't rub your eyes), and the wine. Cook uncovered for 20 to 25 minutes, until you have a spicy sauce.

Tip the sauce into the casserole with the tripe and chick-peas, and stir it in. Cook all together gently for 15 minutes to marry the flavors.

Serve with plenty of bread and wine. My neighbor down the valley would serve the dish with a salad of cos lettuce, freshly picked from her *huerta*, sliced and dressed with chopped onion, vinegar, oil, and salt to clear the palate for a piece of her special goat's cheese. The cheese was her cash crop, and she made it two or three times a week throughout the summer, selling it fresh, or rubbing it with olive oil and paprika and maturing it for a few months on a beam in her lean-to dairy.

◆

BOILED SALT BEEF AND DUMPLINGS

(England)

This is one of the oldest traditional dishes of England. Salted meats carried many a poor household through the winter.

THE BEEF:

1	roast of corned beef (your own or the butcher's)		Parsley stalks
1	onion	3	carrots
6	cloves	2	bay leaves
		1	teaspoon peppercorns

THE DUMPLINGS:

2 ounces (½ cup) flour	1 tablespoon chopped parsley
2 ounces (¼ cup) fresh bread crumbs	½ teaspoon salt
2 ounces suet or the equivalent quantity of fat skimmed from the beef	2 to 3 tablespoons cold water

You will need a stewpan, a strainer, and a saucepan. Wipe the salt beef and put it in a pan which will accommodate it comfortably. Cover the meat with water and bring all to a boil. Turn down to simmer for 10 minutes.

Meanwhile, stick the onion with the cloves, and peel the carrots, reserving the peel. Strip out the stalks from the parsley you will be using in the dumplings.

Taste the beef water which has now been simmering for 10 minutes. If the water is very salty, throw it away, recover the beef with fresh water, and bring back to a boil. If it is not too salty, just skim off the foam and continue with the recipe.

Add the clove-stuck onion to the pot, and the carrot peelings (save the carrots for later), parsley stalks, bay leaves, and peppercorns. Leave it all to simmer. Gentle bubbles are what is required: A rolling boil would toughen the meat. Leave to cook on a low heat: A 4-pound piece will take 2½ hours—add on 20 minutes for each pound thereafter.

Half an hour before you are ready to serve, put a large oval serving dish, preferably of white china, to warm.

When the meat is tender, draw it to the side of the fire and strain off half the stock. Ladle off the yellow fat floating on the surface—you can use this to mix the dumplings instead of the suet, but it must be allowed to cool first. Leave the meat to settle down in its liquid while you cook the sliced carrots in the strained stock. They will take about 20 minutes. Drain them and put them into the serving dish to keep warm.

Meanwhile, make the dumplings by kneading together all the ingredients into a soft dough with light fingers—that and the air in the bread crumbs is the only raising agent. You can include a teaspoon of baking powder if you wish. Roll the dough into marble-sized balls with well-floured hands. Poach them in the simmering-hot stock in which you have cooked the carrots. They will take 10 to 15 minutes to cook. Take them out with a perforated spoon, and give them a quick splash under cold water to stop them from sticking together. Give the stock a final boil to concentrate the flavor while you carve the beef into thick slices.

Serve on the white china dish: slices of deep crimson meat surrounded by the carrots and green-speckled dumplings. Serve with your best beer—the Englishman's diet survived many a crisis when he had enough beer to make up for its deficiencies.

◆

SUGGESTIONS

If you have put an ox tongue in the brine, soak it well before you put it to cook as for the salt beef. It will take 4 hours to be ready. Remove the little bones at the root end, and peel off the thick skin—if the tongue is well cooked, it will come off easily. Serve the tongue hot, cut into slices and bathed in a caper sauce made with its own stock—concentrated by boiling and thickened with flour kneaded with butter, the capers stirred in at the end with a little grated fresh horseradish and a spoonful of mustard. Or serve with a sauce made with some of the stock as before, and flavored with a glass of Madiera or sweet sherry, reduced to half its volume by boiling. If you want to serve the meat cold, pack the peeled and boned cooked tongue into a round bowl or cake tin, neatly curled and pressed under a weight. Leave it to jelly at least overnight.

Leftovers: Serve the salt beef or the cold tongue cut into thin slices. Accompany with baked potatoes (page 95), or with the carrots you have left over sliced and reheated in a white sauce (page 37), or with a French *gratin* of potatoes (page 99).

◆

POTTED MEAT

Lou pastis en pott (France)

This is an unusual potted meat prepared only in the Languedoc. My youngest daughter brought news of it when she stayed with a friend from the school she attended near Toulouse. There were a great many such delicious surprises for her in that particular farmhouse, including a nest of ducklings on the hearth and a pair of lambs who had the freedom of the bedroom.

SERVES: 8 to 10

TIME: Start at least 2 weeks ahead; 30 minutes plus 2 hours cooking, repeated 3 times

FIRST COOKING:

½ *pound lard*	1 *teaspoon juniper berries*
2 *pounds lean beef*	*Salt and pepper*
2 *pounds lean pork*	½ *bottle red wine (the near-black*
3 *bay leaves*	*wine of Cahors or a deep red*
A few sprigs of thyme and rosemary	*Médoc)*

SECOND AND THIRD COOKING:

The same ingredients again each time

You will need a large straight-sided earthenware pot. Scald the earthenware pot and grease it thoroughly with a little of the lard (you can line the bottom with a few fig or walnut leaves if you have them). Cut the beef and pork into slices, trimming the gristle and sinews as you do so. Put the bay leaves on the bottom of the pot. Lay in the meat slices, seasoning with the herbs, salt, and freshly ground pepper as you do so. Pour in the wine—it should just cover the meat.

Simmer the pot uncovered over a very low heat or in a preheated 250°F oven, for 1½ to 2 hours, until the volume is reduced by half. Allow to cool. Seal with a layer of lard, melted and poured over the cool meat. Cover with wax paper tied down with string. Leave the pot on a refrigerator shelf for a week. Then remove the lard seal and add in another 2 pounds pork and 2 pounds beef, the whole covered with wine, seasoned and cooked as before. Repeat the operation at the end of another week. You will now have a delicious dark jelly-meat, which you can eat either hot or cold. If you continue to replace the volume you have removed, the pot can go on forever.

REINDEER

The adventurous traveler Paul du Chaillu, fresh from his explorations in West Africa, observed Laplanders milking their reindeer in 1871:

> I watched the milking with great interest. The women knew every animal around the tent, and if one had been missing they would have been able to designate it at once. Those which were to be milked were approached carefully, and a lasso was thrown gently over the horns, and knotted over the muzzle, to prevent the deer from running away; but they made no effort to escape. Sometimes one would hold the deer while another was milking . . . The process was peculiar: the women held in one hand a wooden scoop, frequently pressing hard with the other, for the thick fluid seemed to come with difficulty; it was poured from the scoop into a keg-like vessel closed by a sliding cover, and so contrived that it could be carried on the back of an animal . . . skin bladders were filled, to be used by the Lapps who were to remain the whole day with the herds. I was surprised at the small yield—some not giving enough to fill a small coffee-cup; but it was very thick and rich—so much so that water had to be added before drinking . . . not unlike goat's milk. The milk of the reindeer forms a very important item in the food of the Lapps . . . butter made from it is like tallow, so they make very little.
>
> While the men were enjoying their pipes the women busied

themselves with cooking. A porridge was made of the dry skimmed milk, stirred into water with a wooden spoon—a palatable and very nutritious dish. Each person had a little bag from which a spoon was taken for table use . . . forks are not used among the Lapps, but some of their silver-ware is very old . . . The Laplanders are very fond of dried powdered blood, which is cooked in a kind of porridge mixed with flour, or diluted with warm water and made into a pancake.

And again on another day:

After the meat was cooked it was put on a wooden platter and the father, as is the custom, divided it into portions for each member of the family. The fattest parts are considered the best, and I noticed that these were set aside for us. Then we began our meal, using our fingers as forks. The fire was kept blazing, for it was 40 degrees below zero; and besides, we wanted the light . . . the men and women smoked their pipes . . . Singing hymns in praise of God, they dressed themselves for the night, putting over their garments a long reindeer gown, extending below the feet—almost a bag. No matter how severe the weather may be, one does not feel cold in such a garb. [*The Land of the Midnight Sun*, Paul du Chaillu, 1881]

◆——————————

REINDEER STEW

Kokt rensdyrkjott (Lapland)

Reindeer are still herded, like cattle in the south, for meat and skins by the Lapp population of northern Scandinavia. The usual cooking method of the nomadic, tent-dwelling Lapps was a heavy iron cauldron suspended over the hearth fire from the crossbar of the tent. The boiling pot could be let up and down on a sophisticated hook-and-pulley system. The tents and implements of the *Same*, as the Lapps call their nation, were always impeccably designed and made. The Lapps were (and still are) accomplished craftsmen—so clever were they at boat building that the Vikings used to employ them to build their long ships. Lapp-carved bone implements, together with their birch bowls and cups, their horn-handled knives and molded bark storage containers, are always exquisitely carved and often inlaid with bone medallions and other decorations.

This recipe comes from a forest Lapp family in Kautokeino, northern Norway, and it was always prepared by the father. In the likely absence of reindeer (or even the alternative, moose), the recipe can be made with beef. The aromatics, with the exception of one trade item, peppercorns, which replaced the myrtle berries, are in plentiful supply in Lapland. The bayberry is the North American representative of the family. Cranberries can replace rowanberries. The tongue of the reindeer, lightly salted and boiled as for ox tongue (page 510) is highly prized throughout Norway and Sweden.

SERVES: 12

TIME: 10 minutes plus 3 to 4 hours cooking

4 *pounds meat plus bones*	1 *tablespoon dried rowanberries or*
2 *quarts water*	*a handful of fresh cranberries*
1 *teaspoon juniper berries*	*A few young fir needles or a handful*
2 *tablespoons myrtle berries or 1*	*of dill or fennel*
tablespoon peppercorns	1 *tablespoon salt*

You will need a heavy stew pot. Crack the bones. Put the bones and the meat, rolled and tied, into the stew pot; cover with the water and bring to a boil. Skim off the froth which rises. Add the aromatics and the salt, and then turn the heat down to simmer for 3 to 4 hours, when the meat should be tender.

Scoop the marrow from the bones into the stew before slicing the meat and serving it with its soup in individual bowls. Accompany with dark rye bread. In Lapland, the accompaniment might be little cakes, thin as dollar pancakes, made from rye flour mixed with blood. Blueberries or wild strawberries in season, served with cream, finish the meal.

SUGGESTION

Cook root vegetables such as potatoes, turnips, and rutabagas in the soup to serve with the meat. Nomadic peoples like the *Same* did not have time to plant harvest vegetables, so this would be a modern addition.

HOT POT

Karjalanpaisti (Finland)

The brick bread ovens which are still to be found in the country districts of Finland were used no more than once every two or three months. Wood fires were lit inside and then the ashes were brushed out, leaving the walls red-hot for batches of bread to be baked. Fuel is always precious in such a climate. The residual heat of the oven was used to prepare slow-stewed dishes. In the north the meat might well be reindeer or moose venison. Beef and pork were more common in the south. Meat baked in the residual heat of the bread oven is a great wedding or celebration dish—the casseroles were put in after the egg-enriched party breads and sugar biscuits had been baked.

SERVES: 8 to 10

TIME: 20 minutes plus 4 hours cooking

4	*pounds mixed meats (a combination of reindeer, venison, pork, lamb, beef, veal, whatever can be obtained)*	2	*ounces (4 tablespoons) lard*
		1	*teaspoon juniper berries*
			Salt and pepper
3	*pounds onions*	2	*cups water*

Preheat the oven to 250°F. You will need a heavy casserole with a lid.

Slice the meat. Slice the onions. Lay the meat and the onions and little bits of lard (unless you're including pork or lamb) in alternate layers, seasoned well with crushed juniper, salt, and pepper, in a casserole. Add the water. Cover tightly, sealing with a paste of flour and water if the cover does not fit very snugly.

Bake in the oven for at least 4 hours. Overnight (at the lowest possible temperature) is not too long. Finish the meal with a fruit soup.

GRILLED MEATS
(Hungary)

The Hungarian fondness for the nomadic Magyar diet of milk, fresh or soured, and grilled meat (fast food for nomads) reflects a taste for the fermented mare's milk and steaks of their hunting ancestors. Dishes called bandit's roast, *zsiványpecsenye* and robber's meat, *rablohus*, testify to ancient carnivorous leanings. As soon as the Magyars settled down, they took to pig keeping with enthusiasm. The meat stews are also throwbacks to the nomadic horsemen, as they were orginally prepared with dried meat and cooked over an open fire in a *bogrács*, a large copper bucket which is still sometimes used in the modern Hungarian kitchen.

Today itinerant food sellers in the market at Gyor in Transdanubia, as in other markets throughout modern Hungary, continue to offer the public what it has enjoyed for so long: meat fast-grilled and accompanied by good country bread. Hungarian street food is served from portable kiosk shelters equipped with bar-height tables for the customers. Here are grilled paprika sausages and black puddings, slabs of fried liver and pork, sold by weight straight from the fire and wrapped in heavy brown paper. A wax paper twist of mustard, a thick slice of pale dense-crumbed bread (also sold by weight), and pickled yellow hot peppers come with it. A mixture of meats is typically Hungarian. Here are three mixed-meat dishes—make them all together and serve them on a big wooden platter as a rather unusual mixed grill. Finish with the alternative street food—doughnuts hot from the frying vat.

◆

HUNGARIAN SAUSAGES

Rachegi (Hungary)

SERVES: 6

TIME: 40 minutes

1	*pound ground veal*		*Salt*
1	*pound ground pork*	1	*tablespoon paprika*
2	*eggs*	1	*tablespoon chopped marjoram*
1	*garlic clove*	1	*tablespoon chopped parsley*

You will need a bowl and a frying pan. Mix the meats and the eggs together well. Crush the garlic in the salt. Add it to the meat mixture, along with the paprika and the herbs. Knead it all into a firm paste. If you have a friendly butcher who will let you have sausage casings, stuff the mixture through a funnel into the well-soaked casings, to make a single long sausage. If you have no casings, shape the mixture by hand (a wet hand is easiest) into sausages about an inch thick. Grill the sausages or fry them in butter. Serve with spiced vegetable pickles (use the Bulgarian recipe on page 522), good bread, and a bowl of mild mustard. Beer or white wine will quench your thirst.

◆

STUFFED PORK CHOPS

Baranya (Hungary)

SERVES: 4

TIME: 30 minutes

8   very thin slices of pork fillet (the
    chop without the bone)
Salt and pepper
1   teaspoon chopped marjoram
1   garlic clove
2   ounces bacon

1   tablespoon lard
One ¼-pound slice of pork, veal, or
    lamb liver
1   tablespoon paprika
1   egg

You will need a frying pan. Lay the slices of pork fillet out on the table.
Sprinkle them with salt, pepper, and some marjoram.

Crush the clove of garlic with a little salt. Mince the bacon and put it to
fry gently in the lard. Add the garlic. Chop the liver small and put it to fry
with the bacon. Cook gently until the liver stiffens and takes color. Off the
fire, stir in the paprika and the teaspoon of marjoram. Allow the liver mixture
to cool a little; then taste, adjust the seasoning, and mix in the egg to bind the
mixture into a stuffing. Sandwich the pork rounds together in pairs with a
mound of the mixture, rather like large ravioli. Fry or grill them until well
browned and cooked through.

Serve with bread, hot pickles, and mild mustard.

FRIED LIVER

Majsult (Hungary)

SERVES: 4

TIME: 20 to 30 minutes

1   pound liver: lamb, veal or pork
2   onions
½   pound tomatoes (or an 8-ounce
    can of tomatoes)

2   ounces (4 tablespoons) lard
1   tablespoon paprika
1   tablespoon chopped marjoram
Salt

You will need a frying pan. Trim the liver of any veins, and then slice it into
strips about half an inch wide by three inches long. Peel and slice finely the
onions. Pour boiling water on the tomatoes to loosen the skins, and then peel
and chop them.

Melt the lard in a frying pan. Add the onions and fry them golden. Push
to one side and stir in the strips of liver. Cook them until they stiffen and take
color. Sprinkle in the paprika and the chopped marjoram. Add the tomatoes
and raise the heat to melt them into a thick sauce. Taste, and adjust the
seasoning.

Serve with a ladelful of *letcho* (page 21) stirred in instead of the tomatoes.

STUFFED STEAK

Kapuvar (Hungary)

SERVES: 4

TIME: 30 minutes

8 *very thin slices of beef steak*	4 *very thin slices of pork steak*
Salt and pepper	4 *slices of slab bacon*
Mild mustard	

You will need a frying pan. Sprinkle the slices of beef with salt and pepper, and spread one side of each with mustard. Sandwich a slice of pork between each two slices of beef. Cut the bacon into larding strips. Make 2 pairs of slits in the beef-and-pork sandwiches, and thread strips of bacon through to hold the sandwiches together.

Fry or grill the sandwich steaks—they will have to be well done because the pork in the middle must be thoroughly cooked. Serve with pickles, bread, and a big tankard of beer to refresh you.

GRILLED MARINATED MEAT OR FISH KABOBS

Kebaps (Turkey)

This is food for nomads and was probably man's first taste of the fire. *Kebāb* is an ancient Indian word meaning "cooked meat"—a modest beginning for a dish which has inspired so many cooks. The secret of good kabobs lies in the marination. Lamb or kid is the usual (and the best) meat: It is delicate enough to respond well to the spices, and tender enough not to harden under the fierce heat of the grill. Liver and lights and other offal also make good kabobs. Pork is another suitable meat, but it must be thoroughly cooked through. Beef is not so suitable, being usually a lean meat and better grilled in larger pieces. Large peeled prawns and monkfish make good kabobs, but need a shorter marination time.

SERVES: 6 to 8

TIME: Start several hours or the night before; 20 to 25 minutes

These marinades are for 2 pounds of meat cut into 1-inch cubes: enough for 6 to 8 people. Make the marinade and turn the cubed meat very thoroughly in it. Leave to absorb the flavors overnight, or for several hours at least. Brush off the larger bits of the marinade before you thread the meat on fine skewers (moisten the wooden ones first so that they do not burn).

The best cooking medium is a charcoal fire, but the oven broiler will do well enough. All but pork kabobs should be cooked quite close to the heat, so that the outside chars but the meat remains juicy. Turn the kabobs once or twice. They will be ready in 10 to 12 minutes over or under not too fierce a heat. Pork kabobs will need 15 to 18 minutes farther away from the heat.

Serve the kabobs with rough chunks of bread or with rice. Accompany with lemon quarters and a few cool, refreshing salads, including a cucumber-and-yogurt salad (page 53).

Greek marinade: 4 tablespoons olive oil, 1 lemon cut into chunks or 2 tablespoons lemon juice or 4 tablespoons white wine, 2 bay leaves, 2 tablespoons marjoram and oregano, and a few grinds of black pepper.

Turkish marinade: 4 tablespoons olive oil, juice of 1 lemon, 2 chopped onions, 1 tablespoon crushed dried mint or 2 tablespoons fresh, 1 teaspoon cinnamon (powder or crushed sticks), and ½ teaspoon freshly milled pepper.

Alternatively, make up your own marinade with your favorite spices. You should have oil plus a sharp element, and such other spices and flavorings as suit your palate. Yogurt and onion are suitable ingredients (the yogurt already has both a fatty and sour element, and it will tenderize the meat). Cumin, coriander, allspice, turmeric, and ground chili are all good seasonings.

SUGGESTION

While the kabobs are in the marinade, make a batch of pita bread to accompany them (page 414).

GRILLED SKEWERED MEAT

Souvlakia (Greece)

These unspiced kabobs can be delicious if the meat is good and the charcoal grill smoke free and hot. Cubes of beef or pork can be alternated with cubes of slab bacon, with squares of a strong hard cheese alternated with cubes of bread, or with chunks of tomato, onion, and green pepper.

Y I E L D : Allow 4 to 5 ounces of meat per person

T I M E : 30 minutes

Thread cubes of beef, and the other ingredients if you are using them, on skewers, brush them with oil, sprinkle with pepper, and grill them over hot charcoal or under a blazing-hot broiler.

When they are ready, sprinkle them with rough salt and serve with quartered lemons, a bowl of *skordalia* (page 56), and plenty of bread. Accompany them with a dish of vegetables, such as *koukia*.

◆

GRILLED SAUSAGES WITH PEPPERS

Mititei (Rumania)

Grills for the cooking of these little sausages are traditionally set up first thing in the morning on market day in town squares all over Rumania, usually within range of a portable beer counter, installed by another traveling salesman, who would provide little chairs and tables. The sausages can be made from virtually any part of any animal; it is an undemanding recipe whose ingredients can still be acquired even in the shortages which plague modern Rumania.

S E R V E S : 4

T I M E : Start the peppers the day before, the sausages 2 to 3 hours before; 25 to 30 minutes

1 *pound green, yellow, or red peppers*	1 *pound finely ground meat (beef is usual; other meat will do fine)*
Oil	
Wine vinegar	1 *tablespoon summer savory*
Salt, pepper, sugar	½ *teaspoon freshly ground allspice*
2 *garlic cloves*	*(a favorite spice in Rumania)*

You will need two bowls and a pestle and mortar. The day before you need them, blacken the peppers under the broiler flame or on top of the stove until all the skins blister and you can peel them easily. Take off the skins; seed and cut the peppers lengthwise into strips. Dress with 3 parts oil to 1 part wine vinegar, and sprinkle with a little salt and pepper and a pinch of sugar. Leave them to marinate overnight.

On serving day: Pound the garlic with ½ teaspoon of salt. Mix it thoroughly with the minced meat, some pepper, the finely chopped savory, and the allspice. Leave the mixture for an hour or two for the flavors to blend.

When you are ready to cook them, make sure that the grill, whether charcoal, gas, or electric, is good and hot. With wet hands, form the meat paste into stubby little skinless sausages about an inch thick. Brush the hot grill with oil, and put the *mititei* to cook about a hand's width away from the heat (that is, not too near). They will take about 7 to 8 minutes, turned once.

They are to be eaten straight from the grill with the side dish of marinated grilled peppers and plenty of bread.

SUGGESTION

Scatter the peppers with a few black olives, little cubes of white cheese, and the chopped green leaves of a scallion or chives.

MINCEMEAT SKEWERS

Raznici (Yugoslavia—Serbia)

The Yugoslavs pride themselves on their grilled meats. These delicious little kabobs are sold on street corners in the markets and from little snack bars all over the towns and villages. Small paprika-flavored sausages are often grilled alongside them. The scent fills the air on warm evenings during the evening promenade, when the population turns out to chat, flirt, or gossip as the mood and age takes them.

SERVES: 4 to 5

TIME: 30 to 40 minutes

1 pound ground meat (pork and beef is the street mix)	½ pound grated or finely chopped onions
½ teaspoon salt	1 to 2 seeded and chopped green chili peppers
Plenty of pepper	

You will need small wooden skewers. Pound the meat with the salt and freshly ground pepper. Knead it thoroughly until you have a soft paste. Form the paste into small sausage shapes with wet hands and push a wooden skewer through the middle of each. Wet the ends of the wooden skewers so that they do not burn over the coals.

Cook over a little charcoal brazier or under a hot broiler. Serve with a dish of grated or chopped onions, the chili peppers, and a thick slab of country bread. That's all: simplicity itself—street food at its best.

For a main meal, serve with a salad of roughly chunked onions, tomatoes, and cucumber dressed with a sprinkling of crumbled strong white cheese and a sliced green chili pepper. Quartered lemons go alongside.

◆

SUGGESTIONS

Further varieties of grilled meat in Yugoslavia include cubes of pork and veal; *pljeskavia*, spiced hamburgers; and *sis cevap*, cubes of lamb.

CHAPTER TWELVE

Breads and Yeast Pastries

The sight and scent of a newly baked loaf have a romantic appeal which transcends all other culinary achievements. William Cobbett, chronicler of things English and rural circa 1830, expressed the traditional view of the English Victorian male: "Give me for a beautiful sight, a neat and smart woman, heating her oven and setting in her bread! And, if the bustle does make the sign of labour glisten on her brow, where is the man that would not kiss that off, rather than lick the plaster from the cheek of a duchess?" [*Rural Rides*, William Cobbett, 1830]

Stirring stuff! However, Mme. Suzanne Llewelyn (an unlikely Welsh name to find in a hill village in the Languedoc, but acquired through a passion for the game of rugby which she, a good daughter of southwestern France, shared with her husband, a son of the distant Rhondda Valley) remembers her own family's pre-1914 baking day somewhat more realistically:

> Our own wheat from our own fields was taken to the miller to be ground into flour, and the miller kept a proportion for his services. More of the flour went to the baker as payment for the use of the oven.
>
> Bread was made at home, once a week, and it never went bad. Never. It went dry of course, but it had a wonderful rough texture that did you good. The oven was communal, a small brick building, no longer used, but still there, on one side of the square. Our mother rose at 2 a.m. to start the leaven. At five, while the oven was being heated with a fire of wood and sagebrush, a crier would go round the neighboring streets calling: "Ladies, time to make your bread." All the ladies would knead and pummel. When the oven was good and hot and the fire had burned down, the master baker scraped out the ashes and hot embers so that the floor would be clean for the bread.
>
> By then the ladies were ready with their big family loaves, oval or round, plump and well-risen and ready for the heat. Such bread!

For a special treat on baking day, you could cut off a hot fresh slice, rub it once with a clove of garlic and then trickle a little olive oil over it. Fresh oil was the best—from that same year, and still cloudy from the press. At winter work in the fields, there was nothing better at midday than a slice off the ham, a piece of cheese and a thick wedge of that bread. Such a meal with a flask of wine and a handful of olives were all anyone could desire.

Charlotte Gower Chapman, young American sociologist studying rural life in the village of Milocca in Sicily in 1928, observed the local housewives at their baking:

> The simplest form is a round loaf, with a long semi-circular gash on the top. More elaborate forms which almost anyone can make are the "fish" and the "pistol." The top of the loaf may be left plain, glazed with white of egg or covered with poppy seeds or sesame.
>
> As soon as they are made, the loaves are put to bed, literally, and covered with all the available blankets and shawls. While they are rising, the oven is heated by a fire of straw and twigs built inside it. When both it and the bread are ready, the oven is swept out, and the loaves put in with a long wooden shovel kept for this purpose. A flat stone door closes the oven and is sealed in place with wet ashes. The sign of the cross is made over the door, and the bread is left for an hour or so to take care of itself. The finished bread is dusted and kept in a basket. It is of a yellowish color and close texture. Butter is not eaten with it, but hot bread may be seasoned with olive oil, salt, pepper and grated cheese, as a treat for the children or for visitors. Every woman is convinced of the superiority of her bread to that of any other woman in the community and of the excellence of the bread of Milocca over that of any other town. Bread is never lightly treated. Before a new loaf is cut the sign of the cross is made on it with the knife and the knife is kissed. No loaf is ever put down bottom-side up. It is the "providence of God" and so to be respected. [*Milocca: A Sicilian Village*, Charlotte Gower Chapman, 1973]

Northern bakers had somewhat less tractable raw materials to hand. Mrs. Tweedie, traveling through Finland with her sister and a Finnish friend in 1898, recorded her own observations of local bread making:

> A servant girl—for well-to-do farmers have servants—made black bread in a huge tub, the dough being so heavy and solid that she could not turn it over at all, and only managed to knead it by doubling her fists and regularly plunging them to the bottom with all her strength. Her sunburnt arms disappeared far above her elbow, and judging by the way the meal stuck to her she found bread making very hard work. Finlanders only bake every few weeks, so the bread is often made with a hole and hung up in rows from the ceiling, or, if not, is placed on the kitchen rafters till wanted. This bread is invaria-

bly sour—the natives like it so—and to get it rightly flavoured they always leave a little in the tub, that it may taste the next batch, as sour cream turns the new cream for butter. [*Through Finland in Carts*, Ethel B. Tweedie, 1898]

YEAST BREADS

COUNTRY YEAST-RAISED BREAD

Pan de campo (Spain)

The Romans held Spanish bakers in high esteem. Spanish bread was delicately white, they wrote home, fine textured, a miracle of flavor and aroma. The Spanish still have not lost their skill, at least in the country districts. All over the Iberian peninsula each little pueblo takes passionate pride in its own master bread maker, whose loaves are highly individual and easily recognizable to his customers, and whose merits are fiercely contested with the neighboring bakeries. This difference is not in shape—which varies from area to area, although usually not within the area: In Andalusia, for instance, convention decrees shape should be either perfectly round and smooth, or oblong and slashed down the top to give a specially crisp crust. Weight ranges from one-pound loaves, suitable for the old grandmother who lives with her unmarried daughter in a Catalan mountain village, to ten-pound special orders taken by the southern cork-tree strippers on their two-week work spells in the forests of Andalusia.

Rather, the difference comes from the bread's texture and taste. Spanish country bread is made with a sourdough starter—which also depends for its efficacy on the bacteria in the kneading trough and other factors difficult to provide in the modern kitchen. A few isolated rural Spanish bakeries (particularly in the undeveloped south) still use the old brick-and-adobe bread oven, and light a brushwood-and-log fire inside to burn until the walls are hot enough for baking. The fire is then raked out and the bread put to bake—such loaves are easy to identify, since they have minute bits of charcoal and a light dusting of wood ash left sticking to their bases. Some bakeries add a trowelful of lime to the mix to whiten the dough.

Even so, Eugenio López, an Andalusian landowner interviewed by Ronald Fraser, was nostalgic in 1958 for the old ways:

> Sometimes I go out in the countryside with a loaf and some lard and a penknife to slice the bread the way the people used to. It reminds me of my childhood and the way everyone lived. How well I remember it! The barley coffee and buñuelos [doughnuts] before going to school when the men and women took down the aguardiente bottle from the dresser to drink a copita to start the day off. The *viva Jesus* I always called it. [*The Pueblo*, Ronald Fraser, 1973]

YIELD: Makes 2 large loaves

TIME: Start 2 to 3 hours ahead; 40 minutes plus 40 minutes cooking

3 *pounds high-gluten unbleached flour*	3 *cups warm water*
1 *ounce fresh yeast or ½ ounce dried yeast*	2 *tablespoons warm milk*
	1 *tablespoon salt*

You will need a large bowl and a baking sheet. An electric mixer with a dough hook would be useful.

Sift the flour into a large warm bowl. All your utensils and ingredients should be around blood temperature to allow the yeast to thrive and work properly. Anything that would scald you will do the same to the little organisms. Mix the yeast into a cupful of the warm water and the milk to liquefy it and start it working. Dried yeast takes an extra 20 minutes. Make a well in the warm flour and pour in the yeast liquid. Sprinkle a handful of the flour over it for the yeast to feed on. Cover and leave in a warm place for half an hour to "set the sponge." This allows the yeast to start working initially on a small quantity of dough, a step which should not be omitted, as it will speed up the process of fermentation.

The mixture is now ready for kneading. Sprinkle in the salt. Have beside you the rest of the warm water. Draw the dry flour into the now-bubbling well with your hand, adding more water as you need it to slake the flour, until it all sticks together in a soft, thick mass. If the dough is too hard, it cannot expand properly. Tip it out onto the floured tabletop, and push and pummel it with your fingers and the heel of your hand. Give it a thorough working until it is elastic. When the dough is smooth and the gluten in the flour well stretched, fold it into a cushion with the tucks underneath and replace it in the bowl. Cover with a clean damp cloth and put in a warm place for an hour to double in size. Experience will tell you where and how long—I put mine in an unlit oven with a tray of boiling water beneath. The dough is ready when it will hold the mark of a finger pushed into it.

Punch it down again by kneading well with clenched fists. This distributes the carbon dioxide manufactured by the yeast evenly through the dough. Knead well and cut the dough in half. Knuckle each piece into a firm plump cushion. Grease a baking sheet and dust it well with flour. Turn the round loaves over so that the creases are underneath.

Put them to double in size in a warm, damp, draft-free place—back in the unlit oven with fresh boiling water. It should take only 20 to 30 minutes this time.

Preheat the oven to 425°F.

Sprinkle the loaves with flour and bake for 20 minutes, then turn the oven down to 400°F for the last 20 to 25 minutes. When the bread is cooked, it will be well risen, crusty, and golden, and the base will sound hollow when you tap it. Dry the loaves upside down in the turned-off oven for 5 minutes.

◆

This dough can be baked in loaf pans or molded into any shape you please—in the north of Spain it would be twisted into a teardrop; other regions have their preferred shapes. Country bakers often prick their loaves with the sign of the cross and their own initials.

Leftovers: Use the stale bread to make bread soups such as *gazpacho*.

Make *migas* with the leftovers: Chop or tear the bread into small rough squares and sprinkle them with water (it could be wine). Wrap the cubes in a damp cloth and leave them to soak up the liquid. Heat olive oil in a frying pan with a clove or two of garlic. Chopped onion, cubes of salt pork, bacon, or little pieces of raw ham can be included, together with a pinch of paprika and that very Moorish spice, cumin. Fry the wet bread very gently for half an hour with the flavorings until it is crisp but not brown, for a kind of fried *gazpacho*, delicious with fried eggs (page 192).

Or cut stale bread into slices and dry in the oven to make *biscottes* for storing in an airtight tin. They are very good with cheese.

Or dry the slices in the oven until crisp, and grate or put them in a blender to make bread crumbs for *croquetas*.

Or follow Thomas Carlyle's recipe, as recorded in *Sartor Resartus:* "On fine evenings I was wont to carry forth my supper (bread-crumb boiled in milk), and eat it out-of-doors. On the coping of the Orchard-wall, which I could reach by climbing, or still more easily if Father Andreas would set up the pruning-ladder, my porringer was placed: there, many a sunset, have I, looking at the distant western Mountains, consumed, not without relish, my evening meal."

◆

SOURDOUGH RYE BREAD

Sauerteig Roggenbrot (Germany and Northern Europe)

This is the classic northern peasant rye bread. Rye is a very hardy early-ripening cereal, which can be cropped successfully where the more delicate wheats cannot survive. It has enough gluten for the making of bread. Oats and barley, although hardy, have a low gluten content and the dough simply will not stick together. A mix of barley and wheat flour is sometimes used—although barley-wheat bread is overly heavy and rather indigestible. Each household would take its own mixture of grain to be milled. Both the highly individual flour and the wooden troughs used for the proving gave a recognizably different flavor and texture to the products of each housewife. A peasant family took great pride in its own household bread.

Rye has a very low gluten content, which makes it exceptionally hard to work. It is characteristic of the Eastern European peasant board, and worth making for its very distinctive flavor and texture. It will never be light, so don't expect miracles. A semi-sourdough seems to work best. If you would like to make it easier for yourself, use half wheat flour—it will give you a much lighter loaf, but it will be a pale ghost of the real thing.

YIELD: Makes 1 large loaf

TIME: Start 2 days ahead; 30 minutes plus 2 hours cooking

THE SOURDOUGH STARTER:
1   *small nugget of yeast*
4   *ounces (1 cup) rye flour*
2   *tablespoons warm milk*

THE BREAD:
2   *pounds rye flour*   2   *cups warm water*
1   *teaspoon salt*   *Sourdough starter*
1   *ounce fresh yeast or ½ ounce*
     dry yeast dissolved in 1
     tablespoon warm milk

You will need a large bowl and an oblong loaf pan. An electric mixer would be very helpful. Mix the starter and leave it to sour in a warm place for 48 hours. This, plus the extra yeast and enough warm water to make a really wet dough, will raise 2 pounds of rye flour.

Put the flour and salt into a warm bowl. Mix the yeast-and-milk mixture with the water. Pour it into a well in the middle of the flour and add the sourdough starter. Beat well with an electric mixer's dough hook for 5 minutes. If you do it by hand, beat with a wooden spoon—rye dough sticks to the fingers like no other. I wish you power to your elbow—it's a tough job.

Leave to double in size—this will take 1 to 2 hours. Punch the dough down and knead it in the mixer again, or with a wooden spoon. Grease a long baking pan and preheat the oven to 375°F. Roll the dough out into an oblong the length of the pan, and then roll it up like a carpet. Settle the dough roll in the baking tin. Leave it to rise again for another hour. Bake the loaf for 30 minutes; then lower the heat to 325°F and bake it for 1½ hours. At the end of this time, take it out and tap the base to see if it rings hollow—the sign that it is ready. Rye bread can take an unconscionable length of time to cook. If your starting mixture was very wet, it will take longer.

Do not cut the bread until the day after you make it, to allow the crumb to settle down. Black bread is dark and sticky and eastern. Eat with a slice of sheep's cheese (soft white *brinza* or firm yellow *kashkaval*) and a plate of fresh raw vegetables: cucumbers, radishes, peppers, sliced onions, quartered tomatoes. Or accompany with pickles and a bowl of thick yogurt. You may then look forward to a long and healthy life: This is the favorite meal of the Georgians, and *they* are practically immortal.

◆

RYE BREAD

Rågbröd (Sweden)

The traditional breads of both the Finns and the Swedes are often leavened, in contrast to those of their neighbors in Norway. This mix includes molasses, a much-prized trade item supplied through the Baltic ports.

> *Rågbrod*, or rye bread, is the ordinary black bread of the country, made in large flat loaves. Halkaka, the peasants' only food in some parts, is baked two or three times a year, so they put the bread away in a loft or upon the kitchen rafters; consequently, by the time the next baking day comes round it is as hard as a brick. A knife often cannot cut it. It is invariably sour, some of the last mixing being always left in the tub or bucket, so that the necessary acidity may be ensured. [*Through Finland in Carts*, Ethel B. Tweedie, 1898]

Y I E L D : Makes 6 rings of *rågbröd* or 3 loaves

T I M E : Start 2 hours ahead; 30 minutes plus 20 to 40 minutes cooking

1½ pounds (5¼ cups) rye flour	Warm milk
½ pound (1¾ cups) plain flour	Warm water or milk and water
1 ounce yeast (or 1 recipe	1 tablespoon salt
sourdough starter as for rye	4 ounces black molasses
bread p. 406)	2 ounces (4 tablespoons) lard

You will need a large bowl and a baking tray. An electric mixer would be helpful. Mix the two flours and put them into a warm bowl. Make a well in the middle. Blend the yeast with 1 tablespoon warm milk, and mix it with a cup of warm water. Or mix the sourdough starter with some warm water. Pour this raising liquid into the well in the flour. Sprinkle the surface with a handful of flour, and put the basin in a warm place for 30 minutes to set the sponge.

Hand beat the sponge into the rest of the flour with 2 ounces warm water or a mixture of milk and water, and the salt, molasses, and melted fat. You may need more or less water—dampness in the air or peculiarities of the mix can influence this. You should have a soft dough which is easy to handle—not so wet that it sticks to your fingers, nor so dry that it cracks when you work it. Knead the dough thoroughly, pulling and knuckling it with warm hands and a closed fist until the dough is smooth and elastic. Knuckle it into a large smooth bun.

Leave until the dough is well risen and has doubled in bulk—do not leave it too long—30 minutes should be sufficient. Putting the dough into a turned-off oven over a baking tray of boiling water speeds up the process.

When the dough is ready, knuckle it down again and divide it into 6 pieces. Pat out each piece into a flat round loaf. Cut a hole in the middle (in the old days, this would allow you to hang the breads by a rope looped across the kitchen rafters for storage). Put them on a greased baking tray to rise again for 30 minutes.

Preheat the oven to 400°F.

Bake the bread in the oven for 20 to 30 minutes, until the buns sound hollow when you tap them underneath. Or shape the dough into 3 thin flat round loaves, lay them on a greased baking tray, prick them firmly all over with a fork, and put to rise again for 30 to 40 minutes. Bake in a medium oven at 375°F for about 40 minutes. Check after half an hour and turn the heat down if the crust is browning too fast.

This bread will keep well.

SUGGESTIONS

For future batches, keep a cupful of the uncooked bread dough, covered with water, in the cupboard until the next baking day. It will keep for 8 days. A greater proportion of white flour can be used to make the bread lighter.

Two teaspoons of whole caraway seeds can be added at the kneading stage.

RYEBREAD RINGS

Knäckebröd (Sweden)

This was the great Swedish pantry standby, still much appreciated in Sweden today.

YIELD: Makes 30 rings

TIME: 45 to 50 minutes plus 20 minutes cooking

2	pounds rye flour	1	tablespoon sugar
6	ounces (¾ cup) butter or lard or both	3	cups warm water
2	ounces fresh yeast or 1 ounce dry yeast	1	teaspoon salt
		1½	pounds (6 cups) sifted rye flour

You will need a large mixing bowl, a rolling pin (the Swedish one for the purpose has diamond-shaped cutouts so that it gives a crenellated surface to the dough), two baking trays, and a wire cooling rack.

Put the unsifted rye flour in a bowl and cut in the fat. Mix it lightly in with the tips of your fingers. Mix the yeast with the sugar and a little of the warm water. Pour this mixture, the rest of the water, and the salt into the rye flour in the bowl, and mix well together. Cover with a cloth and leave for 10 minutes in a warm place.

Pour the sifted rye flour onto the table or a wooden kneading board. Tip the wet dough in the bowl into the mound of sifted flour. Work the new flour well into the dough. You may need more water or less flour to give you a pliable, pastrylike dough. Grease the two baking sheets and flour lightly.

Roll the dough out into a circle about half a finger thick, preferably with your Swedish rolling pin. Otherwise, prick the dough all over with a fork. Using a sharp-edged cake pan about 8 inches in diameter, cut circles in the dough. In the center of each circle cut out and remove a small ½-inch circle. Gather up the leftover dough, and roll it out, and cut it again. You will need to make the *knäckebröd* in two batches anyway, and the dough will come to no harm if it's kept waiting a little.

Let the *knäckebröd* rise for 20 to 30 minutes in a warm place. Meanwhile, preheat the oven to 450°F.

Put the *knäckebröd* in to bake for 10 to 15 minutes, until they are well risen, brown, and sound hollow when you tap the base. Leave them on a wire rack to cool. String them like beads onto a wooden stick, and hang them up in a current of air until you need them.

◆

OPEN SANDWICHES

Smørrebrød (Denmark)

Smørrebrød, literally "buttered bread," is the Dane's favorite meal and perfectly suited to a dairy-farming community. It can be a simple lunchtime sandwich, or it can be served in an infinite variety of ways, a banquet of different flavors and ingredients, for a party. Danish rye is the basic bread used. Otherwise, any good brown bread will do. Do not use German pumpernickel, though; its flavor is too overwhelming and is best kept for cheese.

At home in Denmark for everyday fare, the topping would be simple and wholesome: fish, eggs, or meat spread on top of the buttered rye bread, the meal washed down with beer or milk. There might be spiced herring; or fillet of cold fried plaice; or slices of hard-cooked egg; or liver sausage with pickled cucumber, cheese, and radish; or shrimps, sardines, or smoked eel with scrambled eggs. Again, there might be sliced meat, cold roast pork flanked by a strip of its crackling and a pitted prune, or beef and fried onions. Resist the temptation to garnish with sticky things like canned peaches, pineapple, or glacé cherries. Shavings of fresh horseradish or a slice of beet are just as pretty and much more appropriate.

◆

OAT BREAD

Bara ceirch (Wales)

This is an excellent and light mixed-cereal bread, which is easily made when you are baking a batch of ordinary bread. Welsh baking ovens were, in the old days, often brick-built and peat-fired. There are still a few of these ovens in working order today, and those who use them say they cook a Christmas turkey to perfection. To test the correct temperature to bake bread, the cook must be able to just bear to put her hand in and out eight times. If she cannot do this, or can manage a ninth thrust, the heat must be adjusted. A heavy fruit cake for a wedding will take two days to bake in such an oven, when it is cooling after the weekly bread making. The bricks bleach in the heat to a pale ivory, and it takes days before they give up all their warmth.

Y I E L D : Makes 1 loaf

T I M E : Start 2 to 3 hours ahead; 30 minutes plus 30 minutes cooking

½   *pound (1¾ cups) flour*
¾   *cup water*
½   *ounce fresh yeast or ¼ ounce dry*
     yeast

1   *tablespoon warm milk*
2   *ounces (4 tablespoons) bacon*
     drippings or lard
4   *ounces (½ cup) fine oatmeal*

You will need a large bowl and a baking tray. An electric mixer would save elbow grease. Make the bread dough as in the recipe for the country bread (page 403). Melt the fat, and beat it and the oatmeal into the dough after the first rising. Knead well.

Preheat the oven to 350°F.

Roll the dough out very thin and lay it on a well-greased and flour-dusted baking tray. Mark it into squares and prick it with a fork. Do not put it to rise again. Bake for 25 to 30 minutes, until the cakes are crisp. Delicious eaten hot, spread it with butter and heather honey.

◆

OLIVE BREAD

Elioti (Cyprus)

This bread was originally prepared during Lent by members of the Eastern Orthodox Church. Neither flesh nor eggs nor milk can be consumed during this time, so it is a complete meal in itself.

YIELD: Makes 1 loaf

TIME: Start 2 to 3 hours ahead; 30 minutes plus 1 hour cooking

1	*pound (3½ cups) flour*	*1*	*teaspoon salt*
1	*cup water*	*1*	*onion*
½	*ounce fresh yeast or ¼ ounce dry*	*8*	*ounces black olives*
	yeast	*1*	*tablespoon olive oil*

You will need a large bowl and a baking tray. An electric mixer would be a help. Make the bread dough according to the recipe for country bread (page 403). When you punch the dough down after the first rising, work in this onion-and-olive mixture.

Peel the onion and chop it finely. Pit and chop the olives. Fry the onion in the oil until it is transparent. Add the olives to the pan and then tip the contents onto the bread dough. Work it in well—it will take the full quantity. Shape the dough into a round loaf, and then put it to double its bulk in a warm, damp corner (inside a plastic bag produces the necessary greenhouse effect) for 40 to 60 minutes.

Preheat the oven to 375°F.

Bake the loaf for 30 to 40 minutes, until well risen and golden.

It is to be eaten fresh, or toasted over an olive wood fire, with a trickle of oil to moisten the hot crisp crumbs. With such a feast and a bottle of wine, you will be as tranquil as the scholar-monks of Mount Athos.

SUGGESTION

Serve slices of this bread with a dish of *plaki*, the Greek stew made with olive oil, tomatoes, onions, garlic, and olives, to which fish or meat may be added. Simmer until most of the juices have evaporated and the vegetables, meat, or fish are cooked.

PIZZA AND CALZONE

(Italy)

A specialty of the resourceful bakers of Naples, this is a very simple dish, invented as a filling fast meal for the poor of the teeming city. The true pizza oven is a beehive-shaped brick-built village bread oven. It is fueled with wood in the old-fashioned way: The fire is built inside the oven itself, and the embers are raked out after the walls are thoroughly hot. Pizza baked in such an oven will have a few tiny telltale cinders stuck to its base, where a scattering of embers have escaped the sweeping. The dish sprang from less commercial and more ancient stock—peasant cooks would enrich the ordinary bread dough for special occasions with olive oil and a spoonful of sweet tomato paste, or a few slices of fresh tomato, plus a few onion rings, spread over the top of a rolled-out pancake. This bread would be baked on a special flat clay pan which could be raised to white heat on the cooking fire. These pans can still be bought in rural Italy, but today they are made of concrete. Special breads stuffed with olives, or a bit of *prosciutto* chopped and fried crisp, or merely sprinkled with olive oil and a few leaves of fresh rosemary or sage, are still very popular in country districts.

> The loaves were still abed, literally in the family bed. Many times I have watched Gina Ciccia knead her dough, spread a dark bread blanket on the bed, set her round loaves in rows and cover them with another blanket. Once, when her husband had been driven home from work by rain, I saw him roused from a nap to give place to the batch . . .
> This is the charm to be said over bread: "Crisci, crisci, pastuni, Como crisciu Gesuzzu 'u fasciuni." ("Grow, grow, dough, as grew little Jesus in his swaddling clothes.") [*By-Paths in Sicily*, Eliza Putnam Heaton, 1920]

SERVES: 4

TIME: **Start 90 minutes ahead; 1 hour plus 15 to 20 minutes cooking**

THE DOUGH:

½ *pound (1¾ cups) all-purpose flour*	1 *tablespoon warm milk*
½ *ounce fresh yeast or ¼ ounce dry*	½ *cup warm water*
yeast	1 *teaspoon salt*

THE TOPPING:

2 *pounds ripe tomatoes (or 2*	¼ *pound mozzarella cheese cut into*
pounds canned tomatoes)	*fine slices (any grated cheese*
2 *onions*	*can be used)*
4 *tablespoons olive oil*	*Oregano*

You will need a large bowl, a frying pan, and a baking tray. An electric mixer with a dough hook would be useful.

Make the dough as in the country bread recipe (page 403).

Roll the dough, after its first rising and punching down, into a long sausage shape and cut off short sections about the size of a golf ball. To make single-portion pizzas, roll each ball out into a thin circle of dough about 8 inches across. Press down the middle to give a depth of about ¼ inch, leaving a slightly thicker rim round the outside. If you would like a single large pizza, roll out the whole piece, but it should still be only ¼ inch thick. Put the dough to rise inside a large, loosely tied plastic bag for 10 to 15 minutes.

Preheat the oven to 450°F.

Meanwhile, scald and then peel and chop the tomatoes. If using canned tomatoes, drain and chop them. Peel and chop the onions. Heat the oil gently in a frying pan. Add the chopped onions and fry lightly until transparent. Add the tomatoes with a pinch of sugar if the tomatoes have not ripened to sweet perfection in the Mediterranean sun. Simmer uncovered until the tomatoes melt into a rich, thick sauce—this will take no longer than it takes the dough to rise.

When the oven is good and hot, spread the tomato-and-onion mixture over the dough. Arrange on top of this (if you have chosen to use them) those few extra ingredients of your most discriminating choice. I confess to liking my pizza plain, or at most with a few anchovies and black olives. Lay the slices of mozzarella on the top and sprinkle a little olive oil over all. Grated Gruyère or mature Cheddar or Bel Paese are all possible alternatives if you cannot get fresh mozzarella. Scatter a little chopped oregano on top.

Bake in a very hot oven, 15 to 20 minutes at 450°F, until the bread dough is crisp and the cheese bubbling.

Eat it while it's hot. If you were a ragged customer in a back street of Naples, you would get your pizza straight from the oven and gobble it up sitting on a doorstep in the sun under balconies strung with lines of faded washing.

◆

SUGGESTIONS

Arrange the extra ingredients of your choice over the layer of tomato (the cheese should still be added last): Salted anchovies, black olives, chopped salami, cubed raw ham, mushrooms, sweet peppers, capers, even shellfish are all included in various regions. However, a good pizza should not be an overladen dish. Try and restrain your enthusiasm to no more than three additional ingredients.

Calzone is made by spreading the filling thickly over half the dough, wetting the edge, and then folding the other semicircle over the top, pressing down lightly to seal the two edges together. This arrangement, being twice as thick, will take about half as long again to cook. Make small versions and deep-fry them; children love these "trouser turn-ups."

Pissaladière, the great favorite of Italy's neighbors in Provence, is made in the same fashion. For this quantity of bread dough, peel and slice 4 pounds of onions, fry them gently in olive oil until soft and golden but not brown, and precook the bread dough in a shallow baking pan in a medium oven for 10 minutes. When its surface is well risen and dry, spread on a layer of onion as thick as the dough itself. Scatter with black olives, anchovies, and cheese, and a trickle of olive oil. Finish the cooking in a hot oven, 450°F, for 15 minutes. Keeps well.

◆

PITA BREAD

(Turkey)

This is a yeast-raised flat bread made all over the Middle East and now popular as a sandwich container in Europe and America. Cut in half or slit down one side, it provides a pocket for stuffing with fillings. It is particularly good for kabobs and salads.

YIELD: Makes 20 pitas

TIME: Start 2 to 3 hours ahead; 30 minutes plus 15 minutes cooking

2 pounds (7 cups) all-purpose flour	2 teaspoons salt
1 ounce fresh yeast or ½ ounce dry yeast	2 cups warm water
	Olive oil
3 tablespoons warm milk	

You will need a basin and two baking sheets. A mixer with a dough hook saves energy. Make the dough as for the country bread (page 403)—it should be a little on the soft side. Work in 2 tablespoons of olive oil.

Cut the dough into 20 pieces, knead each into a ball, and then roll each one out into an oval about 8 inches long. Let the pitas rise for half an hour.

Preheat the oven to 475°F.

Flour the baking sheets and put them in the oven to heat. Slap the pitas onto the hot baking sheets and put them into the oven for about 5 minutes. Take them out while they are still soft. Wrap them in a cloth so that they do not harden, and bake the next batch.

◆

PITCHY BREAD

Bara pyglyd (Wales)

This old Welsh recipe for yeast-raised pancakes made the journey across the hills to England, where they are known as "pikelets."

SERVES: 6

TIME: Start 1 hour ahead; 40 minutes plus 20 minutes cooking

½	*ounce fresh yeast or ¼ ounce dry*	*1*	*teaspoon salt*
	yeast	*2*	*cups milk*
1	*teaspoon superfine sugar*	*2*	*eggs*
1	*pound (3½ cups) all-purpose flour*		*Lard for greasing*

You will need a large bowl, a whisk, and a griddle or a heavy iron frying pan. Liquefy the yeast by mixing it with the sugar. Put the flour and the salt in a warm bowl, make a well in the middle and pour in the milk, beaten with the eggs, and the yeast, mixing as you do so. Whisk the batter for 10 minutes, until it is light and frothy. Leave in a warm place for an hour.

Put a griddle (a *planc* in Wales) or a heavy iron pan on to heat. When it is good and hot, grease the surface with a piece of lard held in a rag. Or heat a well-greased baking tray in the oven. Pour spoonfuls of the batter onto the hot surface. Cook on not too fierce a heat on top of the stove or in a preheated 375°F oven for 20 minutes. Turn the pitchy bread once, when holes have formed on the upper surface and it looks dry.

Serve hot, well spread with plenty of Welsh salted butter, piled in a hot dish so that the buttery juices run right through the pyramid.

SUGGESTION

Leftovers: Delicious toasted.

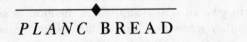

PLANC BREAD

(Wales)

The baking stone or griddle (Gaelic: *greadeal*), a flat piece of iron to be rested over the heat source, sometimes equipped with tripod legs, sometimes with a handle for hanging it up, is often called a *planc* in Wales.

YIELD: Makes 1 loaf

TIME: Start 1½ hours ahead; 20 minutes plus 40 minutes cooking

2	*pounds (7 cups) all-purpose flour*	*1*	*teaspoon sugar*
1	*teaspoon salt*	*1*	*cup each milk and water*
1	*ounce fresh yeast or ½ ounce dry*	*1*	*ounce (2 tablespoons) lard or*
	yeast		*butter*

You will need a large bowl and a griddle or a heavy iron frying pan or (best of all) a Welsh *planc*. Sift the flour with the salt into a warm bowl. Mix the yeast to a liquid with the sugar and the milk and water, warmed to body temperature. Rub the lard or butter into the flour, make a well in the center, and pour in as much of the yeast liquid as you need to make a soft dough and put aside in a warm place for an hour to double in bulk.

Punch the dough down, knuckling well with your fists to distribute the working yeast. Mold the dough into a flat round loaf an inch thick. Leave it to rise again for 15 to 20 minutes. Put on a moderately hot, lightly greased *planc*, heavy iron frying pan, or griddle. Bake gently for 20 minutes on one side; then turn and bake for 20 minutes on the other side. If the *planc* is too hot, the crust will burn before the crumb is cooked.

Split and eat hot with butter. Do not make in quantity—it is much better eaten fresh.

◆

SODA-RAISED BREAD

◆

SODA BREAD

(Ireland)

The daily bread of Ireland, soda bread can be made with white or brown flour and is baked fresh as required, much as the Scots make their scones and pieces. In the days before ovens were usual (that is, until well into this century), the bread would have been baked in a pot with burning turfs on the inverted lid to give all-around heat. The chemical raising agents are a late-nineteenth-century innovation, but without them the bread is rather heavy. See the scone mix (page 423) for a soda bread without baking soda.

YIELD: Makes 1 large or 2 small loaves

TIME: 20 to 25 minutes plus 45 minutes cooking

1½ pounds (5¼ cups) all-purpose flour	1½ cups sour milk or buttermilk (if you cannot get either, fresh
1 teaspoon soda	milk and a teaspoon of cream of
1 teaspoon salt	tartar will have to do)

Preheat the oven to 400°F. You will need a large bowl and a baking tray.

Mix the flour with the soda and the salt, and make a well in the middle. Pour in the liquid in one stream, and knead the dough swiftly and lightly into a ball. The dough should be on the soft side, so you may need extra liquid. Flatten the ball with well-floured hands. Grease a baking sheet and put the dough-cake on it. Make a cross on the top. Bake for 45 minutes. Or make 2 smaller loaves, baking for 30 to 35 minutes.

Eat the soda bread hot or cold with butter. Molasses is good with it too.

◆

SUGGESTION

Leftovers: Store the bread wrapped in a clean tea towel to keep it soft.

◆

LEFTOVER BREAD DISHES

◆

SAVORY TOASTS

Crostini (Italy)

Slices of good leftover bread (French-type bread sticks are good for this) are toasted in the oven, and then either used fresh or stored until needed as the basis for an *antipasto*, the dish served before the pasta. *Crostini* also make an excellent breakfast dish. Either way, they should be warmed and then spread with a savory mixture, which can be as simple as a rub of garlic and a trickle of olive oil.

Spread the *crostini* with chicken livers sautéed in butter or olive oil seasoned with garlic, mashed together with salt and pepper.

Trickle good raw olive oil over the *crostini*, and then top with a slice of cheese; or a salted anchovy, chopped olive paste, and a slice of fresh ripe tomato sprinkled with a few leaves of basil; or a combination of any or all of these; or chopped hard-cooked eggs pounded to a paste with anchovies; or butter and a slice of *prosciutto* or salami.

◆

BREAD-AND-BEER SOUP

Ollebrød (Denmark)

The Danes make particularly good beer and they use it in this beer porridge. Here is enough for a private supper to be enjoyed on a cold winter's night.

SERVES: 2

TIME: Start 2 to 3 hours ahead; 15 minutes plus 30 minutes cooking

1 *pound stale rye bread*	*Heavy cream*
½ *cup water*	*Brown sugar*
2 *cups light Danish beer*	

You will need a saucepan and a bowl. Crumble the bread and soak it for a few hours in a bowl in the water mixed with half the beer.

Put the bread in a saucepan when it is properly soaked, and simmer the mixture until it is a soft, thick mass. Stir in the rest of the beer. Bring back to a boil and simmer gently for half an hour uncovered. It should reduce to half quantity. Eat hot with plenty of heavy cream and brown sugar.

SUGGESTION

Add a little grated lemon rind or a dusting of cinnamon or nutmeg to flavor the soup.

POOR KNIGHTS

Wentelteefjes (Holland)

A delicious way of making use of stale bread, this recipe appears all over Europe under different guises. In France it is called *pain perdu*—"lost bread"; carried across the water to America, it becomes "French toast." Children love it.

SERVES: 4

TIME: 25 to 30 minutes

2 *eggs*	2 *ounces (4 tablespoons) butter*
1 *cup milk*	10 *slices of old bread*
4 *ounces (½ cup) sugar*	

You will need a soup plate and a frying pan. Beat together in a soup plate the eggs, milk, and 2 tablespoons of sugar. Melt a nut of the butter in a frying pan. Soak one piece of bread in the egg-and-milk mixture and fry it golden in the butter, turning once to brown the other side. Continue until bread and batter are all used up.

Serve the Poor Knights immediately, sprinkled with more sugar.

SUGGESTIONS

Sprinkle the slices with grated cinnamon as well, or serve with a spoonful of jam. Syrup—especially maple—is also delicious with Poor Knights, as are fresh strawberries and cream.

UNLEAVENED BREADS

FLATBREAD

Flatbrød (Norway)

Probably the oldest and commonest form of bread in premodern Norway, this is a fine, paper-thin unleavened bread which used to be baked in the farmhouse kitchen only twice a year; it is so fine and dry and indestructible that it could remain fresh stored on a beam in the kitchen for six months at a time. There are still countrywomen around who make their own *flatbrød*. Since oats, rye, and barley are the cereals which can be successfully grown in the cold of northern Scandinavia, these are the grains which are used. The inclusion of wheat in this recipe makes the dough much easier to work. The wide round disks of flatbread are usually factory-baked today. For convenience they are often cut into neat rectangles and packaged in paper to be sold in supermarkets as "extra-thin crispbread."

Each farming household had its own special *flatbrød* mix, depending on the cereals it could produce. The following is a basic modern recipe:

YIELD: Makes 12 to 15 flatbreads

TIME: 1 hour

½ pound (1¾ cups) oat or barley flour	*½ pound (1¾ cups) wheat flour*
	1 teaspoon salt
½ pound (1¾ cups) rye flour	*2 cups skimmed milk*

You will need a griddle or a heavy frying pan, or, best of all, a *takke*. Mix the different flours together with the salt. Pour the skimmed milk into a well in the middle, and knead into an elastic dough. Work it well to develop the gluten. Cut the dough into pieces and roll each one out, preferably with a specially grooved rolling pin, into the widest, thinnest sheets possible (you should aim to achieve a diameter of 18 inches).

Bake on an ungreased metal sheet (a *takke*) on top of your heat source until the flatbreads are quite crisp and dry. Store in an airtight tin. (In the cold, dry air of winter Norway this would not be necessary.)

SUGGESTIONS

Thin flatbread was eaten crumbled into small pieces very much like corn-flakes, with fresh or soured milk or (for special occasions) cream poured over it.

A part of Christmas celebrations is *mølje:* flatbread crumbled into the broth from the boiling of the special Christmas meats.

In certain parts of Norway dry-baked *flatbrød* used to be (and still is in those places where the old traditions hold) the central ingredient of the harvest meal. Moistened to make it as pliable as a pancake, the bread is quartered, spread with fresh sweet butter, and used to wrap up tidbits such as dried mutton, slices of fresh, deep-orange-yolked, hard-cooked egg, a fine slice of the dark-brown sweet cheese, *geitost,* so beloved of the Norwegians, salted herring, and finally a spoonful of cloudberry jam to round off the meal.

POTATO PANCAKE-BREAD

Lompe (Norway)

This excellent soft pancake-wrapper, easily made at home, is eaten in Norway with butter and *geitost* cheese, or used to wrap delicious little morsels of smoked ham, *fenalår*, dried and salted leg of mutton, or a spoonful of berry conserve.

YIELD: Makes 10 to 12 small pancakes

TIME: 1 hour

2 *pounds (6 medium-sized) old potatoes (the older, the better)*
1 *tablespoon salt*
¼ *pound (1 cup) flour*

You will need a griddle or a heavy frying pan, or, best of all, a *takke*. Boil the potatoes in their skins. Peel them as soon as they are cool enough to handle and immediately mash them with the salt. Speed makes light pancakes. Mix with the flour into a dough. (Less or more flour may be needed—potatoes are very variable. The less flour you use, the better.) Form into a long sausage and chop off lengths. Roll these pieces out into pancakes about ⅛ inch thick.

Bake the *lompe* on a hot iron surface.

◆

SUGGESTION

Potato *lompe* have entered the fast-food repertoire of Norway and are sold on street corners as a wrapper for hot dogs: a great improvement on the usual soft white bun.

◆

BREAD PANCAKE

Lefse (Norway)

There are many local variations of this type of *flatbrød*. That of Norway is thicker, today raised with baking powder and sweetened, but the most traditional *lefse* has neither sugar nor baking powder, but is made from a grain flour and mashed boiled potatoes mixed with milk or water. It is made and stored like *flatbrød* itself.

Alette Golden's cookbook (she ran a famous Norwegian cooking school) gives three recipes: equal quantities of oatmeal and rye and boiled mashed potato; equal quantities of barley, oat, and rye flour, with equal quantities of boiled mashed potato; three parts of oatmeal to one part of rye.

Whichever mix you prefer, mash the potato as soon as it is cool enough to handle, and mix in most of the flour, with enough water to mix to a smooth dough. Leave the dough until the following day. Then roll it out into thin wide pancakes. Bake them on top of the stove on a lightly greased griddle. Store as for *flatbrød*.

When you wish to eat your *lefse*, sprinkle both sides with water, and sandwich it between clean linen cloths for an hour or so. Then it will be soft, and can be buttered and folded and cut into neat pieces.

Lefse can be eaten as for the moistened *flatbrød* in the suggestions at the end of the recipe. It can also be layered into a cake with heavy sweet cream or sour cream and sugar.

◆

OATCAKES AND BANNOCKS

(Scotland)

The Scots make a wide variety of oatcakes—no surprise since the main ingredient is the grain most compatible with the cold northerly climate. The original oatcake mix was a simple paste of milled oats worked with cold water. The fishermen of Skye used to dip a handful into seawater and then knead it into a cake for immediate consumption—the most portable of fast food. Even so, to many poor crofters, oatcakes were food for special occasions—daily fare was barley cakes. The instruments for making rolled-out oatcakes are four in number: the spurtle, a flat stick for stirring the water into the oats; the bannock stick, a rolling pin with a crisscross pattern on it like that used in Norway for flatbread, which leaves indentations on the upper side of the cake; the spathe, a flat iron instrument like a palette knife used to flip the cakes onto the hot griddle; and the "banna-rack," used for toasting the oatcakes. Northern England preferred a batter oatcake.

The cooks of Yorkshire and Lancashire needed a deft hand to throw and scrape their preferred version, batter oatcakes. Their utensils were different as well: There was the riddleboard and throwing board and ungreased bake stone, requiring skills which could only be acquired through long apprenticeship, and a ready supply of unstabilized oats—very difficult to come by today. There are Scots oatcake recipes which are raised with yeast, and some which replace the water and fat with buttermilk and cream or with whey. Milk used alone makes them hard. The dough hardens so fast it is wise to make one batch at a time.

Y I E L D : Makes 1 large oatcake or 4 to 5 small ones

T I M E : 40 minutes

¼ pound oatmeal (fine or medium, not the rolled oats sold today to make porridge)	½ tablespoon melted fat: bacon drippings, lard, or butter
1 teaspoon salt	¼ cup hot water

You will need a bowl, a rolling pin, and a griddle or a baking tray or a heavy iron frying pan (the nonstick variety is perfect). Put the oatmeal into a bowl with the salt, and pour the fat and hot water into a well in the center. Mix all the ingredients together as quickly and lightly as possible. You may need more or less liquid. Put the ball of dough on an oatmeal-dusted board, and knuckle it swiftly into a smooth, soft dough. Oatmeal is sticky and thoroughly unruly with a tendency to crack.

Roll the dough out very thin—no more than ⅛ inch in thickness. You will need to dust frequently with extra meal to counter the stickiness, and keep pinching the cracked edges together to keep it whole. Cut the rolled-out dough into rounds—either a large one by cutting around an inverted 6-inch diameter plate, leaving whole to make bannocks, or cutting 6 in quarters to make farls. Or make small ones using a biscuit cutter or a fine-rimmed glass. Rub with oatmeal again and put them to bake on a hot ungreased iron griddle or heavy frying pan. Cook until you see the edges curl—this will only take a few minutes. Remove them and put them either in front of the fire or in a preheated 350°F oven for a few moments to dry the tops.

Or roll the dough out into a square, again about ⅛ inch thick, and put it on a baking sheet. Mark it into squares and prick it all over with a fork. Bake in a 350°F oven until dry and crisp—this will take about 10 to 15 minutes.

Oatcakes are delicious with butter, with cheese, or with butter and marmalade for breakfast. Keep them in an airtight tin. They are best if you warm them again before serving. Oatcakes were often stored buried in the meal chest, where they kept sweet and dry until needed. Robert Burns, Scotland's favorite bard, considered them a delicate relish when eaten warm and washed down with a jug of ale. The west Highlanders liked them with fresh herrings, cold butter, and a sliced raw onion.

◆

SCONES AND PIECES

(Scotland)

The housewives of Scotland have a light hand with the baking which is unrivaled anywhere in the world. Sour milk or buttermilk and very light fingers were the raising agents employed before the appearance of chemical raising agents. This is the most delicious bread Scotland can offer. Scones are at their best made fresh and served straight from the oven. They appear at any and all meals, although they are particularly good for breakfast and tea, with plenty of cold butter to melt into the tender dough and a strong brew of sweet, milky tea to wash them down. A "piece" can be any small bread, and many Highland families used to (and sometimes still do) build all their meals around such "pieces."

SERVES: 4

TIME: 15 minutes plus 15 minutes cooking

10 ounces (2 cups) all-purpose flour	2 ounces (4 tablespoons) butter
½ teaspoon salt	1 cup sour milk, buttermilk, or
½ teaspoon baking powder (optional)	sweet milk

You will need a bowl and a baking tray. Sift the flour, salt, and baking powder (if you are using it—as your fingers grow lighter and more skillful, you will not need the chemical raising agent) into a bowl. Make a well in the center and chop in the butter. Rub the butter into the flour with your fingertips. Knead into a soft dough with the milk.

Preheat the oven to 400°F.

Roll the dough out on a well-floured board and press out small rounds. If you were making scones for tea, you would cut larger triangles instead. Bake them on a hot griddle, although 10 to 15 minutes in a preheated 400°F oven will do very well instead.

◆

Leftovers: Split the scones and toast them. Or split them and fry them on the crumb side only; scones are often served this way at Highland breakfasts.

◆
SHORTBREAD

(Scotland)

This is a celebration bread which is essentially a rich biscuit dough, originally baked for the new year festival of Hogmanay. Only the finest ingredients should be used. Do not skimp on any of them.

YIELD: Makes 2 rounds of shortbread

TIME: 20 minutes plus 1 hour cooking

12 *ounces butter*
¼ *pound (½ cup) superfine sugar*

1 *pound (3½ cups) fine white flour such as Wondra (or, to give even better results, replace 2 ounces of the flour with ground almonds or rice flour)*

You will need a pastry board, a rolling pin, and two cake pans. A food processor and a shortbread mold would be helpful. Cut the butter and the sugar together on a wooden board, and then work with your hand (or in a processor) until thoroughly blended. Sift the flour and then mix it in gradually, not working the pastry too hard or it will toughen, until incorporated into a soft dough like shortcrust pastry. The mixture should not look oily or be overworked, or it will toughen. Cool hands, or better still, a cold northern kitchen, are best for this job.

Preheat the oven to 325°F.

Do not roll out the pastry, but cut it in half, mold it into two flat cakes, and press each gently into either a greased and floured wooden shortbread mold (there are lovely old ones with thistles or other patterns carved into them), which you then reverse onto a baking sheet, or into two 8-inch ungreased cake pans. They should be about ¾ inch in depth. Linings of wax paper are a good safety device to prevent sticking and burning.

Bake the shortbread for 50 to 60 minutes, turning the oven down a little halfway through the baking time. The biscuit will be soft when you take it out, but will crisp as it cools. Transfer it to a cake rack as soon as it firms up a little.

SUGGESTION

Store the leftovers when quite cooled, wrapped in paper and kept in an airtight tin. If you keep the shortbread for long, it can be refreshed and crisped if you heat it in a low oven for 10 minutes.

SWEET BREADS AND YEAST PASTRIES

These special breads are simply the housewife's party breads, made special with the addition of eggs, butter, sugar, spices, and/or fruits. They are the forerunners of all our modern cakes.

For festival meals country wives, particularly those of northern Europe, made their own fruit breads, yeast cakes, cheesecakes, doughnuts, and applecakes. Eggs are used to enrich rather than to lighten dough. Yeast and light fingers are the true peasant raising agents. (Baking powder and chemical raising agents are modern innovations more at home in the bourgeois kitchen.) The use of beaten egg whites as a raising agent was not widely understood even in aristocratic kitchens until the eighteenth century.

PLUM TART

Zwetschkenfleck (Austria)

In Austria and Germany it would not be proper to serve a strudel, a fruit tart, or a dumpling after a heavy meat dish. German country puddings are solid affairs, designed to be the main dish to follow a meatless vegetable-thickened soup. These main-dish pastries conformed to the Catholic rules of Friday fasting and were called *Fastenspeisen*. They include a wide range of delicious sweet dumplings stuffed with fruit or curds, a variety of strudels, and egg noodle dishes baked or served with fruit.

One of the best of fruit tarts, this is also one of the simplest. Make it when you bake a batch of bread—it is quite easy to beat in the extra sugar and butter to an already prepared bread dough.

Y I E L D : Makes 1 large tart

T I M E : Start 2 hours ahead; 30 minutes plus 50 minutes cooking

THE DOUGH:

1	*pound (3½ cups) all-purpose flour*	1	*cup warm milk*
½	*teaspoon salt*	2	*ounces (4 tablespoons) butter or*
1	*ounce fresh yeast or ½ ounce dry*		*lard*
	yeast	1	*ounce sugar*

THE FILLING:

2 *pounds plums*
¼ *pound (½ cup) sugar (more if the fruit is very sour)*

You will need a large bowl, a rolling pin, and a baking sheet. Put the flour in a warm bowl and make a well in the center. Mix the yeast to a liquid in half a cupful of the warm milk. Pour the yeast liquid into the well in the flour and sprinkle a handful of flour over the top. Put aside for 15 minutes in a warm, draft-proof corner for the yeast to develop and set the sponge—a process you can watch if you wish: The yeast, activated by warmth and fed by the starch in the milk and the flour, multiplies its cells and makes oxygen until the surface skin of flour is covered with spongy bubbles. This gets the yeast working well and is a step which should not be left out.

When the sponge is set, melt the butter or lard. Sprinkle the sugar and the salt over the flour. Beat in the liquid butter or lard (it should not be hot, just warm) and as much of the rest of the warm milk as you need to make a smooth, elastic dough. The amount of liquid you require will naturally also depend on the liquid additions. Pummel the dough thoroughly to stretch the gluten.

Knead the dough into a soft white cushion with your fists. Let it rise for about 40 to 50 minutes in a damp, warm, draft-proof place such as an unlit oven over a tray of boiling water or inside a plastic bag in the cupboard.

When the dough has doubled in size, punch it down and knead thoroughly to distribute the oxygen bubbles. Roll the dough out in a circle (or a square—a very usual way of presenting this pie) as thin as for a shortcrust pastry. Butter a baking sheet and lay the yeast pastry on it. Let it rise again for 15 to 20 minutes until the dough is quite puffed up. When the dough has risen, prick it all over with a fork.

Meanwhile, preheat the oven to 450°F and prepare the fruit: Pit the plums neatly without cutting them right through; then place them on end on the dough—then you can be sure they will be tightly packed. Lay a thick layer of fruit over the whole surface. Sprinkle with sugar.

Put the tart to bake for 25 to 30 minutes. When you open the oven door, the tart will look distinctly singed. Don't worry: It will be fragrant, juicy, and delicious. Slip it out onto a large dish.

Serve the country tart warm. Northern French housewives also make this tart, and accompany it with yellow *crème fraîche*. It is at its best after nothing but a soup, while you are still hungry.

Use, instead of the plums, cherries (the little sour wild ones are best of all) or apples.

When the dough has doubled in size and is ready to be punched down and kneaded into its final shape, this is the basic yeast pastry which can be used in any number of ways: Roll it out and use as ordinary pastry for strudels and pies and cheesecake; break off pieces to poach as dumplings; mold it into balls or rings to fry as doughnuts; mix in nuts and raisins to make fruit bread— whatever you please. The dough can be braided or put into a loaf pan to make a tea bread. When settled into its final shape, the dough should be allowed to double its size again before it is baked. This will take about 20 to 30 minutes. Doughnuts are the exception to this—they must not be left so long. Start frying them right away.

POPPY SEED STRUDEL

Mohnstrudel (Austria)

This very popular pastry in country districts throughout Austria and Germany is offered for sale to travelers from roadside stalls in rural Yugoslavia, and is for sale in the markets of Hungary and Rumania. As for the ingredients, markets all over Eastern Europe have their special corner for the nut merchants, on whose stalls mounds of poppy seed, pumice-stone gray as small volcanoes, are flanked by mountains of shelled walnuts, hazelnuts, sultanas, and raisins.

SERVES: 6

TIME: Start 2 hours ahead; 30 minutes plus 45 to 50 minutes cooking

THE DOUGH:

10	*ounces (2 cups) all-purpose flour*	1	*cup warm milk*
½	*teaspoon salt*	1	*ounce sugar*
½	*ounce fresh yeast or ¼ ounce dry yeast*	2	*ounces (4 tablespoons) butter or lard*

THE FILLING:

¼	*pound poppy seeds*
1	*cup milk*
1	*ounce (2 tablespoons) butter*
2	*ounces (¼ cup) sugar*

You will need a large bowl, a rolling pin, a blender or a pestle and mortar, a small saucepan, and a baking tray. Make the dough according to the recipe for the plum tart (page 425). Roll out the yeast pastry on a well-floured board in an oblong to a thickness of ⅛ inch.

Grind the poppy seeds in the blender or crush them in a mortar. Bring the milk to a boil in a small saucepan and add the ground poppy seeds. Boil until the mixture thickens. Remove from the heat and beat in the butter. Stir in the sugar.

Spread the filling over the pastry. Roll it up like a jelly roll. Butter a baking sheet and put the strudel on it, curled into a horseshoe shape. Cover with a damp cloth and put to rise in a warm place for half an hour.

Preheat the oven to 375°F.

Brush the strudel with egg and bake for 45 to 50 minutes. Put it on a rack to cool. Dust the top with powdered sugar.

This strudel is best if it is stored in a cool place for a few days before it is eaten.

◆

SUGGESTIONS

For a special occasion include 2 ounces (¼ cup) of raisins, 2 ounces (¼ cup) of chopped or ground almonds, and grated lemon rind and cinnamon.

Enrich the mix with 2 eggs beaten into the cooled poppy seed filling before it is spread on the dough.

Replace the poppy seeds with a filling of chopped walnuts or hazelnuts (wives and walnut trees, according to the old saying, are better for a good beating: presumably husbands and hazelnut trees are made of more delicate stuff: take your pick) mixed with a handful of bread crumbs or with sweetened curd cheese.

RING DOUGHNUTS

Kucheln (Germany)

A particular favorite at church fairs in Bavaria, all children love them.

YIELD: Makes 20 to 25 doughnuts

TIME: Start 2 hours ahead; 60 minutes

1	pound (3½ cups) all-purpose flour	1 ounce sugar
½	teaspoon salt	2 ounces (4 tablespoons) butter or
1	ounce fresh yeast or ½ ounce dry	lard
	yeast	Oil for frying (this would have been
1	cup warm milk	clarified butter in the old days)

You will need a large bowl and a deep frying pan. Work the dough as for the plum tart (page 425). Doughnut dough must be on the soft side, so you may need a little extra liquid. Allow it to rise once. Then punch the dough down, and cut it into 20 to 25 equal pieces. With these pieces, form spherical flat doughnuts with a diameter of about 2 inches. Brush the tops with melted butter and leave the doughnuts to rise for 10 minutes—they should only be allowed to expand a little.

Pinch each risen doughnut through the middle with your thumb and forefinger. Continue to pinch in concentric circles so that a thin circle of dough remains to hold the outside ring together—rather like the hub of a car wheel.

Heat the oil until a faint blue haze rises. Test with a cube of bread—it should quickly fry golden.

Fry the doughnuts in hot (but not smoking) oil, turning them gently once. The thin web in the middle will be kept clear of the oil by the bouyant ring of dough—and remain pale. The doughnuts will rise as they cook. Fry them for 5 to 6 minutes, until well risen and bronzed as autumn leaves.

Roll the doughnuts in sugar and serve them warm. Hot chocolate with whipped cream accompanies these as a special treat—church fairs come around only once a year.

◆

JAM DOUGHNUTS

Pfannkuchen (Germany)

These doughnuts are party food, particularly around Berlin. They are traditionally served at New Year's Eve celebrations, where they accompany a steaming bowl of wine mulled with orange peel, sugar, and cloves—glühwein.

YIELD: Makes 20 to 25 doughnuts

TIME: Start 2 hours ahead; 60 minutes

1	pound (3½ cups) all-purpose flour	2 ounces (4 tablespoons) butter or
½	teaspoon salt	lard
1	ounce fresh yeast or ½ ounce dry	1 pound scarlet jam (raspberry,
	yeast	strawberry, red currant)
1	cup warm milk	Oil for frying
1	ounce sugar	

You will need a large bowl, a rolling pin, a deep frying pan, and a baking tray. Make the yeast pastry dough as for the plum tart (page 425)—this dough should be on the soft side, so use a little extra liquid if necessary.

Punch it down after its first rising and roll it out. Using a glass tumbler, mark one half of the dough with circles without pressing right through. Put a spoonful of jam in the middle of each circle and then fold the other half of the dough over the top. Press out a circle around each hummock of jam. Put the doughnuts on a well-floured baking tray—spaced out to allow them to expand. Leave to rise for 10 minutes.

Heat the oil in the pan. Fry the doughnuts in the oil for rather longer than the ring doughnuts—7 to 8 minutes, depending on the size. They should have a characteristic pale ring around the circumference, where the dough has risen in the cooking.

◆

SUGGESTION

Austrian carnival doughnuts, *Faschinskrapfen*, are made from the same recipe, but are stuffed with apricot jam before they are fried. Finish them with a dusting of powdered sugar.

◆

HONEYED DOUGHNUTS

Loukoumades (Greece)

The Greeks are justifiably proud of their beautiful honey. On the three-pronged peninsula of Thrace, where the tall peak of Mount Athos shelters an autonomous republic of black-robed monks, the summer air is filled with the hum of millions of honeybees. Their nectar comes from the wild herbs, rosemary and lavender and thyme. Each human village has its captive bee village: long lines of miniature bungalows, numbered like beach chalets, have mostly replaced the old wattle-and-dung baskets. There is an abandoned village in the foothills of Mount Athos whose site is marked by cemetery cypresses; stone rubble walls give shelter to a peregrine falcon and only the bee village is still busy.

Unhusbanded olive trees, pomegranate and walnut trees, and thickets of plums colonize the ancient foundations. Down below, where the village has been resited to be more accessible to the road, there is a village bread oven and a small café. Alexandra (called for the conquering king who passed through so many centuries ago), a handsome woman of some forty summers, works behind the café's counter-cum-kitchen. She serves Greek salad with feta cheese, diced salt-pickled fish dressed with onion, potatoes fried in olive oil, and crisp fried eggs. She also sells 5-kilo tins of the dark, thick honey from the bee village, and on baking days, when the village bread oven is lit, she makes these doughnuts with some of her own bread dough and honey.

YIELD: Makes 20 doughnuts

TIME: Start 2 hours ahead; 60 minutes

1	*pound (3½ cups) all-purpose flour*	1	*tablespoon warm milk*
1	*teaspoon salt*	1	*cup warm water*
1	*ounce fresh yeast or ½ ounce dry*	*Oil for frying*	
	yeast	1	*pound honey*

You will need a large bowl and a deep frying pan. Make a bread dough as in the recipe for the country bread (page 403). The dough should be on the soft side, so you may need an extra tablespoon of liquid. When the bread dough is well risen but still in one piece, put on a panful of oil and heat until a faint blue haze rises. Put the honey jar in a bowl of hot water to liquefy its contents.

This is how Alexandra makes her doughnuts: Wet your hand and pick up a handful of dough. Squeeze it gradually through the top of your fist into short lengths. Slicing them off your fist with a knife, drop the pieces of dough into the hot oil. Allow them to puff up and fry golden. When well risen, take them out and drain them on paper.

Pour the warm honey over the hot doughnuts before you serve them with a tall glass of cold water, a small glass of raki, and a tiny cup of Turkish coffee.

◆

CAKE BREAD

Kugelhupf (Austria)

The *Kugelhupf* has an unusual claim to inclusion in a book on peasant cookery. This cake was a particular favorite of the unfortunate Queen Marie Antoinette of France—casualty of the guillotine and daughter of Francis I and Maria Theresa of Austria. It was Marie Antoinette's reported suggestion that the peasantry should eat her preferred cake as a solution to the bread famine that lit the torch for the French Revolution. Marie Antoinette's *Kugelhupf* might thus be held indirectly responsible for the emancipation of most of Europe's peasantry.

YIELD: Makes one large cake

TIME: Start 2 hours ahead; 30 minutes plus 40 to 45 minutes cooking

1	pound (3½ cups) all-purpose flour	3	ounces (⅓ cup) sugar
1	ounce fresh yeast or ½ ounce dry yeast	1	teaspoon salt
		2	eggs
⅔	cup warm milk	2	ounces (¼ cup) currants
4	ounces (½ cup) butter	2	ounces blanched almonds (optional)

You will need a large bowl and a *Kugelhupf* mold or a Bundt pan. Put the flour in a warm bowl. Make a well in the center. Mix the yeast to a liquid in half a cupful of the warm milk. Pour the yeast liquid into the well in the flour and sprinkle a handful of flour over the top. Put aside for 15 minutes in a warm, draft-proof corner for the yeast to develop and set the sponge.

Warm the butter to soften it. Sprinkle the sugar and the salt over the flour. Beat in the liquid butter, eggs, currants, and as much of the rest of the warm milk as you need to make a smooth, elastic dough. The amount of liquid you require will naturally also depend on the liquid additions. Pummel the dough thoroughly to stretch the gluten.

Knead the dough into a soft white cushion. Let it rise for about 30 minutes in a damp, warm, draft-proof place such as an unlit oven over a tray of boiling water.

When the dough has doubled in size, punch it down and knead it into its final shape. Roll the dough into a long sausage. Butter the mold or Bundt pan and sprinkle it with flour (better still, with ground almonds). Curl the dough sausage around the ring mold, pressing it gently down—it should fill the mold to within two thirds of the top. Cover with a damp cloth and put it to rise in a warm place. It will take about half an hour to rise sufficiently. Preheat the oven to 400°F—you need it hot for this brioche-type bread.

Bake the *Kugelhupf* at 400°F for 20 minutes—then turn the oven down to 375°F and bake it for a further 20 to 25 minutes (check that the crust is not burning—you might have to protect it with foil). Total baking time is 40 to 45 minutes. The *Kugelhupf* should then be perfectly well risen, fragrant and golden. Fit for a queen, if not for a revolution.

SUGGESTIONS

Some cooks use a mixture of butter and lard.

For Easter the *Kugelhupf* is baked in a special fish-shaped mold.

Stollen is the Christmas specialty and the mix is as for the *Kugelhupf*, but with double the quantity of butter and a handful of candied fruit. Grated lemon rind, nutmeg, and cinnamon are sometimes included. Press the dough out into a flat oval and fold the dough over on itself lengthwise to give the classic *Stollen* form. Put it to rise again until it has doubled its bulk. Brush with melted butter. Bake as the *Kugelhupf*. When cool, dust the top of the cake heavily with powdered sugar.

FRUIT BREAD

Kletzenbrot (Austria)

This is a favorite Austrian special treat, made with dried pears or plums—harvested in the late summer and dried spread out on racks in the autumn sun. The plums are dried whole, and the pears are cut in half first.

SERVES: Makes 16 to 20 little buns

TIME: Start 2 hours ahead; 30 minutes plus 30 to 40 minutes cooking

THE DOUGH:

1	pound (3½ cups) all-purpose flour	1	cup warm milk
½	teaspoon salt	1	ounce sugar
1	ounce fresh yeast or ½ ounce dry yeast	2	ounces (4 tablespoons) butter or lard

THE FILLING:

½	pound hazelnuts and/or walnuts	4	ounces (½ cup) sugar
¾	pound dried pears or pitted prunes (dried plums)	1	egg

You will need a small bowl, a large bowl, a rolling pin, and a baking sheet. Put the dried fruit to soak in a little water while you make the dough according to the recipe for plum pie (page 425). When the dough has risen once, roll it out very thin and cut it into 16 to 20 squares.

Chop the nuts and the fruit together, and mix in the sugar and the egg. Put a pile of the nut-and-fruit filling onto each square of pastry dough. Dampen the edges of the pastry and fold over the edges. Turn them so that the seams are underneath. Butter a baking tray and put the buns on it, well spaced to allow them room to rise. Put the tray of buns somewhere warm and draft-free to rise for half an hour (in a turned-off oven over a baking tray full of hot water.)

Preheat the oven to 350°F.

Bake the little buns for 30 to 40 minutes, until they are well risen and golden. While they are still warm, brush them with a syrup of sugar and water (3 spoonfuls of each melted together.) They are delicious for tea.

◆

SUGGESTION

Brandy or lemon juice can be used to soak the fruit.

◆

YEAST CAKE

Bara brith (Wales)

Welsh country cooks are particularly skilled bakers and can boast almost as many varieties of oven as there are recipes for bread and cakes to cook in them.

Bara brith is a rich dough cake and a special treat. Today fashion and speed dictates it be made with chemical raising agents. The yeast-raised version is much more satisfactory. The recipe is to be found all over Europe in various guises and regional variations.

YIELD: Makes 1 large cake

TIME: Start 2 hours ahead; 40 minutes plus 1 hour cooking

1 ounce fresh yeast or ½ ounce dry yeast	1 egg
¼ cup sugar	4 ounces (½ cup) lard or butter
⅔ cup milk	½ pound raisins and currants
1 pound (3½ cups) all-purpose flour	1 tablespoon molasses
1 teaspoon salt	1 teaspoon caraway seeds

You will need a large bowl and an oblong loaf pan. Liquefy the yeast with a teaspoon of the sugar and half a cup of the milk, warmed. Put the flour and the salt in a warm bowl, make a well in the middle, and pour in the yeast mixture. Sprinkle with a little flour and put aside in a warm place for 10 to 15 minutes to set the sponge.

Add the rest of the milk, beaten up with the egg, and mix to a firm, smooth dough. Put aside for an hour to rise in a warm place—inside a plastic bag in the cupboard is a good choice.

Meanwhile, melt the lard or butter to a warm cream, and lightly flour the raisins and the currants so that they do not sink to the bottom of the cake. Butter the loaf pan (if you use butter to grease a cake pan, the cake will taste of butter, whatever fat you have used in the mixture itself).

Preheat the oven to 350°F.

When the dough has doubled in bulk, punch it down, knuckling thoroughly with your fists, and work in the rest of the ingredients: the rest of the sugar, the melted fat, the molasses, and the caraway seeds. Knead the dough into a fat sausage, and press it into the loaf pan. Leave in a warm place for 30 to 40 minutes to double in bulk again.

Bake for 1 hour. It is done when well risen and golden.

SUGGESTION

Leftovers: They are delicious toasted and buttered.

DANISH PASTRIES

Wienerbröd (Denmark)

The country population of Denmark today is largely occupied with dairy farming and meat production. Until a century and a half ago, Danish farming was comparatively undeveloped. Crops were limited to wheat and cereals, and one fifth of the total area of the country was wasteland: heath and swamp. When, during the nineteenth century, the bottom dropped out of the cereals market as the prairie farmers of the United States began to export to Europe, Denmark adapted by importing the cut-price grain herself and feeding it to her livestock. Most Danish farmers today own their own farms, growing cereals and vegetables for both cattle feed and human consumption.

In 1882 the first cooperative was formed, and it is on this system that modern Danish prosperity is founded. There are co-ops for dairy products, bacon factories, egg-exporting societies, and poultry-dressing stations. Each group supplies its neighbors—buttermilk is used to feed the pigs and so on. Although the inspiration of the Danish pastry is acknowledged in its name, never was a marriage more clearly made in Heaven than that between the riches of Denmark's dairy farms and the Ottoman-inspired skills of the Viennese kitchen.

YIELD: Makes about 36 little pastries

TIME: Start 2 hours ahead; 1½ hours plus 20 minutes cooking

THE DOUGH:

1 pound (3½ cups) all-purpose flour	1 ounce (⅛ cup) sugar
1 ounce fresh yeast or ½ ounce dry yeast	8 ounces (1 cup) butter
	1 teaspoon salt
⅔ cup warm milk	1 egg

THE MANDELMASSA (ALMOND PASTE) FILLING:

¼ pound ground almonds
¼ pound confectioner's sugar
1 egg white

THE SPANDAU FILLING:

1 egg yolk	1 cup milk or cream
1 ounce sugar	Jam
1 ounce (¼ cup) flour	

THE HANEKAM (COCK'SCOMB) FILLING:

2   *large cooking apples*
2   *ounces (¼ cup) almonds*

You will need a large bowl, some small bowls, a rolling pin, some saucepans, and a baking tray. Sift the flour into a warm bowl and make a well in the center. Mix the yeast to a liquid in half a cupful of the warm milk. Pour the yeast liquid into the well in the flour and sprinkle a handful of flour over the top. Put aside for 15 minutes in a warm, draft-proof corner for the yeast to develop and to set the sponge.

When the yeast has bubbled up and begun to work, sprinkle the sugar, 4 tablespoons of the butter chopped into little bits, and the salt over the top. Pour the egg beaten in the rest of the milk into the spongy center of the flour. Work the liquid into the flour with a circular motion until you have a smooth, elastic dough. You may need a little extra liquid. Pummel the dough thoroughly with your fists, working the mass up and over itself, to stretch the gluten and make the dough ready for the next stage. It will take a 5 to 10 minute workout—give it all you've got.

Form the dough into a smooth white cushion, with tucked ends underneath.

Flour the table or a wooden board. With a floured rolling pin, roll out the pastry into a large rectangle about half an inch thick. Slice the rest of the butter over the center third of the dough (dough and butter should be alike in consistency). Fold the other two thirds up over it, as for puff pastry. Seal the edges down with the rolling pin. Leave in a cool place for 20 minutes.

Meanwhile, prepare the fillings. These can be simply a spoonful of jam or a piece of fruit sprinkled with sugar, or a more sophisticated egg-custard mix, ground almonds and sugar bound with egg white, a strudel roll filled with soaked raisins—there are many varieties, of which here are three representative versions:

Mandelmassa: Mix the ground almonds, the confectioner's sugar, and as much of the egg white as you need to make a thick paste. Put it aside.

Spandau: Mix all the ingredients together until you have a cream. Put the cream into a small saucepan and heat gently, whisking to avoid lumps, until the custard thickens. Be careful not to overcook the egg. Allow the custard to cool before you use it.

Hanekam: Peel and core the apples, and stew them gently with a little sugar and a spoonful of water until they are soft. Mash them to a purée; peel and chop the almonds, and mix them in. Put the mixture aside to cool. These are known as cockscombs.

Roll and fold the dough again once. Let it rise inside a plastic bag for another 20 minutes. Cut the dough into 3 pieces. Roll each piece into a 12-inch square and then cut it into 4-inch squares, to give you 9 pastries per square. Divide it up into three groups.

Use the first group to make the *mandelmassa:* Put flattened balls of the marzipan paste into the middle of each small square of pastry, and fold two of the opposite edges up to meet over the marzipan.

Use the second group to make *spandau:* Spread a tablespoon of the cold custard over the center of a small square of pastry and put a teaspoon of jam in the middle. Fold all four corners up and pinch them together.

With the last group of little squares, make the *hanekam*: Put a sausage shape of apple puree down one side of each small square. Fold the other side over to make an oblong sandwich. Notch down the seamed side to make a cockscomb effect—fan out the notches by curving the uncut side into a crescent.

When the pastries are filled, put them on a greased baking tray and leave them to rise for 20 minutes—not in too warm a place, or the butter will oil. This pastry has a split personality, being a combination of cold-worked and warm-worked pastes.

Preheat the oven to 425°F

Brush the tops with egg white. Bake the pastries, when nicely risen, for 15 to 20 minutes.

SUGGESTIONS

Don't worry if the pastries don't look very professional the first time—they will still taste delicious and with practice you will soon become more dextrous. The Danes learned in no time.

Make a tea ring by dividing the dough into three strands. Brush each strand with melted butter and sprinkle with cinnamon, sugar, and nuts pounded together. Braid the three strands together and curl the braid into a ring. Sprinkle more nuts over the top. This will take 30 to 40 minutes in a preheated 375°F oven.

CHAPTER THIRTEEN

Sweet Dishes

PIES

APPLE-AND-BLACKBERRY PIE

(England)

The early English system of annual triple-crop rotation in open strip fields made it impracticable for fruit trees, which take far longer than a year to mature, to be planted in fields. The solution, both in England and in Norman France, was to plant semi-wild trees on the edges of the woods, thus giving free access to a fruit orchard to all including the poorest. Blackberries grew wild in any event, as did raspberries, strawberries, and several other varieties of wild berry. These were joined in the woodland by pear, plum, quince, cherry, and medlar. The raw materials for fruit pies and dumplings were thus not difficult to come by, even in years of poor harvest.

SERVES: 6 to 8

TIME: 25 minutes plus 45 minutes cooking

THE SHORTCRUST PASTRY:

½ pound (1¾ cups) all-purpose flour	3 ounces (6 tablespoons) cold butter
1 teaspoon salt	3 ounces (6 tablespoons) cold lard
1 ounce (⅛ cup) sugar	3 to 4 tablespoons cold water

THE FILLING:

1   *pound sharp cooking apples*
½   *pound blackberries*
3   *tablespoons sugar (more if the fruit is very sour)*

You will need a shallow pie dish and a rolling pin. Make the pastry first. Sift the flour with the salt. Add the sugar. Cut the butter and lard into the flour with a sharp knife. When it is all minced fine, finish rubbing the fat into the flour with your fingertips. The secret of light pastry is in keeping it cool—if you use the palms of your hands, the butter will oil and make the pastry tough.

When you have a mix like fine bread crumbs, work in the water one spoonful at a time, still using the tips of your fingers. Knead into a soft round ball. You may need more or less water—it all depends on the weather and the dryness of the flour.

Leave the dough to rest in a cool place for 10 minutes, while you prepare the fruit. Peel and slice the apples. Pick over and hull the blackberries. Put them into a bowl and mix in the sugar. Leave them aside to form juice.

Preheat the oven to 400°F.

Roll out two thirds of the dough into a round base for the pie, and then roll out the rest into a lid. Do this on a well-floured board with a rolling pin, using quick, light strokes, pushing away from you.

Line the pie dish with the larger round of shortcrust pastry. Pile in the fruit. Sprinkle a little water over it—just fingertips dipped in fresh water, enough to help the juice, but not enough to make the pastry soggy. Dampen the edges of the pastry, and lay the lid over the fruit. Crimp the edges together with a fork and cut a steam hole in the top. If you have some scraps of pastry left over, make a few pastry leaves with strips of pastry cut diagonally.

Bake for 15 minutes to set the pastry. Then turn the oven down to 350°F and bake it for another 25 to 30 minutes.

Serve with plenty of thick whipped cream—lovely after a Sunday lunch of roast beef.

◆

SUGGESTION

If you are using a pastry lid only, halve the shortcrust recipe and reduce the cooking time by 10 minutes.

◆

TREACLE TART

(Scotland)

This was my Scottish grandmother's favorite pudding. The Scots have a sweet tooth—and the largest per capita consumption of sugar in the world. Greenock is the sugar center of Scotland, and has been so ever since the first sugar shipments began to arrive in the 1680s direct from the West Indies. Then the tart would have been made with the dark brown molasses from the bottom of the sugar barrels, and would have contained raisins and currants and spices if the cook could afford it. Modern Golden Syrup is more refined and does not need such disguises.

SERVES: 6

TIME: 30 minutes plus 40 minutes cooking

THE SHORTCRUST PASTRY:

6	ounces (1¼ cups) all-purpose flour	1	ounce sugar
1	teaspoon salt	4	ounces (½ cup) cold butter
		3	tablespoons cold water

THE FILLING:

1	pound light corn syrup	1	ounce (2 tablespoons) softened butter
2	ounces (¼ cup) freshly made, untoasted bread crumbs		

You will need two mixing bowls, a rolling pin, and a shallow pie plate. A food processor would be useful. Make the shortcrust pastry as in the recipe for apple-and-blackberry pie (page 438). Roll out two thirds of it to line a pie plate. Roll out the other third and cut it into strips.

Preheat the oven to 400°F.

Mix the syrup with the fresh bread crumbs and the butter. Spread the mixture over the pie base and lay a crisscross lattice of pastry over the top. Bake for 25 to 30 minutes.

My grandmother used to serve the treacle tart hot with thick cream or with a dollop of vanilla ice cream melting into it. Wonderful. She sometimes mixed in the juice of half a lemon to give a little sharpness to the flavor. It was either served after a roast chicken Sunday lunch (see page 289) or on an ordinary winter's day after a thick soup of potatoes and leeks made with the stock from an old boiling hen past its prime. My grandmother was very proud of her henhouse full of Rhode Island Red chickens—and I was sometimes allowed to collect the eggs tucked protectively under their soft marmalade-gold breast feathers.

◆

APPLE STRUDEL

Apfelstrudel (Austria)

A strudel is a whirlpool: The recipe is the cook's whirl of pastry. From the high hills of Yugoslavia to the plains villages of Hungary, each housewife has her special recipe. Mountain village housewives make sturdy strudels with yeast dough spread with curds or poppy seeds. The farmers' wives, their larders stocked with fresh butter and fine-ground wheat, may choose to make theirs with a shortcrust pastry stuffed with sour cherries or plums from the orchard. In the old days, before the advent of ready-made strudel dough, the most delicate recipe was reserved for those households blessed with a cook who had learned her trade in the kitchens of the occupying Turks.

The Ottoman Empire, founded in the thirteenth century and not finally dismantled until the early twentieth century, stretched, in its prime, as far as the battlements of Vienna. On the departure of the invaders, their unemployed cooks took the new skills to the kitchens of the aristocrats of the Austro-Hungarian Empire—and eventually back home to their own valleys. The old-fashioned, heavy strudel, made with yeast dough or pastry, is still widely popular all over Eastern Europe. However, "strudel" now means two different things—it is applied both to the dish itself and to the filolike pastry learned from the Turks. Strudel pastry has come to mean this particular thin dough. Strudels made with the fine filo pastry need patience and time—today most Austrian housewives buy theirs ready-made.

Strudels were most usually made with yeast pastry in the peasant kitchen as everyday fare, although a skilled cook would always prefer to make a filo/strudel pastry for a special occasion. Frozen strudel pastry can be bought in supermarkets and delicatessens—you might have to overlap the sheets to get the width you want. When you make it yourself, remember it must be kept warm to stay flexible.

Apple strudel is the most basic and best loved strudel of all. It is a marriage of the skill of the Ottoman Turks and the fragrant orchards of the northern valleys.

SERVES: 6

TIME: 1 hour (including making the pastry) plus 45 minutes cooking

THE PASTRY:
- ½ pound (1¾ cups) all-purpose flour
- ½ teaspoon of salt
- ½ cup warm water
- 2 tablespoons oil
- 1 ounce (2 tablespoons) melted butter

THE FILLING:
- 3 pounds apples
- 2 ounces (¼ cup) sugar (more if the apples are sour)
- 2 ounces raisins, the juice of 1 lemon, and 1 teaspoon of powdered cinnamon (optional)
- 2 ounces (4 tablespoons) butter
- 4 ounces (½ cup) bread crumbs

You will need a rolling pin, a pastry brush, a large clean cloth, and a baking tray. Pile the flour onto a large pastry board, or, better still straight onto your tabletop. Sprinkle on the salt. Make a well in the center of the flour hill and pour in the warm water and the oil. Mix thoroughly into the flour, from the center outwards. You may need a little more water if the flour or the air is very dry. The paste must be on the soft side. Flour your hands and set about kneading the dough very thoroughly. Feel it grow silky and elastic under your hands as the flour granules absorb the water. When it is smooth and shiny, knead the dough into a cushion, brush with the melted butter, and set it to rest in a warm place under an upside-down bowl for at least 20 minutes—12 hours maximum. At this stage it is a good-natured dough.

While the dough rests, prepare your filling.

Peel and core the apples. Slice them finely and sprinkle the sugar over them. Mix in the raisins, and sprinkle with the lemon juice and the cinnamon, if you are using these. Melt the butter and fry the bread crumbs gently until they turn pale gold. Set aside.

Lay a clean linen cloth out on the table. Flour your hands and the cloth (leave the flour jar out in case you need more). Until you are used to the method, cut the dough in half and make two cushions—a smaller strudel is easier to handle. Put one cushion in the middle of the floured cloth and flatten it with the palm of your hand. Roll the dough out with a floured rolling pin until you have a circle about 9 inches in diameter. That is as far as you go with the rolling pin.

Using the backs of your hands—the fingers loosely bent into a fist, the fists pushed gently under the edge of the dough circle until the outer rim of pastry rests on your knuckles—pull the pastry outwards, stretching it each time. Pull it in all directions until you have a large transparent pancake through which, should you feel inclined, you could read a page of the family Bible. The edges will be comparatively thick. These you tear off as you make the strudel. If the transparent part tears, patch it with trimmings from the edge. The pancake will lap over the edge of the cloth. Brush with melted butter.

Preheat the oven to 450°F and butter the baking sheet.

If you have decided to make two smaller strudels, each one will take half the filling. Spread the filling over two thirds of the dough, leaving a gap around the sides. Tear off the thicker edges of pastry. Fold in the edges of two parallel sides of the dough. Pick up the corners of the cloth, and roll the strudel gently away from you and over itself to curl into a jelly-roll shape.

Pick up the strudel in its cloth sling and roll it out onto the baking sheet. Brush the pastry with melted butter.

Bake the strudel for 45 minutes. Brush with melted butter and serve warm, sprinkled with powdered sugar, for some Austrian-Ottoman magic.

◆───────

SUGGESTIONS

───────────────────────────────

Leftover strudel dough cannot be used again. Instead, gather up the bits into a flat cake and allow it to dry until firm. Grate the cake on a coarse grater to make little scraped noodles called *Reibgerstl*. Dry them in a very low oven and store them in a tin. Sprinkle them into boiling soup—they will only take a few seconds to cook.

Bavarian apple strudel: The housewives of Bavaria like to cook their apple strudel bathed in cream, or egg-and-milk custard, in a deep pan. Settle the strudels side by side in a well-buttered pie dish (if you have made a single large one, curl it around in a hairpin bend), leaving a half inch (a hand's thickness) gap between each strudel. Bake in a preheated 475°F oven for 10 minutes to set the dough. Then pour into the gaps between the strudels a cup of cream, or a cup of milk with a little sugar and two eggs beaten into it. Turn the heat down to 425°F and cook for another 45 minutes (total cooking time, 55 minutes). This is a deliciously juicy and fragrant dish to be served warm. It's very good cold too—but nothing can compare with a freshly baked strudel still warm from the oven.

Cherry, plum, or rhubarb strudel filling: Proceed exactly as for apple strudel, but use pitted cherries, stoned plums, or rhubarb cut into short lengths, instead of the apples. Double the sugar for rhubarb. Be careful not to include too much juice—the mixture should not be too wet.

Curd cheese filling: Proceed exactly as for apple strudel (not forgetting the fried bread crumbs). Beat together 1 pound of cottage cheese or any white fresh cheese, 2 eggs, a tablespoon of raisins, and a tablespoon of sugar. Use this instead of the apple mixture.

All these strudels can be made with shortcrust pastry (as for the *Mürbteig* pastry, which is in the following recipe), or yeast pastry (page 426). They will then, of course, be far more substantial dishes.

◆───────────────────

DEEP-DISH APPLE PIE

Apfelkuchen (Germany)

The everyday version of Mom's apple pie had a basis of yeast pastry and was made as the plum tart on page 425. This recipe is for a special occasion. The dish migrated with immigrants to the New World, and early American cookbooks are full of such recipes. There are no less than eight versions in my American grandmother's *Settlement Cook Book*, circa 1900. The inclusion of almonds is nice but not essential. Germany is too northerly for almond trees to thrive anyway—although these nuts were always part of the traveling spice merchant's stock-in-trade.

SERVES: 6 to 8

TIME: 40 minutes plus 45 minutes cooking

MURBTEIG PASTRY:

¾	*pound (2½ cups) all-purpose flour*	*Yolks of 2 eggs*
2	*ounces (¼ cup) sugar*	*3 to 4 tablespoons cold water*
½	*teaspoon salt*	*1 tablespoon brandy*
8	*ounces (1 cup) butter*	

THE FILLING:

2	*pounds apples*	*1 ounce blanched almonds*
1	*ounce (2 tablespoons) butter*	*(optional)*
2	*ounces raisins*	*Superfine sugar*
1	*tablespoon brandy*	

You will need a mixing bowl, a rolling pin, a small saucepan, and a pie pan with hinged sides (this allows the making of a deep pie). Put the flour, sugar, and salt into a bowl, and cut in the butter with a knife. When your mixture is like fine bread crumbs, mix to a soft dough with the egg yolks, water, and brandy (the alcohol evaporates during the cooking and leaves the pastry short and crisp). Knead the pastry lightly with the tips of your fingers—use more liquid if the mixture is too crumbly. Everything must be kept as cool as possible. The palms of the hands are too warm: Using them will oil the dough and make it tough.

Put the pastry aside to rest while you peel, core, and slice the apples. Fry the apples lightly in the butter. Meanwhile, put the raisins to swell in the brandy—then mix them with the apples. Add the almonds if you are using them.

Preheat the oven to 425°F.

Roll out two thirds of the pastry and use this to line the pie dish. Roll out the remaining third into a circle to fit over the top. Fill the dish with the apple mixture. Dampen the edges of the pastry. Lay on the lid and seal the edges by pressing them together with a fork. Decorate the lid. Make a hole for the steam to escape.

Bake for 45 to 55 minutes, until the pastry is crisp and golden. Scatter thickly with superfine sugar. Serve warm with whipped cream. This is perfection after a good soup.

SUGGESTION

Make the pie in a large ring placed on a baking sheet.

◆

CHEESECAKE

Käsblotz (Germany)

This recipe made the transatlantic crossing most successfully, and a grand total of six alternative mixtures is on offer in my turn-of-the-century *Milwaukee Settlement Cook Book*. This version is from Franconia.

SERVES: 8 to 10

TIME: 45 to 50 minutes plus 30 to 35 minutes cooking

MURBTEIG PASTRY:

¾ pound (2½ cups) all-purpose flour	Yolks of 2 eggs
2 ounces (¼ cup) sugar	3 to 4 tablespoons cold water
½ teaspoon salt	1 tablespoon brandy
8 ounces (1 cup) butter	

THE FILLING:

1 pound cottage cheese	2 ounces (¼ cup) sugar
½ cup heavy or sour cream	Grated rind of 1 lemon (optional)
3 eggs	

You will need two mixing bowls, a rolling pin, and a deep pie pan, 10 inches in diameter. Put the flour, sugar, and salt into a bowl, and cut in the butter with a knife. When the mixture is like fine bread crumbs, mix to a soft dough with the egg yolks, water, and brandy. You may need more or less water. Knead the pastry lightly with the tips of your fingers until you have a soft ball.

Roll out the pastry to fit a 10-inch pie pan. Ease the pastry into it. Put aside to rest while you make the filling. Preheat the oven to 450°F.

Beat the cheese into the cream; then beat in the eggs and the sugar. Stir in the grated lemon rind (if using)—this improves the flavor but is not essential. The top of the cheesecake remains rather pale and anemic unless you glaze it before baking with a spoonful of cream mixed with an egg yolk.

Bake the cheesecake for 30 to 35 minutes. It should be well set and brown on the base when it is done.

Serve the cheesecake warm; it is delicious with fresh berries in season.

◆

SUGGESTION

Spread the mixture over a yeast-pastry base as for the plum tart on page 425.

◆
_____

STRAWBERRY TART

Tarte aux fraises (France)

French bakers prepare these pies all year round with whatever fruit is in season. They may use raspberries; strawberries; split and pitted apricots; sharp little mirabelle plums; and, all winter long, cartwheels of sliced apple, the edges caramelized dark from the oven's heat, and tarts with dried prunes, soaked, stoned, and glistening rich as a plum pudding. In my local market town of Revel they were baked every day and three times on Saturday. When the pies were taken out of the oven, the scented steam curled out into the street and a line of customers would form immediately: French housewives think it no shame to buy their Sunday treat from the *pâtisserie*, provided, it goes without saying, he is unquestionably the best pastry cook in the area. In France, wise patronage reflects as well on the customer as it does on the purveyor.

SERVES: 6 to 8

TIME: 25 minutes plus 30 minutes cooking

THE PASTRY:

4	ounces (1 cup) all-purpose flour	3	ounces (6 tablespoons) butter
½	teaspoon salt	2 to 3	tablespoons cold water
1	ounce superfine sugar		

THE CUSTARD:

1	cup creamy milk (half-and-half is perfect)	2	egg yolks
1	ounce (¼ cup) all-purpose flour	1	ounce sugar
		1	ounce (2 tablespoons) butter

THE FRUIT:

1	pound fresh strawberries, hulled and wiped
½	pound red currant or raspberry jam

You will need a bowl, a rolling pin, and a round 8-inch pie pan, preferably one of those with fluted sides and a removable base. A blender would be helpful. Pour the flour into a bowl with the salt, the sugar, and the butter cut into pieces. Chop the cold butter into the flour and sugar with a knife; then finish by rubbing in with the tips of your fingers. Mix in the minimum amount of cold water to form a soft dough ball. Flatten the ball lightly with a rolling pin dusted with flour; then drape the pastry over the rolling pin to transfer to the tin. Press the circle of pastry out until it covers the base and the sides of the tin. This recipe is nearly as rich as shortbread, which allows it to be baked "blind" (that is, empty) without bubbling. Prick the pastry base all over with a fork, and then put it to rest while you make the filling. You can, if you wish, line the pastry with foil and weight it with beans—then you will need to add 5 minutes to the cooking time.

Preheat the oven to 375°F.

Meanwhile, make the custard cream. Stir the milk into the flour. Whisk in the egg yolks and the sugar. Chop up the butter and stir that in. This is a job that can be done in a blender. Heat the mixture gently until it thickens, stirring all the time. The flour must be cooked, or the custard will taste starchy, and the eggs should not be overcooked, or they will scramble (though not very seriously, as with an egg-only custard). If the mixture does curdle or go lumpy, pour it quickly back in the blender with a little cold milk and beat it up again. When the custard is good and thick, set the bottom of the saucepan in a basin of cold water to cool it down.

Bake the empty pastry shell for 25 to 30 minutes, until the pastry is golden and crisp. Slip off the fluted side piece and leave the pastry shell to cool.

Prepare the fruit. Wipe, twist off the stalks, and halve the strawberries lengthwise. Warm the jam (red currant is best, raspberry is good) with a little water to make a thick syrup. If there are masses of seeds, pass it through a sieve when you pour it over the fruit.

Assemble the pie just before you are ready to eat it—its flavors are as fugitive as ripe strawberries themselves. Spread the now-cooled pastry shell with the cream. Lay the strawberries on their bed of custard, cut sides up, in a single layer of concentric circles. Finally, pour over it all a glazing of warm jam, which releases the irresistible perfume of warm berries. Serve the tart immediately.

◆

LEMON TART

Tarte au citron (France)

These beautiful sharp-flavored lemon tarts kept company with the *pissaldière* on the counter of my local *pâtisserie* in Castelnaudary. The *pâtisserie* stood on one corner of the town square, next to the charcuterie which supplied the locals with their *cassoulet*—one's own earthenware pot to be brought, three days' notice required. Tuesday was market day, and the scent of citrus oil and warm butter would mingle with that of the blossoms on the lemon trees which lined the avenue where the stall holders set up shop.

SERVES: 8 to 10

TIME: 30 to 40 minutes plus 40 minutes cooking

THE PASTRY:

6	ounces (1¼ cups) all-purpose flour	6	ounces (¾ cup) cold butter
1	teaspoon salt	2	egg yolks
1	ounce sugar	3	tablespoons water

THE FILLING:

4 *lemons*

4 *ounces (½ cup) unsalted butter, melted*

5 *eggs, less 2 whites*

5 *ounces superfine sugar*

You will need a 10-inch tart pan (preferably one with a removable base), a rolling pin, a grater, a lemon squeezer, and a whisk or an electric mixer. Sift the flour into a bowl with the salt and sugar. Make a well in the middle and grate in the cold butter. Mix it lightly in. Beat the egg yolks with the water and work them into the flour and butter with the tips of your fingers. Gather into a ball. If you need a little more water to make a soft dough, sprinkle in the minimum. Knead lightly and gently for a short time—this is a very rich pastry and liable to oil. However, the dough should not be too stiff. Flour a board and roll out the pastry dough into a circle to fit the tart pan. Lay the pastry in the pan, easing it into the corners. Cover and put it aside to rest in a cool place while you make the filling.

Preheat the oven to 350°F.

Grate the rind of one lemon, and squeeze the juice from all four. Melt the butter. Beat the eggs and the sugar together (this is much easier with an electric mixer) until they are light, white, and fluffy. Stir in the lemon juice and the butter. Pour the filling into the tart shell immediately, and bake for 40 minutes, until the pastry is crisp.

Serve warm, with an infusion of camomile or lime blossom.

◆

SUGGESTION

Make little tarts from the same recipe. They will need only 20 to 25 minutes cooking time.

◆

CHERRY BATTER

Clafoutis aux cerises (France)

This is a recipe from the Limousin district of France and a true peasant dish—a Yorkshire pudding with cherries. I first encountered it in the Andalusian *finca* of a French woman, long resident in Spain. Her orchard had lemon trees, orange trees, medlars, even avocado—strange hermaphrodite tree—and only one cherry. When it finally fruited in its seventh spring, this is the dish she made with its black harvest. She was a marvelous cook, but I have never seen her put a dish on the table with such pleasure and pride.

SERVES: 6

TIME: 20 minutes plus 40 minutes cooking

1 ounce (2 tablespoons) butter	*4 eggs*
1 pound black cherries	*1 small glass of* eau-de-vie *or*
4 ounces (1 cup) flour	*fruit brandy*
½ teaspoon salt	*Sugar for sprinkling*
1 cup milk	

You will need a large bowl and a 10-inch square baking pan. A blender would be useful. Preheat the oven to 350°F and put the baking dish in with a knob of butter. Pit the cherries.

Mix the flour, salt, milk, and eggs into a smooth batter. Stir in the *eau-de-vie* or brandy. All this is best done in a blender.

Remove the hot pan from the oven, roll the melted butter around it, and pour the batter in. It will sizzle for a moment. Scatter the cherries into the batter and then sprinkle all over with sugar.

Bake for 1 hour.

The *clafoutis* will puff up like a Yorkshire pudding and sink somewhat as it cools. Eat it warm with the thick, yellow, sour *crème fraîche* of France. A little glass from the bottle of *eau-de-vie de fruits—framboise* or Poire William—will echo the ingredients.

◆

SUGGESTIONS

Any other fruit suitable for pies—apples, plums, apricots, pears—can substitute for the cherries. But there is something about the rich dark cherry juice soaking through the golden crust that is particularly special.

You could always marinate the fruit in brandy.

◆

PASTRY WITH NUTS

Baklava (Turkey and Greece)

The best-loved sweet dish of the Middle East, the original *baklava* is claimed by everyone in the region. Bakers from Sophia to Alexandria sell it cut from huge, shiny, golden traysful. The Armenians probably have the best title to its modern identity: The pastry was baked as a Lenten dish, *bahk* being the equivalent of Lent in Armenian and *halva* being the ancient word for "sweet." The ingredients were permitted during the fast, and the layers of pastry were supposed to be forty in number. It was not an association the sponsoring Church necessarily condoned, the flock being more eager to adapt its favorite pagan rituals than the shepherd to countenance their pedigree. The dish appears on the menu at the Ottoman emperor's court no earlier than the end of the fifteenth century. It has made up for its late arrival in popularity ever since.

YIELD: Makes 36 to 40 pieces

TIME: 30 minutes (longer if you make the pastry) plus 40 to 50 minutes cooking

½	pound chopped nuts (almonds or walnuts)	1	pound homemade (or bought) filo pastry (page 441)
8	ounces (1 cup) clarified butter	1	pound honey

You will need a baking sheet (about 12 by 8 inches), a small saucepan, and a pastry brush. Chop the nuts roughly and put them aside. Melt the clarified butter. Brush the baking sheet with butter. Place 2 layers of filo on it—with light fingers so that there is plenty of air between. Don't press on the pastry if you can help it—air between the layers is very important. Sprinkle melted butter over the sheets. Lay on another 2 sheets and sprinkle on more butter. Continue thus until you have 8 sheets in place.

Preheat the oven to 350°F.

Scatter half the nuts over the pastry. Continue with more filo sheets and butter until you have added another 8 sheets. Scatter on the rest of the nuts. Finish with a final layer of 8 sheets. Mark parallel lines across the length and then cut diagonals across to give you diamonds. Pour the rest of the butter over. Sprinkle with water from wet fingers so that the sheets stay flat.

Bake the pastry for 40 to 45 minutes. Meanwhile, make a syrup by melting the honey in a little pan with 3 to 4 tablespoons of water. The syrup must be hot when you pour it over the *baklava*.

When the pastry is well risen and golden, pour the honey syrup over it, trickling it well into the cuts. Put the pie back into the oven for 5 minutes.

Serve the *baklava* hot or cold, with a glass of water and a little cup of thick black Turkish coffee.

SUGGESTIONS

Instead of honey, make the syrup with 1 cup of water, 1 cup of sugar, and the juice of a lemon, simmered together for 10 minutes until the syrup thickens. But it is much nicer with the beautiful honey of Greece.

OIL BISCUITS
Tortas de aceite (Spain)

A treat for both children and adults, these biscuits are characteristically marked with black blisters from the hot oven. They are crisp and delicious—not unlike sweet water biscuits.

Y I E L D : Makes 15 to 20 biscuits

T I M E : 30 minutes

1 *pound (3½ cups) all-purpose flour*	1 *liqueur glass of dry* anis
6 *ounces (¾ cup) sugar*	*(aniseed-flavor liqueur) or 1*
½ *teaspoon salt*	*glass of water and a teaspoon of*
4 *tablespoons oil*	*aniseed (sweet cumin)*
1 *egg*	

Preheat the oven to 425°F. You will need a bowl and a baking sheet.

Mix the flour, ½ cup of the sugar, and the salt together in a bowl. Make a well in the middle, and pour in the oil and the egg beaten into the chosen liquid. Knead into a pliable dough. Roll into a sausage shape and cut into 15 to 20 short lengths. Roll out each piece into a thin circle. Repeat until all the dough is used.

Bake for 10 minutes. Sprinkle the biscuits with the rest of the sugar a minute or two before you take them out. They will keep very well if wrapped in wax paper and stored in a tin. They are delicious for breakfast or as a teatime snack. Children in Spain have them as a special treat during the festival *feria*.

◆

WALNUT TORTE

(Rumania)

The Christmas Eve, the Ajun, the day of the 24th of December, the last of Advent, is a holiday too, and a special dish is eaten in every household, the turte. It is made up of a pile of thin dry leaves of dough, with melted sugar or honey and pounded walnut, the sugar being often replaced by the juice of bruised hemp seed, supposed to be sweet too. These turte are meant to represent the Infant Christ's swaddling clothes. The dough is prepared on the previous evening, and in some places it is used as a means of making the trees bear a rich crop of fruit in the coming summer, a kind of suggestion to Nature by threatenings. The wife, with her fingers full of dough, walks into the garden; the husband, axe in hand, follows close after. They stop at the first tree, and he says "Wife I am going to fell this tree, as it seems to me it bears no fruit." "Oh no," says she. "Don't for I am sure next summer it will be as full of fruit as my fingers are full of dough." And so on with every other tree. [*From Carpathian to Pindus*, Theresa Stratilesco, 1906]

SERVES: 6 to 8

TIME: 30 minutes plus 35 to 40 minutes cooking

THE PASTRY:

8	ounces (1⅔ cups) all-purpose flour	2	egg yolks (the whites go into the filling)
1	ounce sugar		
4	ounces (½ cup) cold butter		

THE FILLING:

½	pound shelled walnuts	6	egg whites
4	egg yolks		Apricot jam mixed with juice of 1 lemon
½	cup sugar		

You will need a bowl, a rolling pin, a pestle and mortar, a whisk or an electric beater, and an 8-inch baking pan. A food processor would be useful. Sift the flour into a bowl with the sugar. Cut the butter into the flour and then finish rubbing the two together with the tips of your fingers—do not use the palm of your hand, as it would oil the butter and make the pastry tough. There are those who freeze the butter and then grate it in and swear this makes the lightest pastry of all. When the mixture is like fine bread crumbs, work in the egg yolks to make a soft dough—you may need extra liquid, in which case use sour cream or cold water. With firm light strokes of a rolling pin, roll out the ball of dough into a thin circle to fit the pie pan. Ease the pastry into the pan—if you stretch it, it will shrink back in the cooking. Put it in a cool place to rest while you make the filling.

Preheat the oven to 350°F.

Finely grind or pulverize the walnuts in a mortar. Whip up the egg yolks with the sugar until you have a fluffy pale mixture. This always takes far longer than you would expect, and is best done with an electric beater. Fold in the ground walnuts. Beat the egg whites with a little more sugar until they hold soft peaks. Fold them into the egg-and-walnut mixture. Spread the jam on the pastry shell and pile in the filling.

Bake for 35 to 40 minutes, until well risen and golden. It should hardly sink at all as it cools.

Serve the pie when cool with hot wine. It is a pie to be enjoyed on a cold winter's night in the Carpathian mountains, by a family huddled around the little crib on Christmas Eve, waiting for the stroke of midnight so that the youngest child of the house can put the tiny figure of Jesus in his hay-lined manger.

◆

PLATE PIES

Teisen lap (Wales)

There's a great skill in the making of a plate pie—cooked on the griddle or *planc* over the fire. These flat pies, a favorite all over Wales, have to be neatly flicked over halfway through the cooking to be baked on the other side. Modern usage adds baking powder to the mix.

SERVES: 5 to 6

TIME: 45 minutes

6 ounces (1¼ cups) flour	3 ounces currants and raisins,
1 teaspoon baking powder (not	mixed
needed by those with light	1 egg
fingers)	½ cup cream or milk
4 ounces (½ cup) salty butter	Superfine sugar
3 ounces sugar	

You will need a mixing bowl, a rolling pin, an 8-inch enamel plate or shallow baking pan, and, if possible, a *planc* or a griddle. The oven may substitute if necessary. Sift the flour and the optional baking powder into a basin, and then rub in the butter lightly with the tips of your fingers. Stir in the sugar and the fruit. Beat the egg with the cream or milk and mix it into the flour. Knead all into a soft dough ball. You may need more or less liquid. Roll the dough out into a circle to fit the plate.

Bake the pie on a medium-hot *planc* or heavy pan placed directly over the fire for 15 to 20 minutes. Then turn it over with great skill and Welsh sleight of hand, and cook it on the other side for 15 minutes.

If you prefer, the pie can be baked in a preheated 350°F oven for 45 minutes. But then you will not be able to show off your skill to the young man who has come courting.

Sprinkle the top with plenty of superfine sugar before serving the pie.

APPLE CAKE

Æblekage (Denmark)

In the old days this Danish party treat would have been made with a yeast dough and be much like the Austrian *Zwetschenfleck*. The arrival of chemical raising agents early in this century gave the Danes an opportunity to lighten the mix.

SERVES: 4 to 6

TIME: 30 minutes plus 35 to 40 minutes cooking

6 ounces (¾ cup) butter	1 teaspoon powdered cinnamon
6 ounces (¾ cup) sugar	mixed with 1 tablespoon sugar
3 eggs	(optional)
6 ounces (1¼ cups) self-rising flour	1 tablespoon chopped blanched almonds (optional)
1 pound cooking apples (2 to 3 large ones)	

Preheat the oven to 350°F. You will need a large mixing bowl and a hinged 10-inch cake pan. An electric mixer would be useful.

Soften the butter and beat it in the mixing bowl with the sugar until light and fluffy (this takes twice as much energy as you would think—the mix has to be really white and airy—it is easiest to achieve with an electric mixer). Beat in the eggs, one at a time. Sift in the flour and fold it in thoroughly (called "tiring"). The mixture will be quite stiff. Grease the baking pan.

Peel the apples and slice them. Spread half the butter mixture in the bottom of the cake pan and lay half the sliced apples over it. Cover with the rest of the butter mixture and then arrange the rest of the apple slices in pretty wheels over the top. Sprinkle the cinnamon, sugar, and chopped almonds over all if you have them.

Put the apple cake to bake in the oven for 35 to 40 minutes, until well risen and golden.

SWEET PUDDINGS AND DUMPLINGS

RHUBARB DUMPLING AND CUSTARD
(England)

Rhubarb, a native of Tibet, was introduced to the English medicinal herb garden in Tudor times, but it was not until the eighteenth century that its scarlet, straw-cosseted early spring shoots became a familiar sight near the manure heap of every English cottage garden. The country poor of northern Europe soon discovered the virtues of a hardy perennial plant which could survive its freezing winters, gave plentiful fruit (albeit in an unfamiliar shape) for its pies, and, most important in Scandinavia, good material for its cottage wines. This dumpling was originally tied in a cloth and suspended, along with the vegetables and the meat, in the soup pot.

SERVES: 6

TIME: 40 to 50 minutes plus 2½ hours cooking

THE SUET PASTRY:
8 ounces (1¾ cups) self-rising flour	4 ounces suet
½ teaspoon salt	½ cup cold water
1 ounce sugar	

THE FILLING:
1 pound rhubarb
3 to 4 ounces sugar
½ cup water

THE CUSTARD:
4 egg yolks
2 ounces (¼ cup) sugar
2 cups milk
½ cup cream

You will need a 1 quart pudding bowl, a rolling pin, wax paper, string, and a clean pudding cloth or foil. You will also need a large boiling pan. Sift the flour into a bowl with the salt and the sugar, and then stir in the suet. Add cold water slowly (you may need more or less liquid) to make a smooth, soft dough which leaves the sides of the bowl clean.

Grease the pudding bowl. Cut off two thirds of the pastry and roll it out on a well-floured board with a rolling pin, until you have a big enough circle to line the bowl. Line the pudding bowl, easing the pastry well down so that it does not shrink too much in the cooking. Roll out the rest to make a lid and put it aside.

Put on to boil a pan of water large enough to accommodate your bowl. Rest the bowl on a metal ring or upturned unbreakable saucer in the bottom of the pan. Wash the rhubarb, and trim the leaves and stalk ends from the sticks—the weight should be 1 pound *after* trimming—the leaves themselves are toxic. Chop the sticks into 1-inch lengths. Pack the rhubarb into the lined pudding bowl, sprinkling with the sugar as you go. Add the water. The filling should come to within a finger's breadth of the top.

Moisten the rim of the pastry and lay the rolled-out lid on top. Pinch the edges of the pastry together to seal. Cover over with a circle of wax paper and the cloth, pleated in the middle and tied around with string. Make a string handle to lift it in and out. Foil can be used instead of the cloth. Steam the pudding for 2 to 2½ hours, checking regularly that it has not boiled dry. Add *boiling* water as necessary. Suet puddings are amiable and easygoing: The only damage that can be done is to let them boil dry or come off the boil while they are cooking.

Meanwhile, make the custard. Beat the egg yolks with the sugar. Bring the milk nearly to a boil, and then pour it over the egg yolk mixture, whisking vigorously. Return it to a gentle heat and stir until the custard thickens enough to coat the back of the spoon. Remove from the heat and stir in the cream. Float a knob of butter to melt over the surface if you are going to keep the custard waiting—this will prevent a skin forming. Beat the butter in just before you serve. The custard should be put on the table in a jug for each diner to take his own.

Serve the suet pudding without delay—it gets heavier as it cools, although an extra half-hour's boiling will do it no harm. The pudding can be made in advance and then reboiled for at least an hour to return it to its former lightness.

Precede a heavy pudding with a dish of plain-boiled meat—perhaps beef boiled with carrots, or a piece of boiled bacon served with stewed apples.

◆

SUGGESTIONS

Fill the dumpling with apples sweetened with honey, or with blackberries, cherries, damsons, or plums. An ounce or two of butter buried in the fruit gives a delicious flavor. Extra ingredients might include raisins, almonds, lemon peel, and ricotta: There is plenty of room for invention.

Suggestions for the custard: Custard is served with steamed puddings in particular, although it also keeps good company with stewed fruit, baked apples, and fruit pies. Flavored with vanilla, coffee, or chocolate, or fresh-fruit purées, it can be frozen into an ice cream. Mix it with a sweetened fruit purée in the proportion of one to one, and fold in the leftover egg whites well beaten to a froth, for the traditional English Fruit Fool.

◆

STEAMED JAM PUDDING

(England)

This is a relatively recent late-Victorian recipe, but it is still the heir to the great English pudding. The inheritors of the peasant tradition in England appear to have retreated to the nursery, and this is where this delicious pudding has been found for many years.

SERVES: 6

TIME: 20 to 25 minutes plus 1½ hours cooking

½	pound (1¾ cups) all-purpose flour	4	ounces (½ cup) sugar
1	teaspoon baking powder (or use self-rising flour)	2	eggs
½	teaspoon salt	½	cup milk
4	ounces (½ cup) butter	½	pound damson or raspberry jam

You will need a mixing bowl, a 1-quart pudding bowl, wax paper, aluminum foil, and a large boiling pan. Sift the flour with the baking powder and the salt. Cut the butter into the flour until the mixture looks like *very* coarse bread crumbs. Or cut the butter in with a knife if your hands are too warm. Add the sugar. Beat the eggs and stir them in. Mix to a soft dropping consistency with the milk.

Put the whole pound of jam into a 1-quart pudding bowl, and spread it up the sides and around the base. The bowl need not be greased. Tip in the pudding mixture. Top with a circle of buttered wax paper. Cover the bowl with a double layer of aluminum foil well folded over the edges. Place the basin on a piece of wood or an upturned saucer in a large pan with a well-fitting lid. Pour in boiling water to come just under halfway up the basin—any higher and you risk a soggy boiled pudding rather than a light steamed one. Bring the water back to a boil and then turn the heat down.

Keep at a steady simmer for an hour and a half, checking every 20 minutes or so that the pan has not boiled dry. Keep adding boiling water to keep up the level. Unmold the pudding onto a hot plate just before you are ready to serve—it is very good-natured and can be kept warm in its simmering water for as long as convenient. Serve with custard as in the previous recipe.

◆

Molasses can be substituted for the jam—use plenty to give a sticky, slightly caramelized coating to the pudding (to weigh syrup, scatter a handful of flour in the scales first). Or add chopped preserved ginger and its syrup (a taste acquired in the Colonies).

The pudding can be baked in the oven in a well-buttered dish for approximately 1 hour (depending on the shape of the dish) at 350°F. Serve after a simple nursery dish such as shepherd's pie or cottage pie (page 363).

◆

SEMOLINA HALVA

(Turkey and the Balkans)

The *halva* made in peasant kitchens all over the Balkans as well as Turkey is a simple affair, made with semolina, and cooked and sweetened with honey or *pekmekz*, a concentrated grape syrup. Sometimes the balls are spiked with pine kernels. Semolina *halva* remains a favorite votive gift among Turkish women. Promised and delivered in gratitude for favors, it combines the most symbolically valuable and the most enjoyable ingredients available.

YIELD: Makes 20 to 25 little balls

TIME: 40 to 50 minutes

THE SYRUP:
 4   *ounces (½ cup) sugar*
 ½   *cup water*
 Juice of 1 lemon

THE PASTE:
 2   *ounces whole nuts: walnuts,*   2   *ounces (4 tablespoons) butter*
     pine kernels, almonds, hazel-   6   *ounces (1½ cups) semolina*
     nuts, whatever grows in your
     woods

You will need two saucepans and a flat dish. Make the syrup by heating together in a small pan the sugar, water, and lemon juice, and simmering for 10 minutes.

Chop the nuts roughly. Melt the butter in a pan and stir in the semolina. Stir it around while it takes a light color—an important step which gives finished *halva* a delicious roasted flavor. Add the nuts. Fry lightly for a moment. Pour in the syrup, stirring vigorously. Simmer gently for 5 minutes to allow the semolina to absorb the liquid. Remove from the heat and pour into a wide, lightly oiled dish. Leave to cool a little and then cut the paste into small squares. Roll each one into a ball in clean hands. You can spear each little ball with a nut if you like, or roll the balls in chopped nuts. Serve them warm, with thick cream.

Take a little glass of raki with the *halva*, a small cup of Turkish coffee, and a long glass of water. They taste like a particularly nutty marzipan.

◆

SUGGESTION

Stir in 2 ounces of raisins when you add the nuts.

SOUR CREAM PORRIDGE

Rømmegrøt (Norway)

Porridge is a favorite time-honored Norwegian country meal. Taken at any time of the day, ordinary porridge is prepared with coarsely milled grains (oats, barley, rye). Special porridge is made with the best the larder holds: rich cream and fine flour. *Rømmegrøt* is served as festival food, at Christmas and on Midsummer Day. Very good *rømmegrøt* is now made and sold deep-frozen by Norwegian dairies. Some confusion arose when nineteenth-century travelers, and indeed twentieth-century sociologists, questioned the inhabitants of isolated communities on their diet. When the reply was universally "*grøt*," it was not appreciated for some time that *grøt* and "food" were synonymous, and that those questioned did not think it necessary to specify that they also ate fish, berries, milk, and meat.

SERVES: 6

TIME: 10 to 15 minutes

    2   *cups sour cream*
    6   *ounces (1¼ cups) flour*
    2   *cups milk (soured or sweet)*
    1   *teaspoon salt*

You will need a roomy saucepan. Bring the sour cream to a boil. Mix half the flour to a liquid with a little cold milk. Stir it into the boiling cream and simmer to allow the butter in the cream to rise. Skim off the butter—it will be served separately. Stir in the rest of the flour and milk.

Simmer for 5 minutes to cook the flour (stirring all the while—it's a devil for sticking and burning). Add the salt.

Serve with a jug of the hot skimmed butter and a bowl of sugar. If berries are in season, serve the porridge with strawberries or raspberries, and raspberry or blackcurrant juice to drink with it.

SUGGESTIONS

Unlock the spice chest for Christmas: Sprinkle cinnamon over the porridge.

The dish can be made with porridge oats, but you will have to increase the cooking time. See page 128 for the porridge recipe.

BAVARIAN CURD DUMPLINGS

Topfennockerl (Germany)

These specially delicate dumplings usually follow a good thick soup. Serve them with a dish of stewed fruit.

Y I E L D : Makes 15 to 20 little dumplings.

T I M E : 30 minutes

½   *pound ricotta or cream cheese*
2   *eggs*
1   *ounce sugar*
1   *ounce (¼ cup) all-purpose flour*

You will need a mixing bowl, a saucepan, and a draining spoon. Beat the cheese, eggs, and sugar together. Beat in the flour—you may need more or less to give you a soft, firm dough. The less you use, the lighter the dumplings.

Bring a pan of salted water to a boil.

Form little dumplings with two wet teaspoons and drop them into the water. Poach them for 5 to 8 minutes at a gentle simmer. They will bounce up to the top of the water. When they are firm, fish them out with a draining spoon.

Serve the *Topfennockerl* with a dish of stewed apricots or plums.

Bury a pitted plum in the middle, or a dark little damson, its seed replaced by a lump of sugar.

Or poach them and serve them in a fruit soup (pages 473–474).

VEILED COUNTRY MAIDEN

Bondepige med slør (Denmark)

This is a favorite Danish country dish, served after a thick soup such as the green pea soup on page 13.

SERVES: 6

TIME: 30 minutes

2	pounds cooking apples	½	teaspoon grated nutmeg
½	cup water	½	teaspoon ground cloves
3	ounces sugar	½	pound raspberry jam or any red
½	pound dry rye bread		jam (optional)
2	ounces (4 tablespoons) butter		

You will need a small saucepan and a pudding dish. A food processor would be useful to make the bread crumbs. Peel, core, and slice the apples. Stew them to a mush in a small pan with the water and a tablespoon of the sugar.

Grate the bread into fine bread crumbs. Fry them in the butter until they are a nutty golden brown. Mix in the rest of the sugar and the spices.

Layer the bread crumbs when cool with the stewed apples and the jam (if you are using it) in a deep dish: bread crumbs on the base, then all the apple, then more bread crumbs, then all the jam, then the rest of the bread crumbs. Serve cool with plenty of thick cream.

The French version is the *Charlotte aux pommes*—a rather grander confection, where a mold is lined with crustless slices of white bread fried golden in butter. The center of the mold is then filled with apples stewed with sugar and butter, and a lid of more fried bread is put over it. The whole mold is then baked in a preheated 350°F oven for 15 to 30 minutes to crisp its exterior. Serve hot or cold. This sophisticated version of the dish is credited to the kitchens of the Emperor Napoleon, who was a great fan of Goethe's heroine Charlotte in the novel *Werther*.

In England, apple Charlotte fills the same gap. Some hold Farmer George's Queen Charlotte responsible for its introduction. The pudding is baked as for the French *Charlotte*, and the jam of the Danes is omitted in favor of two layers of apples.

◆

BREAD PUDDING

Pwdingen Bara (Wales)

This is Watkin Williams-Wynne's recipe for bread pudding. The marmalade is optional.

SERVES: 5 to 6

TIME: 15 to 20 minutes plus 2 hours cooking

6	*ounces (¾ cup) bread crumbs*	2	*eggs*
3	*ounces suet*	2	*tablespoons marmalade*
3	*ounces sugar*		*A little milk*

You will need a mixing bowl, a 2-quart pudding bowl, and wax paper. A food processor would be useful to make the bread crumbs. Make the bread crumbs. Shred and chop the suet finely. Mix all the dry ingredients in a bowl. Beat the eggs and add with the marmalade to the dry ingredients. The mixture should be rather moist, as the bread crumbs swell; therefore, add milk, as required. Turn the mixture into the greased pudding bowl, cover with greased paper, and steam for 2 hours (see recipe on page 457 for steamed pudding). Turn the pudding onto a hot dish, and pour around it either warmed marmalade or melted-butter-and-sugar sauce.

◆

BREAD-AND-BUTTER PUDDING

(England)

The recipe given in E. S. Dallas' idiosyncratic mid-Victorian cookery manual *Kettner's Book of the Table*, says all that need be on the matter of this simple dish:

"Bread Pudding: When one is in the humor to eat bread pudding one wants it very simple—therefore the simplest receipt is the best, and the less we say of currants and candied citron the better. The rule is to pour upon fine breadcrumbs about three times the quantity of liquid—in the form of rich milk and butter. Say there are six ounces of bread, on this put two ounces of fresh butter, and then pour boiling hot 2 cups of the creamiest milk to be obtained. Cover this over, and let it stand until the bread is well soaked—which will take about half an hour. Then mix in three ounces of sugar, the yolks of five eggs, the whites of three, and a little nutmeg. Pour it into a dish and bake it for half an hour."

Set the oven at 350°. I would only add that a jug of cream served with it makes the dish sublime.

SWEET EGG DISHES

EGG NOG

Zabaglione (Italy)

Although this dish frequently appears today as either a sweet dish on its own or to sauce other puddings, it was customarily made by Italian housewives as a restorative for the old and the sick: and a very good restorative it makes too.

SERVES: 4

TIME: 15 to 20 minutes

6   *eggs*
6   *tablespoons sugar*
6   *half eggshells full of Marsala or sweet white wine*

You will need a saucepan, a bowl which can rest comfortably over it, and a whisk. Put a pan of water on to boil. In the bowl, beat the eggs with the sugar until they are light and fluffy. This will take twice as long as you think. Beat in the Marsala.

Rest the bowl over the now-boiling water. Beat until the mixture is firm and holds the mark of the whisk. Serve in glasses with a long spoon.

◆

SUGGESTIONS

If the *zabaglione* is to be eaten immediately, you need not cook it over the boiling water. It freezes (cooked) to make a delicious ice cream.

◆

EGG CUSTARD OR "HEAVENLY BACON"

Tocino del cielo (Spain)

The Moors introduced cane sugar to Europe both directly via their occupation of Spain and indirectly via the returning Crusaders. Sugarcane was planted both in Andalusia and in the Algarve to supply the Arab taste for sweets and syrups. By the time Ferdinand and Isabella finally took Granada and the Moorish occupation was over, the imported taste was centuries old—and centuries-old habits die hard.

The Spanish and Portuguese convents in particular continued with the tradition of sweet making. Confections made with egg yolks (left over from wine clarification, where only the whites are used) and sugar became specialties of various religious festivals. The nun-confectioners gave their products deliciously erotic names: "nun's bellies," "virgin's dew," "angel hair." Recipes for Portuguese egg-yolk-and-sugar sweetmeats soon began to appear in the cookbooks of Europe, including those of England—whose links with Portugal in particular were strong. Sir Kenelm Digby's *Closet Open'd* of 1669 has several recipes for egg-yolk-and-sugar custards. Meanwhile, Portugal was rapidly becoming a successful colonialist and had acquired a clutch of new and sun-drenched territories where her sugarcane could be planted. Limitless supplies of the until-then expensive ingredient further encouraged the confectioners. Rum, spin-off from the sugarcane industry, was added to her cellar (and her rural breakfast table as well).

SERVES: 8 to 10

TIME: 30 to 40 minutes plus 30 minutes cooking

Caramel made with 2 ounces (¼ cup) sugar, 2 teaspoons water, and juice of half a lemon	1 twist of lemon peel
	1 cup cold water
¾ pound (1½ cups) granulated sugar	12 large egg yolks (another 2 if the eggs are small)

You will need an 8-inch-square baking pan, a saucepan, a bowl, a roasting pan somewhat larger than the baking pan to act as a bain-marie, and foil. Make the caramel in the baking pan you will use for the *tocino*. Melt the ingredients together in the pan, turning them over a high flame until the sugar caramelizes a rich golden brown. This will take only a moment or two. Tip to coat the base. Set aside to cool.

Put the sugar with the lemon peel and the water in a heavy pan, and heat over a medium flame until the sugar is dissolved. Boil for about 20 minutes. Stir with a wooden spoon: If the syrup trails a transparent string when you lift the spoon out, it is cooked enough. Remove the lemon peel.

Preheat the oven to 350°F.

Meanwhile, whisk the egg yolks thoroughly. Pour the hot syrup into the eggs, beating as you do so. This will begin the thickening process. Pour the mixture into the caramel-lined baking tin. Cover with foil. Set the baking tin in the roasting tin and pour boiling water all around. Bake for 30 minutes. It should be firm and solid when it is done.

Allow to cool. Cut into squares: sticky, rich, and golden as the sun of heaven—the Moors named Granada, the source of this recipe, the antechamber of paradise. You will need to take a glass of water, Moorish style, with it.

◆

CUSTARD PUDDING

Flan (Belgium)

Egg-and-milk puddings are common all over Europe in dairy-farming lands such as the rich Belgian countryside. *Flan* also appears under the same name as the most universal sweet dish in Spain—where dairy products are by no means widely available. Possibly the recipe traveled south during the sixteenth century, when Spain and the Netherlands were united under the Hapsburg Holy Roman Emperor, Charles V. In modern Spain, however, it is simply a baked caramel custard much like the *tocino del cielo*.

SERVES: 4

TIME: 15 minutes

5	eggs	5	*ounces (1 cup) flour*
1	*quart creamy milk (half-and-half is perfect)*	4	*ounces (½ cup) sugar*

Preheat the oven to 375°F. You will need a bowl, an oval pudding dish, and a saucepan. Beat the eggs together with 1 tablespoon of the milk. Put the flour into the pudding dish, and beat it to a thick paste with the egg mixture.

Bring the rest of the milk and the sugar to a boil in a separate saucepan.

Pour the hot sweetened milk into the dish, over and around the egg-flour paste.

Bake for 20 to 25 minutes.

SUGGESTIONS

Flavor the pudding with a teaspoon of vanilla or a dash of cinnamon.

BUTTERMILK EGG SOUP

Kaernemaelkssuppe (Denmark)

This is a dish from the same stable as the Swedish Christmas porridge. It is a lovely dish for a simple evening meal. I have a friend who always has it as a light supper when he is alone. In Denmark it is eaten before the meat.

SERVES: 4 to 6

TIME: 20 to 25 minutes

    2   ounces (¼ cup) ground rice
    1   quart buttermilk
    2   eggs
    1   tablespoon sugar

You will need a heavy saucepan, a small bowl, a wooden spoon, and a whisk. Mix the ground rice to a paste with some of the milk. Put the rest of the milk in the saucepan. Whisk in the paste, and then stir over gentle heat until the soup thickens and the ground rice loses its raw taste. Keep stirring—milk burns rather easily.

When the soup is ready, mix the eggs with the sugar in a separate bowl. Slowly pour on the hot liquid, whisking steadily. In winter, serve the hot soup sprinkled with chopped almonds.

SUGGESTIONS

A tablespoon of raisins (soaked for a few minutes in boiling water first) can be added, along with a small stick of cinnamon or a piece of lemon peel for flavoring.

On a cold winter's evening stir in small glass of strong liqueur along with the eggs (whiskey will do as well as schnapps).

On a hot summer's day, serve it ice-cold, with slices of lemon and a plate of sweet biscuits.

PANCAKES

SMALL PANCAKES

Plättar (Sweden)

A special frying pan is available in Sweden with little hollows in it for cooking several small pancakes at a time.

YIELD: Makes 25 to 30 pancakes

TIME: 1 hour

½ pound (1¾ cups) all-purpose flour	*3 eggs*
2 tablespoons sugar	*2 cups milk*
Pinch of salt	*Butter for frying*

You will need a bowl, a whisk, and a *plättar* pan or a small frying pan. A blender would be helpful.

Put the flour, sugar, and salt into a bowl. Whisk the eggs and the milk and stir them gradually into the flour until you have a thin cream. This is easily done in a blender. Leave the batter to rest for half an hour or longer. A spoonful of snow lightens the mix in winter.

Melt a knob of butter in each of the dips in the special *plättar* pan, or use a small frying pan. When the butter foams, pour in enough pancake mixture to coat the pan in a thin layer, rolling it around so the coating is as thin as possible. Pancakes are nicest when they are as fine as a lawn handkerchief. Flip it over when one side of the pancake is golden-brown—the sides will peel away from the pan as it cooks. Cook the other side. Continue until all the batter is used up. Serve the pancakes immediately with a spoonful of fresh berries rolled up in each pancake—little wild strawberries, raspberries, blueberries—or best of all in Scandinavia, cloudberries, ripened corn-gold under the midnight sun. Or serve wrapped around a spoonful of berry jam.

◆

Serve the pancakes with sugar and lemon—the English treat for Shrove Tuesday designed to use up all the good things in the larder before Lent.

◆

JAM PANCAKES

Palacinke (Yugoslavia)

Sweet pancakes are a favorite treat throughout the Balkans, as well as throughout Scandinavia, the Low Countries, France, Britain, and practically everywhere else. Each region has its own way of enjoying them, and great pride is taken in the excellence of the raw materials. No housewife would bother to make them unless these were of the best. The Eastern Europeans like their sweets to be sweet and cannot resist stuffing the pancakes with their delicious fruit jams. Buffalo cream would have accompanied—and still does, if you are very fortunate and happen to be passing through Sibiu, or some such town in Hungary or points east, where buffalo are still the beasts of burden.

YIELD: Makes 15 to 20 small pancakes

TIME: 1 hour

4 *ounces (¾ cup) all-purpose flour*	1 *small glass of fruit brandy or*
¼ *teaspoon salt*	*any white alcohol*
1 *tablespoon sugar*	*Butter for frying*
2 *eggs*	½ *pound jam to stuff the pancakes*
1½ *cups milk-and-water*	

You will need a bowl, a whisk, a jug, and a small frying pan. A blender would be useful. Put the flour, salt, and sugar into a bowl. Stir in the eggs and then beat in the milk-and-water mixture gradually until you have a thin cream. This is easily done in a blender. Leave the batter to rest for 20 minutes.

When you are ready to make the pancakes, beat the batter again for a few minutes, adding the plum brandy (the Yugoslavs make an excellent plum brandy—the famous *slivovica*) to lighten the mix. Up in the mountains, a fistful of snow can be used instead. Transfer the batter to a jug.

Heat your smallest frying pan—an omelet pan is very suitable. Throw in a tiny knob of butter (clarified if you have any—it will not splutter and burn). Roll the pan around to spread the melted butter evenly. Pour in a couple of tablespoons of the batter (judged by eye of course: you don't want to be fiddling around with spoons at a moment like this). Roll the batter round the pan—it will stick to it in a thin layer. If you have put in too much, just pour it back into the jug. Cook the pancake over a medium-high flame, keeping a careful eye on it. When the edges are lacy, dry, and curl away from the sides of the pan (the work of a few moments), the pancake is ready to be turned. If you are feeling exuberant and the pan is one of those light raw-iron ones, flip it over in the air. If not, a spatula will do fine. Turn the pancake and cook the other side. Flip it out onto a reversed saucer—pile the pancakes on top of one another as you make them.

Repeat until all the batter is used. Stuff the pancakes with a spoonful of your best homemade jam. Imagine serving them with little rolls of thick yellow buffalo cream. Thick cream will have to do instead.

SUGGESTIONS

Make double quantities: These pancakes freeze beautifully.

Or tuck them into a baking dish in rows, bathe them in 1 cup of thick cream, cover the dish with foil, and put it to bake in a preheated 350°F oven for 20 minutes.

FRITTERS

RAG BISCUITS

Cenci (Italy)

Cenci, Cinderella's fritters, are the northern Italian country child's favorite treat. Michaela, who cooked in the pension in which I stayed as a student in Florence, would make them to keep her little grandchildren happy while she prepared the family's Sunday lunch. She would simply throw scraps of sweetened pastry, left over from the making of a pie, into deep oil and fry them until golden. Transferred to one of her big earthenware dishes, the piping-hot fritters would be sprinkled with powdered sugar. The children never learned to leave them until they were cool enough to handle.

" 'The rich strangers who visit our country pick a little of many things, but we eat all we can get of one or two things—bread and macaroni, or bread and beans. It is only at weddings,' he finished confidentially, 'that we arrive at sweets.' " (Sicilian peasant to Eliza Putnam Heaton in *By-Paths in Sicily*, 1920.)

Sugar appeared in the Italian diet relatively early. The Vatican librarian Bartolomeo Sacchi recorded in 1475 that sugar was being grown in Crete and Sicily as well as in India and Arabia.

YIELD: Makes 20 to 25 fritters

TIME: 30 to 40 minutes

1	*pound (3½ cups) all-purpose flour*	2	*eggs*
2	*ounces (¼ cup) sugar*	1	*small glass of brandy or water*
2	*ounces (4 tablespoons) butter*		*Oil for frying*

You will need a bowl, a rolling pin, and a deep frying pan. A food processor would make the pastry in a moment. If you have no food processor to help make the pastry, put the flour and sugar into a bowl. Cut the butter in with a knife. Mix the eggs together and work them in, adding a little brandy or water as you need it to make a soft dough. Roll the dough out and cut the pastry into ribbons. Twist the ribbons into knots.

Heat the oil in a pan—use a clear olive, sunflower, or other good vegetable oil. Deep fry the knots until they are light and golden. Drain them on paper towels and then pile them up in your best earthenware platter. Sprinkle with sugar and serve hot, just as for the Norwegian Christmas dish of *hjortetakk* (recipe follows).

Children can have their *cenci* with fresh grape juice. For grown-ups, serve the *cenci* with a bottle of cold sweet white, the *vin santo* of Italy.

◆

STAG'S ANTLERS

Hjortetakk (Norway)

Made with luxurious ingredients, these fritters are an absolutely indispensable Christmas treat, as M. du Chaillu discovered when he visited a Norwegian farmhouse in 1871:

> The larder is well stocked; fish, birds, and venison are kept in reserve; the best spige kjod [dry mutton, or either beef or mutton sausage] is now brought forward. A calf or a sheep is slaughtered, and as the day draws near sweet fritters and cakes are made. The humblest household will live well at Christmas . . . The little country stores carry on a thriving trade in coffee, sugar, prunes, raisins, and rice for puddings. Oats are specially bought and put out to feed the birds. [*The Land of the Midnight Sun*, Paul du Chaillu, 1881]

Similar special treats—waffles and pancakes peculiar to the different regions—are made all over Scandinavia at Christmas. *Goro* are made for special occasions, particularly for Christmas and Easter, in a beautifully patterned iron. The *goro* maker used to have an extra-long handle which allowed it to be held straight over the fire. Electric versions are now sold.

YIELD: Makes 25 to 30 fritters.

TIME: Start if possible the day before; 1 hour

3 eggs	1 pound (4 cups) all-purpose flour
6 ounces (¾ cup) sugar	Fat for frying (pork lard was used
2 ounces (4 tablespoons) butter	in Norway; vegetable oil
6 tablespoons heavy cream	usually substitutes today)
2 tablespoons brandy	To finish: extra sugar and cinnamon
Crushed cardamom and grated	
lemon rind (optional)	

You will need several bowls and a pan for deep frying. Beat the eggs thoroughly with the sugar. Melt the butter. Whip the cream. Stir the butter, cream, brandy, and flavorings (if used) into the eggs and sugar. Work in the flour—you may need less or more, depending on the size of the eggs and the absorbency of the flour—to give a soft, workable dough. Allow the dough to rest in a cool place, overnight in the refrigerator if possible.

Roll the dough into a sausage and chop off lengths. Roll each length into pencil-thin ropes, which you can bend to form a ring. Cut a few notches into each ring to make the horn branches.

Heat a pan of deep fat until a faint blue haze rises. Fry the fritters until puffed and golden. Drain on absorbent paper.

Serve sprinkled with sugar and cinnamon in a beautiful golden pile on your best white dish.

SUGGESTION

These biscuits keep well in an airtight tin. In the clear Arctic sunshine of July, I enjoyed a plateful which had somehow escaped the children's attentions the previous Christmas.

WAFFLES

Gauffres de Brussels (Belgium)

The Belgians are very fond of their food and take particular pleasure in their waffles. Belgian kitchen equipment nearly always includes one or several of the square-patterned waffle irons, both the thin ones to make *gauffrettes* and the thicker ones for the *gauffres*. There is considerable debate over the inclusion of yeast in the mix. The alternative raising agent is the egg white beaten to a snow. I give a yeast recipe as more likely to be the peasant version—since the incorporation of air via beaten egg white is a sophisticated and comparatively modern idea.

YIELD: Makes 12 to 15 wafers

TIME: Start 2 hours ahead; 40 to 50 minutes

2	cups milk	2	ounces (¼ cup) sugar
1	ounce yeast or ½ ounce dry yeast	¼	teaspoon salt
6	eggs	1	ounce (2 tablespoons) melted butter
1	pound (3½ cups) all-purpose flour		

You will need two bowls and a waffle iron. Warm half a cup of the milk and dissolve the yeast in it. Beat the eggs with the rest of the milk. Put the flour in a warm basin, make a well in the center, and pour in the yeast mixture, the eggs, and the rest of the milk. Beat until you have a creamy lump-free batter. Put aside in a warm, draft-free cupboard for 2 hours to allow the yeast to develop. Then stir in the sugar, salt, and melted butter.

Cook the waffles in a well-greased waffle iron. Serve with sugar and butter, jam, or syrup.

◆

FRESH CHEESE FRITTERS

Papanasi (Rumania)

A kind of fried dumpling, these little fritters can be served with meat, or, as here, as a sweet dish after a soup.

YIELD: Makes 20 to 25 fritters

TIME: 40 minutes

½	pound ricotta or cottage cheese	Grated zest of 1 lemon or orange (optional)
2	eggs separated and the yolks of two more	1 ounce sugar
2	ounces (4 tablespoons) butter, softened	Oil for frying
4	ounces (1 cup) all-purpose flour	To finish: sour cream and confectioner's sugar
½	teaspoon salt	

You may need a sieve. A food processor would be useful. You will need a bowl and a deep frying pan. Sift or process the cheese if it is the lumpy "cottage" variety, and then beat it into a smooth dough with the 4 egg yolks, butter, flour, salt, and grated rind (if using). Leave the mixture to rest for 15 to 20 minutes. When you are ready to proceed, beat the 2 egg whites with the sugar until they hold peaks. Fold this into the cheese mixture.

Put the oil on to heat. When a faint blue haze rises, drop in tablespoons of the mixture. Fry the fritters gently until puffed up and golden. Drain well on paper towels.

Spoon sour cream over the fritters and sprinkle them with confectioners sugar. Serve them piled in a glorious golden pyramid to be eaten immediately.

SUGGESTIONS

If you would like to serve the *papanasi* to accompany a meat dish, leave out the sugar and the grated peel. The sour cream should be spooned over just the same.

FRUIT SOUPS

BERRY COMPOTE

Rødgrød (Denmark)

One of the best loved of the fruit soups, the best version combines three red fruits in equal measures. Naturally, a single one will do. This is to be served as a soup before the meat dish.

½	pound red currants	2	ounces (½ cup) potato flour,
½	pound cherries		sago flour, or corn flour
½	pound raspberries	2	ounces (¼ cup) sugar
1	quart water		

You will need a heavy saucepan. Stew the three red fruits with the water until the juice has all run out. Press through a fine sieve or jelly cloth. Mix the flour with a little cold water.

Bring the juice back to a boil and stir in the flour liquid and the sugar. Bring back to a boil again, stirring as it thickens. Pour into a bowl, sprinkle with sugar (this stops a skin from forming), and allow it to cool.

Serve with plenty of thick cream.

This makes rather a good summer pudding if accompanied by little hot biscuits.

Serve as a breakfast dish with sour cream or yogurt.

Leftovers: They are delicious as a sauce for ice cream.

RED CURRANT SOUP

Viinamarja Karrpuss (Finland)

The Finns eat their sweet fruit soups and porridges after their meat. The country people do not much like oatmeal—they prefer wheat- and bread-based porridges, or milk preparations such as curds, junkets, and soured cream.

SERVES: 4

TIME: ½ hour plus 15 minutes cooking

4   *thick slices of stale rye bread*
2   *cups water*
2   *cups red currant purée*
2   *ounces (¼ cup) sugar*

You will need a bowl, a blender or a sieve, and a saucepan. Tear up the bread and put it to soak in the water for half an hour. Mix it with the fruit purée. Beat all together with the sugar in a blender, or push it through a vegetable sieve. Pour the soup into a saucepan; heat to boiling and simmer for a few moments to thicken. If you are hungry, serve it with curd dumplings (page 460). Otherwise, eat it with plenty of thick fresh cream and brown sugar.

Raspberry, blueberry, sour apple, and sour cherry are all suitable fruits for this recipe.

A squeeze of lemon juice will sharpen up a purée which is too bland.

It is delicious for a late Sunday breakfast.

WINE AND BEER SOUPS

WINE SOUP

Weinsuppe (Germany)

Sweetened wine, beer, and fruit soups are served before the meat in Germany, in the usual order for soup. In Finland such sweet soups are served at the end of the meal.

SERVES: 2

TIME: 20 to 30 minutes

1	bottle of white wine	1	tablespoon sugar
2	cloves and a small stick of cinnamon for flavoring	2	eggs

You will need a saucepan, a bowl, and a whisk. Bring the wine to a boil with the spices and the sugar. Meanwhile, beat the eggs in a roomy bowl. Take the pan off the heat and pour the soup from a height into the beaten eggs. A slice of Marie Antionette's *Kugelhopf* (page 321) could accompany your delicate meal.

SUGGESTIONS

To make hot beer soup, substitute beer for the wine. Accompany with a slice of toasted cheese (page 211).

COLD BEER SOUP

Bierkaltschale (Germany)

This is one of those little meals to be enjoyed on one's own, a pleasure like that of good bread dunked into strong red wine, as with the southern French habit of *faire chabrot*. The dish has its strong supporters.

SERVES: 1

TIME: 20 minutes

2   *cups light beer*
2   *ounces currants*
4   *ounces brown bread, crumbled*

You will need only a bowl. Put the currants to swell in a bowl in a warm oven for 10 minutes. Take the bowl out of the oven, add the bread crumbs, and pour in the beer. Put the soup in a cool place to soak. It is ready to eat in 10 minutes. Sprinkle it with brown sugar and serve it with cream.

◆

OATMEAL CAUDLE

(England)

A pub drink once very popular in rural England, caudle is digestible and fortifying enough to set a person up for the homeward journey after a long day at market.

SERVES: 4

TIME: 5 minutes plus 30 minutes cooking

1   *quart light beer*   1   *teaspoon powdered ginger*
1   *quart water*   4   *cloves*
4   *ounces (½ cup) oatmeal*   4   *tablespoons brown sugar*
1   *teaspoon grated nutmeg*

You will need a heavy-bottomed saucepan and a wooden spoon. Put all the ingredients in the saucepan and mix well together. Bring to a boil and then turn down the heat immediately. Stir frequently as the caudle simmers gently for half an hour, until it is good and thick. You may need to add a little extra liquid. Set out four heavy mugs and put a spoonful of sugar or syrup in each. Pour the hot caudle in. Stir well and serve while piping-hot.

ALMOND MARZIPAN CREAM

Frangipane (Italy)

Sicily, 1928:

Almonds are raised primarily for exportation and their local consumption is regarded as something of an extravagance. Families in modest circumstances frequently depend on the produce of their few almond trees to provide their supply of ready cash for the year. Other uses are also made for the almond. The outer husk is burned to make a sort of ash soap used in laundering and the hard shell serves as fuel in the braziers. [*Milocca*, Charlotte Gower Chapman, 1973]

3	*eggs*	4	*ounces (½ cup) sugar*
3	*ounces (¾ cup) all-purpose flour*	6	*ounces (¾ cup) ground almonds*
2	*cups milk*		

You will need two bowls, a saucepan, and a baking dish. Beat the eggs together. Mix the flour with a little of the milk, and then stir it into the rest of the milk and the beaten eggs. Cook the mixture over low heat like a custard, whisking steadily and adding the sugar and the almonds little by little. When thick, remove from the heat and pour into an oiled baking dish. When it is cold, cut it into squares like Turkish delight. Serve as a special treat for holidays.

TREATS

PLUM BRANDY

Tuica (Rumania)

Strong alcohol can be distilled from any vegetable matter which will rot, a process of fermentation well known to anyone who has ever gone into an apple loft. The taste for fermented liquor is by no means confined to humans—baboons will feast on rotten fruit which makes them so drunk they lie in helpless heaps; elephants will search out baobab groves where the fruit has fermented on the ground. From the freeze-distilled potato spirits of Finland to the herb-scented liquors of the monasteries of France and Italy, all Europe distills. The peasant community was more accustomed to using its hard liquor as a morning pick-me-up than as an elegant *digestif*.

In Rumania to this day the preferred raw material for fruit brandy is plums. The local village doctor showed D. J. Hall his home still in 1937:

"Have you seen how tuica is made? Come with me and I will show you." So we went down together, the doctor knocking the plums from the trees and filling my hands with them. In a barn were eight enormous barrels about three feet high, standing on their ends. A gentle sizzling came from them, the air was filled with the scent of fermenting plums. "When I make tuica I do not make it straight from the fruit off the trees as the peasants do. I fill these barrels and let the plums lie there fermenting for about six weeks. After that I put them in fabrica. That is in the other shed. There are some there now." I had no idea that tuica could be made so simply. On a brick furnace stood a large copper, a long pipe from it led through a barrel and from the pipe's end fell drop by drop the tuica into a container. "It is primitive, is it not? The fermenting plums are put in the copper, the vapour passes through the pipe. In that barrel is water which is always cold because a stream from the hill flows through it. So the vapour is condensed and there is tuica. So simple, eh?" [*Romanian Furrow*, D. J. Hall, 1939]

There can be no better conclusion to a good meal. *Bon appétit*.

CHAPTER FOURTEEN

The Rustic Kitchen

A well-stocked larder was essential to the peasant household, particularly during the winter months when fresh food was scarce. The larder would usually be protected by a door and a lock, or be safely tucked in the cellar under a heavy flagstone so that its contents could be defended against marauders. Most of the contents would have been home produced, with the few extra essentials such as salt, spices, and, more recently, tea, coffee, and sugar. All would be bought with the housewife's small cash crop—perhaps from the sale of eggs or the nurturing of a crop of silkworms. Pepper was a particularly important ingredient in preserving meat; because of its great popularity, this was imported in bulk and sold reasonably cheaply.

Home-grown staples included not only the usual grains and dried beans, onions, garlic, and storable vegetables, but also fresh cheese, well rubbed with salt, left to mature on a beam, hams and sausages from the annual pig killing, and a wide variety of potted and preserved meats and fish. In northern countries where the ground was often under snow for long periods, the housewife would pickle and salt cabbage and other vegetables, and preserve the berries essential to provide vitamin C throughout the winter. Herbs would be used fresh in spring and summer, and dried for the winter. The prudent housewife could reckon to feed her family "from the drawer"—a term used particularly by those who stored chestnuts in long wooden trays kept under the dresser—for months if necessary.

These basics were the foundation on which many peasant recipes were built. Most of these ingredients, particularly the sausages, are widely available today in our supermarkets. None of the recipes are complicated—peasant methods are essentially simple. There is no reason why we should not make our own frankfurters and salamis if we wish. There is also every reason to be aware of the ingredients which should and should not be included in the recipes when we are shopping for the ready-prepared article.

HERBS

Herbs and wild plants gathered from field and wood have always been a valuable source of both food and medicine to the peasant community. The herb seller occupies to this day a special corner in all Mediterranean and Eastern European marketplaces.

My favorite herb market is held every week in Buis-les-Baronnies in the mountains behind Provence. (Many of its raw materials are gathered from the rocky slopes which surround it, and today the little town boasts a factory for the drying and packaging of its own products.) There, under the medieval arches of the market square, wooden trestles are loaded with sacks of dried aromatic leaves, invitingly open for inspection. Among them are five varieties of thyme, rosemary, bay, sage, and juniper berries gathered wild in the garigue scrub. There is lime tea, green tea, vervain, lemon balm, dried mint, rose petals, marigolds, three varieties of chamomile, cherry stalks, and a hundred different roots and herbs for infusions, each with a special property. The local people demand—as they have always done—great variety. This one for sleep, this for sloth, this for a bad stomach, this for women's ills. Then there are the imported cloves and peppercorns, cinnamon and bundles of licorice root for the children to chew, and bundles of lavender, grown in rows as a crop for the perfume industry.

Herbs for Flavoring

These are grouped here in their botanical families, which I hope will encourage the cook to look for a substitute within the family if a given herb in a recipe is unavailable. There are four main groups in the European wild larder: the mint family, the carrot family, the onion family, and the cabbage family.

The Mint, or Labiatae, Family

All the herbs in this family except sweet basil, which is a native of tropical Africa and Asia, are indigenous to the Mediterranean. Their use was spread throughout Europe by the Roman colonists. If you cannot obtain a specified herb, reach for another in the same group. The results are generally perfectly satisfactory and would be as expected in the peasant kitchen, where the cook would often use whichever herb came easily to hand.

BASIL *(Ocimum basilicum)*: A native of India and tropical Africa but imported into the Mediterranean many centuries ago, basil was used as a charm against the basilisk, or dragon, in ancient Italy, while to the early Greeks it was a royal *(basilikon)* herb. A favorite flavoring in Greece, Italy, and France, it is the dominant herb in the making of Chartreuse. Nip the top leaves of a growing plant to encourage branching. Dry and store after

THE MINT OR LABIATAE FAMILY

1 Basil 2 Marjoram 3 Oregano 4 Spearmint 5 Rosemary 6 Sage 7 Savory 8 Thyme

flowering. Or keep the leaves steeped in vinegar for use in salad dressings. Or store as *pesto* (page 3).

SWEET MARJORAM *(Origanum marjorana):* A native of the Mediterranean and used interchangeably with oregano, or indeed to replace basil in the winter, it is rather more subtle in flavor. In medieval times it was gathered as a strewing herb for the floor. Pick for drying just when it comes into flower—its flavor is strongest when the herb is dried. The American equivalent is *Majorana hortensis.*

WILD MARJORAM OR OREGANO *(Origanum vulgare):* Another native of the Mediterranean, oregano was named "mountain joy" by the Greeks. It is very often used with tomatoes in Italy, particularly in pizzas. Bees love its little white flowers. Dry sprigs of it when it is in flower. There is a Mexican oregano much used in the United States, which has a similar, somewhat stronger, flavor, of the genus *Verbena.*

ROSEMARY *(Rosmarinus officinalis):* The deliciously named "dew-of-the-sea," *rugiado di mare,* does indeed grow best near the seashore. The French burned branches as incense and believed that the flowers were an aphrodisiac. It was used throughout Europe as a protection against the spells of witches. In warm climates its delicate blue flowers blossom all year round and are much loved by bees. It can be picked for drying at any time, although its oil is strongest in August and September.

SAGE *(Salvia officinalis):* An herb used initially as a medicine, sage was planted throughout Europe by the Romans. It was incorporated in the peasant diet for its health-giving properties. The best time to dry it is in the spring, before the plant flowers and its stalks begin to lengthen.

SUMMER AND WINTER SAVORY *(Satureja hortensis* and *S. montana):* These are two very similar species of which the summer variety is a more gently flavored annual and the winter a woody perennial. The flavor of both is somewhere between sage and rosemary. Savory was so popular in medieval England that it was one of the herbs taken by the settlers to be seeded in the New World. Medicinally it was used as an antihistamine to relieve the pain of insect stings. Savory dries well, is an excellent flavoring for meat and fish dishes, particularly trout, and, in England, has the same affinity with beans as mint has with peas.

SPEARMINT *(Mentha spicata):* Growing wild throughout central and southern Europe, spearmint is the best mint for drying and has been in use for thousands of years. Peppermint *(Mentha piperita)* is a stronger variety and is used for oil. Dry mint for storing tied in bunches and hanging in a dry current of air. Then strip and crumble the leaves to keep, like all stored herbs, in an airtight jar out of the light. In pre-refrigeration days mint was believed to prevent milk from turning sour in warm weather. An excellent herb for the digestion, the French use the dried leaves to make an infusion. In England fresh mint is used to sauce lamb and flavor peas. In Eastern Europe and the Middle East it is infused fresh to make a delicious, sugar-sweetened, tea.

THYME (*Thymus vulgaris* plus a great many other varieties): Its name derives from the Greek for "burned offering." Thyme has long been used medicinally, both burned as a fumigant and through its oil as an antiseptic, particularly against fungoid or bacterial infections. Bees love it and collect its delicately perfumed nectar to make the most delicious honey of all. The flavor is strongest when the leaves are dried. Thyme is the principal herb used in the flavoring of Benedictine.

The Carrot, or Umbelliferae, Family

The parts of these plants most usually employed for flavoring are the complete fruits rather than the seeds. The varieties used in Europe are, as with the mint family, native to the Mediterranean. All varieties taste of aniseed in varying degrees.

ANISEED (*Pimpinella anisum*): A white-flowered Eastern Mediterranean annual, aniseed was used as a licoricelike flavoring by the Greeks, the Hebrews, and the Romans, who baked it in cakes which they ate at the end of their gargantuan meals to assist digestion. Anise is still used today as a *digestif*, although more usually now as an ingredient in various strong liquors: Spanish anis, French Pernod and anisette, and the Greek ouzo. Anise shares with its close relation fennel, and with the star anise which is a fruit of the magnolia family, an essential oil, anethole. Aniseeds can be bought from any Mediterranean spice stall and are generally used to flavor sweet biscuits. The seeds are also used in Greece and Turkey to spice stuffed vine leaves and vegetable dishes. They have a particular natural affinity with their cousin the carrot.

CARAWAY (*Carum carvi*): A biennial Mediterranean native, the plant's roots are sometimes eaten as a vegetable as well as the seeds being used for flavoring. Caraway is one of the most ancient spices known to man—it has been found in 10,000-year-old lakeside dwellings in Switzerland. Much liked in central Europe as a universal flavoring, it is used for meat, fish, cheese, pickles, and bread (particularly rye bread), and also for liqueurs like the German *Kümmel*. Caraway has a reputation as a *digestif* and has given its name to seedcake.

CHERVIL (*Anthriscus cerefolium*): A native of Eastern Europe and needing the winter sun to flourish, fresh leaves of chervil were used by the Romans. Chervil continues to be popular in France and Germany as a flavoring for soups, stews, and eggs, often in conjunction with other fresh herbs such as parsley and tarragon. The leaves also appear in the delicious little salads of semi-wild greens at which the French are so adept.

CORIANDER (*Coriandrum sativum*): A pink-flowered native of southern Europe, coriander is used either as dried seeds (the fresh ones have an unpleasant taste rather like the smell of crushed bugs), or fresh in the form of its pungent parsleylike leaves. Another of the most ancient and widespread culinary herbs, it has been employed since at least 5000 B.C., when it

THE CARROT OR UMBELLIFERAE FAMILY

1 Aniseed 2 Caraway 3 Chervil 4 Coriander 5 Cumin 6 Dill 7 Fennel 8 Parsley

appears in Egyptian and Sanskrit records. The seeds are also mentioned in the Old Testament as comparable to manna. Today it is come across most often in Europe in southern Mediterranean recipes. The herb is also used extensively in India and China, and is frequently known by the name "Chinese parsley." Coriander was successfully transplanted to the New World, where the fresh leaves and the seeds alike are now a dominant flavoring in Mexican and South American dishes. The seed is good in soups and stews.

Chinese parsley, as the leaves of coriander, *Coriandrum sativum*, are sometimes called, is rarely seen in its fresh form in the native European kitchen. It is found in Portugal, whose sailors acquired the taste for the fresh leaves from their trade with the Far East. I have also come across the fresh herb used as part of the marinade for *pinchitos* in Moorish Spain. Cypriot cooks also make use of it. The strong aroma of the fresh leaves reminds some people (including me, and I am very fond of the herb) of squashed beetle, and it is not universally appreciated—the name "coriander" derives from the Greek word for bedbug. The mild seeds have been widely used as a spice all over Europe since antiquity, particularly in pickling and preserving mixtures.

CUMIN *(Cuminum cyminum)*: A native of Egypt, it is the dried fruit of the little annual pink-flowered herb which is used in cooking. Another ancient spice, mentioned in both the Old and New Testaments, cumin is much used in Moorish-influenced Spain and in Mediterranean Eastern Europe. In England it was an important item in the medieval spice chest.

DILL *(Anethum graveolens)*: A delicate feathery annual with a flavor much like caraway, dill's popular name derives from the Norse word *dilla*, to soothe. Dill was originally a native of southern Europe and was transplanted over the centuries to northern climes, where it has long been a great favorite and, in particular, a staple of the German and Scandinavian kitchens.

Fruit seeds and leaves are both used, particularly in the flavoring of pickles and the famous Scandinavian *gravlaks*, where it superceded the ancient flavoring of young pine needles. The seeds are widely employed in dried form to flavor cabbage, pork, and potato dishes.

SWEET FENNEL AND FLORENTINE FENNEL *(Foeniculum vulgare* and *F. vulgare dulce)*: The first is a tall, feathery annual native to southern Europe and today to be found growing on every roadside. The second is the annual variety and is grown for its juicy edible celerylike bulb, which is eaten raw in salads or cooked as for celery. Both types of fennel can be used as herbs, fresh or in the form of the dried fruit. The dried stems of the wild variety are gathered in France as an aromatic fuel over which to grill fish. In Spain the same dry branches are used as a flavoring for pickled green olives.

PARSLEY *(Petroselinum crispum* is the well-known curly-leafed variety, followed in popularity by the flat- or fern-leafed parsley, *Crispum filicinum)*: A biennial probably from Sardinia, many varieties of parsley are now cultivated. Grown as a medicinal plant by the Greeks, it is the most widely available herb in today's kitchen and much liked as decoration. The Greeks, from whose word meaning "rock celery" its name derives, used it to adorn their heroes of the Games. The plant was introduced, like so much else, to northern Europe by the Romans. Parsley had many virtues ascribed to it as a medicinal plant and was used to treat several diseases, in particular kidney and liver complaints. It is rich in vitamins, and a spoonful will make up for a deficiency in fresh vegetables. It is best used fresh, although it can be dried. Take care to pinch out the flowering stems if you want the plant to continue in leaf.

The Onion, or Liliaceae, Family

The family includes the genus *allium*, all of whose members (around ninety species in Europe) share a similar familiar pungent odor—many of the wild varieties were used as flavoring by the country people.

CHIVES *(Allium schoenoprasum):* This is a miniature onion which forms a compound bulb, each of which has a bud within it. It is the green shoots from these buds which are used as flavoring and decoration. Chive blossoms make a gorgeous garnish for salads.

GARLIC *(Allium sativum):* The bulb was cultivated at least as far back as the Greeks and Romans. When first harvested in the spring, the plant looks like a juicy white onion. It is not until it has been allowed to dry out (either in the cupboard or in the ground) that the seeds develop into garlic "cloves" by absorbing the moisture from the onionlike layers which enclose them. When the process is complete, which will take two to three weeks, the seed will have grown into a juicy fat clove, and the moisture-filled layers reduced to a fine white protective papery covering. Used in Mediterranean countries as a vegetable as well as a flavoring, garlic when cooked on gentle heat loses its ferocious strength.

LEEK *(Allium porrum):* A particularly hardy member of the family, leeks are usually employed as a vegetable. They can also substitute quite satisfactorily in any recipe which calls for either raw or cooked onion. The tender parts of the green tops finely sliced can replace chives as a garnish.

ONION *(Allium cepa):* In cultivation since preclassical times and used both as a vegetable and as a flavoring, the onion family has a chemical element in its composition which, when cooked, can become at least fifty times sweeter than granulated sugar. The sugar caramelizes on high heat, such as frying, and is very useful in giving color as well as flavoring to stews and sauces. Yellow onions are sweeter than white—and the big purple-tinged salad onions of the Mediterranean are the sweetest of all.

The Cabbage, or Cruciferae, Family

All the brassicas, including cabbage, cauliflower, turnip, rutabaga, and radish, belong to this family, which has the distinction of including no

THE ONION OR LILIACEAE FAMILY

1 Onion 2 Leek 3 Chive 4 Garlic 5 Shallot

members poisonous to humans. The family also includes such garden flowers as candytuft, alyssum, and wallflower—pretty cousins to the fierce horseradish.

HORSERADISH *(Amoracia rusticana):* A naturalized introduction from the East, horseradish now flourishes in the wild, particularly in waste places. A very popular and pungent seasoning in central Europe, Austria, and Germany, horseradish is at its best used fresh and grated on the diagonal to produce long, thin strips—particularly good when stirred into thick or whipped cream in company with its near relation, mustard. Horseradish secretes a volatile oil which is enough of an irritant to be poisonous to livestock. The American cultivated variety is *Amoracia lapa trifolia.*

MUSTARD *(Brassica alba):* A native of Europe and Asia, this is a very widespread plant. The flavor develops only when the seed is crushed and then wetted. Its name comes from the Latin *mustum,* grape juice, with which the Romans were wont to mix it into a paste. Its ancient use as a medicinal plant, in poultices, plasters, and baths, was based on its ability to irritate the skin and thus draw blood to the surface. *Brassica nigra,* the black-seeded one, is the primary American variety.

Miscellaneous Herbs and Spices

BAY LAUREL *(Laurus nobilis):* An evergreen native of Asia Minor now widely cultivated throughout Europe, the leaves of this tree are used both fresh and dried as a flavoring, particularly in many Mediterranean dishes. Wreaths of bay laurel were awarded as trophies in classical times—hence the modern use of the word "laureate." Too much can be poisonous.

CAPER SHRUB *(Capparis spinosa):* The flower buds, the tinier the better, of this native Mediterranean shrub are blanched and pickled in vinegar for use as a seasoning. In Britain, nasturtium buds are sometimes substituted.

CAPSICUM PEPPER (two main species: *Capsicum annuum* and the smaller, hotter *C. frutescens*): Two principal varieties of paprika are grown in Hungary today: those for drying and powdering, and those to be eaten fresh. "Green paprika" denotes the fresh vegetables known as green peppers (if it is red and ripe, it is called a "tomato paprika"). In both its forms it can be "hot" or mild. The hotness lies in the filaments which attach the seeds to the flesh.

The peppers for grinding were traditionally dried in the autumn sunshine, as they still are today in many country districts, hung in garlands under the eaves of the houses until they are so brittle they click and rustle in the breeze. Then they would be further dried in outdoor ovens. In the old days the peppers would be crushed to a fine powder by being trodden with bare feet over a huge sieve or stone mortar, much as grapes are trodden in a wine press. Later the millers of flour took over the job. Toward the end of the nineteenth century a milling device was invented which could leave out, or control the inclusion of, the "hot" element of the paprika, capsaicin, and produce the "noble sweet rose," mild paprika. Thirty years ago a new strain of *Capsicum annuum* was produced which is not naturally fiery, and which can be ground up, seeds, filaments, flesh, and all.

Six categories of varying fierceness are available from the paprika merchants of Budapest today, all ground from *Capsicum annuum var. lingum Szegedense.* They are *Kulonleges,* the most mild; *Edesnemes,* mild; *Feledes,* half mild; *Rozsa,* rose paprika, mild and sweet; and *Eros,* hot paprika. Buy paprika in small quantities and use quickly, while it still has good color.

Fresh ripe peppers contain up to six times as much vitamin C per drop of juice as lemons and oranges. They are also plentifully endowed with other good things, including vitamin A, the source of carotene—which makes flamingo feathers pink, shrimps blush scarlet, gives the carrot its orange hue, and enables good children who eat all their vegetables to see in the dark.

Paprika is considered a cure-all by the peasantry, who cultivate it tenderly and prepare it with immense care. It has come, in fact, to be accorded the same reverence in the European kitchen as it is given in its homeland of Central America. The most effective antidote to the cold winds of the Anatolian plain has long been a shot of brandy with a pinch of hot paprika. Chili paprika is even sometimes sprinkled on wounds to assist in the healing process.

Peppers contain, by weight, between six and nine times the amount of vitamin C found in tomatoes. Their pepperiness derives from the alkaloid capsaicin, which appears to encourage the secretion of gastric juices. It may also have an antibacterial effect. The Mexicans believe it essential to a healthy diet in their own country, where even the most resilient stomach is notoriously vulnerable—a chili a day keeps the doctor away.

The almost universal popularity of chili is a very odd phenomenon: It is now consumed by more people and in larger quantities than any other spice in history, and it has taken only four centuries to reach this preeminence. Recent research suggests that the roots of our passion may lie in the chili's capacity to trigger the body's warning signals. Reactions such as a running nose, watery eyes, and painful sensations in the mouth would normally tell a human not to eat a particular food. Yet this very warning of danger, albeit denied by the intellect, may well encourage the brain to manufacture endorphins, its own natural (and naturally addictive) opiates. Chili devotees may share that lust for excitement which bonds race-car drivers, mountaineers, and addicts of all dangerous sports.

CARDAMOM *(Elettaria cardamomum):* A native of India, it has long been a popular spice in Scandinavia, whose energetic maritime merchants kept her population supplied with such eastern flavorings. It is bought encased in its pod, and the seeds are taken out and crushed before use. Indian cooks roast them before adding them to curries. When buying, check the color of the pod—the paler the pod, the better the seeds. They last virtually forever.

PEPPER *(Piper nigrum):* Pepper, although a native of India, has been prized in Europe since pre-Roman times. It is the dried fruit of a vine. The black variety is picked unripe, and then fermented and dried in the sun. The white variety is produced by allowing the fruits to ripen to scarlet, soaking them in water to loosen the skins, which are rubbed off, then drying the seeds. Pepper, which has the added virtue of keeping virtually forever, accounts for one quarter of the world's spice trade.

POPPY *(Papaver rhoeas):* The corn poppy was originally a native of Asia, but is so ancient and accustomed an immigrant in Europe that it grows wild everywhere. Its seeds are used in cakes and pastries and sprinkled whole on breads and rolls, particularly in Eastern Europe, where tall mounds of the slate-blue seeds are to be seen on sale in all the autumn markets. The seeds are rich in minerals and, pounded into a paste with eggs and sugar, make a delicious filling for strudel pastries and dumplings. They are also ground down into flour and used, mixed with eggs, to make a nourishing wheat-free and fat-free cake. Today, Holland, gardener to Europe, is the major exporter.

SAFFRON *(Crocus sativus):* A native of Asia Minor, saffron has been used certainly since Old Testament days as a dye, food colorant, and medicine. Today it is still widely employed in Mediterranean cooking, particularly with rice. Since 13,000 stigmas go to make an ounce of saffron, and each crocus can produce only 3 stigmas, the spice, wherever labor is the chief cost, is very expensive indeed and turmeric often replaces it (under the name "Indian saffron" or, as I saw it recently in Istanbul's spice market, made from marigold petals and labeled "Mexican saffron"). Saffron was very popular in medieval England, where the aristocracy had a passion for highly colored food. Great fields of *Crocus sativus* blossomed annually, particularly in East Anglia around the eponymous town of Saffron Walden. In Britain it survives in a cake, and sometimes in recipes for sweet buns. In France it is used to color and spice fish soups, including the famous *bouillabaisse*.

◆

MUSHROOMS AND FUNGI

Not all of Europe makes use of its cornucopia of edible fungi. The British are somewhat suspicious of all but the common field mushroom (the variety which is now cultivated). The French, on the other hand, consume a wide variety of theirs, as do the Italians and the Swiss. Yet the real European experts are to be found in the markets of Eastern Europe. A shopping trip for edible fungi on sale by licensed vendors in the markets of Rumania and Hungary during the autumn of 1985 yielded the following varieties. All those I have listed are native throughout Europe, including the British Isles.

Take great care when collecting your own. As a general rule, gather only the ones which are familiar to you. Use a good field guide to make a preliminary identification of new species, but always double-check by taking expert advice before you add them to your basket. The variations caused by sun, rain, temperature, and age can be so wide that the best color photograph— let alone the usually more accurate painting—is often misleading. The penalties for mistakes can be very heavy. Markets in mushroom-gathering areas, like Budapest's superb food market, normally have an expert on hand to check those which are offered for sale, and to give advice to the buyer. In France pharmacies are a common source of guidance during the mushroom-harvesting season.

CÈPE OR "PENNY BUN" *(Boletus edulis)*:* Superb. Mostly found in leafy woods, particularly beech. Looks like a shiny brown bun when damp, and has a diagnostic spongy yellow-ivory underneath. Found from late August to November.

CHANTERELLE *(Cantharellus cibarius)*:* Absolutely delicious. Beautiful apricot-yellow fungi which thrives, half-hidden in fallen leaves and moss, in thick skeins under frondose woods. To be found July to December.

FAIRY RING MUSHROOM *(Marasmium oreades)*:* Delicate small mushrooms which grow in a ring in short grass—particularly on garden lawns. Can be found from June to November.

FIELD MUSHROOM *(Agaricus campestris)*:* Very good eating, this is a close cousin of the original cultivated mushroom, *A. bisporus.** Found in pas-

1 **Agaricus**   2 Boletus   3 Armillaria   4 Cantharellus   5 Craterellus   6 Flammulina
7 Lactarius   8 Lepiota   9 Tricholoma (Lepista)   10 Lycoperdon   11 Marasmium
12 Morchella 13 Pleurotus

tures and meadows away from trees August to November. Cultivated mushrooms are nearly the same.

GIANT PUFFBALL *(Lycoperdon giganteum):* A very large puffball (it can measure one foot in diameter) which makes good eating when young and white. When older, its insides disintegrate into dark powdery spores. Find it almost anywhere, in field, garden, or wood, from August to November.

HORN OF PLENTY *(Craterellus cornucopioides)*:* Excellent eating and dries particularly well. From the same family as the chanterelle whose habitat it shares. This very dark (near black) fungus particularly likes beechwoods. Can be found August to November.

MOREL *(Morchella esculenta)*:* To my mind, the most delicious morsel of all. This mushroom has a distinctive wrinkled dark cap attached to a pale stipe. Can be found all over the place, often as solitary specimens. It likes rich soil—meadows, hedgerows, and grassy banks. Its equally delicious cousin *M. vulgaris* grows in woods and gardens. To be gathered in the spring from March to May.

OYSTER FUNGUS *(Pleurotus ostreatus):* Excellent eating when young and tender, this fungus grows on decaying wood, particularly beech and sometimes conifers. It has pearly gills and a dark gray-blue cap—which makes it look rather like a smooth inverted oyster shell. Grows all year round.

PARASOL MUSHROOM *(Lepiota procera)*:* Excellent eating, this mushroom looks not unlike the cultivated field mushroom, but is taller, has a pronounced double ring around the stipe, and a darker shaggy cap and white gills. Find it at the edges and clearings of frondose woods July to November.

SAFFRON MILK CAP *(Lactarius deliciosus):* Good eating, although not quite as delicious as its name implies. The cap is a bright orange-brown, as are the stipes. It will weep orange tears, so wash its face well before cooking. Can be gathered in conifer woods from August to November.

WINTER FUNGUS *(Flammulina velutipes):* Good eating as long as you discard the stems, which are tough. This may explain why they can survive the winter cold and so are available when supplies of the others have finished. With pale-yellow gills, and a sticky-looking red-brown cap, winter fungus grows in clumps on the stumps of frondose trees. To be found from September to March.

WOOD BLUETT *(Tricholoma nuda):* Both wonderful eating and beautiful to see, this mushroom is tinted a delicate violet. Grows in woods and gardens. Gather from late September to the end of December.

Many of these fungi are also native to North America. Species recommended for gathering in the pastures and woods of the United States by Waverly Root in his encyclopedic *Food* (published by Simon and Schuster, 1980) include the oyster mushroom, *Pleurotus ostreatus;* the beefsteak mushroom, *Fistulina hepatica;* and the Japanese favorite, *matustake,* or pine mushroom, *Armilleria ponderosa,* common in the Pacific Northwest. Others include the giant puffball, the chanterelle, and the horn-of-plenty. A fine wild harvest is available to the knowledgeable American citizen, without setting foot outside his native land.

NOTE: The fungi in the foregoing section marked with an asterisk can be dried successfully. Two ounces of dried mushrooms replaces 1 pound of fresh ones.

Any fungi at all in a wood or a field usually means there's an edible variety around. Pick all mushrooms gently by twisting them loose from their base, like picking an apple from a branch. The fungus plant they grow from—the mycelium, a network of fine threads spreading from the base—can then remain to fruit again.

Wild mushrooms have a remarkable knack of growing a crop of all-devouring grubs if left lying around for a day or two, particularly in a plastic bag in August. Pick them on a dry day and choose only the most perfect, large and maggot free, specimens for drying. Trim, wipe, and brush off the grit from the smaller species, such as chanterelles and morels, which can be dried whole. In the case of *Boletus*, wipe the caps and cut off the stalks; commercial driers pull off the spongy pores underneath—they will come off quite easily. This is, as far as I can gather, done for aesthetic reasons: I leave the sponge on; they dry perfectly well and none of the precious meat is thrown away. Cut the caps into slices. Either thread the fungi, whole or sliced, onto strong thread and hang the strings in an airing cupboard or in a warm current of air to dry thoroughly, or spread them on newspaper and leave them in the lowest possible oven to dry. When they are quite shrunk and brittle, store them in brown paper bags in a dry cupboard until you need them.

To reconstitute, soak them in a little warm water for 20 minutes or so, before using both the fungi and the soaking liquid in recipes for soups, sauces, or stews.

Truffles

There are three edible and esteemed European truffles. These tubers are more localized in their distribution than other fungi.

The Périgord truffle, *Tuber melanosporum*, is the true and legendary black truffle, whose price approaches its weight in gold. The canned version is as ghostly an echo of the fresh tuber as the tinned mushroom of its alter ego plucked fresh and scented from the field in the morning dew. There is no help for it—if you want to taste the true flavor, you will have to find yourself an accommodating pig or a well-trained truffle hound and search out your own in the oak woods of southern France, an activity which would almost certainly bring you into violent conflict with rival hunter-gatherers.

The estimable M. Farnoux, hereditary oil presser to the Provençal village of Mirabelle-aux-Baronnies and in whose olive mill I have often been a guest, told me that he collected baskets of Périgord truffles as a child in the 1940s. Not to sell, you understand. The family ate the treasure themselves, it being wartime in occupied France, and such isolated communities had to survive on minimal imported provisions. He faced no problems with oak trees and truffle hounds: He had but to walk down the avenue of limes that skirted the olive tree plantations which led from the village to the neighboring manse. There, when his sharp child's eyes spotted a little mound of cracked earth by the tree roots, he would stop. If the mounds had a few little flies attending them, that was the place to dig for the truffle. It would take only a morning for him and his brother to fill their basket. (At today's prices they would swiftly have become Provence's youngest millionaires.)

No fancy cooking was necessary, M. Farnoux explained. You had only to roll the truffles, the earth still fresh upon them, into the glowing embers of the wood fire. There they would roast to perfection and need no dressing but a sprinkle of salt. The problem, of course, in those days, he added, was not how to find the black gold—it was how to get the wherewithal to bake a loaf of bread to go with the truffles.

To cook a Périgord truffle—if you are fortunate, knowledgeable, or rich enough for one to come your way—clean off the earth with a little brush, wipe the truffle, then chop it and scramble it delicately with fine fresh eggs from your own or your neighbors' hens—that is, free-range hens of good pedigree whose eggs have been laid in a country garden. (There is no false mystique about eggs from free-range chickens. Like the grapes of the vine—as every experienced wine taster knows—eggs pick up the flavors, colors, and scents of the surroundings which produce them.)

Or leave the truffle in the egg basket overnight to perfume the eggs. Then soft-cook the eggs, slice the raw truffle on the cucumber slicer of the grater, and serve the two together with your best fresh bread.

The creamy-pale Piedmont truffle, *Tuber magnatum*, whose flavor is second only to the black gold of Périgord, should be eaten as nearly raw as possible. Brush off the earth, and then wipe the beech-leaf-brown nugget clean with a damp cloth. The truffle does not need to be peeled. Scatter a careless magnificence of fine slivers over homemade pasta or a dish of Italian rice (page 136), or—best of all—a *fonduta* (page 208). The truffle season opens in September, and by mid-October it is in full swing. November is the best month of all—by January it is all over.

The cook's truffle, *Tuber aestivum*, which is found in calcareous soil, usually under beech trees, is the most common species and the variety native to the British Isles. Although it is not as highly esteemed as the others, the seventeenth-century diarist and epicure, John Evelyn, speaks of it warmly and lists Northamptonshire as fertile soil for truffle hounds. This truffle is to be cooked in any way suitable for ordinary mushrooms.

The *tuber* family is widespread, and there are, says Waverley Root, around thirty members in the United States—none of them particularly good to eat.

OILS

The oils used all over Europe in the peasant kitchen were dictated by climate. They are useful both as a frying medium and as an enrichment of grain-based foods such as pasta and bread. The most important, valued, and ancient of the oils of Europe is that pressed from the fruit of the olive tree. In the north, melted butter or lard was for centuries the most available frying fat. These have largely been replaced in the modern kitchen by lighter vegetable oils—at least for deep-frying.

CORN OIL: This is the staple oil of northern Europe and an introduction from the New World. Good for frying although rather strong flavored. Somewhat heavy on salads.

NUT OILS: Almond oil is produced mainly in Italy and used in sweet making. Walnut and hazelnut are very delicately flavored oils produced in the central districts of France, usually above the olive-growing line, and used today mainly as salad dressings. In those districts such as Berry in central France, where nut oils were locally produced, they were used for both cooking and industrial purposes. Cover and refrigerate once opened— these delicious oils do not stay fresh for long.

OLIVE OIL: In Tuscany and Provence olives are harvested when almost ripe, throughout November and December. They are taken to be ground (whole—pits and all) into a paste at the local press. Oil is then extracted by centrifugal force to give "first-pressing, cold-pressed" oil. The rest of the pulp is then often sold to a factory, which processes it with heat, giving a more fatty oil with a higher acidity, called the "second pressing." This oil goes rancid more quickly when exposed to air. The old unmechanized mills had no facilities for this, and would use the olive pulp as fertilizer or fuel.

Gradings of Italian olive oils are defined by law. The best oil is classified as extra virgin and must be below 1 percent acidity. Second is soprafino virgin, which is allowed up to 1.5 percent acidity. Next is fine virgin—below 3 percent. Last is virgin, which can have up to 4 percent. These oils can be either cold pressed or hot pressed, and factory rectified.

Olives ripen from green to black, and the first oil of the year is always greener than the last-harvested because the early oil has more vegetable matter which has not had time to settle. If you want to use up this delicious *fondo*, give the bottle a shake before you pour the oil. Olives are still largely picked by hand—there being no machinery which can cope with the eccentricities of the trees and the crop. Olive oil will keep for many years if sealed in a container of glass, steel, or tin—plastic is no good for long storage—and kept in a cool, dark larder. It is best in the first year, and at its healthiest when eaten uncooked, being rich in vitamins A, D, and F, low in saturated fats, and high in unsaturated. It has recently been found to have a beneficial effect on cholesterol levels. Many of the recipes of the eastern Mediterranean use olive oil more as a rich juice than as a frying medium.

The olives and oils of different Mediterranean countries are harvested and prepared according to ancient traditions. The Italians make a range of individual *mis en bouteille au château* oils, with more leaf, late- or early-picked olives, and many other factors to differentiate appearance and flavor, specialities which reflect the ancient independence of the Italian farmer. French olive oil is generally of a very high quality, but tends to owe allegiance to cooperative and district rather than individual growers. Spanish olives are of a harder soil and a poorer peasantry who often were obliged to sharecrop and turn in their fruits to a central buyer. The Portuguese like their olive oil stronger than the rest of Europe and allow the fruit to ferment (a matter of hours) before pressing.

Reseal olive oil carefully after opening, and do not leave it too long before using it up. All fruit juices, and olive oil is exactly that, deteriorate on exposure to air. Small containers are more convenient for this reason—although those sweet little jars or pitchers which have no seals should be avoided, as they will not preserve the oil.

POPPYSEED OIL: This oil is much used in Eastern Europe, where poppyseeds are used in cooking and flavoring. A good salad and cooking oil.

RAPESEED OIL: This oil comes from various members of the colza or rape plant, a member of the cabbage family. The familiar sunshine-yellow plants of *Brassica napus* spread bright sheets of color across the fields of Europe.

SUNFLOWER OIL: The favorite oil of Rumania and Bulgaria, this oil is made from the seeds of the beautiful giant sunflower. An excellent all-purpose oil.

◆

STOREHOUSE CHEESES

Cheese is one of the great staples of European peasant larders. It has the advantage of being easily made and stored—needing nothing but ingredients easily on hand in any peasant community. Curd-making agents vary from the preparations, simple or complex, which take advantage of the natural curdling enzyme, rennet, which is present in the digestive lining of dairy animals, to infusions of plants such as butterwort.

Cheeses Used Frequently in Cooking

BEL PAESE (ITALY): A modern commercially prepared cheese first marketed in the 1920s, this cheese is white and mild, melts smoothly, and is used in cooking as a substitute for mozzarella.

CAERPHILLY (WALES): A crumbly white cheese, matured for only three weeks. Known as the most digestible of cheeses, it is difficult to grate but melts well.

CANTAL AND LA FOURME DE CANTAL (FRANCE): A cow's milk cheese, first made in Roman times, from the mountains behind Marseilles. A good matured cheese for melting, somewhere between a Cheddar and a Gruyère.

CHEDDAR (ENGLAND): A matured Cheddar made from unpasteurized milk is one of the finest cheeses for cooking available anywhere. It is elastic enough to be easily grated and melts down beautifully. Farmhouse Cheddar is still made in many dairies, particularly in the neighborhood of Wells in Somerset.

CHESHIRE (ENGLAND): Probably the most ancient cheese made in Britain. Its crumbly quality makes it difficult to grate, but it melts well and can be used in cooking to good effect.

DUNLOP (SCOTLAND): The Scottish variety of Cheddar, which it closely resembles and for which it can substitute in cooking. A very good cheese for melting.

EDAM (HOLLAND): The familiar round ball of cheese encased in red wax. Its imitators are many. A bland cheese, a little soft for grating, but nonetheless a very popular cooking cheese.

EMMENTHALER (SWITZERLAND): One of Switzerland's two great cheeses for melting, this is the one with the holes (the bacteria *Propionibacterim stermanii* is responsible for them). Made in huge wheels, which weigh at least 145 pounds, in the valley of Emmenthal in the canton of Bern, and known since the sixteenth century. It grates superbly, and melts in characteristic long strings.

FETA (GREECE): A soft, salty, strong-flavored cheese, white and crumbly, much used in salads in Greece and the Balkans. Originally made by shepherds from sheep's milk.

FONTINA (ITALY): The cheese from the Val d'Aosta which is used to make a *fonduta*. A very good cheese for melting, which can substitute for Gruyère. The Danish version does not yet match up to the real thing.

GEITOST (NORWAY): The dark brown *geitost* is made from the whey remaining from the common cheese, boiled until the water is evaporated and then shaped into square cakes weighing from two to five pounds.

    Geitost is sold in square bricks and can only be sliced effectively with a Scandinavian cheese slicer—a spatula-shaped instrument with a sharp blade embedded in the middle. *Geitost* melts smoothly and is sometimes eaten thus with *lompe* or *lefse*, one of Norway's soft unleavened pancake-breads.

GRUYÈRE (SWITZERLAND): The second of the two great Swiss cheeses for melting, this is a cow's milk cheese which dates from the eighteenth century. It is made in a smaller wheel (weight only around 80 pounds), has only a few small holes, and has a higher fat content than the Emmenthaler. The best Swiss fondue is made with a mixture of these two cheeses. Both melt in characteristic long strings.

KEFALOTIRI (GREECE): The Greek cheese most used for grating and cooking. A hard, strong, well-flavored goat's milk cheese. Used as a seasoning as much as a food, it is sprinkled on salads, on grilled meat, on rice, and even over a plate of fried potatoes. One of the cheeses, from a group which includes Raclette, Caerphilly, and Cheddar, which are used for roasting.

LAGUIOLE (FRANCE): Made near Bordeaux and belonging to the Gruyère-Cantal family, this is excellent for melting.

MANCHEGO (SPAIN): A hard, salty matured cheese, not unlike a pale Cheddar, with a straw-patterned dark rind. It grates well and cooks tolerably. A shepherd's cheese made with sheep's milk from the central plateau of La Mancha—from where comes its name.

MOZZARELLA (ITALY): The true mozzarella is made from buffalo milk and for cooking is usually used fresh. It is also eaten when dry and matured. This cheese cooks in an interesting fashion: It melts into a delicious rubbery sauce which pulls into characteristic long strings. It provides the best topping for pizzas.

PARMESAN (ITALY): The Italian's favorite cheese for grating, Parmesan is used as an important flavoring agent as well as a food. This universally popular pungent hard cheese is supposed to have originated in the environs of Parma. The large wheels are coated with lampblack and burned umber mixed with wine when it is six months old. After that, the older it is, the better, within reason. *Vecchio* (old) has had two years to come to maturity. *Stravecchio* (extra old) is fully three years old. The oldest is *Stravecchione*, which takes four years before it is ready. Authentic Parmesan has "Parmigiano—Reggiano" tattooed on its rind in small dots.

PECORINO (ITALY): Made from ewe's milk, this cheese is used for grating when it is matured. Often employed instead of Parmesan.

VALAIS RACLETTE (SWITZERLAND): This cheese, made only in the canton of Valais, is used for toasting as *raclette*. A large piece of cheese is speared on a knife and held over an open fire (special little single-bar fires now substitute for this in restaurants), and the crisp sizzling crust is sliced straight onto freshly toasted bread. Eat immediately, of course, with good white wine from neighboring Neuchâtel.

RONCAL (SPAIN): A hard cheese matured and used for grating and cooking. Made in the northern province of Navarre from cow's milk.

RICOTTA (ITALY): A whey cheese which can be eaten as wet white curds, not unlike cottage cheese, or dry, in which case it can be grated like Parmesan. Particularly used when fresh mixed with chopped spinach as a stuffing for pasta, and to make a delicious cheesecake for special occasions. Sometimes taken stirred into strong black coffee.

SARDO (ITALY): The Sardinian version of Pecorino. Now made with ewe's and cow's milk mixed.

PRESERVED MEATS

The autumn pig slaughter was until recently the most important gastronomic event on the European peasant calendar. All over Europe it was a near-ceremonial occasion for those rural households who depended on its products to add flavor and protein to an otherwise somewhat dreary winter diet. The ritual has always fascinated outside observers. Traveling through Rumania toward the end of the nineteenth century, author Theresa Stratilesco observed:

> Even before the beginning of Advent, a pig has been put apart in a cotet, a little pig-sty of his own to fatten . . . The Ignat (the feast of St. Ignacius on 20th Dec) comes at last; the day of reckoning has come; from the early morning you may see the smoke ascending the sky, with its shadow capriciously stretched across the snow-coated hill. Under the burnt-out straw, thrown aside with the iron fork, the pig is discovered in his hard skin, turned ivory after some rubbing and scrubbing, whereupon the cutting out begins. The joints for ham, the sides for the bacon, are carried up to the loft for smoke; the rest of the meat being mostly used for the filling of the traditional *carnati* and *chiste*, the former being the thin ones, filled mostly with meat, the latter, the wider ones, filled with *passat*, the national rice, the seed of the millet. And on a Christmas day there is no peasant table on which the roasted *carnati* will not be grilling in their own fat, beside a golden smoking *mamaliguta* . . . The beggars and gypsies will get their share. [*From Carpathian to Pundus*, Theresa Stratilesco, 1906]

María Avila, farmer's wife from the village of Tajo in Andalusia, recalled for Ronald Fraser in 1958:

> I got married in 1924 . . . My husband's farm was good and he worked hard. So did I. We were able to eat a bit better than most, we had fish more often and every year we killed a pig. From that I cured a couple of legs of serrano ham, made sausages, mortadello, black puddings. When you slaughtered a pig it smelled good for a mile around, not like today when pigs are fattened on artificial foods and garbage and stuff of that sort. Then they were fattened on figs, sweet potatoes, groundnuts, green stuff, and they tasted delicious. [*The Pueblo*, Ronald Fraser, 1973]

Paul du Chaillu remembers the occasion in Norway in 1872:

> With the month of October comes the slaughtering time. The housewife then has a great deal to do in preparing sausages and bacon to last until the following autumn. Meat has to be salted, dried, or smoked. Molja, made of blood mixed with flour, is put up in large quantities, preserved in bladders or cakes; when used it is either boiled or fried. [*The Land of the Midnight Sun*, Paul du Chaillu, 1881]

The most developed repertoires of preserved pork-butchery belong to France, Germany, Italy, and Spain. I include here a brief summary of the most important items in their winter larders. Climate plays a considerable part in the matter—Nordic countries could rely on natural refrigeration to preserve their stores, whereas those with damp or warm climates had to make other arrangements.

Charcuterie

ANDOUILLE: Salted and often smoked as well as precooked sausages. Made from the large intestine and tripe of a pig. Usually sliced and eaten cold.

ANDOUILLETTE: Small precooked sausages made from tripe. Can be split and grilled or fried. Very good slashed and grilled, and served with mustard and creamy mashed potatoes.

BOUDIN BLANC: White puddings, precooked, made with minced chicken, pork, cream, and eggs. Very delicate and delicious. Prick them, baste them with butter, and grill them gently. Serve with a purée of potatoes and celeriac.

BOUDIN NOIR: Black puddings, precooked. Made with blood and pork fat, onions and cream. Cut the *boudin* into lengths and fry them gently in butter. Cook peeled and quartered apples in the pan afterwards, and serve all together.

CERVELAS: Large precooked sausage for boiling. Often smoked. Made with minced pork and beef and flavored with garlic. Nicest if reheated by simmering in red wine. Serve with cabbage or sauerkraut or a hot potato salad. Can be served cold.

CREPINETTE: Fresh sausage mixture wrapped in a caul. Sold raw or cooked for immediate consumption. Bake, fry, or grill.

JAMBON DE BAYONNE: Salted, dried and smoked ham. Eaten as it is. Also used chopped and in small quantites, to give a wonderful distinctive flavor to local dishes. Prepared as the Spanish *jamón serrano* and the Italian *prosciutto*, with the addition of a short smoking.

JAMBON DE PARIS: Salted, if smoked, only very lightly so, and then cooked before sale.

JAMBON DE TOULOUSE: Ham, salted and dried. Uncooked and eaten uncooked, often with a pat of fresh butter. Also used to flavor stews and soups. Prepared as the Spanish *jamón serrano* and the Italian *prosciutto*.

PETIT SALÉ: Pork belly salted, with juniper, peppercorns, bay leaf, and other spices in the cure. Cooked with cabbage, and used in many soups and dried-bean dishes. The favorite larder staple of the French country wife.

RILLETTE: Potted meat. Pork belly cooked so long and so gently that it disintegrates into shreds, then spiced and packed into pots for storage. Eaten cold on bread.

RILLON: Large slabs of *rillette* mixture.

SAUCISSE DE TOULOUSE: A fresh all-meat sausage made with chopped pork—more rough textured than the usual sausage. Sold uncooked. This is the sausage used in the *cassoulet* (page 116). Use proportions of three to one lean pork to hard fatback, season with salt, pepper, and a pinch of saltpeter, and proceed as for the English pork sausages (page 330).

SAUCISSON SEC: A wide variety of regional dried salami-type sausages.

Italian Prosciutto and Salami

BUDINO: Italian blood sausage. There is a semisweet Tuscan variety called *sanguinaccio*, which is mixed with bread crumbs, pine kernels, raisins, and candied fruit, and flavored with cinnamon, coriander, and nutmeg. This is stuffed into a large intestine, tied up, and then boiled for half an hour before storage. It is eaten sliced and fried, or with beaten eggs poured around it in the pan to make an Italian *frittata*, or flat omelet.

COTECHINO: A boiling sausage. Made by stuffing a sewn-up roll of pork skin with spiced chopped meat—a mixture of pork and beef is common. Many Italian delicatessens sell *cotechino*. Cook the sausage whole, pricking it well all over. Bring it to a boil in plenty of cold water. Simmer for 2 hours per 1 pound of sausage. Use the broth to cook 1 pound of lentils for each 4 diners, or serve with mashed potatoes moistened with some of the broth. Serve the sausage cut into slices and placed on top of the lentils or potatoes. The skin is not eaten, but imparts to the broth a strong, delicious fragrance—it can then be used as a basis for good vegetable soups and stews.

PANCETTA: Salted belly of pork, rolled and dried as for *prosciutto*. Used in the same recipes and in much the same way, *pancetta* has a similar flavor, but more fat.

PROSCIUTTO COTO: Italian cooked ham, preserved in brine, and then boiled when needed.

PROSCIUTTO CRUDO: Raw ham, salted and dried for winter stores. Pickled in salt and sometimes garlic for a month, and then hung to dry in a current of air until the brine no longer drips. Then rubbed with pepper and hung in the larder for cutting into slices to eat raw, or cubed for cooking. A staple of the peasant winter larder. Smoked ham is the nearest equivalent—cooked ham does not get anywhere near the correct texture and flavor.

SALAMI: There are many different variations on this well-known spiced and dried pork-and-beef sausage. The mixture is stuffed into the larger intestines of cows rather than pigs. Flavorings vary: salt and pepper always; red or white wine and garlic are usually included; others might be chili pepper and paprika and fennel. The Milan salami has fine-ground meat and fat, which gives a smooth pink sausage; the Tuscans like theirs coarser chopped—with the meat dark red and the fat in snowy lumps, the whole dotted with black peppercorns. All Italy has its own particular preferences.

SALSICCIA: Fresh pork sausages, often flavored with garlic, salt, and black
pepper, and sometimes marjoram, oregano, or some other aromatic herbs.
Can be packed into jars and covered with oil for storage, or eaten fresh,
fried, or grilled crisp.

ZAMPONE: A boiling sausage made with the same stuffing as the *cotechino*, but
stuffed into an empty pig's foreleg complete with trotter. Use as *cotechino*—
the inclusion of the trotter gives a particularly good broth.

Wurst

"*Weck, Wurst und Wein*" load the German peasant farmer's board, and he
has always expected to partake heartily and well of all three. A jug of his own
excellent wine, a thick slice of black bread—country bread, rich and dark and
heavy with rye—keeps comfortable company with the best sausages in the
world. A good helping of mild German mustard, a grating of fresh horseradish, and a dish of sauerkraut or pickled vegetables completes his meal. Schnapps
is the preferred short drink—washed down with a stein or two of magnificent
German beer.

BRATWURST: The basic German sausage is made of finely minced pork flavored
with herbs—usually a mixture of thyme, rosemary, and sage. It is an
all-meat sausage made without bread or rusk, designed to be eaten fresh,
fried in lard or butter.

3	*pounds lean pork (leg or shoulder)*	3	*tablespoons pepper*
1	*pound fatback*	4	*tablespoons chopped herbs: rosemary, thyme, sage*
2	*tablespoons salt*		

You will need a meat mincer or a food processor. Mince all together very fine,
putting the meat through the mincer twice. Stuff the mixture into well-
washed intestines—a butcher who makes his own sausages will be able to sell
you a hank of these, usually preserved in a great deal of salt, so they will need
to be soaked. Failing the casing, the *Bratwurst* meat can be rolled into short
cylinders, lightly floured, and then fried. When working with sausage mixtures, have a basin of cold water beside you so that you can rinse your hands
frequently—this prevents the fat from sticking to your fingers and making you
clumsy.

FRANKFURTER BRATWURST: A smoked sausage for storing. The same composition as the *Bratwurst* sausage, flavored with salt, pepper, coriander seeds,
and nutmeg, the whole moistened with red wine (hence the rose color).
The sausages are smoked to preserve them. To finish, bring them to a boil
in a pan of boiling water, and then turn the heat down and simmer them

gently for five minutes. If you boil them too fiercely, they will split. Frankfurters are very good served with sauerkraut, accompanied by potatoes plain boiled with salt. Or with good black bread, plenty of mild German mustard, and a little pile of freshly grated horseradish.

LEBERWURST: Liver sausage to be eaten cold. Made with pig's liver thoroughly minced with pork fat in proportions of three to one. The mixture is seasoned with salt, pepper, and allspice, and cooked before storage. If you wish to make it yourself and have no sausage casing, bake it in a terrine with foil on the top. Excellent as a simple hors d'oeuvre or picnic dish served with unsalted butter, black rye bread, and radishes. Wash it all down with beer.

RINDFLEISCHWURST: A fresh sausage to be served fried. The meat is beef minced with pork fat, and flavored with garlic and cloves. A little saltpeter is included with the salt. Sometimes called summer sausage, since it lasts longer in warm weather than the pork-based version. Can be smoked and given a preliminary cooking before storage.

SCHWARZWURST: Black sausage, made with pig's blood, cooked to be stored. Fried and eaten hot. An awkward dish to prepare at home unless you slaughter your own pig. All German peasant farmers, in common with most of the old peasant communities, would have kept a couple of pigs for the winter larder. Fed on household scraps such as vegetable peelings and leftovers and stale bread, the omnivorous hogs would be fattened all year for the November pig slaughter. The blood from the neck artery, severed when the animal is killed, must be caught in a pail and stirred so that it does not coagulate before it cools (this is usually the housewife's job). Then the dark-red liquid is thickened with bread crumbs and a small proportion of chopped pork and pork fat. The flavoring is garlic and cloves. The mixture is then stuffed into well-washed intestines, and the sausages are boiled and stored. To serve, cut it into lengths, and fry in butter or lard in company with slices of apples and onions. Accompany with beer or milk curds to wash it down—and a clean napkin tucked under your chin to give you courage. A section of the blood sausage can be poached in a thick vegetable soup to give substance to a main-meal soup-stew.

Spanish Embutidos

BUTIFARRA: A Catalan sausage made from lean and fat pork, chopped together and seasoned with garlic and oregano, cloves, cinnamon, and hot pepper (cayenne). The nearest to the uncooked British banger.

CHORIZO: Chopped pork, equal quantities of fat and lean, flavored with garlic, oregano, and a little chili pepper, and colored with paprika and red wine. Coriander and cumin are also sometimes included. Peasant households prepare their own at the autumn *matanza*, or slaughter. This sausage is sold both dried and fresh for use fried or in stews, where it is an essential flavoring. Saltpeter is included in small quantities in all these pork preparations.

LONGANIZA: My own favorite Spanish sausage, this looks like a long loop of *chorizo* and is made with lean pork flavored with paprika, usually rosemary, and pepper. It is excellent fried with eggs or used in any recipe which needs *chorizo*. It can easily be prepared at home. Fill sausage skins with 1 pound of minced pork mixed with 2 teaspoons of salt, 1 level teaspoon of chopped and pounded rosemary, 2 teaspoons of paprika, a pinch of saltpeter, and a teaspoon of freshly ground pepper. Tie the sausage in a loop and hang it in a dry draft for a day. Keep in the refrigerator.

MORCILLA: The Spanish black pudding, made with fresh pig's blood and chopped pork fat, flavored with paprika (named, in Spain, *pimentón*), salt, and pepper. In rice-growing areas, cooked rice is often included. The casing can be the long, thin intestines, washed thoroughly in running water, or the mixture can be packed into the large intestine to make a single large fat sausage. To be cooked on the day it is made until, as the country people say, it "sings"—that is, the little holes in the intestines expand in the heat and breathe out a faint whistle. To be eaten cold in slices with bread, or fried, or included in a bean stew.

SALCHICHA: Fresh sausage made with minced fresh pork, both fat and lean, lightly spiced with salt, pepper, and paprika. Eaten fresh, fried crisp.

SOBREASADA: A Mallorcan-originated mixture of *chorizo* pounded with chopped fresh pork fat, used as a spread on bread—can be grilled.

◆

PRESERVED PORK

Carne en manteca (Spain)

A product of the autumn *matanza*, or pig killing, this is the standard kitchen standby in rural districts. Town dwellers buy it from the pig-products stall in the market, where the meat preserved in it is often short lengths of *chorizo*. Both the well-flavored lard and the meat itself are used to flavor stews. The bright-orange *manteca* ("butter," as the drippings are named) is often spread on a thick slice of fresh bread—bread-and-drippings—as a sturdy morning meal. The meat can be refried in its own fat and served with plenty of bread as an instant supper. It is a most useful larder item for those who cannot get Spanish *chorizo* and sausages, since it can substitute for them in any recipe, particularly in chick-pea and bean stews.

Y I E L D : Makes a small family's winter supply

T I M E : Start the day before; 1 hour

4	*small red pimento peppers or 2 extra tablespoons paprika*	2	*lemons*
6	*fat garlic cloves*	4	*pounds lean pork*
1	*tablespoon dried oregano or marjoram*	8	*pounds pork fat (kidney fat is best) or 4 pounds clarified lard*
2	*ounces (¼ cup) salt*	2	*tablespoons paprika (the sweet variety, not the hot)*
2	*tablespoons vinegar*		

You will need a pestle and mortar, a bowl, a deep frying pan, and an earthenware pot. Open the peppers and remove the seeds (they will be too fiery if included). Tear the shells of the peppers into small pieces, peel the garlic, and pound the peppers, garlic, oregano or marjoram, and salt together in a small wooden mortar or bowl. Mix the pounded spices with the vinegar. Cut the lemons into thick wedges.

Chop the pork into 1-inch cubes, put it into a roomy bowl, and turn it with the chopped lemons and the vinegar-and-spice mixture until well impregnated. Leave overnight to marinate.

The following morning cube the pork fat (called *pringue*, and sold in sheets in Spanish markets) and put it, adding a few pieces at a time, to render slowly in its own grease in a deep frying pan. Gently does it: The fat itself must not brown but remain pure white and clear. Remove and drain the crisp golden-fried solids. They make delicious little tidbits, lightly salted.

Meanwhile, brush the marinade off the cubed pork. Fry the pork gently in the rendered pork fat or clarified lard for 25 to 30 minutes. It should be very thoroughly cooked. At the end of the cooking time, when the meat is well browned, take the pan off the stove and stir in the paprika. Pour all, meat and bright-orange fat, into an earthenware pot and allow to cool.

Make sure all the pieces of meat are submerged, and store the pot in a cool place—the refrigerator is best of all. The pork will keep for a long time, although care must be taken, if you do keep it for more than a week or two, when you want to remove some of the meat, to melt all down so that the rest of the meat remains sealed.

SUGGESTION

Chorizos (the little red spiced dried sausages) are often prepared in this way for keeping.

SPANISH MOUNTAIN HAM

Jamón serrano (Spain)

The lean, red, half-wild pigs which forage for acorns in the cork-oak forests of Andalusia make the best dried hams. Those who live near the sea, where the breezes are damp with spray and the air is warm all year, send their pigs' haunches up into the sierras to be cured. The Spanish salt and dry their hams in the cold air of their high hills—they do not smoke them. The best hams are cured at Jabugo up in the Sierra Morena (*serrano* means "of the mountains"), which walls the west bank of the mighty river Guadalquivir. This is the river which rises in the foothills of the Sierra Nevada and waters all the rich *vega*, the plain of Andalusia. The salt flats of Cádiz provide plenty of good-quality salt, an important trade item of barter long before the Romans took advantage of the rich deposits.

In Jabugo there are commercial salters as well as the small private farm-house barns. Even the little sheds at the end of the village houses take in the hams of relations who live in less favorable climes. In the big salteries the haunches hang by the trotter in serried ranks. It takes between four and six months to cure them in the snow-cold air, and the price of patience is, as always, high. Up here the pigs glean beneath the chestnut trees as well as in the oak forest, and the best of all are the black pigs. There are long, low attics above the salting sheds where metal braziers glow scarlet on the endless loops of carmine sausages. The *chorizos*, paprika- and garlic-spiced sausages which are used extensively in many recipes, are sometimes very lightly smoked, although the ham is never submitted to heat of any kind.

Jamón serrano is not only appreciated as ham—to be cut into long, thin slices from the haunch as it hangs—but every bit of fat and bone has its recipe. As the ham dries out and less choice morsels are available, the cook will chop up the scraps and cook them with eggs, with vegetables, in soups, to give flavor to any and all dishes. The fat is carefully saved and used to enrich the *cocido* or bean stew. The bones are sawed into lengths and included in any dish which requires long, slow simmering. The Spanish cook needs her *jamón*, and until recently most rural households kept one or two pigs for the year's supply of products of the *matanza*. In urban communities, there is always at least one stall in the market which sells preserved pig products.

BACON AND HAM

(England)

In the days when each household had its pig, tradition dictated that the animal be killed when the moon had just begun to wane: not such an old wives' tale, since free-range pigs graze by moonlight, and therefore would be heavier after a week's feeding in the light of the full moon. The slow ritual process of countryside curing would then begin.

There are still old-fashioned firms who cure good York hams. These are brined, dried, and then aged in sawdust for three months (legend has it that the first sawdust to be used came from the oak beams which went into the building of one of the glories of medieval English church architecture, York Minster).

The York method is certainly very ancient: There is a Roman recipe, recorded in Italy in the second century B.C., which is very similar to the technique used today. In Britain the Romans would have had no difficulty with supplies of salt, the essential agent in the preserving process for hams and bacon, since the valuable commodity had been worked around the coasts from the Celtic Iron Age onwards.

DRY SALT CURE FOR A 14-POUND HAM

(England)

The same method of cure may be used for bacon. A leg of pork severed from the whole side is called a ham. When the leg is left attached to the side, and severed only after the cure, it is called a gammon.

TIME: 3 weeks plus

1	ham (English hams weigh roughly from 14 to 20 pounds)	½	ounce saltpeter (from the drugstore)
1	ounce brown sugar	2	pounds rough salt

You will need a salting pan. Leave the ham unskinned. Rub in the sugar and the saltpeter first, paying particular attention to the bone ends. Then rub on half the salt and put the ham to rest on slats in a salting trough (best if it has a channel for the brine to drain out). Rub in the rest of the salt at the end of a week. Leave the ham to take the salt for a total of 3 weeks (depending on the size of the ham), turning regularly. Then hang the ham to dry in a draft of warm air for a day or two. If you would like to smoke your own, follow the method given for smoking salmon (page 518). Twenty-four hours in the smoke should suffice for a ham; 6 hours is enough for a side of bacon. York hams are then hung to mature for 2 to 3 months in a temperature- and humidity-controlled room.

◆

HONEY CURE FOR HAM

(England)

T I M E : 1 month plus

1	*ham*	*1*	*ounce pepper*
1	*pound rough salt*	*1*	*pound honey*
½	*ounce saltpeter (from the drugstore)*		

You will need a salting pan. Rub the ham all over with the salt, saltpeter, and pepper. Put it in a salting pan. Turn and rub it well with the mixture every day for 4 days. Then pour the honey over the ham and rub it in. Rub the ham with the pickle twice a week for a month before you hang it up to dry.

◆

SALT-CURED LEG OF LAMB

Spekemat (Norway)

Mutton was the meat traditionally used for this storehouse staple. Failing a fine three-year-old wether, a leg of lamb will cure well enough in its place. The meat is chewy and well flavored, much like a dark-fleshed Parma or *serrano* ham. Its preparation was a job for the shepherd's wife during the short cold days of October and November, after the flocks had to be thinned out for the winter. *Spekemat* was expected to last through the winter and provide many a delicious meal into the following summer. At harvest time in particular it came into its own as a mainstay of the midday meal. If urgency to get the crops in required, it could be eaten on foot in the meadows, wrapped in a soft flat bread or *lefse* pancake.

Y I E L D : 4 to 5 pounds dried meat. Allow ¼ pound of dried meat per person

T I M E : Start 3 months before you need it; 20 minutes

3	*pounds salt*	*1*	*tablespoon sugar*
4	*quarts water (less if the leg is smaller)*	*8*	*pounds leg of lamb*

You will need a large saucepan and a large crock. Dissolve the salt in the water to make a brine. Add the sugar. Put the leg of lamb in a large crock and pour enough brine over it to cover it completely. Put a weight on top to keep it underwater. Leave to take the salt in a cool pantry (not below the freezing point, or the salting process comes to a halt) for 2 weeks for a leg weighing 8 pounds (roughly 2 days per pound of meat).

Take the leg out after the allotted time and rinse thoroughly so that you do not get too salty a rind. Hang it out to dry in a well-aired cool pantry, wrapped in a loose bag of cheesecloth or muslin to protect it from flies. It will be dry, delicious, and ready to eat in 2 to 3 months.

Serve, sliced very thin with a sharp knife, as part of an indoor picnic meal, with sweet butter, fresh hard-boiled eggs, a sliver of *geitost* (the Norwegian sweet brown cheese), and flat bread or potato pancakes to wrap around each morsel. A bowl of sour cream and some fresh raspberries can follow as a replacement for Norwegian cloudberries.

◆

SUGGESTION

Serve thin slivers as a first course with sweet butter, or with fresh pears or a juicy southern fig, as for Parma ham.

◆

SALT BEEF AND TONGUE

(England)

Brisket or flank steak is the best cut. Ox tongue goes in as it is, well wiped and trimmed. You will not be able to remove all the bits of bone and gristle from the tongue, or skin it, until it has been cooked. The saltpeter (much reduced in modern cures) acts as a preservative, and gives the meat its characteristic pinkish color.

4 quarts water	½ ounce saltpeter (if your
1 pound salt	drugstore doesn't have it, try
	a good butcher—you can pickle
	without it, but the meat will
	not turn its characteristic pink)
	1 beef brisket or flank steak,
	5 to 8 pounds
	1 ox tongue, trimmed

You will need a brining crock or a plastic bucket, and a saucepan. Scrub a brining crock or plastic bucket very thoroughly with baking soda and rinse it out with boiling water—at the same time sterilize a heavy plate in the same way.

Bring the water to a boil with the salt and the saltpeter, and then let it cool. Pack the meats to be salted in the tub or bucket and put the heavy plate on top. Cover all with the brine and cover the tub.

Ox tongue needs about 5 days in brine. A 5- to 8-pound piece of brisket should be in brine for 6 to 8 days before it is taken out to be cooked. If you wish to leave it longer, it will come to no harm.

◆

SUGGESTIONS

Brown sugar, juniper berries, peppercorns, bay leaf, and cloves are all excellent additions to the brine: Each household would take pride in its own mix. The brine would be topped off with salt and water, and go on from year to year: Once the brine is made and kept well topped off with salted water, it is as sterile as possible and much less likely to grow harmful bacteria than a new one. For a topping-off mix, make a double-strength solution to replace the salt absorbed by the joint you have removed: 2 cups of water to 4 ounces (½ cup) of salt. If white spots of mold appear on the surface, drain out the brine, rescrub and scald the container, and start again with the piece of meat and new brine.

Use the same brine mix to cure pork. A leg or shoulder, trotters, ears, tail, or head (without the brains) can all be pickled to advantage in a salt brine. The larger the piece, the longer salting it will need.

You can also brine meat which is to be roasted. An overnight sojourn in the brine tub will greatly improve its flavor.

◆

SALT PORK BELLY

Petit salé (France)

This is a most useful pantry item now that good store-bought bacon is so hard to come by. It can be kept for months in the salad compartment of the refrigerator and is ideal for soups, stews, and, cut into fine slivers, as a baster for roast meats. Mme. Escrieu, my neighbor in the Languedoc, salted the sides from her annual pig in this fashion, and used it in her fortnightly *cassoulet*. María, my neighbor in the Andalusian valley where I lived before moving to the Languedoc, did not include the aromatics: her pork for salting was simply buried in a heaped mound of salt from the Cádiz flats. She kept her salted meats all through the winter in a drawer in a cool corner of her little kitchen. She did not put in saltpeter, but she would usually include the pig's ear, tail, and trotters in the pile—a kind of culinary grab bag.

YIELD: 8 pounds salted meat

TIME: Start the week before; 30 minutes

8	pounds side of belly pork	4 to 5	bay leaves
1	tablespoon crushed peppercorns	2	pounds salt
1	tablespoon juniper berries	½	ounce saltpeter
1	small bunch of dried thyme		

You will need a pestle and mortar, a large salting tray or plastic container, a very clean board or plate, and a weight. Make sure the pork has not been frozen. Dry the meat thoroughly. Pound the peppercorns and the juniper berries together with the thyme and the bay leaves. Mix the aromatics with the salt and saltpeter (it helps preserve and turns the meat pink). Rub the salt vigorously but carefully into the skin side of the meat. Turn it over and rub salt into the flesh side. Reverse it again and rub more salt into the skin side. Put the meat on a layer of salt in the well-scrubbed and -scalded salting tray. Heap the rest of the salt around and above it. Weight it down with a well-scalded and -scrubbed board, with a 2-pound tin on top. These can be removed after 2 to 3 days.

Turn the meat in the salt every few days. Leave in a cool place and it will be ready to use in a week. The *petit salé* will keep for a long time, and become saltier as it is kept. If it is very salty, throw away the first water in which you cook it. Boil a piece for an hour and it will be very tender. Serve with *choucroute* (sauerkraut) or cold with a salad, as well as using it as an ingredient in dishes such as Mme. Escrieu's *cassoulet* (page 116).

Storehouse Leftovers: Offal and Variety Meats

These were eaten fresh in peasant communities after the autumn slaughter of livestock. They were the portion of those preparing and salting down the winter's larder stores, providing a quick feast at the end of the long day. In towns and cities these off-cuts were sold cheap to the urban poor. There are many recipes (such as the famous *Tripes à la mode de Caen*) which do justice to this abundance but which are essentially city food. The offal of lamb, mutton, pig, and beef are all suitable.

BRAINS: Soak them first in salted water (from 2 to 4 hours, depending on the size of the brain). Remove the covering membrane and wipe the meat carefully. Soak for another hour to get rid of any remaining blood. Finish as for sweetbreads—brains will need an extra 10 minutes' simmering. Store them in their cooking liquid if they are not to be used at once.

FRY: The testicles of male animals, these are reckoned the most delicious morsel of all by those who appreciate such things. Pour boiling water over the fry, skin them, and leave them to soak in cold water with a teaspoon of vinegar for a couple of hours. Then slice them and sauté them gently in butter or oil. Delicious treated in the French manner, with a few sliced mushrooms (wild would be best of all) and cream tossed into the frying pan as the *animelles* cook. In Spain I have had an excellent dish of goat's testicles sliced and cooked in oil and garlic, served with quartered lemons, salt, bread, and fried green peppers.

SWEETBREADS: The two varieties are the pancreas (elongated in shape and found near the stomach) and the thymus glands (rounded and to be found in the animal's throat). Put the sweetbreads in a bowl and cover them with salted water. Leave for 2 hours to soak out any traces of blood. Clean and wipe. Then put them into boiling water with a few peppercorns and a tablespoonful of vinegar. Bring back to a boil and simmer for 15 minutes. Drain and remove all traces of skin and sinew. Press between two weighted plates until cold and firm. Cut into squares. They are now ready to be stewed in butter and sauced with mushrooms and cream, or egg-and-bread crumbed and fried—the choice is yours.

◆

PRESERVED FISH

The Lofoten Islands, a wild and beautiful outpost off the Norwegian coast, lapped by the warmth of the Gulf Stream, have been a center for the preparation of dried and salt cod for at least a thousand years and probably much longer. A rocky archipelago 200 miles inside the Arctic Circle is a long journey from the hills of the Mediterranean, but the Norwegians sprang from Viking stock and their long ships went where they pleased. It is from the cod fishermen of the North Atlantic that the peasant farmers of the Spanish, French, and Italian olive groves get the raw material for many of their favorite dishes.

Recipes for salt cod are so deeply rooted in the southern kitchen that they appear as festival food—an *aïoli* with *morue* is the fast dish traditionally prepared in France for the Christmas Eve supper. Salt cod has such excellent keeping qualities that it became one of the few items for which inland peasant communities were prepared to barter—a storeroom staple which has a very high nutritional value and was often preferred to fresh fish.

Every year toward the end of February, while the snow is still lying in drifts on the pebbled beaches, the cod shoals travel from the Barents Sea to spawn off the coasts of the Lofotens. From early February onwards, the seaside dwellers keep watch on the headlands and in the crows nests of their boats for the darkening patch of troubled water, which heralds the arrival of the fish. When the news breaks, hundreds of fishing boats scramble to sea to reap the harvest. In the old days the boats were small and sturdy single-sailed smacks, painted in combinations of green and blue, red and ocher, which the fishermen built and patched themselves during the long winter months. Today they have company on the waves and have to compete with big oceangoing trawlers supplying modern factory conveyor belts.

Drying racks for *torrfisk* still dominate the fishing harbors of northern Norway—forests of pearl-gray wooden poles, triangular or rectangular stacks of slats which tower over the houses. As soon as the boats return, the villagers set to work preparing the catch. *Torrfisk* requires that the fish are cleaned, gutted, and tied together by the tails in pairs. These are then hung over the poles to dry—with the nets that fished the cod flung over the whole edifice to frustrate the ever-hungry gulls. By June the racks have been cleared, and the fish, now stiff and dry, is on its way for export.

The Norwegians added salt to the curing process during the Middle Ages, and their customers in the Mediterranean soon began to prefer the salty flesh of these *klippfisk*—named after the rocky cliffs on which the cod was laid out to dry. The triangular kite-shaped sheets of fish, coated with coarse gray salt and layered in wooden crates, are still annually dispatched to village shops around the Mediterranean. Today they also reach other, more distant, destinations whose immigrant communities long for the taste of home. Salt cod has a potent nostalgia value. A particularly pungent odor announces the *klippfisk*' arrival to coincide conveniently with the year's first pressings of olive oil. The best Mediterranean salt-cod recipes marry the two ingredients—the harsh pale flesh of the northern ocean and the rich gold fruit of the southern hillsides make a perfect union.

Portugal and Britain entered the trade during the Middle Ages. Today Newfoundland is the major source, and salt cod is now exported by Canada as well as Norway and Iceland.

◆

SALT HERRINGS

Sill (Scandinavia and Northern Europe)

Barrels of salted herrings used to stock one corner of every Swedish farmhouse's winter larder from Jutland to Lapland. The fish was often simply scaled, gutted, and barreled with salt only. The Norwegians kept their barrels of salt herrings in the *stabbur*, a wooden hut on stilts whose raised floor is hung with heavy stones beneath to weight it against the fierce winter gales. A carelessly tethered *stabbur* could be whipped off the hillside and its precious contents flung all over the valley in a flash. The *stabbur* is occasionally still to be found in use in country districts—it provides a cold outside larder whose temperature keeps well below freezing all winter. A salt herring eaten with a slice of rye bread or a piece of Scandinavian crisp bread, together with a handful of the delicious native berries which are still gathered and stored for the winter, made a fast and nourishing meal for the working man, particularly if accompanied by a draft of specially soured milk.

◆

FERMENTED BALTIC HERRING

Surströmming (Sweden)

It is the fishermen of northern Sweden who are responsible for *surströmming*. A certain dependence on geographical peculiarities makes it unsuitable for home cooking, but I include it because it is odd and original and truly peasant.

A catch of Baltic herring (a smaller species of herring than the Altantic variety, with a lower fat content) is barreled up with half the usual quantity of salt and left to ferment in the warm midsummer air—on double time since the midnight sun never sets.

This method of preparation has a legend, recounted by Alan Davidson in his book *North Atlantic Seafood*. He tells how a certain group of fishermen ran low on salt to preserve their catch one year. There being no corner store for a thousand miles, they barreled up the fish regardless—using half-rations. The canny fellows, resourceful as peasants everywhere, managed to convince their clients, a local tribe of reindeer-skin-trading backwoodsmen, to try the new delicacy at a special discount. The customers, to their suppliers' surprise, expressed themselves well satisfied and ordered more of the same for the following season.

The year's supply of *surströmming* is deemed ready for release each August 20. It is then canned and shipped to supermarket cold cabinets all over Sweden. The tins bulge alarmingly and must be opened with care. Devotees eat them with a good helping of chopped onion and the new season's potatoes. Down your supplies before Christmas (it has a four-month "eat by" date on it). It can also be served layered with whey cheese and chopped onion, and topped with bread crumbs and butter. Bake in a preheated 425°F oven for 15 minutes.

◆

SALTED ANCHOVIES

Acciughe (Italy and the Mediterranean)

Barrels of these little fish can be found in every village shop around the Mediterranean. Pungent and salty, they add their own particular character to many Italian dishes. A taste for strong fishy flavors stretches back to Roman kitchens. Apicius, the millionaire voluptuary, was particularly fond of *liquamen*, a powerful pickle brewed from fermented mackerel intestines and used by the Romans as an all-purpose sauce. The process of salting the fish is rather lengthy, but I include it so that the method holds no mysteries. You can then buy the anchovies ready salted and prepare them according to the recipes which follow.

TIME: Start 6 months before; 1 hour

10   *pounds anchovies*
2   *ounces kosher salt (not the dried kitchen salt) per 1 pound of fish*

You will need a wooden barrel or a large plastic bucket. Behead and gut the fish—a quick pinch between thumb and forefinger will do the trick. American anchovies need scaling as well. Sprinkle a thick layer of salt on the base of the container. Place a layer of fish in a circular fan shape, tails to middle. Sprinkle in another layer of salt, then another of fish, and so on, until the fish are all used up. Weight the top. The fish will make their own brine. If they are not submerged within 3 days, make a strong brine [4 ounces (½ cup) salt to 2 cups water] and pour it over them to cover. Store in a cold place. They will be ready in 6 months.

ANCHOVIES IN OIL

Acciughe in olio (Italy and the Mediterranean)

TIME: 20 minutes

1   *pound salted anchovies from your own barrel or the delicatessen's*
½   *cup good olive oil*

You will need a bowl and two to three 2-cup glass jars. Soak the anchovies in milk and water for 10 minutes to desalt them. Fillet them and pack them into glass jars. Cover them with the olive oil. They are wonderful on pizza, on a fresh tomato salad, or on their own on good bread.

ANCHOVY PASTE

Acciughe conservata (Italy and Neighbors)

This is probably the heir to the Roman fermented fish sauce, *garum* or *liquamen*. It can be used as a condiment.

TIME: 20 minutes

1   *pound salted anchovies (barreled or canned)*
½   *cup good olive oil*

You will need a bowl, a blender or a food processor, and two 1-cup glass jars. Soak the anchovies to desalt them in milk and water for 10 minutes. Remove the bones—if you have bought the canned variety, you can omit this step.

In a food processor or blender, blend the anchovies with the olive oil. Seal in small jars under a layer of olive oil. This paste is delicious spread on fresh country bread.

KIPPERED HERRINGS

(Scotland)

It is the dampness of the British climate—it began to deteriorate around 700 B.C.—which led the inhabitants to add other ways of preserving their sea harvest to the more widespread methods of wind-drying and salting. The last was often carried out on the seashore with no preliminary scaling or gutting. Larger fish were very heavily brined indeed, and dried stiff and hard as planks. By the fourteenth century the Dutch had introduced British fishermen to the joys of barreling their catch with salt. Smoking was added to the culinary repertoire at about the same date—the first to benefit from the treatment being the herring catch.

Kippered herrings are cool-smoked. It is quite easy to rig up a small smoker for yourself. You will need a sheltered corner of a shed or outhouse, and an empty forty-gallon barrel or metal drum. Check to see that it never contained dangerous chemicals before you embark on the project. Remove the base and the top of the drum, leaving you with an oversize tube. Cut a semicircle out of the base to allow the smoke to be funneled in. Build a channel with bricks or a piece of wide piping leading into the smoke hole, leaving the other end without a cover so that you can build the smoke fire in it. This arrangement acts like a kind of large tobacco-pipe, except that the fire is at the stem end instead of in the bowl. Light the fire with kindling first. Then feed it with beech, birch, or oak sawdust. The draft will draw the smoke through the pipe, into the drum, and either up the chimney or into the open air.

S E R V E S : 6 to 8

T I M E : 8 hours

12 *fresh herrings*
1   *pound salt*

You will need a barrel smoker or a smoking shed. Clean, split, and wipe the fresh herrings, leaving their heads on. Layer them in a deep dish with plenty of salt and leave them to take the salt for 30 minutes. Take them out and shake off the salt. This cure is very light and will not preserve the fish (even after smoking) for long—no more than a week in the refrigerator, although they will keep much longer if you freeze them.

If you need to preserve them for more than a week, leave them in the salt overnight. Hang the fish for half an hour or so in a draft, until the surface is dry. Smoke the salted herrings by stringing them, tied together in pairs, looped on sticks balanced over the open end of the smoker-barrel. Eight hours' smoking will be sufficient to give them a wonderful flavor and turn them a deep burnished copper. Keep the fire smoldering constantly—it is not good for the cure if you allow changes in temperature.

Eat just as they are, still warm from the smoker, with fresh oatcakes, cold butter, and hot milky tea for breakfast. Or cook them further by grilling with a little butter. Or fry them in a dry pan, sandwiched in pairs with a small pat of butter.

My Edinburgh-born grandmother used to pack her kippers into a roomy jug, so that only the tails poked up. Then she covered them with boiling water straight from the kettle. She would leave them for 5 minutes before taking them out, draining and serving them on a hot plate with a pat of cold butter to melt into them. She liked her kippers with hot buttered toast.

Bones are the trickiest part of kipper eating. The backbone of a freshly smoked kipper pulls free of the flesh and can be hooked out quite easily, bringing the smaller bones with it. There are those who put the grilled fish on the plate flesh side down, tackling the problem by eating their fish from the skin, or nonbone, side.

◆

SMOKED SALMON

(Scotland)

Smoking your own salmon is not a difficult culinary exercise. The salmon is lightly salted before it is smoked—the lighter the cure, the sweeter the flesh. In pre-refrigeration days the fish was salted so heavily and lengthily to ensure its preservation, that it was more like a rigid plank of wood (not unlike salt cod) than a fish by the time it arrived in the southern markets of Britain.

SERVES: 12

TIME: 1 to 2 days

1   salmon (weighing 8 to 10 pounds)
8   ounces salt per side of salmon

You will need a wooden board or large dish, and a barrel smoker. Scale, gut, and wipe the fish carefully. Remove the head, trim the fins, and split the fish down the back.

Sprinkle salt on the board, lay the fish on it skin side down, and spread a layer of salt about ⅛ inch thick on the flesh side of the salmon, with a thicker layer at the thick end of the fish. Leave the fish to take the salt, allowing it to drain as it does so, for 5 or 6 hours. When it is ready, it will feel springy to the touch. The thicker the fish, the longer the salting. Wash thoroughly under running water to remove the surface salt (when you have done so, the surface should still taste salty). Tie a string around the top fin and the hard gill-joint. Hang the salted salmon in an airy room for about 12 hours, until the outside of the fish feels dry to the touch.

Hang in the cold-smoker, as for the kippers (page 516), for 5 to 6 hours. On a windy day it will be smoked more quickly—on a calm day it can be left in overnight. Leave to settle for 2 to 3 days before eating. Slice finely and serve with brown bread and butter. Like all smoked fish, it has an affinity with scrambled eggs. It will keep for a week in the refrigerator. Freeze it if you want to keep it longer.

SMOKED HADDOCK

Finnan Haddie (Scotland)

Finnan is a little fishing hamlet, six miles south of Aberdeen, which acquired a particular reputation for the excellence of its smoked haddock. The fish are smoked over peat, which gives them a highly distinctive flavor.

YIELD: 1 fish serves 1

TIME: 8 hours

Haddocks
2   *ounces salt per fish*

You will need a barrel smoker. Prepare the fish as for kippered herrings (page 516), cleaning the fish thoroughly and splitting them—although here with haddock the heads are removed. (Note the dark prints of St. Peter the fisherman's thumb beside the gills.) The haddock, being larger than the herring, will need longer in the salt—an hour should be quite enough. Smoke the salted and dried fish over the barrel smoker, hung tied by the tails in pairs.

In 5 to 6 hours the haddocks will turn the color of old ivory, pale and delicate. They are a truly delectable dish. Poach them in simmering milk for 15 minutes or put them in a dish, cover with milk (no salt of course), and bake them for 20 minutes in a preheated 350°F oven. Use the milk to make mashed potatoes to serve with them. Haddock has an affinity with cream and eggs, both scrambled and poached, which accounts for the success of Haddock Monte Carlo.

PRESERVED VEGETABLES

FERMENTED CABBAGE

Sauerkraut (Germany and Northern Europe)

Sauerkraut—salted and fermented, or "barrel cabbage"—is an important national dish. It can be served with sausages, with pork, with anything and everything, or on its own with a sprinkling of caraway seeds, a spoonful of sour cream, and a thick slice of black rye bread to mop up the juices. During the summer it may be replaced in the recipes with fresh cabbage—as with all peasant cooking, ingredients are dictated by season.

Sauerkraut substitutes for the fresh cabbage available in the summer, and is made from firm heads of cabbage (Savoy, Drumhead, or Flat Dutch) cut after the first frosts of autumn. The new sauerkraut traditionally used to be eaten with fresh pork after the autumn pig killing. It was eaten again on New Year's Day as an oblation for the year's renewal; with goose for the Christmas festivities; with salt pork and smoked sausages all winter; and then with fresh fish when the spring thaw released the fishing boats. It should be all finished up by the time the young spring cabbage is ready for gathering—the salt content is too low to conserve the pickle in the heat of summer (with today's central heating, it must be stored in the refrigerator).

Sauerkraut can be eaten raw as a salad. It should be thoroughly rinsed in cold water to get rid of excess salt. Then mix it with raw chopped onion and perhaps a little chopped apple. Dress with oil and black pepper.

In Transylvania (now a province of Rumania) I have eaten sauerkraut salad dressed with pumpkin oil. This is a very dark oil with a light nutty flavor which is prepared in the autumn by farmers' wives all over Eastern Europe. The women sit out in their fields in the middle of the pumpkin patch in early October, slashing open the overripe fruit with heavy knives and scooping out seeds into big wire-meshed trays. The pulp goes for winter cattle-fodder and the seeds are pressed for their oil in a hand mill. Pumpkin oil must be stored, tightly corked, in a cool larder—in common with all vegetable oils, it is really a fruit juice and thus volatile, and goes rancid after it has been exposed to air.

Sauerkraut is best made in quantity. I give the recipe as much for interest as in expectation of a practical application. You can always take the easy way out and buy your supplies ready-made.

YIELD: 30 cabbages would have kept a small family going all winter

TIME: 2 hours plus 3 weeks salting

50   *pounds cabbage*
2   *pounds salt*

You will need a large wooden barrel. Scrub the barrel very thoroughly. Set it on boards so that the air can circulate—a cool unheated pantry or dry cellar is ideal.

Pick off the outer leaves of the cabbage and save the perfect ones. Line the bottom of the barrel with ten of these large leaves.

Slice each cabbage head in two and cut out the solid stalk. Put aside three or four heads so that you have some large leaves which you can stuff (replace fresh cabbage with Sauerkraut in stuffed cabbage recipes.) Shred the rest of the cabbage with a very sharp knife. It should look like a mountain of very fine-cut noodles. Mix the salt with the shredded cabbage, and thoroughly salt the halved heads.

Pack into the barrel, pressing each layer down well. (Country women used to tread it down with clean bare feet.) Cover with twenty perfect outside leaves, well salted. Top with a lid or a china plate whose diameter is slightly smaller than the barrel top. Weight the lid down heavily so that it keeps the cabbage pressed down. After a week check to see if the brine is forming well. It should cover the cabbage after 10 days. If not, top off with a brine made with 1 ounce salt to 2 cups water. Replace the lid and weight so that all the sauerkraut is submerged, since sauerkraut, like all pickles, must not be allowed to come into contact with air. The cabbage will now begin to ferment and will be ready to eat in three weeks from the start of the operation. Quite apart from its excellence as food, many blood-cleansing, digestion-aiding properties are ascribed to fermented cabbage.

Check your barrel every week throughout the winter, skim off the foam of the fermentation, and give the sauerkraut a stir every few days. At the same time, rinse off and wipe down the sides and lip of the barrel and the weighted lid. The sauerkraut should then keep sweet and fresh until next season's greens are sprouting.

◆

COOKED SAUERKRAUT

(Germany and Northern Europe)

SERVES: 4

TIME: 10 minutes plus 30 minutes to 3 hours cooking

1 *pound sauerkraut, your own or store-bought (the canned variety, unless precooked, takes the same time; check the instructions on the can)*	1 *cup water or stock* 1 *teaspoon caraway seeds (optional)* *Pepper*

You will need a strainer and a deep saucepan. Drain the sauerkraut, rinse it, and put it in a deep saucepan. Cover with boiling water, or strong clear stock, and cook for an hour, tightly covered. Some households cook their sauerkraut for as long as 3 hours, others for as little as half an hour. I prefer it not too soft. A potato can be grated into the simmering cabbage half an hour before the end of cooking to give a richer sauce. Uncover the dish and turn up the heat for the final 10 minutes to evaporate the remaining liquid. If you are using spices, season with caraway seeds and freshly ground black pepper. If you prefer, cook the sauerkraut in a preheated 350°F oven for an hour.

SUGGESTIONS

Sauerkraut *cooked with white wine:* Substitute half a bottle of white wine for the liquid in the plain *sauerkraut* recipe.

Sauerkraut *cooked with lard:* Melt 2 ounces (¼ cup) of fat (or preferably goose fat) in a roomy saucepan. Add a piece of pork bone or a slice of fatback bacon if you have it. Drain and rinse the sauerkraut and put it in the pan. Cover with stock and simmer as usual.

Sauerkraut *with apples:* Add 1 pound of sharp green apples, cored and sliced, to the sauerkraut with lard recipe. They should go in half an hour before the end of the cooking.

Season the sauerkraut with fennel seeds or crushed juniper berries instead of the caraway.

PICKLED VEGETABLES

Torshi (Bulgaria)

These pickles are made all over Eastern Europe. The Bulgarians, being the best gardeners in the region, make the best pickles. The vegetables should retain a crisp bite, and are often eaten on their own as a salad meal with bread.

YIELD: Enough to make 1 gallon of pickles

TIME: Start 6 weeks ahead; 40 minutes

6 to 7 pounds mixed vegetables: carrots, cauliflower, young turnips, small pickling cucumbers, red, yellow, and green peppers, and green beans—any or all	1 3 3 1½ 2 4	*head of dill* *garlic cloves* *small red chili peppers* *quarts water* *cups white wine vinegar* *ounces (½ cup) salt*

You will need several jars and a saucepan.

Peel and cut the carrots lengthwise into quarters, chopping them in half if they are long. Divide the cauliflower into florets. Peel and quarter the turnips.

Wipe and leave whole the small pickling cucumbers (if you have only large cucumbers, quarter them lengthwise and cut them into convenient pieces). Seed and quarter the peppers. Top-and-tail the beans. Separate the dill into short branches. Peel and halve the garlic. Wipe and leave the chilies whole.

Pack the vegetables neatly into sterilized jars—sterilize them either in a hot (400°F) oven for 10 minutes, or by rinsing them with scalding water.

Bring the water, vinegar, and salt to a boil. Pour the hot brine over the vegetables, and prod the pieces well with a skewer to shake off the air bubbles which might make the pickle go bad. Air is the archenemy of pickles and preserves. Seal the jars tightly and store.

The pickles will be ready to eat in 6 weeks, just as the cold wind begins to sweep the plain. They are very good with fresh bread and a slice of cheese.

SUGGESTION

If you want your pickles to last longer than a few months, use only undiluted vinegar and salt as the brining mixture.

Selected Bibliography

Adam, Hans Karl. *German Cookery*. London: Michael Joseph, 1967.

Aldiss, Brian. *Cities and Stones: A Traveller's Jugoslavia*. London: Faber, 1966.

Arensberg, Conrad M. *The Irish Countryman*. New York: Macmillan, 1937.

Ayrton, Elizabeth. *The Cookery of England*. London: Deutsch, 1974.

Bath, B.H.S. van and Slicher, B. S. *The Agrarian History of Western Europe, A.D. 500–1850*. London: Arnold, 1963.

Beeton, Isabella. *Household Management*. London: Ward Lock, 1912 edition.

Bennett, H.S. *Life on the English Manor: A Study of Peasant Conditions 1150–1400*. Cambridge: University of Cambridge, 1948.

Blum, Jerome. *The End of the Old Order in Rural Europe*. Princeton: Princeton University Press, 1978.

———. *Our Forgotten Past*. (Ed.) London: Thames & Hudson, 1982.

Bonham-Carter, V. *The English Village*. London: Penguin, 1952.

Borrow, George. *The Bible in Spain*. London: Murray, 1843.

———. *Wild Wales*. London: Murray, 1862.

Boswell, James. *Journal of a Tour to the Hebrides*. London, 1785.

Boulay, Juliet du. *Portrait of a Greek Mountain Village: Life in Anbeli in Euboea, 1966–68*. Oxford: Clarendon, 1974.

Brenan, Gerald. *The Face of Spain*. London: Turnstile Press, 1950.

———. *South from Granada*. London: Hamish Hamilton, 1957.

Browning, Ellen. *A Girl's Wanderings in Hungary*. London: Longman, 1896.

Carlyle, Thomas. *Reminiscences*. London: Longman, 1881.

Casas, Penelope. *The Foods and Wines of Spain*. New York: Knopf, 1982.

Chaillu, Paul du. *The Land of the Midnight Sun*. London: Murray, 1881.

Chamoux, Simone. *Les Olives dans la Cuisine*. Lys, France: privately printed, 1985.

Chantiles, Vera L. *The Food of Greece*. New York: Avenal Books, 1979.

Chapman, Charlotte Gower. *Milocca: A Sicilian Village*. London: Allen & Unwin, 1973.

Clair, Colin. *Of Herbs and Spices*. London: Abelard Schuman, 1961.

Cobbett, William. *Rural Rides*. London: 1830.

Dabitesse, M.L. *Révolution Silencieuse*. Paris, 1931.

Dallas, E. S. *Kettner's Book of the Table*. London: Dulau, 1877.

David, Elizabeth. *French Provincial Cooking*. London: Michael Joseph, 1960.

Davidson, Alan. *North Atlantic Seafood*. London: Viking, 1979.

————. *Mediterranean Seafood*. London: Penguin, 1972.

Denton, Rev. W. *Servia and the Servians*. London: Bell and Daldy, 1862.

Dickens, Charles. *The Posthumous Papers of the Pickwick Club*. London: 1936.

Fisher, M.F.K. *The Cooking of Provincial France*. New York: Time-Life Books, 1969.

Franklin, S. H. *The European Peasantry*. London: Methuen, 1969.

Fraser, Ronald. *The Pueblo*. London: Allen Lane, 1973.

Freeman, Bobby. *First Catch Your Peacock*. Gwent, Wales: 1980.

Fytrakis, Eva. *Traditional Greek Cooking* (translated by Diana Reid). Athens, 1981.

Gordon, Jan and Cora. *Two Vagabonds in Sweden and Lapland*. London: Lane, 1926.

Grant, Elizabeth, of Rothiemurchus. *Memoirs of a Highland Lady*. Edinburgh: privately printed, 1830.

Grigson, Jane. *Charcuterie and French Pork Cookery*. London: Michael Joseph, 1967.

Hall, D. J. *Romanian Furrow*. London: Harrap, 1939.

Hardisty, Jytte. *Scandinavian Cooking*. London: Hamlyn, 1970.

Hartley, Dorothy. *Food in England*. London: Macdonald, 1934.

Heaton, Eliza Putnam. *By-Paths in Sicily*. New York: Dutton, 1920.

Hemingway, Ernest. *The Dangerous Summer*. London: Hamish Hamilton, 1985.

Henderson, T. F. *Old World Scotland*. Edinburgh: Adam & Charles Black, 1893.

Hoskins, W. G. *The Midlands Peasant*. London: Hodder, 1957.

Hough, P. H. *Dutch Life in Town and Country*. London: Newnes, 1901.

Howitt, William. *Rural Life of Germany*. London: Longman, 1842.

Johnston, Isobel Christian. *The Cook and Housewife's Manual of Mrs. Margaret Dods*. Edinburgh: Simpkin, 1826.

Kalm, Pehr. *Visit to England on his Way to America*. London, 1892.

Kinglake, A. W. *Eothen: or traces of travel brought home from the East*. London: Longman, 1844.

Le Roy Ladurie, E. *Les Paysans du Languedoc*. Paris: S.E.V.P.E.N., 1966.

Lang, George. *The Cuisine of Hungary*. New York: Atheneum, 1971.

Leib, Ollie. *Bayerische Leibspeisen*. Munich: Kochbuch Verlag, 1979.

Levai, Vera. *Culinary Delights*. Budapest: Corvina Kiado, 1983.

Llanover, Lady. *The First Principles of Good Cookery*. London: Bently, 1867.

Llewellyn, Richard. *How Green Was My Valley*. London: Michael Joseph, 1939.

Lloyd, L. *Peasant Life in Sweden*. London: Tinsley, 1870.

Lovell, M. S. *Edible Mollusks of Great Britain and Ireland*. London: Reeve, 1867.

Luard, Nicholas. *Andalucía*. London: Century, 1984.

Mabey, Richard. *Food for Free*. London: Collins, 1972.

McGee, Harold. *On Food and Cooking*. New York: Scribner, 1985.

McNeill, F. Marian. *The Scots Kitchen*. Edinburgh: Blackie, 1929.

Médecin, Jacques. *Cuisine Niçoise* (translated by Peter Graham). London: Penguin, 1983.

Montagné, Prosper (Editor). *Larousse Gastronomique*. London: Hamlyn, 1961.

Morton, H. V. *In Search of Ireland*. London: Metheun, 1930.

Olsson, Brita. *Baka Matbröd*. Sweden: ICA, 1984.

Oxford Symposium Proceedings, 1981, 1983, and 1985. London: Prospect Books.

Oyler, Philip. *The Generous Earth*. London: Harmondsworth, 1961.

Pagnol, J., Koscher, J., & Mattern, R. *Les Recettes de la Table Provençale*. Strasbourg: Librairie Istra, 1982.

Petis Propos Culinaires, Numbers 1–20. London: Prospect Books, 1979–85.

Pohren, Donn. *Adventures in Taste: The Wines and Folk Food of Spain*. Society of Spanish Studies, 1972.

Pomiane, Edouard de. *La Code de la Bonne Chère*. Paris: Societé Scientifique d'Hygiène Alimantaire, 1930.

———. *Cooking with Pomiane*. London: Faber, 1962.

Raymont, Ladislas. *The Peasants*. New York: Knopf, 1925.

Reboul, J.-b. *La Cuisinière Provençale*. Marseilles: Tacussel, 1895.

Renell of Rodd, Sir James. *Customs and Lore of Modern Greece*. London: Stott, 1892.

Romer, Elizabeth. *The Tuscan Year*. London: Weidenfeld, 1984.

Root, Waverly. *The Food of France*. London: Cassell, 1958.

Rousseau, Jean-Jacques. *La Nouvelle Héloise*. Paris: Firmin Didot, 1866.

Saalfeld, Diedrich. "The Struggle to Survive." Contribution to Blum, *Our Forgotten Past* (op. cit.)

Sava, George. *Donkey Serenade: Travels in Bulgaria*. London, Faber, 1940.

Spink, Reginald. *Denmark*. London: A & C Black, 1957.

Stratilesco, Theresa. *From Carpathian to Pindus*. London: Unwin, 1906.

Stromstad, Aase. *Eat the Norway*. Oslo: Aschehoug, 1984.

Tweedie, Ethel B. *Through Finland in Carts*. London: Black, 1898.

Thackeray, W. M. "The Ballad of Bouillabaisse." *Punch*. London, 1849.

Turney-High, H. H. *The Life and Times of a Walloon Village*. New York: Columbia, 1958.

Viski, Karoly. *Hungarian Peasant Customs*. Budapest: Vajna, 1932.

Warriner, D. *The Economics of Peasant Farming*. London: Frank Cass, 1964.

Weaver, William Woys. *Sauerkraut Yankees*. Philadelphia: University of Pennsylvania, 1983.

Willson, Rev. T. B. *Norway At Home*. London: Newnes, 1908.

Wilson, D. Anne. *Food and Drink in Britain*. London: Constable, 1973.

Windt, Henry de. *Finland As It Is*. London: Murray, 1901.

Woodforde, Rev. James. *The Diary of a Country Parson*. London, Oxford University Press, 1924–31.

Index